ANOTHER THOUSAND
Radio REPLIES
Second Volume

Given from the Catholic Broadcasting Station 2SM
Sydney, Australia

by

THE REV. DR. LESLIE RUMBLE, M.S.C.

Edited in Collaboration with
REV. CHARLES MORTIMER CARTY
Diocesan Missionary

With a Preface by
HIS EXCELLENCY JOHN GREGORY MURRAY, D.D.
Archbishop of St. Paul

•

1422 QUESTIONS and ANSWERS
on
CATHOLICISM AND PROTESTANTISM

These books are now widely used as texts and reference books in Study Clubs, High Schools, Colleges, Universities, Newman Clubs, Novitiates and Seminaries.

Invaluable for the uninformed Catholic—the educated and uneducated lapsed Catholic and Prospective Convert.

WIDE CIRCULATION AT MISSIONS AND RETREATS

•

TAN BOOKS AND PUBLISHERS, INC.
Rockford, Illinois 61105

IMPRIMATUR:

    John Gregory Murray
    Archbishop of St. Paul, Minnesota
    July 10, 1940

Copyright © 1940 by Fathers Rumble and Carty.

Copyright © 1979 by TAN Books and Publishers, Inc.

Originally published in 1940 by Radio Replies Press Society, St. Paul, Minnesota.

Library of Congress Catalog Card Number: 79-51938

ISBN: 0-89555-090-3

Complete and unabridged.

Printed and bound in the United States of America

TAN BOOKS AND PUBLISHERS, INC.
P.O. Box 424
Rockford, Illinois 61105
1979

TABLE OF CONTENTS

CHAPTER		PAGE
	ANALYTICAL INDEX	5
	INTRODUCTION by *Rev. Charles M. Carty*	7
	PREFACE by *Archbishop J. G. Murray, D.D.*	9
	FOREWORD by *Dr. Rumble, M.S.C.*	11
I.	GOD	13
II.	MAN	20
III.	RELIGION	28
IV.	THE RELIGION OF THE BIBLE	35
V.	THE CHRISTIAN FAITH	48
VI.	A DEFINITE CHRISTIAN FAITH	55
VII.	THE PROTESTANT REFORMATION	63
VIII.	THE TRUTH OF CATHOLICISM	78
IX.	THE CHURCH AND THE BIBLE	116
X.	THE DOGMAS OF THE CHURCH	124
XI.	THE CHURCH IN HER MORAL TEACHINGS	220
XII.	THE CHURCH IN HER WORSHIP	254
XIII.	THE CHURCH AND SOCIAL WELFARE	268
XIV.	COMPARATIVE STUDY OF NON-CATHOLIC DENOMINATIONS	303
XV.	TO AND FROM ROME	341
	ALPHABETICAL INDEX	351

FOR COMPLETE ALPHABETICAL INDEX OF ALL THREE VOLUMES, SEE VOLUME ONE.

ANALYTICAL INDEX

(Numbers refer to paragraphs)

CHAPTER ONE—GOD
Proof of God's existence, 1-7; God's nature, 8-11; Supreme control over all things and the problem of suffering and evil, 12-24.

CHAPTER TWO—MAN
Destiny of man, 25-26; Death, 27-30; Immortality of man's soul, 31-36; Pre-existence denied, 37; The human free will, 38-44; Determinism absurd, 45-56.

CHAPTER THREE—RELIGION
Necessity of religion, 57-64; Salvation of the soul, 65-66; Voice of science, 67-69; Religious racketeers, 70-73; Divine revelation, 74-77; Revealed mysteries, 78-81; Existence of miracles, 82-90.

CHAPTER FOUR—THE RELIGION OF THE BIBLE
Gospels historical, 91-95; Missing Books of the Bible, 96-104; The Bible inspired, 105-119; Biblical account of creation, 120-131; New Testament problems, 132-143; Supposed contradictions in Sacred Scripture, 144-149.

CHAPTER FIVE—THE CHRISTIAN FAITH
Source of Christian teaching, 150-151; Jewish rejection of Christ, 152-162; Christianity a new religion, 163-165; Rational foundation for belief, 166-170; Causes of unbelief, 171-175.

CHAPTER SIX—A DEFINITE CHRISTIAN FAITH
Divisions amongst Christians, 176-178; Schisms unjustified, 179-181; Facing the problem, 182-186; The wrong approach, 187-193; Is one religion as good as another?, 194-200; Obligation of inquiry, 201-204; Charity and tolerance, 205-213.

CHAPTER SEVEN—THE PROTESTANT REFORMATION
Meaning of "Protestant," 214-220; Causes of the Reformation, 221-237; Catholic reaction, 238-241; Reformers mistaken, 242-245; The idealization of Protestantism, 246-265; The Catholic estimate, 266-279.

CHAPTER EIGHT—THE TRUTH OF CATHOLICISM
Meaning of the word "Church," 280-282; Origin of the Church, 283-286; The Catholic claim, 287-288; The Roman hierarchy, 289-296; The Pope, 297-315; The Petrine text, 316-328; St. Peter's supremacy, 329-347; St. Peter in Rome, 348-351; Temporal power, 352-360; Infallibility, 361-385; Unity of the Church, 386-387; Holiness of the Church, 388-414; Catholicity of the Church, 415-427; Apostolicity of the Church, 428-434; Indefectibility of the Church, 435-443; Obligation to be a Catholic, 444-451.

CHAPTER NINE—THE CHURCH AND THE BIBLE
Catholic attitude towards the Bible, 452-453; Is Bible reading forbidden to Catholics?, 454-456; Protestant Bibles, 457-463; The Catholic Douay Version, 464-465; Principle of private interpretation, 466-470; Need of Tradition, 471-476; The teaching authority of the Catholic Church, 477-483.

CHAPTER TEN—THE DOGMAS OF THE CHURCH

Revolt against dogma, 484-488; Value of a Creed, 489-490; The divine gift of Faith, 491-494; Faith and reason, 495-511; The "Dark Ages," 512-513; The claims of science, 514-518; The Holy Trinity, 519-533; Creation and evolution, 534-546; Angels, 547-554; Devils, 555-566; Man, 567-591; Reincarnation, 592-595; Sin, 596-621; Christ, 622-667; Mary, 668-696; Grace and salvation, 697-714; The Sacraments, 715; Baptism, 716-735; Confession, 736-760; Holy Eucharist, 761-780; The Sacrifice of the Mass, 781-783; Holy Communion, 784-790; The Catholic Priesthood, 791-792; Marriage and divorce, 793-822; Extreme Unction, 823-828; Judgment, 829-833; Hell, 834-850; Purgatory, 851-862; Indulgences, 863-866; Heaven, 867-876; The resurrection of the body, 877-882; The end of the world, 883-900.

CHAPTER ELEVEN—THE CHURCH IN HER MORAL TEACHINGS

Conscience, 901-902; Truth, 903-904; Charity, 905-908; Scandal, 909-914; Tolerance, 915-916; Censorship, 917-928; The Inquisition, 929-933; Astrology, 934-950; Other superstitions, 951-963; Attendance at Mass, 964-968; Sex education, 969-978; Attitude to "Free Love," 979-999; Abortion, 1000-1033; Suicide, 1034-1040.

CHAPTER TWELVE—THE CHURCH IN HER WORSHIP

Magnificent edifices, 1041-1046; Lavish ritual, 1047-1052; Women in Church, 1053; Catholics and "Mother's Day," 1054-1061; Liturgical Days, 1062-1069; Burial rites, 1070-1073; Candles and votive lamps, 1074-1075; The rosary, 1076-1080; Lourdes water, 1081; The Scapular, 1082-1089.

CHAPTER THIRTEEN—THE CHURCH AND SOCIAL WELFARE.

Social influence of the Church, 1090-1091; The education question, 1092-1095; The Church and world distress, 1096-1112; Catholic attitude towards Capitalism, 1113-1130; The remedy for social ills, 1131-1138; Communism condemned, 1139-1162; The Fascist State, 1163-1177; Morality of war, 1178-1183; May individuals become soldiers?, 1184-1203; The Church and peace, 1204-1230; Capital punishment, 1231-1236; Catholic Action, 1237-1242.

CHAPTER FOURTEEN—COMPARATIVE STUDY OF NON-CATHOLIC DENOMINATIONS

Defections from the Catholic Church, 1243-1244; Gnosticism, 1245; Manichaeism, 1246; Arianism, 1247; Nestorianism, 1248; Eutychianism, 1249; Coptic Church, 1251-1253; Greek Orthodox Church, 1254-1268; Anglican Episcopal Church, 1269-1288; The "Free" or "Nonconformist" Churches, 1289-1290; Presbyterianism, 1291; Methodism, 1292; "Church of Christ," 1293-1296; Baptists, 1297-1300; Seventh Day Adventists, 1301-1304; Plymouth Brethren, 1305-1307; "Catholic Apostolic Church" or Irvingites, 1308-1311; Salvation Army, 1312-1317; Spiritualism, 1318-1327; Christian Science, 1328-1334; Christadelphians, 1335; British Israelism, 1336-1345; "Liberal Catholics," 1346-1350; Witnesses of Jehovah, 1351-1374; Buchmanism or the "Oxford Group Movement," 1375-1387; From Protestantism to Catholicism, 1388-1390.

CHAPTER FIFTEEN—TO AND FROM ROME

Conversion of Cardinal Newman, 1391; Why Gladstone refrained, 1392; The peculiar case of Lord Halifax, 1393-1395; Gibbon the historian, 1396-1398; Secession of Father Chiniquy, 1399-1401; Father Tyrrell, the modernist, 1402-1406; Bishop Garrett's departure, 1407-1409; Judgment on lapsed Catholics, 1410-1413; Protestant apathy towards conversion of Catholics, 1414-1416; Principles for converts to Catholicism, 1417-1421; God's will that all should become Catholics, 1422.

INTRODUCTION TO SECOND VOLUME

The avalanche of letters pouring into my office from every nook and corner of the United States speak in high praise of the valuable and much needed book, Radio Replies, which has been the medium of bringing lapsed Catholics back to the Church and of enlightening those who still remain out of the Church or those who have become converts to Catholicism. Many Protestant Publishing Houses have written in for copies for distribution to Protestant Seminaries.

ITS VALUE FOR MIXED MARRIAGE CASES

The **First Volume** of Radio Replies has cleared away many misconceptions of Catholic claims, especially in so many cases of Mixed Marriages, where the non-Catholic party holds strong grievances against living up to the signed promises. Where religious animosity reigned in the home of the Catholic and non-Catholic parties, many have written in stating that the accidental picking up of a copy of Radio Replies lying around the house and the reading of but a few questions and answers changed the atmosphere of misunderstanding and prejudice towards things Catholic. Wherever religious discussions became nigh intolerable in some Mixed Marriage cases the silent use of the printed word brought about the desired conversion. Converts are made today more through what they **read** than through what they **hear**.

TEACHERS AND PROFESSORS

Teachers and Professors throughout the nation have found this volume of apologetics invaluable as a stimulus to religious study on the part of the high school or university student in the classroom where Radio Replies has been used to divert the student from the monotony of the usually dry Christian Doctrine textbook. In order to equip Seminarians with an understanding of the Protestant mind, many Seminaries have adopted Radio Replies as an official textbook for apologetics. The reading interest of the student or the man in the street in many cases was so aroused that the book was read in one sitting because of the startling sharpness of the quizzes and the clear-cut logical brevity of the replies.

ITS POPULARITY ENCOURAGES PUBLISHING A SECOND AND THIRD VOLUME

The widespread use of the First Volume in hospitals, study clubs, novitiates, retreat houses, seminaries, high schools, academies, colleges and homes throughout the nation has encouraged us to give to the public a Second Volume which amplifies the First Volume by another thousand new and more instructive replies. In **Street Preaching** for the past three summers throughout Minnesota and Wisconsin I have found very few inquiries which are not contained in this handy text and source book. The material presented to me and not found in the First Volume has been embodied in this Second Volume of Replies, which will **soon** be followed by a **Third Volume.** These Three Volumes of five thousand and more replies will serve as a ready encyclopedia for Catholic Apologetics.

IMITATING OUR ENEMIES

I have been campaigning in the spreading of literature in the parish churches through the Archdiocese of St. Paul, speaking at all the Sunday Masses wherever

I go. Getting apologetic literature into the hands of our own Catholic people has reaped great spiritual benefits in bringing many back to the Sacraments and into the Church. This campaign has brought more results for good than I have observed in the years spent in Radio work, Street Preaching and in preaching missions to Catholics and non-Catholics. The printed word has been the weapon of those attacking Catholic claims and it is my conviction that the Apostolate of **Spreading Literature** in imitation of our enemies is very vital today more than ever in brushing aside the false notions about Catholicism and in stimulating Catholics to equip themselves with the proper literature to reply to the questions and charges proposed in the Office, the Shop, the Club, the Street and the Home.

NON-CATHOLIC TRIBUTES

Professors, rabbis, and ministers have personally discussed with me points brought forth in Radio Replies and they after careful perusal of the book confided to me before leaving their locality after a week of street preaching that Radio Replies was the strongest and clearest presentation of Catholic claims they ever studied. It is strange that in spite of open air campaigning in the cause of Catholicism no noteworthy intellectual charge or refutation of any statement in the First Volume has been made by anyone of its readers within or without the Church, and this observation shows that the Catholic Church the world over is suffering most from the great lack of intellectual opposition, and is facing the growing, gnawing cancer of Religious Indifference rather than Differences of Religion.

BEING BOUGHT OVER

Were Dr. Rumble and I offered funds beyond counting to go out and deny the content of these books, we would both be acting against our own consciences in a most dishonest way, did we accept. Only by indulging in a campaign of deliberate lies could we undertake to refute what we have written; and in conscience, therefore, we could take no step but defend the position upheld by these books.

GRATEFUL CONVERTS

Since many readers of Radio Replies who have not even heard Dr. Rumble or myself in the pulpit or on the public platform have come into the Church as a result of studying and debating this work in apologetics, it would be greatly appreciated if these converts would join the long list of those who are sending in a few words of acknowledgment to my office.

WE MEET AT LAST

For many months Dr. Rumble and myself have been corresponding from the extreme ends of the earth concerning the American publication of the First Volume. It is a deeply appreciated privilege to meet at last and to be associated in person with him in getting before the public this Second Volume, and the Third Volume which will be published in the nigh future to complete the series on apologetics.

Rev. Charles Mortimer Carty

PREFACE

HE present volume is a continuation of the fascinating study of problems in religion that engage the attention of all thinking men. Those who have had the privilege of reading the first volume of Radio Replies, which proved so stimulating to Catholic and non-Catholic alike, will find in the present book a more comprehensive study and explanation of subjects that were presented in essential outline in the first volume.

The high motive that has dominated the author is the desire to share with others the treasure of truth that he himself has discovered from personal experience in the process of research in finding his way to the source of truth. Having sought to develop within himself those principles of religion that he had cherished in youth outside the Catholic Church, and finding them inadequate to satisfy all the promptings of his soul, he went through the bypaths that finally led him to the full vision of the personality, the truth and the love of the God-Man, a full vision to be found only in the Catholic Church.

While the topics discussed in his work are necessarily controversial because they were suggested by inquiries from millions of radio listeners all over the world during a period of more than ten years, the method of treatment is not controversial but expository with a view to presenting truth and principle in that objective and inherent value that will bring conviction to an open mind.

Only when men know all the truth that is to be known will they attain that consummate freedom that is based on the possession of all that the mind of man can and should know. While the soul of man instinctively longs for liberty he can never possess it unless he first acquires the knowledge that will enable him to recognize and cherish liberty. The limitation of the human mind that makes it possible for man to indulge in a thousand and one hypotheses concerning essential scientific facts does not permit him to doubt, and continue speculating as to the facts when they are already well established beyond question. When man has developed his knowledge to the point where he is conscious of the possession of truth he experiences a sense of achievement and security in the attainment of the objective that he has sought, and he is no longer disposed to wander afield in the futile adventure of learning whether there may be an order in which the contrary to truth may be acceptable.

In the field of religion the uncertainty and consequent liberty to speculate is due to the limitation of the knowledge of established facts; and only when man has sincerely considered the established facts will he cease from speculation and, by the elimination of his hypotheses in face of scientific facts, accept and enjoy the possession of the truth. There is nothing unscientific in the process by which a man adheres with profound conviction to the truth revealed by the Son of God and preserved in His Church for the temporal and eternal welfare of all humanity.

The exposition of the fundamentals that were involved in the inquiries sent to the author of this volume appeals to the sincerity of all who may find similar problems in their own soul. If the statement of facts may seem to hurt it cannot be attributed to any cause other than the sentiment of those who, in all sincerity, have continued to cherish the conviction that all was well until the physician announces the need of a major operation to save not the body but the soul of the patient.

The unity of the world in the field of human welfare will come only through the unity of the world in the recognition of truth that is basic in the development of human welfare, not only in terms of terrestrial happiness but in the intellectual and spiritual development that is essential to eternal happiness.

JOHN GREGORY MURRAY,
Archbishop of Saint Paul

FOREWORD

This second volume of Radio Replies is new, complete in itself, and quite different in its contents from the first volume which is already so well known and widely distributed. And it has been published in response to innumerable appeals from readers of the first book.

THE FIRST VOLUME

From those readers of the first collection of Radio Replies, bishops, priests, and members of the laity, many of these latter grateful converts, have come very remarkable tributes to the value of the book, both as regards the matters dealt with, and the manner of their presentation. The advantages of such a work of reference should be obvious. When, in 1928, on the occasion of the Eucharistic Congress in Sydney, I commenced a Question Box Radio Session for the purpose of explaining Catholic teaching to non-Catholics, I began by stating two basic principles. Firstly, since God is the Author of all truth, nothing that is definitely true can ever really contradict anything else that is definitely true. Secondly, the Catholic Church is definitely true. It therefore follows that no objection or difficulty, whether drawn from history, Scripture, science, or philosophy, can provide a valid argument against the truth of the Catholic religion.

Stimulated by this clear-cut issue, non-Catholic listeners at once began to submit their difficulties from all points of view. And the fact that the questions are from non-Catholics themselves, and not merely Catholic suppositions as to what they might be expected to think, cannot but prove most useful to all who are called upon to enter into discussion with them.

As to the value of the replies which the Catholic Church can offer to all difficulties proposed against herself or her doctrines, I will let one prominent convert speak. After reading the first volume of Radio Replies he declared: "There is but one answer to the book—to become a Catholic. The only alternative is silence, and the dismissal of the problem of God and of religion altogether from one's thoughts."

The first book, however, summed up the results of my answering over Radio Station 2 SM, Sydney, N.S.W., questions from non-Catholic listeners throughout Australia and New Zealand during the first five years only. Since then, seven further years have elapsed, with an increasing interest amongst listeners, and a continued series of inquiries opening up ever new lines of approach to the problem of religion.

A MORE SEARCHING CHALLENGE

In the first five years I had to deal chiefly with the difficulties of the average man, many of them based on misconceptions of Catholic doctrine and, as often as not, inspired by prejudice. But interest was intensified. Wrong notions were cleared away. The contrast between the actual teachings of the Church and the prevailing sentiments of the secularists, above all in modern non-Catholic Colleges and Universities, became increasingly evident. This was noted by professional men who had sat under the professors in those Colleges and Universities. And there resulted a flood of challenging inquiries, probing far more deeply into the nature, foundations, and consequences of Catholic doctrine.

THIS PRESENT BOOK

From this new material the present volume of Radio Replies has been compiled. For its production, at the invitation of His Excellency the Most Rev. John Gregory Murray, D.D., Archbishop of St. Paul, Minn., U. S. A., I came to America in order to have the personal co-operation of the Rev. Charles Mortimer Carty, Diocesan Missioner, who is so well known throughout the United States as a Catholic Campaigner for Christ, engaging in Street Preaching and a nation-wide distribution of Catholic literature.

As a member of the Australian Province of the Society of the Missionaries of the Sacred Heart—the American Province of which has its headquarters at Geneva, Illinois, U. S. A.—I have for years been engaged throughout Australia in work somewhat similar to that of Father Carty in America. By Radio, by missions in Public Halls, and by instruction classes for converts, my interest has been almost entirely centered in the conversion of non-Catholics whose outlook is very similar to that prevailing amongst the non-Catholics here in America. My being a convert myself of its very nature seemed to indicate such a field of activity.

The selection of the questions and answers in this book, therefore, is the fruit of Father Carty's and my own experience of the needs of today with its denial of the supernatural, its driftage from religion, its adoption of a purely secular basis of life, and its widespread repudiation of those Christian standards of morality which, if not always observed in practice, have at least not hitherto been seriously challenged and denied.

FOR STUDY CLUBS

As far as possible the division of the matter in this second book has been made to correspond with that of the first volume for purposes of reference and comparison. Although this book is complete in itself, it will be found complementary to the first, throwing new light on problems there introduced, and meeting the further angles of approach adopted by those outside the Church who have sought more detailed explanations of her teachings, or have wished to dispute their validity.

ACKNOWLEDGMENTS

It remains for me to thank His Excellency Archbishop Murray for his interest, encouragement, and hospitality during my stay in America; and Father Carty for his valued advice, and a generous co-operation which amounts to blending our labors into a mutual apostolate of the printed word on behalf of the Catholic Faith to those who have not yet attained this greatest of God's blessings. Nor must I forget to thank the many readers of the first volume of Radio Replies who have written gratefully of their indebtedness to it—readers writing, not only from America, Australia, and New Zealand, but from England and Ireland, from India, and Africa, and Canada—and wherever the English language is spoken.

If this second volume accomplishes half the good that has already resulted from the first, it will more than justify its publication, together with the time and labor we have devoted to it.

LESLIE RUMBLE, M.S.C.

CHAPTER ONE

GOD

1. *I am an atheist who wants his difficulties answered without being accused of moral depravity.*

I believe, in the ultimate analysis, with Pascal, that there are two classes of men, those who are afraid to find God, and those who are afraid to lose God. But, to spare you, I will admit that your fear that there might be a God may be perhaps unconscious. Of those who say that they are atheists some are merely unintelligent and do not think; others do think, but merely reject false ideas of God, without knowing how to replace them with the right idea. Since you are not unintelligent I rank you amongst the latter class. Will I accuse you of being morally evil? Of course, I maintain that atheism cannot exist without sin of some kind. If you do not deny God in order to be free from moral restraints, I would have to accuse you at least of a guilty neglect to examine the question as you should. That God exists is certain for everyone with a right conscience.

2. *I have been told that the universe itself is proof of God, on the score that it must have had a Creator.*

That is a sound argument, for as no individual thing in this universe is self-sufficient, the whole collection of individual things cannot be self-sufficient. If each separate atom is unable to explain itself, all together will be as inexplicable as each. Multiplication does not change the nature of things.

3. *Is it not possible that matter itself is eternal?*

I admit that it would be possible for an Eternal Cause to produce eternally some basic created reality. We know from revelation that God did not create from eternity. But it would have been possible for Him to do so. However, you must note this. The appeal to the eternity of matter, which cannot be proved, does not exclude the necessity of an outside Cause. The mere duration of a thing does not explain its existence. You cannot explain a running train by saying innocently, "Why it was always running." In the universe we see a succession of causal mutations, each succeeding stage being caused by a preceding stage, and in turn causing a subsequent stage. Every element is dependent, and no one element can explain itself independently of the rest. And if each link in a chain is dependent, the whole chain is dependent. An eternal series of dependent and caused things can be reasonably explained only by One who is independent and uncaused, who exists with a complete self-sufficiency not to be found in finite things.

In passing, let me call your attention to the problem of life. Even if matter be eternal, there was certainly a time when life did not exist on this earth, and certainly a time when it began to exist. Any belief that it began spontaneously, and without the creative power of God, is credulity, and unworthy of a reasonable man.

4. *Were you to request God to put in an appearance, or manifest His presence beyond doubt to the satisfaction of experimental science, the result would be nil.*

Such a request would be absurd. God, as He is in Himself, is immaterial, and experimental science deals with material things. You might as well offer to believe in the Archangel Gabriel provided I dig up his bones. Experimental science does not cover the whole field of reality. It abstracts from the spiritual field altogether, save indirectly at most.

5. *People may believe that there is a God, but they cannot know it.*

By the use of their reason they can attain to a certain knowledge that God exists. The Vatican Council rightly defined as a dogma of Catholic Faith that natural human reason can know with certainty from the things which He has made that God exists.

6. *Unlike intrinsic evidence, extrinsic evidence is not conclusive.*

Extrinsic evidence is certainly conclusive. I have no intrinsic evidence that Napoleon ever lived. I have the extrinsic evidence of a multitude of documents, and I am historically certain that he did live. Again, if I see the last car of a train disappearing into a tunnel, I have only extrinsic evidence of the existence of an engine at the other end of the train. Meantime, it is intrinsically evident that a thing which does not contain the ultimate reason of its existence within itself, has that ultimate reason in an outside being. That principle is self-evident, and cannot be refuted. On that principle, a being which obviously is not self-caused is evidence of a cause outside itself, and gives sound and certain knowledge of the fact.

7. *The variety of philosophies now extant shows that your conclusion as to the existence of God is not beyond all argument.*

That is true, but it is not to the point. I maintain that the conclusion is beyond all valid and reasonable argument, a very different thing. There is not a single argument against the existence of God which cannot be proved fallacious.

8. *Is not nature itself divine?*

Nature is the effect of a divine creative activity, but it is not itself divine. The word "nature" comes from the Latin "nasci," to be born. It is applied, therefore, to the original character or constitution of some object—a constitution which is the radical principle of all that it is and of all that it does. Thus, by its very "nature" a horse is not a human being. It is not natural to a horse to compose music. That is "natural" which is in accordance with some particular being's nature or constitution. Now we speak of the whole created universe as "Nature" itself. But since it is created—and we speak of it as "Creation"—it cannot be divine in its essential character and constitution.

9. *You insist, then, that God is distinct from nature?*

Yes. The natural world is full of contradictions, and there can be no contradictions in God. The true and the false, good and evil, all manner of imperfections, ignorance, and knowledge, the conscious and the unconscious, constant movement and change—all these cannot possibly be synthesized into one Being called God. We know how different men desire different things and will different things. Men are obviously distinct from one another. They cannot, therefore, be identical with one and the same God. So if you are God, I am not. If I am God, you are not. And it is impossible to say that all is God. Yet if all is not God, all nature is not divine. The whole of creation may be the effect of divine activity, but the effect certainly is distinct from God.

10. *If God is present everywhere in the world, is not creation so inseparable from God as to be part of Him?*

God does exist everywhere. He, therefore, co-exists with all created being. Yet He cannot be identified with created beings. He is in a totally different order of existence. The concept is not difficult. Thought and matter are in different orders of being, yet both co-exist in the same head. A man's material brains could be weighed on a pair of scales; but that would not be weighing the thoughts produced by his soul with the help of those brains. So, too, a current of electricity occupies the same space as solid copper wire; but that mutual presence does not make the copper wire part of the electricity. God's presence everywhere does not make created things part of God. As a matter of fact, God is a purely spiritual Being who cannot have parts. Also, created things are finite or limited, and God is infinite. The finite cannot be part of the infinite. Whilst the universe has its very being "in" God because God is everywhere, God infinitely transcends the universe, differing from it in substance, nature, power, and perfection, and constituting a world of mysterious reality in Himself.

11. *What definition accurately conveys to the human mind an idea of the Deity?*

Many human words convey accurately as far as they go, but not adequately, a notion of some aspect of God's perfections. But for a definition, not of an aspect of God, but simply of God, the most accurate of all human expressions, though still inadequate, is "The Self-existent Being." Thus, God described Himself to Moses in the words, "I am who am." Exod. III., 14. There is an immense depth of meaning in those few words.

God alone exists in His own right. Nothing else "is" of itself and apart from God's causality. All else is but a reflection—a shadow of being; and God is the Author of it. God alone "is"; all else "is dependent."

"I am He who is. Do not seek anywhere else," He may be interpreted to say, "to find the cause of My existence. By this I differ from everything else. This Name is proper to Myself, and I cannot give My glory to another."

God, then, is essential Being. And since every perfection must "be" in order to be a perfection, the plenitude of His Being is the plenitude of perfection. He is. He does not become, progressing from less to greater perfection. Eternal, He never ceases to be what He was, nor does He change to what He was not. He alone is undivided, infinite, identical, essential, and eternal Being; uncaused, yet causing all else to receive being and such degrees of perfection as He chooses to bestow.

God, then, is perfection of Being. He is Truth, for truth is that which is. He is Justice, for justice is the conformity of the will to truth. He is omnipotent, for all else is by Him; good, for evil is the destruction of the true; love, giving benefits to others. He has nothing to fear from any greater than Himself; nothing to envy in any better than Himself. He is Beauty, for beauty is but the splendor of Being, and Truth, and Goodness. All this, and much more, is contained in the simple expression, "I am He who is" as distinguishing God from every other being.

12. *You insist on the existence of God. Do you believe that He is a benevolent God, and that His providence extends to all things?*

Yes, though I admit that you now introduce a problem which has baffled the keenest intelligences of all the centuries, and one the solution of which goes beyond the limits attainable by limited human reason. However, if reason cannot attain to a full and comprehensive explanation of this problem, it can go a certain distance towards a solution, and it can certainly refute objections against God proposed by human reason in view of the evils in this world.

13. *Is everything that happens to man God's will?*

From the negative point of view we can certainly say that those things which happen to men would not happen did God will that they should not happen. But, from the positive point of view, the question arises, "Though nothing can happen against God's will, does God positively will all that does happen?" The answer is—not necessarily.

14. When a person dies, is it God's will that he should do so?

In some cases a death, and all its circumstances, are God's positive will. In other cases, it may be merely God's permissive will. There is a difference between God's positive and God's permissive will. For example, if an employer orders a representative to go from London to Colombo, when the latter goes, he fulfills the positive will of his employer. On the other hand, the employer might express a preference that the representative should go via Capetown rather than via Suez, yet add, "I leave it to yourself to go via Suez if you prefer." If the representative goes via Suez, it is not against the will of his employer. It is at least with the permissive will of that employer, though not a formal command of his positive will. This is merely to show that there is a difference between a positive will and a permissive will; and it is an example which must be kept in mind when dealing with the question of moral and physical evil.

15. If a man is murdered, is it God's will that he should die in that manner?

Since God forbids murder, it cannot be God's positive will that anyone should commit murder. At the same time, whilst people are morally obliged by the commandment, "Thou shalt not kill," they are no more physically compelled to keep that commandment than any other. For God has positively willed that man should be capable of a free choice between good and evil. And God's positive will that man should be free to choose the good must carry with it His permissive will of the evil should man abuse his liberty. If, then, a man commits murder, somebody will be murdered, and that also must be included in God's permissive will. So at least we must say that it was God's permissive will that the murdered man should die in that manner. But I could conceive a case where it would even be God's positive will. If a man were bent on murdering somebody despite God's prohibition, God could positively will that his victim should be one man rather than another. Then it would not be His positive will that the murderer should violate the law, yet it would be His positive will that the victim should meet with such a manner of death rather than another.

16. In the latter case the murderer would be merely the instrument of God's will. How could he be held responsible?

The murderer is responsible because he is doing what God forbids, and what he is not in any way compelled to do. Granted that he insists on his guilty action, God will not prevent it because He cannot do so without depriving him of that free will which God will not take back. But he is not the instrument of God's positive will in his violation of the moral law. From the moral point of view he violates God's positive will, and he is responsible for it. On the other hand, whilst there is moral guilt in committing murder, there is no moral guilt in being murdered against one's will. That is why, if God sees a man bent on committing murder, He could positively will that this man rather than that should be the victim. I have personal knowledge of a case in which the wrong man was certainly chosen by a murderer whose vengeance was as ill directed as it was unlawful. And of all the men I have ever met personally, few would be as well prepared to meet God as the innocent victim, and few as quick to express complete forgiveness of his assailant. He immediately accepted it as God's will that he should die then, and that he should die in such a way. But that did not exempt the murderer from guilt.

17. Why did God put us in a world whose natural disasters, such as earthquakes, can destroy us?

St. Paul replied to this difficulty simply by saying, "Shall the thing formed say to Him that formed it, why hast Thou made me thus?" He stressed the supreme dominion of the Creator, and the limited rights of the creature.

Reason tells us that every created thing by virtue of being created must fall short of infinite perfection. It is bound to be a mixture of perfection and lack of perfection. This world has good features, and bad. We should thank God for the good, and leave to God, without any complaints, the fact that imperfection exists. That is better than forgetting the good, and spending one's life complaining that we do not possess still greater immunity from trials and difficulties.

Let us remember, also, that this life is not all for us. A perfect destiny awaits us after our probation in this world of opportunity.

18. The sight of the evils in this world makes me doubt the existence of God.

Such a doubt is not reasonable. It is because you concentrate on some particular evils, failing to advert to the good, and above all failing to grasp the universal aspect of all creation. The positive evidence for God's existence and of His goodness is certain and solid. If we fail to understand all God's ways, that is evidence, not that God does not exist, but that our human intelligence is finite and limited. To say that we must fully comprehend all God's ways or deny that there is a God is to hold that the human mind is the infinite, ultimate, and infallible criterion of all truth. That is not reasonable.

19. I cannot believe in a God who creates human beings only to know all kinds of physical pain and suffering.

You are not expected to believe in such a God. God did not create men for such a purpose. Two things are certain. There is a God. Pain and suffering are realities. It is foolish to abandon belief in either of these things because we have difficulty in reconciling them. If we find ourselves baffled, the only thing to do is to go on serving God, content to leave the final solution of the problem to Him.

20. I get so indignant when I see suffering that I agree with the axiom, "The only excuse for God is that He does not exist."

Firstly, if there be no God, indignation is absurd. For then suffering is a necessary result of blind material forces. You might just as well get indignant with the sun for rising later in wintertime.

Secondly, the absurdity of the axiom you quote should be evident from the fact that any excusing supposes someone at fault; and if God is at fault, He exists. But let me add that, if He does exist, He cannot be at fault.

Meantime, the only explanation of evil is that God does exist. Evil cannot exist apart from positive beings to experience it. God did not create evil, but He did create all positive beings, permitting them to lack normal perfection at times.

Again, if you say that there is evil, therefore, there is no God; I reply, "There is good, therefore, there is a God." And my reason is stronger than yours, because the good certainly outweighs the evil in this world. And the good cannot be explained without God, whilst the evil can be explained with God. He permitted it only because He was good and powerful enough to draw from it a benefit greater than any harm it can effect.

21. The sight of war, so utterly evil, would make any man indignant. I myself have fallen back on reason, and have become an atheist.

If there be no God, as you now maintain, there would be no men to be at war. And even if there were men, the result of a purely mechanical and necessary evolution, it would not be wrong for them to be at war. If a cog in a machine gets out of place, you are not morally indignant with that cog for its behavior. If there be no God, blind force produced men and produces their conduct. It is as foolish to blame them as to blame an oak tree for not growing straight.

As for the use of reason, take this principle. We must neither belittle nor exaggerate the powers of reason. Reason is powerful enough to prove that there is a God; but it is not powerful enough to understand all God's ways. That reason is not capable of understanding all God's ways does not mean that it is incapable of proving His existence. We cannot argue that, because we neither like nor understand what a fellow human being does, he does not, therefore, exist. You discredit reason even whilst professing to be guided by it.

22. Christian Science tells us that you are trying to solve a problem which does not exist, for pain and suffering are not realities at all.

Both the existence of a good God and of pain and suffering are facts. And since both are facts they are not incompatible. That their complete reconciliation is not possible to the human mind I admit. We, therefore, speak of the mystery of suffering. But it is to behave like a school child to take an answer that pleases one, and then go back and tamper with the facts, adjusting them to fit one's conclusion.

Some people set out with the principle that human reason must be capable of understanding all things. They accept this principle despite the fact that history shows the almost infinite capacity of the human mind to go astray. Working on this unjustified principle they say, "We don't see how to reconcile a good God and suffering." So they go off into two camps, one section with the enthusiastic credulity of atheism, denying that any good God exists, the other section with equally enthusiastic credulity, denying that suffering exists.

The sensible man refuses to deny God or to deny suffering. He has the humility which admits the limitations of human reason, and the faith and trust which continue to serve God in the midst of adversity without tearful protests and moans of despair.

23. If pain and suffering are real, God created them; if they are unreal, they are illusory.

God did not create evil, for evil is the negation of the good. Privations of perfection are not the objective of creative activity. God did create a free will in man capable of failing to do the good dictated by conscience, and positive sense-faculties capable of experiencing pain. Yet pain and moral evil are actual phenomena in this world, and not merely illusions. We do experience an absence of normal health in our bodies, and of moral rectitude in our will. And neither experience is pleasant.

24. Does it not seem strange that God, knowing that would happen, should create man free to please or offend Him? If He could not foresee the future it could be more easily understood.

If God could not foresee the future, instead of being more easily understood, things would be absolutely inexplicable. It is precisely because He foresaw the future, and the greater good He will draw out of these present evils, that He has permitted them.

But, apart from this, why did God, knowing what would happen, create men free to please Him or offend Him?

Firstly, because His foreknowledge in no way makes anyone offend Him. Knowledge does not cause things to happen. Things which happen give rise to the knowledge of them.

Secondly, God gave us free will so that we might have the nobler dignity of being masters of our own destiny, not having to serve Him necessarily and blindly as do trees and inanimate planets and stars. God did not want a forced love from beings capable of an intelligent appreciation of the good. But once God makes man free, man is free either to love God or to reject God; to serve Him, or to rebel against Him. That is, physically. No man is morally free to reject God. God, therefore, forbids that, warning us of its disastrous results.

At any rate, there is a God, and we are free. If we cannot see a satisfactory explanation of the difficulties that occur to us, then we trust God in such matters. Many speculative questions which human curiosity would like to have solved have been left mysteries, either because our minds could not grasp the solution even if they were explained, or simply because God does not choose to justify Himself to His own creatures yet.

See also Radio Replies, Vol. I, Nos. 1-24 for further questions on Existence, Nature, Providence of God and Problem of Evil.

CHAPTER TWO

MAN

25. I would like to ask some question about man's nature and origin, matters over which I have often pondered.

They are important questions, though more important still is the question of man's ultimate destiny. However, it is important that man should know himself. Many people want to know what everything else is, yet have little knowledge of themselves, despite their being so much more important than the lesser things provided for their use and benefit.

26. Even if you prove that the soul is different in origin and nature from the body, what is the gain to humanity?

Immense. Firstly, men would have a right idea of themselves and of a future life awaiting them. Secondly, men would be moved to take the appropriate means to provide for that future. You see, not belonging to the material order, the soul does not follow the course of material things. It does not return to nature and to reabsorption in the universe, but to the great Principle from which it derived its existence by creation. It returns to God, and to a destiny transcending space and time. That eternal destiny will be either good or evil, according to the moral state of the soul when it goes from this world. That surely is an important consideration, and right ideas on the subject cannot but be a gain to humanity.

27. Is it inevitable that the body should die?

Yes, unless a special miracle were to be wrought in some individual case by Almighty God.

28. Surely science in the end will conquer even death.

Science will never free man from the necessity of having to die. Death is as natural to man as it is to all other living things on the face of the earth, whether they be plants or animals. Death is the condition of the continuity of life in this world. The death of preceding generations is the condition for the existence of succeeding generations and in every individual the law of death prevails. Every part of man's bodily organism has its own definite term of vitality. Old cells die and new cells are formed continually. Every movement, and every use of energy means death to a certain amount of tissue. And in the end, should man escape disease or accident, the day must come when the worn-out organism will fail to produce new cells required for continued existence. The entire organism will then die.

29. Even now life is prolonged by scientific means.

Illness may be temporarily arrested, but that does not mean that science can preserve people from ultimate death. To render man immortal in this life science would have to exclude every possible type of disease, all risk of accident, and the whole process of natural decay in every individual human being. Such a thing will never be.

30. Would you regard a scientifically produced immortality as a challenge to God?

There will never be a scientifically produced immortality of the body. By scientific means men may do their best to prolong life against the ravages of disease, but they will never succeed in prolonging it indefinitely. But, whilst a scientifically produced immortality will never be a fact, the man who asserts that science will eliminate the necessity of having to die does issue a challenge to God. For God has told us that "it is appointed unto man once to die, and after that the judgment." Heb. IX., 27. We cannot, therefore, maintain that man will escape death by any natural means and secure an immortal life on earth.

31. Are you sure that, though the body must die, the soul will live on?
Yes, quite sure.

32. If only the fear that death might end all could be replaced by a firm conviction of a future life, many people would be made happy.
That is true. But it is also true that many would be rendered unhappy. There are two classes of people. Some fear that death might be the end of all. Some fear that it might not. Man cannot get away from his moral consciousness. Evil carries with it a sense of impending retribution, and those given to evil are rendered uneasy, not by the thought that death ends all, but by the thought that it might not. They have no desire to meet a just and omnipotent God.

33. What proof is there that the soul will live on?
We have the certainty of God's revelation. Christ said very definitely, "I go to prepare a place for you, that where I am you also may be." Jn. XIV., 3. That you have a prospect of eternal happiness means that you will survive. Again, Christ tells us that He will judge all mankind. Souls will have to be present for that judgment.

34. If a man believed in God, but did not believe in revelation, would not the question of immortality be unaffected?
Even apart from revelation such a man would have to admit immortality.
God is wise. He made man the highest form of creation in this world, and endowed him with reason. Man alone can know his Maker. And as love follows the knowledge of what is good, man can love his Maker. It would be an insult to the wisdom of God to suggest that He made such a being to live but a few years and then to end like a tree or a dog. And God is not only wise; He is just. If there is no future life, what of justice? Good and evil are not balanced in this life. Good people often suffer; the evil often do well. In fact, if there is no future life, there is no true morality, for there is no sufficient sanction. Rob, lie, murder—only be careful! If there be immortality, we can understand God reserving the full manifestation of justice for the next life. But if there be no immortality, then there is no God at all. For the dreadful doctrine that there is no immortality, the proofs should be pretty strong. But what proofs are there? There are none. Moreover, God is good. If you could save the life of a good man you would be glad to do it. Will you admit a God who allows good people to die for justice despite His ability to save them from death? The martyrs went to their death blessing and loving God. Would He let them do that knowing that He had nothing in store for them save the death of dogs? Believe me, the human soul is immortal.

35. How will the soul know anything when separated from the body? When unconscious through an injury to the brain, man knows nothing.
The soul does not depend upon the body for its existence. But for the operation of thought it does need the use of that bodily organ we call the brain, so long as it exists in our present composite state. By the body the soul is linked with this material world. And at present, material impressions drawn from physical experience provide the foundation for thought. Strictly speaking, thought is independent

of the brain. There is no real proportion between thought-activity and brain-activity. Whilst the soul remains united to the body, an affectation of the brain can cripple the thought-activities of the soul; even as a broken instrument can hinder the operations of an expert worker. But, when separated from the body, the soul will be in totally different conditions—conditions adapted entirely to its spiritual character, and independent of material limitations.

36. Psychologically, what will be the nature of a separated soul's experiences?

They will consist in the intellectual vision of purely spiritual realities, and a power to appreciate them. The soul does not see these realities now, because it is immersed in the body, and hindered from seeing in another light. Its proper spiritual light fades before sensitive experience. The light of the sun does not help us to see the stars. It obscures them. Yet the light of the sun is really dim compared with that of the stars. It is merely the nearest light. So death will be but a "revealing night." It will give spiritual freedom to the soul, emancipating it from the chains of mere matter. Then the soul will be immediately conscious of itself and of other beings invisible to us now. It will enter into its own world. It will be conscious of all other spiritual beings, and above all, of God. Here below, we gain fragmentary ideas of God by the study of His work in the whole of creation. After death has released the soul from the body, the soul will come into immediate contact with God as He is in Himself, provided it has deserved to do so. At any rate, God is meant to be the terminus of the soul's journey, so that life will carry us back to the Source of all life. Serious and unrepented sin can alone hinder its doing so, the result then being the disastrous wreckage in hell of all hopes and aspirations.

37. Granted that human souls are immortal, and endowed with intelligence and freewill, do they exist in eternity before their advent to this world?

The soul is created by God at the moment of conception. Prior to its creation it is simply non-existent. Some of the ancient Greek philosophers taught that the human soul had an existence before its union with the body, and that it is imprisoned in the body as a punishment for sins committed in its previous life. Aristotle refuted these opinions, pointing out the absurdity of an intelligent soul continuing its existence, yet having absolutely no memory of its previous doings, discoveries, and aspirations. Again, if we turn to the idea of punishment, it is irrational to have souls punished for unknown crimes in such a way that they can neither correct their faults nor acknowledge the justice of the penalty. Finally, if the soul pre-existed, it would do so as a complete entity in its own right. When united with the body, it could not form one composite personality such as we know man to be. Its presence in the body would be a kind of violent possession by an alien spirit. Such an idea is quite opposed to the naturalness of the union between soul and body—a union whose dissolution awakens so much mental apprehension and anxiety. It is certain, then, that human souls do not pre-exist.

38. You suggest that our eternal fate depends upon ourselves?

Yes. It is certain that man has freewill, and can choose what his eternal fate will be. If a man is in a state of serious sin and dies in such a state, he will go to hell. But he need not have remained in such a state until death took him. At any moment he could have turned to God, repented of his sins, got forgiveness, and chosen a line of conduct which would result in the salvation of his soul.

39. Some people deny freewill.

That is to deny a fact of which we are all quite conscious. I know quite well that, if I am answering these questions for you, it is because I have freely chosen to do so. Had I wished, I could have thrown your letter aside, and simply ignored it. At any moment whilst answering, I am free to cease, and turn to the next letter. To tell me that I haven't freewill would be about as intelligible as telling me that I don't exist. The denial of freewill is absurd, and any position which can be reduced to absurdity collapses by the very fact.

40. Do you not say that God is omnipotent, and that His providence extends to all things? In such a case we have to do as He has planned.

Therefore, since He has planned that we should act in many things according to our free choice, we have no option but to admit the existence of freewill.

41. Then all we do is according to His will?

That we are free is according to His positive will; if we exercise that freedom in an evil direction, it is in accordance with His permissive will. I do not mean that He gives us permission in the moral sense to do evil, for He forbids that. But He permits us to be physically free in the sense that He will not compel us to be good in spite of ourselves.

42. Does not that make God responsible for the evil we do?

No. For example, God wills that I should not commit murder. But He has also willed that I should possess freewill, and be master of my own destiny. That necessarily carries with it the possibility of either obeying God's law, or of rebelling against it. And by the very gift of freedom, God must will to permit my defection from duty, even though He forbids it. In His very omnipotence He does not use His omnipotence to prevent my crime. I see many things done which I feel that I would certainly prevent if I had only half God's power. I feel sure that I wouldn't be strong enough to restrain myself. To be able to do it, yet not to do it, would be too much for me. But if I were God, and absolutely omnipotent, and had His wisdom, then just what God does and permits, I would do and permit. All that happens therefore is in accordance with God's will insofar as that will includes all circumstances, and conditions, and interdependent secondary agents, and the many influences which provide a problem ever bewildering to man.

43. Since God willed both the death of Christ and its attendant circumstances, where was the freedom of Judas in betraying Christ?

In the passion and death of Christ many things were due to God's positive will, but many, on the other hand, were due to God's permissive will. That God merely permitted Judas to indulge an evil will, and did not positively inspire his action, is evident from the Gospel itself. Had Judas been compelled to act as he did against his own will, he would not have been morally responsible. Yet the very Gospels which tell us of the fact that he did betray Christ, tell us also that he was morally guilty in doing so. Therefore he was free not to do so. Thus Christ reproached him, "Judas, dost thou betray the Son of Man with a kiss?" Our Lord did not say, "Judas, you have to do this, so I can scarcely blame you." So, too, in Acts I., 25, we are told that "Judas hath by transgression fallen." It is obvious, therefore, from Scripture, that Judas was responsible for his action.

A difficulty might arise in your mind from the fact that God had predicted through the prophets that Judas would betray Christ. But that does not prove compulsion. It was not predicted that Judas "must" betray Christ. The prediction was based on the fact that he "would" do so by his own free choice. Judas did not do so because it had been predicted. More expressly we are certain that God's will was not impelling Judas because we are clearly told by God's word that "Satan entered into Judas," and that he then went to the chief priests. Lk. XXII., 3-4. Now the will of Satan is radically opposed to the will of God. But this leads to a second possible difficulty. If not compelled by the will of God, was Judas compelled by the will of Satan? It is obvious that he was not, since the Gospels hold him to be personally responsible. If Judas did the will of Satan it was because he freely consented to do so. There was no need for him to do so; and if he obeyed the suggestions of Satan, he did so voluntarily. We know, too, of our Lord's own efforts to win him to better dispositions prior to the crime.

44. God makes man, and also the will of man. Man did not make his own will any more than he gave himself his intelligence.

You are confusing man's will as a radical power of choice with its exercise in a given direction. The two things are not the same. God made man's will, but He did not "make it up" for man, so that it was determined independently of man in a given direction. Man makes the choice his will enables him to make, though he need not make that choice. If man exercises his power in a wrong way, it is not the power that causes him to do so; it is man's own soul and personality which uses its will wrongly. The murderer does not make his own hand; but he makes that hand throttle his victim. There is a difference between the possession of a power and the use of that power.

45. Leaving God out of it, I still do not believe in freewill. I believe in psychological determinism.

There are no facts of psychology which justify the denial of freewill.

46. Medical men say that a man is, for good or evil, what his brain cells make him.

Not all medical men say that. Those who do may know their physiology, but they betray lamentable ignorance of psychology and philosophy. Brain cells are still brain cells, whether they are living or dead. If they are dead, they cannot make a man anything. If they are living, they owe it to a principle of life distinct from themselves. That principle of life is the rational soul of man. Brain cells do not produce thought. The intelligent soul produces thought, using the data provided by the brain as the central exchange recording sense-experiences in the various terminal faculties.

It is quite true that the soul is "conditioned by" the body and by the brain, just as any worker by the quality of his instruments. And in this sense, inherited bodily characteristics or defective bodily qualities can affect a man's character to a great extent. But that does not justify the statement that brain cells make a man good or evil, as if there were no other principles at work in him. Then, too, men equally endowed with well-formed brain cells can employ their capacity in totally different directions, one devoting to a criminal career faculties which would have carried him to the top of the ladder in some honest profession; another devoting intellectual powers to good purposes despite the fact that he could have employed them in criminal pursuits. It is not always a question of heredity. Nor does heredity obey invariable laws.

47. Of course we like to think that we act according to our own deliberate choosing.

There are those who are tainted by an out-of-date materialistic philosophy who like to think that we do not act according to our own deliberate choosing. And they ignore the facts, whilst the normal judgment of the human race is in full accordance with the facts. The most advanced scientists and physicists today are coming back to common sense. In his book, "The Mysteries of the Atom," 1934, Professor Wilson says that in the materialistic conception of the universe prevailing in the nineteenth century, freewill was thought to be impossible, but that the new physics have upset that materialistic conception. "The course of events," he writes, "is not determined by the laws of nature; these merely enable the probability of each possible event to be calculated." What, then, controls the conduct of a human being if natural laws do not? Professor Wilson replies, "The only answer to this question is that we do not know—unless the brain is controlled by spiritual forces not usually included in the physicist's scheme." And he points out that, on the new wave-particle theory of physics, there is always a choice of many possible events for a human being, and that such freedom of will involves no violation of natural law according to the new scientific conception of the universe.

48. *If we know beforehand a person's psychological make-up, we know what he will do or say.*

We do not know the psychological make-up of other people to any great extent. They do not know it themselves. Man is ever a mystery, even to himself. And such faint indications of psychological make-up as we do possess do not enable us to know in advance what our friends will do or say. We have at best a more or less probable conjecture, and our friends are liable at any moment to do the most unexpected things.

49. *We know the number of murders that will be committed next year. How could we know that, if criminals are free?*

We do not "know" the number of murders that will be committed next year. From statistics we can form a probable conjecture. But the conjecture as to what will happen is no proof whatever that it must happen, or that individuals who will commit murder will do so by psychological compulsion. If I know that a man has been working for the last four or five years at a given office, I can form a fairly good idea that he will travel there as usual tomorrow morning. But that does not prove that he cannot choose not to go there tomorrow morning. Nor does a conjecture as to the average number of crimes that will take place next year throw any light on the question of freedom of will, unless one can say which individuals will necessarily commit those crimes—and that cannot be done by any manner of means.

50. *Criminals are products of heredity and environment.*

That is a sweeping and very unscientific assertion. That heredity and environment have an effect upon people to some extent no sensible person will deny. That they necessarily produce a certain type of character is against the facts. Man's reason enables him to perceive the evil character of certain instinctive tendencies, and to conjure up other ideas of his own dignity, personal worth, social standards, and moral values, which neutralize the force of original influences. And man's will enables him to make a free choice of an evil course of conduct, or of a good course of conduct. If heredity and environment determined one's conduct, children of the same family and brought up in the same environment should equally follow the same line of conduct. But they do not. From the most favorable heredity and environment criminals have developed, whilst people have risen above the most unfavorable heredity and environment to become splendid types, through encouragement to take themselves in hand, practice self-control, and to choose deliberately against inherited tendencies. I have met men of the utmost integrity whose brothers have been criminals; deeply religious people from thoroughly irreligious families; children of the same stock and circumstances who have chosen vastly different careers in life, and opposite standards of conduct. It is against the facts to say that heredity and environment determine character by sheer necessity.

Radio Replies—Volume II

51. *The determinist tries to cure criminals where the believer in freewill merely punishes them.*

You take for granted the very thing you must prove. The real difficulty arises for the determinist who attempts to cure a criminal who necessarily acts in a criminal way. You may urge that we can alter the factors that determine his conduct. But that he is determined by such factors supposes the thing you have to prove—that he has no freewill. Granted freewill, attempts to cure the criminal are not excluded. We can try to alter the factors which influence without determining his conduct, and also try to induce a change of will on his own part. And a cure is much more likely on our principles than on the determinist hypothesis.

52. *Naturally in extreme cases, like that of a homicidal maniac, the determinist would probably fail to effect a cure.*

He would fail in a good many other cases, too. Moreover, with his denial of personal responsibility, were his doctrine inculcated in children from their earliest years, he would find that the growing number of criminals would give him more than enough to do. It is significant that, with the driftage from Christian principles, there is becoming more and more evident an increase in crime. A merely secular education which rejoices the materialist far from preventing crime seems but to give it an impetus. In his report on juvenile delinquency to a select Government Committee in London last year, 1939, the appointed expert said, "I consider that a return to the old-fashioned type of religious instruction is essential. I am not a Roman Catholic, but I do honor them for making religious instruction a prime feature in the education of the children of their adherents. A good moral foundation predisposes a young person to eschew evil ways in later life. I would cut out all the fancy stuff in schools, expressionism, pseudo-psychological experimenting, and other foolish 'isms' and 'ologies,' which have no rightful place in a properly run educational establishment." One of the "isms" which should be excluded from any influence in education is psychological determinism.

53. *The correct method of stamping out crime is to attack their causes.*

I agree. But what are the causes? A mechanical deterministic philosophy will never reveal them. It would produce the greatest cause of all—a lack of the sense of personal responsibility and of capability of self-management.

54. *You would punish a criminal because you believe his wickedness to be solely his own fault.*

That is not true. I have never suggested that a criminal's evil conduct is solely his own fault in every case. Believers in freewill make due allowance for such factors as do diminish personal guilt. We certainly say that criminals do deserve punishment insofar as it is their own fault that they have committed crime. That is sensible. But to adopt the attitude of the determinist who denies freewill, and declares that no man is ever morally guilty of any evil he does, violates common sense and the sound principles of reason and observation.

55. *Do you imagine that, if everybody believed in determinism, men would commit crimes with impunity?*

No. I do not hold that the community would appoint no penalties for crime. I agree with Professor Joad's verdict that, if determinism is true, morality must lose its meaning. But, on their own principles, determinists would be determined to act as if determinism was not true, and as if morality was significant, just as they would have to be regarded as determined to think their determinism true when it isn't. That would be the only explanation of their moral indignation with wicked people who, if their theory were right, have no choice but to be wicked. But, if criminals could not escape with impunity, a deterministic philosophy, if adopted, would certainly tend to their multiplication. One is much more likely to develop reliable characters by teaching conscious and deliberate self-control with a sense of moral responsibility than by teaching that people are but the playthings of uncontrollable forces and inclinations. In his book, "The Threshold of Ethics," Dr. Kirk rightly says, "The habit of looking for automatisms, necessities, and compulsions, in our estimates of character, which is generated by the theory of determinism, is a habit which leads wholly in a non-moral direction. The more I treat myself as a plaything of irresistible forces, the more I shall tend to neglect self-criticism and self-discipline; and the less I shall resist the seductive temptations of self-pity, self-excuse, and self-justification."

56. *We cannot escape heredity. You cannot produce a thoroughbred racehorse from a pair of broken-down hacks.*

If man be no more than a beast, your analogy might apply. But if man is no more than a beast, you must not be surprised if he behaves as a beast. However, man is not a mere animal. Nor is character merely a matter of bodily characteristics only. Some of the finest types of men have arisen from the most unimpressive parentage; and from the best stock defective types have resulted. *Freewill is a fact*, and a psychological factor in the development of character which cannot be ignored. And upon the use of man's freewill his eternal destiny will depend.

See also R. R., Vol. I, Nos. 25-56 on the subject of Man.

CHAPTER THREE

RELIGION

57. What can religion do for God?
It enables us to render to Him the acknowledgment due to Him, and inspires us to obey His laws. We can thus respond in some way to His own great love for us.

58. He can need it very little.
He does not need it at all. But He must needs demand that we do what it is right for us to do. We are unjust if we do not return love for love, and gratitude for gifts received. And not God's future well-being, but our future well-being, is inextricably bound up with our fulfillment of religious duties.

59. Service to our fellow men can do a great deal, and they need it badly.
I agree. But religion does not mean the service of God at the expense of our neighbors. The greater one's love of God, the greater and truer will be his love of his neighbors.

60. Reason is enough to tell me what to know and to do.
Reason, when it is right, is good enough as far as it goes. But it is very liable to error, and when right, does not go far enough. We need the additional truth revealed by God and taught us by the Christian religion. Reason cannot refute the claims of Christ, and in fact disposes us to accept them. Certainly reason cannot replace religion. It gives inadequate knowledge only, and cannot give any vital impulse to observe its own moral precepts.

61. Why cannot a man live a good life without religion?
He can do some good things without religion. He can refrain from drunkenness, and pay his debts to his fellow men. But he cannot live a really good life unless he does the main thing for which he was made. And the main thing is that he knows, loves, and serves God, and regulates his conduct towards his fellow men by motives of love for God.

62. I have sound ideas of goodness and morality, and can live up to them without religion.
Your very ideas of what is good and moral are drawn from the general Christian culture of the civilization in which you live. To want your moral standards without the religion which gave rise to them is like wanting rain without wanting the ocean from which it is drawn. Renan admitted that to abolish Christianity, yet to wish to retain its ethics, is merely to inhale a perfume from an empty bottle. Men cannot live on perfumes; and even if they could, the emptiness of the bottle will soon mean the end of the perfume. Again, if the Christian religion is true, as it is, then it is necessary for goodness and morality. For its very acceptance will be part of morality, involving the discharging of our debt to God. Religion is as necessary to good morals as the right course is necessary to good navigation.

63. On the whole, I think religion good for women.
It is. Religion gives them their character and happiness. It gives to that sex which has ever been regarded as frail the nobility of angels, of virtue, of sweetness and devotedness. Such are our mothers. But this does not imply that religion is

not good also for men. When you say that religion is good for women, do you mean that religion is false? Evidently not, because then it would not be good for anyone. Do you mean that women alone have souls to save? Ancient pagans denied that women had any rights in the field of religion on the score that they had no souls. But no one doubted that men had souls. Do you mean that men belong to earth only, and that heaven is reserved for women? A man needs religion every bit as much as a woman. And it is his duty to be religious, rendering to God the acknowledgment and service due to Him from all intelligent creatures.

64. *I have led a happy and contented life, the crux of all human endeavor. Why is religion necessary if this can be attained without religion?*

Firstly, the crux of all human endeavor ought not to be the securing of a happy and contented life in this world. Man's main duty is the religious service of God. If you are able to be happy, you owe it to God that you exist, and that those things exist which give you happiness. You, therefore, owe to God the acknowledgment of your debt to Him by religious worship, offering Him your praise and gratitude. To take all, and enjoy it without the slightest manifestation of gratitude to God, is both unjust and most ill-mannered.

Again, if you seek happiness, seek it properly whilst you are at it. This world is not all. Your soul is immortal, and eternity awaits you. If the sole source of your happiness lies in the things of this world, then you are living in a fool's paradise. No man can escape death, and every cause of happiness for you will be taken from you whether you like it or not. You brought nothing into this world with you, and you will take nothing of it with you when you die. Where then will you find happiness? Religion is our bond with God who made us, and the earnest and fervent practice of religion keeps us in touch with the God whom we are to meet some day, and with whom we are to be forever, if we are to know happiness hereafter. Your own happiness, therefore, is bound up with your religious duties to God, and you owe Him the acknowledgment which you can render Him only by discharging the debt of religion. Neglect that duty, and you are guilty of a great injustice, and you will make wreckage of your eternity. On your deathbed you may say that you "have had" many happinesses during life. But you won't have them then. They came—only to go; and the memory of them will be no compensation for the miseries you will encounter, and which will never go. Be reasonably happy in this life, if you wish. But take up your duties of religion, make sure of your eternal happiness in the next life, and at all costs save your soul.

65. *What precisely do you mean by the saving of one's soul?*

The meaning of that requires a brief analysis of man. Man consists of body and soul. The body is material and perishable; the soul is spiritual and imperishable. But the soul is the real you. It is the soul which knows and loves, is happy or miserable. Now as the soul is immortal, it enters at death into an eternal state, whether it be one of supreme happiness, or of direst misery. By "saving one's soul" I mean going from this world in the grace and friendship of God, so that one avoids eternal misery, and secures eternal happiness.

66. *What are the conditions of salvation?*

That we serve God in this life, doing what He commands, and avoiding what He forbids. That surely is evident. If men have not always done what God commands, or have not always avoided what He forbids, they must at least be sincerely repentant of their sins before they go from this life to meet their eternal Judge.

67. *Religion seems to me to be based on superstition and fear.*

Religion as such is certainly not based on superstition, despite the folly into which some people have fallen where religion is concerned. As regards fear, which is by no means the same thing as superstition, nor necessarily supposes it, all genuine religion is based on a reverential and proper fear of God. For the fear of the Lord is the beginning of wisdom. Craven fear has no place in genuine religion. If any people have adopted religion through motives of craven fear, their conduct would be wrong, and their dispositions would have to be condemned. Their duty would be to rise to higher motives, and seek a proper spirit of religion.

68. *Don't you think that where science advances, religion is rejected?*

No. In some people pretended science can destroy religion either because of their limited mental powers, or because of their pride and self-conceit. Others do not so much love science as hate religion owing to its conflict with their vices. And their continued talk of a love for science (of which they know little or nothing) is a kind of alibi by which they try to conceal their dislike of religion and pretend to impartiality. The really scientific find no tendency to abandon religion on the score of any conflicting evidence. Science has dethroned the sun-god, Jupiter, stone-gods, and other false deities. It has demolished sorcery, incantations, oracles, and other superstitions to some extent. But true religion remains; and the really scientific mind admits willingly that life is a bigger thing than this earth, and that science itself can never satisfy the needs of human nature.

69. *Does not over-concentration on religion tend to insanity?*

To overdo anything is a mistake, and this applies even to religion. A well-balanced man avoids extremes in all departments of life, whether by excess, or by defect. And just as one can damage his health by eating too much, or by not eating at all, so one can injure his mind and soul by religious over-indulgence or by neglect of religion. Over-concentration on any particular subject can lead to extraordinary ideas. Thus over-concentration on gangster stories can give a highly impressionable youth the fixed idea that he must go out and distribute gratuitous bullets. I admit that over-concentration in religious directions is likely to be more dangerous than in other matters. For religion is so much a part of man's very being, and of his complete nature, gripping mind and heart and will, and embracing man's imaginative and emotional tendencies, and reaching deep down into the subconscious recesses of the soul. People disposed to insanity therefore, are ever likely to break out into some form of religious mania. That is why religion needs a rational and common-sense approach as few things else. Yet common sense does not go to the other extreme, and neglect religious obligations altogether. There may be religious cranks. But not every religious man is a crank; and to be without any religion is as much a violation of reason and common sense by defect as it is to fall into excess.

70. *It's my opinion that religion is a racket, designed to provide a living for those who propagate it.*

Do you know anything at all about Christ? Can you find anything in the four Gospels to hint that He designed His religion to provide a living in this world only? When He called His apostles to leave their ordinary means of a livelihood, He did not offer them an easier and more lucrative profession. Religion, of course, like anything else is liable to abuse. Some people undoubtedly have made a money-spinning racket out of religion. And they cannot be too strongly condemned. But that does not justify your sweeping assertion that religion is designed for that purpose. If being provided with a living were the motive, I can assure you that it would never have inspired me to become a Catholic Priest, nor could it inspire me to remain one. Life could offer me much more elsewhere.

71. *If money were completely left out of consideration, there would not be so many advocates of religion.*

There might be more, from one point of view. For a great many people talk religion, but forget about it once there is any mention of self-sacrifice on behalf of religion. Genuine religion requires the fitting worship of God by man both in his social and individual capacity. Public worship requires Churches, and men set apart to devote their lives to the cause of religion. Genuine religion also requires the proper education of children in their duties to God, to themselves, and to mankind; and this requires schools. Genuine religion also demands works of charity to the destitute and to the sick; and this requires orphanages, hospitals and other institutions. All these things require money. And those who subscribe to these things do so from a sense of religion. Meantime, those who lack the same generosity, sneer at the commercialism of religion.

72. *I have all I need, without the aid of any religion.*

Do you mean that you have no religion because you don't see what you would get out of it? If it were profitable, would you adopt it? Your judgment of others really reflects your own attitude in the matter. And your boasting of your possessions is like that of one who boasts of his luxuries and of the fact that he has never paid for them. You are indebted to God for all you have, but leave that debt unpaid, rendering no acknowledgment to Him. There are thousands of people who would never tolerate from their own children the indifference and contempt they expect God to tolerate from them.

73. *Without any formal religion, people should be left to their own quiet thoughts about the Almighty.*

I agree that they would not find that very expensive. It should therefore appeal to all people who are devoid of any spirit of self-sacrifice. But I would suggest that thoughts of the Almighty would be very few and far between in people lacking any education in matters of religion. The substitute you propose in place of religion is very flimsy, unsubstantial, and vague. Quiet thoughts about the Almighty do not constitute religion. Religion requires much more than that.

74. *You claim that not only is religion necessary to man, but that he needs a revealed religion?*

Yes. The world of mysterious reality proper to God is supernatural and inaccessible to us by our own unaided natural powers—a vast ocean of being, as Fr. Sertillanges well remarks, for which we have no boat, and in which all created reality is a kind of lost island on which we live. Revelation by God is necessary if we are to know truths belonging to that mysterious supernatural order of being.

75. *The only source of all our knowledge is the visible and tangible universe about us.*

The universe is the natural source of natural knowledge. But it is not the source of all knowledge. God Himself, who is distinct from all the natural things He has created, and supernatural in comparison with them, can make known to man in a supernatural way certain information about Himself and His relationships with men which could not be naturally acquired. In short, whilst the created universe is the source of natural knowledge, God Himself is the source of supernatural knowledge. He has stepped in, as it were, and given men information they could never have attained had He not so acted.

76. *Even revelation could come only through man's natural powers.*

That is true. But we must not confuse the means by which information comes to us, and the nature and source of that information. I could transmit information to you by telephone. But the information given, as the person giving it, would be in a totally different and higher order of being than the merely material and mechanical instrument used to convey it.

77. It would have to be a spiritual experience coming to us through our senses.

That would be necessary were I, on your own level and in the same order of being as yourself, revealing something to you. I would have to speak, and you would have to hear. For all our normal communications of knowledge are through the senses. But God could communicate to the soul, not as united to the body and the senses, but as an intelligence, whatever ideas He may please. He could do this by immediate interior inspiration, without the senses intervening at all. Of course, in reflecting upon these ideas the soul would use the brain, and try to formulate them in words however inadequately, drawing analogies from sense-data. Any knowledge of supernatural reality thus infused by God, whilst infallibly true, would necessarily remain mysterious to us.

78. The appeal to the mysterious is an appeal to the absurd.

Mysteries revealed by God are truths above the capacity of human reason, but they are not absurd. They are not against reason; they are above reason. If words cannot convey their full sense, no one can prove them to be nonsense. Whatever reason can urge against their truth, reason itself can refute. But reason cannot positively explain their full significance. As a matter of fact, far from being absurd, mysteries are the opposite. The absurd is evidence of the false. But mysteries revealed by God are merely the grandeur of truth itself. They simply bring out the fact that truth is a much greater thing than the small particles of it which the human mind is able to grasp.

79. Does not this mean the abdication of reason?

No. It presupposes the exercise of reason. It is reasonable to believe what God Himself says of Himself and of His purposes. It is quite reasonable, where we can't see clearly, to accept the authority of God who sees all.

80. If we are given the truth about God, I don't see why there should be all this obscurity.

God Himself is not obscure. The trouble lies in our own limitations and in our lack of capacity to understand Him completely. But that does not say that we cannot know that He exists, and that we cannot know quite a lot about Him. Reason, if developed, admits an infinity of things beyond it. If it hasn't got that far it has scarcely commenced work.

81. Would it not have been possible to reveal a clear religion, easy for all to believe?

Granted a revelation of supernatural truth, there is bound to be some obscurity for us. I say for us, because these truths are not obscure in themselves. God sees their full significance as clearly as you see the noonday sun. But the human mind lacks the capacity to see their full significance just as the human eye cannot see infra-red or ultra-violet light rays. By other means we are sure of the reality of these rays. And whilst human reason cannot see for itself that the Trinity, for example, is a fact, by knowledge of God's revelation we are sure that it is a fact.

82. One who accepts revealed religion is expected to believe in miracles.

Revelation includes the fact that miracles have occurred.

MIRACLES AND SCIENTIFIC CERTAINTY

83. *What is a miracle?*

A miracle is an extraordinary event beyond the powers and outside the scope of any created agency, and therefore produced by God Himself. No natural forces could account for it.

84. *When you say that nature cannot account for a miracle, what do you mean by nature?*

Nature can refer to the whole created universe, with all its proper forces and powers; or it can refer to each individual thing in the universe, as when we say that the nature of a man differs from the nature of a beast. But, whether taken in reference to each created thing, or to all created things, nature embraces all that these things can be or do according to the constitution and powers given them by their Creator. And we maintain that the miraculous transcends completely all these powers.

85. *Most people would be very surprised to hear that miracles take place.*

As an extraordinary event not due to natural causes, every miracle is calculated to surprise us to some extent. Of its very nature it is a surprising thing. But, from another point of view, we are not surprised that God should at times work miracles. He is not bound by the secondary laws He Himself appointed as the normal causes of events in this universe.

86. *I am afraid I could never believe in miracles. They are much too strange for me.*

We are naturally inclined to be astonished by the unusual, but we are not justified in denying the truth of an event merely because it is unusual. "The government of the whole universe is a much more wonderful thing than the multiplication of five loaves of bread," says St. Augustine, "but men are not astonished by the former because they are used to it, whilst they are astonished by the latter because it is rare." Granted an omnipotent God, it is absurd to say that miracles cannot happen. Belief in a miracle depends entirely upon the available evidence as to whether it did happen. As a matter of fact, miracles seem strange only to minds which make no allowance for God. He who lives in the presence of God is not surprised to see God act. It is as easy for God to restore life to a dead man as to preserve the life of a living man.

87. *Miracles seem so arbitrary, and so destructive of scientific certainty.*

The God who arbitrarily created all things, and who arbitrarily established the ordinary laws of nature, is not bound to restrict Himself to those ordinary laws. He may arbitrarily intervene and act independently of ordinary natural laws should He wish. Nor are miracles destructive of scientific certainty. After all, no scientist can be certain of what you yourself will choose to do tomorrow. And if that does not destroy scientific certainty, why should it be destroyed by uncertainty as to what God will do? Scientific certainty can be had concerning natural facts. When a supernatural fact occurs, science can testify to the historical occurrence of the event, and then declare that the nature of the event is not within the boundaries of ordinary science. Thus, of a sudden and miraculous cure, science can say, "That person had a broken leg five minutes ago, and now he has not a broken leg. Negatively I can say that no merely natural power can account for the phenomenon." And there natural science stops.

88. *Would your faith be greatly disturbed if the miracles recorded in the Bible never really happened at all?*

It would not only be disturbed. It would be shattered. If any man could prove that the miracles recorded in the Bible did not happen, or that miracles could not happen, I would abandon Christianity altogether. But to disprove miracles you must prove one of three things: You must prove either that there is no God; or that God cannot operate independently of the laws of nature He Himself established; or that the Bible is a lying forgery and not authentic history. No man can prove any of these things.

89. Since people do not believe in miracles today, why should they believe in miracles that happened 2000 years ago?

Some people believe that miracles happen in our own day; others do not. I certainly believe that they can happen; and am prepared to believe that any given event is a miracle provided satisfactory evidence can be produced that it did occur, and that it surpasses the capability of any natural law.

Yet even if miracles did not happen in our own times, that would not be proof that they did not happen 2000 years ago. Events of 2000 years ago must be judged on the evidence of what happened then; not on the evidence of what does not happen now. In other words, the historical evidence for past miracles must be examined on its own merits. It would not be disproved by any absence of miracles now. Otherwise you could prove that women never wore hoop skirts by the fact that the modern woman does not happen to do so.

90. If miracles have ceased to take place, why have they ceased?

Miracles have not ceased to occur. There are three classes of miracles: intellectual, moral, and physical. Prophecy is an intellectual miracle, for it is the prediction with certainty of future events, often dependent upon human liberty. God alone can know with certainty what a given human being will do, say in ten years' time; or what future generations of men will decide to do. A moral miracle is one which does not surpass the inherent capacity of created powers, but which does surpass the ordinary laws regulating them. Thus the unity of some 400 millions of people in the Catholic Faith—people of different nationalities and varying degrees of intelligence; people who probably disagree on almost every other matter, is a moral miracle. God alone can be responsible for their allegiance to the Catholic Church. Physical miracles are sudden external and astonishing events beyond all created powers—an obvious work of God quite outside God's ordinary providence; such as the sudden cure of a broken leg or the instant restoration to perfect health of one suffering from consumption or cancer in an advanced stage. Miracles of all three classes have occurred right through the ages from the time of Christ until our own days. An exhaustive study of the records at Lourdes, or of the lives of the Saints in every century, or of the Archives of the Congregation of Rites, where the most scientific evidence of modern miracles is collected, would convince you of this.

See also R. R., Vol. I, Nos. 57-84.

CHAPTER FOUR

THE RELIGION OF THE BIBLE

91. You regard the Gospel authors as historians?

I insist on the historical value of the Gospels.

92. Critics maintain that the Gospels are not historical in the proper sense of the word.

Similar comments can be found in quite orthodox and excellent Catholic works. For example, in his book, "Christ and the Critics," Felder says that the Evangelists certainly intended to write history, and were subjectively qualified to report correctly the words and deeds of Jesus. But he adds that they had not "a high, scientific education, nor critical precision. But these they did not need. It was not a matter of solving deep problems, or of extracting the truth from old bundles of documents and examining it critically. They merely had to write down perfectly concrete deeds which had been enacted for the most part in public, and were of the utmost simplicity. They were not compiling an account of past centuries; nor did they even pay attention to the chronological sequence of events or the requirements of scientific arrangement. For this reason the Gospels are not historical works in the strictest sense of the term. But, although the Evangelists were not historians in the sense of Thucydides, the father of critical historical composition, they did write down the facts of the Gospel in accordance with the truth."

93. Are not the Gospels entirely set in a theological context to serve theological purposes?

It would be a gross exaggeration to say that. A remarkable feature of the Gospels is their adherence to a bare delineation of facts. Even where we should expect them to make capital out of what they write, they don't. Miraculous events are given without any expressions of astonishment or triumph. Ill-treatment of their Master is recorded without a word of indignation. If the writers were bent on supporting a thesis, having little regard for historical truth, they would have been fools to invent "hard sayings" which could only alienate people; to record that Christ's own relatives thought Him mad; that He was weak enough to pray that the cup of suffering might pass from Him; to paint a picture of a humiliated, mocked, and crucified criminal whom they wanted men to worship; and to insist that His own people rejected Him. If His own rejected Him, why on earth should others accept Him? No. They record what happened as if their only interest were that of observers and narrators. I admit that the idea of theological purpose is not without application to the Fourth Gospel. But that does not hinder the truth of the facts given.

94. The Old Testament penetration of the Gospels is not usually recognized.

All Scripture scholars have recognized the Old Testament penetration of the Gospels. That would naturally be there in books written by Jews educated by the reading and study of the Old Testament, and dealing with One who came to fulfill the religion of the Old Testament. But this has no bearing on the historical value of the Gospels. It is your approach to this question which is at fault. Liberal criticism, in its search for the historical Jesus, does not begin with history and thus try to build up the real Christ. It begins with its own modern views about Christ, and because these do not fit in with the historical records, it does not reach the conclusion that its own views are unhistorical—it argues that the really historical accounts of Christ must be legendary. Critics who do proceed historically recognize more and more the sterling value of the Gospels. Only insofar as they depart from the strictly historical method of research does the legendary theory gain in importance. It is a violation of science to destroy a purely historic question in favor of a philosophic principle. And even were their philosophy not false, the procedure of modern liberal critics would be unscientific. Liberal criticism is guilty of the very error it wants to shift off on to the Gospels. It wants to tamper with history in order to adjust it to a modern agnostic outlook.

95. Critics are unable to say with any confidence who wrote the various books.

That is too sweeping a statement, and already uncritical itself. For, whilst some critics feel that they are unable to do so, other critics are most confident in ascribing the works to very definite authors. Those who profess to be doubtful are themselves to blame for their doubts. For they give too much prominence to purely internal considerations, neglecting outside factors drawn from independent patristic and early ecclesiastical writers. At any rate, it is quite misleading to ascribe any opinion to "the critics" as though there were no diversity of opinion amongst men versed in Biblical criticism.

96. How can the Bible be worthy of credence when it quotes books that are missing, such as the Book of the Wars of the Lord, Book of Jashur, the Acts of Solomon, the Book of Gad the Seer, etc.?

If certain inspired books were missing, that would not be proof that such books as have remained are not inspired and trustworthy. But, secondly, the books you mention were most probably not inspired books at all. The sacred authors could be inspired to quote non-inspired books known to the people of their time, in support of the facts they narrated. If the quoted books have perished, so that we cannot consult them as those could do who were recommended to do so, that does not give us the right to reject the authority of the Old Testament books handed on to us. In fact, we find force in the confidence of a writer who did not hesitate to refer the readers of his own time to outside sources which were then available.

97. Are the Christian Fathers Irenaeus, Chrysostom, Clement of Alexandria, and Theodoret correct when they say that all the Books were burned in the Babylonian captivity?

This opinion which occurs in some of the writings of the Fathers is not correct. They relied upon a passage in the Fourth Book of Esdras, XIV., 18-47. But this book is an apocryphal book written in the First Century A.D. by an unknown Palestinian Jew, five centuries after the time of Esdras. This author gives no authority save his own personal and subjective visions. In the Books of the Old Testament written near the actual time of the real Esdras, or well before the time of Christ, no mention is made of the destruction of the Books by fire. In II Machabees 11, 13, we are told that Nehemias, a contemporary of Esdras, made a collection of the Sacred Books, but we are told nothing about a fire. Neither Josephus nor the Talmud make any mention of it.

98. I wish to suggest that the Books of the Old Testament came into existence for the first time when reputedly found in the Temple.

I realize that; but the references you give fail completely to support your assumption.

99. *Is it not implied in II Kings XXII., 8; and Chronicles, 2nd Book, XXXIV., 14, that the Jews did not know of the existence of the Books of Moses prior to 628 B.C.?*

Most certainly not. Hilkiah, the high priest, immediately recognized the definite Book of the Law, as known in previous times. The king himself did not doubt for a moment that these were the ancient Books which "our fathers" should have heard and obeyed. The people did not for a moment believe that these were new Books, of whose previous existence they had known nothing.

100. *Was Irenaeus correct when he said that the Books of the Old Testament were fabricated seventy years after the Babylonian captivity by Esdras?*

I deny that Irenaeus ever said that. In his Adversus Haereses, Bk. III., c. 21, he says that Esdras collected the words of preceding prophets, and restored to the people the Mosaic law in its original order, just as it was given by Moses. There is no hint of "fabrication" in this classic passage.

101. *James Bruce, in 1774, discovered Ethiopian manuscripts of the lost Book of Enoch, which was in current use in the time of Christ, and from which Christ Himself quoted. Yet that Book is missing from the Old Testament.*

The original Book of Enoch was the work of various Jewish authors who wrote between the years 170 B.C. and 64 B.C. It was originally written in Hebrew. But the Ethiopian translations of the Book were derived from a Greek translation of the Hebrew. The Ethiopian manuscripts found by Bruce were, therefore, post-Christian documents, and there is no doubt that many expressions in them which are identical with the words of our Lord are simply interpolations. Many of the sentences do not fit in with the Ethiopian context at all. In other words, instead of Jesus quoting the Book of Enoch, the Ethiopian translations have incorporated His words borrowed from the Gospels. This, however, does not alter the fact that the original Book of Enoch did influence the New Testament writers. The Book was well known at the time, and both our Lord and St. Paul could have made use of its familiar ideas.

102. *It is incredible that Christ should have used the Book of Enoch yet that it should be missing from the Old Testament.*

There is no particular reason why that should be incredible. Every Book contained in our Canon of the Bible is inspired. That is certain. It is certain, also, that the Church has not included the Book of Enoch in the Canon of the Old Testament. Two questions can here arise. Was the original Book of Enoch inspired? If so, ought it to have been included in our Bible? To the first question we can but say that the original Enoch may or may not have been inspired. The divine inspiration of the Bible would not be affected by its containing quotations from non-inspired sources. To the second question we say that, even were the Book of Enoch inspired, its omission from the Canon of inspired Books affords no difficulty. We are obliged to believe that every Book included in the Canon is inspired. But we have not to believe that every Book that has ever been inspired by God is in the Bible. The preservation of every such Book is not necessary for the preservation of God's revealed religion. God could preserve the substance of revealed truth by means of the Church, permitting inspired Books or parts of them to be lost.

103. *St. Jude quotes the Book of Enoch as inspired.*

St. Jude does not quote the Book of Enoch as inspired. The quotation from St. Jude is as follows: "Now of these Enoch also, the seventh from Adam, **prophesied,** saying: Behold the Lord cometh with thousands of His saints to execute judgment." Jude, I, 14. The Book of Enoch was obviously not written by Enoch, the seventh from Adam, who is mentioned in Genesis, V., 18-24. It was written, as I have said, by Jewish authors between 170 and 64 B.C., who chose the name of Enoch as its title. The prophecy of Enoch, the seventh from Adam, was known by tradition.

104. Why does not the Church restore to the Old Testament this extremely valuable Ethiopian Enoch?

Firstly, the Ethiopian Enoch is not the original Book of Enoch. It is an Ethiopian translation of a Greek translation; and its integrity cannot be accepted.

Secondly, even did we discover an exact copy of the original Book of Enoch, we cannot speak of "restoring" it to the Canon of our Bible, since it has never had a place in the Catholic Canon.

Thirdly, and again provided we discovered an exact copy of the original Book, it would be for the Church to decide this question, and the very Spirit which assisted the Church when she drew up the Canon of the Bible in the first place would guide her in the same way today.

Of one thing you can be certain. Even were the original Enoch inspired, there would be found nothing in it which is not contained substantially in the Canonical Books of our present Bible, and in the traditions and teachings of the Catholic Church.

105. Why should we believe what is written in the Bible at all?

Because it contains the inspired Word of God who can neither fall into error, nor fail in veracity. That leads on, of course, to the question as to how we know the Bible to be the inspired Word of God. The Catholic has no difficulty here, because he accepts the infallible teaching of the Catholic Church that it is indeed inspired. Further discussion from that point of view would lead to a study of the credentials of the Catholic Church as a divinely guaranteed teacher of religious truth. One who does not acknowledge the Catholic Church must fall back on the fact and fulfillment of Biblical prophecies, the extraordinary unity of theme running through so many books by different writers, the supernatural character of the doctrines set forth, and the moral power exercised by the Bible over so many millions of souls who have really studied it and entered into its spirit.

106. We have only the word of Moses for it that he received the ten commandments from God.

That is not true. We have the Word of Christ who personally approved and quoted the teachings of Moses as indeed a prophet of God. Prior to the advent of Christ the Jews had, not only the signs given by God as a guarantee of the mission of Moses, and the actual acceptance of the Law by a people who were reluctant to submit to it, but they also had the continuous history of their people described by many writers—a history recording the divine intervention again and again on their behalf, and ever insisting on the observance of the Mosaic Law. In addition to all this, of course, a Catholic has the authentic and infallible teaching of the Catholic Church as to the divine inspiration of Sacred Scripture. And therefore a Catholic could never say that we have only the word of Moses for it. We Catholics have much more than that.

107. I read recently the statement of a Protestant Bishop that the proof of inspiration rests solely on the power of moral and spiritual appeal in the Bible.

Such a subjective standard alone cannot be accepted. It affords no hope whatever of defending the Bible against modernism and unbelief. One who accepts such a standard would have to reject as uninspired all passages which had no moral or spiritual appeal for him. And an absurd position would arise if others discovered a moral and spiritual appeal in the passages he rejected. Are they to be inspired for them? In that case the passages would be uninspired and inspired simultaneously! They would be the Word of God and not the Word of God at one and the same time.

108. *This Bishop said that Christians are not obliged to believe in the verbal inspiration and literal infallibility of the Bible.*

The Catholic Church, of course, cannot accept a Protestant Bishop as an authority as to what Christians are bound to believe. How the Catholic Church would view this particular utterance depends upon what he meant by "verbal inspiration" and "literal infallibility." If, by verbal inspiration, the Bishop intended a dictation of the very words to the writers by God, as one dictates to a stenographer, Catholics are not obliged to believe in verbal inspiration. But we are obliged to believe that every single word as it left the hands of the original writers was written under the inspiration of God, and infallibly expressed the truth intended by God. God's influence respected the psychological characteristics of the various human instruments He used; and this accounts for differences in method and style. But it is certain that the original authors wrote exactly the things willed by God, so that God is truly the principal Author of the Bible as it left the hands of the original writers, those writers being but the human instruments used by God. Not a word, nor a sentence, belonging to the original writings, could be excluded from the divine influence of God's inspiration.

Secondly, we must ask what the Bishop meant by "literal infallibility." If he meant that not all the Bible is infallible, and that we may distinguish between religious parts and non-religious parts, then no Catholic could agree with him. We Catholics are obliged to believe as infallibly true every single sentence as it left the hands of the original writers. The whole of the Bible is for us the Word of God. We cannot regard the Bible as a mixture of God's Word and merely human thoughts or opinions. The Catholic Church has condemned the doctrine that personal interpolations by the original writers crept into their accounts, interpolations which did not fall under the inspiring influence of God.

109. *The Bishop said that critics too often assume that Christians are committed to verbal inspiration and literal infallibility.*

Catholics are committed to the explanations I have given. And we are prepared to defend the Bible on that understanding, even if others are not. For us, the Bible is wholly and entirely the Word of God, in all its parts. Others may collapse when they see a critic, but the Catholic Church will stand her ground and fight for the truth of the Bible as God's Word throughout. And when the critic is dead and forgotten, the Catholic Church will still be there, and the Bible will still be intact.

110. *He said that it would greatly clarify religious discussions if only the critics would bear these things in mind.*

Certainly a discussion between critics and Protestants would be clarified, if the Protestants marked off all those sections of the Bible which they are prepared to jettison. The critics could then confine their attention to the remainder. But when the critics thought themselves to have settled the Protestant position, they would find themselves still confronted by the Catholic Church with the battle to be fought over every inch of the ground.

111. *Then you cling to the fundamentalist idea that the Bible is infallibly true?*

I must warn you against any idea, if you entertain such an idea, that the term "fundamentalist" is sufficient to discredit the orthodox position. There are fundamental principles in every branch of knowledge—in art, literature, mathematics, and in all other forms of science. Yet no one sneers at those who cling to such fundamental principles as a basis of thought in their respective fields of knowledge. In the field of religion, also, there are fundamental principles; and they are not destroyed by cheap ridicule. If they can be really disproved, well and good. But no one yet has succeeded in disproving the infallible truth of the Bible. Of course, I do not mean that every interpretation individual readers choose to impose upon the Bible is infallibly true. The Bible is true in the sense in which God intended what is said in its pages; not in any alien sense in which mistaken people understand it.

112. *We cannot be expected to regard the Bible as an infallible encyclopedia of general knowledge.*

No one could expect you to do so. The Bible is infallible in what it intends to teach, not in what it does not intend to teach.

113. *The whole conception of the author of Genesis concerning the physical universe was that current in his time. It cannot be regarded as final or unrevisable in the light of later science.*

That is true; but it has no bearing on the question of the infallibility of the Bible. The Bible is not, and does not profess to be a scientific manual. Progress in science, and our further knowledge of the nature and the structure of the universe, may mean the revision of our own views of the universe from time to time. But it does not mean a revision of Biblical teaching. If some people thought that the Bible intended to teach such matters, that was their mistake. It is absurd to suggest that the Bible is mistaken, and therefore not infallible, because it does not teach a scientific view which it never intended to teach, and with which it does not profess to deal.

114. *I do not mind the Bible omitting to tell the scientific truth. But I do object to positively wrong statements.*

To that, I can but ask you to point out a single positively wrong statement. One thing, however, I will ask you to note. There is a difference between a true statement of the universe as it appears to the eye, and a true statement of it as explained by science. Even today it is a perfectly true statement to say in the popular fashion that the sun rose at 6 a. m. But the scientific statement explaining that phenomenon will fall back on the rotation of the earth. The scientist himself will say, "There's a half-moon tonight," and refuse to admit that he is gravely in error because some meticulous lunatic argues that the whole moon is still there, and that nobody has cut it in two. The Biblical writers correctly gave that aspect of the universe which was apparent to their senses, and no later scientific explanations can prove them to have written falsehoods.

115. *If the Bible is the Word of God, it should be perfect.*

If the Bible were miraculously produced by God without the use of human instruments, that is so. But since God made use of human instruments, it will be but relatively perfect. The human writers were living psychological instruments whose personal characteristics God respected, and whose traits are reflected in their writings. The ordinary writing of the same person will vary according to his use of a fine pen or of a broad pen. An imperfect instrument means secondary imperfections. The Bible is relatively perfect insofar as it gives us the revelation of God in accordance with the limitations of human ideas and language, and in as good a way as the various individual human instruments were able to arrange their ideas and express them.

GENESIS AND CREATION

116. *Is that how you account for the errors and contradictions in the Bible?*

I deny that there are any errors and contradictions in the Bible. If you meet with what is apparently an error or a contradiction, then your translation may be at fault, or you have not correctly grasped the sense intended by the writer, or the writer is correctly quoting the errors of others as being errors. But in none of these cases is it the Bible which is at fault.

117. *If the Bible is the work of God, it should be free from errors from cover to cover.*

It is. But it is a fallacy to speak of the Bible as the work of God, abstracting from the human authorship also. The Bible is the joint work of both God and the human instrumental authors He inspired. The work is wholly from God as principal Author; and wholly from the individual writers as instrumental causes. Thus every word in this book comes from myself as principal cause, and from my pen as instrumental cause. Each cause, in its own order, is a complete cause.

118. *If it is the work of man, errors would be easy to understand.*

It is again a fallacy to speak of the Bible as the work of man as if God had nothing to do with it. It is the joint work of both God and man.

119. *Could it be proved to be untrue by showing it to be self-contradictory?*

Yes, for contradictories cannot be simultaneously true. But there are no real contradictions in the Bible.

120. *Truth cannot contradict truth. Yet the account of creation in Genesis certainly contradicts the truth as known by science.*

It does not. It abstracts from science, and deals with the subject from another aspect altogether.

121. *Do you maintain that Genesis gives an authentic account of creation?*

Yes. It gives an authentic account, but not a scientific account.

122. *It is based on a conception of the world as divided into three tiers like a three-storied house, with God on the top floor.*

Since that was the popular notion of the universe around them, Moses could not have done better than use it in speaking to the people on their own level. Two authentic facts would be conveyed in such a conception, namely, that there is a God, and that He is supreme. The conveying of those truths in a setting familiar in current ideas was wisdom itself. If you object to that, you should object to the expression still current despite all our science that the sun rises, on the score that it unscientifically implies the movement of the sun around the earth.

123. *Does not science completely discredit the Genesis story?*

No. It does not affect it. Those people who have talked of the problem of reconciling Genesis with the findings of science have talked of a problem which really does not exist.

124. *Genesis says that, after making the earth, God made two great lights; a greater light to rule the day, and a lesser light to rule the night.*

That is not really true. After *speaking* of the formation of the earth, Moses *speaks* of the formation of the sun and moon—which we know to have been formed earlier than the earth. Moses was not giving the chronological order of creation, but merely allotting to the fourth section of his descriptive scheme the creation of the sun and moon.

125. *To say that Moses did not record the story of creation in its proper order is to belittle Genesis as a divine revelation.*

That is not true. The order in which facts are described has nothing to do with the truth of the facts. The "proper order" can be proper to the sequence of events in themselves, or proper to the scope and purpose of the literary narrative. I could write the biography of a man either according to the time sequence, or according to his accomplishments, dividing the chapters according to his work as a politician, a philanthropist, a litterateur, and so on, despite the fact that the order of years would have to be forsaken. And in both cases the facts would be equally true. Divine inspiration is compatible with any literary style. And the deliberate character of the Mosaic narrative is evident enough to any really intelligent man, indicating clearly that there was no intention of giving the chronological order. Thus eight works are divided into six sections called days. In the first triduum we have the distinction of unmovable things; in the second, their ornamentation. The last day of each triduum contains two works; and each "day" contains a command, its fulfillment, and approbation of the result. This was a literary device by systematic arrangement to arrest the attention, and put the facts more strikingly before hearers. And there is nothing in this arrangement of the narrative to belittle the account as divinely inspired.

126. *Do you hold that the world was made in six days of twenty-four hours each?*

No. Moses described as occurring in six days processes which took long periods. Neither the time nor the order was meant to correspond with the objective reality of the creative process itself.

127. *So you interpret the Hebrew word for day as a period?*

I do not. The Hebrew word "YOM," used absolutely as in the Mosaic account, and in the singular, means a day of twenty-four hours, and nothing else. However long the progressive work of the formation of all things took in itself—and it occupied a very long period—Moses divided his account of the whole process into six sections, allotting each section to a separate "chapter" of his narrative metaphorically called a "day." Vast periods, therefore, were compressed into each chapter. It is one thing to say that a long period was required for the events allotted to each section of an account called for special reasons a "day"; it is quite another to say that the author intended the word day as a long period. The author intended the word "day" as men understood that word; i. e., as consisting of twenty-four hours. The works took a long period in themselves. But the author wished the various sections of his narrative to represent ordinary days of the week.

128. *Why did Moses choose such an artificial classification and literary arrangement?*

That should be evident from the religious lesson he desired to teach. The imagery he employed of six working days for creation was to exemplify the six days of the week on which the Jews should work; and the seventh day was to exemplify the Sabbath, or day of rest and of religious worship.

129. *Are we to believe that God rested?*

No. God is eternal activity. He did not, and does not rest. For the purposes of the narrative God inspired Moses to omit any reference to His works on the seventh day, that men might learn to make that day a day of rest for themselves. In accordance with his literary scheme Moses could say, "Under the inspiration of God, I have narrated in six sections called "days" His various works. I have reserved none for the seventh day. And God wishes you to work on six days only, dedicating every seventh day to rest and worship as though He Himself had rested on that day."

130. *Exodus XXXI., 17, says that God rested on the seventh day, and "was refreshed."*

Speaking in a human way for men Moses had depicted God as resting because of the religious scope of his narrative. But Moses knew quite well that God needed neither rest nor refreshment. Men do, and for them those expressions were used. That the Jews realized that the account was for them, and based on their needs, and not meant to indicate fatigue in God Himself, is evident from the words of Isaiah, XL., 28, saying that God "fainteth not, nor is He weary."

131. *So many of the things recorded are incredible on the face of it. Who could call the account of our first parents historical?*

The account of our first parents, given in the Book of Genesis, truly records the historical facts. The first chapters of Genesis, just as the other chapters of that Book, obviously intend to give history; and the account is quoted throughout the rest of Scripture as historical. But whilst the account is true history, in the sense of excluding fable, legend, and a purely allegorical fantasy, it is a popular, and not a scientific account. This, however, is merely a question of method and style, not of fact. What is described is true, but it is not described according to strict chronology, nor in modern scientific terminology. Many metaphorical and popular expressions occur, adapted to the understanding of the people living at the time the account was written. But the way in which a fact is described does not destroy the historical value of the fact. Most certainly we have to accept as fact a Garden of Eden in which our first parents were placed, and in which they disobeyed God with evil consequences to themselves and to their posterity, the whole human race.

132. *Turning to the New Testament, I would like to suggest that the writers of those books were not relating historical facts, but used the Old Testament to interpret the whole story.*

It is true that the New Testament writers used and quoted the Old Testament. But in no way does this suggest that they forsook historical facts for unhistorical interpretations to suit themselves.

133. *How is it that St. Luke relates two consecutive miracles in exactly the same sequence as Napthali VI.? Is that pure accident?*

No. But St. Luke did not borrow from Napthali VI. Any borrowing was the other way round. Napthali VI. is not part of the Old Testament, but part of an uncanonical book called "The Testimony of the Twelve Patriarchs," and written in the second century B. C. The writings in this book were altered and amplified at various times, and finally in the Christian era were added to by some unknown Christian writer. Scholars, Catholic and non-Catholic alike, admit the later insertion of interpolations into Napthali VI., borrowed from the Gospels. It is significant that many who are unwilling to accept the text of the Gospels are most ready to drop all the rules of criticism concerning other documents which they hope to find helpful in their destructive campaign. At least, if you want to check the Gospels by other documents, apply the same rigid rules of criticism to those other documents, and make sure of their value before using them as a standard of reference.

134. *Is not the writer of the 2nd Gospel patently laboring under the influence of the 22nd Psalm, in recording the mockery, etc., of the man of sorrows? Is that pure accident?*

It was not pure accident. It was due to the fact that the same Holy Spirit was the principal Author of both accounts, despite His making use of two different human instruments; also to the fact that, in both cases, the same events were being described, either as future or as fulfilled.

135. Is there not a parallelism between I Pet., 21-25, describing the suffering servant of Isaianic prophecy, and Isaiah LIII.?

Of course there is. There must necessarily be a parallelism between the fulfillment of a prophecy and the prophecy itself. If there were no parallelism you would say that the prophecy was not fulfilled. If there is a parallelism, you deny the event, and accuse St. Peter of concocting a story borrowed from Isaiah!

136. Is not the parallelism so close that in any other form of literature it would be called plagiarism?

Yes, if St. Peter were not obviously describing what he himself had witnessed, and for which there is abundant other evidence. But granted the fact foreseen by the prophet as he set down its description in anticipation, it is not plagiarism for St. Peter to make use of the same expressions in his portrayal of the same reality. It was not only lawful for him to do so. It would be rather surprising if he did not. And above all when we consider the unity of the prophetic spirit throughout the Old and New Testaments. The same Holy Ghost inspired both Isaiah and St. Peter. One and the same principal Author is responsible for both accounts. And from this point of view there can be no charge of plagiarism at all.

137. May we not assume that St. Luke and St. Matthew had no knowledge of the divine origin of Jesus Christ?

Not unless we wish to ignore evidence, and credulously believe a thing merely because we wish to believe it. St. Luke records the words of the angel to Mary, "The Holy Ghost shall come upon thee, and the power of the Most High shall overshadow thee. And therefore also the Holy which shall be born of thee shall be called the Son of God." Lk. I., 35. St. Matthew I., 20, records the words of the angel to St. Joseph, "Joseph, fear not to take unto thee Mary thy wife, for that which is conceived in her is of the Holy Ghost." Both St. Luke and St. Matthew, therefore, had clear knowledge of the divine origin of Christ.

138. Both give genealogies of Christ in which the names are all different.

Your difficulty arises from the idea that we have to reconcile the two sets of names given by St. Matthew and St. Luke. But that very idea is wrong. The names are meant to be different, and the Evangelists had no intention of giving the same genealogies. One gives the juridical succession through which Davidic rights descended to Joseph and his legal son—Christ. The other abstracts from this legal or juridical succession, and follows the real genealogy according to consanguinity. They therefore approach the question from different viewpoints, and it is a mistake to think that they have to be reconciled. I could deal with the lineage of the Pope either juridically in the papal succession, or really in his own family line; and if a man objected that the lists of names differed, I would merely reply that they were meant to differ.

139. If Joseph was not the father of Jesus, why trouble to give his genealogy at all?

Simply because of the Jewish custom of recording genealogies in the male line. It is certain that Joseph and Mary were relatives in the same line, and fundamentally the lineage of Joseph was that of Mary also. In St. Luke I., 32, the angel told Mary that she would conceive under the direct influence of the Holy Ghost, and that the child born of her would inherit the throne of David his father. That is evidence enough that Mary herself by her own right was in the Davidic line.

140. *If Joseph's blood did not flow in the veins of Jesus, would not the pedigree of Pontius Pilate have been equally relevant?*

No. Firstly, Pontius Pilate was not the legal father of Jesus. Secondly, since the whole point is to prove Davidic descent, the genealogy of the non-Davidic Pontius Pilate would be senseless. Thirdly, Pontius Pilate was not in any way related to Mary.

141. *The nativity stories are certainly unhistorical. St. Luke speaks of the angels and shepherds, but knows nothing of the star and the wise men.*

You mean that he does not mention the star and the wise men. But that is not proof that he knew nothing of them. Each Evangelist wrote a brief account of Christ. The scope of the work forbade treatment of each and every detail of His life. Therefore each author selected what he thought fit to record. I have a copy of Ransome's "History of England." In it he mentions the acquisition of Australia, but makes no mention that Captain Cook landed on its shores. Would you argue that he knew nothing of Captain Cook's arrival in Australia? Or would you reasonably infer that he omitted this point in favor of space for other matters he preferred to record?

142. *St. Luke says that after His birth Jesus was taken to Nazareth and lived there, going with His parents every year to Jerusalem. He knew nothing of the flight into Egypt and the killing of the innocents.*

Omission to record certain events is no argument that an author does not know of them. You would be right, of course, if St. Luke said explicitly, "There was no flight into Egypt, and no killing of any innocents, as my friend Matthew inaccurately asserts." St. Luke nowhere says that. Meantime, there is no conflict. The sequence of events would be the taking of the child to Jerusalem after His birth, the flight into Egypt, the slaughter of the innocents, the return to Nazareth, and thenceforth the visiting of Jerusalem every year. Abbreviation is not proof that omitted items are unknown.

143. *St. Luke says also that Cyrinus was governor at this period, yet as a matter of fact he was not appointed to that position until after the death of Herod.*

St. Luke does say that Cyrinus was governor of Syria at the time of Christ's birth. And, of course, Herod was then living. It is also certain that Cyrinus was not appointed to full legatine control until after the death of Herod, according to reliable historical documents. But St. Luke is not referring to any act of Cyrinus during his term of supreme legatine control. He is referring to actions of Cyrinus in a previous mission before his supreme appointment. According to the Greek text St. Luke refers explicitly to the "first" enrolling made by Cyrinus. You will object that St. Luke expressly calls him "governor of Syria." But in the Greek the word he uses is not the equivalent of Legate at all. It rather indicates an associate procurator. Now are there any grounds to believe that Cyrinus was in Syria in an associate official capacity before he was appointed full legatine administrator? There are. In 1854 Zumpt proved from profane documents and inscriptions only that Cyrinus was employed in Syria between the governorships of Varus and Lollius, which included the year of our Lord's birth. Mommsen says that undoubtedly Cyrinus twice fulfilled public offices in Syria. The evidence is all in support of St. Luke. St. Luke was a highly educated man. He was not entirely a fool. He declares in the beginning of his Gospel that he engaged in extensive inquiry concerning the facts he is going to give. Both in his Gospel and in the Acts of the Apostles he shows a remarkable acquaintance with Graeco-Roman matters. Do you think that, after professing his exact research, he would purposely, or through unpardonable carelessness, commit so gross an error, one so easy to avoid, and one so easily refuted by his first readers? Such a thought puts altogether too great a strain upon one's imagination.

144. In Matt. XI., 14, Jesus says of John the Baptist, "He is Elias." But, according to Jn. I., 21, John said, "I am not." Which are we to believe?

Both, according to the sense intended in each case. St. John the Baptist was not Elias in person, and knowing that his questioners wanted to know whether he was Elias in person, he answered no. On the other hand, Jesus did not intend to say that John was Elias in person. Therefore He said: "If you will receive it, he is Elias that is to come." Matt. XI., 14. In modern English He meant, "If you care to believe it, you may regard him as a sign of Elias whom God, according to the prophet Malachy, has promised to send before the day of the Lord." For our Lord knew that, just as He will come at the end of the world to judge mankind, being then preceded by Elias in person, so now He was ushering in the end of the Jewish dispensation, being preceded by John the Baptist. St. John the Baptist was, therefore, a sign that the end was coming for the Jews as God's chosen people just as Elias will be a sign that the end is coming for the human race. There is, therefore, no contradiction between the two statements. John denied that he was Elias in person. Christ asserted that the future mission of Elias was exemplified before their eyes by the present mission of St. John the Baptist.

145. Jesus said that no man has seen God at any time (Jn. I., 18), yet we are told that the "Lord spake to Moses face to face as a man speaketh to his friend." Exodus, XXXIII., 11.

It is quite certain that no human being, whilst still subject to the conditions of this earthly life, has ever seen God immediately and as He is in His own proper nature. The reference in Exodus is a purely metaphorical way of saying that God communicated knowledge to Moses without any other intermediary. Moses did not have any vision of God as God really is in Himself; and the attributing of a voice to God is but a human way of describing the impressions caused by God and experienced by Moses.

146. St. Matthew says that Jesus rode into Jerusalem on an ass and a colt.

St. Matthew does not say that. He says that "they brought the ass and the colt, and laid their garments upon them, and made Him sit thereon." Matt. XXI., 7. St. Matthew means simply that Jesus sat on the garments which they had placed on one of the animals, namely, the colt.

147. Zachary IX., 9, predicts, "Thy king will come . . . riding upon an ass and upon a colt, the foal of an ass." Does that mean that he will ride into the city upon two animals?

No.

148. Is not the duplication due to parallelism in Semitic poetry?

Yes. Zachary, therefore, merely predicts that Jesus will enter Jerusalem seated on a colt, the foal of an ass, as a symbol of meekness and humility. He does not predict the presence of two animals. But you will notice that St. Matthew (XXI., 5) quotes Zachary, and then, in verse 7, deliberately changes the wording of his own text. If he introduces the mother of the colt, it is not because of the prophecy of Zachary who did not foresee her presence, but because as a matter of fact the mother was brought along with the colt. St. Matthew merely mentioned the mother as being present. And it is quite natural that she should have been brought along to ensure the docility of the colt. Nor did her presence in any way conflict with the prophecy that Jesus would ride into Jerusalem on a colt, the foal of an ass.

149. *The authors of the 2nd. and 3rd. Gospels are more wary; they mention an ass only. But the author of the 4th. Gospel tries to trim the story in accordance with the prophecy by employing a colt only.*

Rather than suspect yourself of being wrong, you would accuse St. Matthew of falling into error, and the authors of the other Gospels you would charge with a wariness which amounts to conscious fraud. But there are a few things to be noticed. The authors of the other Gospels would not have been wary if, knowing what St. Matthew had recorded, they deliberately contradicted him. After all, he was an Evangelist out for the good of the same religion as themselves. Were they thinking of being wary, they would have stood to him at all costs. Again, if the authors of the other Gospels were shrewd tricksters, warily bent on trimming their story to suit their purpose, they may as well have done it right through their accounts, eliminating every awkward, humiliating, and unattractive feature of their description of themselves and of Christ. But no. They were patently honest throughout. The charge of trickery is absurd. You will say that, if they were not stepping warily, they were mistaken, for they contradict one another and St. Matthew. But here it is you yourself who would be mistaken. They do not contradict one another. For whilst St. John speaks of a colt, as you say, St. Mark and St. Luke merely use an alternative Greek word for the same thing. Do they, then, contradict St. Matthew by mentioning one animal only where he mentions two? No. Omission is not denial. They give the essential fact that Jesus rode into Jerusalem on a colt. St. Matthew states the same thing, giving the additional detail that the mother of the colt was brought along with it. There is no contradiction in that.

See also R. R., Vol. I, Nos. 85-166.

CHAPTER FIVE

THE CHRISTIAN FAITH

150. *Granting the necessity of accepting the religion of the Bible, are not Judaism and Christianity fundamentally the same?*

Both religions insist, of course, on the necessity of a religion revealed by God, and of a good moral life. Also both reject idolatry, and urge fidelity to one and the same true God. But, besides these fundamental similarities, there are several fundamental differences. I will mention three. Firstly, religions cannot be fundamentally the same, one of which declares that God Himself came into this world to redeem mankind, whilst the other absolutely denies it. I am speaking, of course, in this latter case of the interpretation modern Judaism imposes upon the Old Testament, not of the real doctrine of the Old Testament. Secondly, Judaism is essentially a national religion. It is true that, theoretically, Israel was meant by God to gather all mankind into one flock, and therefore be a universalist religion. But, in practice, modern Judaism is identical with the Jewish nation. Its national character is more and more emphasized, and the missionary desire to convert non-Jews is almost entirely absent. Christianity, on the other hand, when rightly understood, rises above all merely national considerations, and insists that it is intended for every human soul. Thirdly, the Jewish and Christian outlooks on life are very different. The former is material and temporal, whilst the latter is spiritual and eternal. Neither, of course, is exclusively so. But the difference is certainly fundamental. These points are sufficient to show that the ideals of Judaism and of Christianity cannot be regarded as fundamentally the same.

151. *Is not Christianity a reconciliation of Greek philosophy with Judaism?*

No. That explanation is the refuge of those who begin by rejecting the divine and supernatural origin of Christianity, and who therefore have to find a natural explanation of its appearance in this world. Christianity originated with Christ, and nowhere is there the faintest trace of indication that Christ devoted Himself to the reconciliation of Greek philosophy with Judaism. Nor could Christ possibly have drawn His doctrines from Greek philosophers, who knew absolutely nothing of the great dogmas of Christianity, such as the Trinity, the Incarnation of the Son of God, Redemption by the death of that Son on the Cross, the Resurrection of Christ, and the whole system of supernatural grace. So new and strange to the Greeks was the Christian doctrine that to them it seemed foolishness. When St. Paul preached it to the Athenians, some mocked, whilst others said, "We shall hear you again concerning this." Acts XVII., 32. But it was certainly altogether new to them. The only possible explanation of the doctrine and teaching of Jesus is that given by Himself: "My doctrine is not mine, but His that sent me." Jn. VII., 16. He declared that He had descended from heaven, and was telling men of what He had seen there. And He added, "If I have spoken to you earthly things, and you believe not, how will you believe if I speak to you heavenly things?" Jn. III., 12. It is certain that no one has ever been less of His time than Jesus. No one was less affected by His environment, and by current teachings and prejudices. And it is impossible to find a merely human source for His doctrines, or to argue from them to any natural preparation or human course of study and reading.

152. *Christianity spread because it contained phases of Judaism which commended themselves to the pagan world.*

It would be difficult to indicate those particular phases. However, if there is one thing certain, it is that Christianity had no appeal for the pagan world, which greeted the new religion with centuries of violent hatred and persecution. It was war to the death, and either Christianity or the pagan world had to go under. Christianity wounded the pride of cultured pagans by asking them to worship a crucified Jew. It attacked pagan morals, demanding of men that they should hate what they had previously loved, and love those things against which nature rebelled. The obstacles were immense, and the means at the disposal of Christianity ludicrously inadequate from a human point of view. The only force which can account for this expansion is that correctly given in the Acts of the Apostles. It was the power of the Holy Spirit, promised and sent by Christ. It was the Holy Spirit who strengthened the Apostles, and who enlightened the minds of multitudes who heard them, besides moving their obstinate wills to embrace the lofty doctrines and moral obligations binding upon Christians.

153. *You have said that Christianity is the continuation and fulfillment of the Jewish religion.*

That is so. The Christian religion really rests on a co-ordinated series of facts from Adam to Pope Pius XII, or to any Pope who may succeed him in the future. This series of facts is spread, therefore, over thousands of years, and embraces events, words, declarations of principles, doctrines, and precepts, whether in Jewish or Christian times. The Jewish religion was really preparatory Christianity, its whole genius being a looking forward to the coming of Christ. Christianity is but Judaism fulfilled.

154. *Why, then, is there opposition between the Jewish and the Christian religions?*

From the historical point of view there is opposition insofar as Judaism denies that the real Messiah has come, whilst the Christian religion affirms that he has come in the person of Christ. As a preparatory religion, Judaism was the true religion of God until such time as the Messiah should come. But it was abrogated when all that it foreshadowed was realized. The shadow gave way to the substance. And a religion which still claims to be awaiting the Redeemer of the human race after that Redeemer has come is obviously wrong, and could not retain God's sanction. But apart from the question of time and fulfillment, there is an opposition between the preparatory Jewish religion and Christianity. Literal Judaism was imperfect, and embodied much that was temporal and fleshly, whilst the religion of Christ is perfect, and elevated to the spiritual and eternal plane. Of course, even under the old regime, the true Jew was not one who merely submitted to external rites, but he who loved God,. and was united in spirit with the Savior to come. But many of the Jews had fallen short of this to a very great extent, and were absorbed by worldly and merely human considerations.

155. *Was not Jesus Himself a product of Judaism?*

By birth He was of the Jews. But Judaism could never have produced His character. The character of Christ, as depicted by the Gospels, not only differs from every type of moral perfection which the Jewish mind could conceive. It expressly opposes those types. We have in the writings of the Jews ample material to construct the model Jewish teacher. We have the sayings and actions of Hillel, Gamaliel, Rabbi Samuel, and others—all possessing the impress of national ideas; and descriptions of them are based on ideas most widely apart from the personality and teachings of Christ. Christ was a complete departure from the national type, and from those features which custom, education, patriotism, religion, and nature alike, had consecrated as being the Jewish ideal. In this sense, Jesus Christ was not the product of Judaism. Christ came, not to receive from the Jews, but to give to them that which He gave to the Gentiles, and to such Jews as did accept Him.

156. Jesus was guided by Jewish principles throughout His life.

It was the conflict between the principles of Christ and the guiding principles of the Jewish teachers at that time which ended in the crucifixion of Christ. The Jews wanted a temporal king, whilst Christ came as a spiritual Messiah. The High Priests opposed the teaching and conduct of Christ on every possible occasion.

157. Jesus merely put greater emphasis on the individual and the next life.

He rejected the idea of the absorption of the individual in a nation-religion, taking a universal view which included every individual soul. Likewise, He rejected material and temporal ideals in favor of spiritual and eternal values.

158. If Christ proved His claims so clearly, why did the Jews reject Him?

Not all of them did. Great numbers of Jews were converted in the first years of Christianity. Still, the religious leaders of the Jews, and most of the Jews were not. The first reason for this was the general corruption of moral standards amongst them. Josephus tells us of the prevailing spirit of dishonesty and depravity amongst them. The pride of the Pharisee was not much impressed by the doctrine of meekness and humility preached by Jesus. Nor did the prevailing sensuality respond to a teaching requiring mortification and self-denial. A second reason lies in the distorted idea of the Messiah to be expected. The promise of a spiritual Redeemer had been transformed into an expectation of some mighty temporal prince who would liberate the Jews from Caesar. They did not want a "kingdom not of this world." The chief priests had personal motives also because Jesus denounced their vices and hypocrisy. It is certain that the Jews did not reject Christ for want of evidence. Evidence alone accounts for those who were converted to Him. Those who rejected Him did so for personal reasons based upon their own evil dispositions.

159. It is strange that His claims were so unacceptable to men of light and learning at the time.

It is not strange when one realizes that acceptance of Christ required supernatural faith. Jesus demanded faith in Himself as God. He said to His disciples, "Whom do men say that I am?" They replied, "Some, John the Baptist; others, Elias; others, Jeremias or one of the prophets." But when He asked, "Whom do you say that I am?" Peter replied, "Thou art the Christ, the Son of the living God." And Jesus replied, "Blessed art thou, for flesh and blood hath not revealed this to thee, but My Father in heaven." On another occasion Christ said, "No man can come to Me unless the Father draw him." Matt. XVI., 13-17. Faith in Christ and salvation through Him cannot be made to depend upon natural gifts of education and learning. The intelligent and the educated are not going to have a better chance of salvation than those less fortunate. We can't fill heaven with the intellectuals, and hell with the dull-witted. The men of light and learning who refused to accept Christ may have had some degrees of natural light, but they shut their minds against supernatural light. They may have had natural learning, but they had not spiritual wisdom and insight. If you ask why they lacked such supernatural gifts, I must reply that they rejected such graces as were offered to them through lack of good will and through hardened obstinacy. It was their own fault.

160. For example Caiaphas was a man of great learning, and also at least something of a man of God.

We cannot presume that Caiaphas was a man of deep learning. The office of High Priest had been sadly degraded. Josephus complains that some who were chosen were too ignorant to know the dignity of their position; whilst the Mishna had to include the rubric: "If the High Priest cannot read, let someone read to him." Again, since the High Priests were closely associated with, and at times drawn from the Sadducees, such learning as they did possess was gravely infected by rationalism and materialism. Nor was Caiaphas a man of God save by external profession. The High Priesthood had become subject to Roman political authority. Annas had been deposed by the Roman Governor Valerius Gratus in the year 15 A. D. He was succeeded by Eleazar, and again, after a year's break, by Caiaphas, who was a political time-server, who had a longer run of office than most High Priests, and was determined to keep it. That required, of course, the retaining of Roman patronage.

161. Caiaphas was of the Jews to whom a Messiah had been promised.

That is true. But his religious convictions had been subordinated to political expediency. Richelieu was a Catholic Cardinal who professed that the Catholic Church was the true religion; yet we know how politics dominated him. The case of Caiaphas is no more mysterious.

162. Since the Messiah was then due Jesus did not make such an absurd claim.

The Jews knew that the time of the Messiah was at hand. They had built up quite wrong ideas as to the true character and work of the Messiah, however, and entertained the notion that somehow or other He would be a temporal deliverer of their nation. Even that idea was not welcome to the politically-minded Caiaphas. And when Christ claimed, not only to be the Messiah, but to be God Himself, Caiaphas was overjoyed. He could get rid of one who might disturb his peaceful relations with Rome, and satisfy the religious susceptibilities of the Jews by the charge of blasphemy. The mere claim to Messiahship would not have seemed absurd or blasphemous to the Jews. But they were not prepared to accept a claim to absolute equality with God. Caiaphas knew this, and traded on it. He worked to one end, to get Christ to say that He was God. And seeing Jesus silent under the various accusations, he at last cried, "I adjure thee by the living God that thou tell us if thou be the Christ, the Son of God." Matt. XXVI., 63. The last words were uppermost in his mind. No one was ignorant of the fact that Jesus had spoken and acted as if He were more than a mere man, and as if He were in a unique sense the Son of God. Caiaphas intended his question in this sense. And Christ replied, "Thou hast said it." Then, with pretended horror, but really in triumph, Caiaphas cried blasphemy, and got the verdict he wanted.

163. Did Jesus Himself have any notion of establishing a new religion distinct from the Jewish religion as such?

Yes, insofar as He came to give us that more perfect religion which the Jewish religion had foreshadowed.

164. The Acts of the Apostles tell us that the Apostles still frequented the Synagogues after the ascension of Christ. That is not like the action of men charged to found a new Church.

Acts III., 1, would tell you that Peter and John went to the Temple at the ninth hour of prayer. But why? To tell the Jews, whom they knew to be gathered there, that they had denied the Holy One, and killed the Author of Life; but that He had risen from the dead, and that they must accept the new religion of Christ. Whereupon Peter and John were arrested and thrown into prison. That would scarcely have occurred had they gone there merely to share in the ordinary Jewish worship as of old. Again, Acts V., 42, tell us that "every day they ceased not, in the Temple and from house to house, to teach and preach Jesus Christ." They were certainly devoting themselves to the founding of a new Church.

165. Which Gentile nation first officially adopted the Christian Faith?

In the beginning, of course, the spread of Christianity was due to the conversion of individuals drawn from various nations in the East. Thus, in Acts II., 9-10, we have a catalog of various types, "Parthians and Medes, and Elamites, and inhabitants of Mesopotamia, Judea, and Cappadocia, Pontus and Asia, Phrygia and Pamphylia, Egypt and parts of Libya about Cyrene, and strangers of Rome. Jews, also, and proselytes, Cretes and Arabians." But whilst the Church absorbed units from the various Gentile peoples, the first nation which officially adopted the Christian religion was that of the Romans. And this occurred after the Edict of the Emperor Constantine in 313 A. D., granting tolerance to Christians, and putting an end to the pagan persecutions.

166. I have heard you say that faith is necessary before one can accept Christian beliefs.

Faith is not necessary to arrive at the conviction that God has actually given a revelation to mankind, and that Christianity is that revelation. But, whilst reason can prove the fact of this revelation, faith is necessary for the full acceptance of the contents of that revelation. Quite apart from religion, this holds good in the merely natural order. There is a natural faith with which you yourself could not quarrel, and which you would not dream of branding as unreasonable. For example, reason tells me that there are very good grounds for accepting Professor Haldane as an expert in his own particular branch of natural science. Now he tells me that there are no chromosomes in the simplest living cells. I accept that as a fact by faith in the knowledge and veracity of Professor Haldane in this particular matter. If you asked me to prove that there are no chromosomes in the simplest living cells, I could but show you where Professor Haldane states this to be a definite and certain conclusion of biological science, and advance reasons for the acceptance of Haldane as a competent authority. If you refused to have faith in Haldane in this matter, you would reject his teaching; but the refusal of faith in him in this matter would be unreasonable. So, too, reason can justify the claims of the Christian religion to be the revelation of God. But the teachings of that religion deal with truths of the supernatural order much more above the experience of ordinary human knowledge than Haldane's chromosomes are above the average man's scientific experience. We, therefore, accept Christian teachings by faith; but that act of faith is reasonable in virtue of the reasonable grounds for the Christian religion as the revelation of God.

167. If such proof exists, no reasonable man in the world would remain a non-Christian!

That does not follow. There are reasonable men who have never seriously studied the evidences for Christianity. There are others who have bestowed some attention upon them, but who, although reasonable in other matters, have approached this study with a prejudice which has prevented their appreciating the force of the proofs. Others, again, will admit the force of the proofs, but are not willing to accept by faith the teachings of the Christian religion. Instead of accepting them by faith, they seem to think that an independent proof should be offered for every single doctrine to their satisfaction; and declare that they will accept no religious truth on authority. Yet others are as convinced as I am of the truth of the Christian religion, and of all its teachings; but they will not accept that religion nor those teachings because they are not prepared to fulfill the practical consequences of them. They dismiss all thought of the matter as far as possible—and remain non-Christians.

168. *Would it not have been better for God to have waited until this present time to reveal Himself in the Incarnation?*

You can be quite sure that, despite all human speculations, what God actually chose to do was the better thing.

169. *With the radio and the press and other means of publicity Jesus would have been able to make a greater impression.*

Your suggestion of greater natural means at His disposal would have had little appeal for Christ. Although He could have had them, He deliberately deprived Himself of them even to the extent in which they were available in His own time. And He did this precisely to show that His work was of God. Natural human wisdom would have suggested the entry of the Son of God into this world as a magnificent personage, with striking splendor, and vast resources of earthly wealth. But instead of being born in a palace, He was born in a stable; instead of honor and renown, He was born in obscurity and humiliation; instead of choosing wealth, He chose poverty. To human prudence it seems the road to failure. Had you a desire to establish a world-wide religion, and had the choice of means, you would have chosen just the opposite path as being likely to lead to success. But the more ill advised you declare the means adopted by Jesus, the greater the tribute you pay to His work.

170. *Why did God choose such an apparently unpropitious time?*

The time of Christ was no more unpropitious than today. No time could be more propitious than another on the score that natural means are more readily and abundantly at hand. We are dealing with a supernatural, not a natural religion. Faith in the teachings of Christ cannot be arrived at by any man's unaided efforts. The grace of God is required, giving a supernatural and spiritual enlightenment to the mind. So Jesus Himself said, when the Jews refused to believe in Him, "No man can come to Me unless the Father draw him." Jn. VI., 44. And St. Paul rightly says, "The sensual man perceiveth not these things that are of the Spirit of God." 1 Cor. II., 14. If men could see the works that Jesus did, and hear the words that He said, yet not believe, I do not see how other men would be any better off if they heard a description of His works by radio as they occurred, or heard His words from loud-speakers in their homes. Radio and press publicity would not necessarily have improved matters. Meantime, the printed Gospels are within the reach of all. Of those who read them, some believe; some do not.

171. *Do you think that religion is the one thing in which men deliberately set themselves against the truth?*

Men deliberately set themselves against the truth in many things. But their opposition is certainly more in evidence where religion is concerned. For the more truth a given form of religion contains, the more opposed will that religion be to the corruption of human nature.

172. *Why should there be animosity against the Christian religion?*

It is not because there is anything wrong with Christianity. It is because there is something wrong with the people who experience the animosity.

173. *It seems to me that people are ready to believe almost anything these days, so why don't they lap up your religion?*

Because Christianity does not cater for people ready to believe "almost anything." It demands that they believe a very definite something, to the exclusion of many things which human beings might find more comfortable and pleasant.

174. *If the Christian revelation were really credible, everyone would accept it.*

That is not true. There is more than enough evidence to make acceptance of the fact that God has revealed the Christian religion reasonable. But men do not always behave reasonably. Yet even if a man admitted that the fact of revelation is credible, it does not follow that he would be willing to believe the contents of that revelation. For the contents of Christian revelation include supernatural mysteries which, though not in any way against human reason, are above it. And men, in their pride, can say, "We will not believe anything which is not within the reach of our full comprehension. We accept nothing on trust, no matter who says it." Above all, is this the case when the doctrines in question are not merely theoretical, but involve practical consequences distasteful to human nature.

175. *Surely mankind is anxious to be saved?*

If we take salvation as the promise of eternal happiness, and leave out all other considerations, men would certainly be anxious to get it. But if we view, not the promise of future joy, but the implication that men "need" to be saved, it is a different matter altogether. For the implication is that men have fallen into a rotten and depraved state from which they are incapable of escaping without the help of a savior. Human pride rebels. Men do not like to admit even to themselves that they are evil. They cry out against the doctrine of original sin, and boast that, far from having fallen, the human race has steadily risen, and has a glorious future before it, to be attained by its own efforts. And not only do men banish the thought of original sin. They try to banish the thought of their actual and personal sins. So a man with no religion is full of his own virtues. "I have no religion," he will say, "but I am a better man than many who profess to be religious." Pride is a great force in the world, and God Himself has said that He "resists the proud and gives His grace to the humble." But men do not like humbling themselves; and still less do they like being humbled. Despite their boasting, however, men have their vices and sins which they do not wish to abandon. And they are not prepared to sacrifice present tangible pleasures and interests for future invisible benefits. How many people are blind to future consequences of their actions, even in this life, when in the grip of a present and urgent temptation to alluring self-satisfaction! So mankind is not always anxious to be saved if we consider, not merely the future benefits of salvation, but present implications and the conditions required.

See also R. R., Vol. I, Nos. 167-202.

CHAPTER SIX

A DEFINITE CHRISTIAN FAITH

176. Does the word Christianity refer to religions in general?

It certainly does not refer to religions in general, for there are religions which in no way acknowledge the claims of Christ. You cannot have Christianity without Christ. In popular usage, the word is used in reference to all those forms of religion which profess belief in Christ. But that is a loose way of speaking which lacks all scientific precision, as is often the case with popular expressions. In reality, Christianity rightly signifies only the religion of Christ correctly and completely presented; it cannot signify a multitude of sects blending isolated truths of the Christian religion with various errors which form the basis of division amongst themselves.

177. Why are there so many different religions in this world?

Diversity in religions is due either to the ignorance or to the perversity of men. Men are by nature religiously inclined; and those who lacked knowledge of the true religion invented religions for themselves—religions which differed even as the outlook differed of those who originated them.

178. Why at least are not Christians united?

All who profess to be Christians, of course, ought to be united in one Church. That they are not is due to the world, the flesh, and the devil, besides the fact that human beings are very limited in intelligence, and are endowed with freewill.

The world has had its influence insofar as temporal and national considerations have led men to forsake original unity.

The flesh has taken its toll, men denying the faith they once professed because of its conflict with their passions.

The devil has had his share, sowing cockle amidst the wheat, and choking the good grain in thousands of souls.

That men have been able to yield to these influences is due to the fact that God will not take away the gift of freewill and personal responsibility from any man. As for good people who still adhere to mistaken forms of Christianity, we can account for that only by the limitations of the human mind which render it so liable to error, and so little able to comprehend things in all their aspects. They concentrate on some good element retained in their mistaken form of religion, and lose sight of the aspects wherein it fails.

Christ Himself foresaw and predicted such divisions. "There will arise false Christs," He said, "to deceive if possible even the elect." Matt. XXIV., 24. And St. Paul warned Timothy, "There shall be a time when they will not endure sound doctrine; but, according to their own desires, they will heap to themselves teachers, having itching ears; and will indeed turn away their hearing from the truth, but will be turned unto fables." 2 Tim. IV., 3-4.

179. In view of the different types of mind it seems that different Churches are inevitable.

One question here presents itself. As Christians, are we to believe what Christ taught, or is each man to believe whatever he likes, according to his type of mind? So long as each man arranges for himself what he will believe, making a great act of faith in his own powers of discernment, there will inevitably be different Churches.

But faith in one's own powers of discernment is not faith in Christ. Christ said, "I am the Truth." And we are told, "Let this mind be in you which was also in Christ Jesus." Phil. II., 5. If all had the mind of Christ, that would be the end of diversity. And it is clear that there is something very much wrong with a principle which inevitably leads to different Churches.

180. Different flowers require different soil.

If that be true, it follows that flowers growing from soil other than that intended by Christ are not the flowers He wanted.

181. Is there any likelihood of complete agreement among so many minds as diverse as there are men?

There is no likelihood that complete agreement among men on any religious, philosophical, or even political matter will ever be secured by any merely natural means. But God could certainly enlighten the minds of the most diverse types of men in such a way that they would be in complete agreement on certain given subjects. So, through all the centuries, the most diverse types of men drawn from different nations, men who have disagreed on almost everything else, have been in complete agreement as regards the essential doctrines of the Catholic Church. Today there are over 400 millions amongst various nations who are at one on the fact that Catholic doctrine is correct with the infallible authority of God Himself. The very doubt as to whether this could be done should make the fact that it is accomplished all the more impressive. Robert Hugh Benson, the son of a former Archbishop of Canterbury, became a Catholic. In his book, "Christ in the Church," he writes: "It is impossible to make men of one nation agree even on political matters. Yet the Catholic Church makes men of all nations agree on religious doctrines. When I was a student at Cambridge, I often used to find in one lecture hall, men of one nation and six religions. When I became a student in the University of Rome, I found in the one room, men of six nations and one religion. Is it conceivable that it is a merely human power that makes such a thing possible?"

182. Why are you always talking of divisions amongst Protestants?

It is not one of my regular topics. But when asked to discuss the relative merits of various positions, I point out simply that truth is consistent, and that Christ did insist that unity would be an outstanding characteristic of His Church. The unity of Catholicism is certainly as striking as its absence from Protestantism.

183. These divisions took place 400 years ago, and there is no need to harp upon them now.

The divisions in question have been occurring continuously throughout the 400 years since the Reformation. And the forces tending to division are exemplified in every new sect formed from year to year. But even if all the divisions in Protestantism did occur 400 years ago, surely the question is not one that concerns their remoteness. The question at issue concerns their justification. If divisions are wrong, they were not less wrong 400 years ago than they are now.

184. All the Protestant sects are on the best of terms.

I am afraid that scarcely solves the difficulty, even were it entirely true. The problem concerns their differences in teachings claimed to be revealed by one and the same God. They cannot all be teaching the truth. This is a problem which every intelligent Protestant must face, and not simply dismiss it.

185. Appalled by these divergencies, are not people tempted to reject all the Christian Churches?

Some may be: but to yield to such a temptation would be most unreasonable. If you stood by whilst Christ disputed with a member of the sect of the Pharisees, and another from the sect of the Sadducees, would you say, "I hate sectarianism; and since Christ rejects the Pharisees and Sadducees, whilst the Pharisees and Sadducees reject Christ, I will reject them all, and not submit even to Christ"? If those who were wrong thought Christ wrong, that did not make Christ wrong. In the same way, the Catholic Church rejects the various Protestant sects. They unite in rejecting the Catholic Church. But that does not justify you in rejecting them all, including the Catholic Church.

186. How can we solve the problem as to which is the true religion of Christ?

There are many ways of approaching the problem. But the simplest way is the historical way. Christ founded a Church, said that the gates of hell or forces of evil would never prevail against it, and also said that He would be with it all days till the end of the world. His Church, therefore, must be still in this world, and it must have been in the world all days since His time. That rules out all other Churches except the Catholic Church; for all other Churches came into existence long after Christ, and have not been in the world all days since Christ. But we will see more on this subject later.

187. All the Christian Churches are parts forming between them the one great universal and Catholic Church.

If that be so, you credit Christ with having established a very peculiar kind of Church to teach in His name. For if every Church which professes to be Christian is part of the one true Church, then the Church of Christ teaches simultaneously that Baptism is necessary for salvation, and that it is not necessary; that infants must be baptized, and that they must not be baptized; that the Pope is antichrist, and yet he is the Vicar of Christ; that Confession is an obligation, and yet it is an abomination; that Christ is really present in the Eucharist, but at the same time really absent. It is impossible to believe that Christ, Truth itself, and infinite Wisdom, taught such contradictory doctrines and obligations.

188. May we not regard the different forms of Christianity as so many different angles of the same truth? Do you deny that truth has different angles?

I admit that the truth can be viewed from different angles. But I deny that the truth can be different from itself. We cannot say that people who believe contradictory things are merely viewing the same truth from different angles. Of contradictories, if one is true, the other is false. For example, if a Protestant says that the Sacrifice of the Mass is blasphemy, whilst a Catholic declares it to be the highest act of worship proper to the Christian religion, would you regard those two as merely viewing the same truth from different angles? Reason itself rebels against such a supposition.

189. Cannot we take a kindly view, and see how much the Churches are alike beneath the outward form?

In dealing with the problem of differences between Churches we do not concentrate on the things in which they are alike, but precisely on the things in which they differ. And if we do that, we find that the variations go much deeper than merely outward form. They are constitutional and essential differences which cannot be healed until the constitution and essential doctrines, worship, and discipline of the Catholic Church are accepted by all. No amount of shutting our eyes to this, and speaking kindly of each other will solve this problem. Keeping our kindly dispositions towards each other, we must see all the facts, and work for unity.

190. *There is only one religion in the world, and that is faith in God.*

That cannot be admitted. Mahometanism, Judaism, and Christianity equally believe in God, yet they are three distinct religions.

191. *When asked where His Church would be found, Jesus answered, "Where two or three are gathered together in My name, there am I in the midst of them." Matt. XVIII., 20.*

On the occasion of those words no one was asking Christ where His Church would be found. Our Lord was teaching His Apostles that He would be found in His Church—a very different thing. When the Church legislates, Christ Himself ratifies that legislation. Take the context. In Matt. XVIII., 17-20, our Lord vindicates the authority of His Church when He says, "And if he will not hear them, tell the Church. And if he will not hear the Church, let him be to thee as the heathen and the publican." In the next verse He insists that He invests His authority in the Apostles, saying, "Whatsoever you shall bind upon earth is bound also in heaven." Then He adds the reason for this by saying, "If two of you consent upon earth, it shall be done, for where two or three are gathered together in My name, I am in the midst of them." But even if you take the words as implying Christ's presence with all who meet in His name, you must remember that He laid down many other conditions as well. Those conditions concerning His Church demand unity in doctrine, worship, and discipline. And when He said, "If you love me, keep My commandments," Jn. XIV., 15, not a single one of His commandments can be excluded. Take as a test the commandment to hear and obey the Church. By what Church are you taught? What Church do you obey? The very consideration of those questions forces one to look round in order to find His Church as a preliminary condition.

192. *All are one who are guided by the same Holy Spirit. Jesus said, "I will ask the Father, and He shall give you another Paraclete, that He may abide with you forever." Jn. XIV., 16.*

Christ there promises to send the Holy Spirit as an invisible source of light and strength upon His Church. Whilst that Holy Spirit will operate within the souls of the disciples of Christ, the very promise that He will abide "forever" shows that Christ is speaking of a gift to be granted to the Church collectively, and to remain with the Church till the end of time. As a matter of fact, when Christ spoke, the Holy Spirit was already dwelling in the souls of the Apostles as individuals. But He was not yet dwelling in them as a group, knitting them together in the Church they had to form. For this purpose the Holy Spirit was sent upon them collectively on Pentecost Sunday. It must be insisted upon that, whilst the Holy Spirit dwells within the souls of individual disciples of Christ, His teaching is never at variance with that of the Church. The same Holy Spirit works both in the Church and in individual souls. What the Church says to our ears the Spirit of Truth says in our hearts. The same wind which fills the sails of the ship provides for the breathing of the passengers. If a man says that the Holy Spirit within him tells him something quite opposed to the teaching of the Church, then such a man is mistaking his own vain fancies for the voice of God. That is why Christ said, "If a man will not hear the Church, let him be to thee as the heathen." Matt. XVIII., 17.

193. *It is hard to believe that good Protestant ministers, devoting themselves to Christ's Gospel, are not members of Christ's true Church.*

Their earnestness and devotedness are indeed admirable. But that makes it still sadder that they should be laboring in a mistaken way. They devote themselves to what they believe to be a furtherance of Christ's Gospel, but in reality they have inadequate and wrong notions of Christ's teachings. When they insist upon the love of God, a life of virtue, and devotion to the Person of Our Savior, I am heart and soul with them. But we must not lose sight of the nature of Christ's Church. That Church is one world-wide spiritual society in which all the members profess the same faith, unite in the same worship, and submit to the same Christ-given authority. A man is not a member of that Church unless he accepts the same teachings, participates in the same worship and Sacraments, and submits to the same authority as all other members of it.

194. So long as we are one in spirit, I do not see that variations of form matter very much.

That needs proof. Rev. Dr. Briggs, a Presbyterian scholar, says that, "whilst there can be a unity of the Christian spirit without unity of authority, there can be no Church unity without unity of authority." Yet, as Rev. Dr. Goudge, Regius Professor of Anglican theology at Oxford, has clearly shown, the New Testament absolutely requires Church unity. The various sects adopt isolated aspects of Christianity. But Dr. Goudge rightly remarks that "Christianity *a la carte* will not do. The religion of Christ must be accepted or rejected as a whole."

195. The Protestant Churches tend to unity of action, even if they have not unity of organization.

We cannot make one Church merely by employing the influences of different Churches in the same direction. American troops fought beside British troops in France during the war of 1914-18. They worked together for the same end. But Britain and America were no nearer to forming one nation than before. There is no escaping from the fact of divided and conflicting Churches.

196. Why worry about mere differences in doctrine?

Because truth requires consistency, and God has a right to be believed when He reveals a definite doctrine. No one who understands the New Testament could entertain loose ideas on this subject. St. Paul wrote to the Galatians, "Though we, or an angel from heaven, preach a Gospel to you besides that which we have preached to you, let him be accursed." Gal. I., 8. To Timothy he wrote, "I desired thee to remain at Ephesus that thou mightest charge some not to teach otherwise." I Tim. I., 3. "If any man teach otherwise, and consent not to the sound words of our Lord Jesus Christ, and to that doctrine which is according to godliness, he is proud, knowing nothing." I Tim. VI., 3. It is quite evident from the New Testament that differences in doctrine do matter very much, and that compromise in such things is impossible.

197. Although a Protestant, I think that there is room for all beliefs.

Since the Catholic religion denies that, you can scarcely think that there is room for the Catholic belief. However, let us take your general thought that all religions have a right to exist. Buddhism and Mahometanism are beliefs, yet does not Christianity exclude those? Or was Christ wrong in sending His Apostles to teach and to convert all nations, winning them from their previous beliefs to His doctrines? Christ would never have admitted that there is room for all beliefs. Again, your own remote ancestors were pagans. Had the early Christians accepted your principle that there is room for all beliefs, they would never have sent missionaries to your ancestors. They would have been left in their paganism, and you would have inherited their paganism only. Each link in the chain from them to you would have remained what he was born, and would have died such.

198. All paths lead to God.

That is rather an extreme statement. You believe in the Christian religion, and the Christian religion excludes the idea that all paths lead to God. In fact, it teaches very definitely that some paths do not lead to God. Christ Himself distinguished between two roads, declaring the way leading to life to be narrow and restricted, whilst the way leading to destruction is broad and pleasant to those who are bent on self-satisfaction. St. Paul wrote to the Corinthians, "Know you not that the unjust shall not possess the kingdom of God? Do not err: neither fornicators, nor idolators, nor adulterers, nor the effeminate, nor liers with mankind, nor thieves, nor the covetous, nor drunkards, nor railers, nor extortioners, shall possess the kingdom of God." 1 Cor. VI., 9-10. We cannot therefore say that all paths lead to God.

199. Some climb the steps; others take the longer winding road; but the mountain top comes in view at last—to all of us.

We may hope that it will. We do not know that it will. When Christ put the question, "What does it profit a man to gain the whole world if he suffers the loss of his soul?" Matt. XVI., 26, He at least implied the possibility of not attaining to the mountain top. He warned the Pharisees that their salvation was highly improbable. And of Judas He said, "It were better for him, if that man had not been born." Mk. XIV., 21.

200. I believe in the little saying, "Your truth is not my truth."

On what grounds do you accept that? Truth is neither yours nor mine. It is independent of either of us. We hold things because they are true. They are not true because we happen to believe them. Again, truth is consistent. If you have the truth on a given subject, and my ideas conflict with yours, then I do not possess the truth. And if I am right, you haven't got the truth. If you wanted to go to a certain town by rail, but got into the wrong train, would you ignore the stationmaster's advice, and say, "Your truth is not my truth?" You would not. Why is that axiom valid only when it is a question of the way to heaven?

201. Why can't each choose his own path to God?

Because it is for God to say by what path we will come to Him, and not for man to tell God to be content with whatever men choose to do. How far would you extend your principle? You are a professing Christian. Will you admit the right of every individual to reject Christ and choose his own path to God, even though it be opposed to that prescribed by the very Son of God? If not, then you abandon the principle that every individual has the right to choose his own path. And if you make any restrictions, you cannot object on principle to the restrictions made by the Catholic Church. All you can ask is why the Catholic Church should draw the line in a different place from that chosen by yourself.

202. Every individual must be entitled to his own religious beliefs.

That is a half-truth, and a half-truth is nearly always most dangerous. If, as Christians believe, God has revealed a religion, people are obliged to accept that religion, and no other. They are no longer entitled to their own religious beliefs once God has dictated what they must believe. On the other hand, people are entitled to follow their own conscience, even though their ideas be defective or mistaken. In fact, they are obliged to live according to what they honestly deem to be true and right. Thus, for example, a Protestant, so long as he really thinks his Protestantism to be correct, is entitled and obliged to remain a Protestant. But should he discover the truth of Catholicism, he is certainly no longer entitled to remain a Protestant.

203. Since we all aim at the one destination, it cannot matter by what road we travel.

It must matter, or Christ would not have taught a new and very definite religion. After all, the Jews were aiming at the same destination as ourselves, eternal salvation, and happiness with God. Yet Christ did not say that their road was good enough. Again, if God not only appoints the destination, but also the road by which we must travel, we cannot say that any other road is just as good. The Catholic Church declares hers to be the only right road. Other Churches dispute that, and maintain that any religion will do. It is evident that the Catholic claim, if true, is most important. Study the evidence for it.

204. *Provided we all strive for the one end, why worry as to who is right or wrong?*

Do you really believe that Christ is the Son of God who came down from heaven to teach us the truth in the name of our Creator, and yet that it does not matter whether our ideas of that truth be right or wrong? Is it quite all right for a Church to claim to be that of Christ, yet to teach a whole lot of errors in His name? Do you seriously mean that there is no need to worry about that? And if it does not matter whether one is a Catholic or a Methodist because both Churches are striving for the one end—to serve God, does it matter whether one be a Christian or a Mahometan?

Mahometans also believe in the true God and try to serve Him in their own way. Now just as you would insist that one must strive in the Christian way rather than in the Mahometan way, so I insist that it must be in the Catholic way rather than in the Methodist or any other way. In other words, there is need to worry as to who is right and who is wrong.

205. *All the Churches aim at teaching Christian principles.*

We cannot concentrate on identity of aim only. The Catholic Church will never blame anyone for aiming at teaching Christian principles. But, besides considering the good intention, she also and very wisely considers the principles taught. And she says that, however good the aim or intention of other Churches, that does not alter the fact that they teach many wrong principles.

206. *God is Love, and therefore must be tolerant and impartial.*

Because God is Love, He must love the good and the true. And that excludes the bad and the false. As a Christian, too, you cannot expect God to be tolerant of insults directed against His only-begotten Son. He must be partial to the doctrine taught by His own Son, and He cannot be indifferent to blasphemous denials of the veracity of Christ. Moreover, God must be partial to the exact and complete doctrine of Christ, and not to incomplete or distorted doctrines proposed by men who, with no right to do so, tampered with the teachings of Christ. If you admit this, you admit that God is partial to the Catholic Church, and that He is not pleased with the other Churches which cannot agree amongst themselves save in their opposition to the greatest Church of all—the Catholic Church.

207. *Christ gave broad principles for all to follow.*

He wants all to follow His principles. But if you think that His principles were vague and indefinite, allowing people to believe all kinds of contradictory things, and to indulge in a kind of religious go-as-you-please race, you are very much in error. And you really insult Christ's wisdom as a Teacher.

208. *He taught us all to love one another.*

If you believe it necessary to accept that teaching of Christ, do not forget that He taught much else. And all else that He taught has the same authority.

209. *He did not say that if one is not a Roman Catholic he will not enter heaven.*

He bade the Apostles teach all nations all things whatsoever He had commanded them. In those words we see that He excepts nothing. He also said, "He that believeth and is baptized shall be saved; he that believeth not shall be condemned." Mk. XVI., 16. Therefore once men have had the Gospel of Christ sufficiently put before them, they have to believe it absolutely and completely, under pain of eternal loss. In St. Matthew XVIII., 17, He says, "If a man will not hear the Church, let him be as the heathen." There is then a Church to which we must submit if we wish to belong to Christ. Which is that Church? It is the Church you yourself call the Roman Catholic Church. If you do not think so, you have a twofold duty. You must prove that that Church is not the one intended by Christ, and you must find the Church He did intend.

210. *So long as we worship Christ, we will be saved in the end.*

Why make it necessary to worship Christ? If all are not obliged to adopt the Catholic faith, why should all be obliged to accept Christ? If, in order to escape becoming a Catholic, you argue that one religion is as good as another, you cut the ground from under your feet when it comes to a question of defending the Christian religion against all other forms of religion.

211. *Does it make any difference to people's sincerity, if they follow the Master in their own way?*

It might, or it might not. If they know that it is merely their own way, and not His way, then they cannot be sincere if they say that they follow Christ as their Master. For then He would not be their Master. They would be their own masters. If, however, they really believed that the way in which they were trying to follow Christ is indeed the exact way Christ Himself has prescribed, then they could be sincere, even though mistaken.

212. *If a man is sincere, won't he attain to goodness, no matter what Church he attends?*

It is true that people belonging to different Churches can be equally sincere in their efforts to be good. But that cannot alter the fact that the religions they profess are different. And a man who is seeking the truth will say, "Let me reflect, not on the point in which these good people do not differ, but on the points in which they do differ." In other words, we must abstract from the persons professing the religions, and consider the religions they profess. For it is certain that God, the Supreme Truth, could not have revealed contradictory teachings. Take, for example, the infallibility of the Church. I believe that Christ meant His Church to be infallible. You do not. We cannot both be right. And as we both profess to believe in Christ, the burning problem is whether indeed Christ intended His Church to be infallible. That problem must be solved.

213. *So long as a man tries to be good and to do good, does it really matter what he believes or what religion he accepts?*

Christ said, "Everyone therefore that shall confess Me before men, I will confess him before My Father who is in heaven; but he that shall deny Me before men, I will also deny him before My Father who is in heaven." Matt. X., 10. Evidently it does matter as to whether we profess faith in Christ or not. And that rules out the idea that any non-Christian religions are as good as the Christian religion. Again, if Christ wants His followers to be Catholics and not Protestants, then it cannot be just as good to be a Protestant as a Catholic.

See also R. R., Vol. I, Nos. 203-243.

CHAPTER SEVEN

THE PROTESTANT REFORMATION

214. What is your attitude towards the Protestant Church?

As with Greek Orthodoxy, so with Protestantism—there is no such thing in reality as the Protestant Church. Protestantism is a generic name covering many different sects which agree in protesting against the claims of the Catholic Church.

215. That Protestant means one who protests against Rome is a popularly accepted idea, but it is erroneous.

The Rev. Dr. Goudge, a Protestant, and Regius professor of Divinity at Oxford, writes, "The number of meanings given to the word Protestant is astonishing, as the great Oxford dictionary will show us. It suggests a person whose main interest is opposition to Rome, and possibly there may be such persons. The best use of the word today may be the Roman Catholic and the Eastern Orthodox use, in which a Protestant means a Western Christian who remains outside the Roman Church."

216. Naturally we protest against the errors of Rome.

I deny that what Protestants think to be the erroneous doctrines of Rome are really erroneous, if indeed they be the teachings of the Catholic Church. I add that last condition because many doctrines are attributed to Rome which Rome has never taught. In this case, Protestants simply do not understand the religion they attack. It must be noted, too, that Protestants are anything but agreed amongst themselves as to what should be condemned in Catholic teaching. What one Protestant condemns, another Protestant will vehemently defend.

217. But in reality the word Protestant is positive and means that one witnesses for the great ideals of the Gospel. The prefix "pro" means "for," whilst "testor" means "I witness."

That is a modern interpretation of the word which departs from the historical sense.

218. In the Latin Vulgate translation of the Bible we find the words, "Quos protestantes illi audire nolebant," meaning, "They would not hear them when they protested." 2 Par. XXIV., 19.

Those words refer to the ill will of the Jews who would not listen to the prophets sent by God to protest against their evil practices. They have no reference to the meaning of the word Protestant as applied to the Reformation. It is a dreadful anachronism to connect a word used in a fourth century translation of the Old Testament with a Protestantism which arose only in the sixteenth century. No one could say that St. Jerome had the Protestant Reformation in mind when he translated the Old Testament into Latin so many centuries earlier.

219. Historically the word was derived from the celebrated "Protest" read by the German princes at the Diet of Spires.

That is correct. Here, of course, we approach the real problem. It is the historic meaning of the word according to the events of the period when it arose that really counts, not possible meanings of the word in more remote ages.

220. *The German princes said, "We protest and declare that we neither consent nor adhere in any manner whatsoever to the proposed Decree in anything contrary to God, to His holy Word, to our right conscience, and to the salvation of our souls."*

So spoke the German princes. But what did the Decree demand? These princes had taken advantage of the religious revolt of Luther to secure the political independence of their States. Naturally, in turn, they supported Lutheranism as a great force amongst their people for the breaking of old ties; and they commenced the suppression of Catholic worship in their domains. Now the Decree of the Diet of Spires granted religious liberty to such as had already embraced Lutheranism in the States of the German princes, but demanded toleration for Catholics dwelling within their boundaries. The Lutheran princes protested that they would not grant toleration to Catholics, and said that the religion of their people must be the same as that of their princes. "Cuius regio, illius religio," said these princes. "Whoever is the ruler, his must be the religion." In other words, the German princes demanded the right to impose whatever religion they might please upon their subjects. And their protest was against any obligation to tolerate Catholics. The word Protestant, therefore, according to its historical and religious meaning, was born of a denial of freedom of conscience; and those who thus protested against liberty of worship for Catholics were termed Protestants.

221. *The power of Romanism was shattered by Martin Luther, of immortal memory.*

Martin Luther is undoubtedly an outstanding figure in history. But the immortal memory of Luther will become less and less pleasant as the facts concerning him become known. Those who idealize Luther can do so only by ignoring an immense amount of inconvenient information. He was a priest of the Catholic Church, but one who was not faithful to his obligations even as a Christian. On his own admissions he was a victim of both immorality and drunkenness; and he was the most intolerant of men. Far from granting liberty of conscience, he refused to allow anyone to think differently from himself, and coolly said, "Whoever teaches otherwise than I teach is a child of hell."

222. *When did the Protestant Movement begin?*

In the sixteenth century. Luther, in Germany, broke away from the Catholic Church in 1517, and began to set up a new Church for himself. Henry VIII., in England, abandoned the Catholic Church in 1534, when he brought in the law of his own supremacy over the Church in his own realm. It would take too long to narrate how each of the first Protestants broke away. In various ways, each rebelled against the authority of the Church and was excommunicated by the Church. Luther denied her teaching by preaching heretical doctrines. Henry VIII defended her teachings, but violated the discipline of the Church.

223. *Did not Norway and Sweden adopt Protestantism?*

Lutheranism was imposed on both peoples by their rulers. The princes wanted control of the Church independently of the Pope. In breaking with Rome, they took the nearest form of Protestantism at hand—Lutheranism. Frederic I. of Denmark imposed Lutheranism upon Norway. In Sweden, Gustavus Vasa led a revolt against Denmark, and was crowned king of Sweden. He himself was a Catholic, and the people were much attached to the Catholic faith. But Gustavus needed money for his new kingdom, and to get it he decided to confiscate the estates of the Church. Not from religious conviction, but solely through political expediency, he decided to impose Lutheranism also by civil authority.

PAINTING THE PROTESTANT REFORMATION

224. What made Scotland abandon the Catholic faith?

There were three chief causes: Firstly, most of the people were not instructed in their religion, and were greatly disaffected towards the Catholic Church by the scandalous laxity of the Scottish clergy of the time. The clergy made little pretense at a life in accordance with what they preached, and their disedifying lives left the people ready to back up any preacher who seemed sincere, whether he was right or wrong in matters of doctrine. Secondly, John Knox eventually came from Geneva to preach straight-out Calvinism with a zeal and energy which stood out in marked contrast with the apathy of the Catholic clergy in the cause of the old religion. Thirdly, John Knox had the armed support of the nobles who sought to possess themselves of Church property.

225. So you blame the depravity of the clergy?

I give it as one of the reasons, and even as the main reason. In his book on the "Counter-Reformation in Scotland," Father Pollen says that the depravity and laxity of the clergy were unquestionably the main reasons why the faith of Catholics fell away so suddenly and so completely before the Protestant preachers. This is no argument against the Catholic Church; but it is a terrible indictment of the Catholic clergy in Scotland immediately prior to the advent of Protestantism. As Mr. Joseph Clayton has pointed out, no mass of people will ever be persuaded for long that priests and clerics can justly be exempted from the moral standards prescribed for the laity.

226. This seems to be new history from Catholic lips. Do not most Catholic writers paint the Protestant Reformation in the blackest colors?

They have maintained, and still maintain, that the Protestant Reformation can never be justified. But I admit that most history books written in the past by Catholics have exhibited a good deal of bias against the Protestant Reformers, even as the history books written by Protestants have given a distorted view of the Catholic position—and to a far greater extent.

227. History is history, and the record of truth.

You leave out the fact that historians do not always tell the truth. I admit that the writing of history is a very difficult thing. For, firstly, a man must get the facts, testing his sources rigidly at every stage. Secondly, since no one book can give all the facts, some must be left out. And here the mentality of the writer will decide the omissions. If he has any prejudices, the tendency will be to leave out the facts that tell against his theories. "What has the historian left out?" is one of the first questions to be put in estimating the worth of a textbook. Thirdly, if we consider such undisputed facts as he does give, the question arises as to the interpretation and significance of those facts. Now the textbooks of history in the English language have for the most part been written by men whole-heartedly Protestant, or by conviction anti-Catholic; or at least by those infected by the Protestant tradition, however impartial they may think themselves to be. If only unconsciously, bias and prejudice creep into their writings, and the real truth is not to be found in their works. Our complaint is not against history, but against the historians.

228. You will never undo memories of the past in Protestant minds.

We can correct those memories. We can point out that textbooks perpetuating false views of history do not give a genuine knowledge of the past, and persuade them to cease pulling the bandage off old sores, giving them no chance to heal. In histories of the Protestant Reformation feeling and sentimental loyalties have again and again got the better of dispassionate reason. And the education in history which they have provided has accounted for millions of professing Christians fearing and hating the Catholic Church, and that in a way which is simply baffling to Catholics.

229. Have not Catholic writers distorted history also?

Undoubtedly many have done so. On both sides history has been written in a partisan spirit. Bias, of course, may be quite unconscious. Nevertheless it results in distorted and inadequate presentations of history, and I agree with Mr. Joseph Clayton's advice that, if there is to be any bias where history is concerned, it should be, in both writer and reader, to the truth, the whole truth, and nothing but the truth—and that, both in the presentation of the facts, and in the interpretation of those facts. Of one thing I am certain: the Catholic Church has nothing whatever to fear from the results of such historical research. Truth cannot contradict truth; and the Catholic religion, being the truth, will never find itself in any way disturbed by any facts that history can reveal.

230. Not many people, either Catholic or Protestant, will agree with these views.

Those in a position to give a reliable verdict do so. I have quoted Mr. Clayton, a Catholic writer. In support let me quote a Protestant, Rev. Dr. Goudge, Regius professor of Divinity at Oxford. In a plea for a better understanding between Protestants and Catholics, he begs us to drop the prejudices of the sixteenth century when the Reformation occurred. "The whole spirit of the controversies then," he writes, "was wrong. They were black with hatred and misrepresentation, and largely conducted in theological Billingsgate. If we base our statements upon sixteenth century sources, we generally base them upon poisoned sources. At best they leave out half the truth; and at worst, they are lying." Again he says, "Much of the history written then was not history, but controversy under a thin disguise. Even if the facts recorded are indeed facts—which is not always the case—they are so selected, and so presented, as to give a false idea of what took place. Here there has happily been a great change. The best Catholic and Protestant historians are not far today from agreement about the facts, though they do not regard them in the same way. No instructed Roman Catholic now denies the appalling condition of Western Christendom at the beginning of the sixteenth century, or the failure of the Conciliar and other reforming movements to deal successfully with it. No instructed Protestant now denies that political and personal motives bulked very large in the Protestant Reformation. It is the duty of the better-informed members of all Communions to correct the errors of the less-informed, especially when these errors lead them to misjudge those from whom they are separated." So speaks Dr. Goudge, and I agree with every one of his words in this matter.

231. Don't you find it a mystery that so many millions should fall away from the Catholic Church during the Reformation?

No one with a knowledge of human psychology, and of the conditions of the period, would find it a mystery.

232. Was not the fall of the Roman Catholic Church due to the vilest practices ever recorded against any Church?

The Catholic Church did not fall. Many of her members had fallen from her standards of virtue, and this was made the excuse for their conduct by multitudes who fell from the faith into heresy. And the children of those who then fell away from Catholicism are today falling into indifference to all religion and almost complete unbelief, whilst the Catholic Church is the one great stronghold of Christianity in the world. Even in his own day Luther admitted that the more his teachings progressed, the worse the people became. "It is clear," he wrote, "how much more greedy, cruel, immodest, shameless, and wicked the people now are than they were under the Papacy."

233. Do you deny that the Church was in a state of decay prior to the Reformation?

I deny that. I do not deny that there was a widespread laxity corrupting the lives of many of the clergy and laity alike. St. Thomas More knew the society of his day very well, and he put things pithily when he said, "The world is tired of the clergy, but the clergy are not tired of the world." Yet St. Thomas More did not make the mistake of blaming the Church of Christ for the lax members in it. He blamed the lax members. And it would be a mistake to think that there was nothing but laxity in the Church in the times immediately prior to the Reformation. There were Saints in those days side by side with the sinners. Read that marvellous little book, "The Imitation of Christ," by Thomas a Kempis; and try to realize that that treasure of spirituality was written by a Catholic monk during those very years of supposed universal corruption. That book represents the true ideals of the Catholic Church, and is a strong condemnation of the unchristian lives of those who were a disgrace to the Christian name.

234. The Book of Revelations revealed that many of the hierarchy would fall into gross sins in the Middle Ages. History tells us that they did so.

It is a mistake to restrict the predictions of Revelations to any particular class, or to any particular age. St. John sees the forces of evil ever reviving and renewing their attack against Christ and His Church. Only with the end of the world itself will the influence of antichrist or the Beast come to an end. Through the ages surge upon surge of evil will attack the Church; now prevailing in a greater degree; now beaten back. But we need not go to the Book of Revelations for predictions of evil amongst members of the Church. Christ Himself predicted them. "It must needs be," He said, "that scandals come. But woe to that man by whom the scandal cometh." Matt. XVIII., 7. And He did not make any distinction between clergy and laity. In fact He seems almost to have permitted the fall of Judas, one of the Apostolic hierarchy, to warn us of the possibility of such things, and to preserve us from undue dismay.

235. Pope Innocent III said that the Church of his day suffered from five evils, and that the first of all was the evil conduct of prelates.

Be it so. But notice that Pope Innocent III, whilst aware of the abuses on the part of prelates, did not sanction them. He spoke to condemn them as not in keeping with Catholic ideals. And the obvious cure was the reform of the prelates, and the stamping out of their abuses; not the dynamiting of the whole Church established by Christ, and the creation of new Churches by men who had no authority from God to do so. Certainly Pope Innocent himself never dreamed that such abuses could afford any excuse for leaving the Catholic Church, and setting up other Churches.

236. Reform after reform was instituted by the Popes, only to fail because of strong vested interests.

Despite the exaggerated suggestion of current evils, the admission that reform after reform was attempted shows that the Catholic Church was definitely not evil in itself, but good; that she could not accept with equanimity the violation of her ideals; and that she never remained passive under the sufferings inflicted on her by her own subjects. As a matter of fact, the reforms instituted were not in vain, though in many cases they failed owing to lack of goodwill in the subjects. Eventually the Church did succeed in securing her own internal reform so far as that is possible in a Church consisting of human beings.

237. Will you set out what you consider the main causes for the loss of such multitudes to the Church at the Reformation?

There was nothing whatever wrong with the Catholic religion in itself. But there were a good many things wrong with great numbers of Catholics, or the Reformation would have been impossible. No one simple cause can explain it. The conduct of those who left the Church must be attributed firstly to their infidelity to the grace of God in their own personal lives, and to their own pride and passions. But that so many should follow these leaders demands explanation. Mass defections from the Church were possible only in a given atmosphere. And unfortunately many factors were at hand to contribute to the disaster. Political causes had weakened the authority of the Pope. Their personal ambitions made the German princes of the various small States welcome a movement which would free them from their discordant relations with the Pope altogether—even religiously. The covetous and avaricious also saw the possibility of loot and plunder in the confiscation of Church property. So they supported the Protestant rebellion even by force of arms. In England the Tudor kings had immense power, and Henry VIII, when he could not get his divorce from the Pope, found it comparatively easy to impose his ideas on his subjects, robbing them of the Catholic inheritance. We must remember, too, that the Renaissance had brought the revival of the pagan Greek and Latin classics, and these had corrupted the minds and the hearts of the educated classes. Moreover, many of the bishops and priests, far removed from Rome, had been too subservient to secular authority, and had neglected to enforce the discipline of the Church, thus weakening their hold upon the people. Laxity amongst the clergy had given great disedification; and the delay in their reformation had paved the way for a wrong reformation by breaking away from the Church. Careless priests had left the faithful uninstructed, and incredibly ignorant of their religion; and, not knowing their own faith, great numbers of simple Catholics did not discern the real evil of the separatist movement. Not knowing the truth, they were swayed by the ideas of the Reformers, who denounced Rome without demanding any higher standard of virtue than that which had prevailed. And when the temporal rulers backed up the campaign with violence and oppression, the people simply found themselves Protestants. There were many other factors also, which a brief reply can scarcely describe. But I have said enough to show the possibility of a Reformation, with its disastrous division of Christendom amongst an ignorant, dissatisfied, and disedified laity, above all under pressure by ruling princes, and grasping dukes and earls.

238. In view of all this, was not a Reformation necessary?

Undoubtedly. But there was no need for what is popularly called "The Reformation." Any abuses amongst the members of the Church will always cry out urgently for reform. But Protestantism was not a movement of real reform. It made prevalent abuses an excuse to abandon the Church altogether, instead of remaining with it, and trying to effect the conversion of its lax members to better ways. Moreover, Protestantism retained many of the very abuses, and merely sought to justify them by denying that they were wrong. That the Catholic Church will never do. She may have to admit sadly that her children sin; but she will never say that what is sin, is not sin, as did many of the Reformers.

239. Would the Reformers have had any success had they been dealing with present-day Catholics?

Not with well-instructed and sincere Catholics who are genuinely trying to live up to their religion. Ignorant and careless Catholics would be quite likely to fall away, above all when a less-exacting religion was proposed to them, and if the civil power were employed on behalf of the would-be Reformers. Mexico, Germany,

Russia, and Austria, are proof enough of that in recent times. Where good Catholics have made an heroic stand, and even died for their faith, careless Catholics have fallen away. History contains many useful lessons for all Catholics. The Catholic Church cannot fail. But its members can and do fail. And their greatest safeguards against doing so are a thorough knowledge of their religion, and a life of virtue in accordance with its teachings. Sound education, integrity of character, and a genuine effort to live a life of Christian holiness—and that on the part of both clergy and laity —are necessary for the growth and well-being of the Catholic Church in whatever country it may be established. Catholics can look back with unwavering faith at past ages; but they would be very foolish if they did not profit by the vision of the nemesis that overtook Catholics in those past ages.

240. Did not Martin Luther force the Catholic Church to reform herself?

The multitudes swept from the Catholic Church by Protestantism certainly brought home to her leaders the urgent need for real reform; and that real reform was effected by the Council of Trent. The severe legislation and disciplinary decrees of that Council eradicated the pronounced abuses which gave occasion to the Protestant landslide from the Church; and there has been no such movement since. Protestantism spent its force, so far as the Catholic Church is concerned, in the first years of revolt; and it has not been any real danger to the faith of Catholics since. The notable tendency today is for Protestants to become Catholics; not for Catholics to become Protestants.

241. Surely, then, you owe some thanks to Martin Luther.

Luther we cannot respect. He had no right to leave the Catholic Church, and commence a Church of his own under the pretense of reform. He should have remained in the true Church and labored to reform lax Catholics within it. You wash a plate that needs cleansing; you do not smash it. As a matter of fact, in 1521, the worldly-minded Pope Leo X died, and was succeeded by the German Pope Adrian VI. Adrian was just such a Pope as Luther pretended to demand. He was austere and holy, and at once set to work to reform the members of the Church, beginning with the Cardinals themselves, and battling against Italian laxity. The brave old Pope would have been vastly aided by German support, and the closing of the Northern Schism. But Luther made no effort to help a true reformer set in the very See whence reform ought to have come. Instead of rushing to the aid of a compatriot who was just such a head of the Church as he had declared necessary, he continued to pour forth abuse against the Pope as if he were the devil. Blind passion, and not reason, was Luther's guide. Adrian VI died broken-hearted, and the real Counter-Reformation came with the Council of Trent nearly twenty years later. The widespread chaos compelled action then; but reform was due to the innate power of the living Catholic Church to renew her own vitality.

242. Despite the evils amongst her members, you still insist that the Catholic Church is the true Church?

Yes. Any moral evils which have ever crept in amongst the members of the Catholic Church are a proof, not that the Catholic Church is wrong, but only that her members are human beings ever liable to temptation, and to a lack of generosity in corresponding with the dictates of conscience and the inspirations of divine grace.

243. Since Christ commanded men to carry on His work, were not men free to form new Churches if necessary?

The mere fact that men were ordered to carry on the work of Christ Himself shows that they were not free to form new Churches according to their own ideas. That would be their own work, not Christ's work. Delegates are free to act within the jurisdiction given them by their principals, not to go beyond it. St. Paul denied that he, Apostle though he was, had any right to form a new and different Church. "Though we," he wrote to the Galatians, "or an angel from heaven, preach a gospel differing from what you have received, let him be anathema." Gal. I., 8. And to the Corinthians he wrote, "Let there be no schisms amongst you." 1 Cor. XII., 25. If the Apostles themselves had no right to set up new and independent Churches, they could not possibly have transmitted such a right to others.

244. *You deny that the Reformers had any divine authority for their work?*

Yes. They had no divine authority to commence their new forms of religion, and they did so in opposition to the clear teaching of the New Testament. A reform, not a repudiation of the Church, was needed. Our Lord said that His Church would be like a net holding good and bad fish. At the time of the Reformation there were altogether too many bad fish. But bad fish do not make a bad net. And instead of laboring to turn the bad fish into good ones, the Reformers began to make new nets. That was their mistake. Christ had made the original net, and had said that it would never fail. And it has not failed. The Catholic Church is as vital as ever. It is she today who defends the Bible against Protestant critics; who stands for all the fundamental Christian doctrines; who refuses all compromise where the moral law is in question. But the new nets or Churches made by the Reformers are rapidly going to pieces. The strands are all broken, and the fish are swimming off in any direction they please, losing their faith in Christianity altogether. Those who want the full Christian truth will find it only by returning to that Catholic Church their forefathers should never have left, and from which they themselves are separated through no fault of their own.

245. *Dry rot seems to have set in amongst Christians, and to my mind the Church is dying.*

Many Protestants speak like that, having their own Churches only in mind. They would not do so, if they knew anything of the Catholic Church. Far from being subject to dry rot, that Church is very much alive. Her influence upon souls is exceedingly great. Her Churches are crowded with worshippers four and five times over in the cities, and as often as Mass can be celebrated in country centers. Her schools are crowded with children being taught their religious obligations; and tribute after tribute is paid to her spiritual vitality by people from whom such tributes might least be expected.

246. *Protestants claim to belong to the Apostolic Church.*

The claim cannot be sustained. That Church alone can be truly Apostolic which reaches back to the Apostles by the historical, spiritual, and social bond of uninterrupted succession. Jesus chose and commissioned the Apostles, and they formed the authoritative body in the Church. And in the same Church today there must still be an authoritative body derived from them. This derivation must be historically and socially evident in a visible Church. The whole chain depends on the first link, for that links the Church to Christ.

247. *The Reformation was to restore the Apostolic Church.*

So it is said. But Protestants do not claim an Apostolic character for their Churches in the right sense of the word. As a rule, they seek to attach themselves to Christ directly, without any intermediary society possessing historical continuity. They rather claim to have a religion "like" that of the Apostles, than one given them "by" the Apostles and their lawful successors. The true Christian and Catholic doctrine is that the Eternal Son of God became man in the Incarnation, thus commencing a life at once divine and human. And this life of Christ continues its activity by the Church, which is a kind of permanent social incarnation. As there is one continuous life of humanity by heredity, so the life of the Church is continuous by succession and tradition.

248. We cling to the traditions of the Apostles.

You mean that you have the same doctrines as the Apostles. That is not really true. But even were it true, it would not be enough. To profess someone's doctrine on the grounds of one's own approval of them does not mean social continuity with him. The Church is a society, and its life is collective and organized under one authority. Protestantism has no central authority, and no priesthood properly so-called. It has not an apostolicity such as the true Christian Church requires.

249. The Reformed Church has always acknowledged the Roman Catholic Church as an important branch of the Church Catholic; but that Christian judgment is not reciprocated.

Do all the Protestant Churches constitute the one "Reformed Church"? If so, would Methodists or Presbyterians admit that they are one with Judge Rutherford's Witnesses of Jehovah? After all, Judge Rutherford has as much, or as little right to set up his new Protestant sect as John Knox had to set up Presbyterianism. And it is not true, of course, that the Protestant Churches have always acknowledged the Roman Church as an important branch of the Church Catholic. The first Reformers rejected the Catholic Church as antichrist, and spoke of it with the utmost horror. Preaching in Edinburgh, in 1565, John Knox, the founder of Presbyterianism, declared that the Church is limited to those who profess the Lord Jesus, and have rejected papistry." The Catholic Church must be forgiven for refusing to admit relationship with Protestant Churches which originated with men who denounced her, and left her, and never returned to her. Is it reasonable to suppose that the new Churches set up by the Reformers are really in union with the Church they left? History and logic leave no room for the modern claim of Protestants to belong also to the Catholic Church.

250. Whom do members of Protestant Churches acknowledge as head of their Church on earth?

They have various systems of government. In some, as the Congregationalists, the members of each congregation are a law to themselves. In others, as the Presbyterians, authority is vested by the members in elected office-bearers, different assemblies prevailing in various localities. In these cases there is no universal bond of unity in the strict sense of the word. In Churches which have bishops, as the Catholic, Orthodox Greek, and Episcopal or Anglican, power is vested in those bishops. In the Greek Church the power is ultimately traced back to one or other of almost a dozen different Patriarchs. There is no such thing as one united Greek Church. In the Anglican Church the final authority is traced back to the Crown of England. In the Catholic Church all authority on earth centers in one supreme bishop independent of any national rulers—the Bishop of Rome. Thus we have a genuine ecclesiastical unity side by side with the required universality of one and the same Church throughout the world.

251. Do the Anglican, Presbyterian, and Methodist Churches exist in such foreign countries as Germany, Russia, France, Spain, Norway, etc.?

They may have what may be termed "agencies" in some of those countries to cater for English-speaking tourists of the different denominations. But, insofar as any nationals of these countries profess Protestantism, they usually profess a type of Protestantism peculiar to themselves. Where the Catholic Church unites men of different nationalities in one and the same Christian doctrine, Protestantism permits variations in doctrine to suit the national differences of outlook amongst men.

252. *You habitually speak of your own Church as the Catholic Church. What right have you to drop the prefix "Roman"?*

Either ours is the Catholic Church, or there is no Catholic Church. The expression "Roman Catholic," though frequently used, is really meaningless. Grammatically it involves a contradiction in terms. For the word Catholic means universal or "not limited." To use the word "Roman" as a qualifying adjective of limitation or restriction is like speaking of the "limited unlimited." Again, geographically, the Catholic Church is that Church which exists in all the different countries of the world for members of those different countries. And our Church is alone truly Catholic in that sense of the word. The Church subject to the Bishop of Rome exists in every country precisely for the people of each different country. No other Church is universal in this sense of the word.

253. *I cannot accept your verdict of Protestantism. You seem quite blind to all the positive good it has accomplished.*

I am not blind to the good to be found in Protestantism side by side with its errors. But I am concerned with the Reformation movement as such; and I say that it was not justified.

254. *When the Romish Church rose to power she abandoned the teachings of the Gospel until the people were fed up with the deal given by Rome.*

The Catholic Church never abandoned the teachings of the Gospel. The laxity of many of her members in practice was made one of the excuses for the Protestant Reformation. But the Protestant defection from the Church was a great mistake.

255. *The people gladly accepted the teaching in which the Apostles gloried.*

You would find it very difficult to set out clearly the teachings of the Protestant Reformers which you believe to harmonize with those of the Apostles. For the Reformers themselves were anything but agreed as to what should be believed. They fought against each other's teachings bitterly, indulging in violent mutual recriminations.

256. *Protestantism is a witness to the great truths that have stood the test of time.*

It used to witness to some of them. But unfortunately it is allowing most of them nowadays to be denied without protest, and even by its official teachers and ministers.

257. *Protestants believe the Bible to be the standard of Christian truth, and the very Word of God.*

Many of their leading exponents dispute that today. But even amongst those who still accept the Bible, there is little agreement as to what the Bible means. The Catholic Church defends the Bible as the very Word of God, and is alone capable of giving the authentic interpretation of the sense intended by God.

258. *The Bible gives spiritual freedom such as all Protestants enjoy.*

The Bible nowhere gives freedom to believe as one pleases, or to worship as one pleases. It demands our submission to the truth that we may be free from error, and obedience to the Church that we may be free from false forms of religion.

259. *The Reformation limited the power of priests, and liberated the people from an autocratic hierarchy.*

It abolished the priestly office, limiting the ministry to the preaching of the Word of God and the administration of some of the Sacraments.

260. *It meant a purifying of the ministerial office to an extent that makes it difficult to realize now the evils to which it was subject.*

It is true that there were many evils amongst the clergy at the time of the Reformation. I will go so far as to say that, had the Catholic clergy of the time been all they should have been, the disaster would not have occurred. At the same time, if many were not true to their obligations, many also were strictly faithful, and some were saints fit for canonization. Nor did any really holy priest dream of leaving the Church. I deny, of course, that the ministry was purified by abandoning the priesthood, abolishing its obligations, and adopting definitely lower standards. However, as I have admitted, if the Reformation did not itself purify the ministry, it did occasion a vast movement of reform strictly so-called within the Catholic Church; and the Council of Trent made the most stringent legislation for the better formation of future candidates for the priesthood, and the elimination of abuses. Whilst the Reformation, then, did not purify the ministerial office, it did challenge the Catholic Church to do so.

261. *Protestant Churches are founded on personal trust, and freedom as to how and where we shall meet our Lord in prayer.*

The Catholic Church does not exclude personal trust in our Lord. She insists upon it. And Catholics are perfectly free to seek union with Him in prayer whenever they wish. But the Catholic Church rightly forbids Catholics to seek union with the assemblies of others who profess doctrines other than hers. Whatever charity we have for the persons of others, we cannot extend approval to their erroneous teachings and forms of religious worship. You may be my friend; but your religion is not my religion; and you should not expect me to behave as if it were.

262. *Protestantism at least has meant liberty.*

It liberated people from the Catholic Church. But that was a liberation from the restraints of the truth revealed by Christ, and from His moral laws. In his excellent book on "Luther and His Work," Mr. Joseph Clayton, F.R.H.S. writes, "Whither has Luther led his followers? Into what promised land, after the years of wandering outside the Catholic unity, are now brought the Protestants who date their emancipation from Martin Luther? Four centuries of journeying since Luther started the exodus, and yet the promised land of the Lutheran evangel, so often emergent, fades from sight even as the mirage vanishes in the desert. It is the wasteland of doubt that Protestants have reached—a wasteland littered with abandoned hopes and discarded creeds."

263. *The Reformation meant the restoration of public prayer to its right place as the duty and privilege of every servant of God, and not the monopoly of a select class of monks and nuns called ironically the Religious.*

Such a sneer at those who consecrated their lives to God in the Religious Orders is unworthy of a Christian. Meantime, whilst the suppression of the monasteries meant the suppression of the worship offered to God within them in the name of the whole Church, what have people made of the duty and privilege of public prayer? Protestant clergymen complain regularly of lost congregations, empty Churches, and the neglect of public worship. That scarcely sounds like the restoration of public prayer to its proper place as the right and duty of all the faithful. On the other hand, Catholic Churches are filled to overflowing.

264. *The Reformation meant a purifying of family life.*

In what way? The Catholic Church certainly cannot be blamed for the growth of loose ideas of marriage, easy divorce, the widespread plague of contraceptive birth control, and other acknowledged evils tending to break down family life.

265. How can you escape the evident success of Protestantism?

I deny that its success is evident, at least from the genuinely Christian point of view. Genuine Christianity leads to supernatural rather than to merely natural ideals. Christ said that His kingdom was not of this world, and definitely bade us "love not the world." A spiritual and unworldly outlook is therefore the outstanding characteristic of the Catholic religion. I do not say that it is the outlook of all individual Catholics. But insofar as he has not a spiritual and unworldly outlook, a Catholic has drifted from Catholic ideals. On the other hand, Protestantism does not, of its very nature, lead to a spiritual and unworldly outlook. If some good Protestants are truly spiritual, it is in spite of their religion, not because of it. The contrast is evident in the fact that Catholicism will propose as one of her heroes a St. Francis of Assisi who utterly rejected worldly goods, sought poverty and holiness of life, and ended up as a canonized Saint. But the heroes of the Protestant tradition grow from penniless boys into millionaires, or travel from log cabin to White House.

266. Does exclusive Catholicism make full allowance for our Lord's reference to "other sheep"?

Yes. But you must keep in mind the full text. Christ did not merely say that He had other sheep. He said, "Other sheep I have that are not of this fold." And He added, "Them also I must bring, and they shall hear My voice, and there shall be one fold and one shepherd." Jn. X., 16. That one fold under one shepherd is the Catholic Church only.

267. Would God give a grace converting a person to a sect which held but part of Divine Revelation?

No. God may give the grace of an interior and spiritual conversion to a non-Catholic; but not the impulse to join a non-Catholic Church. The joining of a non-Catholic Church is due to the inadequate knowledge of the person in question. Men can misunderstand the promptings of grace in this matter just as in others. God's ways are mysterious, and beyond our understanding. And it takes two to fulfill His plan—Himself and the individual soul. God patiently allows for the dispositions of each soul, and the realization of His plan is gradual, accordingly. But undoubtedly it is His will that those who seek Him should do so in the Catholic Church, and according to the faith, worship, and discipline prevailing in that Church.

268. Would you approve of Protestant missions in places where their work does not immediately militate against the spread of Catholicism?

Since we cannot approve of Protestantism, we cannot approve of the fact that natives are taught this or that Protestant form of Christianity. But, granted that in certain localities the choice is between their being left in their paganism or converted to Protestantism, I have no hesitation in saying that it would be better for them to be converted to Protestantism. After all, Protestantism preaches the necessity of salvation, and Christ as the means of salvation. This element of truth may be mixed up with many errors. But the element of truth may mean the salvation of souls, whilst the errors are robbed to a great extent of their danger by the ignorance of their character on the part of those who hold them. And half a loaf is better than no bread.

269. Would you admit that such missions do good, and rejoice in it?

There can be no doubt that Protestant missions have done much good. They have improved the morals of the natives, lifted them to higher aspirations, and in many cases inspired genuine virtue and holiness both as ideals and in practice. From Protestant missionaries natives have learned to believe in Christ, to love Him sincerely, and to serve Him most generously. For that, one could not but rejoice.

270. *You do not restrict your approval merely to benefits of civilization?*

No. We are genuinely happy that native pagans are taught to know and love Christ, however inadequately it may be. As a matter of fact, to my mind, the so-called benefits of civilization are the least of the benefits a mission in the name of Christ can confer—if it can be called a benefit at all in some cases! The chief thing is to teach them of God, and how to love and serve God through Jesus Christ, and thus to save their souls. And it is precisely from this viewpoint that we rejoice at such good as Protestant missions accomplish. Undoubtedly we would prefer that the natives should receive the full Catholic truth. But we are discussing the case where natives will be taught Protestantism, or never hear of Christianity at all. To a Catholic, Protestantism includes heresy, and heresy is an evil. But paganism is a greater evil than unconscious heresy. So of two evils we prefer the lesser, and that natives should be Christians unconscious of the heretical elements in the doctrines taught them than that they should remain pagans.

271. *Do you not admit that Baptism administered by Protestants is valid?*

If the right form is used with the normal Christian intention, Protestant baptisms are valid. But here a peculiar position arises. All the Sacraments, of course, were instituted by Christ, and belong to Christ. But He founded the Catholic Church, and committed His religion to her only. Therefore the Sacraments without exception belong to her. Not a single valid Sacrament is proper to any of the Protestant Churches. There is but one Lord, one faith, one baptism. If Protestants can administer baptism validly, it is because one need not be a priest, nor even a Christian, to administer that Sacrament validly, whereas confirmation, confession, the eucharist, extreme unction, and holy orders, require a valid priesthood. Meantime, if baptism administered by Protestants be valid, the subject, though baptized in the Protestant Church, is not baptized into the Protestant Church. Christ instituted baptism into the Catholic Church, not baptism into the Protestant Church. If a child is baptized in a Protestant Church, and the baptism is validly administered, the child is a Catholic, and remains a Catholic until it comes to the age of reason and adopts Protestantism for itself. If I receive an adult Protestant into the Catholic Church together with his infant son, and it is certain that both have been baptized validly, I have to make the father abjure heresy and formally profess his submission to the Catholic Church; but nothing is done as regards the infant son. It is simply taught Catholic doctrine and brought up as a Catholic just as any other Catholic child. Its baptism, although administered in a Protestant Church, made it a member of the Catholic Church.

272. *Is marriage between two baptized Protestants a true Sacrament?*

Yes. For here again, since those who make the contract are the real ministers of the Sacrament, no valid priesthood is required for its administration. The Catholic Church has the right to regulate the conditions governing this Sacrament; and she says that an authorized Catholic priest must be present as her official witness at the marriages of Catholics. But the priest does not administer the Sacrament. The contracting parties minister it mutually by their consent. Validly baptized Protestants therefore contract sacramental marriage amongst themselves as often as they enter into the matrimonial contract, whether it be in their own Church, or in a civil court. (I am speaking of first marriages, not of marriages subsequent to divorce, with the former wife still living.) Here again, as a valid Sacrament, such a marriage is subject to the legislative power of the Catholic Church. But because the parties are in good faith, and unaware of this fact, the Catholic Church exempts Protestants from her own prescriptions for Catholics. Yet they cannot be exempted from the essential prescriptions of Christ. That is why the Catholic Church insists that a valid sacramental marriage between two Protestants can be broken only by the death of one of the parties. Even for them, divorce does not break the bond of marriage and give the right to remarry, in the sight of God.

273. Do you say that those who will not hear the Catholic Church are abandoned as the heathen, yet can administer two of her Sacraments?

Our Lord Himself said, "If a man will not hear the Church, let him be as the heathen." Matt. XVIII., 17. But that obviously applies to people who have realized the authority of the Church, yet have deliberately rejected it. Non-Catholics who have never been Catholics, nor have understood and acknowledged the claims of the Catholic Church, are not guilty of personal sin in their refusal of obedience. They cannot therefore be said to be abandoned as the heathen. In 1927 the late Pope Pius XI. spoke as follows on the Catholic attitude towards the separated Churches: "Catholics are sometimes lacking in a right appreciation of their separated brethren, and are even wanting in brotherly love, because they do not know enough about them. People do not realize how much faith, goodness, and Christianity there is in these bodies now detached from the age-long Catholic truth. But pieces broken from gold-bearing rock themselves bear gold." Those words of the Pope were followed by insistence on the duty of charity towards the separated Churches; which shows that we do not apply to them the words of Christ, "let him be to thee as the heathen."

274. Despite such concessions, Catholics are forbidden to assist with Protestants in prayer and worship.

Yes, but here I must ask you to try to view things from the Catholic standpoint. If someone asked you to join in an important enterprise, and declared that he did so in the name of the State, you would want him to prove that he had the authority of the State, and that the enterprise was within the conditions laid down by the State. If he had no authority from the State, or did not comply with its conditions, you would deny that he was acting in the name of the State. Even though he mistakenly thought he was authorized by the State, he would not really be so authorized. Now a Catholic believes that Christ entrusted the care and administration of His religion to the Catholic Church. If we want to assemble for religious purposes in His name, it must be according to the sanction and direction of His Church, this being one of the conditions laid down by Him. People assembling in the name of other religions are not really assembled in the name of Christ however sincerely they may think it to be so. And a Catholic, granted Catholic principles, cannot sanction by his presence those religious functions organized independently of the authority of Christ, and of the conditions He imposed.

275. You will never get Protestants to see that point of view.

It should not be so difficult. A good Protestant, convinced of the truth of Christianity as he perceives it, has principles which would prevent him from joining in pagan worship. I am not saying that as paganism is to Protestantism, so Protestantism is to Catholicism. I merely want to bring out that Protestants have similar principles to which they will adhere, and that they should make allowances for a Catholic acting on principles which forbid participation in any other forms of worship than those prescribed by the Catholic religion. Every man who has principles and adjusts his conduct to them is liable to be called narrow-minded by others who do not accept those same principles. A Protestant should say to a Catholic, "If you believe that Protestantism is a departure from the Christian religion as intended by Christ, then I cannot blame you for refusing to attend Protestant services. But let us discuss the question as to whether Protestantism is a departure from the precepts of Christ."

276. Rome's laws overlook the higher command of Christ, "Love ye one another."

Love for people of other religions does not exclude acknowledgment of the authority of one's own Church and obedience to it. In fact the very love of Christ which bids us love others also bids us to love His own authority in the Catholic Church and to keep her laws. You, of course, do not see that the authority of the Catholic Church is that of Christ. But if you know that Catholics take that view, you should not blame them for fidelity to the laws of their Church. And you should not blame the Church for making laws to safeguard the religion of Christ, and her own subjects in its profession and practice.

277. Our Protestant ministers do not forbid us to worship with fellow Christians. They trust us.

Catholic exclusiveness is not a matter of not trusting Catholics. It vindicates the right of Jesus Christ to be worshipped only in accordance with the rules of the Church He established.

278. Protestants today at least are not responsible for the divisions brought about by their ancestors, and in which they have been educated.

I admit that the Protestants of today are merely the children of those who broke away from the Catholic Church four centuries ago. But still it is their duty to study the question, and to return to the Church the first Protestants should never have left.

See also R. R., Vol. I, Nos. 244-324.

CHAPTER EIGHT

THE TRUTH OF CATHOLICISM

280. When you speak of the Catholic Church, in what sense do you use the word "Church"?

I intend that organized religious society of all Catholics throughout the world under the Pope as their one visible head on earth.

281. Is not the sense of the word simply "Congregation"?

Originally in Greek the word "ecclesia" meant an assembly of people brought together by a public crier. In Biblical Greek it has many meanings, one of them being that which I usually intend. Thus, in the Old Testament, the Greek word "ecclesia" is used, not to designate a mere assembly, but the whole theocratic society of the Jews as the chosen nation of God. In the New Testament, the word is used also in this same sense of a united and organized body, but transferred to the followers of Christ. It is in this sense that Jesus said, "I will build my Church." Matt. XVI., 18.

282. St. Paul refers to the "ecclesias" in the plural, as when he says, "The Churches of Asia salute you."

That would be quite a correct use of the word. St. Paul uses the word in several senses, knowing that sensible people will be preserved from ambiguity by the context. Sometimes he uses the word to signify a Christian household, as in Col. IV., 15. At other times he uses it to signify all the Christians in a given city, as when he speaks of "the Church which is at Corinth." I Cor., 1, 2. Again he uses the word of the whole body of Christians in general as opposed to non-Christians. Thus he writes, "Be without offense to the Jews, and to the Gentiles, and to the Church of God." I Cor. X., 32. Finally he uses the word to signify the Church as a teaching authority in its divinely appointed officials. Thus he speaks of the "Church of the Living God" as "the pillar and ground of truth." I. Tim. III., 15.

283. When did the Church begin?

When Jesus called the Apostles to follow Him. They were taught by Him, given various necessary powers to act in His name, and finally sent to all the world on Pentecost Sunday, after having received a special communication of the Holy Spirit.

284. Modernists say that it cannot be proved that Christ ever referred to His Church as such, though He did have an idea of calling into being a community of faith.

Modernists dare not admit that Christ actually founded a visible and definite Church. If they did they would have no excuse for not submitting to the Catholic Church. Therefore, so long as they are bent on remaining non-Catholics, they must find some other solution. The concession that Jesus did intend to call into being a community of faith is a suggestion that Christ merely taught some nice moral principles, and that independently of Christ's will, later Christians were led by practical needs to adopt a descipline and establish a visible organization. So the origin of the Catholic Church can be explained by historical and natural evolution—and of course no one is obliged to accept that in the name of Christ!

DID CHRIST ESTABLISH A CHURCH? 79

285. *Jesus refers to the Church only in two texts of doubtful validity, and of course it is tempting to identify the kingdom with it, since the mind of Christ was constantly preoccupied with the kingdom.*

The texts in which Jesus speaks of the Church are not of doubtful validity. It is a modernist trick to hint that troublesome texts are either spurious, or at least of doubtful validity. The texts in question are perfectly sound and authentic; and if modernists reject or doubt them, it is merely because they don't like them. And if modernists do find it tempting to identify the Church with the kingdom, the sooner they yield to that temptation the better, for then they may discover the true Church at last.

286. *If we accept the modernist conclusion, the community of faith is not necessarily identifiable with any present-day Church.*

That is the modernist conclusion. But it is based on the false premise that Christ gave only some nice beliefs and moral teachings and did not establish a definite Church. The kingdom of Christ was not anarchy. He organized it, sending the Apostles as a corporate body to teach the nations and rule them in His name. The denial of this imputes to the early Bishops, trained by the very Apostles themselves, the gravest of sins—the deliberate distorting and perverting of the work of Christ. Those Bishops, most of whom died martyrs for the love of Christ, would have imposed upon the faithful a constitution invented by themselves, yet masquerading as the will of Christ, and to be accepted by an act of divine faith. Moreover, such a denial imputes to the faithful of those early times a bland indifference and a crass folly which would submit without a murmur to so fraudulent and lying an imposition. When St. Paul told the early Christians to obey their prelates, they would have asked what prelates! St. Paul knew that they knew and accepted the constitutional authority he preached. The kingdom of Christ is necessarily identifiable with the Catholic Church today.

287. *Where in the Bible can be found an unequivocal statement by Christ that He was establishing a Church corresponding in any particular to the Catholic Church of today?*

He predicted the advent of His Church. saying, "I must preach the kingdom of God, for therefore am I sent." Lk. IV., 43. He called twelve Apostles, distinct from the rulers of the Synagogue, and appointed them as teachers and rulers in His Church. "Teach men to observe all things whatsoever I have commanded you," He said, "and behold I am with you all days even to the end of the world." Matt. XXVIII., 20. He constituted Peter as head. "Thou art Peter, and upon this rock I will build my Church, and I will give to thee the keys of the kingdom of heaven." Matt. XVI., 18. That kingdom was to be a visible kingdom—as a city set on a hill which cannot be hid. However Christ planted a seed which was to develop. The kingdom of heaven is like a mustard seed, the smallest of seeds, but which grows into a great tree. But it is enough to say that Christ established a Church, prescribed its essential constitution of teachers and taught. rulers and subjects. "Teach what I have taught you. Whatever you bind on earth is bound in heaven—make what further legislation you deem necessary. The gates of hell will not prevail against my Church—I will be with it all days till the end." Such is the message of Christ to the Apostles. Now the only Church which has been all days in the world since Christ is the Catholic Church, and if He did not establish that Church, He established none. If that Church failed, then the gates of hell have prevailed against Christ's Church, and He has not been with her all days since His time until now. The Catholic Church alone has the essential constitution prescribed by Christ, and alone behaves as if possessing the magisterial, sanctifying, and disciplinary authority He conferred upon His Church. There are external differences insofar as the grown tree differs from the seed, but the development is in full accordance with the nature and principles of the seed. And Christ knew that just such a tree as the Catholic Church is today would develop from the seed He planted.

288. Christ converted the Apostles by showing them miracles. Let the Catholic Church show us some miracles if she wants us to accept her claims.

The Apostles were called to follow Christ, and they left all to follow Him prior to any sight of His miracles. And later on, not all who witnessed miracles were converted to Christ by any means. The Pharisees witnessed miracles, and when Christ asked them for which of His good works they desired to stone Him, they replied, "Not for thy good works, but because being a man thou makest thyself God." Jn. X., 33. And even when the Jews, who had hitherto followed Him, abandoned Him, Jesus said, "No man can come to me unless it be given him by my Father." Jn. VI., 66. Miracles do not convert people. Conversion supposes interior consent to an interior grace. Christ said to St. Peter, "Blessed art thou, because flesh and blood have not revealed it to thee, but My Father who is in heaven." Matt. XVI., 17. In any case, the Church herself is a simple fact confronting mankind, and demanding explanation from every thinking human being. The Catholic Church, though composed of poor humanity so liable to human frailty, is so striking in her establishment, her expansion, her unity, and fruitfulness in good works, that she cannot but be of God. No merely human organization could last for two thousand years under the same conditions, and spread through the whole world with the same results. Her preservation has been despite long and terrible persecutions, heresies, schisms, political enemies; frailties and crimes even of Catholics themselves, whether laity, Priests, or Bishops; barbarian invasions, the Reformation, various revolutions, attacks by rationalistic philosophers, and the forces of materialism. The forces of growth and progress in this living Catholic Church can only be from God. She is a divine fact in this world, and if a man does not find this enough, all conceivable miracles will be unable to convert him. Christ said once, "If they hear not Moses and the Prophets, neither will they believe if one rise from the dead." Lk. XVI., 31. And I say that one who is not impressed by the simple fact of the Catholic Church, staring him in the face wherever he goes in this world, would not be moved to take a practical interest in religion even did he see special and occasional miracles.

289. Is not the constitution of your Church monarchial, instead of democratic?

The constitution of the Catholic Church is undoubtedly monarchial. And you are wrong in supposing that it ought to be democratic. The Pope rules the whole Church, and each Bishop is a supreme spiritual ruler in his own diocese. Of course even a democracy must have its officials. But the Catholic Church differs very greatly from any merely human society. It is a society which includes God, who really governs the Church through the Pope and the Bishops. For Christ, God the Son made man, appointed a hierarchy or sacred body of rulers to teach and to regulate the conduct of Christians in His name and with His authority. And the whole Church on earth was to be subject to the supreme authority of St. Peter and his successors. That constitution appointed by Christ cannot be changed by men.

290. There is no room for a hierarchy with supreme governing powers.

That may be the logical position from the Protestant viewpoint. But it is not so in the Church as Christ intended it to be. The true Church is a living organism. In a living human body, next to the soul comes the central nervous system, not the distant cells. In the Catholic Church, Christ is the Head; the Holy Spirit is the soul; and next to the soul comes the Catholic hierarchy. Under the influence of the Holy

Spirit, the Pope and the Bishops are the center of thought and discipline, regulating the activity of the multitude of living cells.

291. *Jesus said He would send us the Holy Spirit to teach us all things.*

That is true. But He also sent the Apostles to teach all nations in His name. If we are going to accept one thing Jesus said, we must accept all. It is the Holy Spirit who teaches us through the Church, and always in accordance with the doctrines of the Church. God does not contradict Himself. He does not send the Holy Spirit to teach us one thing, and the Church to teach us another. If we find ourselves in opposition to the Catholic Church, we can be quite sure that the Holy Spirit is not responsible for our ideas. One thing is certain. The Holy Spirit could not possibly have inspired all the contradictory ideas people insist on attributing to Him.

292. *We read of Bishops ordaining priests; but who ordained the Apostles? There were no Bishops then.*

The Apostles were ordained by Jesus Christ. He personally called them apart from other men to fulfill the sacred duties of the ministry He established. He endowed them with the priestly power to preach, to forgive sin in His name, to offer the Sacrifice of the Mass, and to rule His Church on earth. He also endowed them with the power to ordain other priests to continue the ministry of the Christian religion. They were to be "Bishops" or "Shepherds" of the Christian flock. The "Bishops" are simply those who have received by transmission from the Apostles and from Christ the plenitude of the Christian priesthood. Jesus Himself was the Great High Priest with an absolute plenitude of priestly power. In the First Epistle of St. Peter, II., 25. we find that great Apostle teaching us that Jesus Himself was indeed a Bishop. "Christ," he writes, "suffered for us . . . and you are now converted to the Shepherd and Bishop of your souls." Jesus Himself, therefore, the supreme Bishop of souls, ordained the Apostles and originated episcopal power in the first representatives of the Christian priesthood as we know it today. And the Apostles ordained others to continue the work of the Church. So St. Paul wrote to Titus, "For this cause I left thee in Crete, that thou shouldst ordain priests in every city as I also appointed thee." Titus, I., 5.

293. *The history of the Middle Ages in Europe will prevent men from putting themselves under the domination of priests any more.*

Firstly, by becoming a Catholic, one does not put oneself under the domination of priests in any sense such as that you have in mind. Secondly, you are evidently laboring under the superstition that the middle ages were dark, dismal, and dominated by priestcraft. But educated people have long since grown out of that antiquated notion. Mr. Douglas Jerrold has recently written a book called "England." He may not be a Catholic, but he is not blind to the facts of history. "It is hard," he writes, "in this age of unsatisfied desires to recapture the atmosphere of a century of fulfillment. The faith of the thirteenth century was not our faith; the belief in God had not given place to the belief in man as the mainspring of human hopes. Its economy was not ours. The means of production were, as compared with today, ludicrously poor; but on the other hand, they were in the hands of the many, not of the few. Even its politics were different, for the taxpayer was still a free agent with an effective right to decide the limits of his contribution. In the thirteenth century were laid the intellectual foundations of most of what human wisdom has to tell us of the rights of man and the order of nature, and all that modern wisdom has forgotten of man's duty to God." Such is the estimate of Douglas Jerrold, a writer who does know his subject. And he has indicated the real reasons why people do not wish to become Catholics. It is not really, as you suggest, fear of putting themselves under the "domination of priests." They are at least too sensible to believe in the fears that dread word enkindles in some timid souls. The real reasons are that belief in God has given way to belief in man as the mainspring of human hopes, and that man's duty to God has been forgotten by multitudes who, despite their profession of Christianity, are really indifferent to religion altogether.

294. The historical ecclesiastic has much to live down.

A close examination of history will reveal that ecclesiastics are not the only ones with a skeleton in the cupboard. All groups, classes, and professions, have a past history which is not without blemish. But, confining ourselves to ecclesiastics, if indeed the historical ecclesiastic has much to live down, it is equally true that he has much more that redounds to his credit. The holy, gentle Christ-like priest appears much more frequently on the stage of this world than the one who has proved unworthy of his calling. But the good ecclesiastic is not "news." He is merely what he is expected to be. It is the occasional bad ecclesiastic who is "news" to a world which delights in the abnormal and unexpected. Moreover, evil men resent the goodness of others, if only for the reason that goodness wherever it appears is the condemnation of evil conduct. And as the evilly-disposed do not like being condemned, they watch the Church with malicious eyes, ready to pounce on anything to her discredit, exaggerate it out of bounds, and broadcast it to all who are willing to listen. It is an indictment of our poor human race that the scandalous can always get much more publicity than the edifying.

295. Our poor diseased world has ever suffered from ecclesiasticism.

It has not. An operation involving the complete removal of ecclesiasticism from its midst would not benefit the patient in the least. Its condition would become rapidly worse.

296. If the Church were always ruled by angelic priests it would be ideal.

It would undoubtedly be to the great advantage to the Church were all priests saintly men, though even in that case there is no guarantee that all Catholics would be equally submissive to the directions of those angelic priests. Yet it would not really be ideal for the Church to have only angelic priests. We must face the realities of life, and the essential frailties of human nature. The only way in which all priests could be rendered angelic always would be for God to render them either absolutely immune from all temptations or incapable of yielding to temptation. But surely, even though one is a priest, he should have to meet his own temptations just as any other man, and should be capable of losing his soul as well as of saving it. It is not ideal that a man should have a through-ticket to heaven just because he has been ordained a priest. Priests are subject to the same laws of virtue as all other men. They have to fight for it, doing violence to themselves, and resisting the temptations life itself carries with it. And on the law of averages, it is to be expected that some will fail even whilst some fight their way to the heights of holiness. Others will remain fair average quality. But the Catholic Church remains ever the same, whatever be the variations in the personal holiness of her priests. We cannot say that the Catholic Church is right when we meet a saintly priest, and then say that the same Church is wrong when we meet a careless priest. An unworthy priest may not practice what he preaches; but at least he will not dare to preach what he practices, in those matters at least where he falls short of Christian virtue. And the Church must be judged by those who do live up to her teachings, not by those who do not.

297. As a Protestant I question your statements that it is necessary to have a Pope.

You are not alone in doing so. In fact, if you did not do so, you would not still profess to be a Protestant.

298. Why do we need one?

Because we need the Church Christ thought fit to establish, with just the very constitution He gave it. And since He arranged that we should have a Pope, we need a Pope.

299. Is not Jesus Christ enough?

One does not accept Jesus Christ who refuses to accept the provision made by Jesus Christ for the guidance of His followers through the ages.

300. How did the early Church progress without a Pope?

The Church was never without a Pope. From its very foundation St. Peter had been appointed Pope by Christ Himself when He uttered the words: "Thou art Peter, and upon this rock I will build my Church . . . and I will give to thee the keys of the kingdom of heaven." Matt. XVI., 18-19.

301. In the Acts of the Apostles we read that "they added unto the Church daily such as should be saved." Acts XVI., 5.

Converts to Christ, therefore, submitted to the Church Christ had established. And that Church included its constitution under the primacy of St. Peter. All accepted that.

302. See the manner of government in the early Church. In Acts VIII., 29, we are told that "the Spirit said unto Philip." The Holy Spirit was ruling the Church.

The Holy Spirit is given to the Church, and works in and through the Church, sometimes immediately, as in the case of Philip, sometimes through the channels of visible authorities, as when the Apostles declared of their legislation, "It has seemed good to the Holy Spirit and to us." Acts XV., 28. Never once, of course, could the Holy Spirit inspire any man to act against the lawful authority of the Church, which is the primary object of the Holy Spirit's guidance and influence. The Holy Spirit does not contradict Himself.

303. Why should it be different today?

It is not different today. That is why Catholics accept the same conditions as those which prevailed in the early Church.

304. Is man's moral character so far below the standard of the Apostles that he now needs the Spirit governing second-hand?

I hope you do not imagine that you are on the level of the Apostles! Had you lived in those days, and had you then been a Christian, you would have been as subject to the Apostles in matters of faith and conduct as we Catholics are subject to our Bishops. And when they gave the law, saying, "It has seemed good to the Holy Ghost and to us," you would not have refused obedience on the plea that you would not be governed second-hand even by the Holy Spirit.

305. If Christ gave the Holy Spirit care of the Church, then the Holy Spirit still works in that capacity.

Correct. But you suggest that, although the Holy Spirit was given care of the Church, He allowed the whole Church, Pope, Bishops, and all, to drift to error and deception until the Protestant reformers came along to put it right. If you say that He inspired the Protestant reformers, it is strange that He inspired them with so many different and conflicting ideas! The Holy Spirit knows His own mind. And because she is subject to the Holy Spirit, the Catholic Church knows her own mind. Elsewhere there is chaos.

306. Would you suggest that St. Paul needed a Pope?

Yes; for he needed just that Church which Christ had established; and since that Church was entrusted to the care of a supreme head on earth, St. Paul needed a Pope.

307. He wrote to Timothy that there is one mediator between God and man—Christ Jesus.

That is Catholic doctrine, but it does not obviate the necessity of a Pope. Because Christ is the one Mediator, we have to accept whatever method He appoints for the exercise of His mediation. He chose to dispense the benefits of His mediation through the Church He organized, and He decided that the Pope should be in supreme control of the Church in this world.

308. Paul could go straight to God through Christ Jesus.

Of course he could. So can any Catholic. But we do this by accepting the teachings of the Catholic Church and fulfilling her precepts. That is why our Lord said of His Church, "He who hears you, hears Me." Lk. X., 16. If you think that no agents were ever appointed by Christ to dispense grace to men in His name, the very St. Paul you quote is against you. "Let a man account of us," he wrote to the Corinthians, "as of the ministers of Christ, and the dispensers of the mysteries of God." 1 Cor. IV., 1. Would you reply to him, "I acknowledge no dispenser of any mysteries of God save Christ alone? I go straight to Him, not to you. You can dispense nothing to me—there is one Mediator—Christ Jesus." St. Paul would say to you, "My dear child, I wrote those words, and I ought to know what they mean. They do not exclude His use of us as dispensers of His mediation to mankind. Our power and authority are His power and authority committed to us; and if you want to obey Him, you will account of us as dispensers in His name, and submit to His provision for you." As a matter of fact, St. Paul demanded absolute obedience to his commands. He forgave the sin of the incestuous Corinthian after his repentance, saying, "If I have pardoned anything, I have done it in the person of Christ." 2 Cor. II., 10. Your notion that the supreme mediation of Christ excludes secondary mediators acting in the name of Christ is quite opposed to St. Paul's own teachings.

309. Do not Catholics believe that the Pope is the living Christ?

No. Every Catholic professes in the Apostles' Creed that Christ rose again from the dead, ascended into heaven, and that there He is at "the right hand of God the Father Almighty." No Catholic believes that Christ dwells in the Vatican, clad in the robes of the Pope. We do believe that Christ has delegated His authority to the Pope as supreme visible head of the visible Church in this world, but the Pope is certainly not the living Christ in person.

310. Pope Pius X. made the blasphemous claim that he was "Jesus Christ hidden under the veil of the flesh. Does the Pope speak? It is Jesus Christ who speaks."

A Protestant paper, the "Church Review," in England, Oct. 3, 1895, charged Cardinal Sarto, Archbishop of Venice, with having uttered those words at Venice. Cardinal Sarto was elected Pope in 1903. But as soon as the charge was made in 1895 that Cardinal Sarto had said those words, inquiries were sent from England to Venice, and Cardinal Sarto produced the manuscript of his discourse. And this is what he actually did say: "The Pope represents Jesus Christ Himself, and therefore is a loving father. The life of the Pope is a holocaust of love for the human family. His word is love; love, his weapon; love, the answer he gives to all who hate him; love, his flag, i.e., the Cross, which signed the greatest triumph on earth and in heaven."

311. Pope Nicholas I. said that the Pope, being God, is judged by no man.

Never did Pope Nicholas I. say that the Pope is God. What he does say is this: "Since those in higher authority are not judged by inferiors, it is evident that the Apostolic See, than which no earthly authority is higher, is judged by none." And that is perfectly sound reasoning. Even in civil law, the king is "above the law," and not subject to his own laws. Hence the legal axiom, "The king can do no wrong." Italy itself has acknowledged the justice of the Pope's claim to be independent of all civil jurisdiction, and subject to no earthly authorities.

312. In the "Extravagantes" of Pope John XXII., Roman Canon Law says that it is heresy to deny the power of "Our Lord God the Pope."

That remark is attributed, not to Pope John XXII., but to the Canonist Zenzelinus, in his commentary on Title XIV of the "Extravagantes." But an examination of the original manuscript of Zenzelinus, preserved in the Vatican Library, failed to reveal the words attributed to him; and it has been definitely proved that the reference to God is an interpolation in later copies of his commentary.

313. You say that the Pope is the lawful successor of St. Peter.

That is true.

314. Do you maintain that St. Peter was the first Pope of Rome?

Yes. The word "Pope" simply means "Father," and it is certain that Christ appointed Peter to be the head or spiritual father of the whole Christian family. Also it is certain that he died in Rome.

315. According to your doctrine Peter was appointed Vicar of Christ before he became Bishop of Rome. Why must his successors first become Bishops of Rome before they become Vicars of Christ?

They become simultaneously Vicars of Christ by becoming Bishops of Rome. Christ conferred the Primacy upon St. Peter in such a way that it would continue in his successors. His successors are those who succeed to the episcopal office he held at the time of his death. Now St. Peter presided over the Church at Rome, and died in that city. Therefore the Bishop of Rome succeeds simultaneously to the Episcopal See and the Primacy.

316. Where in the Bible does it say that Peter was the Vicar of God?

The three classical passages in which St. Peter's supremacy over the Church is clearly shown are as follows: In the Gospel of St. Matt. XVI., 18-19, we find Christ saying to Peter, "I say to thee that thou art Peter, and upon this rock I will build my Church; and the gates of hell will not prevail against it. And I will give to thee the keys of the kingdom of heaven. Whatsoever thou shalt bind on earth, it shall be bound also in heaven; and whatsoever thou shalt loose on earth, it shall be loosed also in heaven." Christ there constituted Peter head of the Church in promise, declaring that the office would carry with it the power to act vicariously in the name of God. In St. Luke, XXII., 31-32, we have the words of Christ, "Simon, Simon, behold Satan hath desired to have you, that he might sift you like wheat. But I have prayed for thee, that thy faith fail not; and do thou, being once converted, confirm thy brethren." St. John, XXI., 15-17, tells us how Christ, after His resurrection, commissioned St. Peter to feed His lambs, and to feed His sheep, i.e., to be shepherd over the whole flock.

317. On the strength of the text, "Thou art Peter, and upon this rock I will build my Church," you accord Peter absolute sovereignty over the Church!

Christ alone has absolute sovereignty over the Church. St. Peter had merely a delegated authority from Christ, and it was subject to conditions imposed by Christ.

St. Peter could not change the faith taught by Christ, as he could do had he absolute authority. Had he that, he could have altered things as he pleased. But no. He had to teach what Christ taught. Therefore we do not accord St. Peter absolute authority. But we do say that the fullness of Christ's authority within the limits imposed by Christ was so given to him that all others in the Church were still more secondary in relation to Peter.

318. *Is it not dangerous to base a theory or a dogma upon an isolated prooftext, instead of considering the teaching of Jesus as a whole?*

Do not confuse theories with dogmas. A dogma is a defined and certain teaching lifted far above the realm of mere theories. But now for your question. There would be nothing dangerous in basing a dogma even on one isolated proof-text, provided the meaning of that text was quite clear, and its interpretation in no way opposed to anything else in the teachings of Jesus recorded in the Gospel pages. The one text used, after all, would be as much the Word of God as any other texts. As a matter of fact, however, the doctrine of St. Peter's primacy is not based only on one text. It is borne out by other texts, and also by the teaching of Jesus as a whole.

319. *There are weighty reasons for regarding the words "Thou art Peter, and upon this rock I will build my Church" as a later addition to the text.*

Even were this particular text not genuine, the primacy of St. Peter could be quite satisfactorily proved from many other places in Scripture. However, the text as given in St. Matthew's Gospel is quite authentic.

320. *I think the arguments against its authenticity outweigh those in its support.*

The wish is the father to such a thought. And your anxiety to get rid of the text is a telling tribute to its value on behalf of Rome in your own unconscious estimate.

321. *It seems probable that the words were added in the interests of an ecclesiasticism anxious to discipline those who disputed its claims.*

It is certain that the charge of their addition is made in the interests of those who desire to avoid submission to the authority of the Pope as successor of St. Peter. And they grasp at the flimsiest of excuses to secure their elimination. Your contention will deserve consideration only when you are prepared to say just when they were added and by whom.

322. *St. Matthew alone gives the words, though they occur in a passage taken from St. Mark (the earliest Gospel).*

It is sheer guesswork that St. Mark's was the earliest Gospel or that St. Matthew made any use of it. The Aramaic genius of the wording in the Petrine text in St. Matthew's Gospel and the sequence of thought in the whole of the context forbid the idea that the text does not belong to the original Gospel. The words appear in all the very oldest Codices, and all editors of the Gospel text give them as certain and guaranteed by the rules of scientific criticism. As, for example, Tischendorff, Westcott and Hort, Von Soden, Vogels, and others. Nor can any reasonable explanation of the general acceptance of the text throughout the whole Church be given by those who wish to evade its force by the back-door method of denying its authenticity. I might remark that, by the same method, one could wipe out every single text in Scripture which did not happen to fit in with one's own personal theories.

323. *If it was not a later addition, why did St. Mark omit the words?*

The reasons should be obvious. St. Mark was St. Peter's companion, and wrote chiefly from St. Peter's own teachings. St. Peter had humility enough not to insist on his own prerogatives. Moreover, to the immediate readers of St. Mark the words were already well known both from the Gospel of St. Matthew, and from the oral teaching of the other Apostles.

324. *Granted that the text is genuine, the early Fathers differed from Rome's present interpretation. Most of them see in the "rock" not Peter, but Christ, or Peter's confession of faith.*

You are an optimist in your appeal to "most" of the Fathers. I admit that quite a number of them give different explanations of this text. I have the list of all their various utterances, drawn up for the consideration of the Vatican Council at the time of the definition of papal infallibility. But the point to be noted about the Fathers is this: They were not bent on giving exegetical interpretations, but theological; and they covered the whole ground against early heresies. You would find in their writings their assertions that Peter is the head of the Church, subordinate only to Christ; that the confession or faith of Peter is the rock foundation of the Church insofar as the Church will ever be preserved in the truth through Peter. The Fathers declare also that all the Apostles are the foundation of the Church, but under the authority of Peter. If you have so great a respect for the Fathers, why do you not accept their general verdict, apart from their comments upon this particular text, that St. Peter was given the primacy by Christ over the whole Church?

325. *Peter, of course, does mean rock. But was not Christ's expression a mere play on words?*

In the name of all the Apostles St. Peter had solemnly proclaimed that Jesus was indeed the Son of Almighty God, and in return received the not less solemn words, addressed to him in the singular, "Thou art Peter, and upon this rock I will build my Church." To say that the use of Peter's name was a mere play on words is folly. The text is undoubtedly a proof of the intentions of Christ, initial and persistent, concerning a regular and lasting constitution which He foresees.

326. *The rock cannot refer to Peter, for the original Latin gives "Petros" for Peter, and "Petra" for rock.*

All reputable scholars today, both Catholic and Protestant, admit that no valid argument against the Catholic doctrine can be built up from the different genders of petros and petra. For our Lord spoke in Aramaic, and St. Matthew wrote originally in Aramaic, a Hebrew dialect in current use when Christ lived and spoke to men. From the Aramaic a Greek translation was made. Then from the Greek a Latin translation was made. The Latin has "Petrus" for Peter, not "Petros." "Petros" is not Latin, but Greek. Now in Latin the word for rock, petra, is a feminine noun. Naturally the word was given a masculine form, "Petrus," when applied to the man, Peter. But the external difference in the Latin or Greek forms of the word, due to considerations of gender, do not affect the question. For in the Aramaic language used by Christ there was no such difference. He said, "Thou art 'Kepha,' and upon this 'Kepha' I will build My Church." The word was exactly the same on each occasion. And it was because Christ used the word "Kepha" that we sometimes find Peter called "Cephas," a Greek transliteration of the Aramaic word itself. No argument from the forms employed in the Latin or Greek translations, therefore, can avail in this matter. See also R. R., Vol. I, Nos. 360-376.

327. *When Christ said, "Upon this rock I will build my Church," He was referring to Himself.*

That cannot be accepted. Christ had deliberately changed Simon's name to Peter, which means a rock. And He certainly did not do that merely for the sake of calling him a rock. There was a more profound significance in it than that. Now take the present context. Christ said to His disciples, "Whom do men say that the Son of man is?" Simon Peter replied, "Thou art Christ, the Son of the Living God."

Then Christ said to him in the singular, "Thou art rock, and upon this rock I will build my Church." Even from the grammatical point of view "this" must refer to the nearest noun. If I said, "Paul is an Apostle, and this Apostle will go to the Gentiles," all would know that I was not suddenly changing the reference to myself. Protestant scholars themselves today admit that this is the only really grammatical interpretation, and that other interpretations have been due to theological prejudices.

328. *Christ is the rock. He is called the chief corner stone.*

Dr. Plummer, the Protestant scholar, writes as follows in his commentary on St. Matthew: "The fact that Christ Himself elsewhere, by a different metaphor, is called the 'corner stone' (Eph. II., 20; 1 Pet. II., 4-8), must not lead us to deny that Peter is here the foundation rock or stone. In Eph. II., 20, the Apostles and Christian Prophets are the foundation, as Peter is said to be here. The first ten chapters of Acts show us in what sense Peter was the foundation on which the first stones of the Christian Israel were laid. He was the acknowledged Head of the Apostolic body, and he took the lead in admitting both Jews and Gentiles into the Christian Church. "All attempts to explain the 'rock' in any other way than as referring to Peter have ignominiously failed." (Briggs, North Amer. Rev., Feb., 1907, p. 348).

329. *Could you imagine our Lord building His Church on a mere man, no matter how good he was?*

There is no room for imagining what Christ would do, or would not do, when we know what He did do.

330. *Is it not more consistent with God's plan that His Church should be built on the rock of Peter's confession, and not on Peter?*

That profession of faith by Peter was but a preliminary condition which occasioned the promise of Christ to Peter himself. The attributing to the confession of what should be attributed to Peter himself does violence to the text and context. The Protestant scholar Kuinoel says, "Many interpreters have wrongly understood Christ Himself to be the rock, or the profession of faith by Peter. They would not have taken refuge in these distorted interpretations if the Pope had not wrongly tried to vindicate for the successors of St. Peter a singular and divine authority based upon the words 'upon this rock.'"

331. *That necessary foundation, faith in Christ, is still firm and strong; but Peter is long since dead.*

It is still a firm and strong principle that faith in Christ is necessary to the Christian religion. But many who profess to be Christians are not firm and strong in that faith. The faith cannot look after itself. It is necesary that authorized agents be appointed to teach and preserve the faith. That is the whole genius of the Catholic Church established by Christ, and founded by Him upon the Apostles, of whom the chief was Peter. Meantime, Peter is not long since dead. The office confided to him has persevered in the Church, and Peter still lives on in his successors—the Popes.

332. *If Peter was the rock, and had the supremacy, why the later argument as to which of the Apostles would be the greater?*

Their dispute confirms the Catholic position. As they did not at first understand fully many other things that Christ had said to them, and some of them not until they had received the Holy Ghost on Pentecost Sunday, so they only imperfectly understood the sense of our Lord's words concerning the rock and the keys. Yet they knew that Simon's name only had been changed; that he had been called the rock by our Lord, and that he had been singled out for some pre-eminence. There is nothing more natural than that our Lord's apparently special treatment of some should have occasioned discussion amongst the twelve. And it is still more significant that our Lord, instead of telling them that all were equal, should have contented Himself with inculcating lessons of humility.

333. It certainly needs Roman Catholic spectacles to see Peter as the rock.

You are mistaken. In his book, "The Mission and Message of Jesus," recently published, the Rev. Dr. T. W. Manson, a Protestant authority, declares that the "rock" is Peter himself, and says that verse 19 of Matt. XVI., read in the light of Isaiah XXII., 22, declares that Peter is the ruler of the Church, "God's vicegerent in all the affairs of the kingdom on earth." And he adds, "The authority of Peter is an authority to declare what is right and wrong for the Christian community. His decisions will be confirmed by God." But Dr. Manson adds that, although this is the meaning of the text, the verses afford no justification "for the exaggerated papal claims which have been built upon them." After those last words, no one could accuse Dr. Manson of wearing what you term "Roman Catholic spectacles." Yet he sees clearly that Peter was the rock upon which Christ would build His Church. To preserve his Protestant position, he merely tries to find a new explanation as to "how" Christ built the Church on Peter. But the fact he does not deny, much as it would suit his case to do so.

334. You insist therefore that Matt. XVI., 18, confers a despotic, universal, unlimited power on Peter?

There is no need to bring in the words despotic and unlimited. His authority was universal insofar as it extended to the whole Church. But it was limited by the law of God and the will of Christ. In no sense was it despotic, for Christ never tired of insisting that authority in the Church must be accompanied by humility and saturated with charity. "The princes of the nations," He said, "lord it over them; but it shall not be so among you; but let him that is chief among you be the servant of all." Mk. X., 42-43. Those words condemn despotism, though we must not lose sight of the fact that, by legislating for him that is chief, it arranges for someone to be chief.

335. A few verses after Peter is called the rock, Christ said to him, "Get thee behind me, satan . . . thou savorest not the things of God, but those that be of man." Mk. VIII., 33.

Peter's love for Christ could not bear the thought that his Master should have to endure the things of which He then began to speak. Our Lord appreciated the sympathy which prompted Peter's protest, but insisted strongly that such things must be. In no way did He withdraw any official standing from Peter. If you think He did because these words are subsequent to the promise, then I must draw your attention to the words given by St. Luke XXII., 32, and certainly subsequent to the rebuke you quote, "I have prayed for thee, Simon, that thy faith fail not; and do thou, being converted, confirm thy brethren."

336. If you take the promise literally, why not take it literally that Peter is satan?

The word satan must be taken literally, in its literal sense of adversary. In an appropriated sense it is applied to the devil as "the" adversary of God and man. In this appropriated sense it does not apply to Peter. His proposal, dictated by his love and affection for Christ, that Christ should not suffer, was adverse to the will of God. But it was not dictated by hatred of God. The dispositions of Peter were quite the opposite of those entertained by the devil.

337. Later on Peter denied Christ.

After the denial Christ said to him, "Feed My lambs; feed My sheep." Jn. XXI., 15-17. It is quite certain that Peter's denial did not affect the fulfillment of Christ's promise to him.

338. Is Peter "a" or "the" foundation of the Church?

He is both, for he is one of the foundations, and the chief of them, upon which Christ built His Church.

339. Then how do you account for Ephesians II., 19-20?

The verses are: "You are fellow citizens with the saints, and the domestics of God, built upon the foundation of the Apostles and Prophets, Jesus Christ Himself being the chief corner stone." "Corner stone" is, of course, a different metaphor from "foundation stone." Christ is at once the Builder of the Church and the "corner stone" holding it together. But He built it upon the Apostles and Prophets as foundation stones, Peter being the "foundation rock" upon which Christ based the whole of His building. That is the sense of the words, "Thou art Peter, and upon this rock I will build my Church." And such is the only interpretation sound scholarship will permit. The Protestant Dr. Plummer warns his readers not to be influenced in their interpretation of this text by the conclusion they wish to reach. He himself most decidedly rejects papal authority today. Yet he says of this Petrine text: "The Messiah is going to build His Church, a new Israel, for which Peter is to supply the foundation. It is quite clear that here Christ Himself is not the foundation rock or foundation stone. He is the builder of the edifice." Then he gives the words recorded in 328 above.

340. Matt. XXVIII., 18-20, shows that all the Apostles were equal, and that no one was greater than any other.

The commission to the Apostles to go and to teach all nations, and the promise to be with them all days till the end of the world have no reference to the constitutional authority binding them together amongst themselves. Consequently, the passage you quote does not affect the interpretation of the Petrine texts.

341. In Rev. XXI., 14, John says of the New Jerusalem that the wall had 12 foundations, and on them the names of the 12 Apostles.

That accords with the fact that Christ founded His Church upon the 12 Apostles collectively. But when we come to the relationship prevailing between the Apostles, we notice that whilst all were equal in the special privileges of the apostolate as such, the primacy amongst the Apostles was given as a unique privilege to St. Peter alone. St. Peter was equal with the others as an Apostle. They had no powers he did not possess. But as regards internal authority in the very constitution of the Church, the other Apostles were not equal to Peter, for he had a power they did not possess—that of the primacy over the whole Church.

342. If Peter was head, why didn't he appoint Matthias straight out, instead of joining with the other Apostles in electing him?

If you read Acts I., 15-26, you will notice that St. Peter directed the proceedings. It was he who rose and said, "Scripture must be fulfilled, and one of these who have accompanied us must be made a witness of the resurrection with us." Under his directions the election took place by ballot. St. John Chrysostom, Patriarch of Constantinople in the fourth century, and one of the greatest authorities on Christian doctrine, wrote of this passage: "We see here the providential care of St. Peter for the flock. He has the chief authority in this election, since all were entrusted to him. But although he takes the initiative, he refrains from using his full authority. He alone could have appointed Matthias. But in a spirit of simple humility, and to avoid appearing high handed, he graciously permits all to participate."

343. A Protestant clergyman told me that St. James, Bishop of Jerusalem, was the supreme Bishop in the early Church.

The desire to exalt St. James is born of the wish to depreciate St. Peter. But if St. James was the supreme Bishop in the early Church, who succeeded him in that office? We can point to the successors of St. Peter. Where is the rival lineage derived from St. James? It is intelligible that opponents of the Catholic Church should deny Peter's supremacy, and insist that all the Apostles were equal in all things. That would not be true, but I say that it would be intelligible. But to say that St. James was the superior of all the other Apostles is disastrous to the antipapal position. For thus an office essential to the very constitution of the Church has lapsed!

344. Why did St. James preside at the Council of Jerusalem recorded in Acts XV.?

He did not do so. St. Peter presided. Acts XV., 7, says, "After much disputing Peter rose up and said." He then decided the issue. Verse 12 tells us that after Peter had spoken all held their peace. James then expressed his assent to St. Peter's decision. St. James, as local Bishop of Jerusalem, would naturally have a prominent position at the meeting, since it took place in Jerusalem. But there can be no doubt about his deference to the oecumenical position of St. Peter as chief of the Apostles.

345. If St. Peter was supreme, how could the Apostles send him on a mission?

They could not do so by any command based upon authority over him. Even you will admit that, for if you won't agree that the other Apostles were subject to Peter, you will not go to the other extreme of saying that he was subject to them. The expression is quite easily explained by common counsel and request, based on the general judgment that so important a matter warranted the attention of St. Peter precisely because of his pre-eminence. Much the same thing could occur in a modern Religious Order such as that of the Jesuits. One of the members is appointed in supreme control, and is known as the General. Now it could easily be that, in some important matter, all members would agree that the General himself should attend to it; and published reports would not be wrong in saying that the Jesuits sent their General himself to attend to the affair. And no one would interpret that collective reference as proof that the General was not head of the Order. In much the same way the faithful at Antioch sent Paul and Barnabas to consult the other Apostles at Jerusalem. (Acts XV., 2.) Yet they were subject to the authority of the ones they sent! No argument against the supremacy of St. Peter can be drawn from your suggested difficulty.

346. Paul says, "Other foundation no man can lay than that which is laid, which is Christ Jesus."

If St. Paul believed that Christ was the one and only foundation, why did he write to the Ephesians, "You are built upon the foundation of the Apostles, Jesus Christ Himself being the chief corner stone"? If the place of Christ did not exclude the Apostles as secondary foundations, nor can it exclude the fact that St. Peter was chief of those secondary foundations.

347. In Gal. II., 7, Paul says he had the charge of the Gentiles, whilst Peter was for the Jews. That does not look like universal supremacy for Peter.

The universal commission to St. Peter is evident from Christ's instructions to him to feed lambs and sheep—the whole flock. In the text you quote, St. Paul is speaking of the practical exercise of the Apostolate, with no particular reference to the authority inherent in it; also he intended it as a temporary measure only, and as a general, not as an exclusive commission. St. Paul preached again and again to the Jews, and St. Peter to the Gentiles. But there is no contradiction here of the fact that St. Peter was head of the Church.

348. Is there any indication in Scripture that St. Peter was ever in Rome?

Yes. St. Peter ends his first Epistle with the words, "The Church which is in Babylon salutes you, and so doth my son Mark." Pagan Rome was called Babylon by the early Christians; and St. Peter was writing from that city. Also, St. Paul wrote his Epistle to the Romans in the year 58 A. D. In it he says that he does not want to preach the Gospel where Christ is already known, because he would not build on "another man's foundation." Yet in the Epistle to the Romans he writes to a Church already founded "whose faith was spoken of throughout the whole world." R. I., 8; declares that he himself had not yet visited Rome, R. I., 10-13; XV., 22-23; but that he hoped to do so when he later set out to visit Spain. R. XV., 24. Commenting on these words, the Protestant Dr. B. J. Kidd writes, "Rome, in short, was 'another man's foundation.' No allusion to the 'other man' by name is wanted. The Romans knew well enough whom he meant. Who, then, was the 'other man'? The evidence is early and threefold in favor of St. Peter." Hist. of Ch., p. 52. The Rev. G. Edmundson, in his "Church in Rome in the First Century," p. 28, writes: "There had been a founder of this great Church with whom St. Paul was well acquainted. Who was he? All tradition answers with one voice the name of St. Peter."

349. Why did not Paul mention Peter in writing to the Romans, of all people?

No such mention was necessary, and it would have been positively inexpedient. The most ordinary prudence would make St. Paul avoid mentioning St. Peter as Bishop of Rome in written documents which might fall into the hands of the enemies of the Church. The Christians were most careful not to allow the movements and official acts of their Bishops to become known to the authorities of pagan society. Any hint that the head of the Church had taken up his abode in Rome, or was founding his See in the very heart of the Roman Empire would be disastrous if it came into the hands of enemies. St. Paul's remark that he was not going to build on "another man's foundation" was sufficient reference for those to whom he was writing.

350. Can you prove that Peter was ever Bishop of Rome?

We have a host of early indications that he was, whilst not a single early writer can be quoted as expressing the least doubt on the subject. Heretics and schismatics, as well as Catholics themselves, acknowledged the Bishop of Rome as succeeding to the bishopric of St. Peter. Eusebius wrote as follows: "Peter the Apostle, the first Pontiff of the Christians, when he had first founded the Church at Antioch, proceeds to Rome where, preaching the Gospel, he continues for twenty-five years Bishop of that city." And he adds, "Linus was the first after Peter that obtained the Episcopate of the Church of the Romans." The Protestant Bishop Lightfoot says of Eusebius, "To Eusebius we are indebted for almost all that we know of the lost ecclesiastical literature of the second century . . . in no instance that we can test, does Eusebius give a doubtful testimony. . . . I do not join in the vulgar outcry against the dishonesty of Eusebius. Whenever I have been able to investigate this charge, I have found it baseless."

351. Why should not Antioch, Peter's See, take priority over Rome, Paul's See?

Rome was never the See of St. Paul. St. Paul himself, by his later visit there, his preaching at Rome, and death in that city, earned the title of co-founder of the Mother-See of Christendom. But Rome was ever called the "Chair of Peter," never the "Chair of Paul"; and Eusebius rightly refers to Linus simply as "the first after Peter." The wonderful organization and faith of the Roman Church before St.

Paul went there, and to which he alludes in his Epistle to the Romans, can be accounted for only by Apostolic foundation. And it was undoubtedly St. Peter who founded the Church at Rome, organizing the scattered elements, and placing the Church on a solid basis. Antioch would have had priority had St. Peter remained and died there. But he did not do so. He transferred to Rome, and his successor was naturally the Bishop of Rome, not the Bishop of Antioch.

352. *The Monarch Pope is head, not simply of a religious organization, but also of a political State with temporal interests of its own.*

So far as Catholics throughout the world are concerned, the Pope is the head of a purely religious society known as the Catholic Church. By his control of Vatican City he is politically independent of Italy. But no Catholic in the world, who does not reside in Vatican City, owes political allegiance to the Pope as a temporal ruler.

353. *Christ said that Satan was the prince of this world. Did he give the Pope temporal power, and the right to give away kingdoms?*

You can be quite sure that Satan has never been responsible for any power given to the Pope. You cannot argue that Satan is the prince of this world, and, therefore, every prince of this world must be satanic. Satan inspires evil in this world, but all lawful temporal authority is from God, as the New Testament assures us. Any temporal powers possessed by the Pope in past ages belonged to him either in virtue of his office, or by the legitimate title of donation on the part of Catholic princes.

354. *In the eleventh century one Pope gave England to William of Normandy.*

No Pope ever gave England to William of Normandy. William claimed the right to the English throne on the score that Edward the Confessor had designated him as his heir, and that Harold had sworn fealty to William as his liege lord according to the feudal system. The Pope, after having been appealed to, examined the evidence, and declared that William possessed the true right to the throne. In other words, upon request, Alexander II. merely decided a question of law.

355. *Could the Pope act like that today?*

The eleventh century and the feudal system have gone, never to return. Conditions of those times are no indication of possibilities today under totally different conditions.

356. *Another Pope gave England to Spain.*

That is not true. For political reasons, Philip of Spain determined to attack England. English pirates were plundering the merchant ships of Spain, and Elizabeth was stirring up the Turks in Spain to revolt against Spanish authority. She had also shown great hostility to the Catholic Faith, had murdered Mary, Queen of Scots, and was persecuting Catholics because of their religion. But, whilst Pope Sixtus V. knew that Elizabeth deserved any troubles she might bring upon herself, he told Philip that, if he was victorious, he must nominate some other ruler, who would restore the Catholic religion to England, and protect it in the form in which all Englishmen had acknowledged it prior to the Reformation.

357. *Another Pope gave America to Spain and the East to Portugal—all without regard to the feelings and wishes of the people.*

You have got hold of a few facts without understanding them in the least, and with no idea of how to interpret them correctly. When Columbus discovered America, a hot dispute arose between Spain and Portugal as to the ownership of the new-found territory. Both nations appealed to the Pope to mediate between them in order to avert war. It was a wise move; and, evil as he may have been in his personal life, Pope Alexander VI. handled this matter with supreme justice and prudence. The German historian Pastor says, "This peaceful settlement of thorny questions is justly regarded as one of the great glories of the Papacy. Nothing but complete misunderstanding and blind party spirit could turn it into an accusation against Rome. And it is simply absurd to speak of Alexander VI. as having given away what did not belong to him, taking no account of the liberties of the Americans." In all such negotiations, allowance was always made for the rights and consent of the peoples concerned.

358. Why is the power of Rome declining on the Continent of Europe?

I deny that it is doing so. At various times in certain countries anti-religious minorities may secure political control, but that says nothing about the power of the Church over the hearts and souls of the majority. I have recently read a bitterly anti-Catholic Seventh Day Adventist publication, written by A. L. Baker, in which these words occur: "Today we find the Papacy with more power and prestige throughout the world than at any time since the Protestant Reformation. In Europe the World War turned the wheel of fortune in a most amazing way for the Pope. At the outbreak of the war, fourteen nations were accredited to the Vatican. Now more than thirty-five are represented there. The Papacy has greatly strengthened its position in Europe since the war." Mr. Baker then proceeds to say that her obvious increase in power proves her to be the Beast and the Dragon of Revelations. But you try to spoil it all by denying the very foundation of his argument, and by asserting that her power is declining! However, I suppose you would like it both ways. If the Catholic Church is strong, she must be false because Scripture speaks of the strength of the Beast. If she is not strong, she must be false because she cannot grip the hearts and loyalty of her people. So the enemies of the Catholic Church have spoken for centuries. But it makes little difference. She has been watching old enemies buried and new ones born for two thousand years. They come and go. But she goes on forever.

359. Are anti-Church disturbances due to the improved education of the masses?

No. They have been due to the influence of minority groups of almost entirely irreligious men who have attained to power through the very unpreparedness of the majority. Emancipated from Christian scruples, these irreligious groups have an advantage over those who believe in principled conduct; and they devote much more time to political organizations than those to whom this world is not everything.

360. You refuse to see signs of the diminishing power of Rome?

The history of the Church has varied from age to age, consisting of increases and decreases of influence, now in this country, now in that; but on the whole the Catholic Church throughout the world is ever growing and expanding and in no previous age has shown greater vitality than at present, save, of course, in her initial days when under the extraordinary control of the Holy Spirit, and accompanied by an altogether special dispensation of miraculous phenomena. But the reaction of the world to the Church in any given age has no real bearing on the question as to whether she is the true Church or not. For the solution of that question she must be studied for what she is in herself.

361. What assurance did Christ give that His Church would be preserved from error?

When He said, "I will build my Church," He also said that "the gates of hell would never prevail against it." Matt. XVI., 18. But the forces of evil and of error would have prevailed against the Church had she not been rendered infallible. Again, He commanded men to hear the Church under pain of damnation. He sent the Church to teach in His name, and said, "He who hears you hears me." Lk. X., 16. And again, "He who believes and is baptized shall be saved; he who believes not, shall be condemned." Mk. XVI., 16. He could not order us to believe the Church, with our very salvation at stake, yet not guarantee His Church against the possibility of leading us into disastrous errors quite opposed to His teachings. Moreover, when He commissioned the Church to go and to teach all nations, He promised to be with her all days till the end of the world (Matt. XXVIII., 20), and He sent the Holy Spirit to keep her as the "pillar and ground of truth." All this forbids the possibility of a departure from the revealed truth; or, in other words, constitutes a pledge of perpetual infallibility.

362. In Romans XI., 22, St. Paul wrote to the Church of Rome, telling her to "abide in goodness, otherwise thou also shalt be cut off." That practically says, "You are not infallible. So beware."

St. Paul wrote those words to the ordinary members of the Church at Rome, with no reference to the infallibility of the Apostles and Bishops of the Church. To any and every Christian at Rome he said, "Soul, thou art not impeccable—so beware of pride. Take heed to thyself." Infallibility and impeccability are two very different things. Infallibility means that the Bishops as successors of the Apostles and official teachers of the Church are unable collectively to define erroneous doctrines as dogmas of the faith. Impeccability means that one could not commit sin and fall from grace. Christ was impeccable. But Christians are not impeccable, whether they be members of the laity or of the hierarchy of Bishops. Even the Pope is not impeccable. All can sin; and St. Paul is here particularly warning all against the sin of pride and of boasting against the Jews. He tells them that, as God rejected the Jews, so He will reject Christians also if they are not faithful.

363. In the lifetime of St. John the Lord found it necessary to rebuke the seven Churches in Asia for error. Rev. cc. I-III.

If you study the chapters more closely you will find that there is no hint that the teaching-authority of the Church was guilty of error in doctrine. Infallibility means that the Church cannot officially teach erroneous doctrine. But her officials can err in their conduct, and grow lax and careless in their administration. Infallibility, of course, whilst belonging to the whole Church collectively, belongs specifically in its particular exercise to the "Church-teaching," consisting of the Bishops. Security belongs to the whole Church, including the "Church-taught." But there is no guarantee that all members of the Church will ever retain the humility and docility of true Christians. Individuals can abandon the truth, and fall into error, and into sin. Then it is the duty of the Bishops to correct the wayward subjects. Now you will notice that each of the seven letters are addressed to the "angels" of the Churches. That is, they are addressed to the Bishops in charge of them. And in not one case does the charge concern erroneous doctrine. Thus St. John writes to the angel of the Church at Ephesus, "I know thou canst not bear them that are evil . . . and thou hatest the Nicolaites, which I also hate." To the angel of the Church of Pergamus, "Thou holdest fast my name, and hast not denied my faith." To the angel of the Church of Thyatira, "I know thy works, and thy faith, and thy charity." To the angel at Philadelphia, "Thou hast kept my word, and hast not denied my faith." Nowhere is the orthodoxy of the Bishops denied. Any blame concerns conduct, and carelessness towards others who would introduce wrong doctrine or laxity. As a matter of fact, the letters admit that the Bishops are the custodians of sound doctrine, and should attend to the banishing of error and heresy.

364. *Truth only makes me ask you to consider these things.*

Since you reject not only the infallibility of the Catholic Church, but also, I presume, your own infallibility as well, what guarantee have you that your own ideas are necessarily the truth? I have not the same problem; for, although I do not claim infallibility, I am subject to a Church which is infallible, and which gives me certainty of the truth. But you cannot claim certainty yourself, nor have you any certain guide. If ever a man had reason to pause, and seriously examine his own position, it is yourself.

365. *Should not every individual have the right at a reasonable age to reject what does not appeal to him?*

Certainly not. On that same principle one would have the right to reject what even Christ taught, if it did not happen to suit one's own ideas. How could any Christian consider himself free to challenge the knowledge or the veracity of Christ, or His right to exact obedience to His magisterial authority? The infallibility of Christ is just as much an obstacle to your principle as the infallibility of the Catholic Church. If, however, one never has the right to reject the teaching of Christ and of His Church, a Catholic may and should verify for himself the credentials of the Catholic Church to teach mankind in the name of, and with the authority of God. I would that every Catholic did so.

366. *The Roman Church seems like a schoolmaster who fears to admit that he is wrong lest he lose prestige.*

The Catholic Church is conscious of an infallibility guaranteed by God—an infallibility of which no schoolmaster can be conscious. Christ taught as one having authority, saying, "My doctrine is not mine, but His that sent me." Jn. VII., 16. And the Catholic Church speaks in the same way. Where your schoolmaster knows that he is wrong and fears to admit it, the Catholic Church knows that she is not wrong. There is a world of difference between the two positions. Nor does the Church fear that she will lose her prestige. She dreads only lest any of her subjects should lose their souls.

367. *Has not the Church of Rome sometimes digressed from spiritual matters to matters which did not concern her, as in the Galileo case?*

You have not chosen a good example. The Galileo affair, though directly a matter of science, did indirectly concern the Church and spiritual interests, owing both to the circumstances of the time, and Galileo's own indulgence in theological speculations. The political arena would have provided better examples. But even there the Church as a Church did not digress from spiritual matters. No accepted temporal powers of the Popes in past ages have ever affected the official teachings of the Church in matters of faith and morals.

368. *Did not an infallible Pope pronounce Galileo's theory of the revolution of the earth round the sun to be a damnable heresy?*

No. Your question implies more than can rightly be said. The Committee of Cardinals and theologians appointed by the Pope to inquire into the theories of Galileo gave the verdict that they were false and contrary to Holy Scripture, and that Galileo himself was "gravely suspect of heresy." After the decision was given the Pope sanctioned it. And the decision, of course, was wrong. But the conditions required for infallibility were not present in this case.

369. *Was the infallible Church right then—or now?*

There are no grounds for that question, for the decree against the teaching of Galileo was never issued as an infallible decree. All who understand the conditions required for an infallible decision by the Catholic Church have long since given up the Galileo case as having any bearing on the question at all. Procter, a Protestant astronomer, says this: "It is absolutely certain that the decision in regard to Galileo's teaching, shown now to have been unsound, does not in the slightest degree affect the Catholic doctrine of infallibility whether of the Pope or of the Church." The Protestant historian Karl von Gebler writes, "The two Congregations of the Index, and the Inquisition, and the two Popes who sanctioned their decrees were in error. But no one has ever held that such decisions were infallible even when approved by the Pope, unless specially set forth according to all the conditions of an infallible utterance." Nor was the condemnation of Galileo unintelligible. Although his theory was right, no scientist today will admit that he advanced a single valid proof of the fact. So far as the evidence available was concerned, the old view was just as likely as the new one. Many scientists of the time were opposed to his teachings. And as a matter of fact, ten years before Galileo's condemnation, Kepler, a Protestant scientist, had been condemned for saying the same thing as Galileo by the Protestant theological faculty of Tubingen. The application of the theory to Sacred Scripture was also calculated to have a most disturbing religious effect upon people not prepared for the new knowledge, and from that point of view, efforts to prevent the popular diffusion of the theory were not imprudent. Apart from this judgment in the light of the times, however, the Galileo case has absolutely no bearing on the question of infallibility.

370. *Besides being condemned, was not Galileo brutally tortured by the Inquisition?*

No. Refusal to obey the authorities who forbade him to propagate his doctrines brought on Galileo a sentence of imprisonment, a sentence which was commuted into detention on parole in the Palace of the Grand Duke of Tuscany near Rome. From there he was allowed before long to retire to Siena, where he became the honored guest of the Archbishop. We Catholics do not deny any of the facts in the Galileo case merely because we would prefer that they were not true. But, admitting all the facts of history, we are quite able to show that none of them really militates against the truth of the Catholic Church. If a man says that Galileo was condemned and imprisoned without making any exaggerated statements about his punishment or any allusion to infallibility, we are quite prepared to admit his accuracy.

371. *Does infallibility change to conform to times and circumstances?*

No. Once an infallible decision has been given, it stands for all time. The Catholic Church is committed to that decision, and all Catholics are obliged to accept it as true.

372. *How could a wrong infallible decision be converted into a right one?*

A wrong infallible decision could not occur. It would be absolutely impossible for one Pope to define a given doctrine and for a subsequent Pope to define a contradictory doctrine.

373. *You hold that not only the Catholic Church as a Church is infallible but that the Pope himself is personally so?*

The Pope in his capacity as head of the Church is infallible.

374. *Is the Pope blasphemous enough to call himself infallible?*

He has faith enough to know that the Holy Ghost, the infallible Spirit of Truth, will preserve him from error when defining truths of faith or morals for the guidance of the whole Church.

375. *Then he is bold enough to challenge the very Holy Spirit of God.*

That is not true. He has humility enough to admit that his infallibility when he does exercise his supreme office as teacher of all the faithful is due, not to himself, but to that very Holy Spirit. You yourself are as sure of your own judgment as if you were infallible. Do you claim that the Holy Spirit is surely guiding you to the truth? If so, you are claiming just what the Pope claims, though the Pope claims it under much more limited conditions, and with much greater interests at stake.

376. *I admit that if one could swallow "holus bolus" the doctrine of the infallibility of the Pope, an infallible man elected by fallible men, the rest would be easy.*

We are not asked to swallow anything, as if it did not matter whether it were reasonable or not. We are asked to believe the doctrine of the infallibility of the Pope in matters of faith and morals. And then, indeed, as you say, the rest follows. For if the Pope is infallible, then there is no doubt that men are obliged to join the Catholic Church to which alone the infallible Pope belongs. But that your difficulty against infallibility is based upon a wrong notion of the Catholic doctrine is evident from your words, "an infallible man elected by fallible men." Your idea is that fallible men cannot give what they themselves do not possess. But no Catholic suggests that they do. If a business manager said, "I shall create the position of overseer, and grant the occupant special privileges, yet I will allow the men to elect their own choice," the man elected would derive his authority from the manager, not from those who elected him. Thus Christ instituted the office of head of the Church, and granted the prerogative of infallibility to the occupant of the position when acting in his official capacity in certain matters. The Pope may owe his election to his fellow men; but he owes his infallibility to the Holy Spirit in virtue of the promise of Christ.

377. *On what grounds do you hold that the Pope is infallible?*

Because he is the lawful successor of St. Peter, and, therefore, inherits that privilege of St. Peter according to the will of Christ who declared that the Church would last till the end of the world with the constitutional powers He gave it.

378. *Where do the Gospels say that even St. Peter was to be infallible?*

The doctrine of St. Peter's infallibility is implicitly included in the Petrine texts, given earlier under No. 316. Also, since the whole Catholic Church is infallible, the Pope, as head of the Church, and the last court of appeal, must himself be infallible.

379. *No one could accept the decision of any human being as infallible.*

The infallibility of the Pope does not mean that we must accept as infallible the decision of a human being. You are leaving out the most important factor of all. If a criminal, after being sentenced to jail, cried out, "Why should I be sentenced by a mere fellow man?", the judge could reply, "For the purposes of this judgment I am not a mere fellow man. I am a man endowed with authority and jurisdiction by the State. In omitting reference to my official capacity, you are leaving out the most important factor of all." So with the Pope. We do not accept the decision of a human being as infallible; we accept the decision of a human being who has received authority from God to teach in His name, and whom God has promised to preserve from error when he teaches in his official capacity doctrines concerning faith or morals. Your question is due to an imperfect knowledge of what infallibility means, and the conditions governing its exercise.

380. *The issue narrows down to this, that the Pope is enabled by his infallibility to interpret exactly the Word of God.*

The doctrine is better stated negatively. Infallibility means that God will not permit the Pope to define *ex Cathedra*, or officially, a doctrine not in accordance with the genuine teaching of Christ. Therefore, if the Pope does define a doctrine, that doctrine cannot be against the true intention of Holy Scripture.

381. *What does "Ex Cathedra" mean?*

It means that the Pope must speak, where it is a question of exercising his infal'' .uty, not as a private theologian, but in virtue of his office as supreme head ɪ the whole Church on earth giving a decision for all the members of the Church on a matter of faith or morals.

382. *Does not the prerogative of infallibility suggest that impurity of morals should never have existed amongst the Popes?*

The prerogative of infallibility, rightly understood, has no bearing on this matter at all. The exalted office of supreme head of the Church, quite apart from infallibility, certainly suggests that impurity of morals ought not to have existed amongst the Popes. Hence, the distress of good Catholics when they learn that a few of the Popes led unworthy lives. But not for a moment does infallibility suggest that a Pope could not sin did he choose to do so. Catholics do not maintain that the Pope is necessarily impeccable, or simply unable to sin. We must not confuse impeccability and infallibility. They are two totally different things.

383. *Surely a leader who failed in morals would forfeit his right to be the teacher of others!*

That depends entirely upon the will of the one who appoints him to be the teacher. A bad man can give quite good advice to others. But your judgment is ruled out by our Lord Himself. Christ blamed the Pharisees for not living up to the moral principles appointed by God. He accused them of pride, vanity, injustice, and intolerance—worse sins than the less malicious frailties of the flesh. Yet He denied that they had forfeited the right to be teachers of others in the name of God. In Matt. XXIII., 2-3, He said to the people, "The Scribes and Pharisees have sitten on the chair of Moses. All things, therefore, they shall say to you, observe and do; but according to their works do ye not; for they say and do not." The few bad Popes said, and did not. And the Catholic Church absolutely forbids all Catholics to imitate in any way the wrong personal conduct of any bad Pope. But no bad Pope has ever defined a wrong doctrine, or pretended that his own wrong conduct was in accordance with Catholic moral principles.

384. *If the Pope is infallible, why doesn't he give some straight-out rulings on modern problems?*

What do you intend by modern problems? If they are outside the sphere of faith and moral principles, you have gone beyond the scope of infallibility. And you cannot expect infallibility to operate in a way that the Catholic doctrine does not demand that it should operate. Meantime, the Pope has given many straight-out rulings on modern problems within his competence—as on social justice, marriage, education, birth control, and other aspects of morality.

385. *Is Pope Leo XIII.'s Encyclical on "Labor" an ex Cathedra utterance, and binding on Catholics under pain of sin should they doubt its teachings?*

The Encyclical you mention is not an *ex Cathedra* utterance. But still Catholics are obliged in conscience to accept its teachings. For the authority of the Church is not limited to infallible definitions only. And quite apart from infallibility,

Pope Leo XIII. certainly intended to give an authoritative statement of the moral principles of justice and charity in relation to the workers. Therefore, though we have not to make an act of divine faith in the truth of the Encyclical, we are obliged to accept it in a spirit of reverent obedience. Substantially, at least, we are obliged to take it for granted that the Pope's teaching in that Encyclical is not only not opposed to the doctrines of Christ, but is quite in harmony with them. If doubts come to us in this or that point of his teaching, we must make sure, firstly, that we have indeed understood its proper sense. If we are sure that we have not misunderstood his doctrine, then before allowing ourselves to doubt it, we should make a profound study of the whole subject so that we become competent to form a sound decision. If that study does not confirm our conviction that the Pope is right, then we can submit our difficulties to lawful ecclesiastical authorities, and ask a solution of them. To doubt, or rashly to deny the doctrine of the Encyclical on some given point, without taking these precautions, could become sin in any Catholic who is well instructed enough to know the significance of his conduct.

386. *You think unity in the faith is necessary, and that infallibility is the only way to secure such unity?*

Undoubtedly. Truth is one, and consistent. Contradictory beliefs cannot be equally true. Moreover, Christ, who declared Himself to be the Truth, insisted on unity of doctrine. He gave definite teachings to His Apostles, and ordered them to preach those definite teachings. He declared that there must be one fold and one shepherd. And He prayed for unity, that all His followers might be one as He and His Father were one.

387. *One Church for people of all nations seems, in any case, to be rather a wild dream.*

The fact remains that God has accomplished what you call a wild dream. And the Catholic Church is His masterpiece in this world. One cannot keep the Gospels and reject the Catholic Church. The attempt to do this has led to endless diversity amongst Protestants. They do not grasp the essential teaching of the Gospels. They do not see that the essential work of Christ was to give a system of protection, diffusion, and activity which He established for the service of all times, all peoples great and small, learned and ignorant. That is the marvel, and it is realized in the Catholic Church which embraces over 400 millions drawn from every conceivable nation on the face of the earth.

388. *I agree that the Roman Catholic Church is remarkable for its unity. But should not the true Church of Christ also be holy?*

It should be, and is. Catholics, therefore, are justified in their great act of faith, "I believe in the Holy Catholic Church."

389. *Your Church makes a claim that no other Church dare make.*

That is true; and I am grateful for the admission. No other Church is really conscious of possessing any of the four great marks of the true Church of Christ, or of being one, holy, catholic, and apostolic.

390. *In what particular way is your Church remarkable for holiness?*

She is holy in her Founder, Jesus Christ; in her teachings; in her sacramental system of grace; and in her members. There is no need to dwell on the first point. The Catholic Church alone was founded by Jesus Christ; and there can be do doubt about *His* holiness. On the other points I must ask you to be patient with a rather lengthy explanation. Take first the question of teaching. The Catholic Church has fought everywhere and at all times to spread and defend the full truth revealed by Christ. Where other professing Christian bodies have made outrageous concessions to rationalistic unbelief, she has remained adamant. And there is not a single dogmatic teaching of the Catholic Church which does not tend to confirm in us the will to sanctify our souls; whether it be the dogma of our origin from God by creation; or of our redemption by Christ, His Son and our Lord; or of our going back to God and to our judgment with one of three possibilities awaiting us—heaven, hell, or purgatory. Certainly, the dogma of hell has never yet induced a man to sin. The dogma of purgatory has inculcated the necessity of purifying our lives by Christian mortification and self-denial. The dogma of grace and of the supernatural rules out mere standards of outward respectability, and demands that one's daily life, personal, domestic, and civic, must be inspired by a deep love of God.

If we turn from the dogmatic teachings of the Catholic Church to her moral laws, we can challenge any man to keep them, and not be the better for it. So, too, we can challenge him to violate them, yet not degenerate. There is no Church on earth which so fights to lift man above the natural and the sensual, fighting for purity of morals, the holiness of marriage, and the rights of God in every department of life. So much so that no one joins the Catholic Church sincerely without desiring a loftier standard of living than was previously proposed to him; and no one leaves the Catholic Church save for a lower standard of conduct. If Catholics go, it is not because they have discovered their Church to be untrue, but because they themselves have not been true to their own conscientious obligations.

But the Catholic Church is not only holy in her teachings; she is also holy in her members. The Church certainly has the power to sanctify men in practice. But, naturally, this power will attain its object insofar as men allow themselves to be influenced by it. In general, ordinary holiness prevails amongst the vast majority of Catholics insofar as they usually keep in a state of grace and out of a state of mortal sin. They do try to keep God's laws conscientiously, often making great sacrifices to do so. They are remarkable for their fidelity to their religious duties to God; to their Sunday Mass; to the Sacraments; to prayer; to fasting and other forms of self-denial; to the obligations of alms-giving and charity. Often they are ridiculed as fools and as scrupulous for this fidelity to their religion by those who regard themselves as advocates of liberty. If they sin from time to time, they are never happy in that state, but are most uneasy until they recover God's grace. And always they will admit that sin is sin, acknowledging themselves to be sinners, rather than hypocritically trying to save their faces by pretending that sin is virtue, and that what is unlawful is really lawful.

Turning from "ordinary" holiness, which does allow for lapses through frailty, though the greater part of life is spent in God's grace, there are hosts of Catholics who go further. They not only consistently avoid mortal sin, but they labor earnestly to emancipate themselves from even venial sins. And yet others push on to the practice of heroic Christian virtue. Take the almost interminable list of canonized Saints produced by the Catholic Church. They are her living miracles through the ages, and her true pride and joy as well as the delight and inspiration of Catholics the world over.

That there are bad Catholics does not affect all that I have said. Christ predicted that there would be bad Catholics. The cockle will grow side by side with the wheat. But we can account for the bad Catholics. It is for the critics of the Church to account for the good ones, and above all, for the Saints who have flourished in every age of the Church.

391. *Did not the Roman Church, by its corruption, forfeit its right to be the true Church, so that Christ had to establish the Protestant Churches in its place?*

That cannot be said. Christ declared that His Church would be like a net holding good and bad fish. But any corruption amongst the members of the Catholic Church is not because of her teachings, but against them and in spite of them.

Despite the bad fish within the net, however, the net is quite good. You cannot argue from bad fish to a bad net. And certainly Christ did not establish the Protestant Churches in place of the Catholic Church. It is absurd historically to say that He established them when we know that they were established sixteen centuries after He left this world by men whose names are also well known. It is absurd logically to say that Christ, who is Truth itself, and who said that His Church would be one as He and His Father are one, founded a whole lot of conflicting Churches, each contradicting what the others assert. And it is absurd to say that the forces of evil did prevail against the Catholic Church when Christ said that they would not do so. He said that He would preserve His Church from error and corruption—as a Church—all days from His time till the end of the world. How any one can continue to believe in the Divinity of Christ, yet insist that He could not do as He said He would do, passes comprehension.

392. What is meant in Scripture by "The Scarlet Woman"?

St. John says, in Rev. XVII., that he saw "a woman sitting on a scarlet colored beast full of names of blasphemy." This "woman" has been popularly called "The Scarlet Woman." Many fantastic explanations have been given as to her real character. Some people have said that the Scarlet Woman represents pagan Rome in the days when the Emperors persecuted the early Christians. But that certainly is not completely true, for the "woman and the beast" are described as outlasting pagan Rome. Others, under the influence of religious prejudice, have said that the Scarlet Woman represents Papal Rome. But that is certainly quite untrue. For Papal Rome has ever labored to forward the cause of Christ, whilst the "woman and the beast" are opposed to Christ and the cause of Christ. There is no absolute certainty as to the Scarlet Woman's full significance. Most probably, as the Church is the "Bride of Christ," so the woman represents the "Bride of Satan." I speak, of course in the mystical sense. The "Woman," therefore, stands for the "Antichristian Spirit." The "Beast" upon which the "Woman" is seated, and which she guides and controls, is the material force of this world. The "Woman and the Beast," therefore, signify an antichristian idealism employing the material forces of this world against the cause of Christ, and against all that is holy and spiritual and good. And always through history, in every age, and right to the end, we shall have manifestations of their evil campaign. The campaign is as violent today as ever it was. Officially Christ is banished from commercial, civil, and national life. We see today a wrong nationalism, coupled with a wrong internationalism, which will have none of one thing only—of God revealed in Christ as absolute over all rulers and nations. The unchristian idealism controlling national and international relations on a purely worldly, materialistic, and selfish basis is a re-crucifixion of Christ and of His cause; and it constitutes a manifestation of the "Woman and the Beast" in our own days.

393. Why do some people presume that The Scarlet Woman means the Papacy?

Because they are very ignorant of the Catholic Church, hate it without understanding it, and are enabled by their peculiar mentality to believe whatever they would like to be true without further ado.

394. The Catholic religion, if holy and true, should produce almost invariably a peculiarly excellent type of individual.

You commence with an idea which is only a half-truth. The Catholic religion is able to produce excellent types. If a man seriously wants to be good, the Catholic Church will enable him to be good as no other power on earth. But there cannot be any guarantee that she will invariably produce excellent individuals, because that makes no allowance for the variation in the dispositions of men. Men are not inanimate objects to be sanctified against their will. So Christ compared His religion to seed which falls, some upon good ground, some upon shallow soil, and some upon stone. The seed is always equally good; but its fruit is dependent upon the quality of soil which receives it.

395. Is not Protestantism as well able to give the spiritual outlook as Catholicism?

That cannot be admitted. It is undeniable that Protestantism as such cannot preserve Christian truth intact, and dare not insist upon the fullness of Christian moral teaching. As a result of the Protestant Reformation we find articles of faith denied; fasting and other forms of mortification not taught; the sense of sin diminishing; the evangelical counsels of poverty, chastity, and obedience inspiring monastic life ignored; a clergy unable to rise to the ideals of celibacy, and as unable to give sound spiritual advice as the laity are unwilling to receive it; nationalism displacing the universal outlook of Christianity; materialism supplanting supernaturalism; whilst more and more philanthropy and humanitarianism tend to displace that Christian charity which is in the order of grace, and supposes a pure and disinterested love of God rather than merely of our fellow men.

396. What regulated conduct of Catholics is the least that visible fellowship of the Church requires?

By "visible fellowship" I presume you mean public adherence to the Catholic Church on the part of the person concerned, and acknowledgment by the Catholic Church that he belongs to her fold. For that, the least required is that the person who professes to be a Catholic has not been excommunicated officially by the Church. The Church, of course, insists that all Catholics are obliged to regulate their conduct in accordance with the ten commandments and the precepts of the Church. Insofar as they do not, they sin; and if they sin publicly in serious degrees, they are forbidden the reception of the Sacraments until they sincerely repent and resolve to do their best to observe the laws of God once more. But whatever their sins, and even though interiorly they are not in God's love and friendship, they still retain external membership of the Church, or, as you call it, "visible fellowship." They are sinners, but they are still Catholics; and the Catholic Church, instead of abandoning them, simply pleads with them to abandon their sins. Conscious that part of her duty is to be a kind of hospital in a spiritually sick world, she does not throw the patients out of the window on the score that they are in grave need of spiritual care. So long as a Catholic continues to profess his faith, and has not so directly defied the authority of the Church as to merit excommunication, he is fulfilling at least the minimum required for continued visible fellowship, and will be publicly acknowledged by the Catholic Church as one of hers.

397. What are some of the qualifications of a good Catholic?

A good Catholic is essentially a man of duty. Now we can classify our duties as being towards God, towards ourselves, and towards our fellow men. A good Catholic, therefore, is one who fulfills his duties in all three cases. He loyally accepts and lives up to the religion God has revealed, gladly professing the Catholic Faith, regularly fulfilling the duties of prayer, sacramental life and worship prescribed by the Catholic Church, and obeying the commandments of God and the laws of his religion in all things. In addition to this, he fulfills his duties to himself, controlling his lower passions, avoiding vice and cultivating personal virtue according to the dictates of reason and of conscience. As regards his fellow men, he regulates his relations towards them by the master virtues of justice and charity in all things. A man who fulfills all these duties is a really good Catholic. If he does not do so, then insofar as he professes the Catholic Faith he is a Catholic. But his goodness or badness as a Catholic must be measured by the degree in which he succeeds or fails in living up to the ideals I have given.

398. How is the Roman Church superior to other Churches in the help it gives towards holiness of life?

I have already explained that to some extent under No. 390. But in addition to the ideals and standards of the Catholic Church by which a man knows clearly how to serve God, the worship of the Catholic Church is more helpful than any other Church can offer. The Sacrifice of the Mass, offered in supreme adoration to God, lifts men's souls to Him as nothing else can do. The Sacraments, too,—and all seven—have an immense influence on souls, Baptism conferring the spiritual life; Confirmation strengthening it; Confession destroying later sins which come between the soul and God; Holy Communion bringing Christ to each as the very Guest of the soul; Extreme Unction finally preparing the soul for its meeting with God. The Sacrament of Matrimony is specially ordained to sanctify the duties of the state of marriage, whilst Holy Orders gives a priesthood which has meant an incalculable stream of blessings to the faithful. In addition to those helps, the innumerable practices of piety, prayer, self-denial and abnegation inspired by the Catholic religion result in a greater spirituality and sanctification of men. Finally the discipline of the Catholic Church, based on obedience to the Will of God, has resulted in that general sense of order in the Church which is essential to spiritual progress. In necessarily brief replies I cannot do more than just touch upon the subject; but at least I have said enough to stimulate your own further thoughts.

399. Whatever you may say, I wouldn't join any Church which has priests.

If you became convinced of the truth of the Catholic Church, you would have to join it whether you approved of the conduct of priests or not. It would be ridiculous to neglect your own salvation because all priests were not as holy as you thought they ought to be. You might as well refuse a legacy because all lawyers are not wealthy! However, if you had a right idea of priests and of the Catholic Church, you would not have your present prejudices. And you cannot say what you would do under happier circumstances.

400. Ultimately, if we get down to fundamentals, the priests have been the cause of all the troubles in the Church and from persecutors.

That is not true. The vast majority of priests have been men of moderate and self-sacrificing lives.

401. Is the ideal of chastity for the priests the same as for the nuns?

Yes. The vow of chastity made by both priests and nuns means that any sin against the virtue of purity of morals is also a sacrilege against the virtue of religion. And people who want to live immoral lives do not vow the opposite for the sheer joy of making themselves doubly guilty when they break their vow! It must be remembered too that the vow of chastity does not imply merely a negative obligation to abstain from sins against morality. It implies also that positive obligation of consecrating oneself to God, or of rendering oneself sacred to God, so that the heart and all its affections are reserved for Him alone. Cravings for the consolation of human affections have to be rigidly controlled, never manifested, and elevated by grace to the supernatural and spiritual plane which was characteristic of the love of humanity in the heart of Jesus Christ Himself. The vow of chastity, therefore, demands a very far-reaching and continued renunciation of the sensual in favor of the spiritual.

402. Are you just saying that, or is it the official doctrine of your Church?

In December, 1935, Pope Pius XI. issued an Encyclical on the Catholic Priesthood. In that Encyclical he writes: "A priest should have a loftiness of spirit, a purity of heart, and a sanctity of life befitting the solemnity and holiness of the office he holds. Clerics, therefore, are bound by a grave obligation of chastity. So grave is the obligation in them of its perfect and total observance that a transgression involves the added guilt of sacrilege." Every student for the priesthood has this drilled into him during his years of study and preparation for his ordination; and that is not the way in which people are prepared for an immoral life.

403. *Of course, as a priest yourself, you would defend your fellow priests even at the expense of the Church.*

I certainly would not. The interests of the Church come before the interests of any individual member of the Church. If the conduct of any priest were discreditable to the Church, I would certainly condemn it much more strongly than you would. I give that as a general statement. For in no individual case would I accept the uncorroborated verdict on the conduct of anybody from an anonymous critic.

404. *Are not the outbreaks against the Church in Spain, and Mexico, and other countries due to the selfish lives of priests?*

No. I admit that laxity on the part of some priests may have been a contributing factor towards the discontent of some people. But the chief cause of their discontent lies in the very persons of the disaffected. The good man is saddened by the sight of any disedifying example. It is the evil man who rejoices in it, and makes it the excuse to do still more harm to the Church. Outbreaks against the Church are due to the efforts and propaganda of professed enemies of God and of all religion; and to the apathy or even the bitterness of ignorant and ill-disposed members of the Church, who are only too eager to abandon restraints of their religion.

405. *We have nothing to say against the nuns, who live good, useful, and self-denying lives. We are opposed only to priests.*

Why, then, do the revolutionaries with whom you sympathize, make straight for convents, burn them to the ground, and subject the nuns to shocking ill-treatment?

406. *Even if Catholics knew that the conduct of a priest was not right, they would be afraid to say anything.*

How do you know that? If you were to read the lives of St. Catherine of Siena, or of St. Bernard of Clairvaux, you would find some very straight talk even to Popes —yet both these have been canonized by the Church as Saints. Catholics are not in the least afraid to condemn what is to be condemned; and to report to the Bishop what they believe should be reported. But they do not believe in wholesale condemnations, nor in taking charges for granted without bothering to make sure of the truth. Likewise they know that the law of charity extends not only to calumny, but also to detraction; and they are naturally slow to usurp the right to judge others. But that is not a crime.

407. *Turning from the question of the personal morals of the clergy, is not the power of the Roman Church due to her immense wealth?*

The Catholic Church does not owe her spiritual power to such temporal possessions as belong to her. Rather she owes such temporal possessions to the multitudes of Catholics who, after all, had to be converted to the Church through the ages before they could devote their contributions to the support of their religion. In other words, the Church has not influence because she has temporal possessions; she has temporal possessions because she has influence. Her power over men's souls comes first.

408. *Why is the city of Rome itself crowded with Churches in which are stored up most of the finest and valuable art treasures on earth?*

The number of Churches is due to the fact that, during the last 1900 years many parish Churches, special Shrines, and Chapels to various colleges, Universities, and Central Houses of Religious Orders have been built in that great center of Christendom. Not most of the art treasures on earth are stored in them. One who could suggest that must have sedulously avoided the Museums and Art Galleries throughout the world. If those that do exist in Rome are amongst the finest in the world, that is due to the high level of culture and genius of artists drawn from the Italian people. Their preservation in the Churches is due to the fact that the artists had faith and piety enough to devote their genius to the fitting adornment of this Church or that; and that the death of the artists did not make the authorities feel free to sell these offerings in honor of God's House to wealthy tourists. As a result, travelers from all over the world are still able to see them and appreciate them.

409. *Are not Catholic Churches and institutions built on the best land and in the most expensive style even in our own country, for which the congregations must pay?*

That is not a fact. Such buildings have to be built somewhere; and it is easy to term as the best whatever blocks of land they are built upon—after the event. It is but wisdom, of course, to choose a site suitable and convenient to the uses of the institutions in question. And if good and solid buildings are erected these are not the most expensive in the long run, but really the cheapest. We must take long-sighted views. Finally, those members of the Catholic Church who can afford to to do so, and are willing to do so, will meet the expenses required in due course. Those so burdened with other expenses that they really cannot afford to give, ought not to give; and those not willing to give, are not compelled to give. In most cases the debt is spread out over years, and even over generations, many people giving a little regularly according to their means.

410. *Is not the confessional used to compel people to pay for Church purposes?*

No. Nor has any priest the right to make use of the confessional to compel subscriptions towards Church enterprises over and above one's ordinary duty of normal contributions. And even then, he can but point out one's duty when asked.

411. *Does not the Church compel people to go to Mass so that she can extract wealth from an assured congregation?*

No. Firstly, the obligation to attend Mass is but an application of God's commandment, "Remember that thou keep holy the Sabbath day." Secondly, the Church insists upon the fulfillment of this obligation so that God may receive due acknowledgment from men, not that she may extract wealth from them. Thirdly, if the Church takes advantage of the presence of her people at Mass to appeal for the support of her various works, she appeals to the free generosity of those willing to give, and for works necessary for the good of souls, not from personal or selfish reasons.

412. *Ought not the Pope to go round amongst the poor as Christ did?*

Christ established the Church, saying that it was then as the smallest of seeds. But He predicted that it would grow into a vast tree. The Pope imitates the virtue of Christ, but the administration of a vast Church of over 400 million subjects necessarily involves duties differing from those of Christ Himself. The Pope goes amongst the poor insofar as many of the poor come to the Vatican for an audience with him. Whenever they come at the time appointed for an audience he sees them, speaks with them, and blesses them and their families. But the Pope cannot leave his greater duties to spend his time wandering around the world from city to city, seeking out the poor. Consider his ordinary day's work. He rises at six; says Mass at seven; and is at his desk by eight. With the help of three secretaries he attends to his correspondence until nine. Then he turns to the reports of Papal Nuntios and

Apostolic Delegates throughout the world. At ten he interviews visiting Bishops or accredited diplomats from foreign governments. After that, audiences are granted to groups of visitors until about 2 p. m. After lunch, the Pope returns to similar work until his evening meal, taking one hour off for a walk in the open air within the Vatican gardens. He dines at eight, then says evening prayers with the staff, and after that studies until about 1 a. m. He gives five hours only to sleep. To speak of his going about to visit the poor in their own homes as if he were an ordinary parish priest shows no knowledge whatever of his duties and responsibilities.

413. *Why does he live in such luxury?*

He does not live in luxury. What evidence have you for suggesting that he does? Is it because he dwells in the Vatican which has come down to us through the centuries, and which the Pope does not own? The Pope has to dwell somewhere. He has his room at the Vatican as others have their rooms in their own homes or in boarding houses. You may say that the Pope has a luxurious life inside the Vatican. He has not. He lives very simply, and works very hard. He has the usual Continental breakfast—a cup of coffee and a roll of bread. His dinner, at 2 p. m., consists of boiled meat and vegetables, rice, fruit, and coffee. At 8 p. m., for supper he has boiled eggs, bread and butter, and a cup of hot milk. That can scarcely be called luxury.

414. *Has your disappointment with the Catholics you have met ever made you regret becoming a Catholic?*

I have not met only with disappointments. Some individual Catholics have proved a disappointment insofar as they have failed to live up to their religion. They make a very poor thing of their lives considering the graces at their disposal. On the other hand, I have been greatly edified by good Catholics who do live up to their religion, and who have manifested a holiness and a degree of spirituality in circumstances and places where one would scarcely expect to find a saint. But whatever my disappointment with some Catholics, never have I been disappointed with the Catholic Church. She is the true Church of Jesus Christ, and is rightly described by St. Paul as "a glorious Church, not having spot or wrinkle or any such thing." Eph. V., 27. Her only tendency is to produce saints. Insofar as her children allow her to do so, her one effort is to destroy in them all that could prevent their becoming saints. The Catholic Church is absolutely holy in herself, and she is relatively holy in those whom she influences to the degree in which they submit to her influence. As Catholics withdraw from the practical influence of their Church, less and less, of course, is to be expected of them. But amidst all faults of human frailty, the ideals of Catholics remain as long as they retain the faith. If they know that one who gives bad example is a Catholic, they are more horrified than they would be were he anything else. If a priest gives scandal, their misery and sorrow will scarcely bear description. And the more they love their religion the more broken-hearted they are; for the more they realize how utterly repugnant to Catholic principles and ideals is any deliberate evil in one who shares in the very priesthood of Christ.

415. *You claim that your Church is not only one united Church, and holy, but also that it is Catholic.*

That is true.

416. *Your Church has not been known as Catholic since its foundation; and it has never been universal as the word implies.*

The word "Catholic" is derived from the Greek, and it means whole, complete, and universal. The word was first applied to the Church to which we Catholics belong by St. Ignatius, Bishop of Antioch, who died in the year 107 A.D. He used the word to describe the universality of the Church founded by Christ and subject to the Bishop of Rome. And that Church was truly universal in character from the very beginning. She was commissioned by Christ to go to the ends of the earth and to teach all He had revealed to all nations. She was, therefore, Catholic in scope, though it naturally required time to spread to all localities and peoples in actual fact. Again the Church which Christ established was Catholic in time, since it was to last, as one and the same Church, all days till the end of the world. And the Church to which we Catholics belong is the only Church which has been in the world since the time of Christ. She alone teaches all that Christ taught; she alone gives all the means of salvation and sanctification instituted by Christ; she alone draws her members from all nations without exception, and is alone adapted to the needs of all men independently of their racial and political differences. In a word, she alone is the one true Catholic Church.

417. Which is the largest individual religion in the world today?

The 400 millions of Catholics subject to the Bishop of Rome, Pope Pius XII., constitute the largest religious body in the world. There are about 350 million Confucians and Taoists; 230 million Mahometans; 220 million Hindus; 200 million Buddhists; 200 million Protestants of all kinds; 130 million belonging to the various Greek Orthodox Churches; 16 million Jews; and many smaller forms of isolated pagan religions.

418. Why do you describe your Church as the "Catholic Church," and not as the "Roman Catholic" Church?

Because "Catholic Church" is a sufficient and correct description of our Church. By that title the Church whose chief shepherd is the Bishop of Rome is sufficiently described and identified as distinct from all Protestant, Greek, Unitarian, Jewish, and other religions. The title "Roman Catholic" is an incorrect expression. I refuse to use it because it could confirm Protestants in the mistaken idea that there are other kinds of Catholics. Also it is a contradiction in terms to have a limiting adjective before a word meaning "universal." One cannot limit the unlimited, or localize the universal. To say "Roman Catholic Church" with any idea of restriction is to say "the not-universal universal Church." And that is absurd.

419. You have not the right to drop the word "Roman."

We do not drop the word "Roman." We have never used that word officially as Protestants now want to use it; i. e., as an adjective qualifying "Catholic." Officially, we may say that our Church is the Catholic and Roman Church—Catholic, because it is universal, encircling the world; Roman, because its center is the Apostolic See of Rome. The universal Church must have a center somewhere. It happens to be at Rome, whose Bishop is the successor of St. Peter. In reality, it is for us to ask Protestants why they now want to call themselves "Catholics," qualifying us as "Roman" in order to suggest that we are not the only Catholics. At one time they absolutely repudiated the idea that they were Catholics. The mere suggestion that they might be Catholics would meet with an indignant denial.

420. The word Catholic means universal.

Therefore, it abstracts from all national considerations.

421. Would it not be more universal if the Pope were not always an Italian?

It would be less universal if national considerations had such weight that each nation in turn wanted to exert its influence. We see in the Pope simply the successor of St. Peter, and the Vicar of Christ.

422. One could not imagine a Protestant Archbishop submitting to any foreign control.

Protestants themselves insist that Christ is the Head of the Church. What would they do did He return to earth in His human nature to assert His rights? For nationally He would be a foreigner to them. In His human nature He was a Palestinian Jew, who had not a drop of British blood in His veins, nor the privilege of belonging to the British Empire. The source of your difficulties is your national outlook. You use the word foreigner as opposed to allegiance to a nation in and of this world. But Christ said, "My kingdom is not of this world." He told His disciples, "You are in, but not of this world." He repudiated the blending of religion and nationalism amongst the Jews, and sent His Church to teach all nations. However diverse by nationality, all were to be one in the Church. As an Australian, I am a foreigner to Italians. Italians are foreigners from an Australian point of view. But as Catholics owing the same spiritual allegiance to Christ, there is no room for the word foreigner amongst members of the universal Church. We Catholics can say with St. Paul, "There is neither Jew nor Greek; there is neither bond nor free; there is neither male nor female; for we are all one in Christ Jesus." Gal. III., 28. These earthly differences do not count in the true religion of Christ. We are "Catholic."

423. Is it not because the Catholic Church thinks it her mission to convert the world that she undertakes so many foreign missions?

That is so.

424. A government officer of Papua recently said that unless the missionaries there could give the natives work as well as civilization, it would be better to leave them alone to work out their own destiny.

The question of work and civilization does not really concern the missionaries. If political administrators and commercial exploiters wish to impose their own civic customs and modes of living upon the natives, then these people must see to it that the natives are provided with means of a livelihood in exchange for that abandoned by the natives. The primary duty of the missionaries is to wean the natives from paganism, and substitute the Christian faith, with its worship of the true God, and its loftier moral standards. And the Catholic missionaries are doing their part well. In his book, "Papua Today," Sir Hubert Murray, the Lieutenant-Governor of Papua, says, "The old so-called religion of the Papuan must inevitably go. It is mere self-deception to suppose that it can be kept alive, even if such a thing were desirable. Secondly, something must be put in its place, otherwise the religious development of the Papuan comes to an end. Thirdly, the only thing we have to put in its place is Christianity." Sir Hubert Murray adds that hostility to the missions is possibly merely the expression of an attitude of the "superior person" with a proper contempt of revealed religion, and that it rarely has relation to their considered opinion.

425. He added that if we stop these people in their social progress, we will take away the whole of their life interest.

That does not concern the missionaries who certainly will not interfere with the social progress of the natives. The missionaries will give them the true religion of Christ, merely lifting them to an eternal life-interest without changing their life-interest so far as this world is concerned. Sir Hubert Murray writes on this subject: "It must be remembered that many native customs are cruel and revolting in the extreme, and certainly should not be preserved for a day. But, even taking the best of them, those which are deserving of encouragement, and which one would like to see maintained, it is quite certain that most of them, too, must go, as the result of European influence. It is quite useless to try to bolster them up." And he adds:

"Unprejudiced opinions must admit the great benefits bestowed upon the natives of Papua by missions operating in the Territory. Both boys and girls are cleaner, healthier, better fed and better mannered at the Mission Stations than anywhere else in Papua."

426. *Christianity is not a sufficient exchange. If we are not going to disillusion those people we should leave them alone.*

We have an obligation to free people from the illusions of paganism, giving them a knowledge of the true God, of their Savior Jesus Christ, and of their real destiny. This can be done whilst respecting most of their native customs, and is done by the Catholic Missions, as Sir Hubert Murray has repeatedly insisted. In any case, Christianity is more than sufficient compensation for any temporal disadvantages. The early Christian martyrs thought it sufficient compensation for loss of life itself. It may be that we should not impose our ideas of civic life and commerce upon the natives; but this would not exclude the hope of their exchanging paganism for Christianity.

427. *The white residents are not very favorable to the missions.*

Sir William McGregor, the Administrator prior to the present Lieutenant-Governor, Sir Hubert Murray, wrote as follows: "The two finest and best institutions I left in New Guinea were the constabulary and native police, and the missions. To encourage mission work in every possible way was considered a sacred duty of the Government." Captain C. A. W. Moncton, in his book, "Some Experiences of a New Guinea Magistrate," writes, "I am a Churchman (i. e., Episcopalian) and a Churchman I'll die; but if all Roman Catholics were like the members of the Sacred Heart Mission, there soon wouldn't be any other Church in the world." Sir Hubert Murray, in his book, "Papua, or British New Guinea," says, "So far as one may judge from the ordinary conversation that one hears in Papua, the feeling of the general community is not favorable to missions, and I wish to say that I do not share this feeling. I think that the missions not only do good, but that they are absolutely necessary to the development of backward races. An uncivilized people who come into contact with Europeans will inevitably be led sooner or later to abandon their old beliefs; and when these are gone the native is lost, unless someone is there to put some form of religious teaching in their place. The Government cannot do this, and it is not likely that the majority of the settlers will." He adds that his opinion quite abstracts from the question as to whether Christianity is true or not. But he says, "Personally, I believe that it is; but I cannot help thinking that even if I did not believe it as I do, I should from a purely administrative point of view entertain exactly the same opinion as regards the necessity of some form of missionary teaching at the present stage of Papuan evolution."

428. *You maintain that the true Church must be One, Holy, Catholic, and Apostolic; and that your Church alone complies with these requirements.*

Correct. The Roman Church is not only One, Holy, and Catholic. She is also Apostolic.

429. *How do we know that even the Apostles were Catholics, and that their teaching was Catholic?*

We know that the Apostles were Catholics because Christ not only taught them His doctrine, but told them to go and to teach all nations. The word Catholic means "all." The very commission Christ gave them was a Catholic commission. Again, working backwards, if we take the Catholic Church today, we find that she is the only legitimate successor of the Apostles, and that in virtue of Christ's promise that His Church would never fail, and that He would be with it till the end of the world, the Apostles must have taught then what the Catholic Church teaches now, even as the Catholic Church must teach now what the Apostles taught then. Furthermore, a comparison of the New Testament records of Apostolic teaching with that of the Catholic Church shows perfect conformity, whilst such a comparison with the teachings of other Churches shows departure after departure from the doctrine of the Apostles.

430. I have been told that no Church came into existence until the fourth century!

That was not a correct statement. Christ personally established the Christian Church. He said clearly, "I will build my Church." He did not say, "I will see that my Church is established in the fourth century." In the first century St. Paul wrote to the Philippians blaming himself for having persecuted "the Church." How could he have done so, if the Church did not come into existence until three centuries later? Professor C. A. Briggs, a Presbyterian, in his book on "Church Unity," p. 205, writes, "I cannot undertake to give even a sketch of the history of the Papacy. We shall have to admit that the Christian Church from the earliest times recognized the primacy of the Roman Bishop, and that all other great Sees at times recognized the supreme jurisdiction of Rome in matters of doctrine, government, and discipline. . . . When the whole case has been carefully examined and all the evidence sifted, the statement of Irenaeus stands firm: We put to confusion all unauthorized assemblies by indicating the tradition derived from the Apostles of the great, ancient, and universally known Church founded at Rome by the two most glorious Apostles Peter and Paul . . . for it is a matter of necessity that every Church should agree with this Church on account of its pre-eminent authority." St. Irenaeus wrote that in the second century; and you can be quite sure that the Presbyterian Dr. Briggs would not make the admission he has made in this paragraph unless compelled by the evidence to do so.

431. How do you explain the Apostolic character of your Church?

Christ Himself was its Founder. He prepared the way for it by declaring the fulfillment of the Old Law, announcing His intention to establish a Church, explaining its nature, privileges, and duties, and calling the Apostles whom He appointed to be rulers of the Church, St. Peter being constituted supreme head of the Church on earth. On Pentecost Sunday, or the fiftieth day after His resurrection, He sent the Holy Spirit upon His newly-founded Church in the person of His Apostles, and they commenced their work officially that day of preaching the Gospel to all nations.

432. The commission was to the Apostles; not to any Church.

That cannot stand. Christ established a Church, and the Apostles as the first representatives of that Church received the commission to teach the whole of mankind. It is impossible to restrict the commission to the Apostles only, when the commission was to teach all nations till the end of the world. The Apostles themselves could not go to all nations; nor could they live "all days till the end of the world." The authority was to be exercised in every age thenceforth. There must be some body in the world exercising it now. The commission to the Apostles has survived in the Catholic Church so carefully established and guaranteed by Christ.

433. It is difficult to believe in these Apostolic claims by your Church.

It is impossible to believe in Christ otherwise. If we believe in Christ at all, we must believe that He did establish a definite Church which would last all days from His time till the end of time. But, if you take any other Church except the Catholic Church, you will find that it has not been in the world all days since the time of Christ; and that it was established, not by Christ, but by some later and merely human individual. Yet where we can point to the moment it began in history, and to its originator's name, in the case of every non-Catholic Church, no man can say who founded the Catholic Church and when, if Christ Himself did not. That is why Cardinal Newman, at one time a Protestant clergyman, said, "If the Roman Catholic Church is not the Church of Christ, there never was a Church established by Him."

434. If there was only one Apostolic religion, your own, when and by whom was a breakaway caused?

Breakaways have occurred right through history, beginning in Apostolic times. Simon Magus, mentioned in the New Testament, was really the forerunner of independent men who set up religions of their own. Christ Himself predicted that men would do this, saying, "There will arise false Christs and false prophets to seduce if possible even the elect." Mk. XIII., 22. But in spite of this, He promised to His true Church, "I will be with you all days even to the end of the world." In the first centuries there were heretical founders of rival Churches—men whose names are found only in textbooks of history—Montanus, Manichaeus, Arius, Donatus, etc. In later centuries we find the founders of the Greek Church, Photius and Michael Cerularius. And later still the founders of the various Protestant Churches—Luther, Henry VIII., John Knox, and a host of others. As the years go on, others will arise, linger for a time, and disappear. But the Catholic and Apostolic Church will go on with continued vitality till the end of time. Ever there will be in the world a Church able to trace itself back in an unbroken line to the Apostles; and that Church is the Catholic Church which is subject to the Pope as the successor of St. Peter, the chief of the Apostles.

435. You claim then that your Church is indestructible?

Yes. She can never fail in existence, in doctrine, in continuity of worship, in her unity or in any other of her properties. She is indefectible and unconquerable.

436. Do you imagine that your Church is unassailable?

She is not unassailable, for men do assail her. But no enemies will ever succeed in exterminating her. As the political cartoonist made the devil say to Bismarck, "Well, old man, if you do succeed in smashing the Catholic Church, you'll accomplish what I have failed to do despite my 2000 years' effort."

437. The present state of the world scarcely justifies your confidence in the perseverance of your Church till the end of time.

The present state of the world has nothing to do with it. If not all the forces of hell, certainly not all the forces of this world will prevail against her. Our confidence is not based upon the fluctuating conditions of human society. It is based upon the promise of Christ that He will be with His Church all days till the end of the world. And since Christ is God, He can and will fulfill His promise.

438. Are not all the Christian Churches decaying and dying?

For other Churches I do not speak. As for the Catholic Church, not only does she offer no signs of decay—she is full of life. Never has the position been more favorable and more full of hope for her. In 1874, but four years after the Pope was rendered a prisoner in the Vatican, and when the world might be expected to discount the prospects of the Catholic Church, Disraeli said in the British Parliament, "I cannot disguise the fact. The Catholic religion is a powerful organism; and, if I may say so, the most powerful today." Yet the position now is immensely stronger than when Disraeli spoke. All this, of course, is from the merely human point of view. From the aspect of her divine protection, the Catholic Church is never weak.

439. What of the persecutions in Russia, Germany, Mexico, and elsewhere in the modern world?

What of them? Such things have come and gone all through history. The Church can scarcely have worse things to survive in the future than she has survived in the past. Her enemies die, but she goes on; they a memory, she a fact.

440. I have heard even Catholics admit that things look bad for their Church.

They may say such things at times. Catholics can quite easily have depressing views even whilst they believe in the future of their Church. But I think such Catholics praise the past, forgetting its miseries; and despise the present, forgetting its greatness. It is a tribute, at least, to our ideals of what the Church should be.

441. History is not in favor of your Church by the mere fact that it records so much opposition against her.

History is in favor of the Church, though "historians" have not always appreciated her. The Church is always suspect to someone. But history records what the Church has done, and faith tells us what she will do. She will last till the end of time, ever bringing forth fruits of holiness and virtue, and contributing as no other force towards the welfare of mankind. That men are and have been opposed to her is no fault of the Church. It is the fault of the prejudices and passions of men. Again, the Church differs in her outlook from the ordinary human viewpoint. She judges from the aspect of eternity; and to men she seems always behind the times, or else ahead of the times. There is bound to be opposition, until men can rise to her level.

442. Is it any argument to say, "I am persecuted, therefore I am right?"

Not in itself. But it is, when the Church is persecuted because she vindicates right moral principles, imposes duties, and refuses to condone those vices in which men want to indulge. Once men develop a fever of anti-religion, their first thought is the suppression of the Catholic Church. But by shooting down Catholics for going to Mass, these men give one of the strongest arguments for Catholicism. These persecutors say, "Be quiet about the Catholic religion, or we will kill you." The martyr replies, "My death will be my strongest speech." If they say, "Then all of you will die, except that!" the martyr proudly replies, "Then I shall not die." One thing, however, is certain. Whatever persecutions may arise in this world, the Catholic Church will not die. Christ predicted, "As they persecute Me, they will persecute you." But He also said, "I will be with you all days till the end of the world." He will keep His promise.

443. When you appeal to the past you forget that the very antiquity of your Church is only an additional reason against her being able to continue.

There you are wrong. The antiquity of the Catholic Church does not mean that she is antiquated. As a matter of fact, she is only just beginning. She perfected her constitution only yesterday. Her concentrated organization, the prelude to a vast expansion, is only now coming to maturity. Her recent territorial emancipation from Italy by the Concordat between Mussolini and Pope Pius XI. has but intensified in the eyes of the world her incomparable spiritual prestige. Spirituality and holiness within the Catholic Church are more ardent than ever. And her civilizing influence is so clear that political powers most opposed to her seek her help and use her methods. The future is most promising for the Catholic Church; and whatever her antiquity, she will never be old. Eternal beginnings is the law of that which does not die.

Radio Replies—Volume II

444. Is it necessary for salvation to become a member of the Catholic Church?

Since God sent His only-begotten Son into this world, and that Son established the Catholic Church, sending it to teach all nations, it is certainly necessary to be taught by that Church if one desires to save his soul. Christ said, "If a man will not hear the Church, let him be as the heathen." Matt. XVIII., 17.

445. Do you assert that all people not members of the Roman Church are heathens?

I would not make such an assertion without due qualifications. The Catholic Church, of course, stands foursquare for the teachings of the Gospel. She accepts absolutely all that Christ says. And consequently, she accepts the words of Christ recorded in Matt. XVIII., 17, "If a man will not hear the Church, let him be as the heathen." But to whom does the Church apply those words? She applies them only to those who clearly realize that the Catholic Church is the one true Church, yet who refuse submission and obedience to it. Therefore, she does not regard as heathens the vast majority of non-Catholics, for they have never clearly realized her truth. Full allowance is made for sincere yet mistaken people.

446. Religiously I am just nothing, and have never bothered about religion. Do you say that I am obliged to become a Catholic?

God has declared the Catholic religion to be necessary. And one who becomes aware of that must become a Catholic if he wishes to save his soul. But you adopt a peculiar position. You say you have never bothered about religion. Then it is most necessary that you begin to give your attention to the question. For example, you went to the bother of learning to write. You have bothered to learn the use of various things which are necessary to your earthly welfare. You know what those things are for. But surely it is man's duty to know what he himself is for! And a man cannot know that unless he knows the fundamental truth concerning his origin, his nature, his destiny, and the moral law. The teachings of the true religion alone can provide the necessary knowledge, and a man is obliged to find that true religion. And you are robbed of excuse by the fact that a vast international Church like the Catholic Church is in this world, claiming to speak with the authority of God. Confronted with such a fact, every reasonable man would say, "Such claims are rather tremendous. At least, I'd better look into them and see whether there is any justification for them." One who would note the fact, and simply not bother about it, is violating reason, and has only himself to blame if he wrecks his eternal destiny.

447. There is no need to join the Catholic Church in order to be saved. John III., 15, says, "Whosoever believeth in Him will not perish, but will have life everlasting."

That particular text does not say that non-Catholics will be saved. It might avail if Christ had never said anything else. But He said much else. And whosoever really believes in Christ must accept every single thing He taught, and try to fulfill all that He commanded. For example, He said, "Unless your justice abound more than that of the Scribes and Pharisees, you shall not enter into the kingdom of heaven." Matt. V., 20. One could believe in Christ, yet make no effort to acquire the prescribed justice. That is why Christ said, "Not every one who cries: 'Lord, Lord,' will enter the kingdom of heaven." Matt. VII., 21. It is evident that you cannot attach an unconditional and universal sense to the text you have quoted. They will be saved who so believe in Christ that they are prepared to accept and to fulfill all the conditions prescribed by Him.

448. *There is nothing in those wonderful words of a privileged Church.*

The same Christ who uttered those wonderful words also said, "If a man will not hear the Church, let him be as the heathen and the publican." It is necessary then that those who believe in Christ should hear and obey His Church. And you must ask yourself whether you hear and obey any Church as your teacher and ruler in religious matters. Also you must ask yourself what Church Christ had in mind when He spoke. If you say that it is not necessary to obey any Church, you do not believe Christ's word. And in that case you cannot be ranked amongst those included in the promise, "Whosoever believeth in Him shall not perish." The Church Christ had in mind was the Catholic Church; and once a man adverts to the fact, he must join her if he wishes to save his soul.

449. *Gal. III., 28, says, "There is neither Jew nor Greek, there is neither bond nor free, there is neither male nor female; for ye are all one in Christ Jesus."*

St. Paul was speaking there of the Catholic Church in which national and earthly differences are no obstacle to membership. Insofar as we are members of the Catholic Church, all other Catholics are our brethren. In our mutual faith there is neither Gentile nor Jew, neither German nor Frenchman, nor Italian, nor Irishman, nor American. We Catholics are all one in Christ Jesus, belonging to His mystical body, the Catholic Church. But you, as a Protestant, do not belong to the same Church as Catholics. You should. The text you quote and which says that we should all be one cannot possibly justify our continued separation and your remaining outside the Catholic Church. In reality, it is Protestantism which says that there are Jews and Gentiles, Englishmen and Germans, Dutch and Norwegians, for it permits religion to differ according to nationality. Where Catholicism has one religion for all nations, Protestantism sanctions as many religions as there are nations, and even variations and divisions within the one nation. The text you quote is really suicidal for Protestantism, and proves the necessity of Catholicism.

450. *Would you presume to say that unless a man is a Catholic he is not serving Christ?*

He is not serving Christ as Christ demands. But if he be ignorant of the full teaching of Christ through no fault of his own, he may be trying wholeheartedly to serve Christ, little realizing how mistaken are his ideas.

451. *Surely this is disheartening to many who lead good lives and believe in Christ, yet cannot conscientiously accept the dogmas of Rome.*

Since the Catholic Church is the one true Church to which God wills men to belong, it is impossible to hold out equal hopes of salvation to those who reject that Church and deprive themselves of all the helps she can give. And if some of my statements dishearten those outside the Church sufficiently to make them take an interest, inquire, and discover the truth, leading eventually to their becoming Catholics, I have done them a very great service indeed.

See also R. R., Vol. I, Nos. 325-547.

CHAPTER NINE

THE CHURCH AND THE BIBLE

452. Are not all the Christian Churches based on the Bible?

The Protestant Churches originally insisted that the Bible was the Word of God; but they were based on the various senses their founders read into the Bible and declared to be the meaning intended by God. But the Catholic Church, although she insists that the Bible is indeed the Word of God, does not base her position upon the Bible. She is not so foolish as to say, "Believe the Bible to be inspired because I tell you it is; and believe in me because the Bible, which speaks of me, is inspired." That would be a vicious circle. Of course, if a man already believes the Bible to be the inspired Word of God, the Catholic Church can begin from that in her discussions with him, and show that the very Word of God which he accepts justifies her claims. But if a man does not accept the inspiration of the Bible, then the Catholic Church does not appeal to it as inspired. She will justify herself on the grounds of history and reason alone. Only after the man has acknowledged the reasonable character of her claims, and with the help of God's grace has attained to faith in her as the Church of God, will he be prepared to accept her teaching that the Bible is the inspired Word of God. With such a man the Catholic approach differs radically from that of the Protestant Churches.

453. If you agree that the Roman Catholic Church is not founded on the teachings of the Bible what becomes of her claim to infallibility?

You must not imagine that there could be anything in the Catholic doctrines opposed to the teachings of the Bible. We do not believe that the Catholic Church is founded on the Bible as if men were given the Bible, and then constructed the Catholic Church for themselves according to the ideas they thought the Bible to contain. We believe that the Catholic Church was founded personally by Christ, who built it upon the Apostles, sending them to preach His Gospel and propagate the Christian religion throughout the world. And it was Christ personally who guaranteed the infallibility of the Apostles and of their successors, so that the Church would be unable to err in her official teachings. Since the Church is infallible and the Bible is the inspired Word of God, there will never be a conflict between the two. You must keep in mind, of course, that the Bible is the inspired Word of God in the sense in which God intended all that is written in its pages; not in any false sense which some non-infallible reader desires to impose upon it.

454. Despite the tributes you pay to the Bible, Rome is hostile to it, and does not want her people to read it.

That is not true. In fact the Catholic Church grants special spiritual favors to those who will read Holy Scripture daily.

455. Pope Pius VII. in 1816 denounced Bible Societies as a crafty device by which the very foundations of religion are undermined.

He condemned the circulation of inaccurate translations by Protestant Societies; and the Protestant principle that all should read Scripture for themselves, interpreting it according to their own private judgment, however little qualified they might be to arrive at a sound judgment. He gave as his reason that different readers would arrive at different conclusions, and that the ideal given by St. Paul would be destroyed. For St. Paul wrote, "I beseech you that you all speak the same thing, being of the same mind and the same judgment." 1 Cor. I., 10. And the Pope was right. The chaos in doctrinal beliefs amongst Protestants is experimental proof of it. And Pope Pius VII. justly quoted St. Augustine's words, "Heresies would not have arisen unless men had read good Scripture badly, and rashly asserted their own mistakes to be the truth." But this does not prove that Rome is hostile to the Bible. The Catholic Church most carefully preserved the Bible through the ages—a most foolish procedure did she regard the Bible as evil. In fact, her solicitude for the correct understanding of the Bible, and for its integrity, is obviously dictated by a deep reverence for the Word of God.

456. Pope Pius VIII., Leo XIII., and Pius IX. also warned Catholics against Protestant Bible Societies.

They did so for exactly the same reasons as Pius VII. Catholics believe in a teaching Church. Protestants believe in the reading of the Bible, and its interpretation as each one thinks fit. And this idea is the mainspring of Protestant Societies for the multiplication of Bibles in all languages. And what is the result? We see innumerable Protestant divisions, with many radical differences even within the same sects! Where is the consistency which is the hall-mark of truth? Many, too, are drifting from belief in the Bible altogether, openly denying its value; and the Catholic Church now has to defend it against the very ones who accused her of hostility towards it. It is Protestantism that has proved to be the real enemy of the Bible, not Catholicism.

457. Is there any difference between a Roman Catholic Bible, and a Protestant Bible?

Yes. The Protestant Bible omits several Books of the Old Testament which are contained in the Catholic Bible. It omits the Books of Tobias, Judith, Wisdom, Ecclesiasticus, the two Books of Machabees, and various sections of other Books. Moreover, in those sections of the Bible which the Protestant Version has retained, there are many mistranslations.

458. Has the Protestant Bible undergone any alterations since the Reformation period?

Yes. As soon as Henry VIII. broke away from the Catholic Church in 1534 and established the Church of England under his own supremacy, Cranmer ordered an English translation to be made. The Bible had been translated into English long before this, but he wanted his own special translation. In 1539 the resultant Protestant translation was published, and called the "Great Bible." In the same year also there was published a Version by Richard Taverner. In 1560 another English translation was published at Geneva, to be known as the "Geneva Bible." As these translations revealed many errors, in 1568 a revised edition was published and called the "Bishops' Bible." This Bible was reprinted in 1572 with many corrections and amendments, and called "Matthew Parker's Bible." In 1611 the "King James' Bible," or what is usually called the "Authorized Version" was published; but even this Version was corrected in 1683, 1769, and 1806. Critics, however, pointed out many errors still in the "Authorized Version," and in 1885 a "Revised Version" was completed which contains over 35,000 alterations from the "Authorized Version."

459. You say that Protestants have omitted several Old Testament Books. From what Old Testament is the Catholic Canon taken?

The Books of the Old Testament contained in the Catholic Canon are those contained in the Greek Septuagint translation of the Hebrew Bible—a translation made at Alexandria, in Egypt, by the Jews residing there. This translation was made during the three centuries before the birth of Christ. The Jews, even of Palestine, accepted the Septuagint Canon, or list of Books, and our Lord Himself used it in conversing with them. The Jews began to deny its authenticity only about a century after Christ because they could not resist the arguments drawn from it and used against them by the Christians. They therefore said that it was a bad translation; that it did not agree with the Hebrew text; and they rejected it. But the use the Jews themselves had made of it for nearly four hundred years rendered their rejection of it too late. And their motives, of course, are evident. Their interest was not critical, but polemical.

460. From what Old Testament is the Protestant Canon taken?

When the Protestant reformers abandoned the Catholic Church, they adopted the same policy as the Jews had adopted against the early Christians, and tried to cast doubt upon the Catholic Versions of Scripture. They too, therefore, rejected the Septuagint Canon, and accepted the current Hebrew copies of the Old Testament Books. The Hebrew manuscripts omitted several of the Books contained in the Septuagint, and the Protestants therefore followed suit.

461. Which Bible did Christ and the Apostles treat as the standard version?

Christ and the Apostles used both the Hebrew Palestinian Canon and the Greek Septuagint Canon. Both were familiar to, and were accepted at that time by the Jews.

462. From which Old Testament did the New Testament writers most quote when writing their Books?

They quoted most often from the Greek Septuagint. In fact, of some 350 quotations, nearly 300 are taken from the Septuagint. In his "Introduction to the Sacred Scriptures," Thomas Hartwell Horne, a Protestant writer, says that the New Testament writers had to quote from the Greek Septuagint because many for whom they wrote were ignorant of Hebrew, whereas the Greek Version was generally known and read. If the Septuagint was erroneous, and its Canon false, then far from quoting from it, the Apostles should have denounced it, and warned Christians not to use it, but to use exclusively the Palestinian Canon. The Apostles did not do so. They sanctioned the use of the Canon accepted by the Catholic Church and rejected by the Protestant reformers.

463. Do Catholics say that the Protestant Bible, whether "Authorized" or "Revised," is not a true translation of the originals, and are of no value?

We do not say that they are of no value. And it is certain that, on the whole, they are correct translations. But both Versions omit complete Books from the Old Testament, and both are very imperfect translations, on the admissions of scholars amongst Protestants themselves. The Rev. Frank Ballard, in his book "Which Bible to Read" urges Protestants to use the "Revised Version," and not the "Authorized Version." On page 23 of his book he says that an honest answer admits the imperfections of the "Authorized Version" on the following points—(1) It is based on a faulty text; (2) Words are given wrong meanings; (3) Archaic expressions obscure the sense; (4) Grammatical errors abound; (5) The sacred writers are misrepresented. He rightly says therefore that the "Revised Version" is a great improvement; but Protestant scholars agree that a further revision will have to be made. And it is to be noted that the various corrections of the Protestant Version have been in the direction of closer harmony with the Catholic Douay Version.

464. How did the Catholic Douay Version come about?

It is simply the English translation of the Latin Vulgate translation from the Hebrew and Greek made by St. Jerome in the fourth century. This English translation was made in France between the years 1582 and 1610 by five Oxford scholars who were in charge of the English Ecclesiastical College for the training of Catholic priests at Douay and Rheims. Their names were Allen, Bristoe, Martin, Worthington, and Reynolds.

465. Do Catholics regard the Douay Version as a true translation of the original manuscripts?

Not in every respect. It is certainly a true translation of what is known as the Latin Vulgate. At the time of the Reformation many translations of Scripture from various sources were being spread through different countries, translations often inadequate and in many places positively erroneous. The Council of Trent, therefore, in 1546, sought to avoid all confusion amongst Catholics at least by definitely settling what Version they were to use. The result was a decree selecting and authorizing the Latin Vulgate, or correct translations of that Vulgate. As a matter of obedience to the authority of their Church, Catholics must use this official Version. But, apart from discipline, what is the value of the Vulgate, of which the Douay Bible is a translation? Is the Vulgate itself in perfect accord with the originals? The Catholic Church does not say so. She guarantees that the Vulgate is certainly substantially correct, insofar as it does not differ from the originals in such a way as to lead to any doctrinal error. It is possible that some individual text in the originals may be missing from the Vulgate. It is possible for certain texts in the Vulgate to differ from the originals either in their location, or in their grammatical form. It is also possible for an individual text to have crept into the Vulgate which did not exist in the originals, though never any text which could lead to wrong doctrine. To sum up: Catholics are obliged by virtue of obedience to use the Vulgate—of which the Douay Version is an English translation; and the Catholic Church guarantees the substantial conformity of the Vulgate with the originals so that it must certainly be held to be a sound source of Christian doctrine.

466. Have not Catholics to read even their own Douay Version subject to the direction of their Church?

They read the Bible with the conviction that any sense which would be opposed to the express teaching of the Catholic Church would undoubtedly be an erroneous interpretation. And they know that their Church alone is the only ultimate and infallible interpreter of its pages. Individual readers are ever liable to be mistaken; but the Catholic Church cannot fall into error in any express definitions concerning the contents of Sacred Scripture. Our conviction is that God confided the inspired writings to the guardianship of a living and infallible Church. The written pages cannot explain themselves. The living voice of an authentic interpreter is necessary. And God has provided that in the Catholic Church.

467. Surely any person with the capacity to read and understand the law of our country would be able to read and understand the Bible.

How many men have the capacity to read and understand the law of our country? An ordinary man might manage some of the easier and simpler laws; but highly trained lawyers could wrangle for weeks over individual laws, and even then differ as to their right interpretation. Yet even though the average man could fully understand human legislation, the Bible is God's revelation of a supernatural order of truth far deeper than the product of human thinking; and conflicting conclusions are proof that men have not managed to understand it.

468. Can it be interpreted safely only by Catholic priests?

Not always by them. Priests have made mistakes again and again in the interpretation of Scripture. In many cases the only really safe guide is the authentic ruling of the Catholic Church, to which priests and laity alike must submit. The ordinary priests do not constitute the teaching authority of the Church. The Bishops collectively and in union with the Pope constitute the authoritative Catholic teaching body. And their guidance is often needed, even in what would seem to be most obvious. For example, the few words, "This is my body," seem clear enough. Yet men have proposed a dozen conflicting interpretations of those words!

469. *If God is the Author of Scripture, was He incapable of making it so clear that no one could doubt its meaning?*

To that I must say that even God could not make written words so clear that no one could doubt their meaning. But the fault is not on God's side. It is due to the limitations of men. I have studied Aristotelian philosophy for years, and have taught that subject. Whose fault would it be if I could not write a treatise on the metaphysics of Aristotle totally devoid of obscurity for a class of children whose ages ranged from eight to ten years old? The fault would lie in the lack of capacity in the children. And the distance between the supernatural mysteries of revelation and the highest natural wisdom is infinitely greater than between the metaphysics of Aristotle and the mind of an untrained child.

470. *Did God designedly make the Bible so obscure that people would be forced to seek guidance of the Church to understand it?*

No. The establishing of a teaching Church was not a consequence of the obscurity of Scripture, as if God had really intended the Bible to be the guide of men, but found that it would not work, and then decided to establish the Church. Scripture was never intended to be the final guide of men. God primarily intended to have a body of men appointed to teach in His name. Thus, in the Old Law, He says, "The lips of the priest shall keep knowledge, and they shall seek the law at his mouth." As long as the Old Law obliged, Christ referred the people to that authority. In Matt. XXIII., 2, He says, "The Scribes and Pharisees have sitten on the chair of Moses. All things whatsoever they shall say to you, observe and do." In the New Law He substituted the Apostolic body and their successors as teachers in His name. Some years after the Catholic Church had commenced her work of teaching mankind, a secondary record of some of the events of Christ's life, and of some of His teachings and of those of the Apostles was made. That secondary record is contained in the New Testament; and its collected Books are the "family papers" of the Catholic Church. She owns them, and alone has the right to give the authentic interpretation of their meaning.

471. *I accept the 6th of the Anglican Articles of Religion, as do all good Protestants.*

That Article says: "Holy Scripture containeth all things necessary, so that whatsoever is not read therein, nor may be proved thereby, is not to be required of any man." But that Article is itself quite unscriptural! The last verse of St. John's Gospel tells us that not all concerning our Lord's work is contained in Scripture. St. Paul tells us that much of Christian teaching is contained in oral traditions. Scripture tells us also that the Church must teach all nations whatsoever Christ taught the Apostles. He who believes in Scripture as his only guide ends by believing in his own mistaken interpretations of the Bible, and that means belief in the infallibility of his own judgment—which is not belief in the authority of Christ. The Protestant rule of faith is incomplete, is most uncertain, and has led to hundreds of conflicting sects. The Catholic rule of faith has preserved unity amongst millions of adherents. And Christ surely gave a rule of faith calculated to preserve unity rather than produce diversity.

472. *Do you place more reliance on Catholic dogma and tradition than on the Bible?*

As remote sources of Christian doctrine Catholics accept equally the Bible and authentic Christian tradition. These constitute the written and unwritten Word of

God. The immediate guide of Catholics is the official teaching of the Catholic Church. That Church expresses from time to time in a dogma the exact sense of some doctrine contained either in Scripture or tradition. As divine tradition can never be opposed to Scripture, and Catholic dogma can never be opposed to either Scripture or tradition, there can never be any question of placing more reliance on one than on the others. Of course, where a person's private interpretation of Scripture conflicts with a dogma of the Church, I would certainly place more reliance on the dogma of the Church than upon that person's private interpretation of Scripture.

473. *Tradition is no more reliable as evidence than mere gossip or rumor.*

You are using the word tradition in a sense other than that intended by the Church in this matter. We intend, as a source of Christian truth, that divine tradition which is the collection of doctrines taught by Christ and the Apostles, but which were not written in the New Testament. They have been written in various "Creeds," and "Professions of Faith," and are supported by the unanimous consent of the Fathers who lived in the first centuries and knew the Apostolic teaching. St. Paul said to Timothy, "The things you have heard of me by many witnesses, the same commend to faithful men who will be fit to teach others also." II. Tim. II., 2. The early ecclesiastical writers recorded the teachings of these "faithful men"; and those teachings are an authentic source of the revelation of Christ to be transmitted to posterity. Later, and merely human traditions, have nothing to do with this divine tradition, which has been specially safeguarded by the Holy Spirit.

474. *You admit a misdirection in the Calendar.*

I admit that the various compilers of our Calendar made mistakes in their calculations, and that the year of Christ's birth was earlier than the authors of our Calendar believed. But this error in the computation of time in no way affects Christianity, as a religion, nor the facts of Christianity. If a schoolboy makes a mistake as to the date when King Richard the First died, that makes no difference to the fact that he died when he did.

475. *Does this involve the Catechism's disclosure that Christ lived on earth thirty-three years?*

No. It must be noticed, of course, that the Catechism gives merely the accepted approximate estimate of the life of Christ. It is not a defined Article of Faith that Christ lived exactly thirty-three years. If Christ was born four years before we think He was, then He died four years before we think He did. The thirty-three years would remain as the most probable estimate of the length of His life. However, we do not claim more than probability in this matter, and the question is not of any vital importance.

476. *The misdirection seems eloquent of the inaccuracy of Apostolic tradition as against the handing down of the written word.*

The Calendar, whether accurate or inaccurate, in no way comes under the definition of Apostolic tradition as one of the sources of revelation. No argument based on the Calendar has any bearing, therefore, on the subject of tradition.

477. *Rome's claim to interpretative authority, based on an obviously doctored text of the Bible can only appeal to those who have not heard the voice of the true Shepherd.*

It used to be the Protestant tradition that the Catholic religion is opposed to the Bible. Now when a man has that fixed idea firmly embedded in his mind, he gets a shock when he hears the Bible quoted in favor of Catholicism. The stronger the texts are, the greater his shock. But some people never dream that they may have been laboring under a delusion. They refuse to entertain the idea that they have been wrong all their lives. The texts quoted seem to point to Catholicism all right, but to them it simply cannot be true. So they seek an excuse for not believing what they cannot refute. Every text which seems to favor Catholicism cannot mean what it says, but must obviously be "doctored." And they are so sure that they alone are truly guided by God that anyone impressed by the case for the Catholic religion must be regarded as not having heard the voice of the true Shepherd!

478. *Other Churches claim to have given the Bible equal study, and claim equal value for their interpretation.*

Since no non-Catholic Churches claim to be infallible, but admit their constant liability to error, they cannot even claim equal value for their interpretations. Moreover, apart from their divergence from the Catholic interpretation, they differ amongst themselves. That would not be, had they all equally arrived at the correct sense of the Bible. As a matter of fact, all practically nullify the claims of each as a reliable guide to the meaning of Scripture.

479. *Protestantism and Catholicism are founded on the same basic principles, their differences being due to different interpretations of the Bible.*

They are not founded on the same basic principles. In basic principles they are diametrically opposed. What is the basic principle of Protestantism? It is belief in what one thinks the Bible to mean. If a man thinks the Bible to support this or that doctrine, then it surely does so; for he cannot imagine that he might be wrong. He makes an act of faith in his own judgment. But the Catholic basic principle is very different. Instead of deciding for himself what is or is not the teaching of Christ, the Catholic is taught that teaching by the Catholic Church. He knows that his own judgment is quite likely to be wrong, but that the Catholic Church cannot be wrong. How different are the basic principles of the two religions can be judged from results. For the Protestant principle leads to endless diversity, whilst the Catholic principle leads to a world-wide and international unity.

480. *But the Catholic believes in the Catholic Church because he thinks the Bible supports it.*

That is not so. The Bible does support it, of course. But even if he never saw a Bible, the Catholic would have sufficient ground for his judgment. He knows that the Catholic priest does not preach merely his own opinions, as does the Protestant minister. He knows that his Church is not a particular sect, but a vast united universal Apostolic Church, whose history shows the allegiance of innumerable saints and martyrs. And such a Church is impossible to account for by merely human forces. It is God's work on the very face of it. Merely human institutions have always tended to fluctuation, change, and disintegration. Empires have crumbled. No human being can get even one nation to agree, say, on political matters. How could a mere man persuade over 400 millions drawn from all nations to agree on religious matters—millions who differ on almost every other conceivable subject? The Catholic has reasonable grounds for his acceptance of the Church as the teacher of mankind in religious matters; and he submits to her authoritative teaching in matters of faith and morals, rather than decide for himself what the Bible must mean.

481. *My point is, since Protestantism and Catholicism differ as to what the Bible means, who is to say which is right?*

On Protestant principles, there is no one who could do so. And that is the basic fallacy of Protestantism. It offers no certainty, and can offer no certainty, as to what God does really teach. Yet it is essential that in so grave a matter we should have certainty. The Catholic Church alone can give it.

482. *If you quote the Bible, the Protestant will quote the Bible; so we are back to our point of view of the Bible, and there is no means of deciding the issue.*

For a Catholic the issue does not depend on the Bible, even though the Bible does corroborate Catholicism. No Protestant can prove his beliefs from the Bible, or even that they ought to be proved from the Bible. You say that Protestants cannot prove their position, and that Catholics cannot prove theirs. It's a matter of conjecture and opinion. Protestants may be right or Catholics may be right. Neither has proof, and we must be content to do without proof. I admit that that is the logical result of the Protestant principles on which you argue; and for that reason Protestantism must end in uncertainty and doubt. That in itself should be enough to prove that it cannot be the religion of Christ.

483. *How will the problem be solved?*

Only by abandoning the Protestant principle of personal and private judgment, and accepting the doctrines taught clearly and definitely by the Catholic Church. She is the only tribunal in the world with authority from God to teach all nations, and endowed with infallibility in order that she may not lead men into error. And for two thousand years she has both fulfilled and proved her mission under the protection and guidance of the Holy Ghost.

See also R. R., Vol. I, Nos. 548-592.

CHAPTER TEN

THE DOGMAS OF THE CHURCH

484. Do you not think that the dogmatic demands of the Roman Catholic Church constitute the difficulty for most people?

If so, it is because they have not the right idea of faith, nor the will to submit to the teaching authority of Christ. When Christ, the very Son of God, reveals the truth, that truth must not be accommodated to our mental variations; our own mental outlook must be adjusted to that truth. We cannot take what suits us, and reject what does not. Thus St. Paul wrote, "The knowledge of God brings into captivity every understanding unto the obedience of Christ." II Cor. X., 5. God has the right to demand the obedience of the intelligence as well as of the will; and that obedience is manifested by the acceptance of dogmatic truth revealed by Him.

485. Is not Truth infinite and incomprehensible?

Ontological and Divine Truth as identified with the Being of God is infinite and incomprehensible. But not all logical and derived truth is infinite and incomprehensible. There is a difference between truth of being and truth of thought concerning that being. The created mind can attain and comprehend truth derived from the consideration of created things. It can attain a genuine though inadequate knowledge of uncreated truth insofar as God deigns to reveal that information and insofar as human thought can express it.

486. Is a human being who says that he knows a thing to be the truth with dogmatic certainty capable of comprehending what is truth and what is not?

He is certainly capable of comprehending that a thing is true and its opposite false, even though he cannot comprehend the full inner nature of the thing he knows to be true. For example, I know from historical evidence that Christ lived. I know that He established the Catholic Church. I know that He promised to be with that Church all days till the end of the world. I know that He wrought certain works which proved His claim to be God, and no ordinary man. All that is human knowledge on my own human level. I take His word for it that He has left Himself really present in the Eucharist. I do not fully comprehend the inner nature of His presence there. But I do understand by my human faculties the truth or falsity of facts. It is true to say that He is there; it is false to say that He is not there. I assert the truth with dogmatic certainty—a certainty based on the knowledge that the Infinite and All-perfect God must know the truth, and could not tell a lie.

487. The human mind is limited; acquires knowledge painfully and slowly; and frequently has to renounce what it once thought to be true. Is any religious belief, then, justified in dogmatic assertion?

Not if it be a question of merely human opinions derived by our own processes of thinking from more or less probable premises. But one who is quite conscious that he is preserved by God from error in declaring a truth revealed by God Himself is certainly justified in speaking with dogmatic certainty. And under certain conditions, well known and defined, the Catholic Church has this promised assistance of God where His revelation is concerned, so that her official dogmatic definitions are infallibly correct.

WHAT IS THE VALUE OF A CREED?

488. *All human knowledge (including faith, belief, conviction on any subject, religious or scientific), being human, cannot be anything but partial, incomplete, and fallible.*

That is not universally true even where merely natural knowledge is concerned. A scientifically demonstrated natural truth is human knowledge, and it is not fallible knowledge. For example, it is infallibly true that the earth is a globe. If all human knowledge is fallible then you could not even know for certain that you had sent these questions to me and that I am answering them. Where knowledge of the supernatural is concerned I grant that absolute certainty cannot be had without an infallible teaching authority guaranteed by God.

489. *Christianity demands that we get our hearts right, and our motives clean.*

That cannot be accepted as a complete summary of the teachings of Christ. If there is one thing certain it is that Christ wanted us to get our heads right as well as our hearts. He is not only the way to be followed; He is the truth to be believed. As a matter of fact, one cannot get one's heart right and one's motives clean until he knows what it means to have a right heart and clean motives. Yet the moment he makes any definite statement as to the nature of these things he invades the region of dogma, and is forced to declare a creed. The idea that it is conduct that counts, and that creeds do not matter; that behavior and not belief is what we want, is, of course, a complete reversal of the axiom, "Believe on Christ and be saved." At one time people insisted on faith without works. Now works without faith are demanded. But the Catholic Church opposes both extremes. Faith and works are necessary; belief and behavior are required; the heart must be right, but it must not run away with the head. By all means let us strive after Christian conduct; but we must not make that an excuse for denying the Christian creed.

490. *What is the value of a creed if it does not win the souls of men to Christ?*

It would still have value, even if it did not do that, provided it correctly recorded the teaching of Christ. The truth would still have its value as the truth, even if men did not live up to it. Also, even if men are not living for Christ, it is better for them to have a correct creed than a wrong one. They at least would admit the truth of His teachings even though they did not fulfill His precepts. Surely that is better than rejecting both His teachings and His precepts. Again, the sinner who has a correct creed is in a better position when he does want to yield his soul to Christ than the sinner who has mistaken ideas concerning the nature and duties of Christ's religion.

491. *I have often longed for the faith possessed by Catholics.*

If you have any faith in Christ at all, you can easily have the faith possessed by Catholics. For it is only a question of finding out what Christ taught, and then letting your faith in Christ extend to that also. For example, if you believe in Christ, and find that the Catholic Church is the one He founded, your faith in Him includes faith in the Catholic Church. But I think your trouble is that you misunderstand faith, expecting far more than is required by it.

492. *It is no use trying to make oneself believe what one doesn't believe.*

That exemplifies what I have just said. You imagine that you do not believe a thing unless you fully understand it, seeing all its ins and outs for yourself. But faith is not that. Faith is the acceptance of what Christ has said because He said it. If He tells me that something is true which I would normally have thought incredible, I believe it. And if He but tells me the fact without deigning to explain it to my full satisfaction, it will continue to baffle me. Yet that does not diminish my belief in its reality. Instead of saying, "It is of no use to try to make myself believe what I do not believe," I rather say, "I believe what Christ teaches even though I do not fully comprehend it."

493. Faith has to come to one, and until it does one cannot realize the truth.

It is true that faith in Christ and in all that He taught is a gift of God. And this gift comes to one in answer to prayer. But one has also to come to the faith. That is, one must not have the mere wish, but the will to believe what Christ has taught. We are not asked to realize, or visualize, or see the full significance of what is proposed to us. That would be expecting too much, and is not possible in this life. In such a case we would have "sight," not "faith." I cannot realize that Christ is indeed really present in the Holy Eucharist. I believe it absolutely, because He has said it. Had He not said it, I would have no means of knowing it. I say this to warn you against expecting too much. Wrong and exaggerated ideas of what faith means could conceivably keep you still waiting for a faith you already possess. The conviction that Christ is God and that the Catholic Church is His one true Church, together with the will to accept the teachings of that Church and to obey its laws, are sufficient indications that one possesses the Catholic Faith.

494. If Catholicism does not conflict with sound reason and scientific facts, why is faith necessary?

Because what is believed by faith, though not against reason, is above reason. When God reveals a truth known to Himself alone, and not to be derived from a consideration of the created things around us, we do not know it as a conclusion of human reasoning nor as a consequence of scientific study of created things. We know quite scientifically and historically that God has revealed it, but we know that it is true solely because God has said so; and the conviction of its truth is due to faith in God's knowledge of the subject, and in His absolute veracity. Since revealed truth is above that to be attained by reason and science, it demands in addition to sane reasoning and scientific examination a deep faith in God's knowledge, veracity, and authority; for these are the motives impelling us to accept and believe the additional information in question. So we Catholics accept all the conclusions of sane reasoning; all established scientific facts; and all the defined teachings of the Catholic Church.

495. Did not a Catholic scientist say, "I keep my faith in one pocket, and my science in another"?

If a Catholic scientist used those words with the idea that Catholic doctrine conflicts with science or reason, then either he knew very little of science, or very little of his religion. Instead of adopting the precaution of separate pockets, he should have adopted the precaution of studying a little more deeply either his science or his faith, when he would have found that there is no conflict between science rightly understood and his religion rightly understood.

496. You know that scientists have the unfortunate knack of being able to demonstrate beyond all doubt that anything they say is true.

That is certainly not true. Lord Rayleigh, in a presidential address to the British Association quite recently, said, "The scientific worker knows in his heart that underneath the theories which he constructs there lie contradictions which he cannot reconcile." Professor J. B. S. Haldane writes, "I certainly do not believe all that Darwin wrote, all that Wells, Russell, and Hogben write. Worse still, I do not believe all that I myself have written." He also says, "Much of what passes for scientific psychology seems to me profoundly unscientific. The same is true of eugenics, criminology, and many other ologies." There is not a real scientist who would not laugh at the suggestion that scientists are able to demonstrate beyond doubt all that they say. Many professing scientists have the unfortunate knack of saying that some things are true beyond all doubt, although they are quite unable to demonstrate them. And it is a matter of historical fact that they have had to unsay such things again and again when what they have asserted has been proved false, or what they have denied has been proved true.

497. If you had to choose between faith and reason, which would you choose?

Such a choice will never confront a Catholic. Should there seem to be a conflict, he knows that he has either wrongly conceived a doctrine to be part of the Catholic faith, or else he has wrongly thought the adverse proposition to be reasonable. He therefore re-examines the position, knowing that he will find a mistake in his interpretation of the faith, or a fallacy in his reasoning. If I knew for certain that the Church had defined a given doctrine to be a dogma of faith, and my own ideas seemed at variance with the defined dogma, I would certainly choose to believe my own ideas mistaken rather than charge the Catholic Church with error. After all, Christ guaranteed the infallibility of the teaching Church, not of every individual man. And the history of human thought is as much a history of mistakes as it is a history of truth. Absolute confidence in one's own inability to reason wrongly is itself unreasonable, and against the facts of experience.

498. History shows where reason and the Roman Catholic Faith have clashed.

Not one instance can be produced showing that any article of the Catholic Faith has ever clashed with the conclusions of sound and rightly informed reason.

499. In the past the Roman Catholic Faith has had to bow to reason.

Not one article of Faith has ever had to be tampered with or changed in order to placate what some people have been pleased to call the claims of reason.

500. Bruno the scientist was burned by the Roman Church because he said that the earth revolved around the sun.

He was not. Having been excommunicated by the Calvinists, expelled from England as a disturber of the peace, excommunicated by the Lutherans in Germany, he came to Rome, and was there condemned for blasphemy and heresy, because he denied that Christ was God, and asserted Him to be but a magician. Even then the Church did not burn him. He was burned by the civil authorities as a traitor and as a dangerous enemy of the welfare of the state.

501. Why has the Church always fought against the truth? Is it because she is founded on superstition and lies?

The only answer to that question is another. Why do you not try to find out the truth, instead of taking for granted any assertions you come across, provided they seem to cast a reflection on the Catholic Church? Is it because of prejudice and hate? Two things are necessary when drawing conclusions from history. The first thing is to get your facts right. The second thing is to get your interpretation of the facts right. You have done neither of those things.

502. Through the ages your Church has stood in the way of freedom of thought, even apart from theological matters.

That cannot be accepted. Both in theological and in secular matters she has not only left men free to think, but has urged them to do so. She does take precautions to prevent people from thinking wrongly, in religious matters particularly; but that is a true service to mankind. If at times she has been over-cautious, that was a fault on the right side. Scientists who complain of the restrictions of the Church have had to unsay far more things than those subject to the said restrictions.

503. Why has she exercised such a retarding influence on the advance of civilization?

She has not done so. In fact, the Catholic Church really gave civilization to the world. She is the mother of architecture, music, painting, and sculpture; of ethics, philosophy, and education. Her monks founded schools all over Europe, preserving the literature of the past, and inspiring the literature of the future. She established the great Universities of Europe, including both Oxford and Cambridge. Professor Whitehead, a non-Catholic, says that the middle ages were "pre-eminently an epoch of orderly thought, rationalist through and through ... forming one long training of the intellect of Western Europe in the sense of order." Let me advise you to get the book entitled, "The World's Debt to the Catholic Church," by Dr. James J. Walsh. It will surprise you.

504. History records many instances where the Church opposed lines of thought later proved to be right.

No sound argument can be based on a few isolated cases. Also, if in some individual cases the Church opposed theories later proved to be right, would you blame her for opposing those which later events proved to be wrong? The conservatism of the Church meant the very great benefit of cautious thought; and the modern license has resulted in many things being swallowed as facts which are not facts, and the constant unsaying by "scientists" of what previous "scientists" have said.

505. In the middle ages learning was discouraged for the mass of the people.

It was not. They were taught agriculture and various trades, and were most skilled workers. The glorious buildings they erected shows that. The monks who gave us the most beautifully illuminated manuscripts, and who were devoted to teaching, were drawn from the ordinary people. But book learning is not the only learning, and prior to the inventing of the printing press, the diffusion of literary education as compared with today was impossible. To blame limitations due to lack of facilities as if they implied a deliberate discouragement of learning by the Church is unpardonable.

506. Independent scientific thought was regarded as heresy.

That is not true. In his book, "The Flight from Reason," written by Arnold Lunn before his conversion to the Catholic Church we read these words: "I sympathize with Dr. Walsh's reaction to the popular misrepresentation of the attitude of the mediaeval Church. It is as unreasonable to represent the mediaeval Church as hostile to science, as to suggest that the Popes were keenly interested in the advancement of scientific notions. The mediaeval Church was uninterested in, rather than hostile to science. The intellectual energies of the great mediaeval thinkers were concentrated on philosophy. The neglect of science must be ascribed, not to the active opposition of the Church, but to the fact that the great Churchmen were absorbed in other intellectual interests. The Popes, indeed, were always ready to patronize scientific discovery provided the scientists did not trespass on the province of the theologians."

507. For predicting flying machines Roger Bacon was looked upon as being in league with the devil and was severely punished.

Roger Bacon did not get into any trouble for predicting flying machines. He was a most aggressive and tactless man who caused all his own difficulties. His best friend was Pope Clement IV., who was deeply interested in his first attempts at experimental science. Bacon did not suffer "severe punishment." He was a Franciscan Friar, and his own Order had to keep him in retirement because of his belligerent ways.

508. Copernicus was attacked by the Church as a heretic because he said the earth went round the sun.

Your history is at fault. Copernicus had often spoken of his theories on that subject, and far from being condemned as a heretic, was induced by clerical friends to put them into print. Only 73 years after his death was his book censured; and then merely because of the use Galileo made of it. But these individual cases, even were your interpretation of them correct, would not justify a general indictment of the Church.

509. How can an infallible Church approve such sciences today after bitterly opposing them in the past?

Prudential decrees against a few particular theories in the field of science cannot rightly be construed as opposition to science. Also, such decrees are outside the field to which infallibility is restricted, and consequently do not affect that aspect of the Church.

510. The Church is infallible in her moral teachings, and her opposition was on moral grounds.

The Church is infallible in her official definitions of correct moral teaching. But disciplinary decrees of Roman Congregations are not definitions of doctrine, and are not infallible. It is one thing to define a doctrine concerning moral principles, but quite another to regulate conduct in accordance with such principles as one believes them to apply to particular circumstances in some given period.

511. I am surprised that you should even try to defend the obviously superstitious teachings of Catholicism, and gloss them over.

I am afraid that you begin with the belief that Catholic teaching is "obviously superstitious"; and so strong is this prejudice that any explanation which would show that it is not superstitious must seem wrong to you. Your attitude seems to be this: "As explained by this Catholic priest, Catholic teaching does not seem to be superstitious. But I am quite convinced that it is superstitious. Therefore this Catholic priest must be glossing it over." You put me "between the devil and the deep sea"; for you insist that I am either a knave or a fool. If what I say seems reasonable, then I must be insincere and a knave, because Catholic teaching is superstitious. If I do sincerely believe in it, I am a fool, because Catholic teaching is superstitious. So you have me both ways! But your obligation is to prove Catholic teaching superstitious.

512. You know quite well that in the dark ages immediately preceding the Reformation theology tried to sanctify superstition.

Catholic theology has always classed superstition as sinful, and has labored to stamp it out. That ignorant people are apt to mingle superstition with religion is quite true. But superstition is not necessarily associated with religion. It is a strange tendency in human beings, due to the limitations of the human mind, which is apt to break out at any time. The man who advertises lucky charms today is as sure of a harvest as ever. As regards your estimate of the "dark ages," it is necessary to make a distinction. Intellectually, the thirteenth and fourteenth and fifteenth centuries do not constitute the "dark ages." The real "dark ages" are to be found between the sixth and the eleventh centuries. From the moral point of view I am willing to admit that the fourteenth and fifteenth centuries could rightly be thus called. Side by side with the revival of art and literature due to intense study of the classics there was a revival also of pagan morality in place of Christian virtue. Intellectual interest in a sensual philosophy very easily ends in a greater interest in sensuality. Men, interested in the beautiful style of the pagan classics, absorbed the immoral poison of what they contained and they fell into vices quite at variance with Christian standards. Men began to write filth beautifully only to render their beautiful souls filthy. The Renaissance had very ill effects upon the religious lives of both clergy and laity, and rendered the times very dark indeed from a moral point of view.

513. Did not the Schoolmen spend their time debating such questions as the number of angels that could sit on the point of a needle?

That is a travesty of Scholasticism. Scholasticism, or the philosophy of the Schoolmen of the Middle Ages, can be divided into four periods. It arose between the ninth and the eleventh centuries; developed rapidly during the twelfth century; attained perfection during the thirteenth century with the great St. Thomas of Aquin; and then fell into decline in the fourteenth and fifteenth centuries. In this last period the best traditions of Scholasticism were forgotten, and would-be philosophers were no longer creative thinkers, but rather fought amongst themselves for the honor of the systems they had adopted rather than for the truth. This led to a lot of hair-splitting debates, and when the Renaissance came, men judged Scholasticism by the type they found prevailing, making no distinction between the later and the earlier Schoolmen. It was a superficial judgment; and superficial writers today still repeat the foolish statement that the Schoolmen wasted time debating about the number of angels who could sit on the point of a needle. That is simply a caricature. Men who really know something of history have realized that the Scholastic philosophy must be judged by its uncorrupted form in the golden age of the thirteenth century, and not by those who, in the period of decline, were forsaking its true principles. So Professor Whitehead, Fellow of Trinity College, Cambridge, writes in his book, "Science and the Modern World," that "the greatest contribution of mediaevalism to the formation of the scientific movement was the inexpugnable belief that every detailed occurrence can be correlated in a perfectly definite manner, exemplifying general principles." And he adds that to the Schoolmen is due "faith in the very possibility of science." Those words of Professor Whitehead are more valuable than the verdict of nonentities. It may be that modern materialists wish to live only by their senses which they have in common with animals, and refuse to accept as facts all that is not subject to sense-experience. But the Schoolmen preferred reason, and felt obliged to account for facts made known by a revelation from God which reason justified. Knowing thus of the existence of purely spiritual beings called angels, they quite reasonably discussed their relation to space, just as much a problem as the fact that one can get more and more ideas into his head without having to enlarge his head to provide space-accommodation for them. But the verdict that angels, like ideas, do not occupy space to the exclusion of others is a perfectly rational conclusion which irrational people too easily dismiss with a contemptuous reference to angels sitting on the point of a needle. No Schoolman was such a fool as to think that any bodily posture was proper to an angel. A childish want of thought is the chief characteristic of many modern supposedly wise men when they begin to discuss a Scholastic philosophy of which they know practically nothing.

514. Science leaves no room for an other-worldly religion.

You exemplify my contention that those who suppose a conflict between science and the Catholic religion understand neither science nor Catholicism.

515. Before a thing can exist it must have a definite beginning and an end. Time and space are the only exceptions.

That statement you must try to prove. You do not attempt to do so. I maintain, of course, that it is wrong. God, the Creator of all things, is eternal. He exists, yet He had not to begin to exist, and can never cease to exist. I grant that no created thing exists which had not at least a beginning. And as time and space are co-terminous with created existences, they, too, had a beginning. As for the necessity of created things having an end, that can be disputed; but all I will say here is that whilst the existence of a created thing is dependent upon its beginning to exist, it is certainly not dependent upon its having an end or ceasing to exist!

516. Unless matter can give physical evidence of its presence, it simply does not exist.

That is true. But note two things. You confine your remark to matter, restricting yourself to material things, and omitting reference to non-material being. Secondly, whilst matter does not exist unless it can give physical evidence of its presence, it does not follow that matter is non-existent merely because we fail to detect that evidence. The existence of things does not depend upon our knowledge of them. There are people who have the foolish idea that if they have not seen or heard of a thing, it therefore does not exist. They remind one of the legend of the ostrich which buries its head in the sand and believes that it has no pursuers because it cannot see them.

517. Science has proved the existence of matter by revealing stars thousands of light years away.

The case is not made stronger by appealing to stars thousands of light years away. There is no need to go so far afield to prove the existence of matter. This earth is quite enough for your purpose, as you will find if you try to walk through a brick wall as if it were not there.

518. Yet what evidence has science given us of the existence of what people of all creeds refer to as "the better world"?

I must ask you to define what you mean by science. Do you intend merely experimental science? Do you intend to abandon all reliance upon pure reasoning? Will you deny all value to history? Do you deny for example that Christ ever lived because the fact cannot be discovered with a microscope? Or, granted that He lived, will you deny that His teachings merit credence because you cannot boil those teachings in a test tube? And even if you restrict science to experimental procedure, will you brush aside all the findings of the Society for Psychical Research as being the result of either folly or fraud? You must really decide for yourself more precisely what you mean by science.

519. Let us turn to your abstract and intangible dogmas; and firstly the doctrine of the Trinity.

Though no human mind can fully comprehend the doctrine of the Trinity, yet the concept is not unintelligible. It certainly conveys a definite meaning to Christians. In revealing Himself to us God had to employ terms on our own level which could not but be inadequate to express His infinite perfection. But the terms used are not nevertheless without meaning. We know what a nature is, and we know what a person is. It may be, and in fact must be, that the Divine Nature, and the real character of Personality in God will be mysterious to us. But that does not mean that our ideas are wrong, or that they have nothing in them. It only means that if our ideas are right as far as they go, they do not go far enough to completely exhaust the reality.

520. To the lay mind it seems a hair-splitting of terms which cannot be of supreme importance.

I can but assure you that the matter is of supreme importance. For if the doctrine of the Trinity be false, that would be the end of the Christian religion.

The very essence of the Christian religion is that the Eternal Son of God became man for our salvation. If there is no Trinity of Persons in God, there would be no Eternal Son to become man at all, and the whole of Christianity would be built on a mere flight of fancy. If I believed the doctrine of the Trinity to be false, or in the least uncertain, I would abandon Christianity altogether. That would be the only logical thing to do. So from the Christian point of view you can see that it is no question of hair-splitting, but a matter of supreme importance.

521. Wherein lies the significance?

The doctrine of the Trinity lifts the notion of God, and carries it beyond the most powerful created intelligence, as befits the dignity and majesty of God. By it, God takes life instead of being the great unknown X of the universe. One, He is not solitary. And the multiplicity of the universe is but the shadow of the diversity of God in Himself according to the Trinity of relationships. How conceive of God save as knowing and loving? And how conceive of thought and love in God save as God Himself, yet distinct as operations? How conceive of God as happy without society and reciprocal activity. before the universe; and after its creation, since the universe adds nothing to God Himself? The Trinity gives us a living rather than an abstract God, individualizing Thought and Love in Him, giving interior multiplicity with His eternal unity. If my thought became myself intimately and adequately, and my happiness in myself were essentially identified with myself, I would be a trinity whilst remaining myself. But what is not possible with me is a fact with God; and His living unity is the Trinity.

522. Isn't it merely ways of thinking of God, drawn from Plato?

The philosophy of Plato has contributed towards explanations of the subject, as it has contributed much towards many other departments of human thought. But the dogma of the Trinity in no way came from Plato, or from any other merely human source. The Trinity of Persons in God was taught as a fact by Christ to explain His own Person and work. He gave the dogma, and the dogma gave rise to philosophical explanations of it. Nor does the doctrine merely give ways of thinking of God. Aspects of our own thinking would not be Divine Persons. The dogma tells us of God's own intimate life within the Divine Nature.

523. Are the names Father, Son, and Holy Ghost, merely different titles of the one Being?

They are not merely three different titles of the one Being as if they were names only and in no sense realities. They are three relative personal aspects of one absolute and substantial Being. One and the same Absolute Being can have relative aspects distinct from one another. In God, of course, we meet with what should not be an unexpected mystery. The three relative aspects of the one Divine Nature are Personal. Our experience of finite and created man is of one nature and one person. But our knowledge of finite and created man cannot give us an adequate knowledge of the Infinite Creator unless we are prepared to work on a very crude and anthropomorphic basis. The fact that in the one Absolute God there are three relative Personalities, distinct in virtue of their relationship to each other, yet identically possessing the Divine Nature, is known to us by revelation alone. And we know the fact without being able to comprehend it fully, not because of any defect in God, but because of the defect in our finite selves.

524. Who first promulgated the doctrine that Christ is equal to the Father in power and glory?

That doctrine was first promulgated by Christ Himself, as recorded in the Gospels. Thus Christ said, "I and the Father are one." The doctrine was also clearly taught by St. Paul. Against various heretics in the early Church again and again the Bishops re-declared the truth both implicitly and explicitly. The General Councils of Nicea, and of Ephesus, as well as other Councils, excluded all ambiguity as to what Christ had revealed by their specific definitions and formulas.

525. *Can you find one Scripture text containing the word Trinity?*

No. Nor is there any need to do so.

526. *Can we suppose that the doctrine of the Trinity is taught in the Bible, yet no such word is there?*

There is no question of supposition. The doctrine is clearly given by Christ in His words, "Baptize in the name of the Father and of the Son and of the Holy Ghost." Matt. XXVIII., 19.

527. *The recurring genitive indicates a plurality of names, so that we should say, "In the name of the Father, and in the name of the Son, and in the name of the Holy Ghost." In that case the one name does not indicate one Divine Nature.*

The one name of the Three Persons was certainly meant to indicate the unity of God despite triple Personality.

528. *If you discount grammar in the interests of a particular exegesis words lose the power to prove anything.*

Our exegesis involves no violation of grammar. And all danger of distortion is removed by the use of the usual safeguards of exegesis; namely, the analogy of faith, the interpretations of the Fathers, and the constant tradition of the Catholic Church. No argument based on grammatical form arises where the baptismal formula is concerned; nor can any such considerations rob the words of their trinitarian value.

529. *When St. John says, "In the beginning was the word, and the word was with God, and the word was God," God was the subject of attribution where His word was concerned just as your hand is the instrument of your own conduct.*

The Word of God was personal. My hand is not a person. The Word was with God, because the Second Person of the Trinity is distinct by personality from the Father and the Holy Ghost; yet the Word was God because possessing the same Divine Nature with them. To suggest that the Word of God is no more personal than my hand is quite opposed to the truth. St. John, who declares that the Word was with God, and was God, says also that the Word was made flesh and dwelt amongst us; that in "Him" was life; that "He" was in the world; that "He" dwelt amongst us; that we saw "His" glory, and of "His" fullness we receive grace. The Word was the Eternal Son of God, every bit as personal as the Father.

530. *God the Father is explicitly stated.*

It is also explicitly stated that the Word is "the only-begotten Son who is in the bosom of the Father." God may act in a fatherly way towards us men, but He is a true Father to the only-begotten Son, generated in the same Divine Nature, and equally the uncreated God with the Father and the Holy Spirit.

531. *When Christ said, "My God, why hast Thou forsaken me?", whom did He address? Was He speaking to Himself?*

He was addressing His heavenly Father, and in virtue of the sufferings of His created human nature.

532. *What did the expression imply?*

It did not imply any distinction between Himself and His Father so far as the Divine Nature was concerned. It implied that, in His human nature, He experienced that sense of dereliction by God which man deserved. If man abandons God he deserves to be abandoned by God. Jesus took the place of sinners, and suffered the sense of dereliction deserved by sinners.

533. *I certainly do not understand the mystery of the Trinity.*

Centuries ago St. Augustine replied to a similar complaint with the words, "If you do understand, then that is what God is not." He meant, of course, that no human being can fully comprehend God. We cannot exclude mystery when speaking of God, for if He came within the limits of our finite intelligence He would be finite and not God at all. At the same time, we can understand on our own level what the doctrine of the Trinity means. The idea of personality is not foreign to us, nor is the idea of a given nature. If the Trinity is a mystery it is because both the Nature and the Persons in God transcend all our notions of these things, our ideas giving but a faint and most inadequate reflection of the truth. It is also a mystery because our experience is limited to a single nature with a single personality. A single Divine Nature with a threefold Personality is not on the same plane as any of our ordinary experiences, and is known by revelation alone; and even then only insofar as human words can express the transcendent truth. But the terms are not meaningless, and we do find a profound significance in the doctrine.

534. *Turning to visible things around us, I cannot see what is wrong with eternal evolution.*

If you intend, by eternal evolution, to dispense with God, you would find it a bigger problem to see what is right in it. In dealing with the origin of the universe you will find yourself in deep waters whichever way you turn. We know, however, by revelation that all things less than God were created from nothing by God, and that therefore they are not eternal.

535. *Creation in time is a great mystery to me, and I cannot see how the world could be created.*

To know how the world could be created you would have to comprehend God; and no finite mind can do that. But we do know that God could create by the mere fact of His being God. Creation in time is, I admit, also a mystery. For there was no time before created things came into existence. Creatures began in eternity, and time began with them, and belongs to them because of their successive duration. The universe had a first moment, before which it did not exist. And referring to that moment we say that the world was created at the beginning of time.

536. *Was creation an instantaneous act in the beginning, or does God still create?*

We do not hold that God gave only one beginning to created things, allowing evolution to account for all subsequent developments. God continues to create, or to give new beginnings to new creatures. For example, we admit a new and distinct creation for each human soul. We maintain that new creative activity was required for new species, and for the production of life. Life did not come from brute matter by simple development; nor did intelligence come merely from lower forms of organic life. New creative activities of God could alone account for these things. For the rest we are free to believe, not in an eternal, but in a temporal evolution of created beings. I might point out to you that many thinkers today demand much more creative activity in the world than any Catholic will admit. Bergson, the French philosopher, says that there are always new beginnings in almost every phase of existence. Ever there are new and unforeseen productions, according to him. And he tries to explain all by what he terms "creative evolution." It is impossible to accept his ideas of evolution; but it is significant that he by no means regards evolution as excluding the notion of creation.

THE THEORY OF EVOLUTION

537. You people who believe in the Bible are apparently prepared to repudiate certain scientific facts arrived at by the ceaseless and untiring work of generations of earnest men.

That is not true. We do not reject any scientifically demonstrated facts. Give us any fact that is scientifically demonstrated, and we will accept it at once. But no such fact would, or could, in the least affect our belief in the Bible. We Catholics stand for the principle that truth can never be opposed to truth. God cannot contradict Himself. He is the Author of nature, and He is the Author of the Bible. No truth discoverable from a study of nature will ever be found to contradict a truth set forth in the Bible.

538. One fact you repudiate is that the earth is at least 2000 million years old.

That the earth is at least 2000 million years old is a good conjecture, but not an established fact. Were it an established fact, there would be no difficulty in accepting it, so far as the Bible is concerned. It would not matter were the earth a billion billion years old, taking a billion as a million millions. For the Bible nowhere makes any statement as to the age of the earth at all. We can therefore accept both the truth of the Bible, and any age geology or astronomy can reasonably assign to our planet.

539. You have to repudiate the fact that the earth was not suddenly created out of nothing, but was formed slowly from a mass of molten matter.

The Christian religion does not demand the rejection of that explanation.

540. I refuse to practice any religion until the theory of evolution has been refuted.

There is no such thing as "the" theory of evolution. There are dozens of theories of evolution, whether of the major or of the minor variety. Nor have any of these theories been put forward by any sensible and well-informed men as anything more than a theory, for demonstration is as absent as refutation. And whether any particular theory of evolution be true or not, no one could possibly derive from such considerations any reasonable objection to the practice of religion. There's about as much connection between the theory of evolution, as you term it, and the practice of religion, as there is between the wave theory of light and a pain in one's kidneys.

541. In their book "The Science of Life" Wells and Huxley seem to prove the evolutionary origin of life.

The book in question is not scientific. In it the authors say that "evolution is a fact as well established as the roundness of the earth." Huxley's grandfather, the famous T. H. Huxley, once said that "an assertion which outstrips the evidence is not only a blunder, but a crime." That brands his grandson, together with Wells, as criminal. Sir Ambrose Fleming, President of the Philosophical Society of Great Britain, says, "There are no sufficient reasons for declaring the evolutionary origin of the human race to be a fact." Professor Albert Fleischmann, of Erlangen University, says that "our modern knowledge of animal anatomy is quite incompatible with the leading tenets of the theory of organic evolution." Delage, who accepted the theory of evolution, but who was a real scientist, said frankly that his belief was based less on natural history than on personal opinion. "On facts," he said, "it must be acknowledged that the formation of species one from another has not been demonstrated at all." Popularizers, like Wells and Huxley, are devoid of the scientific temperament. They excel in giving exact descriptions of things which never existed, and for which there is not a shadow of evidence. In the light of the scientists I have quoted what is one to make of the statement in the book you mention that "no denial of the fact of organic evolution except on the part of manifestly ignorant and prejudiced and superstitious minds, exists today"?

542. *Do I understand that you believe only in evolution within the species?*

Your question concerns what is really merely a scientific matter quite independent of the Catholic religion. It is no more relevant to the religious question than would be my opinion as to the nutrition value of cheese. However, since you think it relevant, I will answer your queries. A Catholic is quite free to hold the evolutionary formation of one species from another, or to deny it and hold that evolution has occurred only within specific types. My personal opinion is that there is not a vestige of proof in favor of the transformation of species, and that the probabilities are against it.

543. *Your halting, tame, and tepid faith in the theory of evolution astonishes me. It would have earned for you the martyr's crown in the Middle Ages!*

Firstly, even were one put to death for an opinion concerning any natural department of knowledge, one would not earn a martyr's crown. Secondly, I have no faith at all in any theory of evolution. I am of the opinion that minor evolution has occurred within certain limits, an opinion which is based upon such evidence as science has produced. But that opinion is not faith, for I do not hold it solely upon the authority of others who choose to advance the theory. Thirdly, apart from the martyr's crown, and the nature of my opinion, I would not have been put to death for my views on this subject either in the Middle Ages or in any other Age.

544. *The whole attitude of your Church has changed on this point.*

It has not. It might surprise you to know that St. Augustine, in the fourth century, and St. Thomas Aquinas in the thirteenth century, expressed more advanced views favorable to evolution than those I hold today. And they have been canonized, not crucified.

545. *Your Church says now, "Evolution might be true. We do not know. If it is proved to be true, then we shall believe it." And that is authority speaking in the name of God!*

You absurdly say that the Church now says, though the Church has never said anything else. Then you predict that the Church will "believe" it, as if you imagine that this purely natural matter could become part of the Catholic Faith. It could no more become part of the Catholic Faith than the discovery that gasoline can drive cars. Finally the reference to the "authority" of the Church is ridiculous, for the infallible authority of the Catholic Church concerns matters of faith and morals.

546. *Organic evolutionists can point to visible proofs of their theory which would appear almost overwhelming.*

That is not true. You see, the proofs of organic evolution do not consist in producing isolated and graded fossil remains. What you have to prove is that lower grades evolved into higher grades. You have to prove a process. And to prove that process you need, not what you are able to produce at present, but what you are not able to produce. In other words, you have to produce missing links whose chief characteristic is that they are missing. Professor Berg, in his book "Nomogenesis," speaks as follows: "It is truly remarkable that paleontology in no way displays transitional forms between phyla and classes; and possibly not even between orders. Thus we are ignorant of transitional forms not only between vertebrates and invertebrates, fishes and tetrapods, but even between the cartilaginous (chondrichthyes such as sharks, etc.) and higher fishes (osteichthyes); in spite of a wonderful affinity between reptiles and birds, no transitional forms between them are known. Formerly this was accounted for by the imperfection of the geological record; but the deeper our knowledge penetrates into the domain of fossils, the farther back recede genetic inter-relations, which ever elude our grasp." In the face of that, how can you speak of visible proofs advanced by organic evolutionists?

547. *I believe in God, but I do not believe in the Catholic doctrine that besides this material universe He created angels.*

If you believe in God who is an invisible and purely spiritual Being, it is difficult to see why you should refuse to believe in angels. If one invisible and purely spiritual being can exist, why not others? There is nothing against the possibility of their existence, did God choose to create them. And God has told us that He did create angelic beings.

548. *One can go only by his senses.*

That is not true. You yourself believe in logic and thought; yet you have never had sense experience of these things. You may see printed words as a dog could see them. But you have never seen with your bodily eyes the logic of thought. Then, too, you say that you believe in God. But you have never had sense experience of God.

549. *Would you please tell me what an angel is?*

An angel is a purely spiritual creature endowed with intelligence and will power.

550. *I read a Catholic book once which solemnly and seriously told me that angels are possessed of wonderful agility.*

That information was quite correct, though it was not set down in the book you read any more solemnly and seriously than other matters in it.

551. *Must Catholics believe that angels have the physical agility of an acrobat?*

By God's revelation we have to believe that angels exist. We are not required to believe in any theological explanations about the nature and prerogatives of angels. But that does not forbid our discussing their nature, and setting down what reason tells us concerning them. Now reason compels us to believe in the physical agility of angels. But that has nothing to do with the agility of an acrobat. That agility is bodily and muscular. No one asserts such agility of angels. Bodily and muscular agility, however, do not exhaust the varieties of physical agility. There are other kinds. Wireless waves have tremendous physical agility. They are a physical force, traveling with an incalculable rapidity of motion. Angels are physical, though immaterial and spiritual beings. And they are endowed with an agility proper to themselves.

552. *Perhaps you mean that angels have the same mental agility as clever priests for escaping embarrassing questions!*

Angels have a mental agility far above that possessed by any human mind. Being purely spiritual intelligences, they have immediate intuitions as opposed to human methods of discursive reasoning. Still, the reference to physical agility is concerned with their physical rather than with their intellectual rapidity.

553. *What precisely does the physical agility of angels mean?*

It means that angels are not conditioned by time or space as are men, but that they can operate immediately in widely separated spheres of action. And since angels are created spiritual substances, not possessing the omnipresence of God, they have to be where they operate, which supposes instantaneous transition from one sphere to another. One who believes in angels cannot deny all possible movement to them. And if we admit that angels can act now here and now there, we have no reason to deny that rapid transition is possible to them.

554. Have non-Catholics "Guardian Angels" to protect them?

Most probably, even though they themselves do not think so. After all, our Lord's words could apply to any little children when He said, "Their angels always see the face of my Father in heaven." Matt. XVIII., 10. St. Thomas Aquinas says that God denies to no one the general helps towards salvation. Now amongst the general helps he ranks the assistance of guardian angels, and gives it as his opinion that every human being has a good angel assigned to him for his protection against evil.

555. Are we to suppose an eternal devil as well as an eternal God? Or did God create the devil?

We cannot suppose an eternal uncreated devil. Yet God did not create the devil as a devil. In other words, God did not create any evil spiritual being as evil. He created all things other than Himself, including angels. The angels as created by God were beings of a spiritual nature, endowed with intelligence and free will; and as the terminus of God's creative action they were entirely good. But some angels misused their freedom of will, and rendered themselves evil by their opposition to the God who is goodness itself. Evil is opposed to good. He who is opposed to God is opposed to the good, and renders himself therefore evil. But God is not the cause of such evil. His purpose in giving freedom of will was in order that the angels might have the great dignity of offering Him, not a compulsory love, but a love of free choice. And He forbade that misuse of the gift of freedom which rejects the infinite goodness of its source. God could not forbid sin yet be the cause of it. St. Peter's words that God spared not the angels who sinned show that some angels fell from the good state in which they previously existed into a sinful state; that they were responsible for their own evil choice; that God had that dominion over them which could belong only to their Creator; and that God does punish deliberately chosen and unrepented wickedness.

556. The rebellion of angels in heaven is an enigma to me.

It is a mystery which human reason cannot probe to its full depths, but in no way is there any actual conflict with reasonable principles.

557. These angels had an intelligence immeasurably transcending that of human beings.

That is true. Where men have to secure data through their senses, and reason discursively from premises to conclusions, with liability to error both as regards facts and logical process, the angels, as pure spirits untrammelled by the weight of earthly and material bodies, could perceive truth by an immediate intuition. For this reason their guilt was immeasurably greater than that of human beings. And therefore God showed mercy to men, though He spared not the angels who sinned.

558. They must have known that they were created by God, and that by His very uncreated Nature God infinitely surpassed them.

That is quite true. They fell into no intellectual error on that point.

559. Yet we are told that pride led them to attempt equality with the uncreated God.

They were not so foolish, of course, as to think that they could be equal to the uncreated God. Yet pride did cause their fall. Pride is a sin of the will, not of the intelligence. But every choice of the will, even though it be an evil choice, presupposes at least an intellectual apprehension of the evil thing to be chosen. There must be a theoretical error before a practical error. But how could an angelic intelligence go wrong in its ideas? We must remember that the angels were creatures, and not the Creator. Keener though they were than men in their powers of intuition, their intelligence was yet finite and limited. It was quite possible for them, therefore, to give less attention to one aspect of the truth, and to give more attention to another. It was possible for them to concentrate their attention upon their own natural perfection, and to fail to advert sufficiently to their origin by creation, and to their essential dependence upon God. Granted this, an evil choice of the will by pride was correspondingly possible. Regarding themselves as made for themselves rather than for God, they could pretend to an independence of Him, regarding Him as not necessary to them. And all this without wrongly thinking that they could be absolutely equal to Him and infinitely perfect.

560. *Is not the devil merely an evil influence?*

We cannot say that he *is* an evil influence. Rather he *has* an evil influence, both upon individuals and upon society.

561. *I read recently in a book that possession by devils as recorded in the Gospels was merely lunacy. The book was written by a clergyman.*

It is quite true that those possessed by devils were maddened by them, and exhibited signs of lunacy. But it is not true to conclude that this lunacy was due to merely natural and physical causes. If Protestant clergymen wish to deny the existence of evil spirits as personal enemies of mankind, then they will have to abandon belief in the Gospels and in Christ, if they are logical. Christ spoke of the everlasting fire prepared for the devil and his angels. That would be absurd if the devils were not individual, intelligent, responsible, and personal beings. The effort to find any explanation other than the actual existence of unseen spirits is useless and ridiculous; useless in the light of such texts as St. Peter's words, "God spared not the angels who sinned"; ridiculous in those who still pretend to believe in the Christian religion. The argument can only be, "I do not believe in the devil because he is not seen, and because he is evil." Yet these people believe in God despite His not being visible to bodily eyes; and they have to believe in the existence of moral evil, at least in the case of human beings. There is no reason why they should deny the existence of created spiritual beings who are morally evil, save the prevailing fashion of unbelief in the supernatural altogether.

562. *I fail to see how devils can tempt men.*

How can men tempt each other? They sow evil thoughts into the minds of their fellow men, or impress weaker individuals by the subtle influence of a strong yet evil personality. Devils can do the same. They have but to enter into the current of our own inclinations, or into the smiling appeal of seductive pleasures. They have only to lean on that which is already at breaking-point, or check higher aspirations as they present themselves. The influence of devils can be like that of an undetected poison gas breathed in imperceptibly with the atmosphere.

563. *But why should devils tempt men?*

If a man is evil, he uses even his good powers for evil. We know how evil men can be apostles of evil. Now having fallen themselves, evil spirits want other creatures of God to fall; and they use their powers for this evil purpose.

564. *Men alone are responsible for the evil they do. To blame the devil is a subterfuge of cowardice.*

It is true that men are responsible only for such conduct as is their own deliberate choice. And therefore men alone are responsible for the evil they do. But they are not responsible for all their temptations to do evil. If people blame the devil by saying, "The devil made me do it," that is a subterfuge. The devil cannot "make" people sin against their own will. But it is not a subterfuge to attribute to the devil certain temptations, although I admit that some people are only too ready to declare that he is the source of their temptations. Often enough their own crass stupidity, and lack of care, is the cause of their temptations.

565. What does the "Beast" of Dan. VII. mean?

The beast spoken of by Daniel the prophet means in general the spirit of evil as in bitter opposition to the good. But the vision of Daniel had a very wide and complex significance. It was on four planes at one and the same time. On the cosmic plane he saw, not any particular conflict, but the universal triumph of God in the whole of creation. On the ethical plane he saw the struggle of right and wrong amongst men. On the eschatological plane he saw the consummation of this struggle at the end of the world. On the historical plane he saw Antiochus Epiphanes, king of Syria, who in 172 B. C. took Jerusalem by force, and later desecrated the Temple, setting up a pagan altar which, in the First Book of Machabees is called the "Abomination of Desolation"—an expression used by Daniel himself.

566. Will you explain Rev. XIII., 18?

The verse says, "Here is wisdom. He that hath understanding, let him count the number of the beast. For it is the number of a man; and the number of him is six hundred sixty six." As regards the explanation, we must remember that the Greek and Hebrew alphabets have numerical significance. If the letters of a man's name added up to a certain number, that would be his number. Dozens of names throughout history have been made to add up to 666 by various methods, and no certain solution is possible as to the actual meaning of St. John. The name of Nero Caesar in Hebrew lettering makes 666; and possibly that is as good an explanation as can be given. The number may, of course, refer to some adversary of Christ yet to appear. St. John's words suggest that the correct interpretation will require a wisdom on the plane of his own inspiration when he wrote the Apocalypse. And that, of course, could only be a special gift of God, which the average reader cannot expect to possess.

567. If Adam was the first human being, how long ago was he created?

I do not know. There is no indication whatever in the Bible as to when the first man was created. Nor is it a religious question. It is for science to seek for such evidence as it can discover from geological research. On such indications as science has so far been able to offer, it is probable enough that the first man was created perhaps 35,000 years ago. It would certainly be rash to go beyond 50,000.

568. You have granted that the world may be 2000 million years old!

The problem of the age of the earth itself differs from that of man. In relation to the probable existence of the earth man has lived upon it for a very short time.

569. Do those who speak of pre-Adamites mean animals with a certain degree of likeness to men?

The pre-Adamite theory was first put forward seriously by a Calvinist named Isaac de la Peyrere in 1655. But Isaac de la Peyrere himself ended by renouncing Calvinism and becoming a Catholic; and he also renounced his pre-Adamite theory. The pre-Adamite theory did not mean animals with a degree of likeness to men, but men truly human beings equally as developed as Adam himself. Adam, therefore, was not the first man, but merely the first remote ancestor of the Jewish race, the Gentiles being descended from other and previous human stock. This doctrine is condemned by the Catholic Church as opposed to the Scriptural teaching that all men without exception are descended from Adam even as Christ, the second Adam, died for the redemption of all.

570. Who lived before the Jews?

Various peoples descended from our first parents, Adam and Eve. Definite historical details of the Jews can scarcely go back beyond 2094 B. C. when Abraham went from his native land in Babylonia down into Palestine. Egyptian historical records can be traced back to 4000 B. C. We have evidences of a Chinese civilization back to 2000 B. C. Records of the Persians, Indians, Greeks and Romans, of later periods, yet contemporary with the Jews of the Old Testament are also available. History, of course, does not go back very far. The earliest fixed date in history is about 4200 B. C. In the absence of records we have nothing but conjectures to go upon for pre-historic periods. But this gives no reason for doubt as to what we do know. What we know of Christ and of His teachings is not invalidated by obscurity as to the history of dispersed mankind during the period which elapsed between the creation of Adam and the earliest historical records of subsequent generations.

571. Why does the Bible mention the Jews only?

Other peoples besides the Jews are mentioned in the Bible. But since the Old Testament is the inspired record of God's chosen people, it cannot be expected to contain exhaustive accounts of other peoples. Other peoples are mentioned only insofar as they came into contact with, and affected the Jews.

572. Isn't Christianity rather narrow-minded, to make our earth the center of existence and forget the millions of spheres like our own upon which life most probably exists?

Whatever may be said of possibility, there is no probability that life exists upon millions of other spheres. Probability demands at least some shred of evidence, and there is no such evidence in existence. It is possible that life exists on other spheres; but Christianity has never denied that. It is illogical to attribute to Christianity a teaching you think narrow-minded, and then to transfer your epithet to Christianity whether it contains that teaching or not.

573. If life existed on another planet, would that affect the Christian religion?

Not in the least.

574. Would Christ have redeemed such people on other worlds by His death on Calvary?

To that I can but give a conditional reply. If there be living beings on other planets; and if they be endowed with free will; and if they have sinned against the moral law of God; and if God did attach their salvation to the death of Christ on the Cross, then Christ died for their salvation also. But who could verify all those "ifs"? Meantime God has revealed to us on this earth all that we need to know for our own needs; and such speculations concerning other possibilities are of little practical importance. The lack of such knowledge is no hindrance to our own salvation, and will not excuse us if we fail to attain it.

575. Are all human beings now on this earth descended from the one couple—Adam and Eve?

Yes.

576. Adam and Eve had two children, Cain and Abel. Cain killed Abel, and afterwards took a wife. Whence came that wife?

We are told three things in the Bible concerning this matter, and there is no other source of information. The three things are these: Firstly, that Adam and Eve were the first two human beings on earth. Secondly, that the days of Adam were 800 years, and that he begot sons and daughters. Thirdly, that Cain took a wife. The only possible conclusion is that Cain married a female descendant of Adam. Cain most probably married a sister. He could have married a niece, although that would have involved the prior marriage of a brother and sister.

577. *It is against all laws that a brother should marry his sister.*

The marriage of brothers and sisters is against the natural moral law in the present state of the human race. But laws which are normal now need not have obliged when conditions were abnormal. Special conditions demand special laws. And the beginning of the human race is an abnormal thing. God Himself created two human beings and commanded them to increase and multiply. The only possibility was by the intermarriage of their children. And God permitted this as long as it was necessary. He who could create human beings could easily preserve them from the evils usually associated with close intermarriage by a special act of His providence; and, in any case, the children of our first parents were not so closely related to each other as Eve was to Adam.

578. *Could it be said that Cain married a female of a pre-existent lower animal species?*

That could not reasonably be maintained. A mother drawn from a lower species would not be capable of producing children fulfilling all the requirements of a higher species. The offspring of such a marriage would not be human beings at all. The only explanation which does not violate reason is that Cain married a female descendant of Adam and Eve within his own species.

579. *If there were no other people except Adam and Eve and their family, who were the people that Cain was afraid of in the land of Nod?*

The Bible tells us that Cain went out to dwell in the land of Nod. But this does not mean that he went to an inhabited place. In Hebrew the expression "land of Nod" merely means "land of exile." The verse intends only that Cain fled from the others into exile. He took his wife with him, having married one of the daughters of Adam. Knowing of the command to increase and multiply, he feared that future men, hearing that he had murdered his own brother, would kill him if they found him.

580. *If we are all descended from Adam and Eve, how account for essential racial differences, diverse languages, and dispersion to isolated places?*

Essentially all human beings are similar. Racial differences afford no real difficulty against humanity's unity of origin. In fact, all such differences are accidental, not essential. The geographical distribution of peoples even to the most isolated places from a common center is easily accounted for whether by land routes, or by primitive rafts and boats. And the mere fact of such dispersion would give rise to differences in language.

581. *If our first parents were white, how did the black races originate?*

There is no evidence to tell us whether Adam was white, black, or between the two, much as the Arabs today. It is certain that all human beings are descended from Adam, whatever their color. How then account for the colors of different peoples? Simply by natural factors, such as climate, operating through thousands of years, the effects becoming permanently ingrained by heredity. As regards color, it is certain that it depends neither upon the blood nor upon the skin itself. Beneath the skin there are pigment cells which are the sources of color, and which are affected by many things, heat, cold, mode of life, etc. Darwin himself admits, in his book "The Descent of Man," that diversity of color is no sound argument at all against the derivation of all men from a common first parent.

582. *According to the Bible the primitive Patriarchs lived for very long periods. Did their year correspond with the present twelve months, or was it shorter?*

There are no indications that it differed in length from the year as we know it. The attempt to diminish the length of the years lived by our earliest ancestors leads to formidable difficulties—far more formidable than the long lives granted to them. That men could live such long lives did God will them to do so affords little difficulty. And there are good reasons why they should do so, both for the purpose of the multiplication of the race, and for the preservation of primitive revelation through successive ages. That man does not live so long now can be due in no small way to the advent of sin and moral depravity. Vitality and vigor diminish in a degenerate race; and the general laws of heredity help to explain a progressive enfeeblement of humanity as a whole through the many thousands of years since its creation.

583. *What does your Church teach concerning the nature of man?*

Her teaching on that subject is that of all sound philosophy. Man consists of body and soul, the body being material and perishable, the soul spiritual and immortal.

584. *Have not the words "soul" and "spirit" in the Hebrew and Greek many different meanings throughout the Bible?*

They have; and therefore the sense in which the words are used must be determined from the context in which they appear. The same thing is true of the English language. Both words are still used with very many different meanings. If we say of a sick person "poor soul," we do not imply that he is without a body. If we say that some friend was "the soul" of the party, we do not imply that others present had no souls of their own. If we quote the hackneyed lines, "Breathes there a man with soul so dead," we do not intend that his living body is animated by a soul that is actually dead. In the same way we can speak of the "spirit" of a man, intending the spiritual principle of his very being, or merely his mentality, or character, or intentions, or motives, or his influence, or a dozen other aspects of his person. But the fact that a word can be used in many ways does not destroy its value when it is used in a particular way. All that we have to ask ourselves is in what particular way the word is used in a given context. And when Christ said, "Fear not them that can kill the body, but who cannot kill the soul," Matt. X., 28, He obviously intended that the death of the body does not involve the death of the soul. And the only reason for that is the totally different nature of the soul from that of material objects. The soul is non-material, spiritual, and immortal, or not subject to physical death. It can be morally dead by sin; but that does not mean that it ceases to exist.

585. *In my opinion the soul is only the mind or conscience.*

The mind or the conscience is not the soul itself, but a power possessed by the soul. The soul is a created spiritual being made in the image and likeness of God, the Supreme and Infinite Spirit. And just as we speak of the "Divine Mind" in God, or of an "angelic mind" in the angels, so the "human mind" is the power of intelligence in human souls. Conscience is merely a judgment of the human mind concerning the moral goodness or badness of conduct. So long as the soul is united with the body in this life, the soul exercises its intelligence or mind with the help of the material brain, which is like a telephone exchange linking it with all the bodily senses—senses which put us into contact with the material world around us.

586. You speak of man's twofold composition of soul and body. But St. Paul speaks of "spirit, soul, and body." I Thess. V., 23.

In that text spirit and soul are the same thing considered under different aspects. As giving life to this body of ours it exercises the functions of a soul, and is the principle of sensitive life in us in conjunction with the sense faculties. But that same soul is, in its intrinsic nature, spiritual and in the image and likeness of God, capable of purely intellectual operations. Whilst the soul is immersed in a material body it must regulate the lower passions with God's help; but as purely spiritual its mind and will must be united to God by truth and love; and when the soul is separated from the body these last operations are the ones that will persist. Therefore St. Paul speaks of our animating principle first in virtue of its higher and more important capacity as spirit; then in virtue of its lesser capacity as soul informing the body; and finally of the body itself. St. Paul, therefore, does not intend three principles in man, but two; one of which, the soul, he takes according to its two different functions.

587. Are we strictly masters of our eternal destiny?

Yes. Eternal destiny is but the manifestation of the true state of conscience in a saint or in a sinner at the moment of death. All that happens is that this state is fixed eternally. One is either in God's grace and friendship or not at the moment of death. What you are now would be your eternity were you to die now. "The Kingdom of Heaven" is within you—if you be in the grace of God. The life given by Christ to those who love Him and serve Him simply continues. Our earthly existence merely serves to enable us to get God's grace if we lack it; or to recover it, should we lose it.

588. Does the soul, immediately after death, make contact with another body?

No. So long as it is in this material body it needs the help of material bodily powers to exercise its intelligence. But once the soul is liberated from the body by death, it enters into a completely different state; and under the new conditions the mind or intelligence of the spiritual soul will be able to operate without the aid of a material brain and senses which are adapted to this world. Neither God nor the angels have any need of a body to exercise their spiritual powers. Nor will the human soul once it enters into the realm of the spirit beyond the portals of death. Therefore you can dismiss the idea that, immediately after death, the soul makes contact with another body. It will exist in a state of separation until the last day, when it will be united in the resurrection with the body it possessed in this life.

589. I read recently where a doctor restored a man to life by massaging his heart after he had been dead for some hours. As it could not return from heaven or hell, where was that man's soul during those hours?

The patient was not really, but only apparently dead. His soul, therefore, was still united with his body. Normally speaking actual death does not occur until some hours after the heart has stopped beating. Death really and finally takes place when the soul has left the body; and no one maintains that the soul loses its association with the body the moment the heart stops beating. So long as any cells remain in a state of animation the soul can be present. For that reason the Catholic Church permits the anointing of the apparently dead up to two hours after the heart has stopped.

590. Lazarus at least, who had been brought back to life by Christ, was dead. If his soul had survived, why couldn't he tell us what things were like after death?

It is certain, of course, that Lazarus had really died, and that his soul had separated from his body. Then why couldn't he tell of his experiences? If we dealt with this question from the mere viewpoint of fact, we could say that there is no evidence that he could not have done so. However, it is not recorded that he ever did so. Personally I do not think that he had any conscious experiences to tell. God knew that the death of Lazarus was to be but for a few days, and that he was to be restored to life again. At once we see that his soul could not have encountered the fate of those whose term of probation in this life is definitely over. Some special provision had to be made for the soul of Lazarus. And I think it very probable that, just as the soul is inoperative as regards knowledge whilst still in a body under the influence of chloroform, so the soul of Lazarus, though separated from his body, was preserved in being, but with its normal operations suspended. Under such conditions Lazarus would simply know that he was restored to life, finding out from others how long he had been dead, four days.

591. Do departed souls retain memories of us, and know what is still going on in this world?

There is every probability that they retain memories of those whom they loved or met during their life on earth. But there is no real probability that they are aware of things which have occurred since their death, except insofar as God may choose to manifest such knowledge to them. The human soul secures its information concerning this world through the bodily senses—seeing, hearing, and touching things. Those senses are its normal means of contact with this earthly life. But when the soul leaves the body, it is separated from these sense-faculties, and therefore loses the normal means of contact with the life we still experience.

592. Does your Church allow belief in reincarnation?

Catholic dogmatic teaching absolutely excludes belief in the doctrine of reincarnation, or the transmigration of souls, with their consequent reappearance in this world in other bodies.

593. Is it not possible that Mussolini is Nero?

Not in the least.

594. Could not Henry VIII. have been Judas Iscariot?

No. Henry VIII. was Henry VIII., and no one else. And Judas was Judas. Under no circumstances could the one become the other. Nor could I imagine either wishing to be the other, even were it possible.

595. May not another Christ appear in some other form, or even be living in this world today?

No. Jesus Christ is "the same yesterday, today, and forever." He is the Eternal Son of God, who became man, was crucified, died, and was buried. He rose from the dead and ascended into heaven in His glorified human nature. There will be no further incarnations of the Son of God in this world; but He will appear in all His glory and majesty at the end of time to judge mankind. And He will appear in the one human nature He took from the Blessed Virgin Mary. He will never acknowledge any other human nature as His.

596. In the Apostles' Creed Christians profess belief "in the forgiveness of sins."

Sin is undoubtedly a fact in this world; and if the true religion be for men, it cannot overlook that fact. Religion cannot abandon the sinner to himself. It is there to do something for him, and chiefly to destroy sin. The word "sin" is from the Latin word "sons" meaning "guilty"; and he who is guilty of moral evil is a sinner. Such moral evil is an offense against God.

597. *No man can hurt God; and I am sure that people who do wrong have no thought of offending God.*

Inability to do actual harm to God personally does not mean innocence and irresponsibility. As a matter of fact, One whom we cannot hurt because of His greatness and majesty deserves the greater reverence. And one does offend God in His designs by opposing His will of perfection and order. Moral evil introduces discord and abominations into the harmony of God's work. You say that evil-doers do not intend this, and have no thought of offending God. It may be that sinners rarely think of this aspect. Some do. But the majority rather seek to have whatever they desire, and merely ignore God's will. They would prefer to be able to sin without offending God. But that is not the wish to avoid evil. It is merely to wish that evil were good. That, however, cannot be; and they deliberately choose evil, despite God's prohibition.

598. *Would you take literally Christ's words, "If thy right eye scandalize thee, pluck it out; for it is better that one of thy members should perish than that thy whole body be cast into hell"?*

Those words are certainly not meant to be taken literally, for such mutilation of self would be sinful; and one can avoid sin without having to do that. Christ was driving home the lesson that sin as such, and above all grave sin, is the greatest of all evils. Speaking to the Jews He used a mode of speech with which they were quite familiar. He meant: "The salvation of your soul is your chief work." He chose a metaphor from surgery which, to save the body, has at times to amputate a limb or remove an organ—in those days a most painful business. And He meant, "Be ready to endure any suffering or trial rather than sin. Even had you to pluck out your eye or cut off your limbs—a thing which will never be necessary—deliberate sin would still be the worse alternative."

599. *I heard a Catholic speak of two kinds of sin—mortal and venial. I couldn't believe my ears.*

There certainly are two kinds of sin, some of a very grave character called mortal sin; others of a less grave character called venial. Mortal sins rob the soul of grace, and forfeit one's union and friendship with God. The man who deliberately disobeys the known law of God in grave and serious matters sets himself up against God, turns away from Him, and renounces His friendship. By doing so he turns his back on his eternal destiny in favor of a futile and transitory pleasure or advantage. Venial sins do not have such a far-reaching effect; but they do render one less pleasing in God's sight. The man who respects God's will in serious matters, but who offends in smaller matters, does not forfeit God's friendship altogether; and, therefore, by retaining His friendship, he maintains the true direction of his life towards God. But he does stray from the direct path of the good; and for that he will need forgiveness, and have to undergo proportionate purification of soul.

600. *Evil cannot be a sin more or less; it is either a sin or it is not.*

Venial sin is a sin—not "more or less" a sin. But there can be sins of more or less gravity. Sin is a crime insofar as it is a violation of God's laws. Now God is not less just than men. And crimes against human laws are of more or less gravity. Thus, we have capital crimes and penal crimes. Some offenses against civil law are so venial that the highest penalty for them is a small fine. The Judge may not inflict more. Murder, however, is in a different category altogether. It is a capital or mortal sin against the law, and can merit deprivation of life itself. Your own sense of justice will tell you that these distinctions between crimes against state laws are justified. And the same principle must apply to crimes against God's laws.

Radio Replies—Volume II

Mortal sin puts one beyond the pale of God's friendship; venial sin does not do so, but it carries with it its just penalties.

601. I don't agree that there are big sins and little sins before God, as if He did not regard stealing a stamp as being just as much stealing as taking a hundred dollars!

It may be just as much stealing, but it is not stealing just as much—even in God's sight. We do not say that venial sins are little sins as if they were negligible. Though they are not so grave as mortal sins, Catholic doctrine insists that no sins, grave or less grave, are ever justified.

602. The Bible certainly gives no grounds for saying that there are two kinds of sins.

That is not so. Keep in mind that mortal sin cuts one off from God's grace and friendship, whilst venial sin does not, even though it renders the soul less pleasing in God's sight. Now the Book of Eccleciasticus, in warning us against sin, says, "He that contemneth small things shall fall little by little." XIX., I. That is, succeeding sins tend to become greater as the conscience is deadened. Proverbs XXIV., 16, tells us that even the just man falls often. In other words, whilst remaining just or justified by grace, he still has his small sins. Christ said that it would be more tolerable for Tyre and Sidon in the day of judgment than for Bethsaida, clearly indicating degrees in guilt. Matt. XI., 21. So, too, in Jn. XIX., 11, Christ said to Pilate, "He that hath delivered me to you hath the greater sin." We cannot say the "sin is sin," and there are no different kinds of gravity.

603. The principle is at fault. All theft is sin, and hideous in God's sight. One sin is as much a sin as another.

No one suggests that lesser sins are not sins; nor that any sin is pleasing to God. All sin is hateful to Him. But some sins are more hateful than others. You say that the principle behind this distinction is at fault. But take the principle that we owe obedience to the laws of the state. One who violates a traffic law violates the principle of obedience to law. So does the gangster who murders a fellow citizen. Will you say that one is just as much a violation of the law as the other, and hang them both? Or if we take simply theft, can you see no difference between the child who steals a cake from the cupboard and the cold-blooded miser who robs a widow of her lifesavings?

604. If there are two kinds of sins, how do you distinguish one kind from another?

By the very nature of the thing forbidden; by the necessity of particular virtues to which particular vices are opposed; and also by the extent of damage done to others where justice is concerned. For example, according to the nature of the thing forbidden, some sins are always mortal, as direct hatred of God, deliberate blasphemy, murder, adultery, etc. When measured by the necessity of virtue, a deliberate denial of one's faith is a mortal sin because it implicitly denies God. Sins against justice are measured by the seriousness of the injury done to others. The more grave the injury the graver the sin. In addition to these factors, circumstances must be taken into account, as the degree of knowledge possessed by the person offending; the degree of advertence to the law before breaking it; the extent of really malicious will entering into the evil conduct.

605. Do all Catholics understand these things?

Yes. In particular cases difficulties can arise, of course. But in all doubts the Catholic knows that he has but to submit his case to the priest who is well trained in moral theology, and the priest will tell him what is lawful or not lawful;

and what is a grave violation of the law, or a venial offense. It is because they lack such help and training that non-Catholics are so confused in this matter. Where they would consult a civil lawyer in difficulties of civil law, they consult no one as to whether their conduct is within the law of God or not, and as to the gravity of that law. So they speak of one sin being just as much a sin as another, making no allowance for degrees of guilt. If such ideas were transferred from moral disease to physical disease, one would have to say: "One disease is just as much a disease as another. There are no mortal diseases as cancer and consumption, and lesser diseases as measles and mumps. The principle is the same—all diseases are opposed to the law of physical health just as all sins are opposed to the law of spiritual health." These analogies from civil law with its varying degrees of guilt, and from physical diseases with the variations in intensity, show how inadequate are your ideas of sin.

606. Does a Catholic who commits mortal sin still belong to your Church?

Yes; but as a dead member. He receives no blood from the heart of the Church, which is Divine Love. He does not obey the directing inspiration of the Church, which is the spirit of Christ. He has no right to the Eucharist, which is the bread of life, and which should be nourishing the life he lacks. Though he still associates with living members, and kneels side by side with them in the Church he attends, he is like a paralyzed limb. He has cut himself off from communion with the Church from within. And it is his duty to recover the life of grace by Confession and repentance, and thus become a living member of the Church once more.

607. Besides distinguishing between mortal sin and venial sin, you also make a distinction between original sin and actual sin?

Yes. Original sin is the inherited guilt by which we participate in the first sin committed by Adam as representative of the whole human race. Actual sins are all sins subsequent to that first sin, whether in itself or in its derivation.

608. Was the original sin a mortal sin?

Yes; that is evident from the drastic consequences.

609. You maintain that the doctrine of the fall and that of the atonement are interdependent?

That is so.

610. Since the sin of Adam was necessary to produce the atonement, why did God blame Adam?

The sin of our first parents did not produce the atonement. God produced the atonement in order to repair the sin of our parents and of all subsequent generations. And as the sin of our first parents was not necessary, but was their own morally evil choice, God rightly blamed them.

611. Were not our first parents somewhat harshly treated, to say nothing of subsequent generations?

No one would deny the severity of the treatment. And that should at least impress upon us how grave an evil in God's sight must be the moral disease called sin. But, whilst not called upon to deny the severity of the treatment, I do deny that God has treated the human race unjustly. It has deserved far more suffering than it has received, and has not deserved the great blessings God has designed to bestow upon it.

612. In making man, why did not God make a better job of it, if He did not want man to fall into sin?

A better job could not be made of it, in view of what God wanted man to be. God's will, of course, is the ultimate criterion of the qualities and perfections to be bestowed upon His various creatures. A cabbage has not the right to complain that it is not a horse; a dog has no right to complain that it is not a man. We cannot say that God would have made a better job of a cabbage had He made it a cat instead. Since He wanted to make a cabbage, it must be content to be a cabbage. Had God wanted to make a cat, and only a cabbage resulted from His work, there might be some room to complain that a better job might have been made of it. So, in the case of a human being, endowed with intelligence and free will.

Man was as perfect as possible in accordance with God's plan for him. But the gift of free will, of course, left man's destiny in his own keeping; and that included the possibility of an evil moral choice. Had that possibility not been present, man would not have had the honor and dignity of a free being; and no better job would have been made of man by depriving him of this honor and dignity.

613. *If God wanted man to attain heaven, could He not have placed man there in the first place?*

That would not have been in keeping with God's plan that man's destiny should be in his own hands. By his nature, man is made for earth rather than for heaven, and could have no natural right to be in heaven. God gave him all that his nature could rightly demand. In addition, God offered freely to man the prospect of an eternal supernatural happiness in heaven, provided man made a correct use of his mind and will by obedience to God's law. And He offered the help of Divine Grace for this purpose. Far from complaining that God did not do more for them, men should be grateful that He should have done so much in their favor.

614. *The whole idea of the Catholic dogma concerning the fall of man and its patching up by the redemption implies folly in God, and merciless injustice.*

If you think so, you cannot have a right apprehension of Catholic dogma.

615. *God gave man a very weak will and provided a very strong devil to test it.*

That is not true. If you wish to attack a teaching of any religion, you must first correctly state that teaching. That man's will was "very weak" and the devil "very strong" is your own invention. Again, it is opposed to Catholic teaching that God provided any devil at all. The devil, as evil, was not the work of God. An objection based on a wrong statement of Christian doctrine requires no answer save an indication that it is an effort to refute what the Christian religion does not teach.

616. *Before creating Adam, God knew that he would fall.*

That is true. But that was not the only thing that God knew. He knew that Adam would not be compelled to fall; and He knew also that, granted sin, side by side with His justice, His mercy would so provide for mankind that good would result from the evil; so much so that it would be infinitely better for mankind to have been created, and to fall from grace, than not to have been created at all.

617. *Then God drove Adam out of the comparative safety of the Garden of Eden into a world abounding in pitfalls and dangers.*

That is not a correct presentation of the case. Adam forfeited graces and privileges which were above the normal requirements of human nature, and never really due to man at all. He went from a privileged state to an unprivileged state.

618. *When our first parents fell victims to an enemy far stronger than themselves, true mercy would have forgiven them.*

Firstly, Adam did not fall a victim to an enemy far stronger than himself. We are dealing with sin, and sin is an evil choice of a free will. Now, even as God

Himself would not coerce the will of Adam in favor of fidelity, so the devil could not coerce the will of Adam in favor of sin. He might tempt, suggest, allure; but he could not touch the will of Adam or Eve. Our first parents remained in control of their own destinies, and they were fully responsible for their choice. Secondly, mercy did grant ultimate forgiveness to them, for Scripture tells us that God drew them from their sin. (Wisd. X., 2.) But mercy itself demanded that this should be only after they had learned humility from consequent miseries. Physical sufferings are secondary when compared with wreckage of character. And if such sufferings contribute to the restoration of character they are not an unmitigated evil. Emotional pity and sentiment often lead human beings to mistake weakness for mercy. Parents who say they are too merciful to punish wrongdoing in their children are not really merciful to their children at all. They are too weak to do their duty; and how cruel they have really been is evident from the miserable and spoiled characters of those children throughout all their later years. There is something in being "cruel in order to be kind"; and God knows what is best for the welfare of human souls, whatever their circumstances.

619. *True justice would have weakened the enemy to prevent further occurrence of such a catastrophe.*

Your notion of weakening the enemy is based on the wrong idea that the devil had or has some compelling power over the human will, or that the human will is fully guilty where there may be present a diminished responsibility. In reality, justice does not demand the removal of the sources of temptation. Man's destiny is in his own keeping, and he must attain that destiny by the service of God and the practice of virtue. But there could be no just reward for a service of God which costs us nothing; and virtue is exercised in the midst of temptation. There is no particular virtue in being good when there is no inducement to be otherwise. It was quite just to leave us the opportunity of practicing true virtue in the midst of temptation; and it was merciful that forgiveness should be available for failures of which we repent.

620. *Do you mean that we are all born in a guilty state before God?*

We all commence our earthly existence without that life of Grace which would have been ours had Adam not sinned. Spiritual death is the state of every soul as individuals are born into this world. For we are all born children of wrath, as St. Paul says in Eph. II., 3. In other words, we are all born in a state of original or inherited sin.

621. *Why did God give men their freedom, when He knew beforehand that so many would misuse it and be lost for eternity?*

Because He knew that men need not sin; and that His knowledge of what would eventuate did not cause them to sin. Also, included in His knowledge of the fall of man was His knowledge of the Incarnation of His own Son by whose redemptive merits every single sinner from the time of Adam would have a true opportunity of salvation from eternal loss. Finally, God knew that, however many people do lose their souls, viewing creation as a whole and relatively to human beings, the sum total of good will far outweigh the sum total of evil. It is a mistake to concentrate on the thought of individuals who are lost. God had not to choose between creating only those who are lost, and not creating at all. He had to choose between not creating, and creating a whole human race, not one of whom need go to hell, and of which, if some do lose their souls, multitudes do not. Why should those who save their souls be deprived of eternal happiness because others, who need not do so, choose to sin and to die without repenting?

TEACHING OF JESUS

622. *Is it Catholic dogma that, in order to accomplish mankind's redemption, God became man for thirty-three years?*

It is Catholic dogma that God the Son, the Second Person of the Holy Trinity, became man in order to redeem us; and from the moment of His Incarnation, He retains both His Divinity and His assumed humanity for all eternity. His death meant the separation temporarily of His human soul from His earthly body, but not the separation of either His soul or His body from its union with His Divinity. In the resurrection, His human soul and body were reunited; and having risen from the grave, Christ ascended body and soul into heaven, there to continue for eternity in His glorified humanity. In His human nature, of course, God the Son took the name of Jesus Christ.

623. *Why should the Son of God have to come to earth to save sinners? Could they not have been saved by believing in God only?*

Under no conditions could any sinner be saved by believing in God only. Mere belief will save no one. The sinner would at least have to repent of his sins. But even so, your question will come—why could not sinners be saved by belief and repentance, without the necessity of the Incarnation? The answer is that they could have been saved in that way had God decided on that plan of salvation. But God did not. He decided to send His own Son for our redemption, and that because it was the better thing from every point of view. He thus manifested in a special way how greatly He loved us. He made things easier for us merely human beings who depend so much on visible manifestations. Faith in an unseen God is not so easy as faith in a God who has been in our midst, proving His power and His mercy in a way which human history can record. Our hopes are immeasurably lifted and stimulated, for man need not despair of attaining to God when God is willing to stoop to man's own level. And justice is safeguarded when reparation for our sins is made to God in a human nature drawn from a race which had offended God in the first place.

624. *I have not been able to find any new teaching on ethics or morals given by Jesus.*

He gave much new teaching on ethics and morals, both in matter and spirit. For example, His teachings on poverty, humility, simplicity, virginity, marriage, love of one's neighbor, supernatural motives of conduct, and the ordaining of moral conduct to spiritual as opposed to temporal ends—these, and much else, were new.

625. *Is there a single moral aphorism attributed to Jesus which cannot be paralleled in Rabbinical literature?*

Yes. Jesus quoted Rabbinical standards when He said, "You have heard that it hath been said: Thou shalt love thy neighbor and hate thy enemy. But I say to you: Love your enemies; do good to them that hate you; and pray for them that persecute and calumniate you." Matt. V., 43-44. It is true that much of the moral teaching of Christ finds a counterpart in the Rabbinical writings. The teachings of Jesus included those of natural morality and of the Old Testament. Rabbinical literature, therefore, had but to set down the ethical ideals of the natural moral law, or of their own religious precepts, and they could not but record much that Jesus would teach. But Jesus instilled a far greater significance into common teachings, and laid quite a new emphasis upon them. Moreover, He went beyond them again and again, and came into conflict with the Pharisees repeatedly because He did so.

626. *Most of the recorded sayings of Jesus can be paralleled verbally in the Rabbinical writings, and even the Golden Rule is there.*

Merely verbal and external similarity of expression means little. Where the moral law is concerned, two things have to be considered—the statement of the law, and the sense in which it is interpreted. Now, in comparison with the ethical teachings of Jesus, Rabbinical literature gives a most inadequate statement, and fails almost entirely to rise to the level attained by Christ. As for the Golden Rule, it cannot be said that the form in which Christ taught it was already familiar to the Rabbinical writers. In its negative form the saying is found in both Jewish and pagan sources before the Christian era; i. e., "Do not do to another what you would not wish him to do to you." Yet even in this negative form, no one insisted upon it, giving it the urgency imposed upon it by Christ. But when we leave the negative form, and turn to the positive form, "Do to others as you would have them do to you," we are given a distinct advance upon other teachings, and carried forward to the region of an all-embracing charity in the order of faith and divine grace. This is beyond the order of natural ethics; and no man can fulfill it without an interior power impelling him to put it into practice.

627. *Will any scholar admit your verdict?*

Undoubtedly. I have based it on the study of expert writers on the subject. Let me quote one unimpeachable authority, the Jewish scholar, Joseph Klausner, who published a "Life of Jesus of Nazareth" in Hebrew in 1922. An English translation of this book was published by Danby, of London, in 1925. Klausner admits that the moral teaching of Jesus transcends that of any other master. Here are his words: "Jesus was a wandering preacher, differing from others in certain aspects, such as His emphasis on the moral commandments to the exclusion of formalism, in the original and direct nature of His teaching, and the miraculous element of His mission. He was not a mere teacher among the teachers of His day; His originality was incomparable; and as a moralist and as a spiritual leader no man in Israel has ever approached Him. But considered from the Jewish standpoint Jesus is not, and cannot be the Messiah; the Kingdom of Heaven and the days of the Messiah have not yet come. But Jesus still remains, even for the Jews, a moralist without a peer; and the moral teaching contained in the Gospel of Jesus, if it is separated from the rest, is one of the most glorious jewels in the literature of Israel throughout the ages."

628. *Isn't it just the advance of years that makes for a man's greatness such as Jesus Christ?*

No. Far more often the advance of years makes for a man's complete disappearance from history and the memory of man. A man has to be of striking personality and accomplishments before his contemporaries or posterity will magnify him and enshrine him in the gallery of fame. Where religion is concerned, I admit that there is always the tendency to a growing idealization of a striking personality, often with the creation of an almost completely unhistorical tradition concerning him. But the check on that is historical research. And research has shown that Christ was just as we know Him to be. The Gospels were written by eyewitnesses; and their integrity is certain.

629. *Look at Mahomet, Buddha, and Confucius, each with his thousands of worshippers.*

Not one of these is worshipped as Christ is worshipped. Not one, whether in personal character, or in teaching, or in work, accomplished anything inexplicable by ordinary human and natural powers. Nor will the records of any of them stand intensive critical research. A mass of legends and myths has grown up around them. That they have thousands of followers is but natural. Men are incurably religious; and, if unaware of the true religion, they will grasp at some substitute religion offered by almost any dominant personality, provided it does not demand too much self-denial.

630. *Does it matter whether Christ was God, or merely the Divine Son of God?*

What do you mean by the distinction you make? If I were to say, "So-and-so is not a man, but merely the human son of a man," I am sure you would ask me to explain myself more clearly. A son is one who is generated in the same nature as his father. A human father has a son possessing human nature also. And if Christ is the Divine Son of God, He possesses the Divine Nature also, and is God. The only alternative is that He is not the Divine Son of God, but merely a human creature made by God on the same level with other human beings.

631. *I cannot accept more than that Christ was the Divine Son of God.*

You really mean that you do not believe Christ to be God at all. But that is a complete denial of the Christian Faith, for when St. Thomas the Apostle addressed Christ as "My Lord and my God" he would have been quite mistaken, and Christ's acceptance of such a tribute would have been blasphemous.

632. *What more can be demanded than the acceptance of the Divine Sonship of Jesus Christ?*

The expression "Divine Sonship" can be ambiguous. It is necessary to accept the Deity of the Person of Christ without any half measures. Jesus is God in virtue of His Divine Nature possessed in union with and equally with the Father and the Holy Spirit. The expression "Divine Sonship" can be ambiguous because both words have been employed by men with various grades of meaning. People speak of a "divine poet," or of a "divinely beautiful character." A Protestant friend once told me that he believed in the divinity of Christ, but not that He is God. Now when we Catholics use the word "Divine" of Christ, we mean absolutely that He is God. Again, the word "Sonship" can be ambiguous. We sometimes speak of our being the children of God by creation. At other times we may speak of sonship by adoption as opposed to actual generation. Or one may simply mean sonship by a mutual paternal and filial affection. But none of these senses means what we intend by the "Divine Sonship" of Jesus. We mean by that expression that the Person of Jesus is the Second Person of the Holy Trinity, eternally generated by the Father in one and the same Divine Nature, equal with the Father and the Holy Spirit in all things, infinitely perfect, and as truly God as the Father Himself. Jesus is not only the Son of God. He is God the Son.

633. *Christ often spoke of "My Father in heaven." He would not do that if He was God.*

Precisely because He shared in the same Divine Nature as His heavenly Father of Whom He was begotten from all eternity long before He appeared on this earth in human form, that is just as one would expect Him to speak.

634. *In Matt. XXIII., 9-10, He says, "Call none your father upon earth, for one is your Father who is in heaven. Neither be ye called masters, for one is your master, Christ."*

That does not prove that Christ is not God. In the first part of this text He is teaching His listeners that no earthly parental authority can supplant the authority of God. In reference to Himself, however, He did not hesitate to say, "I and the Father are one." And even whilst saying that God alone is the supreme Father and Master, He puts Himself on the same level as God by saying, "One is your Master, Christ." If Christ were not God, He should have said, "One is your Master—God."

635. *In Matt. XXIV., 36, He says, "Of that day and hour no one knoweth, no, not the angels of heaven, but the Father alone."*

Christ was there speaking in virtue of His assumed human nature. The knowledge was proper to Him as God, but not proper to Him as man. He did not know

God's moment in virtue of the human nature in which He had come to teach mankind, and He merely brought out the fact that this particular piece of information was not part of the message He had to reveal to men. Briefly, it was but a way of saying, "That is God's secret." The text in no way disproves the identity of our Lord's Divine Nature with that of the Father.

636. Christ did say, "Why callest thou Me good? One only is good—God."

Christ said much else also. Nor do these words imply that Christ is not God. He would not contradict Himself. He knew, however, that those around Him saw only His human nature or created humanity, and that they had not yet attained the faith to see beyond merely human appearances to His Divinity. And He once more tried to lift their thoughts to God as the Source of all created goodness. It was a warning that we must not stop at any created goodness which is but a reflection of the infinite goodness of God, and meant to lead us to Him. On another occasion, when Philip said to Him, "Lord, show us the Father," Christ rebuked him also for not rising above thoughts of His merely human characteristics, and said, "Philip, he who sees me sees the Father also. Do you not believe that I am in the Father, and the Father in me?" Jn. XIV., 8-11.

637. Christ said, "The Father is greater than I." Jn. XIV., 28.

The Eternal Son of God, after the Incarnation, possessed two natures, the uncreated Divine Nature, and the created human nature born of the Virgin Mary. When He said, "I and the Father are one," He referred to His Divine Nature. When He said, "The Father is greater than I," He referred to the created visible human nature which appeared before the eyes of those to whom He was speaking.

638. When Christ said, "I and the Father are one," He meant no more than in purpose and desire.

The unity prevailing between Himself and His Father, of which Christ spoke, was more than a merely moral union of purpose and desire. It was a unity in one and the same Divine Nature. It was on the occasion of these words that the Jews declared themselves determined to stone Him because, as they said, "Being a man, thou makest thyself God." They knew quite well that Jesus was claiming much more than a merely moral union with God by purpose and desire. Had Christ merely intended that, they would not have accused Him of blasphemy; nor would they have wanted to stone Him to death.

639. Later on Christ prayed that His disciples would be one with Himself as He and His Father were one. Were His disciples one with Him in any other sense than by accord?

Yes. They were one with Him by the reality called grace which incorporated them all in one and the same Christ by a physical even though spiritual union; He the vine; they the branches. At the same time, in the words you quote, Christ was stressing the necessity of complete unity, not the nature of that unity, which necessarily differs in God from that possible to man. Christ prayed that His disciples would be one in the way possible to them, as He and His Father were one in the way proper to God.

640. He said, "I came to do the will of My Father." Also, "The words I speak are not mine, but His that sent Me." Also, "Of Myself I can do nothing; but if you ask the Father anything in My name He will give it to you."

All those expressions were proper to Christ in His mission on earth and in virtue of the created human nature in which He fulfilled that mission. They also suppose the distinction between the Eternal Father, Son, and Holy Ghost, taught by

Catholic theology. But they do not exclude Christ's participation in the Divine Nature, nor His claim to be God.

641. On the Cross Jesus cried, "My God, My God, why hast Thou forsaken Me?"

That is true. Since mankind had forsaken God by sin, it was but just that mankind should be forsaken by God. But the Eternal Son of God took a human nature in which to expiate man's sin. On the Cross, He allowed that human nature to experience the bitter sense of dereliction by God. Hence the cry. But such an experience in His human nature has no bearing at all upon the question of His identity in the Divine Nature with the Father and the Holy Spirit.

642. Would God forsake His own Son?

Not in the sense you have in mind. But, since men deserve to be forsaken by God, then if the Eternal Son of God takes to Himself a human nature in which to expiate sin, it is not surprising that in that human nature He should experience an overwhelming sense of that dereliction by God which sin deserves. And that sense of dereliction in His human soul was more than enough to justify the momentary expression, "My God, My God, why hast Thou forsaken me?" That this sense of dereliction, though so intense, was but a transitory sword of anguish is evident from the confidence in our Lord's later words, "Father, into Thy hands I commend my spirit."

643. If Christ was God the cry would mean, "Myself, Myself, why hast Thou forsaken Myself?" Rather absurd!

The cry from the lips of Christ expressed that sense of abandonment which He willed to experience in His human nature only. There could be no question of abandonment insofar as He shared in the Divine Nature with the Father, the first Person of the Most Holy Trinity. But in His human nature He could certainly undergo the experience of the pain and misery and sense of dereliction which abandonment by God will involve for those people who die estranged from their Maker. And that temporary experience was quite properly expressed from the human point of view by the cry, "My God, My God, why hast Thou forsaken me."

644. If we take Jesus merely as a perfect man, what do we lose?

I knew it would come to that in the end. Jesus is to be merely a man, and not Divine at all! And you ask what do we lose by such a belief? We lose our Christian religion. We lose the Faith of the ages. We lose all hope of ever being redeemed by Christ, for if He be not God His work was in vain. We lose the conviction that "God so loved the world as to give His only-begotten Son." We lose the right to call ourselves Christians any longer. We join the rationalists and other enemies of Christ, and brand ourselves as guilty of false pretenses so often as we lay claim to the Christian name.

645. If Jesus Christ was in mortality, whilst the other Divine Persons remained in the celestial sphere, what difference was there between Jesus and an ordinary man?

We cannot say that, when the Second Divine Person became man, the other Divine Persons remained in the celestial sphere. There can be no question of the Second Divine Person being somewhere whilst the other Divine Persons are elsewhere. In fact, since the three Divine Persons in the one Divine Nature constitute God, then, because God is everywhere, the three Divine Persons must be simultaneously everywhere. The difference between Jesus and an ordinary man is this: An ordinary man is a created personality in one created human nature. Jesus is an uncreated personality in two natures, one Eternal and Divine, the other created and human, existing only from the moment of its conception in time. Take yourself. You are an ordinary man. You are an entirely created personality, consisting of a material body and an intelligent spiritual soul. That body and soul make "you," rejoicing in an independent and responsible existence. Beyond your body and soul, the principles of your created being, "you" would not exist. Nor did "you" exist prior to the creation of your soul which, together with your body, constitutes "you." Now Jesus vastly differs from this. You are an entirely created personality. The personality of Jesus is uncreated. The human body and soul of Jesus, though created, never had an independent and responsible existence. The Second Person of the Trinity took that body and soul to Himself in personal union, so that both body and soul were ever dependent upon Him and He was responsible for all that resulted from His activities in them. Apart from your body and soul there would be no "you." "You" did not exist prior to their production. But the Person manifested to us in Jesus did exist before the Incarnation. For Jesus is the name given to a unique and Divine Personality, pre-existing eternally as God, yet possessing also from the moment of the Incarnation a created human nature without in any way ceasing to retain His eternal participation in the Divine Nature. Surely, then, there is a vast difference between Jesus and an ordinary man.

646. *If God is everywhere, He must fill every man even as He filled Jesus. What was the difference between the relationship of Jesus to God, and that of other men? God must be part of all.*

It does not follow that, because God is everywhere, He must be part of man's being. Man's being is finite and created. The Infinite and Uncreated God could not be a component part of created finite being. God and man are in two totally different orders of being, and their co-existence in the same place or space could not make them part of each other. As a matter of fact, God is not even conditioned by space as are creatures. But even in the natural and physical order, thought and brain co-exist in a human head without thought becoming part of the brain. The brain belongs to the material order; thought to the spiritual order. If thought were part of the brain, the brain would increase or diminish as thought increased or diminished. But it does not. And just as thought can co-exist in one's head with a material brain without becoming a component part of that brain, so God's existence everywhere does not make Him a part of man's being. What then was the difference between the relationship of Jesus to God, and that of ordinary men? It cannot consist in any aspect of God's omnipresence, since the human nature assumed by the Second Person existed as much within the immensity and omnipresence of God as you do. It must consist in something over and above that relationship to the omnipresence of God; in something proper to Jesus, and not possessed by any other human being. What was it? It was this: Apart from the Divine Attribute of omnipresence possessed by the Divine Nature, the Second Person of the Holy Trinity entered into possession of, and controlled the human nature born of Mary, so that this human nature never became a created human personality as you or I, but remained the created instrument of a Divine Personality. Thus, within the omnipresence of God, which no created being can escape, a new bond is established between the human nature of Christ and God, a bond which does not exist in the case of any other human nature. It is a personal bond, enabling the one Person of the Eternal Son to say equally, "I am God," or "I am man," according to His possession of both a Divine and a human nature. Other human beings can never say, "I am God." They are restricted to the expression, "I am a man." But the human nature of Christ was gripped into a bond of personal union with the eternal and Divine Son who possessed and controlled it, making it integral to His one Personality for the purposes of our redemption in a nature drawn from that human race which was to be redeemed.

647. Did Christ's death on the Cross have to be?

It had to be by what is known as a conditional necessity. God could have exercised His mercy only, and condoned our sins without exacting expiation on the part of the human race. But if God wished to satisfy the claims of justice even whilst exercising His mercy, then the Incarnation and death of Christ were necessary. The Son of God freely chose to offer Himself in sacrifice, and that sacrifice was the logical necessity consequent upon His choice. He need not have chosen to die, and to die in such a way; but having chosen to do so, the fact necessarily followed.

648. Had no one attempted to crucify Christ, what would have become of our salvation?

I do not know. Nor does anyone else save God alone. In dealing with God's work for the salvation of souls, our knowledge is limited to what He has revealed and actually accomplished. It is impossible to say what would have been done by God if what has happened did not happen. We must take things as they are, and be content to let curious speculations go unanswered.

649. If it was ordained that Christ should die, why does any blame attach to those who put Him to death?

Just as the sins of mankind in general from which Christ came to redeem us were not willed by God, so the evil dispositions of those who actually put Christ to death were not willed by God. Thus, the treachery of Judas, the injustice of Pilate, the hatred and malice of the Jews—these things were evil and opposed to God's will. And those guilty of such evil dispositions were blameworthy before God. You must not think of God as planning that Christ should die, and then arranging that some men will be evil enough to kill Him. Where we think one thing after another, God sees all things simultaneously. He sent His Son to a world which He knew was wicked, and needed redeeming; and into the midst of men who would, as a matter of fact, be evil enough at heart to condemn Him to death. But the evil was the fault of men, not of God. God did not ordain, nor cause the evil; but he permitted it to be the death of His Son who had undertaken to expiate it.

650. If the Second Divine Person suffered only in His human nature, how was the atonement made by God? Catholic doctrine makes it a purely human sacrifice.

The sacrifice of Calvary was not a purely human sacrifice. The atonement was made by God because the Person, whose human nature was nailed to the cross, was God. The Person, and not the nature under the control of that Person, is the terminus of attribution. If I commit murder, I do it. It's no use saying, "My hand did it." The human nature which was nailed to the cross was His who was and is the Second Person of the Holy Trinity. And the sacrifice, though directly involving the death of the human nature, derived its dignity from the Person to whom it belonged. It was, therefore, an atonement of infinite value derived from the infinite dignity of the Second Person of the Holy Trinity. One may or may not agree with our explanation; but in no sense can one say that on this explanation a purely human sacrifice took place on Calvary. That could follow only if we admitted that Jesus was a purely and merely human person. That we have never admitted.

651. You hold that Christ died to save sinners.

The Catholic doctrine says that Christ died for the purpose of saving sinners. But note this: Christ did not die to save sinners unconditionally, as if His death means that all sinners are necessarily saved. His death provides salvation for all who are willing to comply with the conditions laid down by Himself.

652. One clergyman told me that Christ died for me personally.

That is true. But Christ did not die to force salvation upon anybody. He did die to offer the means of salvation to all mankind, and, therefore, to every single member of the human race. In that sense His death will avail for you personally, if you personally comply with the conditions prescribed by Christ. It is as if you personally were in debt, and I lodged sufficient money in the bank to discharge that debt, giving you a checkbook to draw upon the money. I could truly say that I had done enough to save you from beggary. But if you refused to put your name to a single check, and would not walk a step towards the bank, despising my arrangements, you would not be saved from beggary. That would be your own fault, however, and no proof that my provision for you was not efficacious in itself. Christ did not die for sinners so that they could go on being sinners, yet be sure of salvation in spite of themselves.

653. Can you tell me from what He saved sinners?

People who are now dead, who were sinners during life, but who repented of their sins, and did their best to comply with the conditions imposed by Christ, have been saved by Him from hell. People who are still living have not yet been saved by Christ. He has paid the price necessary for their salvation, if they choose to avail themselves of it. Those who are actually sinners in grave matters are not availing themselves of it at present; and if they die without changing their dispositions they will not be saved at all. Those sinners who do abandon their sins, repenting of them, and die in a state of such repentance, appealing to Christ for salvation, will be saved by Him—from hell.

654. Did Christ die to save sinners from death in the ordinary sense of the word, or from hell?

He did not die to save sinners or anyone from death in the ordinary physical sense of the word. Even those who will be saved and who have been saved, were not intended to be freed from the necessity of death as the termination of this earthly life. Their salvation is from a future and eternal hell—that living death of all man's hopes and aspirations for happiness.

655. If I do not escape hell, does the atonement apply to me?

It will not be applied to you. But the fact will remain true for all eternity that Christ did do His part to atone for your sins, and the privilege of salvation was possible for you. The atonement was there, but you did not avail yourself of it.

656. My reason abhors the thought that another should suffer for my shortcomings.

One who has no faith in Christ, as Christ really was and is, could alone speak like that. If Christ be reduced to the merely human level, and emptied of His Divinity, then it becomes a question of merely man and man; and we all admit that, where man and man are concerned, no mere man could satisfy for the sins of another man; and that he who sins should do so, if it be possible to him. But in reality, no mere man can satisfy adequately for sin against God, however well able he may be to repair injuries against his fellow creatures. And only the true Christian doctrine solves the problem of reparation of sin against God.

657. We would be base and cowardly, knowingly to allow the existence of such a position.

We have no choice in the matter. For it is an accomplished fact that Christ died for the redemption of mankind. The only choice left to us is rejection of Christ's sacrifice, or acceptance of His redeeming work. He who has no faith in

God's revelation and no sense of sin or real understanding of what sin means will reject it.

658. *Such a doctrine does not strengthen, but weakens the Christian religion.*

You would not say that, did you have a right idea of the doctrine. Try to grasp the position. The gravity of an offense is intensified by the worth of the person offended. Precisely because one's own mother has a special claim upon the respect and reverence of her child, ill-treatment of her is worse than that of another. But sin is against the infinite dignity and majesty and authority of God. No mere creature could make adequate atonement or reparation to the Creator for such an offense. Yet since human nature gave such offense, one in a human nature should make reparation. So the Eternal Son of God became man. Because of His Divinity He could make adequate reparation; because of His humanity, He could make it in our name. Man did not love God enough to keep God's law, but broke that law and became worthy of death. Why should God preserve man in life only that man might offend him? So Christ endured death, expiating our sinful pleasures by His sufferings, and compensating for our own lack of love by the immense love in His human heart for God. And in order that this might not be just one isolated individual suffering for another, even as He blended Himself with our humanity in the Incarnation, so He blends us with Himself by grace. He is the Head and we are the members; and Head and members are one. So Christ sacrificed Himself, making those for whom He did so one with Himself. By this very union of love between Himself and us Christ could say to His Father, "Father, what I offer, they offer; and the love you have for me will be your love for them also." Thus God "so loved the world as to give His only-begotten Son." That Son, by shedding His blood for us, atoned for our sins, exemplifying His own words, "Greater love no man has than that he should lay down his life for his friend." Jn. XV., 13. One who sees no spiritual significance in this does not understand ordinary gratitude which cries, "I'll never forget what you have done for me this day; never can I thank you enough; and if ever I can render you a service ask it of me." It is this doctrine of Christ's death on the Cross for us, of His vicarious death, that the Saints found their greatest inspiration, even as St. Paul, who said, "I live in the faith of the Son of God who loved me and delivered Himself for me." Gal. II., 20.

659. *You have said that after His death, Christ resumed the life He sacrificed on the cross.*

Catholics believe that. And the man who rejects it must shut his eyes to the historical evidence available.

660. *Such a statement is due to your confusion as to the nature of factual proof.*

That is not so. Factual proof may be either by personal experimental knowledge, or by the evidence of history. If I say that historically a man must shut his eyes to the evidence, or believe that the Battle of Waterloo took place, you cannot say that I am blind to the nature of factual proof.

661. *Of course you may possess evidence other than that of the Gospels: evidence which leaves no shadow of doubt as to the resurrection being a fact.*

The Gospels and St. Paul's Epistles constitute five independent historical documents which leave no shadow of doubt. Their being bound in one volume does not affect their independence of each other. You begin by rejecting the resurrection on the score that you will not believe in what seems to you so incredible a thing. You doubt the Gospels precisely because they record what you deem incredible.

Did I produce any other documents recording the resurrection, you would have the same reason for doubting their reliability as you make your excuse for denying the reliability of the Gospels! It is not reasonable to refuse to believe unless I can produce evidence other than that contained in the documents which contain the evidence. If I produce five documents, instead of refusing to believe until I can produce more documents, your duty is to disprove the historical value of the five documents produced. Merely to ignore them is to shut one's eyes to the evidence.

662. *The only unquestionable fact is that certain contemporaries of Christ have given accounts of the resurrection which may or may not be sincere; or which, if sincere, may or may not be mistaken.*

You do not doubt, therefore, that the accounts were written by contemporaries of Christ. You base your doubts on the possibility of the writers being insincere; or, granted their sincerity, on the possibility of their being mistaken. Now the possibility that they were insincere has long been abandoned as quite unreasonable by even the bitterest enemies of Christianity. Firstly, it would be so pointless to conspire to impose on the world a religion in which the Apostles themselves did not believe. They had nothing to gain. Men do not break with all their friends, and invite persecution and death, for a lie which they know to be a lie. Nor were the cowardly Apostles rendered suddenly courageous by a conviction they knew to be unfounded. If they were liars, they were not conscious liars. They were sincere. That leaves your second possibility. Were they mistaken? That supposes them to have been deranged, and suffering from some strange hallucination. But that is impossible. It is so evident that they were not expecting Christ to rise. Their tendency was to unbelief, not to belief. And also, there were too many witnesses for them all to be subject to precisely the same hallucination. Nor is it reasonable to admit their sanity on things you are willing to accept, and arbitrarily declare them insane whenever you do not happen to like what they have to say. To make your likes and dislikes the test of credibility is prejudice—not reason.

663. *Before such an event is accepted as historical, it must satisfy the strictest tests imposed by the laws of evidence.*

Quite so. And the historical evidence for the resurrection is better than that for the greater number of events of those times accepted as historical by scholarly men. The only reasons you have advanced against the value of the evidence are suggestions that the writers were either liars or insane. And neither suggestion is reasonable.

664. *We are too inclined to take someone else's word for things; i.e., to depart from the strict laws of evidence.*

All historical evidence consists in the acceptance of the recorded word of others. Such acceptance is not a departure from the strict laws of historical evidence, provided we make sure that the documents are authentic, that there are sufficient witnesses to preclude the possibility of derangement, and that the witnesses were men of unimpeachable honesty.

665. *Unless evidence as disinterested as an entry in a birth register were forthcoming, one must hold that no real proof exists.*

That is foolish. The fact that an account of an event has been written voluntarily, and not at the instigation of State officials, cannot invalidate the account. We cannot reject history merely because the authors were interested enough to want to write it. I admit that, when extraordinary events are recorded, we must inquire more carefully into the nature of the interest prompting the writers. In the case of the Gospels, there is no interest other than the desire to record the truth.

666. *Even in an official record the chances of faked entry and human error would have to be considered.*

In the case of the Gospel and Pauline accounts of the resurrection they have been considered, and with a thoroughness with which no one who is familiar with the subject could quarrel. The chances of faked entry are excluded by the very independence of the records. And that human error is responsible for the narration of the event is impossible.

667. *Catholics may think it worth their while to believe it, but they must not therefore pretend that a proof exists.*

They do not pretend that a proof exists. They say that the historical proofs of the resurrection as a fact render its denial a violation of reason. It is the man who does not want to believe who pretends that the evidence is not sufficient. Yet he has nothing to advance against that evidence except his prejudice against anything supernatural. He practically says, "I do not think that it would happen, and I refuse to accept any evidence that it did happen." But preconceived ideas of the probable and improbable must yield to facts.

668. *Why do Catholics believe that Mary prays for them and helps them?*

Because they believe that she is their spiritual Mother, and that she has not lost her interest in those for whom her Son died, merely because she is in heaven. It is the Christian law, according to St. James, that we should pray for one another. The Saints in heaven pray for us who are on earth and still endeavoring to work out our salvation. And Mary is the greatest of the Saints. It is but an application in practice of our belief in the Communion of Saints, a doctrine we profess every time we say the Apostles' Creed.

669. *Why do they pray to her instead of to God, as Protestants do?*

We do not pray to Mary instead of to God, but we pray to her as well as to God. And those who retain devotion to Mary are in the habit of offering more prayers directly to God than those who have repudiated devotion to Mary. Moreover, prayers to Mary are prayers to God through her intercession. And you cannot deny that at times it is good to have our Lady praying with us rather than to pray alone to God. Two prayers are better than one, above all when the other whom I have asked to join in my petition is the very Mother of Christ.

670. *To my Protestant mind your worship of Mary is little short of idolatry.*

That can only be because you have not understood Catholic doctrine on the subject. The Creator alone is God. Mary is as much a creature as any other human being. But whilst she is as much a creature as we are, we have not been honored by God nearly as much as she.

671. *Does not the elevation of Mary, Mother of Jesus Christ, to a rank quasi-divine, find an illuminating analogue in the ancient Egyptian cult which gave Isis the divine rank of Mother of Heaven?*

Firstly, Mary has not been elevated by the Catholic Church to a rank quasi-divine, or even remotely divine. In Catholic theology she falls as far short of divinity as I do, and that's infinitely. Secondly, there is no true analogue between the historical Mother of Christ and the purely mythological Isis, and still less can any illumination be derived from a comparison of the two.

672. *Catholicism says Mary is omnipotent in power and infinite in mercy.*

It does not say that Mary is omnipotent in power and infinite in mercy. It says that her prayer and intercession have a special efficacy in winning for us the protection of the Omnipotent power of God and His infinite mercy.

673. "Since by man came death, by man came also the resurrection." Nowhere in Scripture do we find that by man and woman came the resurrection.

The resurrection was but the complement of the redemptive work. Essentially that work was accomplished on Calvary by the death of Jesus on the Cross. And Mary was there, standing at the foot of the Cross, identifying herself with the offering of her Son. By man and woman came our death. Both sexes co-operated in our downfall, and both sexes co-operated in our redemption. God Himself predicted that this would be so. After the sin of our first parents, God said to Satan, "I will put enmity between thee and the woman, and thou shalt lie in wait for her heel, and she shall crush thy head." Gen. III., 15. Mary is the second Eve as Christ is the second Adam. And both repaired the evil of our first parents, Christ principally and Mary secondarily and subordinately to Christ.

674. *I have even read in a Catholic book that Mary is co-redemptress of mankind!*

Mary's work was to be our co-redemptress, and to mediate for us together with Christ, but of course in subordination to Him. He is the one principal Mediator to whom we owe all. Do not be disturbed by this association of Mary with the redemptive work of Christ. If all Christians are members of Christ, and are called upon, as St. Paul says, to fill up what is wanting to the suffering of Christ, then you can be sure that as Mary, His Mother, was more closely associated with Christ than we are, so she is more closely associated with His redemptive work. By a special title, therefore, we call her co-redemptress. We call her "Our life, our sweetness, and our hope." For, in bringing forth Christ she brought us forth to life, she is the model of every virtue, and above all should be the glory of all women; and she is our hope as Eve was our despair. All this tells us what she is for. She is our spiritual Mother in heaven, and she fulfills the duties of a Mother, winning for us by her intercession that grace of Christ which is life to our souls and which, please God, will mean eternal life in the end.

675. *What do you mean by her Immaculate Conception?*

The Immaculate Conception does not mean that Mary was conceived miraculously, or that there was anything abnormal in her physical origin. It simply means that her soul was preserved from that taint of original sin which all others inherit from our first parents. It was really an anticipated baptism, a redemption of Mary's soul by prevention of sin's contamination and through the merits of Christ. The Eternal Son of God would not enter this world through a defiled doorway.

676. *Mary said, "My spirit hath rejoiced in God my Savior." Lk. I., 47. Would Mary have said this if she were already immaculate, and in no need of a Savior?*

She owed her preservation from sin to the anticipated merits of Christ. Christ, therefore, was her Savior by prevention as He is ours by subsequent cleansing.

677. *Mary also said, "He hath regarded the lowliness of His handmaiden." How could she be lowly if she were the highest person ever in existence since Adam before his fall from grace?*

Mary was not the highest person in existence since Adam. Christ was infinitely higher than Mary. But sin is not the only motive of lowliness or humility. The purest and most innocent of creatures, by the mere fact of being a creature, is infinitely lowly before the Creator. Adam, before his fall from grace, was the lowly servant of God. Jesus Himself, in virtue of the limitations of His created human nature, said, "Learn of Me, that I am meek and humble of heart." Our Lord was certainly without sin, and if He described Himself as lowly of heart, the use of the same expression by Mary is no argument against her sinlessness.

678. *If Mary was free from sin and immaculate, how could she die? Death is the wages of sin.*

Death is the wages of sin in a very special sense. Sin or no sin, it is natural to man to die. The human body, just as the bodies of animals, has a natural process of growth to maturity followed by age, decay, and death. Naturally, therefore, even Adam and Eve, had they never sinned, would have encountered a natural physical death if no other provision had been made for them. But God promised them a supernatural exemption from any natural process of death if they remained faithful to Him. They fell, forfeited their supernatural immunity from physical death, and nature was allowed to have its way. Therefore death is the wages of sin not as if death were abnormal, but as a normal conclusion of earthly life from which men had lost their exemption. Since Mary was human, it was not unnatural that she should die. But you will ask, "If she was supernaturally preserved from sin, why was she not supernaturally preserved from death?" That we shall see.

679. *No one except Christ could possibly be without original sin, and yet see death, unless he or she were God.*

I am afraid your thought is here a little obscure. Christ was without original sin, yet saw death, not because He was God, but because He was man. In His Divine Nature He could not die. In His human nature He could. Keep in mind that death is natural to a human nature, quite apart from original or any other sin. A human nature could not be God, and it could, and normally should die, quite apart from sin. By a special privilege God had exempted man from the normal process of death on the condition that he refrained from sin. Man sinned, and lost the privilege. Mary was preserved from all taint of sin, and by that, at least, deserved to be preserved from the natural process of death. But her life and her vocation were so intimately blended with the life and vocation of Christ, that both she and He endured an undeserved death. As when mankind fell, both sexes were represented in Adam and Eve, so both sexes were represented in our redemption. Mary, the second Eve shared death with Christ, the second Adam. The death of Christ was our redemption, but included in the redemptive work of Christ, though subordinate to it, was the death of Mary. The primitive traditions which tell us of the assumption also tell us of the "falling asleep of the Virgin Mary," an expression used to denote the transitory character of her death.

680. *Why does the Catholic Church maintain that Mary was "ever a virgin," when Scripture clearly states that she was a virgin only until the birth of Christ?*

The Catholic Church has defined as an article of faith that Mary remained always a virgin. Every Catholic in the world is obliged under pain of serious sin to believe that on the very authority of God's knowledge and veracity. Now cannot you see that the Catholic Church would be very, very foolish to define such a doctrine, if the opposite were clearly stated in Scripture? Anyone can get hold of a copy of Sacred Scripture. If the opposite of the Catholic dogma were clearly stated there, one would only have to quote the passage to refute the defined doctrine, and the whole case for the Catholic Church would collapse. Should you not suspect that if the Catholic Church has defined that Mary remained ever a virgin, then, to say the least, there cannot be anything in Scripture against it? Don't you think the Church would have made sure of that, before defining what otherwise could so easily be proved to be erroneous?

681. *If Joseph was not His father why do they trace His descent from David through him?*

Because the Jews always kept their genealogies in the male line, and since Mary was of the same tribe as Joseph, his line of ancestry was also hers.

682. *You say Jesus was descended from David through Mary, but the Bible says He is descended from David through Joseph.*

The Bible does not say that. St. Matthew says, "Joseph, the husband of Mary, of whom was born Jesus." That says no more than that Joseph was related by marriage to Mary, who, as a matter of fact, gave birth to Christ. St. Luke says at the beginning of his account, "Jesus, being (as it was supposed) the son of Joseph." He knew quite well that Jesus was not the son of Joseph in reality, though Joseph was the legal head of the Holy Family.

683. *Did Jesus or Mary ever deny that Joseph was His father?*

The whole of the New Testament is the written Word of God, and as Jesus is the Eternal Word, every utterance in the New Testament is His. When St. Luke writes, "Jesus, being (as it was supposed) the son of Joseph," Jesus accepts full responsibility for those words. No direct utterance from His own lips whilst on earth is recorded, though that is not proof that He never spoke of it. Not every word Jesus ever said was written down. Indirectly His words in John VIII., 14, 23, certainly indicate an origin differing from that of ordinary men. "I know whence I came," He said, "but you know not whence I come. You are from beneath; I am from above." Mary certainly spoke of the fact that Jesus was not the son of Joseph, for all scholars admit that St. Luke got his account of the birth and infancy of Jesus from Mary. But Matthew I., 19, 25, shows clearly that Joseph knew that he was not the father of Jesus. Mary being found with child, Joseph being a just man was minded to put her away privately. But the Angel appeared to him and said, "Joseph, son of David, fear not, for that which is conceived in her is of the Holy Ghost." Reassured that the child of which he knew he was not the father had been miraculously conceived, Joseph did as the Angel of the Lord commanded him.

684. *The Sinaitic Code, or maybe one of the Neutral Texts, is that "Joseph begat Jesus." How reconcile this with the Catholic concept of a Virgin Birth?*

That reading does not occur in what are known as the Neutral Texts, nor in the Codex Sinaiticus. It occurs in a Syrian translation found on Mt. Sinai some few years ago, and which has been called the Sinaitic Syriac. Now as regards the wording you quote, i.e., "Joseph begat Jesus," I reply that whether it is correct or not it would not necessarily affect the Catholic concept of the Virgin Birth. But also I say that, whilst it would not affect the doctrine whether correct or not, it is not correct. Firstly, even if it were correct, it would not affect our doctrine. For such an expression would be quite normal even when referring to legal paternity as opposed to real and natural paternity. And parallel passages compel the acceptance of legal paternity only. Secondly, however, it is not correct. This isolated Syrian translation must yield to the Codex Sinaiticus and the Codex Vaticanus. Vod Soden admitted the reading you quote into his edition of the Greek text, and met with protests from scholars the world over. His action was against all the principles of Biblical textual criticism, and Lagrange did not hesitate to call it a "critical enormity." The reading, therefore, cannot be accepted as correct, and even if it were, it would not affect the Catholic doctrine of the Virgin Birth.

685. *From the medical standpoint a virgin birth is impossible.*

The medical standpoint is that children normally result from the activities of both a father and a mother. And with that standpoint I am in full agreement. But then, we have never said that the birth of Christ was a normal event. And no medical standpoint demands the admission that God is bound always to observe normal procedure according to the natural laws we usually observe. Once we assert a miraculous birth outside the normal teachings of medical experience, there is no medical standpoint left. There is a philosophical standpoint, as to whether an Infinite Creator could do immediately what He usually does mediately by secondary causes of His own making. And, granted the philosophic possibility of His doing so, there arises the historical standpoint as to whether He did so. And the Virgin Birth is an historical certainty.

686. *If Joseph was not the father of Jesus, then Jesus was illegitimate.*

That is not so. What is an illegitimate child? An illegitimate child is one born as the result of unlawful relations between two people not married, and who is not legally accepted in the eyes of the state as belonging to a lawfully married couple. But the Child Jesus was not the result of any unlawful relations on Mary's part with any person to whom she was not married. The very Bible which says that St. Joseph was not the natural father of Jesus also makes it clear that no other created human being was the father. St. Joseph was told that God Himself had miraculously caused Mary to be with child; and it is as legitimate for God to dispense with the need of a human father as to allow normal processes of generation. So, from the viewpoint of His conception Christ was certainly not illegitimate. Secondly, Joseph and Mary were lawfully married, and the Child born of Mary was legally accepted by the State as belonging to a lawfully married couple. In the external order, therefore, Jesus was legitimate also in civil law. Both by origin and public acceptance, then, He was quite legitimate.

687. *In what category would you place the Gospel of Nicodemus?*

The author of that uncanonical Gospel was orthodox in his faith, and in no way intended to discredit that faith.

688. *He mentions that the Jewish contemporaries of Jesus chided Him with being of illegitimate birth.*

It is not improbable that the Jews thus slandered Christ. And the author mentions it as a slander. If the Gospel of Nicodemus has any value for you, you can get nothing more out of it than that the enemies of Christ made a charge against Him and that the charge was false. But you, apparently, wish to accept the record of a false charge as sufficient evidence that the charge was true.

689. *Is not such a matter supported by a second century writer, Celsus, who enlarges this into the charge that Joseph divorced Mary for adultery because she had borne a child to a certain soldier named Pantheras?*

The matter is not supported by Celsus. Celsus, the pagan, and the bitter enemy of the Christian Church, repeated and amplified whatever slanders he could find. And the fact that Celsus slandered Christ in the second century no more militates against the historical character of the Gospels than the fact that you approve of those slanders in the twentieth century. Origen refuted Celsus centuries ago, showing the obviously fictitious nature of his calumnies. No reputable scholar attaches any weight to the utterances of that bitter pagan.

690. *Further, was not this charge also carried into Jewish writings, from quite an early date, which state that Jesus was actually the son of a Greek officer in the Roman Army named Pantheras?*

It was. And such was to be expected. Bitter enemies of the Church in those days no more hesitated to indulge in the propaganda of lies and calumnies than they do in these days. But, as Origen points out, the enemies of the Church had no sources of information against Jesus save the Gospels themselves. The very name of your Greek officer, Pantheras, was probably no more than a corruption of the Greek word for Virgin, "Parthenos." The attacks of these early opponents of the Christian religion have but one real value only. In their own perverted way they furnish important evidence of how essential to the Christian Faith was the doctrine of the Virgin Birth in the estimate of all the early Christians. But you repeat very old charges when you fall back on the objections of early Jewish and pagan enemies of Christianity. Do you really think that, after surviving those for nearly two thousand years, the authenticity of the Gospels is going to collapse under them now?

691. What is there that is essential in a belief in the Virgin Birth?

For a Christian it is essential to believe all that God has revealed. To deny the truth of what God reveals is to accuse God of not knowing what He is talking about, or of being a deliberate liar, surely not a very Christian attitude towards God! In the Apostles' Creed Christians for centuries have professed their faith that Jesus Christ was "conceived by the Holy Ghost, and born of the Virgin Mary." The Gospels very clearly state God's promise to Mary that her Child would be due to the immediate operation of the Holy Ghost and the Divine Omnipotence without the necessity of any relations with the opposite sex. They also show that St. Joseph knew quite well that he was not the father of Jesus, and that he was told that the Child to be born of Mary was "of the Holy Ghost." To repudiate the fact that Jesus was born of a Virgin Mother is, therefore, to repudiate the direct teaching of Sacred Scripture.

692. Is it possible that the holding of such a belief can strengthen one's character?

It would not matter in the least if it could not! What is true does not cease to be true, merely because it does not prove useful for every purpose. The truth that there are other planets besides this earth does not serve to strengthen one's character. But men do not deny the truth because of that. However, belief in the Virgin Birth of Christ does strengthen one's character, for it is due to one's faith in God, and the man of deep faith in God is strong where others are weak. To deny what God has revealed to be true is the rebellion of pride, and pride is the beginning of all sin and corruption of human character.

693. Can the belief encourage one to stronger Christian living?

Most decidedly. For if indeed Christ be God coming to seek us, instead of our merely seeking God, then an impetus is given to our love of God which cannot rest content without reciprocal generosity. It may be said that the doctrine of the Divinity of Christ could be independent of that concerning the Virgin Birth. But not so. Is it not significant that attacks on the Virgin Birth come from those who reject all the supernatural and miraculous aspects of Christ? True Christians have ever held fast to the doctrine of the Virgin Birth, not only as a fact revealed by God, but as a guarantee of the real humanity of Christ because born of a human mother, yet not less decisively as a guarantee of His super-human dignity because born without the agency of a human father. The conviction that Jesus is my God is the greatest possible encouragement to Christian living. And His supernatural Virgin Birth, having for its end the founding of a new and regenerated humanity, and the introduction of a Redeemer with the divine forces needed for the world's salvation, is the normal corollary of the doctrine of Christ's Divinity. Natural generation has never resulted in a truly human, yet at the same time, a super-human being. Therefore those who have lost faith in the super-human character of Christ attack the Virgin Birth, and insist that His was a merely natural generation by an ordinary father and mother in the ordinary way. But their rejection of the Virgin Birth is a mutilation of Scripture, a contradiction of the Christian Faith from Apostolic times, and a surrender of Christian teaching into the hands of advocates of a non-miraculous, purely humanitarian Christ who may be ranked only with Buddha, or Confucius, or Mahomet, as each may wish.

694. How do you know the Virgin Mary is in heaven yet?

I will reply to that question as Christ replied to His adversaries on another matter. Do you remember how the chief priests said to Him one day, "Tell us by what authority Thou dost these things?" and He replied, "Answer Me one question, and then I will tell you. The baptism of John, whence was it, from heaven or from earth?" They would not answer. Now let me ask you a question. If the Virgin Mary is not in heaven yet, where is she? Will you suggest that our Savior did not save His own Mother, and that she is in hell? Or, if you won't admit that, will you suggest that she is not in heaven yet because she is still in purgatory?

695. Please explain fully the Assumption of the Blessed Virgin Mary.

The doctrine merely says that, after the Blessed Virgin Mary died, her body was not allowed by God to corrupt as is the case with others. This was prevented by the resurrection of her body before corruption could set in. Reunited with her soul, her body was spiritualized and glorified; at once being assumed into heaven. In other words, God anticipated for the Blessed Virgin Mary what is going to happen to all the saved on the last day.

696. What reasons are there for her bodily assumption?

Death and corruption are penalties of original sin. But Mary, by her Immaculate Conception, was preserved free from all taint of original sin. You may ask, "Why, then, did she die?" Though innocent, she died in union with her innocent Son. She shared in the whole work of redemption, identifying herself with Jesus in all His sorrows and sufferings. And she accepted death as He accepted death. But, as she shared in His redemptive work, so also she shared in the privilege of His resurrection and glory. After all, it was just as easy for God to take her glorified body to heaven at once as it will be to take the glorified bodies of all the saved at the last day.

697. Does Catholic dogma admit our Protestant doctrine that since Christ has paid the price of man's salvation, man is no longer in danger of losing his soul?

No. And you will find no support for your belief in the Bible. Christ Himself warns us to watch and pray lest we enter into temptation. That is meaningless, if temptation in no way endangers the soul. He said, "Blessed is that man who, when his lord cometh, is found watching." Lk. XII., 37. That implies that it is possible not to be in a fit state when called to judgment. Again and again He warns us of the danger of losing our souls, and puts the question, "What does it profit a man if he gain the whole world, and suffer the loss of his soul?" St. Paul tells us to work out our salvation in fear and trembling. Those who think themselves to stand are told to beware lest they fall. Your once saved, always saved idea finds no justification in the Bible.

698. I say that Christ saved us by His death once and for all.

In other words, no man can be lost, in whatever wickedness he may indulge, and even though he persists in evil dispositions until his last conscious moments! According to your doctrine, therefore, it does not matter whether a man tries to live a good life or not. Whether he wants it or not, he's got to be saved. There is no other alternative. Christ was talking folly, according to you, when He said, "Fear not those who can kill the body, but who cannot kill the soul; but I will tell you whom to fear. Fear ye him who has power to destroy both body and soul in hell." Matt. X., 28. If all men are necessarily saved, there's no need to fear anything at all. Again, why does our Lord tell us that, on the last day, all men will be judged, the good being rewarded, and the wicked sent to the everlasting fire prepared for the devil and his angels? Your ideas do not harmonize with the Bible at all.

Radio Replies—Volume II

699. *Our truly Protestant position is that the "just shall live by faith."*

If that text is rightly interpreted as meaning that the just man must have faith, and must live in practice according to the requirements of his faith, it expresses the truly Catholic position. But the original Protestant position was that good works were in no way necessary for salvation, and that man is saved by faith alone. I call that the original Protestant position, for not one in a hundred Protestants today accepts it. Where the first Protestants said, "Not what a man does but what a man believes is the test of salvation," the modern Protestant says just the opposite. "Not what a man believes, but what he does," is the slogan among Protestants now. When Protestants say they will never lose their Protestant inheritance, I say they have lost it. The original Reformers, men like Luther, and Calvin, and Knox, would denounce their present position with violent rebuke.

700. *Faith alone makes a man good. As soon as the idea arises that we become good and are saved by good works, they become utterly damnable.*

If we turn to the real teaching of the New Testament, we find St. James saying, "Faith without works is dead. Do you not see that by works a man is justified, and not by faith only?" Jas. II., 20-24. Thus speaks St. James. He taught that both faith and works are required, and that both are taken into account at our judgment. But even if we take, not New Testament teaching, but Protestant teaching, we cannot say that good works fulfilled in order to obtain salvation are today regarded as utterly damnable by Protestants. That was Protestant teaching. It is not now.

701. *I very much pity Roman Catholics.*

Compassion for those whom you believe to be unfortunate is certainly to your credit. But your belief that Catholics are unfortunate is not justified by anything you urge in your letter. When the women of Jerusalem wept over our Lord during His passion, He said to them gently, "Weep not for Me. Weep for yourselves and your children." Lk. XXIII., 28. And I say the same to you, because, whilst believing in Christ, you pity Catholics precisely because their conduct is in accordance with Christian principles.

702. *They always have to be striving to be good Roman Catholics.*

That certainly is our doctrine. Surely if one is a Catholic, he ought to strive to be a good one. But your difficulty is concerned with the idea of striving. And you think that all this striving to be good is not in the spirit of Christianity. But did not Christ Himself say, "If you will enter into life, keep the commandments." Matt. XIX., 17; and again, later, "If you love Me, keep My commandments"? Now one who wishes to be a good Catholic is told that he must strive to keep these commandments. And it is not always easy. It is easier to follow temptations opposed to them. Christ said, therefore, "Strive to enter by the narrow gate." Lk. XIII., 24. He evidently believed in striving to be good Christians. St. Paul writes to the Galatians, VI., 7, "Be not deceived. God is not mocked. For what things a man shall sow, those also shall he reap. In doing good, let us not fail. Whilst we have time, let us work good to all men." And as if he had not insisted sufficiently on the necessity of striving to be good, he wrote to the Philippians, II., 12, "With fear and trembling, work out your salvation." To the Corinthians 1, IX., 25, he said, "Know you not that they who run in a race, all run indeed, but one receiveth the prize? So run, that you may obtain. And everyone who striveth for the victory, refraineth himself from various things. I run, but not carelessly; I fight, but not as one beating the air. But I chastise my body and bring it into subjection." What is all that but striving! In 1 Timothy VI., 11, he writes, "But thou, O man of God, pursue justice, godliness, faith, charity, patience, mildness. Fight the good fight." Add to all this our Lord's constant warnings to us to be vigilant, to watch and pray, to pray without ceasing, and it is very difficult to see what you can find to condemn in our doctrine that one has always to be striving to be good.

703. *Good works will never save anyone.*

Natural good works, performed without any motive of love for God, and by one not in God's grace and friendship, will save no one. That is why St. Paul says, "If I should distribute all my goods to feed the poor and have not charity, it profiteth me nothing." 1 Cor. XIII., 3. But good works inspired by love of God and performed by one in God's grace and friendship do contribute towards one's salvation. That is why the New Testament, in James II., 24, says, "By works a man is justified, and not by faith only." In fact, such good works are necessary for salvation, for St. James says in V., 26, "For even as the body without the spirit is dead, so also faith without works is dead."

704. *St. Paul says, "Not of works, lest any man should boast." Eph. II., 9.*

St. Paul excludes works performed by one's own efforts, independently of God's grace. No man will be able to boast that he saved himself by his own efforts, and that he did not need the grace of Christ. But St. Paul did not contradict St. James who declared that, "By works a man is justified, and not by faith only." And this is the teaching of Christ who said, "If any man love Me, he will keep My commandments," and the keeping of Christ's commands means good works. We do need, besides good works, both faith and charity, and in the text you quote St. Paul is insisting upon faith as one necessary condition, a faith which is a gratuitous gift from God. But not for a moment does St. Paul mean that a man is saved by faith only, to the exclusion of good works.

705. *As Christ died He said, "It is finished." He completed our salvation, and we believe in His finished work.*

Christ's words, "It is finished," do not show that our salvation is completed in one glorious act. They indicate that He had fulfilled His part in the essential work of our redemption. But our part still remains. He has paid the price, but we shall be saved only if we fulfill the conditions necessary to profit by His death for us. And it is not enough to believe in the finished work of Christ by simple faith in order to secure eternal salvation in heaven with Him. Christ said to the Apostles, "Teach men to observe all things whatsoever I have commanded you." Matt. XXVIII., 20.

706. *Did not St. Peter champion salvation by works of the Jewish Law, whilst St. Paul demanded salvation by faith?*

Both St. Peter and St. Paul insisted upon salvation both by faith and good works. Did St. Peter insist on salvation by works only, when he wrote, "There is an inheritance reserved in heaven for you who, by the power of God, are kept by faith unto salvation"? I. Peter 1, 5. And how can people say that St. Paul championed salvation by faith to the exclusion of good works, when he wrote to the Galatians, "Be not deceived. God is not mocked. What things a man shall sow, those also shall he reap. For he that soweth in his flesh, of the flesh also shall reap corruption. But he that soweth in the spirit, of the spirit shall reap life everlasting. In doing good let us not fail. Whilst we have time, let us work good to all men." Galatians VI., 8. He is a very shallow reader of Scripture who would confine St. Peter's teaching of salvation to works, and St. Paul's to faith. But, above all, it is a mystery how anyone can say that St. Peter based salvation on works of the Jewish Law, when we find him writing in his first epistle, I., 18, "You were not redeemed by your vain mode of living and the tradition of your fathers, but by the precious blood of Christ."

707. God must know beforehand whether a soul is born to be damned or otherwise.

No soul is born to be damned. God sincerely wills the salvation of all men, and gives all men sufficient grace to be saved. In fact He warns us all by conscience and by His commandments against the very things that could destroy our eternal happiness. He would not warn us against the things that take us to hell if He wanted us to go there. He would keep silent about them and let us go over the precipice.

708. If God knows a soul is to be damned, it is useless for that soul to try to attain salvation.

There is no predestination for damnation. Nor is it futile for an individual to endeavor to save his soul. God says even to the worst sinners, "Repent, and if your sins be as scarlet, they shall be made white as snow." Isaiah I., 18. If a man is lost, it will be solely through his own fault. God may know that certain souls will choose to damn themselves, but He knows they have not got to do so, nor does His knowledge make them do so. Knowledge doesn't cause an event, the event causes knowledge. Because Jack is running I know that he is running. But he certainly isn't running because I know it. God knows that a man will choose to lose his soul only because that man will so choose. There is no need for him to choose so disastrously. He receives sufficient grace for his conversion. Let him correspond with the voice of God and of conscience, repenting of his sins, and he will be saved. It is not futile for him to endeavor to save his soul, and if he is lost it will be precisely because he did not endeavor to do so. Just imagine a farmer who says: God knows whether I'm going to have a crop or not. If He knows, I'll have it, whatever I do. If He knows that I won't have it, I won't have it, whatever I do. So I won't plough, I won't sow any seed, it's futile. Such a man is working on the absurd idea that knowledge causes the event instead of realizing that the event causes knowledge of it. Let us all do our best in the service of God, the practice of extra virtue, the avoiding of sin and the desire of holiness. If we do, the practical result will be our salvation. The solution of the speculative problems can safely be left to God.

709. Was not St. Augustine, an orthodox Catholic bishop, author of the Calvinistic doctrine of predestination to hell?

No. Calvin certainly did not get that doctrine from St. Augustine, though he may have pretended to do so. G. P. Fisher, Protestant professor of Ecclesiastical History at Yale University, in his standard work "The History of the Christian Church," page 321, says that Calvin, in his "Institutes," went further than Augustine, declaring that sin, and consequently damnation, are the effect of an efficient decree of God. Now St. Augustine could not have taught that doctrine, if Calvin had to go further than Augustine in order to teach it! But let us go to St. Augustine himself. A man who believed that some men are predestined to hell no matter what they might do, could not possibly write as follows. In his book on "Catechizing the Ignorant," St. Augustine writes, "The merciful God wishes to liberate men from eternal ruin, if they are not enemies to themselves, and do not resist the mercy of their Creator. For this purpose He sent His only-begotten Son." Again he writes in his book "On the Spirit and the Letter," "God wills all men to be saved, and to come to the knowledge of the truth; but not in such a way as to take away their free will, according to the good or bad use of which they will be most justly judged." No man who believed that God predestines some men to hell could write those words. Those who claim St. Augustine as the author of Calvinistic predestination to hell have never understood St. Augustine; and perhaps have never made anything like a serious study of his works. The Pelagian heretics denied the necessity of grace for salvation. St. Augustine insisted that man cannot save himself without the grace of God. He insisted, too, that grace, being grace, must be a gratuitous gift of God which, though given to all men, could not be due under any title of justice to them. Calvinists made the unwarranted conclusion for themselves that, because it was not due in justice, therefore it was not given to some; and that God therefore created some souls intending them for hell. But St. Augustine never taught that.

710. Why should a good-living Catholic go to hell because he dies without repentance after committing mortal sin, whilst a bad Catholic, sinful all his life, repents at the last moment, and goes to heaven?

Take the good Catholic first. To live his good life he kept the commandments of God. But no observance of God's commandments gives any subsequent right to break them. If he breaks God's commandments by later mortal sin and refuses to repent, he dies in a state of mortal sin and at enmity with God. He necessarily goes to hell, though he need not necessarily have fallen into a state of sin, and further, need not necessarily have remained in such a state. A previous good life in no way justifies later sins. If a man commits murder on Wednesday, is it any defense that he did not commit adultery on the preceding Tuesday? Now take your poor sinner, who, after living a bad life, repents and saves his soul. By repentance, he recovers God's grace. And he is saved, because he availed himself of God's mercy, asked for forgiveness, and died in God's friendship. The one-time good man is not lost because of his previous good life, and this man is not saved because of his previous bad life. There would be injustice if that were the case. But it is not. The one-time good man is lost because he nullified his good life by subsequent sin; the bad man is saved because he nullified his bad life by subsequent repentance and a request to share in the merits of Christ.

711. What value has a deathbed repentance when a soul has steadfastly refused to submit to God's will during life?

If there be a sincere deathbed repentance the soul would be saved, provided the sorrow were perfect, or, if imperfect, it had the assistance of the Sacraments of the Church. But steadfast refusal during life to do God's will does not give much hope of a deathbed repentance. Firstly, God has promised forgiveness to those who do repent. But He has never promised time to repent. He says Himself that death may come to us at any moment and blessed is the one who is found to be watching. That does not augur well for the unprepared. Secondly, even granted some form of regret, the ingrained dispositions of a soul which has steadfastly refused to do God's will during life do not give much hope of suddenly attaining to a perfect love of God and perfect sorrow for past sins. And if such a soul dies without the Sacraments, it is lost. Yet such a soul has done nothing to deserve the happiness of the Sacraments. We are warned over and over again by God against the presumption of delay in our conversion to Him. To carry on in sinful dispositions, determined to go on with them, is the conduct of a fool. The only safe preparation for a good death is a good life.

712. What value has repentance when a soul decides to conform to God's will only when this life offers no further hopes of self-indulgence. The only motive is expediency and fear of the fate awaiting the wicked.

If such repentance proceeds from a purely natural dread it is not really repentance at all, and has no value whatever. If it proceeds solely from a supernatural fear based upon faith in the revealed doctrine of hell, it would have sufficient value to save a soul provided the Sacraments were received. Otherwise it would not save the soul. And there is no guarantee that a priest could be obtained in time for the administration of the Sacraments. We do not know whether we are to die of a slow illness, giving us plenty of time to prepare to meet God, or suddenly of heart failure. God could take me as I am talking to you at this moment, and without the slightest warning. Mere fear of what will happen to us will not of itself save us. Perfect sorrow without the Sacraments will save us. Imperfect sorrow with the Sacraments will save us. But imperfect sorrow without the Sacraments is powerless to do so. The persistent and habitual sinner cannot rely on salvation except by taking it for granted that he will have the opportunity to receive the Sacraments, or that he will suddenly attain to perfect dispositions of love and sorrow which are absolutely alien to his distorted and warped nature. It is clear that there is no justification for his taking these things for granted. The only real security is the security of a good conscience, and the only possible advice to the man who is not running straight with God is that he should square up, repent sincerely of the past, and begin to serve God. Let us remember the words of Christ, "Thou fool, this night thy soul shall be required of thee," Lk. XII., 20, and His estimate, "What does it profit a man if he gain the whole world and lose his soul." Matt. XVI., 26. Our Lord made both. And He ought to know. To risk one's soul for anything this life can offer is to be a fool. To be prepared to make any sacrifice rather than jeopardize one's eternal salvation is wisdom.

713. I heard a Missioner say that God is not satisfied with the last miserable year of a sinner's life. That is, it is no use accepting Christ in the last year of life.

You are making the priest say more than he did say. He did not say that it was no use repenting of one's sins at the end of life. God has promised forgiveness whenever a man sincerely repents of his sins, even though it be with his very last breath. A man who thus repents will at least save his soul, and God is more satisfied with that than He would be, did the man not repent at all. The mission priest you heard was trying to bring home the fact that, if God is worth serving in the last year of a man's life, He is worth serving throughout life. Scripture itself says that it is indeed good to have served God from one's youth. Nobility of soul rebels against the thought of spending all one's best years in sin, and offering God the dregs of one's life. And that is certainly not the way to serve God as God must wish. But we cannot conclude from that that it is no use turning to God at the last. If one has not served God as he should, it is of the utmost use to die at least repenting of one's sins; and the more one's sins the greater one's obligation to repent of them.

714. According to Catholic doctrine a murderer can repent and save his soul. But what of his victim, killed with no time to repent? That does not seem fair to me.

It is certain that the murderer can repent and save his soul, though he will have to expiate in Purgatory the injustice of taking his neighbor's life, so much greater than the mere taking of his property. Meantime we have to remember that if the victim were in a state of mortal sin at the moment of the tragedy, the murderer was not responsible for his being in such a state. Death may come to a man in any one of many ways, whether slowly by disease, or suddenly by accident, or even by the ill will of some fellow human being. But whenever death comes, and however it comes, no man has a right to be in a state of sin at that decisive moment. Every man has the obligation to be ready to meet God just when God takes him, and by whatever means he is taken. So Christ warns us, "Watch ye, therefore, because you know not what hour your Lord will come." Matt. XXIV., 42. And again, "If the householder did know at what hour the thief would come, he would surely watch and not suffer his house to be broken open. Be ye then also ready, for at what hour you think not the Son of man will come." Lk. XII., 39. In actual practice, of course, we cannot say that any man has been killed with no time for repentance. In a flash, quicker than the speed of any bullet, God could offer a man all the graces necessary for a complete reconciliation with Him. We cannot therefore form any certain judgment concerning the actual fate of any soul, and must leave that question to God. He alone knows the interior dispositions of each soul as He recalls it to Himself. Of one thing we are sure. Every soul receives sufficient grace for its salvation. Of one thing we are ignorant—of the manner in which God dispenses that grace. And we must leave each soul to God, refusing to judge concerning its eternal destiny.

715. Do you think that a sacramental system is truly useful?

Since Christ chose to establish a sacramental system, it matters little what I think. However, apart from our Lord's obvious will, I do see that a sacramental system is the best possible. The Sacraments are so in keeping with human nature, they so fit in with life, and are so adapted to our tendencies and limitations. Again they offer us a certainty of supernatural grace which others never have, and which gives us such tranquillity of conscience and peace of soul. Socially, also, they express the bond of unity amongst all members of the visible Catholic Church, and strengthen that bond. But no reasons which I can advance in favor of a sacramental system can add weight to the fact that Christ actually established His religion on sacramental principles. For one who accepts the religion of Christ it is enough that He should have given it to us just as it is.

716. Why do you say that when we are baptized we are born again?

Because Christ came to redeem us from the death of sin, and to give us a new life of grace derived from Him. So He said, "I am the way, the truth, and the life"; and again, "I am the vine, ye are the branches." As surely as the branches derive their life from the vine, we must derive our life from Christ. Now every life supposes a birth, and as no human being gets the life of grace given by Christ merely by being born of his earthly parents, a new birth is required. And it is by the rebirth of Baptism that we secure the supernatural life of grace which is derived from Christ and incorporates us with Him.

717. We Protestants are taught that when Christ said, "Ye must be born again," He meant a change of heart.

That would be a most inadequate explanation. For a change of heart means conversion from unbelief to belief in Christ, and from morally evil ways to morally good conduct. It therefore means repentance. Now our Lord did insist on repentance or a change of heart in all who sought baptism, but He did not identify it with baptism. He said, "He that believeth and is baptized shall be saved." Mk. XVI., 16. When speaking of the rite of baptism itself, He said, "Unless one is born again of water and the Holy Ghost, he cannot enter the kingdom of heaven." Jn. III., 3. You will notice here that, whilst conversion or change of heart is an interior change in our own dispositions, the new principle of life comes from forces outside us. It is something put into us, and signified by an external rite. The good preparatory dispositions are from us; but the new life is not from us, but from God. The washing with baptismal water signifies the cleansing of the soul from the disease of sin belonging to children of a guilty race; and the Spirit of the Living God is mentioned as infusing into our souls a principle of new life altogether which is rightly said to regenerate us, and give us a new birth to a spiritual life of grace far beyond and above the merely natural life secured by natural birth.

718. What did Christ mean by "being born again"?

The life He gives us is quite distinct from the life we secured at birth, and is derived from another source. Our very nature is changed and lifted to a higher plane, a plane therefore called supernatural. The starting point for Christians is the fact that the Eternal Son of God became man. But He descended to our level and shared our human nature by His human birth that He might lift us to His level and enable us to share His nature by a supernatural birth. In Him, God is given to us that we may become one with God. And as surely as His human life enabled the Son of God to live and experience our life in this world, so by our rebirth into the Christ-life we are to live and experience the life of God through grace in this world and through glory in heaven. It is obvious that such an experience is proper to God and not to man, just as an intellectual life in this world is proper to man and not to a tree. A tree would have to be elevated far above its natural life to be able to converse with man and share in man's activities. The human level would be supernatural in comparison with the level of mere vegetation. Far more is the God-level supernatural in comparison with man's level. For us to live the life of God, to know as He knows, love as He loves, and be happy with His happiness, we certainly will need a new principle of life, and new powers which are beyond those got by natural birth. And Christ communicates that new life to us by a baptismal rebirth which enables us to share in the Divine Nature, and gives a thought, love, action, and destiny in common with God. And we receive the principle of that life by the Sacrament of Baptism in which we are born again of water and the Holy Ghost. That life is in us by grace as the life of the oak tree is in the acorn; and it is that life of grace which will attain its full development and perfection in the glorious life of eternal association with God in heaven itself under conditions infinitely above the natural conditions of life in this world. That is what Christ meant when He said, "Ye must be born again."

719. *Would not the general tenor of Paul's teaching suggest that the Gospel of Christ was the power of God unto salvation, to all them that believe?*

Yes. But the word "believe" there, is not to be taken in the restrictive sense of a theoretical faith in Christ, but in the universal and practical sense of one accepting the full religion of Christ, which includes the necessity of receiving that Sacrament of Baptism instituted by Christ. Nowhere did St. Paul ever suggest a dispensation from the necessity of baptism.

720. *Is not the application of water merely symbolic, testifying an inward regeneration?*

No. The sacramental external rite does not merely testify to an inward regeneration. It causes that regeneration. The Sacraments, as instituted by Christ and deriving all their power from Christ, are the very actions of Christ. He uses the Sacraments as instruments in the effecting of His work of grace, just as He used His humanity on earth as a medium of His power. We know that a woman touched but the hem of Christ's garments, and was healed. And Jesus felt virtue go out from Him. That was but an image of the conferring of grace by visible and tangible Sacraments instituted by Christ, of which baptism is one.

721. *Is not the inward regeneration the result of believing and receiving the Gospel?*

Yes, in the inclusive sense as implying the fulfillment of all the conditions laid down in the Gospel; including, therefore, the reception of baptism.

722. *Does Catholic doctrine allow that the soul of an unbaptized heathen can enter heaven?*

Not in the case of unbaptized infants who die before coming to the use of reason and the stage of personal responsibility. The heathens who do come to the age of personal responsibility can attain to the supernatural order of grace and inherit that very heaven for which baptism is normally required on certain conditions. For example, a pagan may never have heard of the Gospel, or having heard of it, may have quite failed to grasp its significance. He remains a heathen, knowing no better, and dies without receiving the actual Sacrament of Baptism. In such a case God will not blame him for that for which he is really not responsible. At the same time, God wills all men to be saved, and will certainly give that heathen sufficient grace for his salvation according to the condition in which he is. If that heathen, under the influence of interior promptings of conscience and the actual inspirations of grace given by God, repents sincerely before death of such moral lapses as he has committed during life, he will secure forgiveness, and save his soul in view of the Baptism he would have been willing to receive had he known it to be necessary, and could he have done so. We Catholics say that such a heathen has been saved by Baptism of Desire. The desire, of course, is implicit only.

723. Will the soul of a still-born child go to heaven?

Not unless the doctor or nurse was able to baptize the child before the actual separation of its soul and body. Granted complete lack of baptism, or baptism administered too late, the soul of such a child will be given by God all the natural happiness of which it is capable; but it will lack that fullness of happiness possible only to those who have been made one with Christ by the divine grace He alone can give. Since such a little one, of course, has been guilty of no personal sin, it will never have to endure any positive suffering. It will have all the natural happiness it is able to enjoy, and will not miss an additional happiness which it knows to be beyond the realm of possibility for it. No one ever wastes time or tears hoping for the impossible. Baptism alone makes the very Vision of God as He is in Himself possible for infants, and that Vision of God is the heaven to be shared by Christ our Lord with all who have been incorporated with Him, and die united to Him by sanctifying grace.

724. This miserable teaching is an unscriptural invention.

Even though you regard the teaching as miserable, the infant at least will not be miserable, but as happy as it is possible for it to be. I admit that it will not attain to the full happiness of heaven itself. Now is that teaching unscriptural? Scripture teaches that only by regeneration or by being born again, one becomes a member of Christ. Now an infant who dies without being baptized has been born, but not born again; generated, but not regenerated. And Christ Himself has said, "Unless one is born again of water and the Holy Ghost, he cannot enter the Kingdom of God." Jn. III., 3. It is the clear teaching of Scripture that compels the Catholic Church to say that unbaptized infants who die before attaining personal responsibility cannot enter heaven. God will render them happy with natural human happiness, but they cannot share in the supernatural happiness of heaven which is proper to God Himself, and not proper to a created human nature.

725. Such a doctrine strikes at the character of God, His justice, His love, and also at the Gospel of Christ.

The Catholic doctrine is based on the Gospel of Christ, and would never have been dreamed of but for that Gospel. And it safeguards the character of God who, in His justice and love, gives such an infant all the happiness of which it is capable for all enternity. It merely lacks the supernatural happiness of which baptism would have rendered it capable, a baptism it failed to receive.

726. Do you maintain that there is a kind of intermediate heaven of endless happiness for unbaptized children?

I have never used the word heaven in this connection, for the term heaven is reserved for the state of those who attain to the beatific Vision of God. I do maintain, however, that there is a state of endless natural happiness in store for the souls of infants who have never attained to personal responsibility, and who have died without baptism.

727. Are Purgatory and Limbo one and the same place?

Limbo is a general term which can mean any intermediate state between heaven and hell. The word Limbo comes from the Latin word Limbus, which means border. The term, therefore, means a state bordering on some other state. In other words, it means an intermediate state between heaven and hell, being neither the one nor the other. We could speak, therefore, of the Limbo of the Fathers, when dealing with the souls of those who died before Christ and were awaiting the opening of heaven to mankind by the redemption. So, too, we could speak of the Limbo of Unbaptized Children, when referring to the souls of infants who have never committed personal sins yet have lacked Baptism. Purgatory is but a Limbo of Purification. By common usage, however, people intend by Limbo the state of natural happiness reserved for unbaptized children, and in this sense Limbo is not to be identified with Purgatory. In Catholic usage, where Purgatory means an intermediate state of painful purification, Limbo means an intermediate state without any positive suffering.

728. Where is Limbo?

I can no more answer that question than you can say where is heaven, or where is hell. If you do not reject heaven because you cannot say where it is, you cannot reject Limbo for that reason. Geographical terms based on calculations of material locality cannot do justice to the mysterious realities of the next life. Yet if we are not to be silent about them altogether, we must speak of them in terms of what we know already from this world. All we have to realize is that our speech is inadequate to convey a full idea of such things, and that they give only some idea. But some idea is better than no idea.

729. What is the state of an unbaptized infant in Limbo?

It is a state of such happiness as is demanded by a human being who has been guilty of no personal sin, yet who has not received the supernatural destiny which comes only with incorporation in Christ by divine grace. In other words, it attains a happiness which is proportionate to a purely natural condition, not that which is proper to one who has been elevated to the loftier supernatural level given by Christ. And the deprivation of the higher happiness fills it with no more regret than a man experiences because he cannot have a week-end cottage on the moon. However nice a thing may be, if we know that it is beyond our capacity, was never due to us, and is quite impossible of attainment, we do not worry in the least about it. So will it be with the unbaptized child in its state of natural happiness.

730. What evidence have you that such souls are in Limbo?

The evidence that such souls did exist; that they are immortal; that, according to the Gospels they can't be in heaven; and that, according to God's justice they can't be in hell. Where will you declare them to be? In heaven? If so, have they attained heaven without the grace of Christ? If not, how did they get the grace of Christ? What authority have you from Scripture to endow them with this grace without baptismal rebirth by water and the Holy Ghost? If you dispute our reasons for believing them to be in Limbo, you have much less reason for believing them to be anywhere else.

731. Which is the correct way, to be immersed entirely under water, or to have water poured on the head?

Either way is correct. In both cases the significance of washing or cleansing is retained. There is nothing in the New Testament to show that baptism must be conferred exclusively by immersion. In fact the baptism in one day of the three thousand converts in Jerusalem on the occasion of St. Peter's first sermon would have been impossible had it been by immersion. Research has shown that there was no sufficient water supply available in the city at that time for the purpose. Again, when St. Paul baptized his jailor in prison it could only have been by pouring. Bedridden invalids, and the dying, who desired baptism could not be immersed; yet they could not be denied so important a Sacrament. Water poured on their foreheads retained the significance of grace washing their souls as the water washed their bodies. Ablution is possible without taking a plunge bath. From the very times of the Apostles, therefore, baptism has been administered either by immersion, or by pouring water on the person to be baptized. If I were away out in the center of Australia far from any stream of water, and a dying companion begged me to baptize him, a cup of water would certainly be sufficient for the purpose.

732. Can infants fulfill the conditions of baptism?

Yes, at least passively, insofar as they are quite capable of receiving baptism. Actively, they can fulfill the promises made in their name at baptism, when they come to the age of personal responsibility.

733. I argued with a friend that infants should be baptized because original sin must be destroyed in order to enter the life of grace. Was I right?

You correctly interpreted the mind of Christ. The significance of the Christian religion is much more profound than many non-Catholics think. For most Protestants baptism is merely an external act associating the subject with their Church, and implying a profession of the Christian faith. They do not think of it as actually giving a new principle of life interiorly and within the soul of the recipient. Yet that is the Catholic idea, and the real doctrine of Christ, and it is essential. Christ was God who descended to our level, shared our human nature, and did so in order to lift us to His level, give us a share in the Divine Nature, and render a heavenly destiny possible to us. As He took our life, He gives His life. He gives His by our baptismal regeneration. It means a new and spiritual vital principle within us which our natural birth could not give us. And children who have had no more than their merely natural birth are without it. They could never, therefore, experience the happiness of heaven should they die in their unbaptized state. Astronomers say that human beings as at present constituted could not possibly live on the planet Mars. They would have to be given altogether new capabilities adapted to Martian conditions before they could do so. Much more will man's soul have to be reconstituted in order to live the life of God in conditions which are infinitely above natural capabilities. The additional and new principle of life given by baptismal rebirth means just such a regeneration or reconstitution of the soul.

734. But infants are quite unaware of this.

They are just as unaware of their acquisition of a merely natural life principle. But that does not prevent them getting it.

735. How, then, can they accept the Christian Faith? That requires belief, and they are incapable of believing.

The belief of the parents is sufficient here just as it is sufficient for so much in the natural life. The parents believe on their child's behalf that food is necessary, and give it food. They believe that instruction is necessary, and give it. They believe that sound morals are necessary, and teach the good principles they know. They don't wait for the child to make up its own mind on all these things. Later the child will know and accept for itself the wisdom of these things. In the same way, parents who know that Christ is the way, the truth and the life, choose Christ on their child's behalf. They set their child, who is a continuation of their own life, and in whom they live over again, upon the right way; they teach their child the truth of Christ; and at the earliest possible moment secure the implantation of the life of Christ in the child's soul by baptism. Later on, the child gladly accepts and ratifies this gift of itself to Christ as it grows into an understanding of its faith and begins to live consciously according to its precepts. And it is a real tragedy that, owing to mistaken notions, the Baptists and others allow so many little children to die without baptismal regeneration, lacking the life Christ alone can give, and which no earthly birth can confer, with the result that such children are forever incapable of attaining the supernatural destiny reserved for those to whom a share in the divine nature has been communicated by water and the Holy Ghost. Professing Christian parents who neglect to have their children baptized do an injury both to Christ and to the children they deprive of the life He desires to give them.

736. *On what Scriptural authority does the Catholic Church base its practice of Confession?*

On the promise of Christ, as recorded in Matthew XVI., that He would give the keys of the Kingdom of Heaven, and the power of binding and loosing to His Apostles and the Church. And again, on the fulfillment of that promise, with specific reference to absolution from sin, as recorded in John XX., 23. There we are told that, having breathed upon the Apostles, Christ said to them: "Receive the Holy Ghost. Whose sins you forgive, they are forgiven; and whose sins you retain, they are retained." By those words He gave the power to the official representatives of the Church of forgiving or not forgiving sin as they judged fit; and promised to sanction and ratify their decision.

737. *I have been told that "Whose sins you forgive," means that the Christian minister has the right only to assure people that God has forgiven sins of which we repent. Do you accept that interpretation?*

It is an altogether inadequate and erroneous interpretation. Christ did not say, "When you assure people that God has forgiven people because of their repentance and faith, those people have been forgiven." He breathed upon the Apostles and said, "Receive ye the Holy Ghost." The action and the words indicate, not a promise of future guidance, but an actual communication of the Holy Spirit to them, by whose power they would be able to effect what He was telling them to do. We must note also that Christ had just declared that He was giving the Apostles a mission identical with that which He Himself had received from His Father. "As the Father sent Me," He said, "I also send you." Now Christ did not merely assure people that God had forgiven them when they showed signs of faith and repentance. He Himself came into this world to destroy sin, and He directly forgave sin in individual cases at His discretion. We must note, too, that the Greek word used for forgive is active, and signifies a positive and efficacious influence, not a mere declaration of a forgiveness which has already been effected by God. The interpretation given you, therefore, does not agree with the correct sense of Sacred Scripture.

738. *Christ gave the power to the Apostles, not to the Bishops and priests of today.*

As Christ conferred this power upon the Apostles, they conferred it in turn upon those whom they ordained and consecrated. These, in turn, ordained others; and by an uninterrupted succession of lawfully consecrated Bishops, the power has been retained and transmitted in the Church. Normally the Church comes into contact with individual subjects through her priests, not through her Bishops who preside over large sections of the Church. And the Church exercises her absolving powers through priests. That is why St. Paul wrote to Titus, "For this cause I left thee in Crete that thou shouldst ordain priests in every city, as I also have appointed thee." Titus I., 5. As a matter of fact, the Sacrament of Penance, if it is to be available to all men, as it must be, simply has to be exercised by priests, for no Bishop would be able to deal with all the faithful of a whole diocese. Christ instituted this Sacrament for the necessities of men, and He certainly did so in a way in which it could be applied to them in their necessities. Never in the history of the Church from earliest Apostolic times was it ever questioned that priests as well as Bishops possessed this power in virtue of their ordination.

739. In John XX., 23, Christ spoke to His Apostles, not to any pastors of today. I cannot therefore believe the Catholic teaching.

To that I must say, firstly, that you ask an absolutely impossible condition before you will believe. You would believe only provided all the priests of all succeeding ages could have been present simultaneously when Christ gave the power of forgiving sin. Secondly, you forget that Christ established a Church which He said would last all days even to the end of the world. And that Church had to continue just as He established it, retaining all the powers He intended its pastors to possess. And in John XX., 23, you see Him endowing the pastors of the infant Church with the essential power to forgive sin. The same Church through the ages must retain within herself that same power.

740. By saying our prayers each evening, and telling our sins directly to God, they are just as surely forgiven as telling them to a priest.

Are you sure of that? How much time do you devote to the examination of your conscience, to the discovery of your sins, and to the realization of their guilt? Do you know what dispositions of soul are required for the forgiveness of sin? And do you understand your obligations of restitution and reparation of harm done to others by your sins? Again, if forgiveness is obtained privately, and without recourse to a priest, why did Christ so solemnly confer upon the Apostles the power to forgive sins, saying, "Receive the Holy Ghost: whose sins you forgive, they are forgiven"? That was quite unnecessary if the power was not to be exercised. And Christ did not confer unnecessary powers upon the Church. As a matter of fact your idea springs from an inadequate notion, not only of Scripture, but also of the Christian character. The Christian who sins is guilty against himself, against the Church and against God. He recovers grace by his own actions, by the action of the Church, and by the action of God. Within himself he repents, to the Church he confesses and is warned of his duties; and, through the priest, God forgives. I might add that a favorite charge against the Catholic Church used to be that it is a great advantage to get rid of all one's sins in a moment by one Confession. But you at least realize that Confession is an uncomfortable penalty. And you wish an easier method still by wanting to get rid of your sins in a moment without Confession. You will never taunt Catholics, therefore, with choosing an easier way out than is available to Protestants.

741. The forgiveness of sin is an act that can only be done by God.

Correct. But God can do it personally and immediately, or He can exercise His power through chosen human instruments. In either case it remains His own power. The only real question to be solved is as to whether God did ever delegate His power to forgive sin to human beings. I have shown that Christ said to His very human Apostles, "Whose sins you forgive, they are forgiven." Will you accept the truth of those words, or will you reject belief in Christ? If you reject belief in Christ, you must cease to be a Protestant. If you accept the fact that He left to His Church the power to forgive sin, then you must become a Catholic. The choice, of course, must be left to yourself, and to the grace of God.

742. To apply to a priest seems like snubbing the Almighty.

It is no more like snubbing God than it would be like snubbing the King to respect and submit to the authority of an Ambassador fully accredited by the King. In fact, to refuse to acknowledge the spiritual authority of those men who have been commissioned by God to exercise it, is to snub God. That is why Christ said to His Apostles, "He that despiseth you, despiseth Me, and he that despiseth Me despiseth Him that sent Me." Lk. X., 16.

743. What advantage have Catholics in the practice of Confession to a priest?

They have at least the advantage of fulfilling Christ's definite will. But the practice of Confession has immense advantages. It steadies the flood of evil by imposing a real and periodical check. It forces men to recollect themselves, and pay attention to their spiritual state in order to give an account of it. It unmasks sin, robbing it of its charm, and showing up its true malice and hypocrisy. It restores to people the control of their souls, revives their resources, and helps to break their perverse inclinations. At the same time, it is a great consolation. It lightens the soul's worries and anxieties, and gives certainty of pardon. Even though heaven seems mute, it assures the soul that God still loves and offers only encouragement. It guarantees a clean sheet on which one may yet write holiness and virtue. Hundreds of Protestants have regretted the loss of the confessional, and write wistfully and longingly of the boon it must be to Catholics.

744. If a man wanted to confess his sins, but died unexpectedly before he could do so, surely his sins would not be held against him because of his inability.

On your very hypothesis, such a man would go to Confession if he could. Since he cannot, God forgives him in virtue of his will to go to Confession, giving him the necessary graces to enable him to make an act of perfect contrition.

745. If this sin is not held against him, why the need of the confessional?

Since Christ instituted Confession as the normal means of forgiveness, the actual use of this Sacrament is normally necessary. If a Catholic secures forgiveness apart from Confession, it is only insofar as he is unable to confess, and insofar as he has the will to do so, were it possible. If he were in such dispositions that he would not confess, did the opportunity present itself, he would not be forgiven. It is one thing to be forgiven because one has the will to fulfill all that God requires, yet does not do so only because prevented by circumstances beyond one's control. It is quite another to demand forgiveness on one's own terms, deliberately rejecting the normal means instituted by Christ.

746. What justification is there for imposing penances in Confession?

Protestants, of course, deny not only the necessity of confessing one's sins, but also the obligation to make personal satisfaction for them by penitential works. For a Catholic, sufficient justification for the imposition of penances is found in the fact that the Catholic Church requires it as part of the Sacrament of Confession. For to that Church our Lord has said, "Whatever you bind upon earth is bound also in heaven." We accept the laws of our religion because they have the authority of Christ latent within them, not because we ourselves happen to approve of their wisdom or of the reasons for them. However, there are reasons for the law that penances must be imposed upon those who seek forgiveness of sin in Confession; and those reasons are based upon the known will of God in relation to the forgiveness of sins in general, and also upon the very nature of the Sacrament of Confession as instituted by Christ.

747. Could you give me the reasons for this discipline?

As I have said, they are based upon God's own procedure in dealing with sin, the teachings of Christ, and the very nature of the Sacrament of Confession. In the Old Testament God Himself couples the forgiving of sin with the imposing of penances. The very sufferings and miseries that came upon the human race because of sin show that sin must be expiated. God forgave David the great sin that king had committed, yet despite the forgiveness, exacted a penalty. "Because thou hast repented," He said, "thy sin is forgiven thee. Nevertheless, because thou hast done this thing, thy own son shall die, and shall not live." II. Kings XII., 13-14. Through the Prophet Joel, God gave the general law, "Be converted to Me with all your heart, in fasting and mourning." Joel II., 13. In addition to sorrow, the people had to inflict the penance of fasting upon themselves. Again God said, "Redeem thy sins by alms-giving." By depriving themselves of their goods in favor of the poor people can compensate the unlawful pleasures they have taken at the expense of God's law. Protestants admit that these principles held good in the Old Law, but say that Christ has expiated our sins on the Cross, and that we are exempt from such expiation. But this is not true. The New Testament does not exempt us from the need of penitential expiation of sin. It insists that we take up our cross as Christ carried His; that we suffer with Christ, and fill up in ourselves what is wanting to the sufferings of Christ.

Christ did not suffer so as to free us from the need of expiating our own sins, but that we might be able to expiate them with greater success and merit in union with Him. Finally, Christ instituted the Sacrament of Penance, sanctifying the whole penitential process. He said to the Apostles, "Whose sins you shall forgive, they are forgiven." He gave them a truly judicial power, requiring the hearing of the case, a sentence of forgiveness or otherwise, and the imposition of due reparation.

748. *I should think that with perfect contrition for one's sins, the priest's absolution should be enough.*

Firstly, I might ask how you could be sure that any particular penitent's contrition is perfect. There are many degrees of sorrow, and many variations of motive. Again, even though the sorrow were perfect, remember that God said, "Be converted to Me with all your heart, in fasting and mourning." You would say that to be converted with all one's heart should be enough! Finally, if one has really perfect contrition he wants to make reparation for his offences against God. He feels that he can never do enough to expiate them. Thus the Saints, who excelled all others in loving contrition and sorrow, excelled others also in their spirit of penance, self-denial, and mortifications. The more deeply men plunge into sin, and the weaker their spirit of contrition, the less they see the need of self-accusation and penitential expiation. Those who fight against sin, emancipate themselves from it, and develop perfect sorrow for their own past infidelities, see how evil sin is, and how it does deserve, not only the sufferings permitted by God, but self-inflicted penances as well.

749. *Must a priest keep silent about the sin of a murderer confessed to him, if an innocent man is condemned for the crime?*

The priest would violate his Christian obligations did he betray his penitent under any circumstances whatever from knowledge secured in the confessional. Firstly, evidence in civil law courts is given by witnesses in their capacity as citizens. But the criminal did not confess to the priest in his capacity as a citizen of the State, but in his capacity as the agent of God. And as God Himself keeps silent, allowing even mistaken human procedure to take its course, so must the priest keep silent. Secondly, the priest's silence is not the cause of the innocent man's arrest and punishment. That would have occurred whether the real criminal went to Confession or not. Thirdly, if the priest did act as you suggest he should, far greater evils would arise from his conduct than the one you think he could avert. If Catholics are subject to the obligation of confessing their sins in order to secure God's forgiveness, they must know that they can do so with absolute confidence and security. Any betrayal of a penitent who has come to Confession in order to fulfill a conscientious obligation imposed by God would be outrageous. And the Catholic law that the seal of Confession obliges everywhere and always, and permits of no exceptions whatever, is the only just law.

750. *This seems a mockery to me.*

That is because you have little knowledge of comparative moral obligations.

751. *To my mind the priest should be treated as an ordinary accessory after the fact.*

Since God knows, even as the priest shares in the knowledge proper to God, would you hold God as equally guilty for His silence?

752. *What if the priest's own innocent father or brother or mother were condemned? Could he expose the real murderer then?*

If the priest had no other knowledge from external sources independently of the murderer's Confession he would be bound to absolute silence. No sin submitted for absolution in the confessional may be used in any way at all by the priest outside of Confession. This law admits of no exception. If a man confessed to me that he had sinned by resolving to shoot me, I would simply have to commend myself to God's protection. Did I know where the man kept his revolver, I could not even go and remove it; for I would be making external use of knowledge secured in the Sacrament of Confession. There are many grave reasons for this severe legislation. Firstly, every penitent who manifests his sins to a priest in order to obtain absolution, does so only on the understanding that the priest will respect his confidence absolutely. And the moment a priest agrees to hear anyone's Confession, he practically enters into a contract to preserve silence concerning all sins manifested to him. Secondly, besides this contract, Christ intended the Sacrament to be in favor of the penitent. If people thought that, under certain circumstances, the priest could reveal what he hears in the confessional, they would either stay away, or be gravely tempted to conceal their sins; which would turn a Sacrament meant for their good into an occasion of grave spiritual injury. Thirdly, the legislation of the Church demands obedience. And the Fourth Lateran Council manifested clearly how strict is the mind of the Church in this matter. That Council decreed as follows: "Let the priest be most careful not to betray any penitent, by word, or sign, or in any other way. Any priest who presumes to reveal a sin manifested to him in Confession must not only be deposed from his priestly office, but must be sent to an enclosed monastery, there to do penance for the rest of his life." And the law, as I have said, permits of no exception.

753. *But if the priest does not speak, would he not be morally guilty of his innocent mother's death?*

No. It would, of course, be a terrible trial for any priest. But he would have to accept the trial, and permit things to take their course. He is not morally guilty of his mother's death, for that death would take place just the same, had the murderer not gone to him for Confession. Therefore, the priest's hearing of the murderer's Confession does not cause his mother's death. Her death is unfortunately due to the mistake of the civil authorities. If you say that at least the priest could save his mother by speaking, I can but reply that he is not morally free to speak, and that he would not therefore be morally guilty of her death. He is not morally free to speak, because he has no information as a human being, and in his capacity as a citizen of this world. St. Thomas Aquinas, one of the greatest of theologians, thus explains the matter. "Whilst hearing Confessions, the priest acts in the name of God, and should behave as God Himself behaves. But God does not reveal, but keeps silent concerning sins manifested in Confession." The priest may use only that knowledge which he acquires in the ordinary way in which other men acquire knowledge. But what he hears in Confession is to be regarded as unknown, since he does not know as a man, but shares in a knowledge proper to God alone. After all, God knows all things. And God is not morally guilty of the poor woman's death owing to the mistakes of men. Nor is God obliged to work a miracle to save her. He has entrusted the administration of justice to men in this world; and He will rectify all errors in His own good time. An innocent person may die through an accident of law, just as other innocent persons die through the accident of a motorist's false judgment, or the geological accident of an earthquake. And the priest, in the case you give, is unable to prevent the accident of his mother's death, and is certainly not morally guilty of that miscarriage of justice. Whatever you think of this reasoning, however, the fact remains that, according to the laws of the Catholic Church, no priest could betray the sin told him in the confessional.

754. Does not your Church easily reconcile itself to sin?

No. She is ever ready to reconcile the repentant sinner to God. But never can the Catholic Church justify sin of any kind. In her eyes sin is the greatest of evils. But it is not an irreparable evil. After sin, all is not finished. All can and should be put right with God. The sinner can be purified and rise as high as before. And Christ has sent His Church precisely to save people from their sins.

755. My observations suggest that your Church has quite a special love for sinners.

Your observations have led you into error. The Catholic Church has a special love for those of her members who make special efforts to live a life of virtue and holiness. At the same time, whilst she has not a special love for sinners, she does extend to them a special mercy and gentleness. They have more need of sympathy than others, and Christ Himself said that He came, not for those who need not the physician, but for the sick.

756. If a criminal is pardoned by the State, society never fully esteems him again.

Society does not see the heart, and scarcely has a heart. Jesus set the example to His Church by making His friends from amongst sinners.

757. Despite their frequent Confessions Catholics frequently fall into the same sins? How often can they get forgiveness?

You omit reference to the hosts of Catholics who have gradually grown out of their sins with the help of frequent Confession. Meantime, those who do not make much progress may lack earnest effort, but more often their sins are due, not to malice, but to frailty. By temperament and heredity they may have very strong tendencies to sinful attractions, or they may be subject to the force of habits, habits which may be due to past guilt, yet which may diminish present guilt. When you ask how often they can secure forgiveness, I say as often as they are truly repentant at the moment they seek absolution. God's love is such that even the obstinate infidelity of His children cannot exhaust His mercy. And He is ever ready to pardon even a multitude of sins. Jesus spoke of forgiveness, not seven times, but seventy times seven times. He knows our weakness, and supplies for it. To all sinners He says, "Come to Me, and I will refresh you." And in promising forgiveness, He does not add, "Unless, of course, your sins be your own fault."

758. Catholics are thus encouraged to think that they can go on sinning with impunity.

Can a Protestant who commits a sin secure forgiveness of that sin? You will have to say yes, or all Protestants are damned, for they all commit sin. Now does the thought that they can get forgiveness lead them to think they can commit further sin with impunity? Again, which is likely to prove the greater deterrent against future sin, the thought that one can get forgiveness without Confession, or the thought that one will be able to get forgiveness only provided one is willing to confess that sin to a priest? Tell me, would you find the thought of having to confess all your own sins to a priest pleasant or repugnant? If repugnant, would not the inducement be not to sin, rather than have to confess it? And cannot Protestants, therefore, get away with sin more easily than Catholics? Furthermore, is Confession an inducement to sin when no priest can forgive any sin unless the penitent is resolved to try to avoid it in the future and is prepared to repair the harm done to others, if any? And are Catholics lulled into the false idea that they can sin with impunity when they are told that, whilst the guilt of their sin is forgiven by sacramental absolution, they will yet have to expiate their sins in purgatory, and that accumulated sins will mean accumulated sufferings there? If there is one thing you cannot say, it is that the Catholic Church encourages the idea that people can sin with impunity.

759. Do you believe it is right to ask a girl at Confession all the filthy questions on immorality that the teaching of St. Ligouri advises and the Church upholds?

I don't believe it is right to ask any penitent at Confession any filthy questions. The teaching of St. Alphonsus Liguori does not advise such questions nor does the Church sanction such questions. As you have no experience whatever of this matter, whereas I have heard thousands of Confessions and am quite conversant with the principles of moral theology, including the teaching of St. Alphonsus Liguori, concerning the duties of a confessor towards his penitents, you will excuse my saying that you do not know what you are talking about. Every priest knows how to ask any information necessary for an adequate Confession, or the spiritual advice of a penitent, without trespassing against the requirements of delicacy and propriety, and without offending against the susceptibilities of any who seek his advice and help. If the confessional should be abolished because of the peculiar notions invented concerning it by the diseased imaginations of bigots who know nothing of it, then there is scarcely an institution for the spiritual, mental, or even physical welfare of human beings that should not be blown up with gelignite.

760. The recital of sins and their details must involve the moral corruption of both priest and penitent.

That's just what it must not do. Do you imagine that there are no rules governing the conduct of priests in the confessional? No one is ordained a priest without long training in moral theology, and the principles governing all his duties. If a penitent commences to go into unnecessary details, he forbids further explanation. If he has to interrogate penitents, he is guided by rules of prudence, keeping ever before his eyes the rule given by all theologians that it is better to err by defect in many things than to exceed even by one question in that which is indelicate. But I have said enough to show that your preconceived notions afford no sufficient ground for your opinion.

761. What is the Host? Where, when, and by whom was it originated?

The word Host comes from the Latin word Hostia, meaning a victim. Now the victim in the sacrifice of Calvary was Jesus Christ, and He is forever the propitiation offering Himself to His father for our sins. And because He, our victim and offering to God, is in the Holy Eucharist, the consecrated wafer is often called simply the Host. The Host, then, is the Holy Sacrament of the Eucharist in which Jesus Christ is really and substantially present under the appearances of bread. The Host, or in other words, the Blessed Sacrament, was originated by Jesus Christ in the Supper Room at Jerusalem the night before He died, when He took bread into His hands and said, "This is My Body." Matt. XXVI., 26.

762. *Is it possible for the Roman Catholic Priesthood to change bread and wine into the Body and Blood of Christ?*

It is. For the Catholic Priesthood is the Priesthood of Christ Himself communicated to those who are duly ordained as Catholic priests. It was Christ who took bread and wine, and said, "This is My Body," and "This is My Blood." After which He said to His Apostles, "Do this in commemoration of Me." Christ thus first effected the change, and gave to others the power to effect the same change.

763. *So priests are really the creators of their Creator!*

They are not. In the first place, to create is to produce something from nothing. Obviously the conversion of the substance of bread into the substance of Christ's Body is not creation. Secondly, you still speak as if a priest, in his official capacity, were exercising his own proper and merely human powers. That is not so. It is the power and priesthood of Christ, communicated to him, which effects this sacramental change. If Christ could do it at the Last Supper, He is still able to do it by means of such human instruments as He deigns to choose. Here the Creator obeys His own power insofar as that power has been committed to, and has been exercised by a priest.

764. *Are the priests mightier or more powerful than God?*

Most decidedly not. Your question is based upon the idea of a power independent of God, and in possible conflict with God. But the power by which a priest causes the presence of the Creator in the Eucharist is not a power independent of God; nor can it be opposed to God. It is God's own power vested in the priest, and it is operative only when the priest fulfills duties appointed by God according to conditions established by God. To help you to understand this take the following example: If the King had a most trusted ambassador, and commissioned him to make certain arrangements in his name, agreeing to abide by those arrangements, and do whatever the ambassador might decide, the ambassador could say truly that he had full power, even over the King. Yet his power would be derived from the King, and, in fact, be the King's own power exercised through Him.

765. *It is absurd to say that Christ's body and blood can be in a wafer made by nuns from flour and water.*

The fact that nuns make the wafers from flour and water has nothing to do with the case. No Catholic dreams that the Presence of Christ is due to any influence of the nuns, or those who make the wafers. Nor is it due to the activity of the flour and water employed. But God, Who is Omnipotent, can easily change the substance of bread into the substance of the human nature of Christ, leaving unchanged the appearances that are the object of our sense-perceptions, should He so desire. No one can deny this power to God. The only point is, does God do so? He Himself says that He does. For the Gospels clearly show that Christ left Himself under the appearances of bread and wine in the Eucharist. Well I remember how a Wesleyan clergyman tried to convert a well-read Agnostic. The Agnostic asked him whether he believed in the Gospels and that God really did come to earth, and appear at Bethlehem under the outward appearance of a little wriggling baby in Mary's lap! "Of course, I do," replied the minister. "Then if I could believe that," said the Agnostic, "I would at once join the Catholic Church. It is no more difficult to believe that God is present in the Eucharist as Catholics believe, and their doctrine is equally clearly taught in the Gospels you say you accept." He was not a Christian, unfortunately. But he was logical in this particular matter. You profess to believe in Christianity but you are not logical.

766. *It is totally against all Scripture teachings to say that the bread becomes actually the body of Christ.*

I fail to see how the teaching that it becomes His body is opposed to His words, "This is My body." In St. John VI., 47-67, you will find our Lord very emphatic about it. Like yourself, the Jews said, "How can this man give us His flesh to eat?"; and Jesus did not begin to mitigate His doctrine and say, "Of course, I don't really intend to do that. What I will give you will be ordinary bread in a kind of little memorial ceremony. You really won't have to eat my flesh in reality." Listen to what our Lord did say, "Amen, Amen, I say unto you: Except you eat the flesh of the Son of Man, and drink His blood, you shall not have life in you. He that eateth my flesh and drinketh my blood hath everlasting life." And He goes on to drive home the actual sense of His words. "For My flesh is meat indeed: and My blood is drink indeed. He that eateth My flesh, and drinketh My blood, abideth in Me, and I in him." You see how He left the Jews no loophole. Nor were they under any misapprehension. They knew what He meant, and He knew that they were thinking exactly what we Catholics hold now. They said, as you say, "This is a hard saying. Who can hear it?" And many of them left Him from that moment. He saw them going, and knew why they were going. But He would not unsay His words in order to keep them. He let them go.

767. *If Jesus said, "This is My body," He also said, "I am the true vine," and "I am the door." In those cases it was metaphorical, for our Lord is not a vine or a door in reality. Logically, therefore, we should say, "This represents My body."*

That is not a logical conclusion. In fact, it is a dreadfully shallow fallacy, and quite opposed to our Lord's clear statements which I have just given you. There is no logical parallel between the words, "This is My body," and "I am the vine," or "I am the door." For the images of the vine and the door can have, of their very nature, a symbolical sense, Christ is like a vine because all the sap of my spiritual life comes from Him. He is like a door, since I go to heaven through Him. But a piece of bread is in no way like His flesh. Of its very nature it cannot symbolize the actual body of Christ. And He excludes that Himself by saying, "The bread that I will give is My flesh for the life of the world, and My flesh is meat indeed." That is, it is to be actually eaten, not merely commemorated in some symbolical way.

768. *The use of the word "is," is explained by the fact that in the Aramaic language spoken by Jesus, there was no word for represents.*

That was a favorite argument of the early Protestants. But it has been abandoned now. For, firstly, research has shown that there were nearly forty different ways in which Christ could have said, "This represents My body," in the Aramaic language. Secondly, even prior to this research, the fact was pointed out that the Greek language abounded in symbolical expressions, and St. Mark, St. Luke, and St. Paul, who wrote in Greek under the inspiration of the Holy Spirit, should have expressed the figurative sense in that language, had the figurative sense been intended by Christ. Instead, even whilst using Greek, they select words which exclude the symbolical sense.

769. *The Apostles must have taken the symbolical sense, for they did not remark on the repugnant literal sense.*

You overlook two points: At the Last Supper it is far more likely that the Apostles would have remarked upon our Lord's words if He had meant them symbolically rather than in a literal sense. There were many other alternative expressions by which our Lord could have made it clear that He did not intend to give His actual body, but merely a symbolical memento. If Christ intended to give merely a symbol of His body, and not His body at all in reality, He chose the very worst words to convey His meaning when He said without any qualification, "This is My body." It was so unnecessary to choose that expression, and so absurd, that the Apostles would certainly have demanded an explanation of what He meant. But they did not. They knew that He meant what He said. You must remember that, long before the actual giving of His body to be eaten at the Last Supper, our Lord had given the Apostles the opportunity to express any notions of repugnance His doctrine might awaken within them. In John VI., we read of our Lord's promise to do what He did at the Last Supper. "The bread that I will give is My flesh." "Except you eat the flesh of the Son of Man," etc. Many of His listeners, rightly understanding that He meant His actual flesh, expressed their repugnance. "This saying is hard. Who can hear it?" And they left Him. Then Jesus turned to His Apostles, and gave them the opportunity to express their repugnance also, and to leave Him if they wished. "Will you also go away?" St. Peter replied, in magnificent faith, "Lord, to whom shall we go? Thou hast the words of eternal life." St. Peter did not pretend to comprehend the mystery. But he knew that our Lord meant to give His very flesh in the one way which those who went had understood, and he simply accepted our Lord's assurance because of his firm faith in Christ. But the point to note is this: Having overcome any ideas of repugnance then when our Lord promised to give His very flesh as food, there is no reason to expect expressions of repugnance from the Apostles when the promise was fulfilled at the Last Supper.

770. *Is not Christ, since His resurrection, a spirit?*

Christ rose in His complete human nature, and, therefore, in His material body. It was after His resurrection that He said to the Apostles, "See My hands and My feet, that it is I Myself; handle and see: for a spirit hath not flesh and bones, as you see Me to have." Lk. XXIV., 39. At the same time it is certain that, whilst Christ rose with the same body and blood, His material substance had undergone a radical change, and had been endowed with quite new qualities proper rather to spiritual entities than to matter as we know it. So His body could enter a closed room without any hindrance from doors and walls. But, though subject to different conditions, it was still that same body in which He had lived and died.

771. *Where does the blood come from? A spirit has no blood.*

Christ did not rise from the dead in a purely spiritual state. He rose in His material body, even though His material substance was subject to new conditions and qualities. And He retained the very substance of His flesh and blood. But your question, "Where does His blood come from?" is dictated by a grossly materialistic outlook on the merely natural plane from which the Catholic doctrine completely abstracts. Any notion of a liquid stream of blood flowing from Christ now must be put aside altogether. For the idea of liquid, or of flowing, has to do, not with the substantial reality of blood in itself, but with qualities and space-time notions which are inapplicable to the Eucharistic Presence. The substance of Christ's body and blood is present without the manifestation of those ordinary external qualities we usually associate with a body or with blood in a merely natural state. So it's useless to appeal to natural external qualities.

772. *Has your Church ever proved her claim by chemical analysis of a Host?*

No chemical test could possibly prove or disprove the Catholic doctrine. Chemicals could affect only the qualities of bread, and at best would prove that the qualities of bread remain. As the Catholic Church declares that they do remain, no progress is made by chemical tests. The inner substantial reality cannot be reached by chemicals.

Radio Replies—Volume II

773. How would the process of decay act in a consecrated and an unconsecrated Host?

In exactly the same way, since the qualities of bread remain the same before and after consecration.

774. Would there be any material difference between the two substances after decomposition?

Possibly not. In the process of decomposition, as the proper qualities of bread undergo their change and cease to be the qualities of bread as such, the substantial presence of Christ's body is withdrawn by Divine Power, God providing the connatural substance suitable to the new character of the corrupted qualities.

775. Is there a separate presence of God in the Eucharist?

There is not a separate presence of God in the Blessed Sacrament; but there is a new and distinct mode of presence. He is equally present there, but in a new and additional way. Thus, since God is everywhere, in Him we all live and move and have our being. And the humanity of Christ did this just as the human nature of any other individual man. But there was an additional mode of God's presence in Christ which has never been realized in others, insofar as the very personality of Christ was the Second Person of the Blessed Trinity. And the complete Christ, body, blood, soul and divinity, is present in a new substantial and sacramental way in the Blessed Sacrament.

776. Where and what is this human soul of our Lord at this present time?

It is still His human soul, forming an integral part together with His body of His glorified human nature. As Christ ascended into heaven in His human nature, His human soul is in heaven as part of that human nature.

777. We are told that, in the Eucharist, we receive His body and soul, as well as His divinity.

That is true. The substantial presence of Christ in the Eucharist requires that. But we must note that in the Eucharist we have the presence of the body and soul of the risen and glorified Christ, which abstracts from merely earthly conditions as we know them. And also, our Lord's presence is according to His substantial being in a way which further abstracts from accidental modifications such as those which enable us to calculate dimensions, shape, color, resistance and other phenomenal manifestations of ordinary material things.

778. How many persons are there present in the Holy Eucharist?

All three Divine Persons are present in the Holy Eucharist, for God is there present. But the Father and the Holy Spirit are there by association. When the priest consecrates the Host, the immediate effect is the presence of the body of Christ. By direct association His soul and His divinity are present. By indirect association owing to His divinity, the First and Third Persons are present together with the Second Person of the Blessed Trinity.

779. Is the Trinity received in Communion, or the Second Person only?

Since we receive Christ in Holy Communion, and since Christ is God, we receive God. And in receiving God, we receive all three Divine Persons. But where we receive the Second Person directly by reason of His immediate union with the body of Christ, we receive the Father and Holy Spirit indirectly by reason of Their association with the Second Person in the Divine Nature.

780. What relation arises between the soul of the communicant and the First and Third Persons of the Trinity?

The whole idea of Communion is to bring us into a special union with God, and that means into a more intimate union with all Three Persons of the Blessed Trinity. The Blessed Sacrament is the medium by which, in virtue of our Lord's humanity, we attain that union. His humanity links us with His divinity because itself is united with that divinity in an indestructible and personal union. And in that divinity we are brought equally into relation with all three Divine Persons. What is this relationship given by Sacramental Communion? God is present everywhere by His immensity, knowledge and power. But that is His natural presence. No one can escape it. Yet, if men cannot escape God's immensity, knowledge and power, they can escape His love, forfeiting it by sin. If a man repents of his sins and recovers God's grace, God is united to that man in a new way, no longer natural but supernatural. He is one with such a man, not only by the contact of power, but by the far more intimate contact of love. That there is a difference between these two modes of presence and union all men admit. Two people, physically present to each other in a room, could be miles apart in quite another sense. There may be nothing in common between them. They are not drawn to each other. We even say that they behave distantly to each other. There is a chasm between the spirit of one and the spirit of the other. Now it is this chasm between the soul and God which is eliminated when grace replaces sin, and when a man ceases to rebel against God's will in order to love Him. And that means a union of intimate and personal friendship with all three Persons of the Holy Trinity. Thus, Christ said, "If anyone love Me, My Father will love him, and We will come to him, and will make Our abode with him." Jn. XIV., 23. The plural indicates a new mode of presence of the Persons of the Blessed Trinity. Now this new relationship, or union, with all three Divine Persons exists in all who are in God's grace. But, as is evident, such a union can be ever intensified. One can grow in grace, and in the love of God. Now I can answer your question. Every Sacramental Communion intensifies our degree of grace, and, consequently, the intimacy of our union equally with all three Divine Persons of the Blessed Trinity.

781. What is the Mass?

The Mass is the sacrifice of the Christian dispensation in which the very body and blood of Jesus Christ under the appearances of bread and wine are offered to God by a lawfully ordained priest. This sacrifice of the Mass is offered to render honor and glory to God, to thank Him for His benefits, to make reparation for the sins of mankind, and to beg of God the graces and blessings we need. It represents and continues in our midst the one great sacrifice of Jesus on the Cross, and is offered for all the purposes for which He died.

782. Christ meant His disciples, each time they broke bread, to remember His death, and so renew their love for Him each time.

He meant that, but far more also. Not only were we to remember His death for us, but He left His very body under the appearances of bread so that we might reoffer to the Father, Him who was our victim on the Cross. Not only were we to remember His death; we were to show His death as often as the celebration occurred, thus fulfilling the prophecy of Malachy. "For from the rising of the sun even to the going down, My name is great among the Gentiles, and in every place there is sacrifice, and there is offered to My name a clean oblation; for My name is great among the Gentiles, saith the Lord of hosts." Mal. I., 11. Nor were we merely to renew our love for Him. He was to renew His life in us. So He said, "As the living Father hath sent Me, and I live by the Father, so he that eateth Me, the same also shall live by Me." Jn. VI., 58. It is difficult to understand why you should wish to belittle the greatness of His gift.

783. Hebrew X., 12, says that Christ's was a finished or perfected work or sacrifice.

The Catholic Church teaches that the Sacrifice of the Cross was a complete and perfect Sacrifice. The Mass is not a new sacrificing of Christ in the same sense, but is a new offering and application of the Christ sacrificed on Calvary. The absolute Sacrifice occurred on Calvary, the Mass is a relative Sacrifice, deriving its value from the Cross. Just as prior to His death on Calvary, Christ offered His Body and Blood at the Last Supper saying, "This is My Body which is given for you, this My Blood which is shed for you," so in the Mass, not now by anticipation but in retrospect, Christ the Victim is offered to His Father.

784. What did our Lord mean when He said, "He that eateth Me, the same also shall live by Me." Jn. VI., 58. Is not our eternal life due to the death of Christ on the Cross?

It is true that our Lord merited eternal life for us by His death on the Cross. But the fruit and grace of that sacrifice are applied to our souls by the Sacraments. Now the central Sacrament of all is the Holy Eucharist. We receive the principle of supernatural life by Baptism, but the Eucharist is ordained for the preservation of that life. The most important function for a living being is to live. And it lives by nutrition. The growth and development of a tree is an act of continuous nutrition. Now the Eucharist is for the spiritual nourishment of the spiritual life. And it does all for the life of the soul that ordinary food does for the life of the body. It sustains the life of grace. It repairs loss of spiritual vitality. It promotes progress towards a perfect development in holiness. And it gives the joy of health in the spiritual order. And since the Eucharist is the very Body, Blood, Soul and Divinity of Christ, our Lord rightly said, "He that eateth Me, the same shall live by Me." There is one essential difference, of course, between the activity of the Eucharist, and that of ordinary food. Ordinary food nourishes our bodies by becoming absorbed and transformed into our own living tissues and cells. But the opposite process occurs in the Eucharist. Holy Communion absorbs us into a unity with Christ. It is a greater and stronger food than any merely natural food. Instead of merely fostering our natural life, it intensifies our participation in a higher and supernatural life.

785. He added, "He that eateth this bread shall live forever." Yet the Eucharist does not stop death. Those who have received Holy Communion die just as those who have not.

The Eucharist is opposed chiefly to the forces which lead to the death of the supernatural life of grace within the soul. But it also robs the natural death of the body of all permanent power, since it will lead to the restoration of bodily life in a glorious resurrection. Even though Christ died, He overcame the power of death by His resurrection. Death could not keep Him in the tomb. By receiving the Body of Christ in Holy Communion, you receive the right and title to your own glorious resurrection. In the Eucharist our Lord continues His work for you.

786. I would like you to explain also what St. Paul meant when he wrote, "We, being many, are one bread, one body, all who partake of one bread." I Cor. X., 17.

The explanation of those words lies in the fact that the Eucharist is not only an individual rite, but essentially social. Holy Communion unites you in Christ with all others who also receive that wonderful Sacrament. And all being united in Christ, all should be united by the bond of charity. The Eucharist is a communion with Christ and a Common Union of all who partake of it. Thus, as bread is made from a multitude of individual grains brought into unity, so the Church is built up by a multitude of individual members held together in the unity of Christ's mystical body by the Holy Eucharist. St. Paul, therefore, insists on the special bond of loyalty and love which should prevail amongst all who have the great privilege of kneeling at the altar rails in the Catholic Church.

787. When did it become universal for the priest only to receive Communion under both kinds, and what circumstances led to this law?

The general law really dates from the Council of Constance in the year 1415. The circumstances leading up to this law were as follows. From the earliest times, Communion was given to the laity under both kinds, or under either kind. The general rule was to give Communion under both kinds, but at times, Communion was given under the form of bread only, or from the chalice only. All admitted that Christ was entirely present under either kind, and never was there any law commanding reception under both kinds by the laity. As years went on, variations in practice arose, and there was no uniformity. The Church permitted local customs to be observed. The custom of giving Communion under the form of bread only, however, became more and more widespread, chiefly for reasons of reverence and convenience. About the twelfth century, however, two erroneous doctrines began to manifest themselves. One declared that the custom of giving Communion under one kind only was a sacrilegious abuse; the other, that Christ was not completely present under either kind. It was the growth of these errors which led the Council of Constance in 1415 to define that the complete Christ is present under either the appearances of bread or the appearances of wine; that the custom of giving Communion under the form of bread only was most reasonably and wisely introduced; and that it is heretical to say that Communion must be given under both kinds. Three years later, in 1418, amongst the list of questions to be put to the Wycliffites and Hussites in order to test their orthodoxy, the following was included: "Do you believe that the custom observed by the universal Church, and approved by the Council of Constance, by which Communion is given to the laity under the form of bread only is to be so observed that no one may condemn it, nor, without the authority of the Church, depart from it?" From this it is clear that the law dates from the beginning of the fifteenth century.

788. You admit that the early Christians received Communion under both kinds?

In the early Christian Church it was the normal practice to give Communion under both kinds. But the discretionary power of the Church was in use even then. Sick people, prisoners, and martyrs received Communion under the form of bread only. Infants often received under the form of wine only, a drop or two being placed upon the tongue. All knew that the practice was perfectly valid in these cases, despite the normal custom being otherwise.

789. Christ gave both in remembrance of Him.

Quite so. And both kinds must be used in the commemorative Sacrifice of the Mass. But Communion deals with the Sacramental, not the Sacrificial aspect of the Eucharist. Therefore, St. Paul says, "He who eats or drinks unworthily is guilty of the body and of the blood of Christ." 1 Cor. XI., 27.

790. If we can receive both body and blood under the one form of bread, why should our Lord have instituted the two forms at all?

Because the Holy Eucharist was instituted not only as a Sacrament, but also as a Sacrifice. For the Sacramental reception of Christ, one kind only is sufficient. But as a Sacrifice representing the separation of Christ's body and blood on the

Cross, the Eucharist requires the external significance of separate consecrations under the solid appearances of bread and the liquid appearances of wine. Though there can be no real separation of Christ's body and blood, now that He has risen to die no more, the separation which took place on Calvary is symbolized by the apparent separation of the two elements in the separate consecrations. Thus, our Lord said, "As often as you do this you shall show the death of the Lord until He come." 1 Cor. XI., 26. Both kinds are necessary, therefore, for the Sacrifice of the Mass; either kind will do for Sacramental Communion. If a priest offers Mass, he must receive under both kinds; but if he does not wish to say Mass, yet desires to receive Holy Communion, he receives under one kind only, just as the laity, and is quite content to do so.

791. The Catholic doctrine of the Sacrifice and the Sacrament of the Eucharist supposes the correlative Sacrament of priestly orders.

That is true.

792. I find no mention of an earthly Priesthood in the New Testament.

There is plenty of evidence in the New Testament that Christ established a priestly office to be undertaken by human beings. What is a priest? He is one chosen from among men, dedicated to God by consecration, and deputed to teach and sanctify men, and to offer sacrifice to God. Now did Christ choose men, consecrate them and command them to teach and sanctify others and to offer sacrifice to God? Most emphatically, yes. He chose men. St. Luke VI., 13, says, "He called together His followers, and chose twelve." He consecrated them. Christ certainly was a priest, in fact, the great High Priest, who mediated between His Divine Father and the human race. For that priestly mission He came into the world. Very well. Now in St. John XX., 21, He said these remarkable words to those He had chosen, "As the Father hath sent Me, I also send you," i. e., you must continue in My Name My priestly mission. Then He consecrated them, communicating to them His own power, for Verse 22 says, "He breathed on them, and said 'Receive ye the Holy Ghost.'" Having chosen and consecrated them, He commanded them to teach men heavenly doctrine and to sanctify them. In St. Matthew 28, 19, He said to them, "Go, teach all nations." As regards sanctifying men, He said, in Matthew 28, 19, "Baptize them in the Name of the Father, and of the Son and of the Holy Ghost." In John XX., 23, "Whose sins you shall forgive they are forgiven them." St. James V., 14, writes, "Is any man sick? Let him call in the priests of the Church, and let them pray over him, anointing him with oil and if he have committed sins, they shall be forgiven him." Finally, Christ ordered them to offer sacrifice to God. At the Last Supper He said, "This is My body which is given for you, this is My blood which is shed for you, do this in commemoration of Me and as often as you do it you shall show the death of the Lord." As often as a lawfully ordained priest celebrates the Mass he offers this sacrifice. The same victim is offered, Jesus Christ, and by the Priesthood of Christ in the celebrant. Only by a successive and perpetual priesthood by choice, consecration and divine commission can this be done. And thus only is fulfilled the prophecy of Malachy I., 11, where he tells the Jews that the Messiah will abandon them and turn to the Gentiles predicting, "From the rising of the sun even to its going down My name will be great among the Gentiles and in every place there is sacrifice and there is offered to My name a clean oblation." Mal. I., 11. The Sacrifice of the Cross took place not in every place but on Calvary only. The Sacrifice of the Mass is offered in every place, in all countries and among all nations by the priests of the Catholic Church. So now you have the reasons for the priesthood derived from and instituted by Christ, and still existent in the Catholic Church.

793. *Did Christ institute the marriage ceremony as we have it today?*

He instituted marriage as a Sacrament. The ceremonies of today accompanying that Sacrament have been instituted by the Church in virtue of the authority to do so, given her by Christ.

794. *Does the Roman Church forbid divorce under any circumstances?*

A civil divorce on the understanding that it gives a legal right to separation, but that it in no way dissolves the latent bond of marriage and gives no right to remarriage whilst both parties still live, is permitted at times for very grave reasons. But under no circumstances does the Catholic Church permit divorce in the sense of abolishing the bond of marriage and as giving a right to remarry, where baptized people are concerned.

795. *If two Protestants marry in the Protestant Church, get a divorce, and then marry other Protestants, again in the Protestant Church, are their second marriages valid in the sight of God?*

No. When two Protestants marry, their marriage is valid in the sight of God. Now it is certain that Christ absolutely forbade divorce, and remarriage whilst the former partner is still living. Protestants, therefore, cannot, any more than Catholics, contract a second marriage valid in God's sight whilst a former wife or husband is still living. No civil divorce can give them the right to do so as far as God is concerned, for no legislation of men is really valid when it is opposed to the legislation of God. The State may tell Protestants that they are free to contract second marriages after getting a civil divorce. But if Protestants accept that permission, then they accept the principle that human laws have higher authority than the legislation of Christ Himself. We Catholics can never admit that, and to your question I must reply that, whatever civil law may say about it, a second marriage of a divorced Protestant whilst his first wife is still living, is simply null and void in the sight of God.

796. *I cannot understand the refusal of your Church to sanction divorce and remarriage.*

I am afraid that is because you are a humanitarian rather than a Christian. Christ forbade divorce and remarriage; and the Catholic Church has no option save to maintain His law. Marriage is the foundation of collective life, and symbolizes the life-giving union of Christ with His Catholic Church, a permanent union never to be broken, but to last all days till the end of the world. And the union of two Christian people who marry should last till the end of their lives.

797. *I am sure that many people who would otherwise join your Church refuse to consider it because of its attitude to this question.*

I am sure of that also. But the Catholic Church cannot water down Christian obligations in order to gain converts. She is not here to adjust Christian teaching to the desires of men. She is here to lift men to Christian ideals.

798. *Protestant Churches permit divorce and remarriage. Why does your Church stand apart, and demand more than others?*

Protestant Churches, I admit, have failed hopelessly to safeguard Christian ideals of marriage. The stability of marriage is recognized practically, and firmly defended, only by the Catholic Church. And she stands apart from the laxity of other Churches because she sees more clearly than they, and knows by divine wisdom what is the right attitude in this matter. She knows that she is divine and that she must watch over the world in the name of God. She is charged with the care of morality, and makes her stand where others give way. Her prohibition of divorce safeguards the moral welfare of the married; prevents thoughtless marriages and easy separations; protects women, so unequal to men in the contract by fragility and need of support; and benefits the children, future humanity itself, by securing for them a permanent home and continuous education. Divorce is bad for society, for individual morality, and for human life in its totality.

799. You must admit that unhappy marriages benefit no one, and do great harm.

Unhappy marriages are likely to be far fewer where possibilities of divorce and remarriage are excluded. People accuse the Catholic Church of not recognizing the real conditions of life. But in reality, she knows the best conditions of life, takes higher views, and refuses to allow that a valid marriage can be broken by divorce. Where marriage is an absolute failure and grave evils can result from continued relations, the Church permits separation; and, if necessary, civil divorce for the sake of legal obligations. But this civil divorce gives the right to separation only, not to remarriage whilst both parties still live. It is absurd to want a law safeguarding good marriages and breaking up bad ones. Such a law would react on the minds of those contemplating marriage, of parents, married couples, and children. It leads to doubt, instability, and infidelity. It is no use saying that civil divorce laws take precautions. People easily find a way through such precautionary measures, and it ends in the rule of pleasure, with the tide of divorces ever increasing.

800. What Scripture support is there for the absolute indissolubility of Catholic marriages?

Marriage is dissolved by death. But apart from that, a perfected marriage in the Christian law cannot be dissolved. Thus, in St. Mark X., 11, 12, our Lord says, "Whosoever shall put away his wife and marry another, committeth adultery against her. And if the wife put away her husband, and be married to another, she committeth adultery." In 1 Cor. VII., 39, St. Paul says, "A woman is bound by the law so long as her husband liveth; but if her husband die, she is at liberty."

801. In Matthew V., 31, 32, Christ said, "Whosoever shall put away his wife, excepting for the cause of fornication, maketh her to commit adultery."

That text does not mean, as some people seem to think, that Christ allowed divorce where adultery has been committed. We get the right interpretation from the context and from parallel passages. The context shows us that Christ was abolishing previous permissions of divorce. Parallel passages give us absolute prohibitions with no conditional clause thrown in by way of parenthesis. The passages quoted in the preceding reply leave no loophole of escape. Death alone really breaks the bond of marriage. How, then, is the text from St. Matthew to be understood? There is but one possible interpretation. Our Lord indeed intends to forbid divorce, but He does not intend to forbid permanent separation when adultery has been committed. He, therefore, takes care to exclude this latter case from His decree, throwing in the exception by way of parenthesis. The correct sense, then, is this: "Whosoever shall put away his wife (I am not speaking of mere separation without remarriage, for that is lawful in the case of fornication), but whosoever shall put away his wife and marry another commits adultery." The Christian law absolutely forbids divorce and remarriage whilst the first partner still lives. Those who accept such divorce abandon Christianity and deny the authority of Christ. No permission given by civil legislation can avail against the prohibition imposed by God. According to the teachings of Christ, divorced and remarried people are simply living in adultery.

802. *Modern Biblical criticism has made more involved the dispute between the wide and narrow concepts of divorce expressed in differing passages from Matthew and Mark.*

I deny that the differing passages of Matthew and Mark express wide and narrow concepts of divorce. They do not. They both express the same equally strict Christian concept that marriage between Christians is binding until death. Some modernist critics may claim that there is a conflict between the passages in Matthew and Mark. But that says nothing. These criticis say and unsay all kinds of things. And their verdicts are confounded by wiser critics than themselves. Moreover, the wrangling of critics outside the Catholic Church avails nothing against the authoritative teaching of that Church on the subject; save, of course, for those seeking an escape from Christian obligations. These people make much of the critics, not because they are convinced of the worth of what the critics say, but because it gives them an excuse to do what they want to do. Moral weakness is intelligible, but at least let us be straight and honest.

803. *The tendency of the times is to recognize that the matter must be treated not through the letter but in the broad spirit of Christianity.*

Christianity, then, must be adjusted to the tendency of the times. As the times change, Christianity must change. But if it changes, it is no longer the Christian religion. It will be another religion masquerading under the name of Christian. As for recognizing that the matter must be treated in the broad spirit of Christianity, the advice must be: "First catch your hare." In other words, it is necessary to recognize the broad spirit of Christianity before one can be guided by its light. The whole dispute is between the sacramental and secular views of marriage. The Christian view is the sacramental; the un-Christian view is the secular. And the spirit of Christianity will have to be broad indeed when it can accept the un-Christian view without any qualms of conscience.

804. *The peoples of the civilized world have recognized through the law of the land the civil concept of marriage.*

In their estimate, therefore, the civil concept has supplanted the Christian concept. And the source of authority for this change is simply that people want it, and that the law of the land approves it, with no reference to God's authority. One hears the echo of the old cry, "We have no king but Caesar!"

805. *I am a Protestant, but my Protestant wife has divorced me, and married again.*

She had no right to do that, of course. And so far as the Catholic Church is concerned, her bond of marriage with you is still binding.

806. *I would now like to marry a Catholic girl, but the Catholic Church will not marry us.*

You are not free to marry again whilst your wife still lives. And the Catholic Church has no option in this matter. She is here to see that the law of Christ is observed; not broken.

807. *Personally I am opposed to easy divorce laws, and think it a great mistake for any Government to enable people to get a divorce whenever it suits them, and over trifling disturbances.*

I agree with that wholeheartedly. But I cannot agree with your further remarks.

808. *If, however, a man has been divorced through what is really no fault of his, I think that the Catholic Church should permit remarriage.*

The Catholic Church is not free to permit it. Christ Himself has given the law, "What God has joined together let not man put asunder." Matt. XIX., 6.

Once two people have validly received the Christian Sacrament of Matrimony, they have entered into a contract binding until death. The Church must insist upon the necessity of observing that law. And the matter is so serious, that exceptions cannot be made. There is scarcely a general law in existence which does not hurt somebody. But if the common good demands a rigid general law in important matters, the general good must prevail over the occasional hard cases. But, in any case, the Catholic Church lacks the right to tamper with this positive law of Christ.

809. *Surely the Catholic Church should make an exception for a good Catholic who has been fervent in her religion, has always given good example, and done many services to the Church!*

Previous fervor in one's religion does not give the right to later laxity. Nor can any years of good example give the right to set a bad example; whilst former service of God and the Church cannot justify any subsequent offense against God, or subsequent violations of the laws of the Church.

810. *By refusing to marry us the Catholic Church robs us of mutual companionship and comforts of home life.*

The appeal to what is expedient from your point of view cannot outweigh that which is right from God's point of view. The girl must look elsewhere for a husband. You yourself are not free to marry whilst your wife still lives. This probably sounds hard to you. And it is hard. Not for a moment would I deny that. But do not blame me for your difficulty. I am but stating the law of Christ, and Christ never promised that the observance of His laws would always be easy. Nor did He say that we are dispensed from it when it becomes difficult. When Christ gave the law that one who puts away wife or husband, and marries another, commits adultery, the disciples saw the possibility of such hard cases, and said, "If the case of a man with his wife be so, it is not expedient to marry at all." Matt. X., 10. But our Lord did not mitigate His prohibition. I have deep sympathy for you in the trial God has permitted to come upon you. But there is only one thing to do, take up your cross and carry it for the love of Christ, faithfully keeping His law, even though your wife has violated it.

811. *If the Catholic Church won't marry such people, and they marry elsewhere, you know that they and their children will be lost to the Catholic Faith.*

Where before you appealed to expediency from your point of view, you now appeal to expediency from the viewpoint of the Catholic Church. But the case is in no way improved. We must stand to principle, even though the heavens fall. What is merely expedient cannot dispense us from what is known to be right. The Catholic Church cannot adjust the teachings of Christ to the will of men. She must persuade men to adjust their conduct to the teachings of Christ. If the girl you mention marries you outside her Church, she will know in her own heart that before God and in conscience she is not married to you at all. She will also be deprived of the rights and consolations of her religion, and all that you can offer to take the place of God in her soul is yourself. And I am sure you do not think that any human being could be a sufficient substitute for God in any human soul. If you wish to make the girl happy, you will not do so by marrying her. If you desire her good, you will rather advise her to look elsewhere for someone who is free to marry her.

812. *What advice can you give which will satisfy both the Catholic Church and myself?*

You might have brought the girl into it, too. However, the only advice I can give you which accords with the laws of the Catholic Church is that you should cease to contemplate any further marriage whilst your wife still lives. I cannot offer you the satisfaction of your own wishes in this case. I can but offer you the opportunity of Christian self-denial for the love of God.

813. Will you kindly say whether the Catholic Church has ever granted a special dispensation for the annullment of a marriage?

The Catholic Church has often declared marriages thought to be valid to be in reality null and void. These declarations of nullity merely say that no real matrimonial bond ever existed, owing to some invalidating impediment at the time of the matrimonial contract. But you evidently have in mind the case where a marriage was not null and void from the very beginning, yet where the Catholic Church has granted a decree nullifying an existent marriage bond. The Church has the power to dissolve such a marriage, and has done so, but never in the case of two baptized Christians who have both contracted and consummated their marriage. The death of one of the parties can alone dissolve such a marriage, and the Catholic Church declares that neither she nor any other power on earth can do so. Where other types of marriage are concerned, those who desire a decision can but submit their particular cases to the proper ecclesiastical tribunals which are appointed to consider whether the Church has the power to annul them, and whether there are sufficient reasons to justify her use of that power.

814. Was Napoleon's marriage to Josephine performed by a Catholic priest in a Catholic Church?

Napoleon first contracted a merely civil marriage with Josephine. This marriage being invalid in the eyes of the Catholic Church, Napoleon decided to put things right, and married her according to the requirements of the Church.

815. When Napoleon divorced Josephine and married Marie Louise of Austria, was this second marriage performed by a Catholic priest in a Catholic Church?

Napoleon's union with Marie Louise cannot be called a marriage. He forced a decree of nullity from some subservient and unauthorized clerics, and compelled others to officiate at his marriage ceremony with Marie Louise according to the religious rites of the Catholic Church. But this attempted marriage was a mockery, and has never been acknowledged by the Catholic Church as valid. His first marriage with Josephine had been rectified, was valid, and could be broken only by his or her death.

816. You say that the Roman Church does not allow divorce and remarriage, yet the Pope gave Marconi a dispensation for a divorce, and allowed him to marry again.

That is not correct. In 1905 Marconi went through a marriage ceremony with Miss Beatrice O'Brien. Miss O'Brien, despite her name, was a Protestant, and Marconi was a very ill-instructed Catholic at the time. Neither of them intended marriage in the Christian sense of the word at all. Christian marriage is a permanent contract until death. Yet these two intended marriage only until they should grow tired of each other. They may have thought that was all right, but it wasn't all right; and what they thought to be a marriage was simply null and void as a Christian Sacrament. Eventually they grew tired of each other, and got a civil divorce. Long after their civil divorce, the case was put to Rome, and a verdict was sought as to how the former experimental marriage was regarded in the eyes of the Catholic Church. The verdict was, "Null and void from the very beginning." This was not a decree of divorce breaking any existent bond of matrimony, but a decision of nullity, declaring that no bond of matrimony had ever existed, and that the parties had really been single people, however erroneously they might have thought themselves to be married. And being single people, they were free to marry whom they might please.

817. Does not the Marconi case refute Rome's boast that she does not tolerate divorce?

The decision really emphasizes how rigid the Catholic Church is in her vindication of marriage against divorce, and in her doctrine that death alone can break the bond of a valid marriage. For here she declares that a marriage is no marriage at all unless the parties do enter into the contract on the understanding that death alone can terminate it. The Marconi case, far from showing that the Catholic Church does permit divorce, is but a further indication of the rigid attitude of that Church against divorce.

818. Am I to infer that the first alliance was merely a Companionate Marriage? If so, of course, your explanation holds good.

In reality it was no more than a Companionate Marriage, though the ceremony took place in an Anglican Church, and was recognized by civil law.

819. If the marriage was civil, it was perfectly legal.

The State declared that they were to be treated legally as husband and wife. But they were not husband and wife in reality and before God. The only form of marriage recognized for Christians by the Christian religion is a permanent contract binding until death. If two Christians go through a marriage ceremony intending a temporary contract or a trial marriage only, they do not contract a true marriage at all before God, whether their marriage is acknowledged by civil law or not. Now Marconi's first marriage was a temporary contract only. The State regarded them as married, but in reality and before God they were not married at all. The State ceased to regard them as married when it granted them a civil divorce. And then they were legally, as they had been all along in reality, single people.

820. If their marriage was legal, the annulling of the same by the Pope is only divorce under another name.

That does not follow. The fact that a marriage is legal does not mean that it is a true and binding marriage in the sight of God. The civil law will accept the marriages of divorced Christians as legal, though such marriages are forbidden by God, and not recognized by Him as marriages at all. Christ said clearly, "He that puts away his wife and marries another commits adultery." If the second marriage were valid, he would not be living in adultery. It is evident, therefore, that not every legal marriage is a true marriage from the Christian point of view. Now after Marconi had secured a civil divorce releasing him from civil obligations, the case was put to Rome, asking whether the marriage had ever been a true marriage from the Christian point of view. The reply was, no. This was not a divorce annulling any existent bond, but a declaration that there had never been any bond in the sight of God at all. Surely you can see the difference between the breaking of a bond, and the declaration that no bond had ever existed.

821. Because the parties merely agreed between themselves privately that the marriage would last only as long as they wished, the Church declares it null and void.

Here you are mistaken. It is certain that Christian marriage is essentially a permanent union until death. A condition made by the parties against this essential requirement would invalidate the marriage, even though made privately. But here is the point to be noted. If a declaration of nullity is sought from the courts of the Church, the Church will not accept the word of the parties concerned that they agreed privately to limit their consent to a given period. If they went through the form of marriage, the presumption stands for the validity of that marriage until outside proof is forthcoming that the parties did agree to a temporary contract only. In the Marconi case, outside proof was available; for prior to the marriage, the girl's mother extracted a promise from Marconi that the girl was to be freed as soon as she found that she was not happy, and that she was to be granted a divorce in order that she might marry somebody else. If the two had merely agreed privately, and no evidence was available save their own, they would not have secured any decree of nullity. They would have been told that if, indeed, they had limited their consent, their marriage would be invalid before God. But as they could not prove that in the external order, the marriage must stand, and their obligation would be to rectify their defective consent at once, and render the marriage valid in conscience by mutual agreement of permanency until death.

822. Then people have only to say afterwards that they did not intend a permanent union, and ask the Church to declare it null and void!

I think I have already shown that your impression is not justified. Of course, since the parties make the contract, and it is essential that they intend a permanent contract, the parties could invalidate the marriage by refusing to intend a permanent contract. But the Church teaches that this would be gravely sinful, and that such a mock marriage would be no marriage at all, and that any attempt to live as married people would be mortal sin. So that she leaves no one free to make such a contract. If a couple did contemplate such a temporary contract, and the Church knew of the conditions beforehand, the Church would refuse absolutely to perform the marriage. If the parties made the condition privately, and the Church did not know, the Church can but take it for granted that they intend a true and permanent marriage in the Christian sense of the word, and perform the ceremony. But their merely saying afterwards, as you suggest, that they really didn't mean a permanent marriage, and will the Church please give them a decree of nullity will be of no use. The Church won't take their word for it, will refuse the decree, and order them to rectify their defective consent.

823. When a Roman Catholic dies, the priest anoints his sense-faculties with blessed oil to keep away the evil spirits, some say.

Whoever asserts that to be the purpose is wrong.

824. Or perhaps it is to purify those organs from all evil.

You are nearer the mark now, but not quite right yet. The last anointing is to purify the soul of those sins it has committed through the misuse of the various bodily senses.

825. Would you explain something about the Sacrament of Extreme Unction?

Extreme Unction is that last of the Sacraments for the individual, by which those who are seriously ill and in danger of death, are anointed by the priest for the remission of their sins and, if it be God's will, for their restoration to health. The Sacrament of Extreme Unction gives special sacramental graces; and these in turn give an altogether special strength and peace of soul just when they are most needed. This Sacrament also, by the power of Christ, eradicates any lingering traces of sin; and partially, where it does not completely, fulfils the expiation due to sin in the next life.

826. Why does the priest have to anoint all the bodily senses?

Because so often it is by the bodily senses that people are led into sin. Now those bodily senses are five: sight, hearing, smell, taste and touch. The priest therefore anoints the body according to these senses, the eyes, the ears, the nostrils, the mouth and the hands. At each anointing he says the appropriate prayer. For example, when anointing the ears he says, "By this holy anointing and through His most loving mercy, may the Lord forgive you whatever sins you have committed through the sense of hearing." And so on, with the others. The Greek Orthodox Church has this same Sacrament of Extreme Unction, but differs slightly in its method of anointing the body, choosing the forehead, the chin, the cheeks, the hands and the feet. But the Sacrament is essentially the same, a bodily anointing with oil in the name of the Lord. In cases of urgent necessity, when there is no time to fulfil all the anointings, the Catholic priest may give one only, anointing the sick person on the forehead, and saying, "Through this holy anointing may the Lord forgive you whatever sins you have committed."

827. May I ask you of what use is such anointing when the spirit has fled?

It is of no use when the spirit has fled. It is of use only on the supposition that the soul has not yet departed from the body. Priests are forbidden to anoint a dead body from which the soul has certainly departed.

828. Where does man go after death?

His body will go temporarily back to the dust. His soul goes to the judgment of God, and thence to one of three possible states. If the soul is quite fit for heaven, it enters heaven. If it is not quite fit for heaven, it goes to purgatory. If quite unfit for heaven, it goes to hell. Thus Scripture says, "It is appointed unto men once to die, and after this the judgment." Heb. IX., 27. It tells us also that one who has been fully faithful to God will receive the invitation, "Enter thou into the joy of thy Lord." One who dies in God's grace and friendship, but who has not been fully faithful, will be saved, according to Holy Scripture, but so as by fire. One who dies rejecting God will be rejected by God and will be buried in hell.

829. Is not a man judged by his conscience?

He is. But by his true conscience. Many men during this life warp their conscience by continual self-deception. They pretend that what they want to do is right, and gradually lull themselves into a sense of security. But when the soul goes from this world, all pressure will be removed, and the true conscience will speak, and the voice of God will not be denied. Conscience warns people now. Then it will judge them.

830. Can you establish the particular judgment of each soul at death, proving it from Scripture?

The doctrine is sufficiently established by the fact that it is the official teaching of the Catholic Church; and it would not really matter whether the doctrine were contained in Scripture or not. However there are more than enough indications in Scripture. Christ described the deaths of the rich man and Lazarus the beggar as resulting in an eternally fixed state for each, the one in hell, the other in heaven. And that this was prior to the general judgment is clear from the fact that the rich man is made to plead that his relatives yet living be warned in time. St. Paul declares that the just receive their heavenly reward immediately after death, without waiting for the general judgment, and said that he desired to die and thus to be with Christ which is far better. St. John declares in the Apocalypse that the souls of the martyrs are living and reigning with Christ, adding that for them the general judgment has no terrors. And in XIV., 13, he says, "Blessed are the dead who die in the Lord. From henceforth now, saith the Spirit, they rest from their labors, for their works follow them."

831. If the particular judgment is an infallible doctrine, are not all the references to the last day, and a resurrection, and also a judgment by Christ, just pure fiction?

Not in the least. The particular judgment is in no way incompatible with those truths. I cannot understand why you should think it so. At the last day the bodies of the dead will be raised from the tomb and from the dust into which they have returned. Souls already judged in the particular judgment will be reunited with their respective bodies, and in the general judgment by Christ in His majesty and glory the sentences they have already received will be publicly confirmed and proclaimed. No real difficulty presents itself in this matter. Nor is the general judgment useless. The particular judgment is for each soul in turn; the general judgment is not for us, but for the universal vindication and glory of Christ.

832. Will Christ have power in the general judgment to reverse the results of the previous particular judgment?

No. For God cannot contradict Himself. In each case it is a question of the infallible decision of God. In the particular judgment His decision is given; in the general judgment it is publicly reaffirmed.

833. Should not people serve God now, instead of staking all on the state they will be in at the moment of judgment?

The only way of being sure of right dispositions at the moment of judgment is to serve God now. He who is right at every moment is right at any moment. All the same, death is a dramatic moment. No drama penned by any playwright has ever had so critical and astonishing an ending as that which every soul will encounter when it leaves the stage of this world. However familiar we may be with the idea, the realization that eternity was wrapped up in our fifty or sixty years in this world will prove rather staggering.

834. What is hell?

According to Christ, it is a state of eternal misery and suffering, the pain of which is best likened to that caused by fire. As there is both good and evil in this world, so do their counterparts exist in eternity. And as evil is the opposite of good, so hell is the opposite of heaven. If heaven is light and happiness, liberty and peace, hell is darkness and misery, servitude and torment. As a man sows, so shall he reap. If a man dies identified with the good, he will save his soul and attain heaven. If he dies identifying himself with evil, he will lose his soul. By God's mercy, however, there is no need for any man to do that. However greatly one has sinned, by sincere repentance he can obtain forgiveness and salvation through the merits of Jesus Christ and by fulfilling the conditions prescribed by Christ. When we speak of Jesus as Our Savior we mean that He saves us from the eternal ruin of the hell we have deserved. Those who deny the existence of hell can find no real significance in the title of Savior which belongs to Jesus Christ.

835. I find hell an awful proposition.

So do I, as well as all thinking men. The best thing we can do is to make sure that hell never becomes anything more than an awful proposition. If a man fell into the awful reality of hell, he would see at once that no proposition formulated by men could possibly do justice to the grim actuality.

836. If there is a hell, God can't be there; and if He is not there, He is not everywhere. Therefore God is limited, and not infinite.

That argument begins with the false premise that God is not present in hell. For not even hell can escape God's presence. But whilst God is so present everywhere that even hell cannot be exempted, He is not so present in hell that He could be affected by hell. His very mode of presence is proper to Himself, and different from any notion we can form of it adequately by ideas drawn from created relationships. He will certainly be present there by His being, and knowledge, and power. But it will be a physical presence only, affording no consolation to those enduring the sufferings of hell. We can form a faint idea of what this means by our own present experience. Two persons can be physically present to each other in the same room. But there can be a chasm between them from another point of view. They have nothing in common; feel not sympathy but antipathy for one another; and are, in fact, said to behave distantly to one another. In other words, in the moral order, there is a distance between them which physical presence can but accentuate. In hell, of course, the misery will be on one side only, that of the soul estranged from God. At any rate, God is everywhere, even in hell, however our limited ideas may fail to explain the nature of His presence. And human souls must cry with David, "Whither shall I go from Thy spirit? Or whither shall I flee from Thy face? If I ascend into heaven Thou art there; if I descend into hell Thou art present." Psalm 138, 8.

837. *God, who is all-merciful, would not wish to torture anything for all eternity.*

Correct. Therefore He warns us that there is an eternal hell, and forbids us to do the things that could take us there. If He wanted us to go to hell, He would not do that. If I want a man to fall into a trap, I don't carefully explain its presence and tell him how to avoid it. Also that God does not want us to go to hell is evident from the fact that He sent His only-begotten Son to die for our very salvation from so dreadful a fate. But, in appealing to God's mercy, there is one point you overlook. What if a soul rejects God's mercy, won't appeal to it, doesn't want it? It can't refuse God's mercy and have it. Such a soul will encounter God's justice, and Scripture tells us that it is a terrible thing to fall into the hands of the living God. And Jesus tells us that the sentence of the wicked will be, "Depart from Me ye cursed into everlasting fire, which was prepared for the devil and his angels." There is no hint in Scripture that lost souls will ever cease to exist.

838. *Boundless mercy seems to contradict eternal misery, don't you think?*

I don't. Boundless mercy supposes the possibility of eternal misery. There is no room for mercy unless there be misery, and no room for boundless mercy unless we suppose boundless misery. Boundless mercy is a mercy which forgives that which does deserve boundless misery. But mercy is not forced upon people. It must be asked for and accepted. It cannot be rejected and at the same time be enjoyed. And if a person is in a state of sin deserving boundless or eternal misery, yet rejects the offer of boundless mercy, what is there left but hell? If you assert that because God is boundless in His mercy, as He is, no one could go to eternal misery, will you say that there is no hell? Or that God has made a hell knowing that it was quite unnecessary as it is to be eternally untenanted? And what will you do with Satan? Is he not in that everlasting suffering prepared for him and his angels? He who proves too much, proves nothing. There is something wrong with an argument which ends in the denial of known facts. God is a God of boundless mercy. He has revealed that there is a hell of eternal misery. There is no contradiction. People can escape the boundless misery by a sincere appeal to God's boundless mercy.

839. *Would a man be good if he built a bridge knowing that many would fall through it and get drowned?*

If he built a bridge knowing that many would have to fall through it, he would scarcely be good. But if he built a bridge through which no one need fall, and warned people not to fling themselves over, he would be good in providing a bridge. But people who say they do not believe in hell because God is good are talking thoughtlessly. They believe in a good God. Now that God through Christ His Son has taught us that there is a hell. He would not be good if He taught us a deliberate lie. A good God tells the truth. And if there is a hell it is good of Him to tell us. If there is a hell, it is well to know that there is one.

840. *I prefer to believe in a good God.*

No one can believe in a good God and logically refuse to believe in hell. If love of the good be infinite, it demands an equally intense hatred of evil, the negation of good. Good and evil exist in this world and both have their counterparts in eternity, heaven or hell. To accept heaven because we like it, and reject hell because we don't like it, is going by feeling and sentiment, not by reason.

841. *Would it not be better not to create than to punish some souls forever in hell?*

Even did that seem better to us, our petty ideas are not the measure of all that is truly wise. Creation is a fact. Hell is a fact. That souls can be lost is a fact. If we find it hard to reconcile these facts with our human ideas we can only conclude that our ideas must be limited and inadequate, and that God's infinite wisdom must perceive more aspects than those to which we advert. God has, in fact, revealed this truth in the words, "My thoughts are not your thoughts, nor your ways My ways." We are too prone to concentrate on individual details and lose sight of the whole scheme. God had not to choose between creating this or that individual, but a race of beings propagating its kind. And He saw that the general good far outweighed individual losses. After all, if my great-grandfather lost his soul, that would be his own fault. There was no need for him to do so. But if he had not been allowed to exist, my grandfather, my father and myself would not have had the opportunity of saving our souls. There is no reason why I should be deprived of eternal happiness (if I attain it) because my great-grandfather chose to throw away his eternal happiness (if he did).

842. *Do you think that all serious sins deserve hell?*

Undoubtedly they deserve it. But that is not to say that they will necessarily get it. God's mercy is such that sin can always be forgiven. Only unrepented sin can keep a soul out of heaven. Paradox as it may seem, there are mortal sins permitted by God for a man's very salvation. Christ has said, "He who humbles himself shall be exalted." Matt. XXIII., 12. Ever He insists on humility. "Unless you become as little children, you shall not enter into the kingdom of heaven." Matt. XVIII., 3. Children believe without question, and instinctively obey. We must have child-like faith in Christ, and child-like obedience to His will. Yet where Christ says, "He who humbles himself shall be exalted," He also says, "He who exalts himself shall be humbled." If men exalt themselves, whether by pride of intelligence or independence of will, then God will break them by humiliation after humiliation, if He loves them. Again and again He has ground the intellectually proud down to the very dust, permitting them to fall into the most humiliating sins, whether through drink or sensuality, sins smashing up their self-esteem, and, as I have said, meant for their salvation, not for their damnation. St. Augustine, with all his great intellectual gifts, was thus brought low. Had God not permitted his early sins, he would never have shed his later and saving tears of humility. So I say that all serious sins deserve hell, but through God's mercy, not all serious sins are thus punished.

843. *A small boy commits his first mortal sin and dies unrepenting next day. He goes to hell. An old man after a lifetime of sin repents at the last and goes to heaven. Why is this not an injustice on God's part?*

Because God's granting of salvation to one who does fulfill the necessary conditions cannot possibly oblige Him in justice to grant salvation to one who does not fulfill those conditions. Apart from your hypothetical description of the differences in ages and the quantity of iniquity, you say in substance that one human being dies in grave sin, and another does not. Keep in mind all the conditions necessary for a mortal sin, clear knowledge, serious matter, deliberate choice, and full moral responsibility. No human being at any stage in his life has any right to be in such a state of mortal sin, and if anyone is in that state when death comes, his blood is on his own head. But in such theoretical cases there is danger of a false idea of God. We must not reason as if God were a God of vengeance only, and not a vigilant and good Providence. He is present at the decisive hour and human beings are under His influence even when they are to give their eternal yes or no. He does not wait to catch small boys in a state of mortal sin. And mortal sin does not create in God the will to damn forever in hell, but to convert. He says Himself, "I will not the death of the sinner, but that He be converted and live." To everyone therefore He offers graces of conversion, and those graces must be refused in a decisive manner, if a soul is to be lost. Your small boy is pure hypothesis. Of its nature one only mortal sin deserves hell. But that God would not give the boy a chance to repent, or that the boy would not correspond with last graces, is pure supposition. However, if any soul does go from this world in a state of unrepented personal mortal sin, that soul goes to hell.

844. *You think the offense suffered by God merits such a terrible sentence. But why?*

The fact that there is a hell we know by revelation. But it is a mystery just as the revealed doctrine of the Trinity, or of heaven itself. However, we know at least that hell is misery and for eternity. Now why does a grave and deliberate offense against God merit such a terrible sentence? In the abstract it does, because it is the insulting of an infinite goodness and of an infinite majesty. The justice of hell depends on the injustice of sin. And here we must be content not to comprehend. For our ideas of justice are associated with relations of man to man. There is an infinite lack of proportion between human justice, and the justice between an infinite Creator and the finite creature. But all that is a matter of abstract principles. In the concrete, hell is a terribly logical consequence of actual realities. There is but one God, one Savior, one source of eternal life and one salvation. If a man forfeits this, hell alone can be the result. He who dies rejecting an infinite good deserves to experience the loss of that infinite good. In other words, if a man rejects God, he should experience rejection by God. And hell is eternal, not so much because sin is infinite, but because it is without remedy. The lost cannot escape hell because they do not repent. They do not repent because they are out of that state in which change is possible. They are out of time, out of probation, and beyond the reach of grace. They are always punished because always evil.

845. *Would not one hundred years reckoned by earthly standards of time be quite sufficient?*

Ideas of successive moments according to our experience of time in this world cannot possibly give us an adequate standard of comparison. Hell is a mystery outside our time and space notions. And we must realize that we are talking like children on our own little level and in our own little way. It is as if a child were to go into a shop and ask for eight ounces of misery. Time and eternity are in two different orders of being. But taking your analogy for what it is worth, I would say that the only thing which can destroy sin is repentance with the help of God's grace. For by that one makes his own the expiation of sin offered by Christ on the Cross. And that is the only possible expiation of sin. Without that, sin can never be expiated. Therefore a soul in hell, unable to repent and deprived of grace, never can succeed in expiating his sins, whether in one hundred years or a million. But as I have said, our reckoning by time and years is inadequate. Eternity is a mystery to us, and we can but say that the soul which goes from this world in mortal sin never attains happiness.

846. If a man were born a lunatic, was never baptized, committed murder, and would murder again, yet dies without repenting, would he go to hell?

Such a man could not go to hell. If he has been a lunatic from birth owing to defective brain-formation, he has never really attained the normal use of reason, and therefore has never been responsible for his conduct. Murder would be a crime for one in possession of his faculties. But a lunatic is not responsible for, and guilty of, what would constitute a crime for others. Lunatics from birth, who have never been baptized, meet with a fate similar to that of unbaptized infants, who are debarred from entering heaven because they lack Baptism, yet who cannot be sent to hell, because they lack responsibility. They attain to a state of eternal natural happiness. I have said that the brain cells do not make a man good or evil, although they do condition the activities of the soul. An imperfect brain lessens both the capacity of the soul for good operations, but also the responsibility of the soul before God. A completely disordered brain which involves straight-out lunacy, does not make a man morally good or morally evil. It leaves him without any moral responsibility at all. And such a lunatic ranks as an infant which has never come to the use of reason.

847. Why base our religion on fear?

There is no need to do so, and it would be wrong to do so. Our religion is based upon faith, hope and charity. But these very virtues make you believe in hell, hope to escape it, and do all you can to help others escape it. In other words, the mere fact that we are not obliged to be thinking day and night of hell does not give us the right to deny it. Hell is not the sum total of the religion, taught to Catholics, at least. Out of three hundred and fifty-seven questions in the ordinary Catechism, three deal directly with the doctrine of hell. Hell is one doctrine of the Christian religion; a doctrine not to be viewed in isolation, but in the light and perspective of the whole Christian economy. There is no need for any soul to go to hell, but one of the surest inspirations to make use of the means to avoid hell arises from the thought of its existence.

848. I have heard Roman Catholic talks and sermons several times, and each time they essentially pertained to hell fires and how to avoid them.

I do not think you could have heard many sermons by Catholic priests. For sermons on hell are certainly rare. Indirectly, of course, priests will stress the necessity of saving one's soul and the inevitability of each human being's judgment by God with the twofold possibility of either heaven or hell for eternity. But, whilst the fear of the Lord is the beginning of wisdom, there is no need to remain in that fear without rising to the wisdom and the love of God which is so much more positive and precious. The Christian life does not consist only in avoiding sin. It requires also the practice of virtue. Not only salvation, but sanctification of one's soul is important. Still we must never lose sight of the bedrock necessity of saving our souls. When the rich young man said to Christ, "Master, what must I do to possess eternal life?" Lk. X., 25. Our Lord replied, "If thou wilt enter into life, keep the commandments." He did not warn the young man about any overanxiety as to the saving of his soul. In fact, again and again He Himself stressed the necessity of retaining very serious views on the subject.

849. This factor naturally makes me, an outsider, think that priests attempt to instill fear into their parishioners.

Catholic priests must preach the Gospel of Christ, and all of it. And I certainly do not think they preach the severer truths of the Gospel out of proportion to their place in the preaching of Christ Himself. Again and again our Lord, who said that He came to save that which was lost, dwelt on the dread fate of those who continued in their sins. To the Pharisees He said, "Ye fools, ye blind guides, ye whited sepulchres, ye serpents and generation of vipers, how can ye escape the damnation of hell?" He spoke of the worm of remorse that dieth not, of weeping and gnashing of teeth, of the everlasting fire prepared for the devil and his angels, and declared that it would be more tolerable for Sodom in the day of judgment than for those who rejected Him. And to all of us His question stands as a challenge, "What does it profit a man to gain the whole world and lose his soul? What will a man give in exchange for his soul? Better go blind and lame to heaven than seeing and whole to hell. Fear not those who can kill the body, but cannot kill the soul. But I will tell you whom to fear. Fear ye Him who can destroy both body and soul in hell. Yea, fear ye Him."

850. By this means priests force their people to go to Church.

That is not true. You must not judge Catholics to be so devoid of the love of God that they do not personally want to go to Church for the positive spiritual blessings He gives them, and the consolation of His special presence. If, however, some individual Catholic had not enough personal love of God to induce him to attend Mass, and did so chiefly from the fear of losing his soul, that would certainly be better than not going at all. Nor could you say that the priest forced him to go by preaching the severe doctrine of hell. It is the faith of that individual man in the doctrine preached by the priest that takes him to Mass. As a matter of fact, the priest no more forces a Catholic to be faithful by preaching the doctrine of hell than Christ can be said to have forced His disciples to be true to Him by so insisting upon that doctrine in the first place.

851. What Scriptural authority has the Catholic Church for teaching that there is a purgatory?

The Catholic Church has Scriptural authority for whatever doctrines she teaches, insofar as she was appointed to be the teacher of mankind by Christ. It would not really matter whether a given doctrine were contained in Scripture or not. Whilst everything in the Bible is true, not everything true is in the Bible. I am getting rather tired of being asked to prove everything from the Bible, as if the Bible were the only test of what we must accept or reject. And even if you insist that the Bible only is the guide, you could not quote any Scriptural authority to show that there is no purgatory. However, after these preliminary remarks, whilst Scripture says nothing against purgatory, does it indicate that there is a purgatory? It does. Don't be baffled by a mere name. It is the thing, not its name, which is in question. Purgatory is an intermediate state, which is neither heaven nor hell, and in which souls are purified from the stains of sin contracted in this world. To prove purgatory, therefore, I have to prove that there is an intermediate state, and that souls are purified after death. Now that the intermediate state is a reality is evident from 1 Peter III., 18. St. Peter there says that Christ died in the flesh, but that His living soul went to preach to those spirits that were in prison. Those souls were in a state which was after this life, yet which was neither heaven nor hell. St. Paul tells us in 1 Cor. III., 15, that if, at a man's judgment after death, his lifework proves to be imperfect, he shall be saved, yet only by fire, i. e., after being purified as by fire. This cannot refer to the eternal punishment of hell, for out of hell there is no redemption. It refers, then, to a temporary loss of the Vision of God, and the enduring of a purifying expiation for a time, the soul being ultimately saved and admitted to heaven. This is practically the definition of purgatory.

852. A Catholic booklet on purgatory says that, if all the sufferings of this world were visited upon one human body, the slightest pain of purgatory would be much greater.

That statement is based on the truth that after death the pain of the privation of seeing God is worse than any physical pain. This is the essential suffering of purgatory wherein souls are purified from stains of sin. Naturally, the lesson is driven home that sins will have to be expiated sooner or later, and that they are not worth while, even though we do secure forgiveness of them as far as guilt is concerned. But in meditating or in preaching upon this basic fact, some room must be allowed for amplification and imaginative description. If not, we would have to give up talking about most things. The idea that the least pain in purgatory is worse than all bodily sufferings in this life is quite a possibility, insofar as the soul alone goes to purgatory and, therefore, endures spiritual sufferings which are worse than merely bodily afflictions. We must note, too, that in this life there are always distractions lessening advertence to one's state; but death will have removed all earthly interests from the soul. Writers who dwell on the intensity of sufferings in purgatory are rightly impressing the idea that intense efforts should be made to avoid sin. We should do our utmost to avoid increasing our own purgatory, even as we pray for those souls actually undergoing such dread purifications. Purification of soul will not be an easy and pleasant thing, to say the least. Sin is easy and pleasant, its reparation is quite the contrary.

853. *No one has returned from the dead to tell anyone of the existence of purgatory.*

You believe in heaven; but has anyone returned from the dead to tell you of the existence of heaven? You believe in heaven because it is the teaching of Scripture that there is a heaven. So also is it the teaching of Scripture that there is a purgatory.

854. *I admire the Salvation Army which speaks of its dead as promoted to glory.*

I, too, admire much in sincere members of the Salvation Army. But the idea that a soul is promoted to glory, or enters heaven immediately after death, has no foundation beyond their desire that it should be so. The extravagant belief does credit to their hearts, but it is a case of their wish being father to their thought. They have not a scrap of evidence that things are really so.

855. *Would not the blood of Christ shed for all sinners cleanse their souls?*

It could do so, did souls make full and perfect use of it. But the precious blood of Christ does not cleanse the souls of men in spite of themselves. Men have to do their part by sincere repentance and by the yielding of their souls to Christ in faith and love. But there are degrees of repentance, and faith, and love. Granted perfect repentance, and faith, and love, a soul participates fully in the effects of the precious blood of Christ. All sins are then expiated, and no further expiation in purgatory will be required. But some souls have very imperfect repentance, and faith, and love; whilst others have none at all. The precious blood of Christ does its work in a soul proportionately to the dispositions of that soul.

856. *Has any religious body other than yours made it an article of faith?*

Other religious bodies are not in the habit of defining where they stand, or of declaring any certain allegiance to any doctrine, save perhaps to the doctrine that there is a God of some sort. They change with every wind of doctrine, and feel the need of being able to repudiate their previous teachings, whenever it becomes expedient to do so. I refer, of course, to Protestant Churches in general. The Greek Orthodox Church is more stable, though it, too, is becoming affected by modernistic tendencies, and abandoning rigid adherence to original Christian teachings. However, it is part of the Greek Orthodox faith that there is a purgatory in which souls are detained in order to expiate their sins, and in which they can be helped by our prayers, and by the Holy Sacrifice of the Eucharist. The Anglo-

Catholic section of the Church of England is also reviving this doctrine, declaring it to be a part of Christian teaching which was mistakenly rejected by Protestants at the time of the Reformation. As a matter of fact, although Protestants rejected purgatory at the Reformation, choosing to keep only an eternal heaven and an eternal hell, they are now rejecting the eternal hell idea, and teaching a purgatory of progressive purification and improvement after death until one does attain the perfection required for heaven.

857. I have even heard Catholics speak of purgatory as a consoling doctrine, though the Protestant idea of going straight to heaven is much more comfortable.

The existence of the intermediate state of purification called purgatory is not only a reasonable doctrine, but it is a doctrine revealed by Almighty God. And since it is true, the doctrine is bound to be more consoling than its denial. There is more consolation in knowing the truth than in being ignorant of it. But even apart from this, the consolation of the doctrine is apparent all along the line. The Protestant doctrine is most uncomfortable. Protestants admit only heaven and hell. I speak in general, for many don't admit heaven, still more don't admit hell, and yet more do not admit anything at all where religion is concerned. But let us take those who profess at least orthodox Protestantism. These deny purgatory, and admit only heaven and hell. Right. Then if a man is not quite good enough for heaven, he's got only one place left to go, and that's hell. The Catholic doctrine gives an extra chance. The poor beggar might not be good enough for heaven, but we deny that he is necessarily bad enough for hell. He may go to purgatory until he is fit for heaven. And certainly our doctrine that there is a purgatory is more consoling than the doctrine that there is no purgatory. Again, it is more consoling to know that I will be forgiven and purified, than to believe that my sins will be overlooked, but that I shall be left as I am, intrinsically unchanged. I know that I would not like to be thrust into God's presence just as I am. The contrast would be more painful than any purgatory imaginable. Those who talk so glibly of no purgatory, besides ignoring God's own teaching, have either a very poor idea of God's majesty and perfection, or else a very extravagant idea of their own goodness.

858. How do you know when any particular soul goes to purgatory?

If he goes there, we know that he goes there immediately after death. Whether he goes there we cannot say for certain. If he were a Saint, he would not go there. But Saints are so rare, that all the chances are that the vast majority have some faults to be expiated in purgatory.

859. Who is the judge to say what souls are in purgatory?

God alone. The Catholic Church does not claim to be able to say what particular souls are in purgatory, and which ones are not, save in the case of the canonized Saints. Those she knows to be in heaven. It may happen, of course, that people will pray for one who is no longer in purgatory but who has been released and admitted to heaven. But Catholics don't mind the extra prayers. It's better to say more than are necessary than deny to our departed loved ones the help we can give them. And, as no prayers are wasted, if we offer them for souls who are not in purgatory, they will benefit others who are there, and that in virtue of the communion of Saints in which we profess belief every time we say the Apostles' Creed.

860. If a man is sentenced and hanged for wilful murder, but dies truly repentant, will he enter purgatory before going to heaven?

All would depend on the degree of his repentance, and the intensity of his love for God prior to and at the moment of his death. If, by some miracle of grace, he attained to an utterly unselfish and perfect love of God, he would go straight to heaven. For such love covers a multitude of sins. "Because she has loved much," said our Lord of the sinful woman, "many sins have been forgiven her." Lk. VII., 47. The reason for this is that perfect love secures perfect identification with Christ, and a complete participation in the merits of His death and sufferings on the Cross. His expiation of sin, therefore, abrogates the necessity of the soul's own personal expiation of its sins in purgatory. However, the attaining of such perfect love of God after a life so little disposing one to it would be a miracle of grace, and not normal. Normally, even though a soul repented sufficiently for its salvation, it would yet have to expiate its sin in purgatory according to St. Paul's teaching that, if one has done evil, one will answer for it; and if saved, will be saved so as by fire. Naturally, we must take the normal for granted, and pray for the souls of the departed, rather than fondly take it for granted that they attained to dispositions of perfect love which may not have been theirs at all.

861. Are the prayers for the dead derived from the Old Testament?

The duty to pray for the souls of the dead is inculcated in the Old Testament, and it is again taught in the New Testament. Christ Himself tells us that there are sins which secure their full remission only after death; that men, far from being able to sin with impunity, will expiate their sins, and will not be liberated from their expiation till they have paid the last farthing. St. James tells us that we must pray for one another that we may be saved, and that the continual prayer of a just man avails much. If we can pray for those undergoing trials in this life, we can pray for those undergoing trials in the next life after their day of judgment has brought them before the tribunal of God's justice. You accept the New Testament. Yet there we find St. Paul, in writing to Timothy, offering a prayer for the repose of the soul of his dead friend, Onesiphorus. "The Lord grant unto him to find mercy," he prayed. 2 Tim. I., 18. Commenting on those words, the Reverend M. F. Sadler, an Anglican scholar, says, "Onesiphorus was dead. But we have no reason at all to believe that the moment a soul dies it is perfected. And in every Christian Liturgy that has come down to us there are prayers for the departed, asking of God peace and rest for them." In an Anglican manual of doctrine by the Reverend Vernon Staley which I have by me at the present moment, I find this statement, "It is quite right to pray for the departed."

862. Christ never told anyone to pray for the dead.

Not all that Christ said or did is recorded in the Gospels. They are fragmentary accounts only. Meantime, those who believe in Christ accept both Old and New Testaments as the Word of God. Now in the Old Testament we read, "It is a holy and wholesome thought to pray for the dead that they may be loosed from their sins." 2 (Mach. XII., 46. In the New Testament St. Paul tells us that Christians are members of Christ and members, therefore, of one another, so that if one member suffer anything, all the members suffer with it. And St. James tells us to pray for one another, advice certainly not limited to this life only. So we find St. Paul praying for the departed soul of his fellow laborer, Onesiphorus.

863. What does an indulgence mean? I am a non-Catholic, and feel that many other non-Catholics must wonder what it means.

You can be quite sure that many other non-Catholics have no idea what is the meaning of an indulgence according to the Catholic teaching. It is the remission of the temporal punishment due to sin after the sin itself has been forgiven. For example, let us suppose that a child disobeyed his father and was to be put in a dark room without supper. But he showed such remorse that his father forgave him the offense but insisted on his going to bed supperless as a punishment. The child accepted his punishment so submissively and said his prayers so fervently that his mother was permitted by the father to give him a cookie in bed. Now apply that to any soul. By our sins we both offend God, and deserve punishment. Even after the offense against God is forgiven, we still have to expiate our sins, either in this world or in the next. But the Church grants us a remission of the expiation we should undergo, provided we do certain good works such as prayer, fasting, or almsgiving. Scripture itself warns us to redeem our sins by almsgiving. That is, even after being forgiven, we should remember our past sins, and try to compensate for them by works of charity. An indulgence, therefore, is a remission by the Church of the penalties due to our sins even after they have been forgiven.

864. Do not indulgences give Catholics permission to commit sin?

No. No such indulgences are available in the Catholic Church. The only people who ever granted indulgences of that nature were the early Protestant reformers. For they said that people are saved by faith only. And they declared themselves saved, and unable to be lost whatever they might do. Such a doctrine, denying the necessity of good works, was logically an indulgence to do as one pleased. In the Catholic Church, however, sin is held to be essentially evil. At all costs it must be avoided. Never can any permission be granted to sin. And no matter how holy a person may be, if he does sin gravely and dies without repentance and conversion to God, he will lose his soul. Moreover, one who is in a state of grave sin can never gain an indulgence whilst in that state. One must be in God's grace and friendship before an indulgence can be gained. So, far from being an inducement to sin, an indulgence is an inducement not to sin, but to keep in a state of grace.

865. On what grounds does the Church claim to be able to grant indulgences?

On the grounds that a mutual communication of spiritual goods exists between Christ and the Christian, as also between the Saints, together with all others in heaven, and the Church militant on earth. This is simply an application of the doctrine of the Communion of Saints in which all who recite the Apostles' Creed profess to believe. And that the Church has the power to apply the satisfactory value of our Lord's sufferings, and of those of the Saints and Martyrs, to her children on earth, is evident from the fact that Christ gave her the power both to bind and loose in His Name. He said to her, not only, "Whatsoever you shall bind upon earth, shall be bound also in heaven," but also, "Whatsoever you shall loose on earth, shall be loosed also in heaven." Matt. XVIII., 18. By an indulgence the Church remits to us a certain amount of the expiation we must offer for our sins either in this life or in purgatory.

866. It seems absurd that the Pope could remit punishment in purgatory for the sake of a few Our Fathers and Hail Marys.

In the first place, Christ left to His Church the power of forgiving sin. Now if it is not absurd that the Church can forgive by the power of Christ, the greater evil, the very guilt of sin, why is it absurd to say that she can remit the lesser evil, the temporal punishment due to sin? If there be any absurdity, it is your comparison between the remission of punishment in purgatory, and the offering of a few Our Fathers and Hail Marys. You would suggest that there is no proportion between the two things. But there is no need that there should be a proportion. If the conditions prescribed had to equal the benefit conferred, there would be no real indulgence at all. We would merely have an exchange of one form of expiation for another. The prayers required by the Church are but a condition she demands for the obtaining of a remission of expiation out of all proportion to what we do. An indulgence is an act of leniency and mercy, sharing out to us the satisfactory value of others, those others being Christ, and the Saints and Martyrs whose merits constitute the spiritual treasury of the whole Church.

HOW DO YOU KNOW HEAVEN EXISTS?

867. You speak of life as a preparation for heaven. But what is this heaven, and how do you know it exists?

The Catholic teaching is that heaven is an eternal state of perfect happiness rendered possible by the very Vision of God Himself, and that this happiness will be granted to such of mankind as attain the salvation of their souls. The justification of this teaching lies in the fact that God Himself has promised such a destiny, a promise reiterated and confirmed by Christ during His life in the midst of men.

868. We have no destiny beyond this world, and Christ never promised any other. He ascended to the heavens and disappeared.

I am afraid you do not quite understand what we mean by heaven. If you have the idea that we intend the visible heavens, I beg you to put the idea aside at once. For we do not mean that. Heaven is an eternal state of happiness resulting from the very Vision of God just as He really is in Himself with all His infinite perfection. And Christ definitely promised heaven in this sense. Read through the beatitudes in the fifth chapter of St. Matthew. There our Lord tells us of the poor in spirit, and of those persecuted for justice sake, that theirs is the kingdom of heaven. He says that their reward will be very great in heaven. And also, "Blessed are the clean of heart, for they shall see God." Matt. V., 8. He also said distinctly, "I shall go and prepare a place for you; that where I am you also may be." Jn. XIV., 3. He declared that those who love and serve God will be invited to come and possess the kingdom prepared for them, and He describes the new state as everlasting life. In John XVI., 20-24, the words of Christ are recorded wherein He says, "Amen, amen, I say to you, that you shall lament and weep, but the world shall rejoice; and you shall be made sorrowful; but your sorrow shall be turned into joy. I will see you again, and your heart shall rejoice; and your joy no man shall take from you. Ask, and you shall receive, that your joy may be full." St. Paul tells us that we shall know God even as we are known by God, for we shall see Him face to face, and not merely obscurely as now by reasoning from the beauties of creation as one might gain knowledge of an author by reading his books.

869. Is heaven a place where there are land, rivers, mountains, and the utilities of life, such as there are in this world?

No. St. Paul tells us that eye has not seen, nor ear heard, nor has it entered into the heart of man, what things God has prepared for those who love Him. Therefore, so surely as you have seen, or heard, or touched things in this visible universe which are the objects of your senses, those things will not be constitutive elements of heaven. What heaven will be like I cannot, therefore, describe in human language, for our concepts are all derived from the visible universe, and cannot convey adequate views of the next life. But at least I can say that there is a heaven, and that it will mean everlasting happiness. God must intend life to lead to happiness rather than to misery, and He, therefore, intends virtue, as leading to that happiness. The purpose of a Christian life, said Christ Himself, is "that My joy may be in you, and that your joy may be full." Jn. XVI., 24. The chief happiness of heaven will be eternal union with God, and the immediate Vision of God. As surely as the eye can now see some transcendently beautiful natural scene, so will the mind be immediately conscious of God's infinite perfection and beauty in Himself.

870. Don't you think it absurd to say that God will be our reward, exceedingly great? At best a purely spiritual God could be apprehended only by the mind, and our complex human nature demands more than that.

Despite our complexity, all our happiness even in this world is by means of knowledge secured in various ways. We may know by intellectual understanding, or by sight, or hearing, or touch. Knowledge is the source of happiness insofar as we experience joyous reactions when we are conscious of truth or beauty or pleasure, whether by our senses or by our intelligence. The desire to possess things is merely to insure the continuance of this consciousness. In heaven, God will be all to us, since He contains all. We will find still better in Him all that we may rightly look for in created nature, or in self. And in the measure in which we possess God, we shall possess all else.

871. *What is the substance of heaven?*

It will be an everlasting experience rendering the complete human being happy, not merely with human happiness, but with divine happiness. Just as the eye now sees the things of this world, so the mind will see God's own personal perfections. Instead of being merely self-conscious, the soul will become God-conscious; and in God we shall find in an ever so much better way all that we ever found to be good in created things or in self. And, of course, ever so much more besides. Heaven, then, is not a place to be described in terms of longitude and latitude, nor by ideas of scenery drawn from this earth. It is a spiritual state of perpetual existence which escapes limitations of time and space concepts. For further knowledge of the conditions that prevail in heaven I can only advise you to live in such a way as to go there. Then you will know all.

872. *Doesn't the idea of contemplating God year after year, and century after century, suggest frightful monotony?*

That idea does. But it is a wrong idea. Eternity is not time, and is not to be described in terms of time. When you speak of century after century, you are thinking of a succession of years. But eternity is not a question of a long time. It is outside time altogether. This is a great mystery, I know. But I can't help that. We who measure all things by time cannot understand a state of existence without time. But reason itself tells us that God's own existence must be independent of the flux of time. One can get a faint idea of happiness without time from occasional experiences in this life. An artist entranced by a scene of ravishing beauty can be utterly forgetful of time. His mind has gone off into realms not conditioned by time, and he finds it hard to believe that he has been so long inactive, when he comes to himself, and, as we say, back to earth. Of course, that is but an analogy, and has merely the force of an analogy, no more. But it helps to throw some light on the problem.

873. *The eternally fixed state of heaven would be unbearable to mankind.*

Heaven is eternally fixed insofar as it is a permanent as opposed to a temporary happiness. But to imagine that, because it is permanent, it must consist of a never-ending monotonous passivity is ludicrous. It is a fallacy to judge of heavenly occupations and joys in the light of earthly pleasure in finite and created things which are too trivial for the human soul and must begin to pall sooner or later. That is why people seek change, and think that there can be no real happiness without constant change, even, nowadays to the changing of wives in many cases. This attitude is due to loss of faith in the spiritual and supernatural, with a consequent adoption of a merely materialistic outlook. Yet whilst they have come to think only in terms of materialism, men are quite confident that they understand the Christian heaven despite the fact that it cannot be interpreted in terms of materialism.

874. *Shall we have a new kind of knowledge altogether in heaven, different from ordinary human methods of knowing things?*

Certainly there will be a new way of knowing things in heaven. Here we know created things by personal experience, and we find God reflected in them. In heaven we shall know God as the first object of our experience, and we shall know all created beings by their reflection in Him. Here, too, we form representative ideas of things, and know things insofar as these representative ideas of them are within our minds. But in heaven we shall not have an idea of God. We will not have to form a representation of Him, thinking God by ideas of God. We shall think God by God; for being in the spiritual order, God will immediately unite Himself with our intelligence, flooding our souls with supreme and eternal happiness.

875. *Men must have some form of employment to develop further their personality and gain richer experience.*

Evolutionary philosophy wrongly dreams of eternal developing. When a photographer goes into his darkroom to develop his picture his purpose is to attain definite results, not to stay there forever developing. Development and progress are not ends in themselves, but are ordained to perfect fulfillment of all capabilities. It is absurd to want to develop yet to be afraid of developing into anything definite. One might just as well set out on a journey with only one dread, the dread lest one should arrive at one's destination. In heaven our personality arrives at its fullest perfection. But that perfection, instead of excluding activity and experience, demands these things, and offers a greater capability of them than is possible in any earlier stages of development. There the object of our experience will be, not any finite created thing, but the infinite and inexhaustible truth, goodness, and beauty of God Himself. He will be more than enough to absorb us, and the experience will be so rich, profound, and significant that no richer will be possible. If men say that they find this concept beyond them, I can only remind them that, in their present imperfect stage they are not capable of comprehending fully those conditions which require perfect development for their full appreciation. Owls can't see in daylight, not because there is no daylight, but because their visual powers are not adapted to daylight.

876. *If heaven is eternal, it can never cease or be lost. Yet the angels in heaven sinned and lost it.*

We say that heaven, once attained, can never be lost. Yet we also say that some angels rebelled in heaven, and lost their right to happiness. But a right idea of Christian teaching on this subject shows that there is no trace of contradiction. Heaven is not used in the same sense in the two expressions. God created men upon earth, and angels in heaven. Heaven is used there merely to designate a spiritual state of a higher nature than that we know on earth. God gave us men a half-material, half-spiritual nature. He gave the angels a purely spiritual nature. Both men and angels were capable of operations proportionate to the nature they possessed. And those operations were natural. Now it is not natural to any created being to see God immediately and intimately, as God sees Himself. An angel by its natural powers could no more comprehend the vastly superior being of God, than a horse could comprehend the psychology of man. Any immediate knowledge of God must be above a created nature, and, therefore, supernatural. The angels, therefore, though in heaven in the sense that they were not of earth, did not have the immediate Vision of God. They were not, by virtue of their mere creation, in that full and permanent happiness which the Vision of God alone can give. And they had to earn that full happiness by conforming to God's will in all things. Some did not, and in that sense they rebelled and forfeited the additional supernatural and essentially permanent happiness given to the good angels. When we speak of our attaining heaven, we mean the attaining of the supernatural and immediate Vision of God as He is in Himself. The moment one sees God, sin becomes impossible. Yet sin alone could interfere with one's happiness. Sin is due to our being attracted by wrong things. We deliberately exclude our consideration of the good we should do; refuse to weigh the evil aspect of our proposed conduct; and concentrate upon some prospective apparent advantage. But the moment we see God as He is in Himself, it will be impossible not to advert to His infinite goodness, and sin will become impossible.

877. What is the sense of the doctrine that our bodies will rise from the dead? Where will be the need for a material body in heaven?

The sense and the need of the human body in heaven follow from the necessity of the survival of man. Man is not his soul only. He is a composite being, consisting of both body and soul, and must survive in his complete nature. Even though the soul attains happiness before its reunion with the body, it will be in an abnormal and unnatural state, its full powers lacking their operations. Then, too, the death of the body is a punishment of sin, and the full reparation of sin demands that the body be restored to life once more, even as Christ's own body rose from the grave.

878. A spiritual religion should not be bothered with a future for the body.

The Christian religion is at once spiritual and human. It is a spiritual religion adapted to the needs and demands of our complete nature. It is founded on the Incarnation of the spiritual God, the Eternal Son taking flesh to lift flesh to His own spiritual heights. The visible and social character of the Church, and the tangible Sacraments show the consideration for man's bodily nature which is in perfect harmony with the doctrine of the resurrection of the body.

879. Will the body united to the soul on the day of the resurrection be a physical body?

It will be a physical body, but not subject to its present conditions. It will have undergone a vast change, adapting it to altogether new circumstances. St. Paul tells us that the body will be transfigured and spiritualized, and that we will no longer have an animal body living and dying by the senses.

880. Will it require food and clothing, assuming of course that one goes to heaven?

Not being subject to the conditions of this life, it will not need the nourishment necessary in a material world, nor protection against unfavorable elements. The spirit will give its own life to the body which will not need to be ever repairing a constantly failing vitality. Therefore, even for the body there will be a complete change of state, the glorified soul infusing new powers into it of which we can form no adequate idea now.

881. Bodies are subject to constant evolutions and fluctuations. It is impossible to imagine a body in an eternally fixed condition. Will it be mummified?

The body will not be in any eternally fixed condition of stagnation; nor will it be mummified. There are more things in heaven and earth than are dreamed of in your philosophy. I grant that the vital functions of the body will not be as we know them now. But the body will experience its own activities and pleasures, not in the Mahometan sense, but according to the new conditions of heaven. Life in this world is a perpetual struggle against decay and death. The sequence of abstinence from food and of taking food is a dying and a being reborn daily. In its immortal state our body will not be subject to evolutions and fluctuations. The spirit will give its own mode of life to the flesh, and food will not be necessary. This will not mean the destruction of our human nature. It will mean a change of state.

882. Will their resurrected bodies add to the happiness of souls already in heaven?

They will not add to the essential happiness of souls which have attained already to the beatific Vision of God. But they will mean a further extension of that happiness, and add a new secondary happiness. The possession of their essential happiness, of course, forbids our applying any notion of unhappiness to souls already in heaven.

883. Do Catholics believe in the Second Coming of Christ?

Yes.

884. What does the expression in the Creed mean: From thence He shall come to judge both the living and the dead?

Those words refer to the general judgment of the whole human race at the end of the world. God has revealed that, in due time, our Lord will come in great power and majesty to judge all mankind.

885. An atheist friend of mine says that, if that be true, we should not believe that a person is judged the moment he dies.

That does not follow. Each individual soul is judged by God as it leaves this world. So Scripture tells us, "It is appointed unto men once to die, and after this the judgment." Heb. IX., 27. Your friend will say, "If each soul has its particular judgment as it goes from this world, then why the general judgment of all collectively at the end?" There are many reasons for that. The first and particular judgment is for us; the second and general judgment is for God, whose justice will then be manifested to all creatures. Again, at the particular judgment the soul only, in a state of separation from the body, is judged; at the last judgment the souls of men will be reunited to their bodies, and they will experience a reiteration of their judgment in their complete personalities, and the bodies in which men have served God or sinned will share in the happiness or misery which is the lot of the soul. Furthermore, man is not only individual; he is essentially a social being. We live in society, a common life in which mutual influences, good and evil, are constantly in evidence. Now a common life should have a common ending. Our Lord tells us that there is nothing hidden which shall not be revealed. For wise reasons time keeps its secrets; but time, at the end, will reveal all to all under the eyes of the great Judge. And all that God has done or permitted will be justified before the whole universe. Those who have died in the grace and friendship of God will find this general judgment to their glory and happiness. But those who have died at enmity with God will find it to their disgrace and misery. So God will triumph either in His mercy or in His justice.

886. Scientists say that the earth will last for millions of years, gradually cooling down till all life is frozen out.

If we allow for purely natural factors that is most probable. That is, the earth will probably go on for millions of years, gradually cooling down, provided God

Himself does not step in and bring the existing state of affairs to an end in a way beyond the comprehension of men.

887. Is it after this scientific conclusion that the Day of Judgment is expected?

The Catholic Church teaches that Christ will certainly come again to judge the living and the dead and that will end the present era as far as mankind is concerned. And that will be before all life is frozen out from this globe. When it shall occur is not known to men and not included in the teachings of the Church. Also, whilst this coming of Christ will affect the human beings who inhabit the earth, the Church has nothing to say as to what will happen to the globe itself. It may go on cooling till it is as cold as the moon, perhaps by some cataclysm to be reduced to a nebulous vapor once more and begin a cycle of condensation all over again. That all rests with God, and matters little to men whose fate will long have been decided ere such possibilities can materialize. The scientists would say: Judging by the apparent natural laws we observe, and abstracting from any untoward and supernatural intervention by God, we think the world will go on for millions of years, and eventually grow so cold as to freeze all life out of existence. If you ask them: But is there any likelihood of a supernatural intervention by God? they would reply: Speaking purely as natural scientists, we don't know. Natural science is not competent to speak on such a subject positively. Christ has revealed that such an intervention will take place at some future time, and we scientists cannot say that it will not happen, nor can we say that there are any reasonable grounds for refusing to believe in the authority and capacity of Christ to fulfill His predictions.

888. St. Paul speaks of "That Day," of the crown of justice laid up for him, and of the blessed hope which looks forward to the glorious appearing of the great God, and our Savior Jesus Christ. When will this appearing take place?

There are two judgments, the particular judgment of each individual which takes place immediately after death; and the general judgment which will occur at the end of the world. In the particular judgment, each soul will answer for its life on earth, and will be rewarded or punished accordingly. St. Paul knew that our Lord is not outdone in generosity, and after all his labors and sufferings, knew that he could confidently expect a crown of justice to be received as soon as his life was over. Therefore, he said, "Having a desire to be dissolved and to be with Christ, a thing by far the better." Phil. I., 23. The day of each one's death, therefore, is "That Day" from the viewpoint of the individual's eternal fate. But the glorious appearing of our Savior Jesus Christ refers to the general judgment of all mankind at the end of the world, when Christ will come in all His majesty and power to manifest His triumph in the sight of men and angels. When this final consummation of the ages will occur no man can say. God has revealed that it will occur, but purposely refrained from revealing when. Jesus, therefore, said expressly, "Of that day and hour no one knoweth, no not the angels of heaven, but the Father alone." Matt. XXIV., 36.

889. What did our Lord mean when He said, "Heaven and earth shall pass away; but My word shall not pass away." Matt. XXIV., 35.

He primarily meant that His teachings were eternally true. It is as if He said: Though all else should fail, My doctrine can never fail. It will last forever.

890. Will this earth ever be destroyed?

Certainly in its present form and structure. Our Lord Himself has said that the heavens and earth will pass away, but that His words never fail. In speaking to men, He was speaking of the heavens and of the earth as they saw them, meaning that things as they are now will cease to be so. We are told that all is to end in a vast cataclysm, both material and moral. An extraordinary transformation will come over the whole material universe, and Christ, who came as an infant in mercy, will appear as a Judge to administer justice.

891. *Will heaven pass away?*

No. Our Lord was referring to the heavens, not to heaven as a state of eternal happiness. The visible universe as we see it now is in a state of transition. At least in its present formation it will pass away sooner or later, even by merely natural processes. But apart from this, the final coming of Christ will mean a shock to the existing visible order of things, and a vast change in it. Through all such changes, however, the doctrine of Christ remains unchangeably true, and all that He has taught will most certainly be verified.

892. *What is meant by a new heavens and a new earth?*

Even were the present universe left as it is, every soul that goes out of this life must see a new heavens and a new earth, if only because it will see things from a completely different aspect. Science tells us that the atoms and molecules of even the most rigid objects are in motion and at an incalculable speed. If the soul could get a truly scientific vision of the dance of atoms and molecules, and of the very stars, it would certainly see the universe under a very new aspect. But the change to come should not only be attributed to the changed condition of the soul. There will be a change in the actual scheme of earth and the heavens. There will be a new order, and a perfect adaptation of all things to a new end. Christ will be the organizer, as He has organized the Church and humanity. It is quite possible that all may be spiritualized and submitted to the elect, the elect to Christ, and Christ to God. Thus, St. Paul himself says that all creation waits for the manifestation of the children of God. Exactly what will occur, of course, is a mystery which God has not deigned to reveal. But He has revealed the fact that Christ will come again in some glorious way to judge mankind. And we Catholics accept that fact on the authority of God's word.

893. *What is meant by the New Jerusalem?*

The very word Jerusalem means City of Peace. The New Jerusalem means the finally established and spiritual Kingdom of Christ, in which He will reign in eternal happiness and peace with those who are saved.

894. *Let us suppose that the whole drama of existence has been played out to its conclusion, and the curtain has fallen.*

I will take your supposition, but must compliment you upon your imaginative powers, so evident in a description which cold dry reason could have expressed in the four words, the world has ended.

895. *Then there are some souls in heaven and some souls in hell.*

Some will be in heaven, and some will be in hell.

896. *On the one hand some will be enjoying unlimited happiness; on the other, enjoying unlimited misery.*

Neither the happiness nor the misery will be without limits. Likewise, those in misery won't be enjoying it. A better word would be suffering. If you want reasoning you should try to show that you allow reason to influence your own statements. Inaccurate and exaggerated statements invite easy dismissal rather than serious discussion.

897. What do you suppose God will have got out of it?

I do not go in for suppositions. I know that God will get this much out of it. The very goodness which diffused itself generously in the creation of human beings will be acknowledged and proclaimed by those human beings whether they are in heaven or in hell. And that, not because it will be of any essential advantage to God, but because it is right that it should be so. You will not find it difficult to conceive this of those who attain heaven. Your difficulty will be to conceive it of those who lose their souls and go to hell. Let me try to help you. God's goodness not only gave man the gift of existence, but also the dignity of a free will by which he would be master of his own destiny. If man, however, yields to pride, rebels against God, and dies still obstinately refusing to make his peace with God, then unrepentant pride will by its very eternal punishment proclaim the eternal rights of the Supreme Good to be loved above all things. Hell is a proclamation of those rights, exemplifying as it will that supreme hatred of evil which is a necessary consequence of a supreme love of good. Love and hatred are really one and the same movement in reference to opposite objects. For evil is opposed to the good, and hatred is the reaction of love for what is good against the evil opposed to that good. Were there no love for good there would be no hatred of evil. And hell, by the very grimness of its penalties upon evil, will proclaim for eternity that the good should have been loved.

898. How much better off will God be than if the thing had never taken place?

Creation, and the consequences of creation, could not add to God's perfection and happiness. But God is just and will vindicate the rights of justice. Meantime, you have been created. And your chief concern is to fulfill the will of the God who made you. Instead of asking how much better off God will be whether you save your soul or lose it, the practical problem for you is to ask how much better off you will be if you save your soul and avoid hell. So Christ puts the question to you, as to all of us, "For what doth it profit a man, if he gain the whole world, and suffer the loss of his own soul." Matt. XVI., 26. You cannot ask yourself that question too often.

899. If it had to be, to satisfy Himself in some way, then He is deficient in some respect.

We cannot say that God had to create anybody. God was free to create or not to create. Granted, however, that He freely chose to create you, endowing you with intelligence, free will, and immortality of soul, then if you abuse the gifts God gave you, use them to offend God rather than to serve God, and die without being reconciled to God, God will have to send you to hell. And He will do this to vindicate the claims of justice. Far from this implying a deficiency in God, there would be a deficiency in Him if, having given the moral law, He did not vindicate that law. Men too easily assume that God's dominion over creatures must not under any circumstances involve inconvenience for those creatures. Their liberty must be supreme, even if God is to be deprived of the liberty to appoint the moral laws regulating their conduct. Men must be allowed to flout those laws, and do as they like, and even God has no right to threaten retribution. So men deny hell, and if they acknowledge religion at all, it is to be allowed no office but to soothe and comfort them. Genuine love of God casts out fear. But men want to cast out fear, without bothering about the love of God. And then they talk about a deficiency in God if they are not allowed to do so.

900. *If God is really the All in All, it is rank foolishness to imagine that He would be complimented in any sense by the scheme you attribute to Him.*

It is not I who attribute any scheme to God. I declare what He has revealed to be the eternal counterparts of the good and evil not only possible, but so evident in human life. And if we take the three great motives of conduct, what is useful, what is pleasant, and what is right, I have already said that God's treatment of creatures will not be based upon utility or pleasure, but upon what is right and just in itself. And the rank foolishness is to imagine that God must abandon what is right and just because a creature in rebellion against Him whines about the sacrilegious violation of its own utility and pleasure.

See also R. R., Vol. I., Nos. 593-1023.

CHAPTER ELEVEN

THE CHURCH IN HER MORAL TEACHINGS

901. *I should be grateful if you would define conscience for me.*

Conscience is simply a judgment of the intelligence applied to moral matters. In mathematics the mind concludes that two and two make four. In music it will judge as to whether the notes harmonize with one another or not. In moral conduct, it judges that good must be done, and evil avoided. And when some particular course of action presents itself, it will decide as to whether that course of action is in harmony with good principles or not. Whence come the principles with which conduct is to be compared? They are part of our very nature, impressed upon us by the Creator Himself. And in this sense conscience is the voice of God within us. Every human being is born with an urge to tend to a perfect development. But this will be possible only if life be well ordered. Hence, the innate conviction that the order of nature itself must be respected. As a creature, man has an innate tendency to respect the rights of the Creator; as social, he has an innate tendency to respect the rights of his fellow men; as intelligent and self-regulating, he tends to respect his own dignity. And conscience manifests itself by interior approval or reproach according to his observance or violation of these natural obligations imposed by the God who made man as he is.

902. *I know I can always say, "Follow your conscience. Conscience is the last court of appeal."*

You cannot say that. Conscience is not the last court of appeal as the guide of conduct, whatever may be its value in relation to one's judgment by God. The last court of appeal, where right or wrong conduct is concerned, is the revealed law of God. The individual conscience can be objectively erroneous through lack of knowledge, or through malice. For example, God says, "Thou shalt not commit adultery." Yet there are people who say that they cannot conscientiously see any wrong in adultery. If they are telling the truth, then their conscience is wrong. They have distorted their conscience. God's law is the standard of right and wrong just as the sun is the standard of time. And conscience is right if it is conformed to God's law, just as a watch is right if it is in harmony with the sun.

903. *How would you define a lie?*

I would define it as the uttering of what one knows to be false, and that whether by speech, writing, or gesture.

904. *Would it be a lie to say what is untrue to a person who has no right whatever to the information sought?*

Yes. A lie is wrong in itself, not merely in reference to the rights of others. If others have a right to the truth, a lie is by that fact a still graver sin. But, even if they have no right, to say what one knows to be untrue is still a lie, and sinful before God.

The idea that men may tell lies provided the listeners or readers have no right to the truth leads to immense evils. Each man constitutes himself as the judge concerning the extent of other people's rights, and soon ends by saying what he thinks will be for their good, or his own good, whether it be true or false. Thus, we have official lies in war time, political untruths, newspaper dishonesties, and a general spirit of mistrust which renders social peace and confidence impossible. In December, 1935, a statement by a Polish doctor on the scene in Abyssinia was sent to the League of Nations, declaring that the Italians had deliberately bombed the Red Cross hospital at Dessye.

That news at once got headlines in the newspapers, so that all the world could read of Italian brutality, and work up suitable feelings of indignation and disgust. The item was quoted and re-quoted, and as it went from lip to lip it left in its wake a train of ill-will, hatred, anger, and contempt in people of a dozen countries.

Two months later the news was cabled that the doctor in question had retracted his statement, saying that he signed it without reading it, being forced to do so while performing an operation in the presence of the Abyssinian Emperor. But this retraction does not alter the fact that the original lie had had two months' liberty to enkindle ill-will and hatred; nor was it possible to undo the harm already caused. This is but one instance of the evils wrought by lies.

905. *Is there any true charity without a supernatural motive?*

We might say that there is no "supernatural" charity without a supernatural motive. The word "charity" comes from the Latin word "carus" which means "dear;" and not primarily in the "moonlight" sense of the word, but rather as "expensive," something for which I am willing to sacrifice quite a lot. Now it is possible to do good to others at one's own expense without a supernatural motive. But such natural kindness has no supernatural value. St. Paul rightly says, "If I should distribute all my goods to feed the poor, and if I should deliver my body to be burned, and have not charity, it profiteth me nothing." 1 Cor. XIII., 3. It is obvious that he here intends supernatural charity, prompted by the love of God. Mere kindness to human beings, whether for the love of those human beings, or for the sake of self-esteem, is profitless; and in any case based upon the error that man and not God is an adequate motive for doing good. Such kindness, therefore, should not be called "charity," but rather "philanthropy," which means love of man for humanity's sake; or "humanitarianism," the cult of humanity.

906. *What is the greatest manifestation of charity in relation to our fellow men?*

The edification given by a personal life of virtue, and the avoiding of the scandal that leads others into sin.

907. *Will you please explain for me and reconcile two conflicting passages in St. Matthew's Gospel, Matt. VI., 1, and Matt. V., 16?*

There is no real conflict in the passages you mention, as we shall see. In St. Matt. VI., 1, we read, "Take heed that you do not your justice before men, to be seen by them." And our Lord adds that we should not let our left hand know what our right hand does. Our Lord is not there forbidding us to do good, even publicly. He is dealing with the question of motives. In the twenty-third chapter, verse 5, St. Matthew records our Lord's condemnation of the Pharisees because "all their works they do," He said, "in order to be seen by men." Some people do good almost entirely in order to secure praise from their fellow men, not with any idea of fulfilling a duty to God, nor really with any true desire to benefit their neighbors. They hope to benefit self. Other people may be fairly indifferent to praise from others, but find self-satisfaction in telling themselves how wonderful they are; and their motive is but vanity and pride. Our Lord condemns both attitudes, and forbids us to do good merely in order to impress our fellow men, or in order to feed our own vanity and self-esteem. But He does not forbid us to do good.

908. *In Matt. V., 16, our Lord says, "So let your light shine before men that they may see your good works, and glorify your Father who is in heaven."*

Here our Lord imposes the obligation to give edification to others. But again He insists on the same motive as in the former passage you quoted. Our intention must be that others may see our good works, but not us; and that they may glorify God, and not flatter us by their praise. Unless our conduct corresponds with our religious teaching, we will never win anyone to God. So our Lord had to insist on both precept and example. He says, "You are the light of the world." Matt. V., 14. Every Christian should be a living opposition to the darkness and spiritual blindness which are bred by evil conduct and the warping of conscience to suit the world's desires. So, too, our Lord tells us, "You are the salt of the earth." Matt. V., 13. Every Christian should be a preservative against the spread of moral corruption. And Jesus added, "If the salt lose its savor, it is good for nothing save to be cast out." If, by wrong teaching and advice, or by evil example, one corrupts others instead of preserving them, one is good for nothing before God and man. Such a one is cast away by God in the sense that the cure of so perverse a being is almost hopeless. In both the passages you quote, therefore, our Lord insists on good behavior, but with the one intention of fulfilling one's duty to God, banishing merely natural motives.

909. *In Matt. XVIII., 7, we read, "It must needs be that scandals come; but nevertheless woe to that man by whom the scandal cometh." St. Luke XVII., 1, records our Lord as saying, "It is impossible that scandals should not come, but woe to him through whom they come." Why does He threaten men for what they cannot possibly avoid?*

He does not do so. Knowing the malice of men in general, He predicts that some will, as a matter of fact, give scandal. But the prediction that scandals will occur does not impose any necessity upon this or that individual to give scandal. Every single individual is quite able to avoid giving scandal, even though all will not practice sufficient self-control in order to avoid doing so. And you must keep in mind the fact that such scandals as do occur, do not occur because Christ foretold them. He foretold them because He foresaw that they would arise.

910. *What is the scandal of which Jesus spoke? To shock others, or to indulge in "scandal-mongering," does not seem to deserve such indignation.*

The scandal of which Jesus spoke is not to be understood in the ordinary every-day sense of the word to which we are accustomed. If only everyone were "shocked" by the bad conduct of others, it would be all to the good. "Scandal-mongering," of course, could deserve the anger of God, should it mean serious injury to a neighbor's person or reputation. But the scandal of which our Lord spoke so indignantly is the act by which one person persuades or causes another to commit sin, seeking an end at the price of the corruption of another soul's ideals and virtue.

911. *Did Christ use the word "woe" in this case with the same sense as that He intended when He said "Woe" to the Scribes and Pharisees?*

Where Christians are concerned it is certain that He meant it in a much stronger sense. On few occasions was He more vehement. We know that capital punishment is a grim thing which makes criminals tremble. "You'll swing for this," has a deadly effect on their minds. Yet more terrible is it to hear Jesus, the Divine Legislator, threaten eternal penalties for scandal. He has for it only a curse, and a real curse. Of Judas He said, "It were better for him, if that man had not been born." Matt.

XXVI., 24. But of the scandal-giver, the corrupter of souls, He says, not better had he been left non-existent, but better if he had a millstone tied round his neck, and were flung into the sea. He quoted a punishment which was inflicted on noted criminals amongst the Jews and Syrians to impress upon us that the punishment to be inflicted by God for such a crime will be as certain as death by drowning like a cat with a stone tied round its neck. Evil influence is a crime before God, however indifferent it may seem in civil law. And the dreadful penalties threatened by God are not a dead letter.

912. What is the peculiar guilt of scandal as opposed to other sins?

No sin is so opposed to Christianity. For to love God and one's neighbor, according to Christ is the whole of the law. Yet scandal directly attacks these two principles. It is the real enemy of God, for God created the souls of all human beings in His own image and likeness, and owns them all. But scandal disfigures His image and likeness in other souls, and robs God of them by causing them to abandon Him by sin. In addition every Christian believes that Christ died for the salvation and sanctification of souls, yet by evil influence the scandal-giver would ruin that for which Christ died. The blood of Christ is on such a man's hands. And if Christ will have to say to the lost, "Depart, ye cursed," ten thousand times will He curse the cause of such ruin.

The injury to one's neighbor should be evident. Scandal ruins the friend one pretends to love. He who leads others into sin on the pretext of giving pleasure, gives not happiness but misery even in this life. Where is the happiness in years of remorse? History has revealed blinding misery and tortured consciences as a legacy of agony for years amongst souls, due to a complete lack of principle in those who have ruined them. The scandal-giver may go his way, apparently respectable, and even revered by men who know nothing of his victims. But God knows, and will exact an account some day.

913. After all, if a person does lead another into sin, that other person agrees to it, and is just as responsible, no matter what the crime may be.

The person who is induced to do wrong is not "just as responsible." I admit that he or she is responsible before God for agreeing to the evil suggested. Christ therefore pointed out the punishment of both the giver and receiver of evil suggestions, and earnestly exhorted His disciples not to yield to corrupting influences. As people need not give scandal, so others need not yield to it. And our Lord warns us, "If thy right eye scandalize thee, pluck it out; if thy right hand, cut it off." Matt. V., 29-30. He did not literally intend self-mutilation. It was but a strong way of saying, "However attractive the proposal made to you, however pleasant or useful it may seem, reject it whatever the cost, or the pain, or the sacrifice involved."

But still, if the tempted person does yield, his or her responsibility is not so great as that of the seducer. In fact, it would be better for the scandal-giver if his victim did not yield. For then he would have his own guilt only to answer for. But if the victim yields, then he is responsible for that other person's sins also. Without his sin, the victim's sins would never have occurred. It is a fearful responsibility. If any soul goes to hell through another's corrupting influence, such a soul would be a perpetual appeal to justice that a similar fate should overtake its corrupter. Cursing the day of their meeting, many a soul could cry out against the cause of her sins, "I had no idea of wickedness till you taught me. But for you I would be in heaven." But even if ultimately saved, the victim can lay at the door of the scandal-giver long years of gnawing-remorse, and mental wreckage bordering on lunacy at times. Not without reason does Sacred Scripture tell us, "He that deceiveth the just into a wicked way shall perish."

914. *Is scandal the sin against the Holy Ghost, which is forgiven neither in this world nor the next? If not, could not the scandal-giver secure his salvation and blot out his crime by perfect repentance and contrition?*

Scandal is not the sin against the Holy Ghost. The sin against the Holy Ghost is a positive contempt for all the means of salvation offered by God. However much scandal a man has given, God will offer him the graces necessary for his salvation, and it is quite possible that the unhappy wretch will accept them. But whilst scandal can be forgiven, it is not like other sins. Those guilty of corrupting others must answer to God both for their own souls and the souls of others. They forfeit the right to special graces, and all the chances are against their attaining that perfection of contrition which would transfer the whole of their expiation to Christ on the Cross. God is not mocked. And if the scandal-giver is fortunate enough to escape hell, he will endure a purgatory of inexpressible suffering until the last farthing which he owes to the justice of God and the souls of his victims has been paid.

915. *Is it the policy of the Roman Church to indulge in a campaign of hatred, abuse, and criticism of everything that savors of Protestantism?*

No. The policy of Catholics, insofar as they are Catholics, is to seek first the Kingdom of God and His justice. Primarily they must sanctify their own souls, clothing themselves with the virtues of Christ. Secondarily they must labor to save other souls by prayer, good example, and a readiness to give an account of their own faith to all who desire a knowledge of it. But in all their relations with others their policy is charity. As a matter of fact, Catholics have nothing whatever to gain by the mere destruction of Protestantism anywhere. For it is more than likely that Protestants who lose a belief in their own religion will drift simply to indifference, unbelief in Christianity at all, and almost complete irreligion. No Catholic wants that. If we point out the things in which we believe Protestantism to be mistaken, we have no desire whatever to destroy belief in those doctrines in which it is not mistaken. Our one purpose is that non-Catholics should progress from partial views to complete views, and receive that fullness of the Christian religion which is to be found in the Catholic Church. And any efforts we make in that direction are prompted, not by hatred, but by love of our neighbors whom we want to be benefited by graces and blessings of which they are as yet unaware.

916. *Is it true that all Catholics take an oath never to buy from a Protestant what they can obtain from a Catholic? Or do you believe in the verse, "Let brethren dwell together in unity?"*

If any Catholic takes an oath injurious even to an enemy, he commits a sin. Catholics are quite free to deal with Catholics or Protestants in business. They certainly agree with the verse—"Let brethren dwell together in unity." As citizens we are all brothers and should dwell together in civic unity. But those of our citizens who have broken unity with the Catholic Church are not our brethren in religion. The Catholic Church did not break with them; they, or their ancestors, broke with the Catholic Church, and their duty is to return. But meantime as fellow citizens, let us maintain national fraternal unity and not let differences in religion affect our purely civic relations. Our religious beliefs are an affair between our own conscience and Almighty God. By being a Protestant you do not offend me personally and I have no reason to get upset about it. Likewise by being a Catholic, I have not done you any injury and you have no reason to feel personally offended. We stand shoulder to shoulder in love of our country and our country's people.

917. *Why should the Catholic Church prescribe what its members are to read?*

The Catholic Church does not prescribe the literature Catholics are to read. She does at times prescribe the literature they are not to read. She was sent by Christ to teach and preserve the true faith in this world. Just as the State forbids the sale of injurious chemicals and poisons, the Church forbids that literature which can poison the mind and soul. She would not be doing her duty if she did not.

918. *If your Church has the truth, what have you to fear?*

That those who possess the truth may, through their own imprudence, lose the truth. Your question is like saying, "Cocoa is nourishing, so we need not fear to drink arsenic."

919. *Is it a venial or a mortal sin to read a book forbidden by the Church?*

It would be a mortal sin to disobey the disciplinary law of the Church in this matter; for no book is placed on the Index without very grave reasons for the prohibition.

920. *I heard a Catholic say that, during all the years the Index has been in existence, only one mistake has been made; i.e. the banning of Galileo's books.*

Even the banning of Galileo's books was not a mistake. The ecclesiastical authorities were wrong in declaring Galileo's theory of the movement of the earth round the sun to be erroneous. But it must be remembered that, though correct, Galileo's theory was at the time no more than a hypothesis. Galileo could not prove it; and not one of the arguments he advanced for it is accepted to-day as scientifically demonstrative. All his arguments gave a probability only. In the present state of general education we all know now that there is no doubt on the subject, and that the movement of the earth is in no way opposed to Sacred Scripture rightly understood. But people did not know that then, and they were not ready for the new knowledge. Its general publication could result only in widespread disturbance due to a lack of preparatory knowledge; and Galileo himself made the mistake of going outside the realm of science to invade the field of theology. He set up as an exegete of Scripture, and thus brought upon himself the censures of lawful religious authorities. The conservatism of the Church was prudence itself in the face of these novelties not yet proved, and likely to result, owing to the circumstances then prevailing, in widespread disturbance and harm to souls.

921. *It was not merely a mistake, but bold-faced effrontery.*

If a man wishes to prove that the legislative authority of the Catholic Church is effrontery, he must disprove her claim to have been commissioned by God to legislate in His name for the religious and moral welfare of men. He will find that a formidable task. He may not believe it. That is beside the point. Let him produce proof that it is invalid.

922. *"The mere banning is a mistake from the scientific point of view."*

The banning by responsible authorities of what is likely to be harmful to the welfare of those under their control, whether it is likely to be to their physical harm, or their mental harm, or to their moral and spiritual harm, is not in the least an unscientific proceeding.

923. *The scientist must reject all authority in truth or falsity; for accepting authority means rejecting inquiry.*

If the scientist must reject all authority in truth or falsity, then, for one thing, he must deny the value of all historical records. He must declare, for example, that no one can be certain that Napoleon ever lived; for the truth of that is known only from the authority of historical records. As for the absurd dictum that the acceptance of authority means the rejection of inquiry, scientists themselves accept a thousand things on the authority of previous scientists in order that they may pursue their own inquiries either in other fields, or in the same field to a further extent. Truth however we may know it, whether by personal discovery or by authority of experts, is always an advantage. It saves us from waste of time inquiring along lines already known to be wrong and enables us to inquire still more deeply into the truth already known.

924. *A man does not discover truth by authority. He discovers it by research, analysis, and experiment.*

A man can obtain the truth, either by personal discovery, or by being told it by others who already know the truth. In the latter case he attains knowledge by authority. Now when God reveals the truth through Christ, we have no option but to believe it. The alternative is to accuse God of ignorance or of a want of truthfulness. Either is an insult to God. We therefore, acknowledging His authority, accept what He says by faith. From the very nature of things one must submit to the authority of God, or he will learn nothing much about God, or man's destiny in the light of God. The attitude of those who refuse to do this is rather ridiculous. The very foundation of their own education came to them by authority. They went to school, and accepted an immense amount of truth in natural things on the authority of their teachers. They built on that knowledge, and discovered further things for themselves. Can you imagine a person deciding to take up the study of chemistry, yet completely ignoring all that former chemists have discovered on the subject! Faith in the authority of experts is a perfectly valid source of knowledge. And religion, with its demand for faith, is based on that principle. Those who won't submit to any authority in religion demand a license in respect to that subject which they do not ask in any other field of knowledge.

925. *Since censorship limits freedom of inquiry it is immoral—ethically bad.*

The statement as it stands is self-contradictory. For to condemn anything as ethically bad is to uphold a censorship of conduct. It matters not whether that censorship forbids harmful reading, or harmful drugs, or any other occasions of injury to individuals or society. You, of course, have in mind the censorship of books. Would you say that censorship is immoral when it forbids the reading of immoral books? If the books are immoral, the law forbidding them is by the very fact moral. Unlimited liberty does not exist as a right either before God or in reason. One cannot support such an unlimited liberty without denying the exclusive right of truth and virtue to exist. Forgers of evil thoughts and of error have no more right to circulate their wares than forgers of bad money have the right to circulate their bogus coins. If you insist that truth has the right to exist, you deny the right of error to exist. And I am quite sure that, if you had the power, you would put on your own list of prohibited books all Catholic books teaching that books ought to be prohibited. You would forbid the teaching of all that you choose to regard as "ethically bad" in Catholicism.

926. *Censorship prevents "inquiring for the sake of inquiring," which is the same thing as inquiring for truth's sake.*

That is absurd. One might as well say that a man running to catch a train is running for the sake of running. The purpose of a censorship is to prevent the pursuit of inquiries which wiser people know will result only in harm to the ill-informed, and to those incapable of arriving at a right judgment in grave matters. Is every human being capable of forming a sound judgment on any subject at all? Have parents the right to regulate the reading of their children? Besides intelligence, have not human beings passions which affect their judgment every bit as much as evidence, and often much more? The Catholic Church, having the right to teach religion and morals, has the correlative duty to watch over the education of her subjects in these matters. "Evil communications corrupt good manners." A man's thoughts are moulded by what he reads. Bad companions exert an evil influence on those frequenting their company. The State rightly has a consorting act forbidding such associations. A book is a companion; and a bad book is a bad companion. And it is immoral, and ethically bad, for responsible guardians not to forbid evil to those under their care. Nor can any occasional imprudence in the exercise of the duty affect the principle that they have the duty, and the right to exact obedience from those committed to their care.

927. *In our democracy there is no room for restrictions of any kind on our liberty in this matter.*

In other words, you object to censorship of any kind where reading matter is concerned. Democracy must not be allowed to defend itself and its children against indecent filth, or even against literature calculated to undermine democracy itself! You are a great and wise defender of democracy indeed! We must remember that there is mental poison as well as chemical poison. And it would be as foolish to abolish all restrictions on corrupt and dangerous literature as to abolish all restrictions on the sale of dangerous drugs. To grant everybody access to everything, even though it be to their harm, is merely extreme folly.

928. *A faith, like anything else, is of poor quality if it cannot meet its rivals in open competition.*

The truth of the Catholic religion can stand the test of anything that may be opposed to it. But you forget that there are various degrees of intelligence in people who may happen to know the truth. And in an argument between two people, far more often than not, it is not the truth that is being tested, but their relative wits. A less-intelligent man with a good case can easily lose in a debate with a more-intelligent man who is supporting a bad case. And such a debate would reveal, not the merits of the case, but the merits of the disputants. In the same way, if a poorly equipped Catholic failed to justify his faith in an argument with a clever atheist, that would not prove any poor quality in the Catholic Faith itself. It would prove only that the Catholic in question was not well-up enough in his religion to defend it. And even though a good Catholic had not the erudition necessary to refute the arguments of a more highly educated unbeliever, his own faith would be unimpaired by his failure to do so.

929. *Does the Church give its tacit approval to the Inquisition?*

It explicitly condemns the extravagances and unwarranted cruelty of certain individuals who held office in the Inquisition. On the other hand, it explicitly approves the Inquisition as it should have been administered according to the social conditions prevailing in those times, and according to the particular evils to be eradicated. She would not approve the same measures in the present era. Changed conditions of society require a different approach to its various problems.

930. *As the Church is responsible for religious zeal inculcated in its majority membership, how came the Inquisition to let loose something the Church was unable to govern?*

Firstly, not a majority membership, but relatively few of the members of the Catholic Church were responsible for inexcusable excesses during the dominant days of the Inquisition.

Secondly, whilst the Church is responsible in inculcating religious zeal, she is not responsible for any excesses of such zeal in individual members. She did not inspire such excess, and she condemned it over and over again. Her legislation was often unheeded, but her inability to control wayward members is an inherent difficulty in all societies composed of human beings. God Himself, who gave the Ten Commandments, does not compel men willy-nilly to keep them. The State takes upon itself the responsibility of educating its future citizens; but always it will find that it lets loose upon society some whom it is unable to govern, and who will respond to no appeals for law and order. Even in the Church, as a religious society, men still retain their freedom. If obedient to the Church, men are voluntarily obedient. And once you bring in the voluntary element, you must be prepared for individual failures.

931. Does the Church condemn today the matter—as apart from the manner—of those Inquisitional executions?

She does not condemn the principle that the State has the right to safeguard the common good even, if necessary, by inflicting the penalty of death upon its enemies. However the application of the principle must vary according to the type of society prevailing in any given age. Apart from the manner, which the Church had often to condemn, the Church does not condemn the matter of Inquisitorial executions in the times when they occurred. For, as I have so often pointed out, the State then, as a State, professed Catholicism and the disturbance of Catholic principles meant the destruction of the existent form of society. The propagation of heresy was, by the very fact, an offence against the State and the common good. The State could, therefore, defend itself against such sedition. But much water has gone under the bridge since then. We live in very different times. And whilst the Church does not condemn to-day the matter of Inquisitorial executions then, she would condemn such executions were they suggested to-day. Circumstances alter cases.

932. If the Church has not deviated from the course set for it by Christ, and has not altered its practices and teachings in any way, would not its treatment of defaulters remain the same?

Firstly, and by the way, non-Catholics today are not defaulters. They have never professed to belong to the Catholic Church; and were born to non-Catholic parents, so that their being outside the Church is no fault of their own. But let us take your main difficulty. The Church would deviate from the course set for it by Christ, if it did not alter its practices and discipline from time to time. Of course it could not alter any defined teachings as to what is to be believed by faith, or as to principles of morality. But in her relations with the changing conditions of this world, the Church must be able to legislate to meet new emergencies, and to relax that legislation when such emergencies have passed—probably to give place to new ones. For this reason Christ said to His Church "Whatsoever you shall bind on earth, shall be bound also in heaven; and whatsoever you shall loose on earth, shall be loosed also in heaven." Matt. XXVIII., 18. This power of binding and loosing allows for a fluctuating disciplinary legislation according to the necessities of various ages.

Again you must note this. The application of the principles and legislation of the Church is in the hands of human beings. At times the very officials may fail to discern the mind of the Church; or may exceed the authority given them by the Church; or even ignore the laws of the Church. In such cases one should blame the individuals responsible, and not the Church whose laws they violate. Thus the Popes protested again and again against abuses in the Spanish Inquisition. Thus, too, a recalcitrant Bishop in France handed over Joan of Arc to be burned at the stake. The Church absolutely disowns his conduct. Many practices of clerics horrify us as we study the history of the ages, but such practices cannot rightly be called practices of the Church. And, in any case, the disciplinary laws of the Church need not be the same in one age, as in another whose conditions are very different. Nor does the alteration of such legislation mean that the Church has deviated from the course set for it by Christ.

933. Why would you advocate State toleration of all religions even though the State were 95% Catholic? Can you explain that?

Quite easily. The Reformation period is over. Protestants today are children of Protestants and are not therefore personally renegade Catholics. Most Protestants sincerely take their religion for granted, and are honestly convinced that the Catholic Church is wrong.

Now let us suppose that 95% of the population were Catholic—the other 5% Protestant.

The Catholic Church declares that no one can be received into her fold *against his will*. The Catholic Church then, on her own principles, cannot compel the 5% to become Catholics if they don't want to do so. Therefore, even in a Catholic State, they must be tolerated in the sense that they be allowed to worship God in their own mistaken way and according to their personal, if erroneous, conscience.

934. *What does the Church teach concerning belief in astrology?*

That it is superstitious nonsense, and that it is sinful to place any serious reliance upon it.

935. *How much is harmless, and how much dangerous?*

None of it is really harmless, for even if one were to indulge in astrology jocosely there would always be a danger of beginning to take oneself seriously. Real danger commences the moment one begins to entertain the thought that "there might be something in it." And there are many gullible and easily impressed people who do this. The end of the road is complete abandonment of both reason and religion. I have recently read a book by a prominent English "astrologer" in which he says that the sun itself is really God, and that the planets are angels. He declares that the sun and the moon and the planets deserve our reverence and our worship, though people are not educated up to the stage of realizing that yet! However, according to him, as astrology becomes more popular, more and more people will come to discern its spiritual and religious significance. Catholics are bound in conscience to have nothing to do with astrology.

936. *What reason would you give for not believing in the assertion that we are influenced by the stars?*

I would give three reasons: the first based on an analysis of the stars; the second on an analysis of man; and the third on a study of history. Astronomy, by spectroscopic analysis reveals the purely material constitution of the stars, and reason insists that there is no more reason why they, rather than any other material elements in the universe, should have any control over man's conduct. Reasonable people no more believe that they are influenced by stars than by starfish.

Secondly, an analysis of man reveals that he lives not only by bodily senses which can be affected by material influences, but also by intelligence and will. And only the infinite intelligence of God can know what the free will of man will choose in the future. That cannot be known by us from a study of the stars.

Thirdly, a study of history shows a complete lack of consistency in the life and conduct of people born in the same astrological circumstances, and no trace of uniformity which should be present were the stars a reliable influence upon them.

937. *I have friends who firmly believe that we are influenced by stars.*

Their belief is due to their own credulity. I admit that such credulity is growing more and more widespread in these days. But that does not justify it. The ancient pagans were profoundly given to such superstitions, and the general driftage of the world around us from religion is leading to a revival of these pagan tendencies.

938. *They were born in August, under Leo, and say they have the gifts and traits peculiar to those born in that month.*

Strangely enough, I myself was born in August; but apparently I didn't get the gifts and traits required for a belief in astrology. It is really absurd to think that the forces of heredity must adjust themselves to a given month and constellation before they dare to operate in a given child. However, I cannot go more deeply into the subject now, and can but suggest that you tell your friends to use their reason rather than blindly follow imagination and credulity inspired by futile curiosity.

939. Dr. Korsch, of Dusseldorf, writes in the Nov. 1938 issue of "Demain" concerning astrology and the Catholic Church.

He would have been much wiser had he not done so, rather than pen such nonsense.

940. "He points out that the Church rejects fatalism, and the idea that stars have a soul; but astrology itself is not condemned."

That is absolutely false. From the very first days of its existence the Catholic Church condemned astrology. Astrology was rife amongst the Jews when Christianity commenced. The Jews had picked up the superstition from the Babylonians; and in the Old Testament the prophets sent by God denounced it again and again. The Catholic Church took up the same stand. In the year 120, Aquila Ponticus was excommunicated from the Church for practicing astrology. How can Dr. Korsch say the Church did not condemn it? Under the firm stand taken by the Church, and as Christianity grew, the astrologers of pagan Rome lost their reputation and influence, and were reduced to the position of mere quacks deceiving the credulous and gullible. In the Middle Ages, Arabs and Jews kept astrology going, whilst both Church and State in Catholic Christendom condemned it absolutely as a heathen superstition. That condemnation has never been withdrawn.

941. "Lactantius and Augustine did not doubt the existence of demoniac forces coming from the stars, but they believed that man's free will and divine grace could overcome these forces."

The latter concession does not make reparation for the error in the first part of the statement. Astrological demonology was a Jewish and pagan product against which the early Fathers fought in every possible way. St. Jerome, who lived at the same time as St. Augustine, when writing his Commentary on the prophet Micheas, declared the teaching of the Church by saying that indulgence in such superstition is always sinful. St. Augustine himself writes in his "Confessions" that, before his conversion to Catholicism, he was addicted to astrology—a "thing which true Christian piety rejects and condemns." And never did he teach that demoniac forces are located in the stars.

942. "Albertus Magnus wrote many astrological treatises."

He did not. He wrote on astronomy and philosophy. Unfortunately, the term astrology was used with much wider significance than now to include even astronomy in those days. But what must be noted was the distinction between superstitious astrology and astrology as the purely natural science of astronomy. Albertus Magnus confined his attention to the latter, and emphatically subscribed to the Church's condemnation of the former.

943. "Roger Bacon (1214-1292) was, of all Catholics, the greatest defender of astrology."

He would have been the greatest opponent of astrology as understood by advocates of it today, were he still alive. No man living would have poured more merciless ridicule upon it. Bacon was most interested in astronomy and philosophy, not in astrology as a superstition so much in vogue amongst moderns who, deprived of the Catholic Faith, are drifting from all genuine Christian religion and turning to old pagan, Arabian, and Jewish superstitions.

944. "St. Thomas Aquinas (1225-1274) declared in his 'Summa Theologica' that man's body and character were fixed by the stars."

St. Thomas Aquinas expressly condemns that idea; and declares that divination of the future by the stars, save where purely astronomical phenomena are concerned, is both impossible and sinful as an attempted practice. He concludes his explanation of this matter in his "Summa Theologica" by saying that if anyone uses a consideration of the stars in order to fortell future accidental events or the future conduct of men, he is indulging in a vain and false opinion, and his divination is superstitious and sinful. II, II, Q. 95, art V. It is an insult to St. Thomas to say that anywhere in his writings he declares that man's character is fixed by the stars. If men cannot even read aright the written words of those they quote, what is the value of their astrological guesswork when they pretend to read the stars!

945. "The Council of Trent (1545-1563) prohibited genethliacal and judicial astrology, but permitted natural astrology."

The term "natural astrology" meant ordinary scientific astronomy. The Council of Trent permitted no astrology at all as that word is understood today. The "genethliacal astrology" condemned by the Council of Trent is defined as "the prediction of the future from the consideration of birthdays and the relative positions and movements of the stars." That is the condemnation of what is today known as astrology.

946. Dr. Korsch concludes: "Astrology does not contradict the tenets of the Roman Catholic Church; and the Church has never taken up a position opposed to the tenets of astrology."

That is quite false. How he could come to such a conclusion it is impossible to imagine. On his own words it stands condemned! And all the misquotations and ambiguities of which he has been guilty in his efforts to arrive at such a conclusion argue either to a colossal ignorance of history, or to a dishonesty one is loath to attribute to any man, even to an astrologer.

947. Can fortune tellers really tell the future of the persons consulting them?

No. Whether they give mere conjectures, or have actually got in touch with occult sources of information, there is no certainty that what they predict will eventuate. Fortune telling is not a reliable source of knowledge, but must be ranked as superstition.

948. Does the Church forbid Catholics to consult fortune tellers.

Yes. By doing so, people seek a knowledge of the future which has not been revealed by God, and which cannot be known in a natural way. Apart from revelation by God, we can know events in this world either by their actual occurrence, or in their natural causes—as an astronomer predicts future rain from present atmospheric conditions. But future events dependent upon the providence of God and the free will of men are not contained in the lines on one's hand or in the throwing of dice, or in crystals and tea cups.

Any serious intention of discovering the hidden future by such means is forbidden by the Catholic Church as superstition and a sin against religion. And the Church is here repeating God's own law. In Deut. XVIII., 10-11, we read, "Neither let there be found among you anyone . . . that consulteth soothsayers, or observeth dreams and omens . . . neither let there be anyone that consulteth pythonic spirits or fortune tellers." Such is the clear law given by Almighty God.

949. Would it be a serious sin to consult fortune tellers?

I have said that it would be a sin. If you ask concerning the gravity of the sin, I would say that it is gravely sinful to do so with a serious intention of thus discovering the future.

950. What would you say of a Catholic mother who consults fortune tellers, and declares in the presence of her family that she believes in them, that the Church does not forbid Catholics to consult them, and that some of the things they have told her have come true?

Firstly, the Church does forbid Catholics to consult fortune tellers; and this mother either knows it, and is in bad faith; or else she is ignorant of her religion on this point.

Secondly, her serious consultation of fortune tellers is a gravely sinful thing, and she is obliged in conscience to give it up.

Thirdly, her boasting of her belief and practice in the presence of her family is a grave scandal, and she must cease giving such bad example, doing all she can to correct the wrong impressions already given.

Fourthly, that some things fortune tellers predict have come true in no way justifies her conduct. That some, and not all of the things told her have come true, suggests mere guesswork; and serious reliance upon such predictions is superstition. If she denies that the replies are mere guesswork, and asserts that the fortune teller really does know the hidden things of the future, then the case is worse. Whence would such a fortune teller derive such knowledge? Certainly not from any natural means. The knowledge would come either from God, or good spirits, or from evil spirits. It can't come from God, for He has forbidden the seeking of knowledge from fortune tellers. It can't come from good spirits, for they are obedient to God. It can only come from evil spirits with whom Christians are forbidden to have any communication. Whatever be the results, and however they be obtained, Catholics are forbidden by God and by the Church to place any superstitious reliance on fortune tellers, or to consult them seriously concerning their affairs, temporal or eternal.

951. Can cup readers really see the future of the person whose cup they are reading?

No.

952. I have met people who really believe in these things.

You would do them a kindness in referring them to a mental specialist.

953. I would like to know what you think about it.

It's a lot of silly nonsense.

954. Does the Catholic Church forbid dreams?

The Church can hardly forbid a man to dream, for dreams can arise from purely mechanical and involuntary excitation of the imagination. But the Church does forbid people to regard dreams as certain manifestations of knowledge or reliable sources of information. Belief in dreams is ordinarily superstition, and they should be ignored, not taken as a guide to conduct.

955. If so, on what authority?

God Himself declares that dreams are to be disregarded, and that it is wrong to trust in them.

Thus, we read in Deut. XVIII., 10, "Neither let there be found among you anyone that observeth dreams and omens." And again in Jer. XXIX., 8, "For thus saith the Lord of Hosts . . . give no heed to your dreams which you dream."

956. In Genesis XXXVII., we read of Joseph's dream of the sheaves, by which his future was indicated.

That prophetical dream was certainly sent by God. Aware of that, and of other similar cases, I said that ordinarily a belief in dreams is superstition.

Dreams can arise from four possible causes, and the first test of the value of dreams is negative, i. e., we must exhaust possibilities.

Two possible causes are within ourselves; and two external to ourselves.

Within ourselves we have mind and body. Anxious thought or strong impressions of soul can react during sleep by mechanical excitation of the imagination. Such dreams are natural psychological events, reflecting past mental states, and in no way indicating the future. They should not be regarded as reliable sources of knowledge of the future. Again, the body can cause dreams by indisposition owing to food, indigestion, nerves, etc. Such dreams, whilst indicating perhaps present ill health, cannot be relied upon as signs of the future without superstition.

External to us we have either evil or good spirits. The vast majority, if not all our dreams will be traced to natural dispositions of soul or body. But when neither of these natural causes could account for them, then we must test whether they are of God or of evil spirits.

If they are of God, the object of which one dreams will be good and pure in itself and in no way unworthy of God. The dream will impel the recipient to holiness of life and give rise to no evil impulses. The soul will remain in that tranquility of peace which God gives, and not be perturbed, anxious and upset. Even so, the individual soul is not a judge in its own case. If one believes that God has manifested His Will by means of a dream, he should submit the whole matter to his spiritual adviser, whether during or apart from Confession, and be guided by the prudent directions of an experienced Priest.

957. What is the nature of a curse?

In the strict sense of the word, a curse is the invoking of evils upon another in the name of God. In other words, it is an implicit prayer to God that He will afflict the person cursed with certain specified or unspecified evils.

958. What is the power or probable effect of a curse?

None whatever, if it proceeds from human ill will or malice. God certainly will not answer prayers inviting Him to fulfill the sinful aims of men.

On the other hand a curse might proceed, not from ill will, but from good will, and for the good of some malefactor. Not malice, but a love of justice, and a desire to prevent further iniquity, might impel an indignant man to say to one who has willfully shot another, "May God wither your arm that you may never shoot again." God could certainly make that curse realize its purpose, even though normally He would not do so. Under the inspiration of God the prophets of old have cursed sinners, but in those cases they have merely pronounced the sentence of God in the name of God.

959. May an ordinary individual call down the curse of God upon another?

To wish any evil to another with malice and the evil desire of seeing him suffer would be sinful. The gravity of the sin would depend upon the intensity of one's evil dispositions, and the character of the affliction invoked. Normally speaking, it is mortal sin to curse a fellow human being. It could be a venial or lighter sin, if no really serious evil were intended or the curse were uttered only impulsively and in a sudden rush of temper.

It could be lawful for an ordinary individual to wish evil to another provided he intended only the good of that other, and the good intended outweighs the evil invoked upon him. But it is better to abstain altogether from expressing such wishes. Human wisdom does not always rightly judge as to what is best. There is always danger of self-deception as to the motives prompting our actions, and it is easy to interpret our own ill will in terms of lofty disinterested ideals. Also the invocation of God's name involves a great risk of irreverence and blasphemy.

960. *Is it likely that one cursed by another without any justifying reason would meet with misfortune, and bring misfortune upon his immediate associates?*

Not in the least.

961. *Would people who frequent a place cursed by an ordinary individual without justifying reason incur a misfortune?*

No.

962. *If a person frequenting such a place did meet with misfortune, to what would you attribute it?*

Certainly not to the unjustified curse. To attribute the misfortune to that would be sheer superstition. If a misfortune should occur, it would be one which would have occurred in any case, and it should be regarded as a mere coincidence that it took place after visiting a supposedly cursed locality. It might possibly also be attributable to one's own mental state. Highly strung and superstitious people, on hearing of the curse, could work themselves up into a state of worry and illness, and attribute these evil effects to the curse instead of attributing them to their own psychological conditions. No reasonable person should pay any attention to curses invoked on persons, places, or things, by irresponsible people. Misfortunes don't happen merely because evilly disposed people wish them to occur.

963. *Is it lawful to take an oath on the Bible in a court of law?*

There is nothing wrong with such a practice. It is dictated by faith in God, as also by a love of truth and justice. In no way is it intended to be a contempt of God, or an expression of irreverence. If men were always truthful so that one could always rely with absolute confidence upon their testimony, the oath in court would be quite unnecessary. But men are not always truthful, and in very grave matters involving the administration of justice, the State has the right to impress upon men their obligation to tell the truth. By his oath on the Holy Bible, a man calls upon Almighty God to witness that he is telling the truth. If he commits perjury, he has solemnly called upon God to witness that a lie is the truth—inviting Almighty God to share in his prevarication. The average man, at least, finds this consideration a sobering thought. If he would not stop at a lie, he hardly desires to go so far as sacrilege and blasphemy. God Himself sanctioned this use of His name and authority in the cause of truth. In Deut. VI., 13, we read, "Thou shalt fear the Lord thy God; and thou shalt swear by His Name." St. Paul wrote to the Corinthians, "I call God to witness upon my soul that to spare you I came not to Corinth." 2 Cor. I., 23.

An oath, taken for a grave reason, and observed in a spirit of reverence is a good thing. Evil appears when people take oaths flippantly and without cause; or when they do not observe their lawful oaths.

964. *Why are Catholics compelled to go to Mass on Sundays and Holy Days of Obligation?*

Because they owe to God the definite, regular, and public acknowledgment of their indebtedness to Him by the practice of their religion, and because the Sacrifice of the Mass is the highest act of worship in their religion.

You must remember that religion is a form of justice, by which we render to God what we owe to Him. Catholics are compelled to fulfill the duties of their religion just as honest people feel compelled to pay their just debts to their fellow men. Honest people want to discharge their obligations. And the fact that they have real obligations does not affect the fact that their fulfillment of them is voluntary. God exacts religious acknowledgment. He tells us to remember to keep holy the Sabbath day; and that is not permission to forget. Now Catholics don't want to be unjust to God, and their Church tells them that they will be unjust to God unless they attend Mass on the days appointed. They are glad to know their obligations, and attend Mass on those days rather than be guilty of serious injustice towards the One to Whom they owe so much. As a matter of fact, God is good in Himself; He has been good to us; we have not been very good to Him; and we need His constant help. So we owe God adoration, thanksgiving, expiation of our sins, and the acknowledgment of our dependence on Him by offering prayers of petition. And all four obligations are fulfilled by fervent assistance at Mass. The wisdom of the Catholic Church in appointing definite times for the fulfillment of these obligations should be evident. A general obligation never to be fulfilled at any particular time is often not fulfilled at all. So we see many non-Catholics omitting duties of religion altogether; or fulfilling them when they happen to feel like it, or turning to God only when things go wrong. But Catholics say, "It's not a matter of what is pleasant, nor merely of what is useful; it's a matter of what is right." Religion is a debt to be paid regularly. We want to pay that debt regularly. The Church is there to tell us how regularly we should do so, and we are grateful to her for giving us the information. And, in a spirit of justice to God and obedience to our Church we feel compelled to fulfill the obligations of our religion. I hope that clears the matter up for you.

965. *Why must Catholics be present at Church on Sundays or a mortal sin committed?*

Because the Catholic Church, to which God said, "Whatever you bind on earth is bound in heaven" says that any Catholic who culpably neglects to sanctify Sunday by attendance at Mass is guilty of a mortal sin, refusing to pay his debt of religion to God and violating a strict law of the Church.

966. *Catholics go to Church only because they are frightened.*

People who have no notion of the faith and love and sense of justice towards God which the Catholic religion inspires are given to saying things like that. But we must be patient with them. They simply do not understand.

967. *You have said that the person who goes to Church because he fears punishment by the Church is better than the person who does not attend Church at all.*

I have never said that. People have often said to me that Catholics go to Mass on Sundays only because they are taught that they commit mortal sin if they do not. The sin is against God, and punishment by the Church does not, and did not enter into the question. In reply to the suggestion I have said that it is mortal sin for a Catholic to miss Mass on Sundays through his own fault; that mere fear of committing that mortal sin, where the majority of Catholics are concerned, is supplanted by their love of God and positive desire to fulfill their religious duties to Him; but that, if any individual Catholic went to Mass only because he feared to commit mortal sin, that would certainly be better than not going at all. For undoubtedly it is better to do right through fear to do wrong, than to do wrong.

968. *The person who attends Church in this spirit is a hypocrite.*

He is not. Hypocrisy is a lying pretense at a goodness one does not possess. The man we are considering possesses a genuine reverence for God at least to the extent of being unwilling to offend Him seriously. And that unwillingness to offend

God takes him to Mass. That there are higher motives, I admit. But I deny that the man has an evil motive. His motive is good as far as it goes, even if it does not go far enough.

969. *The Catholic Church seems very much behind the times where the training of children in sex psychology is concerned.*

Experts are against you.

970. *Psychology tells us that a child's sense of responsibility simply does not develop in its childhood.*

That is not true. The conscience of a child or its sense of responsibility, begins to develop from the moment it attains to its first conscious ideas. The basic general intuition that good ought to be done and evil avoided has not to be taught to the child at all, for it is the innate characteristic of every soul. Precisely what is the good to be done, and the evil to be avoided begins to be understood from the moment a child becomes aware that parents approve or disapprove of some of its actions. The apprehension that some actions are right and others wrong may be fairly vague at first, and insufficient for any serious degree of moral guilt. But a diminished sense of responsibility is not a complete lack of responsibility, and it is ridiculous to make the sweeping statement that a child's sense of responsibility "simply does not develop in its childhood."

971. *Therefore, the child has no morals. Its notions of wrong are not distinct to itself from the moral point of view.*

Such an assertion makes no allowance for degrees of knowledge and corresponding degrees of moral responsibility. Does it follow that, because a child has less apprehension of moral values than a guilty adult, therefore a child has no moral responsibility at all?

972. *Moral training is evil because it hampers the free development of the child, and thus leads to delinquency.*

That is an example of the folly to which your theories lead in the end.

973. *A child with no moral training would not develop a conscience; and thus he would not know the difference between right and wrong because he would not do any wrong.*

Comment upon that is scarcely necessary. The "reductio ad absurdum" will be patent to all. When a man's theories arrive at such a conclusion they have refuted themselves. What is conscience? It is the human judgment applied to moral matters. The primary judgment that good ought to be done, and that evil should be avoided is natural to a human being—as natural as the judgment that the mouth is the proper receptacle for food. Moral training does not create conscience, it teaches what is the evil that should be avoided. It makes the difference between a rightly informed conscience, and a wrongly informed conscience. To say that a child's judgment in moral matters should receive no training, and that it should not be taught the nature and the obligation of virtue, is a disgraceful utterance to offer in the name of education. That "the child would not know the difference between right and wrong because he would not do any wrong" is absurd. The most that could be said is that the child, not knowing the difference between right and wrong through lack of moral training, would do wrong without knowing it to be wrong. Do you advocate that as an excellent result to be attained?

974. *A science like biology should be introduced in the ordinary timetable.*

Do you think it a pity that innocent children should be left in dismal ignorance of reproductive functions for so many years before nature has fitted them for such capabilities?

975. *The sexual functions should be treated quite openly, and the sense of mystery should be done away with.*

To that let an expert in such matters reply. Dr. F. W. Foerster, who was lecturer in Psychology and Ethics at the University of Zurich, and Professor of Education at the University of Vienna, says of himself, "I come from the ranks of those who dispense with all religion." That profession of unbelief will possibly appeal to you. But it is too much to hope that the balance of Professor Foerster's remarks will do so. Here they are: "The foundation of all sound education in sex must consist in distracting the mind from sexual matters, not in directing it towards them. Moral preservation is a question of power far more than of knowledge. Our modern educators are no more than beginners in the great problem of the care of souls and the development of conscience; and they would have done well to have learned in this difficult sphere from the great spiritual and psychological knowledge and pedagogical experience of the Catholic Church, instead of attempting to act on their own ideas and on their own fragmentary knowledge. The more realistically the teacher grasps human nature in his study of the problem of sex, the more he will be constrained to abandon the materialistic standpoint, and to recognize the indispensability of the Christian ethic. The time is only too soon coming when those who are now the victims of folly and blindness will be compelled to realize that there are eternal truths which cannot be set aside with impunity by any would-be wisdom of today. The old idea of loyalty with its immense educational power, one of the pillars of all higher culture and civilization, has become a thing of mockery, and sexual purity is looked upon as unhealthy. All these concessions to the natural man not only tend to undermine character in the sphere of sex, but they help to destroy the authority of spiritual ideals in every other sphere of life." So speaks Dr. Foerster. When some fellow freethinkers condemned him for paying a tribute to Catholic principles, Dr. Foerster replied, "Is it in accordance with the spirit of free inquiry to reject a genuine scientific opinion because it happens to be in agreement with the stand of the Catholic Church?"

976. *The attitudes of fear and shame should be entirely eradicated.*

Is there no such thing as a proper sense of shame and modesty, that all sense of shame should be entirely eradicated? The virtue of purity or chastity is so important that God Himself has implanted in human nature a particularly strong sense of shyness and delicacy concerning sex matters, and shame in sins against virtue. This sense of decency is one of the strongest preservatives against depravity. But with the loss of religion, modern so-called psychologists and educators are attacking this sense of modesty in every mood and tense. Dr. Richard Cabot, a non-Catholic medical man, has this to say on the subject: "Nowadays it is said that there is nothing improper in itself, and there is no reason why we should not deal with anything in any company. The answer to that is contained in the relationship of our minds to our bodies. It is a general law that if our minds interfere in a province where they do not belong, we get into trouble. For example, we are not meant to be conscious that we have a heart. As physicians go through their work they see a good many sick people who are sick because they have been made conscious that they have a heart. As soon as a person turns the full light of consciousness on the state of his heart he begins to have trouble. The enormous effect of many advertisements we see in the papers is to dislocate consciousness. Concentration of attention in itself makes things actually work wrong. We are not meant to think, or speak, or write of everything in heaven or earth, in every company and at every time. A great deal said today contains the silent implication that the virtue of modesty is an outgrown affair, and that we today, in accordance with the revelations of science, have no use for it. As a result of this idea much is said under the name 'frankness' that does not deserve praise."

977. *The "sex-drive," like all others, must, of course, be controlled.*

Sex inclinations are not "drives." Such terms convey a wrong impression, as determinists, of course, wish them to do. Sex inclinations are innate tendencies, if you like, or passions.

978. *Though we should do our best to eradicate fear in this matter, it must be confessed that the reactions to fear often help one to get out of danger.*

Out of what danger? Physical danger? That is denied. Moral danger? That is not admitted. Determinists at best can speak of "the good of society." But what influence upon a child will be exercised by the thought of the "good of society"? That awakens no fears in the individual where the sex problem is concerned. Dr. Cabot, the non-Catholic medical authority whom I have already quoted, writes as follows: "Those who are trying to prosecute the campaign for purity without manifesting at every point the Christian religion are acting to a very considerable extent upon the assumption that the motive of fear is the most important motive of which we can make use. But this is not only ineffective teaching. It does positive harm because it teaches us to believe in a morality of consequences. There is already too much tendency to believe that to be found out is the great sin. Christians have a special duty to insist on the religious view of this matter. Immorality is not primarily a matter of social disorder or inconvenience, nor a matter of personal misfortune or disease, but a rupture of the relation between the soul and God; and ultimately, nothing else." In other words, immorality is sin, and a violation of God's laws. But Christ would lift men's thoughts from the vice to the virtue, inculcating ideals of chastity, and giving the promise, "Blessed are the clean of heart, for they shall see God."

979. *I do not understand all this talk about chastity. Personally, I can see no harm in people seeking outside marriage the pleasures you call sensual and immoral. I am an honest searcher after truth.*

In other words, immorality for you is not a vice, and chastity is not a virtue. You see no harm in unbridled lust, and think pleasure the only standard of conduct. No wonder you cannot appreciate the Catholic religion! But tell me, honest searcher after truth as you are, if later you do marry and have children, would you advise one of your own daughters to become a prostitute? Would you assure her that she would thus be entering a quite honorable profession, nobly contributing to the legitimate pleasure and happiness of mankind, and at the same time embracing a profitable career?

980. *I can understand that stealing, murder, and such crimes must be avoided because they harm our neighbors, but sexual pleasures harm no one.*

You are talking arrant nonsense. You give as a reason for avoiding stealing and murder the fact that they harm our neighbors. Do you deny that they are wrong in themselves? If you steal $100, is the only thing wrong the fact that your victim has lost the $100? Was there no dishonesty and moral depravity in your action considered in itself? And if you say your action was not wrong in itself, will you tell me why it is wrong in itself to harm your neighbor? What precisely is your standard of morality—if you have one? Your assertion that promiscuous sexual pleasures harm no one is, of course, merely stupid. Individually and socially they have caused untold harm. The man who has not learned to control his passions in accordance with the purpose intended by God will end by descending to a level lower than that of the brute beast. And in no passion is this more quickly verified than in the case of sensuality and lust. The man who thinks sensual pleasures an end in themselves to be sought quite lawfully whenever desired will himself end in a corrupt heart, an enfeebled intelligence, and a paralyzed will, his whole character ruined.

931. *Of course, if I could get what Catholics call the "gift of faith," I would become a Catholic tomorrow.*

You say you would become a Catholic if you could get the conviction we call "Faith." But the light of Faith is as little likely to shine in a mind which entertains such views as a candle is likely to burn in the depths of a well whose atmosphere is thoroughly foul and corrupt. Christ Himself indicated the relation between morals and faith when He said that they who love the works of darkness come not to the light.

932. *No one seems to be able to tell me why it is wrong to have sex relations with a woman before marriage.*

I will leave you with little doubt on the subject, I hope, by the time I have finished commenting on your letter.

933. *I have often had discussions with other men trying to find out why.*

You almost make me despair of humanity when you say that. The very first man you met should have been able to tell you. We are indeed reaping the fruits of secularism and driftage from Christianity! The Victorian rationalists attacked the Christian religion, and Protestantism was not able to resist that attack. Protestant writers compromised, and watered down the Christian Creed. Then the rationalists turned their guns on the Christian Code. There exists today a vast conspiracy of modern intellectuals to destroy the very principles of sexual morality. And your letter is evidence of the extent to which their doctrines have percolated to the masses. You are one of those who have discovered that, having lost the Christian Creed, you cannot keep the Christian Moral Code. As belief in a future life becomes dim, and God, and sin, and punishment for sin, pass into the region of fairy tales, pleasure becomes the rule of conduct. At the foot of the Cross of Christ men found strength to deny themselves, and take up their own cross. But, having lost faith in Christ, well, they are off to amuse themselves. But the state of affairs today is particularly depressing. History records that great wars were followed by loose morals for a period, after which there was a reaction to decent standards. But there are grave reasons to fear that there will be no reaction this time. In former ages the moral law was broken; but its truth was not questioned. But now thousands like yourself have lost the moral sense. You rank the old standards as outworn conventions. And denying virtue to be virtue, you will never want to recover it.

934. *Sexual relations custom permits only in the married state.*

So that is how far you have drifted! Moral obligations are a matter of custom only. There is to be no God to Whom we owe a duty; no Christ Whose law we must acknowledge; not even reason to control our conduct. Morality is merely "custom," and men are as sheep who all follow one another through a break in the fence merely because others are doing it! Your ignorance is simply appalling. For not only are you quite unaware of Christian teaching; you do not realize that, on this matter of sex, Christian moral standards have a majestic philosophy behind them which includes the best thoughts of Plato and Aristotle, the Stoics, and the most enlightened of Jewish thinkers. But more of this later.

935. *I think the custom arose out of the necessity of having a family unit to support children.*

It is good that you should make some attempt to find out the reasons for the custom, instead of merely declaring the custom to be accepted because it is the custom.

But you are wrong if you imagine that the custom arose merely by human agreement; and that it is a convention made by men, and therefore able to be abolished by them at their own sweet will. It is God Himself who forbids sex-relations outside the married state, and that both by revelation, and by the innate moral law He has stamped upon our very being, a law of which all normal people are aware. Those not aware of it are either mentally deficient, or have distorted and warped their characters by conscious depravity.

986. What other reason could there be for restricting sex-relations to the married state?

In other words, why is deliberate indulgence in sexual pleasure immoral, apart from marriage? Because chastity happens to be a virtue; and the opposite of virtue is vice. God forbids vicious conduct. Christ forbids it, and says, "Blessed are the clean of heart, for they shall see God." Matt. VIII., 8. If you advocate impurity as being quite all right in itself, you fall lower than the ancient pagans. They at least were not blind to the beauty of chastity. Chastity is a virtue, which controls in the married, and altogether excludes in the unmarried, all voluntary indulgence in the sensual and passionate pleasures associated with functions ordained by God for the reproduction of the human race. God implanted in us two great bodily appetites, the one for food to preserve the individual life; the other for sex-relations to preserve the life of the race. The pleasure attached to these appetites is to induce people to do what is necessary for God's purpose. To enjoy the pleasure whilst fulfilling the duty is lawful. But the purpose, and not the pleasure, is the main thing. Take food. The virtuous man eats in order to live. The man given to the vice of gluttony lives in order to eat. He is ruled by his senses instead of controlling them; and that is immoral. Against his health the drunkard makes use of a function which should serve for health. The sex appetite is for social health. To seek indulgence in it without regard to its end or purpose is a crime against nature, and a degradation. And the end or purpose is lawfully sought only in the state appointed by God for that purpose, the state of marriage.

987. Surely our natural inclinations give natural rights to enjoy sexual love.

That is natural to man which is in accordance with his complete nature. Now man consists of both body and soul. He is both animal and spiritual. He has senses, but he has reason also. And his soul, the spiritual in man, should control by reason the lower animal passions, and not be controlled by them. The soul must rule the body. The body must not rule the soul. That which accords only with the blind passions of man's lower animal self, but which is opposed to the dictates of reason and conscience, is not natural, but unnatural to man. A mere animal gratification of the appetites is not the purpose of life. It is puerile because unreasoning; and it is degrading, for, as Cicero says, "Human nobility lies in that quality by which he differs from animals—his mind." The Christian, at least, is bound to fight for virtue; he must struggle to control blind passions. Unregulated self-indulgence is to grow flabby in one's character, and impair one's will. The pleasure lover who talks of "self-expression," and laughs at the idea of "self-repression," ends in utter depravity. Chastity is the only law which has ever lifted life above the tyranny and bondage of the lusts of the flesh. It may be difficult, but to say that it is right to violate chastity because it is difficult is a complete renunciation of human dignity and nobility.

988. If we can avoid having children, why should we deny ourselves the union?

You are progressing! Contraceptives can be so easily obtained now that unfortunate consequences of immorality can be obviated. Therefore the immorality itself ceases to be immoral. Is that what you mean? Do you think it the new ideal that men and women, boys and girls, should be free to secure any pleasure they can give each other without any restrictions at all—because contraceptives are procurable? Can't you see that there is much more against securing sex-pleasures from a girl to whom you are not married than against securing them by solitary vice? Or do you deny that there is any such vice as impurity at all? If one addicted to solitary acts of impurity is corrupt and depraved, is it quite all right for him to corrupt others? Such apologies for sin are simply disgusting, and I can only hope that there are not many who take the outlook you are trying to express.

989. Married people perhaps cultivate the idea that sex-relations are not lawful except for them, because they are jealous that their rights should be infringed.

In other words, you imagine that the moral law in this matter is due to a kind of "dog-in-the-manger" attitude on the part of married people! But the law is not due to that at all. All single people, with a natural sense of morality, maintain the same thing. God Himself has said, "Thou shalt not commit adultery," forbidding any indulgence outside marriage. Christ said that if a man looks after a woman in the street to lust after her, he has already committed adultery in his heart. The natural moral law itself tells us that sex is for reproductive purposes, and that its exercise is lawful only in the state nature itself ordains for those purposes. Sex is essentially a function of the family. There is a whole world of meaning and value in the family. The relation of husband and wife is the highest form of personal union. This union is sacred, not only in itself, but also in its character as the creative source of life for both individuals and society. The family is the vital foundation by which life is handed on from generation to generation; it is the nursery of all social virtues; the only safeguard of the deeper values of human life against the vulgarities of license. If your licentious theories are adopted, women will find love stripped of all romance, all decency, all reserve, and all fidelity. In declaring all indulgence outside marriage to be gravely immoral and wrong, in forbidding irregular unions because they separate sex from its proper social function, Christianity adopts standards which are based on a true conception of human nature, and in full accordance with the genuine discoveries of biology and sociology.

990. If our actions have no harmful effects on ourselves or on others how can they be wrong?

Do you mean to say that the only harmful effect you can see in what you propose is the possibility of a girl becoming an unmarried mother; and that therefore all is well provided she be preserved from that external consequence by the use of contraceptives? But take yourself first. Is not the loss of your own virtue a harmful effect? Once commence such conduct, and how far will you go? Until you become a debauched rake, and utterly depraved? You may say no, but that you confine your suggestions only to relations before marriage with the particular girl you intend to marry. Then is it no harm to her to rob her of her greatest treasure—her virtue? An indescribably pure and clear atmosphere surrounds the chaste. If a girl has other faults, yet preserves her purity, all honor seems to remain to her. If she loses that, she joins the ranks of all other "fallen women." Would you do that in the name of love? Love seeks the good of the one loved even at the expense of self. A good man who sees the girl he loves in danger of her life will risk his to save her. But you are not talking "love," you are talking "lust"—a lust which seeks personal gratification at the expense of a deceived victim. It is lust which lays waste all the nobler instincts of manhood, and all the special beauty and charm of womanhood. And should you not marry the particular girl after all, will you seek to ruin others, leaving her with a life-long consciousness of pre-marital infidelity, the more torturing the better the man she does marry in the end—if she does so at all? Your suggestion is that of a man who has no moral standards, and does not even see the need of them. You express the standards of those who want merely a thoroughly selfish gratification at the price of a good woman's virtue. God help all good women, if your views ever become prevalent amongst men. The only way to protect the higher interests of all human beings, both individually and socially is to cling to or return to Christian standards. Sex has duties as well as privileges. It is an opportunity of self-sacrifice, and the serving of God as well as the best interests of the human race. The procreation of children is the explanation and justification of sex indulgence. That is lawful only in the married state. Outside marriage, therefore, all indulgence in sex pleasure deliberately sought is a perversion, immoral, and sinful before God.

991. *If the Catholic Church condemns free love, what can you do to stop it?*

I can but explain the moral law, and urge people to keep it. But instruction of itself does not convert people. The grace of God and their own good will are also required. Still I agree with you that the growing tide of immorality is an anxious problem. And loose ideas on the whole subject of petting, flirtation, and love-making are growing more and more widespread as moral restraints are abandoned. And these loose ideas have led to the wholesale breaking of God's commandment, "Thou shalt not commit adultery." Morally, of course, free love can never be justified. By free love I mean free indulgence in love-making between a man and a woman for its own sake, without any honorable purpose of marriage in view, and with no sense of further obligations to one another. Many people understand by free love straight-out adultery. But I go further back than that. For just as honorable love leads to marriage, so dishonorable love is the road that leads to adultery. And dishonorable love-making is already sinful, and immoral in itself.

992. *Too many are losing themselves in love for one another.*

If people lose themselves, it is not from love for one another, but from selfish indulgence of their own passions regardless of the welfare of the one they pretend to love. Such conduct does not deserve the name of love at all. The only love-making which is morally justified is that of lawful courtship, with possible marriage in view, and with all the restraints of respect and modesty. Courtship begins by a man singling out a girl for special attention, and by the manifestation of affection for her. And this is justified only provided the man and the girl are free to marry, and have at least a remote intention of possible marriage. So parents have the right to ask any man who seeks to bestow his attentions upon their daughter whether he intends possible marriage. And if two young people have *genuine* love for one another, there is not much danger of their losing themselves. For true love is not dominated by sensuality. It is something deeper than mere emotion and flesh, passion and lust. It is a firm mutual affection based on mutual respect for each other's character. It is unselfish, thinking of the good of the other, and would rather endure any self-restraint than harm the other in any way. Certainly if love-making does not rise above the mere thrill of bodily sensations, it can be no more than indulgence in passion. And a woman makes herself very cheap who is ready to give herself to anyone, or even various and different men who happen to reach out for her. It is, of course, flattering to a girl to be singled out for special attention and demonstrations of affection. Her natural inclination may be to grasp at the joy of being loved. But she should ask herself a few questions. Is the man free to marry her? If not, he is merely one of those men who can't keep his hands off women. If he is free to marry, does he merely want her to be his plaything for the moment? If so, he does not love her at all, but wants her merely to pander to his passions, a thing any good girl will indignantly reject. Already his very attempt to break through her reserve and bestow his ardent attentions upon her is immoral; and if she accepts them, and allows them to continue, she will find that they are but a prelude to graver sins threatening complete moral wreckage.

993. Do you mean that the only love-making which is morally justified is that of lawful courtship with possible marriage in view?

Correct. The instinct of love between male and female is implanted by God primarily for the production of children. The mutual attraction of the sexes towards one another, and its expression by love-making, kissing, and embracing gravitate of their very nature towards that complete bodily union which terminates in the child. There is no love between persons of opposite sex which does not spontaneously and consistently aim at this design of nature, however ignorant of the fact young people may be. Any couple indulging in flirting, love-making, kissing, petting, and cuddling, is already inviting the prospective child, however remotely. And since parenthood is unlawful outside marriage, indulgence in free love for its own sake outside marriage and apart from all intentions of marriage, is unlawful and sinful. Whoever is not in a position to meet nature's purposes in lawful wedlock is not morally free to indulge in exchanges of love primarily intended for the procreation of children and the conservation of the human race.

994. If this is the Catholic teaching, how can many young Catholic boys and girls of 15, 16, 17 years of age engage in boy and girl friendships with passionate love-making of the cinema or magazine type, with or without their parents' knowledge?

Such passionate love-making in mere boys and girls, who cannot be seriously thinking of marriage, is in itself gravely sinful conduct. Such young people are neither able to appreciate nor to fulfill the heavy responsibilities of fatherhood or motherhood. If any such young boys and girls do indulge in such love-making, it is either because they lack instruction, or because they lack any real character formation. They seem to think that as soon as they experience the love urge towards the opposite sex, as soon as those first dawning inclinations come to them, it must be right to indulge them merely because experienced. So they yield to their impulses, and wallow in fervent endearments and caresses which are merely the indulgence of blind sex instinct. The end is only too often both moral and social disaster. Such boys and girls have never been taught that blind inclinations and passions must be controlled in accordance with reason and conscience; or, if they have been told that, they have not been trained in self-control even in other departments of life. I need scarcely say that if boys and girls indulge in passionate love-making with their parents' consent, then such parents are either criminals or lunatics. If without their parents' knowledge, then the parents have never been true parents to those children at all. They have neither exercised proper supervision, nor have they instilled into their children the right principles of obedience and confidence.

995. Ostensibly these boys and girls are regular at their religious duties, but apparently priests do not stop a boy from having his "girl-friend."

You must remember that a priest can give advice only according to such facts as are submitted to him for the purpose. It is quite possible that boys and girls indulging in love-making as a pastime drown their uneasiness of conscience, persuade themselves that it is not so wrong, and fail to mention the matter in confession. They have a false conscience on the subject, to which many things contribute. Finding the topic delicate, teachers at school avoid it, and give little instruction on the matter. Parents at home are careless in the general upbringing of such children. And at the pictures the children sit with an obviously approving audience whilst the sweetness and delights of women in men's arms are graphically depicted. It is not surprising that so many children should deceive themselves into thinking that it is not so wrong for them also to indulge their artificially stimulated instincts.

996. *It seems to be one thing in theory, but another in practice.*

There is no difference between theory and practice, so far as the Catholic Church is concerned. The moral theology of the Catholic Church is clear on the subject, and the priest will apply it in practice by rightly assessing the guilt of conduct about which he is interrogated, and by forbidding in the name of God what is to be forbidden. Catholic theology teaches that conventional demonstrations of love by kissing and embracing between parents and children, relatives and friends, which abstract altogether from sex interest are not sins. Such behavior between persons of opposite sex for the mere sake of the sensual thrill is venially sinful at least, provided there be no honorable intentions of courtship and possible marriage. Ardent and prolonged embracing between detached persons of the opposite sex who have no intention of marriage is ranked as mortal sin by Catholic theology almost invariably. But, whilst a priest applies these principles in practice and advises people accordingly, he has no means of making everybody live up to them any more than he can ensure the observance of any of the commandments by merely stating them. But I do admit that adolescent boys and girls should have these principles put more clearly before them than is commonly done; and that parents should exercise much more control and take much more interest in their sons and daughters during the earlier years of their development than most parents do.

997. *What are the duties of husband and wife as regards free love?*

That should be obvious. I have already said that free love-making is morally wrong even for single people. It is still more gravely wrong for married people. For Christian people marriage is a state in which a man and woman, who are free in conscience to do so, give themselves to each other permanently for the sake of children, and mutual love and companionship. They vow absolute fidelity to each other, and each obtains exclusive rights to the other's love and affection. Any alienation of affection is a great sin. Any third party who would seek to bestow his attentions on a person vowed to another in an existent marriage commits grave sin. So would any married person who would either bestow his or her attentions elsewhere, or accept such attentions. Injustice is measured by the reasonable resentment of the owner. And how greatly a good man would resent the injustice did he find his wife in the arms of another man can be imagined without any great effort. The intruding party would not long be left in doubt, nor the wife. Unfaithfullness of heart is already a sin, and it is most frequently followed by straight-out adultery, and not seldom by the divorce court.

998. *You absolutely forbid to married people indulgence in free love?*

The very terms are contradictory. For by the mere fact of being married, people are no longer free to accept love from others or bestow their love upon others. No wife can exchange affection, or yield to the embraces of men other than her husband without sin. Nor can a husband exchange affection with other women, or reach out to embrace them without sin. Husband and wife must reserve themselves for each other. And that reserve cannot be broken through without sin. Their persons are sacred to each other, even as every person is sacred according to civil law. If a business man places his hand affectionately on the shoulder of a typist, she can sue him at law, and get damages, if she resents the liberty he has presumed to take. Quite recently a Judge stated in a court case that every intentional touch by one person of another against that person's will is an assault according to law, however trivial and technical it may be. And I say that if civil law justly safeguards each individual from assault, then married people, since they have given themselves to each other, have the right to demand that each will reject and resist every intentional liberty attempted by any third party. Certainly no man has the right to lay his hand upon the wife of another man; and no woman upon the husband of another woman. The moral sense may be so dead in some people that they will persuade themselves that there is nothing wrong with such conduct. But that does not make such conduct right. And Catholic theology definitely teaches that such liberties are sinful. Free love is immoral in itself; where people are concerned who are vowed to one another, it involves the additional sin of injustice.

999. Why not permit companionate marriage for a time, instead of binding people to a mistaken union for life?

Firstly I quarrel with the very expression "Companionate Marriage." Since the parties to such cohabitation are not married, why call it marriage? The expression is merely an effort to give a respectable name to a disreputable union. It is not a marriage, and the parties will soon be looking round for other companions. Secondly, such unions could not possibly prevent unhappy marriages. They might prevent any marriage, but they cannot guarantee freedom from unhappiness, should a marriage really take place. Marriage is not a momentary thing, but a durable state. And things can go wrong despite a long companionate experiment just as they can go wrong despite an equally long and quite honorable courtship. Thirdly, Christ declared marriage to be a permanent sacramental contract binding people until death. That is the only kind of marriage possible for Christians. If you want to substitute illicit and immoral temporary relationships, at least have the honesty not to call them marriages, or Christian, or progress. Finally, the Church does not bind people to a mistaken union for life. The Church merely declares the Christian character of marriage as a permanent state in life. They are those who enter this state who bind themselves one to the other. And to avoid making a mistake they should give due thought and consideration to the matter. If they do contract marriage, future difficulties and trials do not mean that the marriage was a mistake. They are incidental to life in this world, and provide scope for the exercise of Christian virtue. Of course this is the crux of the whole question. People who are not really Christians, and have no will to practice virtue, desire to abolish Christian standards. They would prefer a series of immoral companionships, hypocritically tacking on to them the title of marriage to preserve some outward appearance of respectability. It is to the credit of the Catholic Church that she condemns absolutely such retrogressive and pagan ideas of morality.

1000. Wide publicity has been given to the case of a doctor who was acquitted on a charge involving an illegal operation.

That is true.

1001. What is the law or teaching of the Catholic Church on the right or otherwise of a doctor to perform an operation such as he admitted he carried out?

The Catholic Church teaches, and ever will teach, that no doctor has any right before God and in conscience to perform such an operation. The deliberate and direct destruction of innocent human life is forbidden by the commandment, "Thou shalt not kill." Another principle insisted upon by the Catholic Church is that the end does not justify any morally evil means. And the commandment, "Thou shalt not kill," forbids the direct killing of an innocent human being before birth as well as after birth.

1002. Does the law or teaching differ from accepted medical ethics?

No. But if it did, accepted medical ethics would be wrong. However no medical man who observes the ethical principles generally acknowledged by the profession would perform such an operation. Doctors exist to save life, not to destroy it. And there are thousands of doctors, men of honor and integrity, who will have nothing to do with an operation to secure the deliberate abortion of a living child at any stage prior to viability. Even if the choice seems to be between the life of the mother or of the child, they will not deliberately destroy the life of the one in order to save the other. Admitting the equal rights of both to existence, they do their utmost to save both, leaving the issue to God's providence. And very often they do save both, finding their earlier opinion most happily mistaken.

1003. The public may construe the jury's verdict in the case as a change in a principle of criminal law.

It was not. The doctor believed that the law forbade what he did, and argued that he wanted the law changed. But when the case actually came to court, his legal advisers really dodged the issue, and pleaded that his action was really remotely in accordance with the law. And the jury accepted the plea, and gave a verdict of not guilty. But, whatever the attitude of civil law on this matter, in the light of God's law, "Thou shalt not kill," operations similar to that performed rank as the sin of murder. No human legislation can change the law of God, nor can human reasons of expediency justify its violation. The Catholic Church, therefore, will always insist that such operations are morally wrong and unjustified before God.

1004. At what stage of its development does a child receive its individual soul?

The soul is present the moment the active and passive principles of germination coalesce to form a definite entity. We therefore say that from the moment of conception, the soul is present. Our very doctrine of the Immaculate Conception of the Blessed Virgin Mary implies that doctrine. For we say that, from the moment of her conception, her soul was preserved immaculate, or free from any taint of original or inherited sin. Her soul, therefore, was created by God at the moment of her conception, and long before human activity in the sense of discernible physical movement. In St. Luke we read that, when Our Blessed Lady visited Elizabeth, the latter cried, "Behold, as soon as the voice of thy salutation sounded in my ears, the infant in my womb leaped for joy." I., 44. Even before his birth, St. John the Baptist was able to know by revelation of the presence of the also yet-unborn Christ. And the souls of others are also created at the moment of their conception. The unborn child possesses an "earthly existence" every bit as much as the child lying in a cradle or romping in the streets. It is a living human being from the moment of conception.

1005. You condemn abortion even when strongly recommended by a doctor?

Correct. No doctor has a moral right to recommend unjustifiable homicide. And the killing of a living unborn child is that.

1006. Apparently it is unjustified because (1) to take the child's life in order to save the mother is opposed to moral principles, since the end does not justify the means; (2) because the taking of the child's life violates the commandment: "Thou shalt not kill"; (3) because the doctor can never be certain that the mother's life will be lost by allowing normal processes to continue.

You last point is not quite correctly put. Normal processes may be accelerated where necessary, provided the prematurely born child is able to live. That would be after the twenty-eighth week. Also whilst uncertainty on the part of the doctor would make it still more unjustified to take the life of the child, that factor is not really material to the case. For even were he certain that the mother would die unless he destroyed the child, he would not be morally free to take that living child's life. He must simply do all that he can for both within the moral law, and hope for the best. But that last point does not affect your argument. The two vital factors are the commandment: "Thou shalt not kill," and the moral principle that the end does not justify the means.

1007. *Let us now consider that form of "self-defense" where one man kills another to save his own life.*

Very well.

1008. *The taking of this other life is a violation of the commandment: "Thou shalt not kill."*

That is not so, if there be no other way out. If an unjust aggressor seriously threatens to wound or even kill another man, that other has the right of self-defense. If less than death, such as wounding or disabling, is sufficient, to do more is sinful and against justice. But the right to defend one's own life is valid always against an unjust aggressor; and by his criminal conduct he encompasses his own death if he goes so far as to render so violent a defense necessary.

1009. *One can never be certain that the other person would have taken one's life. The facts, reasonably interpreted, pointed to it.*

No more than that is wanted in the case of self-defense against an unjust aggressor.

1010. *Now I submit that, if the extreme form of self-defense is justified, then abortion is justified.*

That does not follow, for the child is not an unjust aggressor, is guilty of no crime in being in its natural place, and is actuated by no malevolence towards the mother. The cases are not parallel, and the transition from one to the other is illogical.

1011. *Both involve the taking of life to preserve life, and are opposed to the fifth commandment.*

That is not true. In abortion the doctor directly intends the killing of an innocent child as a means to the end he desires to attain. He does not merely permit the child to die. He definitely kills it. The child is not responsible for its own death, unjustifiably exposing its life to danger. But in self-defense against an unjust aggressor, the attacked person intends directly his own protection, opposing violence to violence. The aggressor unjustifiably exposes his own life to danger if he walks into the zone of protection his sinister intentions have forced the attacked person to set up. The attacked person does not intend his aggressor to be an aggressor, nor to be killed. He intends his own safety and permits the aggressor to kill himself should he be so evil as to render his death necessary and put himself in the way of it. If the aggressor chooses to throw his own life away, it is he who breaks the fifth commandment. But the unborn child is not an unjust aggressor; is not choosing to throw its own life away; and, in abortion, is killed deliberately as a means to an end.

1012. *As to the uncertainty, the doctor performs abortion because he has both inductively and deductively reached the conclusion that if this course is not adopted, the mother's life will be lost; but in self-defense the decision to take another's life, though formed in much the same way, is usually taken in a disturbed and emotional state vastly different from the impersonal, disinterested and scientific attitude of the legally qualified medical practitioner.*

In self-defense the decision is to defend one's own life even by extreme measures, permitting the aggressor to encompass his own death if he persists in his murderous intentions. In the case of abortion, it is the doctor who is the unjust aggressor. It is he who is attacking an innocent life, and you are not making his case any better by saying that he is not doing it in the heat of the moment and in a disturbed state of mind, but with cool, calculating deliberation. As a matter of fact the human being he is going to kill has the right of self-defense. And if only that living child were big enough, and able to do it, the right would be there to defend itself by violence if necessary, even though the doctor met his death by persisting in his decision to kill the child. And surely you will not say that the defenselessness of the child makes the case of the would-be killer any better!

1013. *If it be agreed that "Thou shalt not kill" is not categorical, but means, "Thou shalt not kill except in certain circumstances," or, "Thou shalt not unlawfully kill," surely we could interpret the other commandments in the same way.*

I do not argue that the commandment "Thou shalt not kill," is not categorical. It categorically forbids man, on his own responsibility, to take his own life or that of anybody else. Therefore I have pointed out that an unjust aggressor has no right either to indulge in his criminal aggression, or to risk encompassing his own death by encountering the means of self-protection adopted by his intended victim.

1014. *For example, why not say, "Thou shalt not commit adultery except in certain circumstances"?*

Just as a man is categorically forbidden to kill, so he is categorically forbidden to commit adultery. Apart from that, there is no parity between the two cases. The commandment "Thou shalt not kill" vindicates the individual's right to life and to self-defense which others ignore to their cost. But it would be impossible to vindicate the law "Thou shalt not commit adultery" by committing or permitting adultery.

1015. *If the fifth commandment does not mean what it seems clearly and explicitly to state, why should the other commandments?*

The fifth commandment means what it clearly and explicitly states.

1016. *The extreme form of self-defense is, I know, sanctioned by the law of the land; but so also is divorce which is granted on many grounds which you maintain are opposed to the law of God.*

The State officially acknowledges neither God nor the laws of God. Nor would it for a moment claim that its own legislation is a necessary indication of the right interpretation to be imposed upon God's ordinances. It's no use quoting the decrees of human legislative bodies composed of men professing any religion or no religion.

1017. *As a lawyer I would be very interested if you would analyze my remarks.*

I have complied with your request. Your questions certainly bring out the need of an authentic interpreter of God's laws just as the State appoints courts for the authentic interpretation of civil law. You know what difficulties arise in civil life where the sense and application of civil laws are concerned. A civilian will consult a lawyer. Lawyers themselves will differ. Appeals will be carried from court to court until perhaps the final authoritative decision of the State will be given in a judgment in which the sense of the law is crystallized, and which is quoted henceforth as a precedent. Where the Divine Law is concerned the Catholic Church is the authentic organ of interpretation. You may consult me as a kind of "ecclesiastical attorney." And I have been explaining to you the sense and interpretation of God's law, "Thou shalt not kill" in reference to abortion. Actually the

Catholic Church has officially passed judgment on the matter—a judgment which anticipates any appeal from this "fallible attorney" to an official tribunal. For the Catholic Code of Canon Law declares that where abortion is concerned excommunication is incurred by the very fact by any Catholic who cooperates in bringing about an abortion or the killing of an unborn living child at any stage of its development. The excommunication falls upon those who persuade or advise another to have it done, who commission an abortionist to do it, and upon the abortionist who performs the operation. No Catholic priest could ever sanction such an operation, and if he actually advised one who sought his advice to have an abortion performed, Canon Law declares that he is to be deposed from office. That legislation, so strict and so far-reaching, settles the question for Catholics. Abortion is murder, forbidden by the commandment: "Thou shalt not kill." And no amount of human speculation about the pros and cons of the case can avail against this authentic decision of the Catholic Church. If one disputes the authority of the Catholic Church to adjudicate in such matters, then the discussion moves on to another topic altogether, namely, the credentials of the Catholic Church as the divinely appointed guardian of faith and morals in this world.

1018. *As a woman listener, I object to your assertion that abortion is murder.*

The deliberate destruction of a living child prior to its birth is as much murder in the sight of God as its deliberate destruction after its birth.

1019. *So if a woman will lose her life if she has to bear a child you say it is a sin to relieve her?*

I never said that it would be a sin to relieve her. We are discussing the means to be taken in order to give her relief. I simply say that it would be sinful to destroy deliberately the life of her child as a means to the end desired. What you must face is the question as to whether it is a sin or not to kill an innocent living child. Will you answer that with a yes or no? Or will you say, "Of course that would be murder unless we had good reasons for it." Would you then say that murder ceases to be murder as soon as it happens to be expedient?

1020. *A woman may not have known until too late that she cannot safely give birth to a child.*

She may have certain fears, and they may be fostered by an accommodating doctor. But neither the woman nor the doctor has absolute certainty that both mother and child will not survive. Yet even if they had, will you admit the principle that the end justifies the means, and that it is lawful to do evil that good may result? The child is living, and it is a perfectly innocent human being so far as personal conduct is concerned. On what score has it forfeited its right to life? On what grounds do you think that the commandment no longer obliges—"Thou shalt not kill"?

1021. *I am told that, if a Roman Catholic husband is informed by a doctor that it is a case of losing either the mother or the child, he "must" say that the mother is to be sacrificed no matter how many other little ones need her care.*

You have been wrongly advised. No Catholic man, nor any other man, has any more right to say that the mother "is to be sacrificed" than to say that the child has "to be sacrificed." He must ask the doctor to do his utmost to save both lives without resorting to the direct killing of the child. In hundreds of cases, despite fears and conjectures, both lives have been saved. Should one life, or even both be lost, despite all morally lawful precautions, then death is due to unavoidable causes. No human being can be accused of having sacrificed either life. But if the living and innocent child is deliberately killed as a means towards saving the mother, then indeed one without any right to do so has chosen to sacrifice an innocent human life.

1022. Truly you are a ruthless Church.

You do not know what you are saying. The Catholic Church forbids the direct killing of either mother or child. You advocate the deliberate murder of the child. Who is ruthless?

1023. *I know of a splendid Roman Catholic mother who lost her life, and her child was lost, too; and she left another little one of about 3 years to the care of a careless heartless father. I am rather inclined to think that was breaking the fifth commandment.*

I would be glad if you would say who, in that case, broke the fifth commandment. If that Catholic mother gave her life rather than allow her child to be killed, she was indeed a splendid Catholic—as splendid as the early martyrs of the Christian religion who also died rather than violate other laws of God. The sad consequences you mention do not affect the point at issue. Fidelity to what is right often has uncomfortable consequences. But the appeal to convenience or expediency is ethically invalid where an action is evil and immoral in itself. We cannot do evil that good may come. The deliberate murder of the child cannot be justified in that way.

1024. *What would be your remedy for a wife who knows that another child will mean danger of death?*

I can but explain the sound moral principles affecting the case. If the wife's fears are indeed well founded, and it is certain her life will be gravely endangered, then the husband should refrain from asking those privileges ordained to the procreation of children. If he does not, the wife would be justified in refusing his requests, though she may, if she chooses, discount the risk, and face the possible dangers, trusting in God to preserve her, should it be His Holy Will.

1025. *If she refused, would your Church make that a reason for granting the husband a divorce, permitting him to marry again?*

Most certainly not.

1026. *Good, loving, tolerant, God-fearing women who have to suffer the pangs of childbirth should make these laws, not men who have shirked the responsibilities of fatherhood and know nothing of what they are talking about, save in theory.*

Neither women nor men may make any laws concerning this matter. It is for God to make the laws. You speak of "good, tolerant, God-fearing women." If they are God-fearing, they will respect His laws, and certainly will not tolerate the abortion you advocate, involving the murder of an innocent child as a means to some other end. As for priests not knowing what they are talking about, one does not have to be married in order to know the implications of the law, "Thou shalt not kill." If you think that priests do not understand the difficulties which the observance of God's law will cost in certain individual cases, you are very much mistaken. And if you think the priest devoid of sympathy you are still more mistaken. But the priest knows that, even as he did not make the law, so he cannot abrogate it. He knows that it is useless for him to give a permission he has no authority to give and which God will not ratify. God has given the law. The priest must declare that law. Men may not do evil that good may come. It is morally evil in itself to destroy an innocent child's life. One may not do it, therefore, even to save the life of another. Abortion is murder, forbidden by the commandment, "Thou shalt not kill."

1027. *Who are you, may I inquire, who dares to make such a statement?*

I am a Catholic priest giving the only statement possible so long as the law of God stands. "Thou shalt not kill."

1028. *You are a priest of a Church whose very foundation is bathed in the blood of so-called "heretics" whom the Church ruthlessly put to death.*

The Catholic Church has never put anyone to death for being a heretic. She has declared certain of her renegade subjects to be heretics or deniers of the faith; and in ages which differed from our own in social structure, the State put militant heretics to death as enemies to the general civic welfare. But what has all that to do with my declaration now that the killing of an innocent child is murder? Your vehement denunciation of what you regard as murder in the Middle Ages should make you grateful for our milder views now, and a staunch supporter of our doctrine that innocent children must not be killed.

1029. *Yet you said it is a sin to take the life of an unborn child to save the life of the mother.*

Will you say that it is not a sin to destroy the life of an innocent unborn child? If to that question just as it stands you reply, "Yes, it would be a sin to kill such an unborn child," will you hold that it is lawful to do a morally wicked thing provided you can foresee some apparent good to be got by doing so? If you say, "No. I don't believe you may do a sinful thing as a means to a good end—I do not believe that the end justifies evil means," then you may not plead the safety of a mother as justification for the murder of her child.

1030. *Now be consistent. Why is this wrong, when the wholesale slaughter of heretics was right?*

The wholesale slaughter of heretics can never be right. But even if it were, it would not affect the case of an innocent unborn child who has not been guilty of heresy.

1031. *Has the priesthood killed all the human feeling you once possessed that you wouldn't say, "Save the mother"?*

Not at all. I would beg the doctors to move heaven and earth to save both mother and child. But the law of God compels me to say that they may not resort to the deliberate murder of either in order to save the other.

1032. *Are you a mere dispenser of doctrine, a cog in the ruthless machinery of the Catholic Church, devoid of all human feelings, that you say, "Let the mother take her chance"?*

You do not abolish the grave law of Almighty God, "Thou shalt not kill" by calling the man who repeats it a "mere dispenser of doctrine." Nor is this law, which the Catholic Church did not make, nor can unmake, an indication of her "ruthless character." God made the law, and God forbids ruthless murder. My human feelings do not really affect the matter; but still I am not devoid of them. And they do protest against the deliberate murder even of an unborn child. Will you tell me why your human feelings are indifferent to that? Also why the child should have certain death inflicted upon it rather than that the mother should "take her chance," facing only a possibility? Time and again doctors have expressed their opinion that a mother will not survive, yet care and skill have saved both lives.

1033. *Perhaps in the future you may be man enough to have the courage of your real convictions and say, "Save the mother."*

I go further. I say, "Save both." You say, "Murder the child." Think the whole matter over again. And don't imagine for a moment that I am simply refusing to understand your position. You mean well, but you have let your heart run away with your head. Concentrating on one aspect of the case you have lost sight of other aspects, and sentiment has obscured your vision of all the principles at stake. Owing to the limitations of the human mind absorption by one idea can blot out all advertence to others, as in the case of the man who laughed uproariously whilst being flogged, and gave as the reason for it, "You're flogging the wrong man." Concentration on the ludicrous aspect made him oblivious of physical pain. In your case thoughts only of pity for the mother (quite noble in themselves) have excluded from your mind all thoughts of the life of the child and its inalienable right to existence. And it is to that right I call your attention—a right vindicated by God's commandment: "Thou shalt not kill."

1034. Is suicide a mortal sin?

In itself, the action of taking one's own life is mortally sinful. God is the Author of life and of death, and He has never delegated to each individual the right to take his own life. The commandment, "Thou shalt not kill" extends to one's own life as well as that of others; and to take one's own life is to usurp an authority which belongs to God alone. But whilst I say that suicide is a mortally sinful action in itself, it does not follow that every man who commits suicide is guilty of mortal sin. To be guilty of mortal sin a man must not only do what is seriously forbidden by God; he must also know clearly that it is so forbidden, and be so in possession of his reason that the choice of his will is made with full freedom and deliberation. If we consider, not the action, but the man, charity demands that we give him the benefit of any doubts, and believe that he was not quite himself at the time.

1035. Does the Catholic Church grant burial to one who takes his own life?

The normal law of the Church forbids the Christian burial of a suicide, when there is no reason at all to think that he was not in his proper senses at the time. She refuses her rites in such cases to impress upon people the gravity of such a crime against oneself, society, and Almighty God. But when there are good reasons to believe that a suicide was not in his normal senses, and it is fairly common knowledge that the person was in ill-health or oppressed by worries, the Church permits Catholic burial.

1036. What penalties does the Catholic Church inflict upon relatives of a suicide?

None. The additional trial and the greater sorrow of relatives demand still more charity and sympathy than that extended to those who have suffered an ordinary and normal bereavement. And this law of charity holds whether the suicide were in his proper senses or not. No fault attaches to his relatives, and it would be both unchristian and inhuman to make their trial harder to bear by any unkind treatment of them in word or deed.

1037. You said that, according to the Catholic view, we must refrain from judging that any given soul has actually forfeited salvation.

Correct. We cannot, in any given case, say that God's mercy has not found a way to secure the repentance and salvation of a soul.

1038. I once attended the funeral of a suicide who was buried outside consecrated ground, and who was denied Catholic burial rites.

The laws of the Church forbid Catholic burial to suicides unless there are sufficient signs to warrant a prudent judgment either that they were not sane at the time, or that they repented of their crime between the attempt at self-destruction and their actual death.

1039. *The refusal of Catholic rites shows the contradiction between the attitude of the Church, and your verdict that Catholics are forbidden to judge that any particular individual has actually died in mortal sin, and lost his soul.*

There is no contradiction between the two things in question. The law of the Church forbids Catholic burial to deliberate suicides in order to inspire Catholics with horror of such a crime. In the administration of that law in the external order, the authorities, being human, must form their judgment according to the external circumstances. If a suicide gives no external signs warranting a human judgment of insanity or subsequent repentance, then men cannot but admit that, to all appearances, it was a deliberate and unrepented violation of God's law in a very serious matter. To counteract any impression that she is indifferent to such conduct, the Church forbids any external religious privileges due to those of her children who observe her laws.

But, when we go from the external order to the invisible order of grace and the interior dispositions of a soul, the Church admits that this is beyond her external cognizance. There is always the possibility that factors have been at work of which the Church is unable to judge. And it is because of this possibility that the Church, although she must administer her laws in accordance with the external realities, refuses to judge for certain that the soul of any suicide is actually lost.

1040. *As a Catholic I found it painful to witness such a burial.*

It is precisely because all who still retain the Catholic faith would find it painful to see a Catholic deprived of religious burial rites that the Church has appointed such a penalty. Most penalties create a painful impression. We can never check a grave evil by rewarding it with pleasant consequences; nor, for that matter, by merely being passive. Equal treatment of those who die natural deaths and of those who die by suicide would leave the impression that the Church did not mind how human life is terminated. But she does mind; and the more painful the impression created in Catholic hearts, the more they will realize how very much the Church deplores suicide. But she expects us to realize also that the really painful thing is not so much the penalty as the evil action which deserves such a penalty; and we should be saddened indeed by the sight of any human being taking his own life in defiance of God's law.

See also R.R., Vol. I., Nos. 1024-1334, for other moral problems.

CHAPTER TWELVE

THE CHURCH IN HER WORSHIP

1041. *Travelers have told me that the streets of Roman Catholic European countries reek with beggars and starving animals, whilst the Churches have the most lavish adornment. Would Christ agree with that?*

You should not readily believe all "Travelers' Tales." I, too, have traveled in Catholic countries of Europe. I have met many beggars in my time at home and abroad. It is quite an exaggeration to say that the streets of Catholic countries abroad "reek" with beggars. And the starving animals are a myth. Some of the Churches are very, very beautiful; some are not, but rather poor and plain. But even supposing that you had made an accurate statement of the position, your question is pointless. Christ would certainly agree with the beautifying of God's House.

1042. *Have you no thought of how the money for these Churches is squeezed out of innocent people who have had this disease drummed into them since early childhood?*

Have you ever thought that generosity towards God might not be a disease? And has it never occurred to you that Catholics might love their religion enough to give gladly and spontaneously what they can afford towards its support? Do not conclude that generous dispositions which are foreign to you are necessarily foreign to all other human beings. It is a mean-spirited man who, feeling the reproach of another's generosity, seeks to rob him of all credit by attributing it to unworthy motives or to a craven submission to compulsion. The only good thing in such a man is that he does feel the reproach.

1043. *You call a donation to a Church a sacrifice. Why?*

Not because such a donation leaves the giver impoverished. It does not. Many a man has said to me, "I have never missed what I have given to the Church." It is a sacrifice in a positive sense insofar as it is an offering to God to Whom we owe the sacrifice of worship, honor, and praise. At times it can involve an element of self-sacrifice insofar as one deprives himself of some little pleasure he could have had, did he not give the price of that pleasure to a religious work. But even that does not mean that a man reduces himself to beggary.

1044. *If Christ came to earth again, how would you explain to Him the reason for your beautiful Cathedrals and mansions for the "Trustees of the Truth"?*

Christ would know that, if Catholics have erected beautiful buildings and Cathedrals, those buildings have not been erected for any earthly "Trustees of the Truth." They have been erected to the honor and glory of Christ Himself, so much do Catholics think of Him, and so ready are they for self-sacrifice in His cause. Neither priests nor bishops own those buildings. They cannot will them away. They themselves are drawn from the very Catholic families of workers, families which have given their donations toward Churches, and schools, and rectories and convents, and hospitals; families which have given their sons and daughters to fulfill the duties of religion and charity within them. Opposed to your own narrow outlook, listen to these verdicts of two fellow non-Catholics who were not quite so blind. In his book "English Traits," Ralph Waldo Emerson wrote, "In seeing the old Cathedrals I sometimes say: This was built by another and a better race than any that now look upon it. The architecture still glows with faith. Good Churches were not built by bad men." But those old Cathedrals were built by Catholics, and the generation that looks upon them is a generation that has forsaken the Catholic Faith in England. Now listen to another of your fellow non-Catholics, William Force Stead, in his book, "In the Shadow of Mt. Carmel." "We do right," he says, "to seek God in a Church. Some say they can worship better out-of-doors. They enjoy the idea of being 'in tune with the Infinite.' But it is almost always a lazy and hazy idea. Real worship demands a focussing of the attention and effort. There is no better focus than the lighted altar. Out-of-doors our ideas of God are diffused, and God Himself is diffused. At Church our ideas of God become concentrated. Enter a dim Cathedral—and wait, and things will grow clearer. The divine discovery begins in darkness. We must find God, because the market place is not enough for us. We cannot live by bread alone. Men in terror and despair fled away from the work-a-day world, and built their heavily-shadowed Cathedrals,—not in terror of the unknown—but of the things they did know—the petty and the commonplace, the dreadful inadequacy of it all. The stones had no meaning until the spirit of man took hold of them. They have undergone a transfiguration. All that the Cathedral stands for is hidden in the human heart, as the stones were hidden in the earth; and it leads to the Supreme Spirit—God."

But I am afraid these thoughts will have little appeal for you. Yet let me remind you that the niggardly spirit which begrudges generosity in the cause of religion to the honor and glory of Christ is depicted in the Gospels where a certain man complained that the precious alabaster box of ointment lavished upon Christ could have been sold, and the price given to the poor. You know the name of that man. His name was Judas.

1045. *I have no religion, but recently for the first time in my life I entered a Catholic Church. I never thought a Church could be so beautiful.*

Not all Catholic Churches are beautiful. In mission countries they will often be of bamboo and grass; in other isolated places, of wood, or of galvanized iron; or even if of brick or stone, they will often lack the beautiful ornamentation of a Cathedral. Of course, on the principle that nothing can be too good for God, we Catholics would wish to contribute in every possible way to the beauty of God's House. But it is not always possible to realize our desires. Catholic Churches in this country are for the most part plain serviceable buildings, lacking any particular attraction by "decorative beauty."

1046. *Now I know why Catholics attend Church so regularly.*

If you do know why Catholics attend their Church so regularly, you give no indication of your knowledge in this question. If you think that a sentimental attraction for the beauty of their Churches can account for it, you are mistaken. For you will find Catholics just as faithful to their Sunday Mass when Mass has to be offered in a plain brick hall as in a Cathedral. Catholics do not go to Mass because they find a kind of entertainment or pleasure for themselves in doing so. They go rather to please God, and to fulfill a duty towards Him by public acknowledgement of Him. They do not go so much to get, as to give. They have been getting from Him all through their lives, week by week; and on Sundays they attend Mass to render their duty of praise and gratitude to Him. They know that they owe their duties of religion to God every bit as much as they owe a due return to their creditors in business and civil life. Remember, too, that the beauty of a Cathedral was an unaccustomed novelty to you, but not to regular Catholic worshippers there; and it would hardly carry them there week in and week out, year after year, and all through life. There must be more in it than you have imagined. It is the conviction that they have a grave obligation to render the debt of religion to God.

Radio Replies—Volume II

1047. *All the liturgy of the Catholic Church seems very different from the simple teaching of Jesus, doesn't it?*

The teachings of Jesus were not so simple as many people suppose. Only an inadequate knowledge of those teachings can speak like that. His doctrines are most profound, and many people profess that they cannot solve what seems to them so involved and at times paradoxical.

But the teachings of Jesus are not really involved in your question. The liturgy of the Church concerns her forms of worship. Now I admit that the forms of worship in the Catholic Church today are much more elaborate than in the time of Christ. But they are in full keeping with the principles He laid down. An oak tree is a much more elaborate thing than an acorn; but its development is in full accordance with the potentialities of the acorn. The growth and development of the Catholic Church through two thousand years must affect her in all aspects of her being. But essentially and fundamentally she remains the same. Outwardly, to take one example of her liturgy, the Mass seems very different from the simple Last Supper. But precisely what was done at the Last Supper is done during the Mass.

1048. *Does not all human history and experience reveal a tendency to a form of religion which appeals to the senses rather than the spiritual side of human nature?*

Yes. But surely you will admit that the tendency to overemphasize what I might call the "sensible furniture of religion" is an excess which must be corrected without our going to the other extreme of wanting to neglect the senses altogether.

1049. *Is not the Christian religion (and incidentally the Jewish, of which the Christian is the culmination) a religion where the material gives place to the spiritual?*

We must not say that, in the Christian religion, the material "gives place" to the spiritual as if there were no room for the material in our religion. It is better to say that, in His revealed religion, God insisted that the material side of it should be kept in its proper place. Yet never, either in the Jewish or the Christian Law, did He exclude it. He merely demanded that, in the midst of external observances, the invisible spirit of religion should be regarded as the chief thing to be attended to. Remember that God is the Author of both the body and the soul of man, and has the right that both should be employed in divine worship. Both senses and spirit can be occupied with divine things. Again, from our point of view, though God is a pure Spirit, we are not pure spirits. We are composed of body and soul, and live both by our senses and our intelligence. And if religion is to be adapted to the human nature called upon to exercise it, religion must cater for both elements in man. As man's soul is enshrined in a material body, so the spirit of religion is embodied in outward and visible signs. Thus our very Christian religion is centered in the visible Incarnation of the invisible God. God deliberately put Himself within the reach of man's sense-perceptions.

1050. *Christ was not concerned with ceremonies and doctrines, but with men's souls.*

Precisely because He was concerned with men's souls He was very much concerned with ceremonies and doctrines. By ceremonies religion is adapted to the needs of men who are so conditioned by their senses, and so dependent upon visible and tangible manifestations of realities. Therefore Christ constantly made use of ceremonies, and prescribed ceremonies.

Again, He came to teach truth; and it is impossible to teach a truth without giving a doctrine. A doctrine is merely a teaching. Why did Christ tell the Apostles to teach all nations all things whatsoever He had made known to them, saying that he who believes not, shall be condemned? The very welfare of men's souls depends upon their acceptance of the doctrines taught them by the Son of God.

1051. In Jn. IV., Christ told the Samaritan woman that the time had come for the true adorers to adore the Father in spirit and in truth.

Those words in no way deny the necessity of external and sensible helps to religion. Christ denied that true religion would be confined to a particular place, such as Jerusalem or Mt. Garizim, or to a particular people such as the Jews or Samaritans. And when He added, "God is a Spirit, and they that adore Him, must adore Him in spirit and in truth," He was insisting on the necessity of interior spiritual dispositions without which external observances are of no value.

1052. It is tragic to see Romanism bound and shackled under the burden of obsolete ritualism and ceremonial, claiming to be the Church of Christ.

To me it is astonishing that such blind prejudice, and such an utter lack of understanding can still exist in these days. Let me quote for you the significant words of Ralph Adams Cram, published last year in a remarkable essay on Religion and Beauty. Ralph Adams Cram is a Protestant, an artist, and a philosopher. He is the author of twenty books on art, architecture, politics, and sociology; and he holds doctorates from Princeton, Yale, Williams and Notre Dame Universities. Here is what he has to say: "From the outbreak of the Protestant revolution, the old kinship between beauty and religion was deprecated and often forgotten. Not only was there, amongst the reformers and their adherents, a definite hatred of beauty and a determination to destroy it when found; there was also a conscientious elimination of everything of the sort from the formularies, services, and structures that applied to their new religion. This unprecedented break between religion and beauty had a good deal to do with that waning interest in religion itself. Protestantism, with its derivative materialistic rationalism, divested religion of its essential elements of mystery and wonder, and worship of its equally essential elements of beauty. Under this powerful combination of destructive influences, it is not to be wondered at that, of the once faithful, many have fallen away. Man is, by instinct, not only a lover of beauty, he is also by nature a 'ritualist,' that is to say, he does, when left alone, desire form and ceremony, if significant. If this instinctive craving for ceremonial is denied to man in religion, where it preeminently belongs, he takes it on for himself in secular fields; elaborates ritual in secret societies, in the fashion of his dress, in the details of social custom. He also, in desperation, invents new religions and curious sects working up for them strange rituals . . . extravagant and vulgar devices that are now the sardonic delight of the ungodly. . . . If once more beauty can be restored to the offices of religion, many who are now self-excommunicated from their Church will thankfully find their way back to the House they have abandoned. The whole Catholic Faith is shot through and through with this vital and essential quality of beauty. It is this beauty implicit in the Christian revelation and its operative system that was explicit in the material and visible Churches and their art. We must contend against the strongest imaginable combination of prejudices and superstitions. These are of two sorts. There is first, the heritage of ignorance and fear from the dark ages of the sixteenth century. I am speaking of non-Catholic Christianity. Ignorance of authentic history, instigated by protagonists of propaganda; fear of beauty, because all that we now have in Christian art was engendered and formulated by and through Catholicism; fear that the acceptance of beauty means that awful thing—'surrender to superstition.' It is fear that lies at the root of the matter, as it does in so many other fields of mental activity." So speaks Ralph Adams Cram, who, as I have said, is not a Catholic, but who thus pleads with his fellow Protestants to return to the Catholic wisdom their forefathers so mistakenly abandoned.

1053. Why must women have their heads covered when in a Church?

That women should cover their heads when in Church is a Christian custom based upon the words of St. Paul in 1 Cor. XI., 6. There he definitely gives the instruction that Christian women must cover their heads during divine worship. He gives two reasons for his decree, one theological, the other moral. The theological reason is as follows: Every being's true glory and honor is to keep the place assigned to him or her by God. Now God Himself differentiated between the sexes, and that difference should be manifested during our public religious acknowledgment of Him. Man was created first, and woman dependently upon man. The covering of a woman's head was to be a sign of this dependence. Both men and women are created, of course, for God; and their souls are equally precious to Him. But secondarily, women were created as the helpmates of men, so that secondarily women were created for men, rather than men for women. The moral reason given by St. Paul deals with Christian modesty. Loose women of ill repute went to their temples without any head covering, not veiling their beauty, but bent on a vain display of their attractions. St. Paul would have none of this in a Christian Church. "Therefore, ought the woman to have a power (i.e., a veil) over her head," he writes, "because of the angels." 1 Cor. XI., 10. He mentions these pure spirits to bring home the fact that spiritual considerations alone should prevail in our worship of God, and not sensual vanity. A woman's hair is the object of her vanity and earthly glory—and she knows it. Let her at least veil it in Church, giving her attention to higher things, and allowing others to do so also. Thus you have the legislation of St. Paul, and the reasons for it.

1054. Is the Catholic Church opposed to the observance of "Mother's Day"?

All depends upon the manner of its observance. The modern "Mother's Day" celebration was originated by an American girl named Miss Anna Jarvis of Philadelphia, U.S.A. On one occasion, whilst placing a wreath of flowers on her mother's grave, she got the notion that people should wear a white flower on some yearly anniversary in honor of a living mother, instead of waiting to pay the tribute of putting flowers on her grave. It was a pretty sentiment, though quite detached from religious motives. In May, 1913, the United States Congress declared the second Sunday in May to be a day of national observance in America; and the idea spread to other parts of the world. Now a celebration in honor of mothers is the expression of a naturally noble sentiment, and with such a manifestation of filial piety the Catholic Church could not quarrel. Unfortunately, the selection of a Sunday, and the adoption of the idea by many Protestant Churches have invested the celebration with a non-Catholic religious atmosphere. The day has become almost a Protestant substitute for our Catholic religious Feast Days. That aspect naturally does not appeal to the Catholic Church.

1055. Is not "Mother's Day," of American origin, another beautiful custom filched from the Catholic Church and put to base commercial ends?

I certainly do not think so. I do not agree that the celebration of "Mother's Day" is intended to serve any "base commercial ends." It is intended as an expression of a naturally noble human sentiment, and to foster that sentiment. But the celebration is not of Catholic origin, nor is it drawn from Catholic sources. The Feasts of the Catholic Church are concerned with the very highest nobility of man which results from his elevation to the supernatural order by divine grace. But those who have rejected the Catholic Church, and who have lost their supernatural ideals, find themselves confined to the infinitely lower, and merely natural plane. Finding no significance in the Feast Days, and the celebrations promoted by the beautiful liturgy of the Catholic Church, they are driven to the invention of new festivities for themselves. Having forsaken the divine for the merely human level, they celebrate what all admit to be the noble human relationship between mother and child. "Mother's Day" is a kind of humanitarian substitute for the great Christian Feasts of the Catholic Church. And many will find a significance in it who have long since ceased to find any real significance in Christmas, or Easter, or the Feasts of the Ascension of Christ and of the Assumption of our Blessed Lady.

1056. Is it not more than a coincidence that Mid-Lent or "Laetare" Sunday has long been known in the Catholic Church as "Mothering Sunday"?

It is not more than a coincidence. The American originators of the present "Mother's Day" were certainly not moved by the fact that Mid-Lent Sunday used to be known in England as "Mothering Sunday." They themselves would not admit that they drew their ideas from Catholic sources.

1057. The fourth Sunday in Lent was called "Mothering Sunday" from a reference in the Epistle of the Mass for that day.

That is true. But the primary sense of the expression was not merely natural. The Epistle in question has a deep supernatural sense. St. Paul contrasts the Jewish Dispensation with the Christian Dispensation. In other words, he contrasts the Synagogue with the Catholic Church. And he shows that the Church will be a mother for far more children than the Synagogue, bringing forth those children to eternal life in Christ. In the Middle Ages Catholics so well understood this supernatural fact that the faithful used to go in procession to the Cathedral or "Mother Church" of their various dioceses, carrying gifts and offerings as tokens of love and gratitude. Surely you can see how far elevated this celebration of "Mothering Sunday" was above the present non-Catholic celebration of a merely natural and earthly relationship.

1058. "Mothering Sunday" was a day of reunion in Church and Home of our Catholic forefathers. A bunch of Spring violets was given to the mother, and the blessed Simnel cake was eaten in common.

It is true that, besides the visits to the Cathedral "Mother Church," the day was celebrated in the family circle, with the presentation of Simnel cakes in honor of the mother of the household. The English poet Herrick alludes to this custom in the well-known lines:

> "I'll to thee a Simnel bring
> 'Gainst thou goest a-mothering,
> So that, when she blesses thee
> Half that blessing thou'lt give me."

But even the festive celebrations at home on Mid-Lent Sunday, when the table was adorned with the rich plum Simnel cake, was intended as an encouragement to continue the strict observance of the Lenten Fast on weekdays.

1059. If there is any connection between the present "Mother's Day" and the ancient "Mothering Sunday," I think the beautiful custom should be rescued from distortion, and be given its true place and significance in our Catholic life.

As I have pointed out, there is no connection between the two celebrations. When all Christendom was Catholic, there was a succession of beautiful festivities and celebrations of deep religious significance. And we Catholics still have a most inspiring succession of liturgical Feast Days. But non-Catholics, who have abandoned the Catholic Church and her festivities in honor of the great mysteries of the Christian religion, have to look round for other things to celebrate. And as their vision does not rise above the merely natural level, they have invented "Mother's Day" to celebrate the noblest of purely human relationships. We Catholics, however, must remember that human sentiments are not everything. And wonderful as mothers may be, still more wonderful is the story of our supernatural life of grace derived from Christ our Lord. "Mother's Day" may be all right in itself, and good as far as it goes. But as a humanitarian substitute for the beautiful festivities of supernatural significance in the Catholic Church, it can have little appeals for Catholics. As citizens, we join most heartily in the celebration of national holidays. As human beings we are prepared to do honor to all good mothers. But as Catholics our bond is one of supernatural grace with Christ, and it is not possible to find a place and significance in our religion for a purely humanitarian institution.

1060. *Would a Catholic be a hypocrite were he to wear a white flower in honor of his mother on that day?*

He certainly could not be called a hypocrite. If he wore a white flower, it would be in all sincerity as a tribute to the memory of his mother, and for no other reason. But like many other normally good things, the wearing of the white flower on "Mother's Day" has suspicious associations from the Catholic point of view. Miss Jarvis conceived that idea one day when visiting her mother's grave in order to place some flowers there. This to her seemed rather futile, and she suggested that it would be better to wear a white flower in honor of a living mother than to wait until it could be placed on her grave. The very thought carries the vague implication that we can do no more for our dead when death takes them from this world, and that, of course, is quite opposed to the Catholic outlook. By our prayers we can follow our loved ones, and still help them; and a prayer for a departed mother is of infinitely more value than the putting of flowers on her grave, even as a prayer for a living mother is far better than wearing a white flower in her honor. If the white flower is to be worn on the supposition that we can do no more for mother when she is dead than put flowers on her grave, then the Catholic Church could not but object to the practice. If, however, this implication be not in the least intended and the wearing of the white flower be a merely natural tribute to one's respect for mothers, the practice would be harmless.

1061. *I cannot see any harm in setting aside one day in the year to do special honor to mothers. It would not mean that we should forget her on other days.*

There is no harm whatever in setting aside a special day in honor of mothers. It was the practice of medieval Catholics in England to do so. The only difficulty for Catholics in the modern celebration lies in the circumstances surrounding the observance today. The fact that a Sunday was chosen as an explicitly religious day, and that Protestant Churches have invested the day with additional religious significance, and that the honoring of a living mother was prompted by the thought that nothing of any practical benefit could be done for a dead mother—these things make Catholics hesitant about adopting the practice; and above all since, however their own motives may exclude such ideas, there is always a danger of their participation being misinterpreted. I think, therefore, that I have made things clear. In itself, there is no harm in the observance of "Mother's Day." But its origin and circumstances rather rob it of its appeal for Catholics.

1062. *Christmas Day is always on December 25th. Why are not our Lord's death and resurrection celebrated on the same day each year?*

For the sake of convenience, the world has forsaken the Jewish Calendar, which is based on the movement of the moon round the earth, in favor of the Roman Calendar, based on the movement of the earth round the sun. Now the normal procedure of the Church is to arrange her festival days according to the accepted

Roman Calendar. By way of exception, however, the Church retains the Jewish Calendar for the celebration of Christ's death and resurrection. Since the movement of the moon round the earth does not keep proportionate time with that of the earth round the sun, Easter necessarily becomes variable in relation to the Roman Calendar. Easter Sunday is always the Sunday after the first full moon to occur after March 21st. It can fall on any day between March 22nd and April 25th. The reason why the Church has retained the Jewish method in the case of the death and resurrection of Christ is chiefly based upon the religious significance of these events. The paschal lamb of the Old Law, celebrating the liberation of the Jews from captivity in Egypt by the slaying of a lamb to preserve them from the slaughter of the children of the Egyptians, was but a type or figure of Christ, the true Lamb of God. By His death and resurrection we are liberated from the captivity of Satan. In order to bring out the identity between the figurative paschal lamb of the Old Law, and the true Lamb of God in the New, the Church insists that Easter be celebrated at that very time when the Jews used to celebrate the passover. In other festivals the Church follows the Roman, or rather, the Gregorian Calendar, which is a modification of the Roman Calendar.

1063. *What is Ash Wednesday?*

Ash Wednesday is the first day of Lent, ushering in the forty days of fasting and penance prior to the celebration of Easter and the Resurrection of Christ.

1064. *Why is it called "Ash Wednesday"?*

Because on that day the Catholic priest blesses some powdered ashes, and signs the foreheads of the people with them as they come to the Altar Rails. As he marks them with the ashes, he says over each, "Remember, man, that thou art dust, and into dust thou shalt return." Gen. III., 19. The ashes remind us of the shortness of life, enkindle serious thoughts of eternity, and are a symbol of repentance.

1065. *How many years old is the celebration of Ash Wednesday?*

The special celebration of the Wednesday which introduces the forty days before Easter Sunday can be traced back some 1600 years. In the fourth century it is certain from documentary evidence that the early Christians used to regard it as a special day of penance, though it was not the custom then to make use of ashes. The additional ceremony of sprinkling ashes upon the heads of the people originated most probably in the seventh century, at the time of Pope Gregory the Great.

1066. *The assembly of the Free Presbyterian Church strongly protests against the recognition of Good Friday as a holy day, there being no Scriptural authority for so regarding it.*

A strong protest against things offensive to Christ would be a little more intelligible. But a protest against an effort to honor Christ from a body of professing Christians is an enigma. The authority of Scripture for the fact that our Lord died for us on Good Friday is more than enough warrant for our regarding the day as one demanding special reverence. Would the Free Presbyterians quarrel with the recognition of their own birthdays as having an importance not belonging to other days? And do they, or do they not, believe that the death of their Savior has meant more to them than their birth into a state from which they needed redemption?

Or again, is Christmas Day, the very birthday of Christ, sacred to the Free Presbyterians? Yet they have no more, and no less, Scriptural warrant for its observance.

1067. *This protest is in accord with our recognition of Holy Scripture as our supreme guide in matters of faith and morals.*

This bears out what I have always said—that Holy Scripture alone cannot be the supreme guide in faith and morals intended by Christ. All Protestants accept this rule—yet it leads one group to protest against the desecration of Good Friday, and it leads another group to protest against that very protest. It is an insult to the wisdom of Christ to suggest that He made no better provision than this for the guidance of men. However, in reality, He established the Catholic Church, and sent it to teach all nations. That Church does so, and all Catholics at least know where they stand. Outside the Catholic Church it is chaos, and dreary protests against each other's very protests.

1068. In days of almost general desecration of the authorized Sabbath day, we regret that there is a growing tendency to attribute a fictitious sanctity to the day known as Good Friday.

Christ's death on the Cross was not fictitious. All that it has meant to us is not fictitious. That the death of Christ occurred on Good Friday is not fictitious. I scarcely think the Free Presbyterians knew precisely what they themselves meant when they used that word. And a few questions suggest themselves. Will these Protestant Ministers protest carefully against the attributing of a fictitious sanctity to Christmas Day, when its observance draws near once more? And do they think they will block the desecration of the Sabbath day by asking people not even to recall all that Christ did for them on Good Friday? It is a weird idea to propose that, since Christ is not honored as He should be on Sundays, we must see to it that He is not honored as He should be on Good Friday.

But I have said enough. The Catholic Church at least remains loyal to all that our Lord's death has meant to those who love Him. Every Friday throughout the year she calls upon Catholics to give up the pleasure of taking meat on the day Christ gave up His very life for them. She prepares for the annual commemoration of the death of Jesus on Good Friday by the forty days of Lenten observance, and devotes the whole of Holy Week to recollection, prayer, and fitting religious services. If people want fidelity to the memory of Christ they will find it nowhere as they will find it in the Catholic Church.

1069. What is meant by "Corpus Christi," and why is it held each year?

The Feast of Corpus Christi is celebrated yearly. The words "Corpus Christi" mean the "Body of Christ." And the Feast of Corpus Christi is a yearly celebration of the great privilege possessed by Catholics in the Holy Eucharist which contains the very Body of Christ. We celebrate this religious festival each year just as we celebrate the Feast of Christmas in honor of Christ's birth in Bethlehem. It is a great thing for us that Christ should be born, and certainly deserving of an annual commemoration. So also, it is a great thing that we should have our Lord in the Eucharist. And that, too, we celebrate annually by the Feast of Corpus Christi. Shortly before the Reformation came along, when all England was Catholic, one of the colleges at Oxford University was established, and named "Corpus Christi College." It still retains that name, though many do not advert to its significance.

1070. Is the Catholic burial service in any way designed to benefit the soul of the departed?

Most decidedly. In fact, abstracting from the fact that it is essentially a part of our liturgical worship offered to God and a bond of union between living members of the visible Church on earth, the whole of the service is one of prayer for the soul of the departed person, imploring God's mercy for that soul, forgiveness of his sins, an early deliverance from expiations due to past infidelities, and a more generous share in the happiness of heaven insofar as our intercession can secure these things for him according to our fellowship in the Communion of Saints.

1071. What is the meaning of absolution given to the dead?

Strictly speaking, there is no such thing as absolution given to the dead. If we take absolution in the sacramental sense, as part of the Sacrament of Penance, it is evident that the person to be absolved must still be a living subject of the Church in this world. At times, however, you may hear of the "last absolution" being given at a Requiem Mass, that "absolution" being pronounced over the dead person lying before the Altar. But that "absolution" is not to be taken in the strict sense of the word, as if it had sacramental efficacy. Rather it is a liturgical prayer for the repose of the soul of the departed person—a prayer which would be of no avail to that person, did he die in a state of mortal sin.

1072. *I thought absolution could be given only to the living insofar as they are disposed to receive it.*

That is correct. Sacramental absolution cannot be given to dead people. If people are unconscious, or have even apparently died but a short time before the arrival of a priest, the priest can give but conditional absolution, which would avail only insofar as the subject is capable of responding to it, in the sight of God. God alone can know whether such a conditional absolution has its effect or not. But in any doubt, the priest gives the benefit of the doubt to the unconscious person, and absolves conditionally in the hope that the Sacrament may be of actual benefit.

1073. *What difference is there if a dead person is buried by a layman instead of a priest?*

In the actual burial of the dead person, no difference. In the blessings obtained for the soul of the dead person there would be a great difference. In the first place, the layman might, or might not read the official prayers of the Church on behalf of the deceased. If he did not, his own prayers, were he to substitute any, would lack the efficacy of the official liturgical prayers of the Church. On the other hand, even were he to offer all the official liturgical prayers of the Church, those prayers would not have the same value as they would were they offered by a priest. For, as distinct from the layman, the priest is, by his very ordination, a consecrated element in the worship of the Church; and through the priesthood officially, independently of the personal merits of individual priests, the Church dispenses liturgical blessings and graces which are not so dispensed through laymen. There is a difference, therefore, between the Church officially praying her own liturgical prayers through the lips of one of her priests, and the reading even of those same prayers by a layman who is unable to act officially in the name of the Church.

1074. *Where in the Bible did Jesus tell His disciples to teach us to burn candles for our dead?*

Nowhere. Yet the Bible recommends prayer for the dead, and nowhere forbids the burning of a candle from religious motives as an expression of prayer and a symbol of our belief in Christ as the Light of the World.

1075. *I have read in a Catholic paper of the Votive Lamp system, and would like to know something about it.*

You are welcome to ask any questions you wish about Catholic teachings or practices. But there is no such thing in the Catholic religion as "Votive Lamp system." In itself, the lighting of a lamp before an altar or a shrine as an expression of piety is quite a legitimate practice. A person, unable to give himself continuously to prayer, may leave a lamp burning as a tangible expression of his faith, and love and devotedness to God. And he may even regard it as a silent prayer to God, asking God's blessing and protection. A modern writer has recently said, "I am always strangely moved when I see the white beams of the votive candles in a Church, modestly crowded together in some corner by the altar—as if they were living souls shining there, and consuming away in their own fire; the faithful candles which we put there. We have to go; but they remain in our place in the sacred building, until their service has wasted them to the last drop." As a simple religious practice, therefore, votive candles are quite justifiable. But, as with all religious practices, excess is possible, and excesses are always to be condemned. Moderation is necessary in all things.

1076. Why is the Rosary so necessary in the Roman Catholic religion?

The Rosary is not a necessary part of the Catholic religion. It is a very useful form of devotion which Catholics are free to adopt or not. Most Catholics are wise enough to adopt it, and the Church makes use of it in her evening devotions very often.

1077. For what reasons are Rosary Beads used by Catholics?

In what is known as the Rosary, one undertakes to meditate on each of several aspects of the life and sufferings of Christ, each meditation lasting as long as it takes to recite one Our Father and ten Hail Marys. To save us from the distraction of counting these prayers we quietly allow beads, divided accordingly, to slip through our fingers, our lips repeating the prayers, our minds pondering over the significant mysteries of our Lord's life on earth.

1078. Why do they count Rosary Beads?

They don't. They know just how many beads there are in a Rosary, without having to count them. To save any attention to the counting of their prayers they use Rosary Beads, so that they can attend to their meditation on the Gospels during the time it takes them to say the usual prayers proper to the Rosary. The beads are thus a help to avoid distraction. They also symbolize a spiritual garland of prayers to be laid at our Lord's feet just as one would place a garland of flowers on the Cenotaph for lesser and merely natural reasons of reverence and gratitude. Just because you don't do things, or because they are strange to you, you must not think them foolish, or that there is nothing in them.

1079. The "Rosary symbol" was borrowed from the Hindus and Moslems, and it symbolizes the name of Mahomet.

No "Rosary symbol" exists among the Hindus or Moslems. The use of beads for the counting of their prayers may exist, and they may attach a symbolical meaning to their beads. But they have not the symbolism of the Rosary. The Catholic Church attaches no symbolism to beads. They have a purely utilitarian value, as a help to completing a certain number of prayers without the distraction of counting them. The Rosary is a series of vocal prayers counted on the beads, accompanied by meditation on the mysteries of the life of Jesus Christ. Its symbolism is that of a garland of spiritual roses offered to God, and this symbolism refers to the prayers, not to the beads. The beads as such stand for nothing. I might point out that the Rosary did not come into existence until the twelfth century, though beads for purposes of other prayers undoubtedly existed before that. But if the Rosary did not exist until the twelfth century, it is not correct to speak of "Rosary symbols" prior to that date.

1080. The Roman Catholic Christians took over this fetish from the Moslems 560 B.C.

Firstly, the Rosary is not a fetish. A fetish is an object with a spirit inhabiting it, whose services are at the disposal of the one who possesses that object. Now no Catholic has ever believed Rosary Beads to be inhabited by any spirit or spirits; nor are the beads worshipped in any way at all. Therefore, the Rosary cannot be a fetish. Secondly, how could Catholics take over the Rosary from the Moslems in 560 B.C.? No Christians existed before Christ Himself existed. But perhaps you mean 560 A.D. Yet here again you will be in no small difficulty. For no Moslems existed before 622 A.D., and the Rosary was unknown to Catholics until 600 years after that.

1081. *What is Lourdes Water? And can it cure people anywhere?*

What is known as Lourdes Water, is quite ordinary water, except that it has been brought from Lourdes, in France, being taken from the flowing spring there where God has wrought so many undoubted miracles. Lourdes Water, therefore, contains no naturally curative or medicinal properties. The waters do not cause the cures. It is God who does so, on certain occasions when the waters are applied to sick people.

Now God is everywhere, and just as present to people here in our country as to people who actually go to Lourdes. It follows that God *could* certainly cure people who make use of Lourdes Water here, just as He *has* cured them there.

But *is* God *likely* to do so? The answer is—Not as a rule. Why not? Because any cure will be due, *not* to natural causes, but to a miraculous interference of God's Omnipotence with the ordinary course of nature, and the ordinary course of nature is ordinary, whilst a miracle is extraordinary—and the extraordinary is necessarily rare. I do not say that miracles are unlikely in general. They occur too often and in every age, for us to say that. But a miracle in some particular case is more likely not to be granted than to be granted. But it is not impossible and one *is* justified in making use of Lourdes Water, not superstitiously as if expecting some magical effect, but with faith in God, sincere devotion, and complete resignation to whatever His Holy Will may be. In such a case God could, if He thought fit, grant our desire, in order to honor our Blessed Lady, from whose shrine the waters came. And even if God did not grant the actual cure, He *may* grant some alleviation, and will *certainly* grant spiritual graces and blessings proportionate to the faith, piety and devotion of those who manifest such belief and confidence in Him and in the dear Lady Mother of Christ.

Catholics understand these principles. When they make use of Lourdes Water with fervent prayer and devotion, they *would* be overjoyed *if* God granted a cure.

But knowing that miracles are necessarily rare, they are not in the least surprised or disappointed if He does not. In this case they find consolation in the thought that God knows their faith and piety and that He will grant them other spiritual graces and blessings much more precious than any temporal favor. And their love of God brings to their lips at once the words of Christ, "Not My Will, but Thine be done," whatever God may decree.

1082. *I read in a Catholic paper that those who wear the brown scapular of our Lady will not go to hell and will be released from purgatory the first Saturday after their death.*

Your difficulties show that this brief statement was given without the explanation with which Catholics are familiar.

1083. *Now I ask you, do you believe, as a man and a priest, that a scapular has such magic power?*

I certainly do not believe that a scapular has any magic power. Nor does any Catholic. Nevertheless, I myself wear a brown scapular, and hope to benefit by its blessings.

1084. *Why prayers for the dead, if a scapular, valued at 10 cents, releases the soul automatically from purgatory on the Saturday after one's death, merely provided you wear it?*

No Catholic believes that the mere wearing of the scapular has that effect.

1085. *All a Catholic needs to do is to wear the scapular!*

Again, no Catholic believes that that is all that is needed. Now let me explain, briefly. The scapular is a small piece of cloth which is part of the religious habit of the Carmelite Order. Those who join the Confraternity of the Scapular are in a certain degree affiliated with that Order and share in all their prayers and good works. And as the Carmelite Order is established in honor of the Mother of Christ, those who wear the scapular in a spirit of true devotion and love have a special claim to her intercession and protection. Historical documents tell us that our Lady appeared to St. Simon Stock, an English Monk, and promised a special protection of all who would wear the badge known as the scapular. But the promise that one's soul would be preserved from hell supposes sincere dispositions and excludes absolutely the sin of presumption. If anyone were to wear the scapular and presumptuously think that enough, and that despite any and every sin salvation would be secure, such a one would certainly not be preserved from hell. And every Catholic knows this. But granted sincere devotion to our Lady and sincere efforts to live a life worthy of Christ her Son, the scapular does give the well-founded hope that Mary will obtain for one the privilege of death in God's grace and friendship, and consequently preservation from hell, even though the soul must yet endure purification in purgatory. The additional promise of release from purgatory on the Saturday following one's death—it is called the Sabbatine Privilege—supposes additional conditions of prayer and Christian mortification throughout life, conditions not easily fulfilled.

However, it is enough to say that all presumption is excluded; that no magic power attaches to the scapular or the wearing of it; and that the spiritual privileges are strictly dependent upon the dispositions of soul with which one adopts the scapular and tries to live a good Christian life.

1086. *I would be surprised if you could show me where this is mentioned in Scripture.*

You would have more cause for wonder if I could, since the scapular devotion arose in the Church some thousand years after the Scriptures were written. But there is nothing in the idea of scapulars which in any way contradicts any principle in Scripture. It is in perfect harmony with Gospel principles. A piece of cloth worn with piety and devotion is just as able to convey a blessing to the wearer as clay made from earth and spittle was able to be an agent of blessings to the blind man cured by Christ, or as the handkerchiefs and aprons which had touched the body of St. Paul were able to heal the sick and convey spiritual benefits. Acts XIX., 12.

1087. *Was not the Sabbatine Indulgence granted by our Lady through Pope John XXIII., to whom she is said to have appeared?*

You have got the wrong Pope. The report attributes the apparition of our Lady, not to Pope John XXIII., but to Pope John XXII., who was said to have published a Papal Bull proclaiming the Sabbatine Privilege, popularly believed to mean that the soul of one faithful to certain conditions would be released from purgatory through our Lady's intercession on the first Saturday after death.

1088. *Was not John XXIII., an anti-Pope? If so, would our Lady grant an Indulgence through an imposter?*

John XXIII. was an anti-Pope. But he is not connected with this matter. As I have said, the Bull was attributed to Pope John XXII., who certainly was not an anti-Pope. So even if all were historically true, there would be no question of our Lady appearing to an anti-Pope. But, as a matter of fact, all is not historically true. It is certain that the supposed Papal Bull was never issued even by Pope John XXII. He was said to have issued the document in 1322. But the document is first heard of in the collected works of Leersius, who lived 100 years after Pope John XXII. Some unknown author, overendowed with imagination, probably ascribed the vision of our Lady, and the Sabbatine Privilege to Pope John XXII.; and Leersius, coming across it, embodied it in his work without critical examination, and taking it for granted. So, not only is there no question of our Lady appearing to an imposter, she did not even grant the Sabbatine Privilege to her people through the lawful Pope, John XXII.

1089. Why is this Indulgence of doubtful origin commended today by the Congregation of Indulgences and modern Popes?

The Papal Bull attributed to Pope John XXII., is not of doubtful origin. It is certainly not authentic. It did give rise to the popular idea of release from purgatory on the first Saturday after one's death. Later Popes never asserted the Bull to be genuine. But, owing to the widespread belief of so many people in good faith, they decided on their own proper authority to grant certain indulgences, and to sanction the devotion to a limited extent.

To get an idea that is really authentic we must go, not to the spurious document attributed to Pope John XXII., but to the authentic decrees of later Popes, and above all, to the decree issued by Pope Gregory XIII. in 1577. That decree has been ratified by the Congregation of Indulgences, and by several modern Popes. And it makes no mention of any certain release of the soul from purgatory on the first Saturday after death. It simply says that people who manifest a special devotion to Mary, the Mother of Christ, by wearing the Brown Scapular of Mt. Carmel, by ever observing chastity according to their state, by reciting daily the Office of our Lady, or, alternatively, by abstaining from meat on Wednesdays and Saturdays, may reasonably hope for her special protection, and a particular share in her merits both in this life and the next, above all on Saturdays. Whether the departed soul would be released from purgatory in virtue of these special favors is not stated, though it would not be an unreasonable hope, were the conditions I have mentioned fulfilled throughout life.

In view of later literature on the subject, we add this to the above answers.

In 1923, P. E. Magennis, O. Carm., Prior General, published *"The Sabbatine Privilege"* New York: Connolly, 1923. And there have been several articles in the *"Analecta Ordinis Carmelitarum,"* and the *"Analecta Ordinis Carmelitarum Discalceatorum,"* both official organs.

Leersius wrote in 1483 — therefore some 161 years after 1322. He refers to copies of the Bull of John XXII — and *these were found about 1575*. John XXII did give the Sabbatine Bull on March 3, 1322. Alex. V in 1409 *repeated its contents* and confirmed it. A copy of Alexander's Bull was made in 1421, sealed and signed by public notaries and Carmelite officials. In 1430 a copy of the 1421 was made, signed and sealed, and other copies have been discovered in the Vatican archives. If such official copies cannot be trusted, actum est de historia. Another document, written in 1461, has also been discovered recently — so Leersius is not the first to mention the Sabbatine Bull. Although no original copy of John XXII's Bull is extant, there are unquestionable legal duplicates.

When Pope Pius XI allowed the Medal to be worn in place of the Scapular, he specified that all the indulgences of the Scapular "That which is called the Sabbatine, not excepted" could be gained with the Medal.

See also R. R., Vol. I., Nos. 1335-1440.

CHAPTER THIRTEEN

THE CHURCH AND SOCIAL WELFARE

1090. Why is it that countries in which Roman Catholicism predominates as a religion are now socially and economically decadent?

That question is far too vague, and takes altogether too much for granted. I must ask you to state precisely which countries you have in mind. It is possible that there is a country in which "Roman Catholicism" predominates, yet which is not socially and economically decadent. It is possible that there are countries which are socially and economically decadent, but in which non-Catholic forms of religion predominate. And it is even possible that there are socially and economically decadent countries which know no other form of Christianity in the main save Roman Catholicism, but in which that religion has ceased to have any predominating influence in their administration. You see how impossible it is to answer a question which gives rise to so many possibilities.

But it is only fair to warn you now, before you submit more precise questions, that the line of thought prompting your inquiry will lead you nowhere. For you are associating two ideas which have no necessary bearing one upon the other. Firstly, "if" a Catholic country were decadent, it would not be "because" the people professed the Catholic religion. Secondly, and quite apart from the question of cause and effect, the truth, or otherwise, of a religion is not to be discerned from the alternating material prosperity and adversity of individuals or nations. For these reasons, I say that your line of thought will lead nowhere as an effort to solve any question as to the truth of Catholicism.

1091. Everybody knows that the Roman Catholic countries have steadily deteriorated, whilst Protestant countries have prospered.

No one can know that; for Catholic countries have not really deteriorated. They have, perhaps, been at a standstill from *certain points of view*, whilst some Protestant countries have forged ahead in those specific directions.

The judgment upon which the question is based is erroneous, because too sweeping.

Men invariably tend to think their own nation superior to others; and even if they are superior in some things, they are apt to claim superiority in all things. We make our test of comparison the thing in which we happen perhaps to excel. An American will boast that his country possesses the mighty dollar in abundance and undoubtedly leads the world. If Australia produces more wheat and wool we tend to make those the test of greatness. Did we produce more battleships, battleships would be the test. But it is a fallacy to see our good points and overlook the good points others possess and which we do not possess. In Spain, the trains are slower than in England, but national proficiency in music is far higher. In material and industrial progress, apart from its disastrous consequences, England and Germany had the coal and iron. The Southern countries had not. The age of inventions was bound to benefit more the better adapted countries from a geographical and geological point of view. The Reformation, above all, helped in England. The confiscation of Church lands and property enriched the few, and had Capitalists ready to finance the great industrial enterprises. In Catholic countries the wealth was more evenly distributed and no group of individuals was in the position of the wealthy of England.

But the swing of the pendulum is altering things under our very eyes. Industrialism and Capitalism are failing. Italy is rising, still remaining Catholic. England is falling. No one could maintain that she holds the dominant place amongst the powers she once held. And her internal miseries are much greater than many suspect, with the poverty of the masses, vast unemployment, and indescribable slums in all her greater cities. I am just facing facts impartially. The material and industrial progress of Northern European Protestant countries was due chiefly to geographical, political, and racial factors. If religion had any influence at all, it was because Protestantism not only made men lose faith in the supernatural claims of the Catholic Church, but tended to unbelief in the supernatural altogether. Protestantism has certainly tended to make men lose sight of spiritual things, diverting their attention to natural and material things as being more important. I confine this to material and industrial progress. In other matters, there has been retrogression and a deterioration not found in Catholic countries, above all in domestic and social ethical standards. I have no time to give you more, but I have indicated something of the vastness of the question.

This matter, of course, has no bearing on the truth or otherwise of the Catholic religion. We can't have the Catholic religion true when Spain was dominant in the sixteenth century, and the same religion false when England happened to be dominant in the nineteenth century. I am sure you see that. Catholicism must be judged on its own merits as a religion, not from the material fluctuations of nations in things mutable of their very nature.

1092. *Speaking of education, what is the real reason for Catholic antipathy to our state schools?*

Whatever others may think of our public policy of free, compulsory, and secular education, Catholics cannot in conscience accept that system as being suitable for the education of Catholic children. The real reason is that the religious training of the children is not sufficiently provided for, the time allotted for religion being quite inadequate, even were it utilized. The State system demands the "3 R's," reading, writing and arithmetic. Catholic principles demand the "4 R's," religion, reading, writing and arithmetic; and religion first, not merely a third-rate item. Again, even granted that religion *were* taught adequately in the school, education is as much a matter of environment and atmosphere as of anything else. You can't have a Catholic atmosphere in a school, where 75% of the children are non-Catholics. Children's convictions are formed or deformed in the playground every bit as much as in the classroom. For children are impressionable and greatly influenced by the opinions and assertions of their companions. And a Catholic child who constantly hears non-Catholic children giving utterance to their parents' peculiar religious or irreligious opinions is certainly not being well grounded in the Catholic Faith. If Catholic parents want to bring up their children as good Catholics, they *must* send them to a school where they will come into contact with a consistent Catholic teaching, both in classroom and playground.

1093. *I know that the Bible says, "Bring up a child in the way it should go, and it will not depart from it." But that merely means that the child will lose the power to think for itself, believing only what it has been taught in childhood.*

That is a foolish interpretation of the words you quote. There is no reference whatever to any loss of power to think for oneself. The words say that the child is to be brought up in the way it *should* go, obviously in the right way; not in the wrong way in which it should not go. And if one has been taught the right thing in childhood, he will continue to believe it, if he has any sense, in later life. Any Catholic who thinks for himself in later life, will find only reasons to confirm the truth of the Catholic Faith taught him in his youth, provided he thinks soundly, and avoids packing his mind with false ideas derived from unreliable and partisan sources.

1094. Why the Catholic idea of teaching religion every day in religious schools? Christianity is a simple religion.

It is simple in its principles, but it has to be taught in its fullness in accordance with our Lord's command, "Teach all things whatsoever I have commanded you." Also, Catholic education is as much a matter of atmosphere as of classes in religious doctrine. To put any child in the midst of hundreds of others who never mention religion, scarcely think of it outside Sunday school hours, or if they do speak of it, do so according to systems utterly opposed to Catholic teaching, is no way to give a *Catholic* education to a *Catholic* child. Where it is possible, Catholic parents are obliged to secure a truly Catholic education for the children God gives them.

1095. Is Rome finding it difficult to keep the flock together, and Catholics from finding out too much in these modern times?

The Church is doing her duty in trying to keep the "flock" within the sheepfold. Surely you are not going to blame the shepherds for doing their strict duty in the name of Christ. Also, it is not to prevent Catholic children from finding out too much. It is to prevent them from knowing too little of the truth, from acquiring too many erroneous notions, and from modeling their lives upon those of sheep wandering without a shepherd.

1096. The real business of life is to alter the form of society, by revolution if necessary, and give everybody a fair share of the good things kept by the lucky few. So please discuss that.

Altering the form of society will be useless unless you alter the human beings composing that society. Give everybody an equal share of the "good things of this world" tomorrow, and inequalities will at once begin to develop. Envy, jealousy, dishonesty, laziness, dissipation, immorality, imprudence, and every kind of excess, will still be there. Some will accumulate, others recklessly scatter and waste their possessions. Moreover, a sudden and radical change by revolution is more certain to cause immense suffering than it is likely to produce any benefits for anybody. Christianity, which works on the innermost heart of man, is the only thing that can remedy the ills of the world today. And it is significant that the multiplication of miseries we all deplore has accompanied a wholesale driftage from the Christian religion in practice. A return to genuine Christianity is the one real remedy. And that means a return to the Catholic Faith and the observance of its moral obligations.

1097. Will you agree that the masses are in a starving condition after the preaching of the wonderful Gospel for 2000 years?

No. I agree that sections of the masses are poverty stricken, and that some members of these sections are reduced practically to starvation point. But it is an obvious exaggeration to say, without any qualification, that the masses are starving. Again, the fact that many—and far too many—are not so well provided for as they should be after 2000 years of Gospel preaching does not necessarily argue to any fault in the Gospel preached. At most it argues to the fact that many ignore the Gospel; or that, whilst acknowledging its truth, they fail to put its principles into practice. But I am not called upon to defend the conduct of those who don't believe in the Gospel, nor of those who do profess to believe, yet don't attempt to live up to it. If you condemn them, I can only join you in condemning them for their attitude. And that, just as I would have to condemn you if, whilst blaming others, you yourself failed to observe personally what the Gospel demands of you.

1098. *Is not poverty the enemy of God?*

Not necessarily. When the Eternal Son of God came into this world He embraced poverty, and promised special blessings to the poor. If anything, He condemned the other extreme of wealth, and declared that riches are much more likely to take men from God than poverty.

At the same time, a great deal of the poverty in this world is due to the injustice of the rich. And that injustice is undoubtedly the enemy of God. Again, abject poverty can be, and often is, the occasion of temptations to crime. And in this sense, poverty could be regarded as the enemy of God.

1099. *If poverty be in any way the enemy of God, why do we Christians hesitate in abolishing it?*

Men will never succeed in abolishing poverty entirely. Our Lord has said, "The poor you will always have with you." But that does not alter the fact that there are far too many poor, and that the cause of their poverty is not according to God's will. Why, then, do we Christians hesitate in abolishing this excessive poverty of so many people? For the simple reason that the vast majority of those who are really Christians are amongst the very poor whose lot is to be remedied. In other words, we Christians have not within our hands the means whereby we can abolish such injustice. Our Lord warned us that the more money a man gets, the less likely he is to be a good Christian. And the wealth of the world is concentrated in the hands of rich men who have no Christian inspiration to use their power for the alleviation of poverty, and the bettering of the lot of the poor at what they regard as their own expense. It is because they won't obey Christian principles that the poor also abandon Christian principles, turn Communist, and proceed to take by force what the rich unjustly reserve for themselves. It takes a lot of Christian principle on the part of the poor to refrain from Communism, and appeal to social justice by constitutional means, whilst those who control the goods of this world are quite deaf to the claims of social justice.

1100. *In a recent reply you said that the poor shall be always with us. Why? Is it because the Churches want the poor to be kept poor?*

That is not the reason. I was not expressing a wish. I was stating a fact; or rather, I was quoting the very words of Christ predicting the fact that there would always be poverty for some people in this world.

1101. *The evidence I have shows no benefits conferred on society by the Church.*

If that be so, the evidence you have is inadequate, and secured from non-Catholic sources only. And you cannot expect non-Catholic authors to give space to Catholic beneficial activities.

1102. *I mean not only the Church of Rome, but Protestant Churches, too.*

I am not here to defend any form of professed Christianity other than the Catholic Church.

1103. *The worst blots on our society have been agitated against by those outside the Churches, including my own—the Church of England.*

When you say "our society" you are probably judging in the light of that section of the world which is predominantly Protestant. People have often boasted that Protestantism ushered in a new and glorious society, and that Protestantism was responsible for building up our present civilization. If people want to flog that civilization and dwell upon its evils, let them be consistent and still exclude the

Catholic Church from responsibility. Since the Reformation, at least, the voice of the Catholic Church has been consistently ignored in Protestant countries. The Church of England was the creation of the English throne, and a state department, with more affinity for the Lords than for the commoners, and with little interest in the workers and the downtrodden. Catholics were despised and persecuted, and excluded from all influential political positions. They were not in a position to agitate against the blots in the post-reformation society of Protestant countries.

1104. I have in mind child labor, and the abolition of slavery.

Child labor flourished chiefly in England where Protestantism had the influence. Against it, Catholic authorities uttered protests to which Protestants would not listen, and wrote books which Protestants would not read. The first real recognition the Catholic attitude received in England was in the person of Cardinal Manning—who merely dwelt upon principles formulated by the Pope.

As regards slavery, you can have no objection to the Catholic Church when you advert to the facts.

Slavery was deeply interwoven with the Roman civilization when the Church first began her work. The Church labored to better the lot of slaves from the beginning. She taught their equal human dignity; worked for their emancipation; ordained them as priests; and by the year 225 had a fugitive slave as Pope. She urged those owners who were converted to Christianity to release their slaves; and within 200 years of Constantine's conversion she had practically eradicated the pagan concept of slavery. Later in history the inroads of Mahometanism revived slavery, for the Moors regarded it as a duty to enslave captive Christians. Religious Orders sprang up dedicated to the ransom of slaves, and from 1198 to 1632 the Trinitarians and the Order of Mercy redeemed from slavery over 1,400,000 slaves.

When Spain and Portugal captured their American colonies, the Popes did their utmost to prevent slavery. Pius II., in 1482, Paul III., in 1537, Urban VIII., in 1639, and Benedict XIV. in 1741—all actively denounced and resisted slavery. Gregory XVI. and Leo XIII. both fought the later African slave trade. But it was chiefly being fostered in American colonies founded from Protestant England; and remember that Catholics themselves were not emancipated from penal laws in England until 1829.

1105. When these evils were rife, the Church was in a powerful position, yet did not denounce these tragedies.

The Catholic Church was not in a powerful position, and had little opportunity in the Protestant atmosphere of England and America at the time of which you speak. In fact, Catholics were treated practically as the slaves whose lot you bemoan. The Catholic Church denounced the abuses you mention; but her denunciations received no attention in Protestant countries. I do not defend the Protestant Church which was dominant, but I deny that it was truly representative of Christianity.

1106. The Church adopts the same attitude today towards social evils; or only touches them when they affect her as an institution.

That remark shows that you are quite unfamiliar with what the Catholic Church has done and is doing in the social sphere today.

1107. The Church will be forced to take cognizance of these evils, or lose her status entirely.

The Catholic Church is fully cognizant of all the evils you have in mind. Nor is she in the least fearful for her own future. She is conscious that she was established some 2000 years ago by Jesus Christ Who promised that by His divine power and protection she would last all days even to the end of the world. And I scarcely think she will have greater obstacles to meet in the future than those she has survived in the past.

1108. *The Christian Churches of the world, including the Roman Catholic Church, have a more or less large following in the so-called civilized countries.*

They have.

1109. *Presumably they have a first-hand knowledge of the terrible conditions of the poor in those countries.*

They have.

1110. *Why do not all the Churches in general, and the Roman Catholic Church in particular, make some real effort to eradicate these evils?*

I cannot speak on behalf of other Churches. The Catholic Church in particular has made real efforts to eradicate the evil. But pronouncements by the Catholic Church are not heeded nor given publicity in non-Catholic countries, nor in Capitalist countries. Religious prejudice and the resentment of Capitalists whose injustice has been condemned combine in a conspiracy to silence. And for the most part the Catholic protest reaches only Catholics amongst those whose lot should be remedied, not those able to remedy it.

1111. *Why not bring pressure to bear on the respective Governments?*

In what way? Moral condemnation leaves them cold. Would you advise the Church to organize political opposition or armed rebellion? And if she did either, would you undertake her defense against the howl of execration from her enemies, or join in with them?

1112. *Instead, they are happy to say prayers, hand out a little charity here and there, and do much talking, with little or no real action.*

Can you really blame any Church for happiness at prayer, the chief act of religion? The reference to "handing out a little charity here and there" is a niggardly tribute above all to the Catholic body which distributes millions of dollars yearly subscribed by people already bled dry by the unjust burden of double taxation for the education of their children. The "real action" you think the Church should undertake I cannot discuss until you inform me of the nature of the activity you have in mind.

1113. *Is it not a fact that the Church even opposes many wise reforms merely from ignorance or unwillingness to accept up-to-date ideas?*

That is not a fact. The Church has many of her clergy devoting their lives to sociological study, who are experts in such subjects. They are neither ignorant, nor in the least unwilling to abandon out-of-date ideas. But they insist upon weighing new ideas on their own merits and if they oppose some of them, they but seem to be opposing wise ideas to those who have not sufficiently studied the matter.

1114. *Since 75% of the crimes in the world are caused by capitalism, is not capitalism sinful in itself?*

The capitalistic system as such is not sinful. In some form or other capital and labor will have to co-operate. The present form of capitalism has developd in certain evil directions, and those evil tendencies must be corrected. The inequalities, poverty and suffering of many today have resulted from lack of due control of the capitalistic system; and these sufferings have certainly been the occasion, though not the cause, of crimes and of violence. Your estimate that 75% of the crimes of the world are occasioned by evils due to a badly regulated capitalism is probably excessive, but it would be very difficult to give any precise estimate.

1115. Is it true that all men have equal rights to the use and enjoyment of the elements provided by nature?

Of some of them—yes. For example, no one has any right to prevent another from breathing the good fresh air that nature has provided for the use of all living creatures. In other cases, it is not true that all men have equal rights to the use and enjoyment of the elements provided by nature. At most, they have equal rights to acquire by a just title such natural goods as their capacity and initiative render possible. Once a man has acquired property, equal rights of others to that property are excluded. At the same time, the use and enjoyment of property by those who possess it are not unconditional. The exercise of the right of private ownership is limited by the duties of justice and charity to one's fellow men, and by the right of the State in certain cases to safeguard the common good.

1116. Is it true that each man has an exclusive right to the use and enjoyment of what is produced by his own labor?

That is not true as it stands. It would be too sweeping an assertion. For a thing could be produced by a man's labor from goods owned by another, and even with the assistance of capital provided by others. In some cases, however, one's own labor could give rise to a just and exclusive title of ownership; in which cases, ownership would be subject to the conditions I have already mentioned as regards the use and enjoyment of the goods in question.

1117. Does not the Catholic Church favor capitalism and the employing class in her social doctrines?

No. The Church was born poor, has ever honored the poor, inspires the love and practice of poverty in hundreds of Religious Houses, and teaches that riches are rather a hindrance than a help to salvation.

1118. Has it not been said that the Catholic Church is the religion of beggars but that she dines in palaces?

Christ Himself was born in poverty, and ever loved the poor. Yet often He dined with the rich. The Church, like her Master, is all things to all men. All have souls to be saved, and the Church appeals to all to fulfill their respective duties.

1119. Would you deny that the Church suspects social reform which favors the lower classes?

I would certainly deny that. She is most anxious for a social reform which will result in the betterment of the poor. But you cannot expect the Church to give her blessing to social theories which preach a false materialistic doctrine of life, and which urge rebellion against the natural rights of man as well as against God and religion. Reform in favor of the workers which restricts itself to social economy within the limits of justice and charity will meet with nothing but encouragement at the hands of the Catholic Church.

1120. Don't you think that, if the working classes believe in a hereafter, they do not struggle to better their own social conditions?

No. They may refrain from unlawful measures. But their Catholic religion and their belief in a future life do not hinder them from lawful prudential measures in this life. In fact, they know that God expects them to use their faculties, and make suitable provision for their earthly necessities as long as they are in this world.

1121. In Catholic countries where workers are taught to view things in the light of an eternal destiny are not their conditions deplorable?

In the modern industrial conditions these countries may be suffering as others are suffering. But prior to the industrialization of the world, the workers of Catholic countries were not in a deplorable condition. For example, the guilds of operative masons were entirely Catholic in origin and were protective measures for those stone workers. These guilds have no connection whatever with speculative masonry as embodied in the Masonic Lodges.

Again, with the rise of industrialism, Pope Leo XIII. was one of the first to demand favorable conditions for the workers, and he was regarded as an innovator and attacked right, left and center by the capitalist world of the day. That world is at last beginning to see that he was right. If Catholic principles were put into practice, the lot of the workers would certainly not be deplorable.

1122. If a foreign armed force invaded our country and evicted people from their homes, would your Church forbid the people to resist by force, if necessary?

No.

1123. If the police of this country evict workers from their homes on behalf of capitalist owners, does your Church forbid those workers to resist by force?

Yes. In the preceding case you have a foreign nation invading a country not theirs and evicting people from their own homes. In this present case, you have legitimate authority in our country evicting people, not from their own homes, but from houses lawfully owned by others. If you think these cases parallel, you have a strange idea of similarity.

Again, your imagination insists on supposing that the landlords are wealthy people. There are many people who have saved just enough to own one other house besides the one they live in. The rent is often their only means of support, and they have a right to that revenue. They cannot be obliged to allow a family to live in their house who will not, or who cannot, pay, when they can let the house to others who can. And the law protects their rights—a law citizens must uphold, not resist.

If a thug wanted to sandbag you and rob you of your personal possessions in the street, you would be glad enough to secure the protection of the law and the help of near-by police. Yet the owners of a house have as much right to the rent as you have to your watch and chain, and to your loose cash.

I admit that it is the duty of the State to make suitable provision for the families of workers who, through no fault of their own, cannot secure work or sufficient remuneration. The State can do this, either by paying the rent, and leaving the poor in the homes they at present occupy, or by providing them with other accommodation. But private owners of houses have no obligation to make provision for those who wish to occupy homes rent-free; and there is no justification in attacking the police who fulfill their duty, and who are not responsible for the laws they have to apply. To forestall a further difficulty, let us suppose that the landlord is already a wealthy man who does not need the rent. If the tenants cannot pay the rent, is he obliged to allow them to occupy his house? And we can make the case as black as possible by supposing that, if he turns them out, he will be able to get no other tenant, the house will remain unoccupied, and the evicted people will have nowhere to go. Even here, he is not in debt to those people, and is not bound in strict justice to allow them to remain. It is the social duty of the State to provide for them, not the duty of an individual owner. I would say this, however: If the owner knows that the State will make no provision for them, and that the evicted people will actually be left in dire straits, then he would sin, not against justice, but against charity, did he refuse to allow them to continue in a house for which he had no other use himself, or the rent of which he could easily do without for the time being.

1124. *If you forbid violent resistance against eviction, you confirm the growing belief that the Church exists to protect landlords and capitalists.*

Not everyone who owns a house is a capitalist by any means. The Church asserts the principle of justice to all, and insists most strongly upon justice to the workers who have less means of defense than those with wealth at their disposal. Your talk of the growing belief among the workers is a general assumption on your part. If it be the growing belief amongst some workers, that belief receives no reasonable confirmation from the doctrine I have given.

1125. *If not, why does the Church command the workers to protect their own oppressors against foreigners, but sternly forbid them to protect themselves?*

You are begging the question in your every utterance. The Church does not command workers to defend their oppressors against an invading foreigner. If a people desire to be incorporated in the invading nation, they may submit without resistance and be thus incorporated. But the Church says that they are not obliged to do so, and may as a nation defend their right to independent existence. In this case, workers do not defend their oppressors against the invader. They defend themselves in union with all others also contributing to national defense.

Again, you wrongly assert that the Church forbids workers to protect themselves in time of peace against their capitalist oppressors. She does not. She urges them to unite, and make use of all lawful means to better their lot. She has ever been in favor of unions and combined action. She does forbid the use of any unjust and morally wrong means, but that is a totally different thing.

1126. *The Church has declared many times that "human authority represents that of God," and that it is therefore sinful to rebel against it.*

The Church certainly says that human authority is of God, for St. Paul tells us very clearly, "Let every soul be subject to higher powers: for there is no power but from God: and those that are, are ordained of God." Rom. XIII., 1. But this applies only in the case of the just exercise of authority. To all the just laws of a de facto government, whether it be monarchial or republican, we owe obedience in conscience.

But does the Church say that it is sinful to rebel against a constituted government? The Church says that it is certainly lawful to resist any unjust and tyrannical exercise of authority. Even rebellion is lawful as a last resort. But this is such an extreme measure and productive of so much evil, that it is lawful only on the following conditions:

(1) If the government is habitually and continuously tyrannical, pursuing a selfish object to the manifest detriment of the people.

(2) When all legal and peaceful measures have been tried in vain, by published criticism, meetings of protest, and deputations to the authorities.

(3) When there is a reasonable hope of success and the rebellion will not cause greater evils than those to be remedied.

(4) When the judgment of the government's injustice is not merely a private or party judgment, but that of the majority of the citizens.

Granted these conditions, rebellion would be lawful.

1127. *How are the workers to know when the authority of their oppressors comes from the Lord, and when it does not?*

If a law is manifestly opposed to the law of God, citizens do not owe obedience to that individual law. But if a law passed by a government for the common good entails some hardship upon a section of the community—that section may take all just means to secure some amelioration. They would not be justified, however, in organizing a rebellion. Not all workers agree that they are oppressed. Many are quite comfortable. Those who are in unfortunate circumstances should take all lawful means to awaken the public conscience, and secure some amelioration of their conditions. But the conditions I have outlined as being necessary to justify armed rebellion are certainly not verified in our country. Workers are obliged to submit to the just legislation of the present government, and organize to pull their full weight for the abolition of such legislation as they feel to be unjust. But they must proceed by constitutional means.

1128. *The Church says that State authority is of God, but Karl Marx denies State authority, calling the State merely a machine to oppress the worker.*

Karl Marx does not deny State authority by any means. He says that the Capitalist State is a machine for the oppression of the worker. He advocates class struggle, the overthrow of the Capitalist State, of religion, family and school as at present constituted. The proletarian State, with collective ownership, is to follow, with its own rigid discipline and authority.

1129. *Which explanation will the worker find most reasonable, after coming into collision with the gun, the baton, and the boot, wielded by State authority?*

The most reasonable explanation for the workingman as for every other man, is the Catholic explanation. If workingmen unite and work by constitutional means to better their conditions, they won't come into collision with authority. They will mould its legislation. But if they refuse to pull together, and small groups break out into spasmodic rebellions they will accomplish nothing, and force the government to take all necessary measures for the preservation of public order. Meantime, whilst some impulsive workers may overstep the bounds of lawful procedure here and come into conflict with State authority, in Russia the workers are in an infinitely worse plight. The Soviet's own official figures admit over a million and a half executions during the past ten years, chiefly of starving workers who have taken collectively-owned food to keep their bodies and souls together. The gun, the baton, and the boot prevail in Russia as in no other country in the world.

Conditions generally under our present form of government do not warrant the Russian experiment here.

1130. *Why does not your Church teach honesty and equality, instead of deference to the rich, calling it loyalty and religion?*

The Catholic Church teaches honesty, insisting that dishonesty is always sinful. She does not teach equality in this world, though she does teach that Christ died equally for all men.

Yet she does not teach deference to the rich calling it loyalty and religion. Wealth as such is no title to deference. True virtue is, and also lawful authority. Loyalty dictates the duty of respect for authority, and it is dishonest to refuse. Religion dictates respect for virtue. I have immense respect for the poor man who is a good man; none whatever for the wealthy man who is unjust and depraved. But not all poor people are good, and not all wealthy people are evil. Anyway, wealth as such is not a title to any particular deference.

1131. *Will the Catholic Church tell us how we can get peace on earth whilst the material conditions of the present economic order pit men against men and nations against nations?*

The material conditions of the present economic order are not alone to blame for social discord. The psychological factor of selfishness enters largely into the question. But the faults and the injustice of the present economic order do occasion immense distress, and the peace of all is not possible whilst things remain as they are. Let me quote to you Pope Pius XI. In his Encyclical on Labor and Capital he writes, "The immense number of property-less wage earners on the one hand, and the superabundant riches of the fortunate few on the other, are an unanswerable argument that the earthly goods so abundantly produced in this age of industrialism are far from rightly distributed amongst the various classes of men. Every effort must be made that a just share only be permitted to accumulate in the hands of the wealthy, and that an ample sufficiency be supplied to the workers." The Pope then goes on to insist that there must be a reconstruction of the present social order, thereby clearly indicating that peace is not possible in the present social order. He rejects the program of socialism, and lays down the moral principles which must govern true social reform, demanding the mutual co-operation of all men, whether employers or workers, together with the just intervention of State authority. But his chief point is that the laboring classes have genuine grievances, which must be remedied in accordance with all the principles of social justice.

1132. *What prevents our Church leaders from devising a technique which would make the fullness of the earth available to the people?*

If all the professors in this world who have devoted their lives to the study of political economy have failed to devise such a technique, why should Church leaders who have to devote their lives to another matter altogether succeed where the economists have failed? You might as well ask why the leading members of the legal profession have not devised a technique for the immediate destruction of cancer throughout the world.

1133. *What alternative policy would you suggest to replace the Capitalistic one which comprises the platforms of the Labor and Liberal Parties of today?*

It is not possible to give here an adequate answer to so general a question as that. However, I can give a brief indication of the direction along which genuine reforms should move. I would suggest a Co-operative State, with vocational groups carrying on all present necessary works and businesses, and taking over many of the functions the State has taken upon itself. The State should give more time to regulation, and less to enterprises it has tended to assume and control. A redistribution of wealth is necessary by lifting wages from their actual condition to those necessary for a decent living, with opportunities of comfort and culture. Wages must not be sacrificed to profits—profits must, if anything, be sacrificed to wages. The first charge of an employer should be the persons of his employees. The business should be run for the employee as well as for the employer. State authority, and the functions of capital and labor, will have to exist, of course, in any form of society. But, in the "Co-operative State" all three would undergo modifications in the direction of a better distribution of this world's goods, a greater respect for human personality, and general contentment and happiness.

1134. *I have been told that the Roman Catholic view on reconstructing the social order is expressed in the great Encyclical Letter of the Pope entitled "Quadragesimo Anno."*

The basic principles upon which any sound policy of reconstruction must rest are clearly set out in that Encyclical.

1135. *I am told that the solution there given is not only Christian and suited to human nature, but more practical than the doctrines of Karl Marx.*

A solution based on the principles of the Pope's Encyclical would be more practical than an attempt based on the doctrines of Karl Marx precisely because the

Catholic solution is Christian and adapted to the full requirements of human nature. As a matter of fact the principles of Karl Marx can never lead to a solution of social evils. They can end only in causing greater social evils than those they are intended to remedy, for they are based upon a wrong interpretation of history, an erroneous philosophy of human nature, and a fatal divorce from God, the very Author and supreme Master of the human race. Such fundamental errors cannot but vitiate a system built upon them. And those who are not blind can detect the evil effects already manifest where attempts have been made to apply the principles of Karl Marx.

1136. In his book, "The Risen Sun," Martindale says, "I am convinced that the only well-thought-out theory besides the Catholic interpretation of life is the Communist Bolshevik one."

Father Martindale expresses that opinion. He absolutely denies the truth and value of the Communist theory, of course. It is based on wrong premises, and ends in disastrous results. But, granting that its views of life in terms of the material, mechanical, and complete irreligion, are false, it is true that the wrong theories of Communism have been more carefully elaborated than any other non-Catholic philosophies, and more fervently reduced to practice. Others scarcely know what they want, and still less how to get it. Communists know what they want, and are not in the least undecided as to the means they should adopt. But they want the wrong thing, and in any case will never realize their own ideals, erroneous as they are.

1137. What exactly does Martindale mean by the Catholic interpretation of life.

The Catholic interpretation of life insists on full recognition of all the elements making up the human personality, material, intellectual, and spiritual; it declares that the end or destiny to be attained by man is not temporal and confined to this world only, but eternal and linked with the very happiness of God in heaven; and it demands that man should take the means both for his temporal welfare in this world, and for the attaining of his eternal destiny in heaven.

But, as the eternal is more important than the temporal, heaven above earth, and the intelligent soul nobler than the material body, so all earthly concerns must be subordinated to eternal and spiritual principles, and regulated in the light of those principles. Christ Himself put the great question which is fundamental in the Catholic interpretation of life, "What doth it profit a man if he gain the whole world, and suffer the loss of his own soul?" Matt. XVI., 26. And St. Ignatius Loyola gave the practical application when he said, "Man is created to praise, reverence, and serve God, and by this means to save his soul. All else on the face of the earth is to help man attain this end. Therefore man should use things insofar as they help him to this end, and avoid them insofar as they are a hindrance."

Whilst men, then, must bestow reasonable attention upon the problems of this world, they must not exclude attention to the more important religious, spiritual and eternal principles. If they do, they will not attain even the purely earthly happiness they seek.

1138. Do the Encyclicals provide a really practical social program of reform?

They contain the principles of a new social order, but when it comes to a question of hours of labor, rates of wages, economic planning and similar matters, there are all kinds of practical applications which remain to be made. But the work of adaptation won't go on until people become familiar with the principles laid down by the Pope in order to apply them for the regulation of both rights and duties in domestic, national and international life. In a recent discourse M. Van Zeeland, the Prime Minister of Belgium, said, "I do not know any doctrine which by its coherence, definiteness, and adaptability gets to such close grips with reality as that of the Encyclical "Quadragesimo Anno." After a careful and detached study of the leading economic and social doctrines elaborated in the last century, I have reached the conclusion that none of them keeps abreast of the facts, or is sufficiently broad to satisfy aspirations which, one after another, the nations experience today. I do not pretend that in the Encyclical you will find a literal solution of all our economic and social difficulties. Far from it. What I am convinced of, however, is that the general indications it contains give us the most reliable guide and the most coherent body of doctrine at present existing in the world." Those words of the Belgian Prime Minister are well worth our attention.

1139. Why does not the Church accept Socialism?

She cannot accept a system which is based upon merely materialistic views of humanity, as if man were composed of body only, and did not possess an immortal soul, nor have any prospects of a future life. Also Socialism in practice, instead of making your lot any better, would reduce thousands of others to the same distressing state. The Church advocates strongly both social justice and social charity, two things conspicuously absent from the world today. Her principles would mean many reforms in the socialistic direction. But she cannot sanction the program or system of Socialism in its entirety. That would be completely destructive of Christian civilization.

1140. Has not Karl Marx done more for the uplift of the working classes than Jesus by all His teachings?

Most decidedly not. Few men have done more to give the working class a purely material outlook than Karl Marx. And to give any man a purely material outlook is not to uplift him, but to degrade him. Man consists of a spiritual soul and a material body. The spiritual soul can lift the material body to heaven; the material body can drag the spiritual soul to hell. In the teaching of Jesus the soul is all-important and must lift man to God. In the teaching of Karl Marx the material body is most important and must be attended to—even if the soul be dragged down to hell.

Where is the uplift in substituting materialistic mud for man's true spiritual nobility? Karl Marx would have man to be a crawler in the dust—perhaps a fat well-nourished and comfortable crawler—but nevertheless—a crawler in the dust.

1141. Why is the Roman Catholic Church so vehemently opposed to Communism?

Because that Church is exceedingly anxious to vindicate the rights of God, and to secure the salvation and sanctification of men.

1142. On what grounds do you condemn Communism?

I could reply in a few words by saying, "On the ground of insanity." But you will want the insanity proved. Does Communism violate reason to such an extent that it can be called madness? I maintain that it does. It is bad for the individual, for the family, and for society itself. The individual right of ownership is destroyed. Communism restricts or even abolishes the right to private property sanctioned by the natural law and positive legislation of God. No true incentive to self-development and progress is left. Liberty, so prized by every reasonable human being, is abolished. Men are but cogs in a machine, and the so-called will of the people ends in the will of a tyrannical group of leaders. In addition, the family is broken, and children are deprived of true parental care and education. Russia, in great part, is a huge foundling home; if it can be called a home at all. The State itself cannot provide for its own citizens. It cannot regulate supplies in accordance with demands, and people starve in outlying quarters if only because overlooked by authorities. Few people realize the immense flood of misery and suffering Communism has meant in Russia. But, in addition to the dictates of reason prompted by the thought of the individual, the family, and the State itself, Communism is the declared enemy of religion. And religion is absolutely essential to the welfare of man, quite independently of the fact that God has the foremost right to man's acknowledgment and service. Also because Communism seeks to place all man's happiness in material things only, it is a denial of the true spiritual nobility of man. A Catholic who supports Communism is supporting a force which aims at the destruction of religion and above all of the Catholic Church. Your question is really like asking, "Why cannot a child assist the murderer of its mother?"

1143. Would one be right in suggesting that the Roman Catholic Church is the richest in the world in worldly wealth, and is opposed to Communism because the confiscation of its wealth would reduce its power?

One would not be right in suggesting that. The Catholic Church does not want any power for the mere sake of having it. If she desires any influence in this world it is only insofar as that influence will enable her to do good on behalf of the souls of men.

Naturally she would dread any confiscation of the means at her disposal which would diminish or cripple her work. The confiscation of her Churches, hospitals, orphanages, and other charitable institutions, together with her schools, would undoubtedly interfere with her worship of God and service of mankind. And it would be unjust, of course. For if Catholics have chosen to make sacrifices on behalf of their religion, it is pretty cool for others who have not made similar sacrifices to step in and say, "Let us confiscate all your savings on behalf of your religion for our own use and benefit."

Yet these effects of Communism are not the real worry of the Church. The Church condemns Communism because it is based on principles concerning man's personal, religious, social and political destiny which are directly opposed to the teachings of Christ. These false principles are of the very essence of Communism. Of its very nature it must fight against God, against religion, and against every moral code outside its materialistic horizon.

1144. Why sound the note of alarm concerning Communism?

I utter a warning, giving reasons to show that it is not ill-founded.

1145. If your Church is, as alleged, founded by the Son of God who promised to be with it all days, why should you fear the Communists?

I do not fear that they will succeed in nullifying the promise of Christ to be with the Catholic Church all days till the end of the world. But I do fear that they will destroy both the temporal and eternal happiness of far more of my fellow human beings than I can bear to think.

1146. Why should you fear the effects of an anti-God Campaign?

Because I cannot be indifferent to the insulting of God by the very creatures who owe their existence to Him; nor can I be indifferent to the misery of fellow human beings who, by their deliberate rejection of God, deserve rejection by Him for all eternity.

1147. Surely God can look after His own—if they be His own.

Here you wish to imply that, if there be a God, an anti-God campaign should have no effects. But you omit consideration of the fact that men have their own responsibilities. God may command them to serve Him, but He will not compel them to do so. He won't take back the gift of freewill. And since each man is confronted with a choice, it is quite possible for the urging of motives in favor of an evil choice to have an evil effect. And Christians have a duty to expose the evil character of motives which are wrapped up in a sugar-coating of apparent good to deceive the undiscerning. God certainly can look after His own if they allow Him to do so. But even those who are now His own will not necessarily do their part in looking after themselves.

1148. *You said that, if Communism triumphed, religion would be persecuted and driven underground.*

That is true.

1149. *I have always understood that Jesus promised suffering and persecution to His followers. Is there not a want of faith in your complaints?*

I did not complain of any prospective persecution. I did complain of the apathy of professing Christians by which they tolerate the causes of Communism and even foster its growth. And if I predict an intensified attack on religion, I do so as an appeal to zeal for the welfare of the religion of Christ in human hearts, rather than from any desire to escape altogether the sufferings and persecution promised by Jesus. Not want of faith, but a spirit of faith prompts zeal for the extension of the Kingdom of Christ in human souls.

1150. *You have frequently complained that the press, whether in books or newspapers, has given a distorted account of Catholicism and its activities.*

I have. Both religious and political bias have been evident over and over again in published reports concerning the Catholic Church.

1151. *Is it not conceivable, then, that the Capitalist Press will also twist things in their favor against Socialism and Communism—their deadliest enemies?*

It is not only conceivable, but it is morally certain that the Capitalist Press as well as the Communist Press will be guided, not by a love of truth, but by expediency in its presentation of matter for its readers. That is why, to form a just estimate of what we read, we must watch the trend of world events, and discern the motives of various parties and systems in the world. Then, in the light of those motives, we can estimate the worth of the information put before us by the various journals devoted to the interests of any given party. You see I not only maintain that the "Capitalistic Press" misrepresents issues on Catholicism, it will misrepresent almost anything should the expediency of the moment require it. And so will any newspapers published by any parties or systems in which the prudence of this world only is accepted as a standard. The materialistic outlook, whether of Capitalism or Communism, has little in common with any ideas of moral obligation.

1152. *There has been much propaganda put out by the Capitalist Press to indicate that Communism in Russia is anti-Christ.*

I don't think the Capitalist Press knows very much on the subject of anti-Christ. Nor is it very interested in that subject. When political expediency seemed to require it, the Press sought to enkindle antipathy to Russian Communism by dwelling on its anti-religious character, hoping to appeal to such religious susceptibilities as its readers might possess. But you can be sure that the Press had no more love for religion than it manifested for Russian Communism.

1153. *Is not Communism in Russia rather anti—"The Orthodox Russian Church"; a "spur" I believe from the Catholic Church.*

The Orthodox Russian Church is no more a "spur" from the Catholic Church than any Protestant Church. It is both heretical and schismatical, and entirely independent of the Catholic Church. Meantime Communism in Russia, and everywhere so long as it remains Communism, is not only anti—"The Orthodox Russian Church," but anti-God, and anti all religion. It has to be, of its very nature, which is essentially materialistic. Lenin's dictum still stands for all Communists, namely, "All religious ideas are an unspeakable abomination."

1154. *It is well-known history that the Russian Orthodox Church was on the side of the ruling powers in keeping down the working classes prior to the 1917 revolution.*

That is true. For the Russian Orthodox Church was essentially a National Church subject to the control of the ruling powers. And the ruling powers used it practically as a State Department for the securing of their own ends.

1155. *Is it not natural for the now liberated working people to feel strongly against so-called Christian activities?*

We can speak of the Russian workers as liberated from the old regime. But they are certainly not liberated under the present regime.

Letting that go, however, it was natural that, in reacting against the old political regime, they should react against the Church identified with that regime. And as practically the only professing form of Christianity they knew was that of the Russian Orthodox Church, it is not surprising that they termed themselves anti-Christian. I say that that was natural. But I do not admit that it was justified. For the heretical and schismatical Russian Church was not truly representative of Christianity.

1156. *In denying that a good Christian could be a Communist, you may point to the trials and shootings in Russia.*

In giving my reasons for my assertion I did not mention those.

1157. *I cannot accept that as an answer, for in our so-called Christian countries the ruthless Capitalist States murder thousands of people physically and mentally in poverty and suffering.*

Firstly, if I say that Communist Russia is not Christian, you do not disprove my statement by saying that Capitalist countries are not Christian.

Secondly, you yourself eliminate any reference to Christianity by terming those Capitalist States "so-called Christian countries." If they are not truly, but only "so-called Christian countries," your argument is not against Christianity, but against those unchristian Capitalist States.

Thirdly, whilst you apparently don't agree with my estimate of Communism, I do agree with your estimate of Capitalism. You see, its a three-cornered fight—Catholicism, Capitalism, and Communism. Catholicism is opposed to the materialistic outlook and the injustice of both Capitalism and Communism. But you fail to see that. You see only the opposition of the Catholic Church to Communism, and at once proceed to identify her with Capitalism. In that you are much mistaken.

1158. *In his Encyclical letter Quadragesimo Anno of May 15th, 1931, Pope Pius XI., said, "No one can be at the same time a sincere Catholic and a true Socialist." Does the Pope's infallibility apply to this particular statement?*

Yes. It is not a definition, but it is an infallible judgment on a matter connected with Christian morality in which the Pope speaks as Supreme Head of the Church with the intention of deciding the matter definitely for the benefit of the whole Catholic world.

Thus he says clearly—"This question is holding many minds in suspense. Catholics are raising their eyes towards the Holy See earnestly beseeching Us to decide.

In our paternal solicitude we desire to satisfy these petitions and we pronounce as follows: 'Whilst Socialism really remains Socialism, it cannot be brought into harmony with the dogmas of the Catholic Church—the reason being that it conceives human society in a way utterly alien to Christian truth.'"

A few lines later the Pope says, "All that we have thus far laid down and established by our Sovereign Authority."

The utterance therefore is certainly to be classed as an infallible judgment. The Pope explains the sense of his condemnation by saying that even moderate Socialism which refuses to make use of physical force and which condemns class-warfare and the abolition of private property, is yet incompatible with Catholic doctrine. Why? Because it acts on the principle that material welfare is the purpose of man's existence or at least the purpose of social organization, whilst the Catholic Church declares that men both individually and socially must primarily consider the praise and glory of the Creator by the fulfilling of individual and social duties for the love of God and in accordance with His laws. And this in order to attain not only temporal but eternal happiness. If a policy of social reform includes all these principles of the Catholic religion it is no longer real Socialism in the accepted sense of that word. Therefore no man can be truly Catholic and truly Socialist at the same time.

1159. *Granted that this decision be infallible, is it a sin for a good Catholic to be a true Socialist?*

If he supports real Socialism he is no longer a good Catholic. Any Catholic who supports a truly Socialistic program adopts conduct which is sinful, and he is guilty of sin once he realizes the decision of the Catholic Church. Thus the Pope says "With grief we perceive certain Catholics joining the ranks of Socialism—deserting the Church. We have wondered why they are going so far astray—for any real injustice they denounce *We* denounce. They are unhappily deceived and wandering far from the paths of truth and salvation." It is therefore sinful—gravely so, for a Catholic to support Socialism.

1160. *After a lifetime of study of the Capitalist System, I am firmly convinced, although a Catholic, that Socialism is the only right system.*

By saying that you but afford a further proof of the necessity of being guided by the Catholic Church where principles of morality are concerned. A study of the evils and abuses in Capitalism cannot possibly prove that Socialism is the only system.

1161. *Pope Innocent III. taught that whatever a person does against his conscience leads to hell.*

He certainly did not teach that. Venial sins are contrary to conscience, but they do not take people to hell. The Church certainly does teach, however, that a man is obliged to follow a right and normal conscience.

1162. *If my conscience tells me to be a Socialist, and Pope Innocent III. tells me I must follow my conscience, how explain the contradiction when Pope Pius XI. declares that no Catholic can be a Socialist?*

There is no contradiction. Pope Innocent does not say that you must follow your conscience as you have formed it at present. A man can have an erroneous conscience, either because he has deliberately warped it by self-deception, or because he is inadequately informed. There are external tests by which a man can tell whether his conscience is right or wrong. Conscience is certainly wrong if it bids conduct opposed to God's known law, or opposed to the obedience due to the authority of Christ in His Church. A right conscience in a Catholic dictates obedience to the teachings of the Church, and you would follow your real conscience if you renounced opinions opposed to her definite teachings and allowed yourself to be guided by her in this matter. Pope Pius XI. said that no Catholic can be a Socialist. Pope Innocent III. says that you must obey your conscience. If you do, you will not be a Socialist, but adhere to the teaching of the Pope.

1163. Do Roman Catholics place the Pope before the King?

What would you say were I to ask you, "Does a Protestant boy place his father before the King?" If you reasoned rightly you would say, "In some things he does; in other things he does not." You see, two different factors come into the case, and it is illogical to jump from one to the other in the same breath. The boy would owe filial piety to his father, and civic loyalty to his King. So, too, Catholics owe spiritual allegiance to the Pope, and civic loyalty to the King. In spiritual matters, they place the Pope before the King. In the civic order, they place the King before the Pope.

1164. Do Roman Catholics believe that the Pope is greater than the King?

I have just said that in spiritual matters the authority of the Pope comes before that of the King. In temporal and national matters, the authority of the King is supreme. If you ask me whether the spiritual and religious sphere is of greater dignity and importance than the temporal and national sphere, I must reply that it is. And as the Pope is the supreme ruler in the higher sphere, his office is greater than that of the King.

1165. Is local and national patriotism possible to a Catholic who accepts such views of the Pope?

It is not only possible. The Pope himself tells Catholics that it is their bounden duty.

1166. Do not the ruling classes find the Catholic doctrine that the faithful must submit to civil authority a very convenient one?

Not always, by any means. We have to obey rulers for the love of God—and that can be done only in lawful matters. If rulers exceed their authority and demand obedience to unlawful commands—then the love of God forbids us to obey. The law of obedience in a spirit of loyalty to God imposes definite restrictions upon them. Thus Catholics can never admit that the State has any right to allow divorced people to re-marry if the previous and lawful partners are still living. And the fact that the State *does* allow it, in no way frees the conscience of a Christian from guilt.

1167. If the Catholic Church teaches patriotism, why does she forbid Catholics to be loyal to the "Totalitarian States"?

She does not. She bids them to be loyal to their countries insofar as the law of God permits. But they cannot accept those doctrines specifically which are opposed to God's law, religious freedom, and rightful individual liberties.

1168. Does the Catholic Church recognize the countries Italy, Russia, and Germany, to be "Totalitarian States"?

She does, and she repudiates their totalitarian principles. All three countries demand State Absolutism, Russia on a communistic basis, Italy and Germany on the basis of a fascist dictatorship. Italy, however, professes to exclude State authority in religious matters, though its tendency is ever to trespass on the religious field and conflict with the rights of the Church. Hitler, in Germany, would like to suppress the rights of the Church altogether, and repeatedly violates the guarantees he gave in his Concordat with the Vatican.

1169. Is the Catholic Church opposed to the "Totalitarian State" merely because that system seeks to subjugate the individual to the State, to the detriment of the individual?

Not merely because of that, although that is one good and sound reason for the opposition of the Catholic Church to "State Absolutism." The "Totalitarian State" is also an invasion of domestic rights, and most dangerous to the freedom and independence of religion. Moreover, it is essentially wrong in itself. It supposes unlimited power vested in a dictator, or a ruling group, not constrained by law, and basing its power on force and violence. This means in practice the servile State, with a tyranny established which was unknown even in ancient Sparta. The Catholic Church insists that justice will never be done unless government is truly representative in which the people's affairs are managed by men chosen by the people, and answerable to the people for their policy. On February 11th, 1929, the Lateran Concordat between Italy and the Vatican was signed. On May 13th, 1929, Mussolini declared that the education of youth belonged to the State; and that, whilst they would be taught the Catholic religion, they must be moulded according to Fascist ideals with a sense of virility and power of conquest. Next day, May 14th, the Pope denounced Mussolini's doctrine of State absolutism, his principle that children belonged to the State, and denied the right to instill aggressive nationalism and ideas of conquest. And he reminded Mussolini that the powers of the State are conferred upon it by those it governs. "Hence," he said, "the State must use its powers on behalf of those who conferred them." These words of the Pope show the wide gap between the democratic social principles of the Catholic Church, and the anti-democratic ideas of Fascism.

1170. In the light of these questions I am interested in the status of Catholics in Germany under the present National Socialist Regime.

It is a very unhappy one.

1171. Friends returned from Germany say that practically the whole nation, including the Catholic section, is wholeheartedly behind Hitler's regime.

That is the only impression which the ruling tyranny allows to be published in German papers. But it is not true.

1172. It is intelligible that all would support an unselfish effort to rebuild the nation after the hopeless post-war years.

That is true. But Catholics cannot wholeheartedly support the methods adopted. The "Totalitarian State," whether on Communistic or Fascist lines, is opposed to Catholic principles.

1173. I admit that the Church has had setbacks at the hands of the Nazi party, but not severe ones, and only in certain provinces.

The attacks on the Church, and on Catholics generally, have been most severe, and throughout Germany.

1174. I fail to see, therefore, how the present system of government in Germany can be detrimental to a Catholic either as a member of the Church or as a son of the Fatherland.

The essential tendency of the present regime in Germany, if it can accomplish it, is to rob a Catholic of his Faith, and to turn him from a son of the Fatherland into a slave of a Fascist dictatorship.

1175. Are the Catholics of Germany bound to refuse to support this order of government which alone offers hope to them?

I deny that the present form of government in Germany alone offers hope even from the national point of view. From the viewpoint of their religion, it offers Catholics but death and destruction. Yet it means persecution, misery, and death, if they do not submit in general to the prevailing tyranny. And I can but say of Catholics in Germany what the Pope himself said of Catholics in Italy as regards the Fascist regime. Here are his words: "We must say that one is not a Catholic—except in Baptism and by name as opposed to his obligations—who adopts and develops a program so opposed to the rights of the Church of Jesus Christ, and of souls." But he adds that he realizes how, for countless persons, daily bread and life itself, are at stake. So he says that, if they are compelled externally to support the "Totalitarian State," they must in their own consciences make the reservation "insofar as the laws of God and the Church permit," or "in accordance with the duties of a good Christian." And they must be prepared, if need be, to declare their reservation externally should they be asked to choose between the State and their religion. That judgment concerning the position of Catholics in Fascist Italy could apply to Catholics in Fascist Germany. The only difference is that Catholics in Germany are much the more likely to meet with the necessity of rejecting State demands in the name of God, and of suffering the consequences of their fidelity to conscience.

1176. Is it not well known that the Church of Rome accepts Fascism, which is akin to Communism?

Fascism is not essentially akin to Communism, although it can be perverted in the Communistic direction, as in Germany. The Catholic Church prescribes no political policy, and sanctions any form of government within the bounds of social justice. She does not accept Fascism any more than she accepts the present British constitution. She tolerates both, and would be quite prepared to condemn any abuses which might arise in these different forms of government.

1177. Yet Fascism is as great a curse as Communism, aiming to destroy the worker where the latter wants to destroy Capitalists.

Fascism does not aim at the destruction of the worker. Mussolini's Fascism sanctions and supports religion, and aims at the well-being of every individual in the State; and for that purpose demands that every individual must contribute towards the service, discipline, and progressive construction of the national well-being. Remonstrance by the Church against a few initial abuses, secured their rectification. Hitler's imitation of Fascism in Germany is no true indication of what real Fascism is. He has not understood at all the aims and principles of Fascism. Meantime, whilst Communism's objective has been to dethrone both religion and capitalism, it has succeeded in destroying the worker, and has merely imposed a new and worse tyranny. Nor only that. The Soviet is rapidly turning back towards capitalism, and is working on Capitalistic principles in its own name.

1178. Is war justifiable under any circumstances according to the will of Christ?

If all men did the will of Christ there would be no war. But if some people refuse to do the will of Christ, those who desire to fulfill His will may be compelled to fight and may quite lawfully do so.

1179. Did not Christ counsel meekness, and say that if we are smitten on one cheek, we should turn the other?

An individual is free to practice heroic meekness where his own rights are concerned, if he so desires. But, when smitten on one cheek, it must be his own cheek he turns to endure further injuries, not somebody else's. If you saw some bully flogging an innocent child, it would not be virtue on your part to allow the bully to go on doing so. Whatever you might be prepared to suffer on your own part, it would be your duty to prevent the continued suffering of the child, even though you had to attack and damage the bully.

1180. Would not that counsel of Christ extend to states as well as to individuals?

No. The father of a family may have the patience of Job in his own trials, but he has the duty to defend his wife and children from harm at the hands of others. If he neglects to do so he cannot claim that he is imitating the meekness of Christ. Christ nowhere teaches that we must allow others to suffer unjustly. Now civil society is simply domestic society on a larger scale. And the responsible leaders or guardians of the State are obliged to see that the lives and property and welfare of the citizens are preserved from danger. If, owing to the malice of others, there is no means of doing this save by taking up arms, opposing violence to violence, war is lawful.

1181. The fact is that your Church, and all its stepchildren, officially proclaim that warfare is not incompatible with the mind of Christ.

Firstly, I object to your description of non-Catholic Churches as stepchildren of the Catholic Church. A stepchild is born of one party to a subsequent legitimate marriage. Now the original union between Christ and the Catholic Church has never been broken; and neither the Catholic Church nor Christ ever gave birth to any non-Catholic Churches. Therefore those Chuches cannot be described as stepchildren of the Catholic Church. Secondly, you are in error when you say that the Church officially proclaims that warfare is not incompatible with the mind of Christ. You ought to be aware that the Pope has officially proclaimed again and again that peace is the only thing compatible with the mind of Christ, and that he has declared his one ambition to be the securing of the peace of Christ in the Kingdom of Christ prevailing in all human hearts. And he has declared that it is his prayer that God may scatter those nations that delight in war.

1182. How is it that members of your Church—an international or Catholic Church—can be justified by the leaders of that Church, and even urged on, in various opposing countries, in fighting and killing one another?

I could reply simply by denying the fact. Your very question begs the question. However I will give you this much explanation. By being members of the international Catholic Church, people do not cease to belong to their own countries and retain duties in the sphere of national loyalty. And the leaders of the Catholic Church in any given country are as justified in urging their spiritual subjects to fulfill what they believe to be duty to the country as they are justified in urging men to be honest in business, or in urging children to fulfill their duties to their parents. It used to be the charge that Catholics, because of their international religion, could not be loyal to their respective countries. You quarrel with them for exhibiting loyalty. In no case do Catholic leaders, however, urge men on "to fight and kill one another." They may urge men to vindicate their country's cause, to defend it against defeat, to secure its rights. The purpose is, not to kill others, but to safeguard one's own national welfare. If this is impossible without war, and the death of enemies, then that may have to be unfortunately tolerated. But to concentrate on that unhappy consequence and speak as if it were the primary intention is a fallacy. You might just as well blame Surgical Schools for training men "to butcher people with knives." They have a higher purpose than that—the welfare of their patients.

And the primary purpose of an army is the welfare of the country whose cause it must defend, and to join which can easily be a duty in times of national danger.

1183. Who is the authority which decides about the justice of wars?

Catholic theology sets out all the principles according to which a war is just or unjust. If, however, two nations engage in war, we pass from the juridical order to the factual order. The decision now will concern the application of the principles to an actual case. Who is the authority which decides which party has acted in accordance with just principles, and which party has violated them? Unfortunately, the nations today acknowledge no competent international authority. The Pope could, and would be willing to give a sound judgment, did the conflicting parties submit their cases to him, with full documentary evidence of the matters in dispute. But they will not submit to his arbitration, and, therefore, must be content with such tribunals as they do acknowledge. They have established the "League of Nations," and the "Hague Court"; but these are not satisfactory because the nation which receives an unfavorable verdict will not accept it. However, since these are the only authorities the nations will acknowledge, they must restrict complaints of failure to themselves and their accepted tribunals. Certainly it is not reasonable to blame the Catholic Church, whose judgment is not even sought.

1184. What view does the Church take of a soldier killing another so-called enemy soldier?

The Catholic Church takes the view that if the soldier knew quite well that the cause of his own country was unjust, he would be guilty of murder, unless he were acting solely in individual self-defense against some individual soldier of the enemy forces. If, however, he did not have certain knowledge that his own country's cause was unjust, he would be free from personal guilt in obeying his officers and fighting for victory, even though it meant his killing enemy soldiers.

1185. Was Christ incapable of taking life in the same sense?

Had He been an ordinary human being, and not the Son of God come into this world for the salvation of souls, and had He been a soldier in the employ of His country, He would not have been incapable of fulfilling the duties of a soldier, even if it meant killing enemy soldiers in actual warfare. But you must notice the two suppositions. In reality Christ, who was the Son of God, and the Eternal King with a Kingdom not of this world, cannot be made the standard of such a comparison with an ordinary soldier, who is obviously the subject of a Kingdom which is of this world, and to which he has duties in the natural order, besides his duties to Christ in the spiritual order. You will notice in the Gospels that Christ met several military men, yet never once did He condemn their occupation; nor did He ever condemn war. He abstracted from the temporal concerns of this world, and preached the Kingdom of God, bidding men to attend to the spiritual welfare of their souls, and to make sure of securing their eternal welfare, whatever might be their success or disasters in this life. So, for example, in a somewhat similar way, He refused to interfere in the litigation of two brothers over a legacy from their parents. One of them said to Him, "Speak to my brother, that he divide the inheritance with me." But our Lord replied, "Who hath appointed Me judge, or divider, over you?" And He simply took the occasion to say, "Beware of covetousness, for a man's life doth not consist in the abundance of things he possesseth." Lk. XII., 14. In other words, Christ refused to decide who was right and who was wrong in this dispute over interests concerned with this world. He left that to be solved by the ordinary human administration of justice. From the contentions of nations He also abstracted, and condemned neither the military profession, nor its employment, when deemed necessary by the countries concerned in actual warfare.

1186. *If so, could you imagine Jesus with a bayonet dripping with blood, which He had just withdrawn from the entrails of another individual?*

I cannot. But why? Is it because all war is necessarily wrong? No. If you had no weapon but a bayonet, and you could not stop an unjust aggressor from killing you save by running the bayonet through him, you would not be guilty of any crime before God by doing so. You are not obliged to sacrifice your innocent life for the sake of sparing his guilty life. And the same principle can be extended to nations. Nor did Jesus ever condemn war in a just cause. His condemnation of all injustice would, of course, exclude an unjust war.

But, even though it could be lawful to engage in war, why cannot I imagine Jesus engaged in such strife? For the simple reason that, whilst fighting for one's temporal well-being can be lawful, Jesus came for our eternal rather than our temporal welfare. He came to teach us detachment from earthly concerns, and to set an example of that detachment. He never condemned a moderate and necessary interest in earthly concerns, but He Himself was not interested in them, and bade us to seek first the Kingdom of God. He abstracted from the material bodily pursuits of men, and concentrated on spiritual welfare of their souls. I can no more imagine Him wielding a bayonet than I can imagine Him frequenting the Stock Exchange in order to try to amass an earthly fortune. His Kingdom might be in this world, but it was not to be of this world. And it is impossible to imagine Him absorbed by any of the affairs of this world.

1187. *Is it not the fact that Jesus was immovably a pacifist?*

It is not a fact. Though temporal, political, and national matters were outside the scope of His mission, He did not condemn them. His mission was to teach men spiritual truths for the good of their souls, and to redeem them from sin. Without any condemnation of earthly warfare, He even chose analogies from it in order to illustrate His higher teachings. And He treated war as quite a normal event, incidental to the imperfections of this worldly existence given over to the administration of men. Thus in Lk. XIV., 31, He says, "What king, about to make war upon another king, does not first think whether he be able with 10,000 to meet him that, with 20,000, cometh against him?" Accepting this as human prudence, He warns us to use similar prudence with God.

1188. *If Jesus was not a pacifist, can you picture Him with a gas mask, decked out in all the equipment of civilized warfare?*

There is no need to do so.

1189. *Would you pray to such a conception of Christ?*

Since Christ is God, I would pray to Him no matter what He might choose to do, or not to do. But as my conception of Christ does not happen to include your fanciful hypothesis, I am not called upon to pray to Him under such conditions.

1190. *Could He, under any circumstances, in such a conception, be admitted also to sonship, or even cousinship, with a merciful God?*

Since, by His Person, He is and ever was the Eternal Son of God, and by nature identical with the merciful God, all talk of His being admitted to the sonship of God is absurd. One is admitted to what he was not previously. The only sensible way to put your question would be, "Could Jesus, as the Son of God, be conceived of under such circumstances?" In reality, no. The Jews made the vast mistake of thinking that the Messiah would be a kind of temporal military king to deliver them from oppression. Jesus effectively showed that the Son of God would not come into this world for so paltry an object. Worldly campaigns and leadership were nothing to Him. He came for other and far more lofty interests.

1191. *Yet you can picture followers, or alleged followers of Jesus, with bayonets, killing their fellow Christians.*

I can picture a citizen of one country, who happens to be a follower of Jesus, fulfilling military duties in his country's cause, against the soldiers of another opposing country, even though those soldiers also happen to profess the Christian religion. A man engages in war, not precisely as a follower of Jesus, but as a citizen of his own country; and his intention is in no way to kill fellow Christians. His intention is to put the soldiers of enemy forces out of action. If he wanted to kill fellow Christians, he would have to interrogate every enemy he met regarding his religion on the score that he was looking for fellow Christians in order to exterminate them. Your introduction of the Christian religion in such a way is quite irrelevant, and a violation of reason.

1192. *Jesus of Nazareth Himself did actually have to face a situation in which force could have been used for defense.*

I am glad to notice your acceptance of the historical value of the Gospels on this matter at least.

1193. *This was, of course, at Gethsemane, when He bade Peter sheathe the sword by means of which he might have defended the "Son of God."*

That incident occurred. Christ forbade Peter to defend Him by means of the sword.

1194. *Now Peter surely loved his Master.*

He did.

1195. *If Peter was not justified in fighting on such an occasion, how can any group of people be justified in killing, even to defend human life?*

That question is inconsequent. The fact that Christ forbade Peter to use his sword in the particular circumstances mentioned affords no basis for any conclusion concerning the morality of war. For Christ did not forbid Peter to use his sword on the score that violent defense against unjust aggressors was wrong in itself. He forbade Peter to use the sword on this particular occasion for several reasons. Firstly, Christ knew that the time had come according to God's Will when He should enter upon His passion, and it was not right to seek to escape it. Secondly, and in any case, Peter and the Apostles were utterly unequal to the armed throng which had come to secure Him, and thought for them urged Christ to advise the prudent course. Thirdly, their defense of Christ was really unnecessary, for He told them that, if He really wanted to escape He could easily do so, if only by commanding "12 legions of Angels" to defend Him. It should be obvious to you that Christ was not attacking the right of armed self-defense in general.

1196. *Taking the traditional character of Jesus, as accepted by your Church, what would He say in reference to my previous questions?*

What I have said.

1197. *What would be His ruling in the matter of international war generally—regardless of alleged reasons of provocation by the warring parties?*

He would not solve the question regardless of the reasons alleged. Certainly He would say that a nation which had tried all possible means to preserve peace, yet despite that had war forced upon it by an unscrupulous enemy, would be justified in taking up arms and engaging in international war rather than go out of existence as a nation.

1198. *He could not but condemn war.*

Nowhere in the Gospels will you find a single passage in which Christ denied that war could ever be lawful; nor, though He met with many soldiers, and even wrought miracles for some of them, will you find one word of His condemning the military profession.

1199. *After all, according to the Christian conception, all are sons of God.*

All who are in the grace of Christ are sons of God by a spiritual regeneration on a spiritual plane which far transcends any earthly relationships. This does not emancipate us from earthly duties arising from our natural condition whilst in this world.

1200. *According to this, any sort of war would be a civil war.*

That does not follow. For our supernatural sonship of God through Christ is by grace in the spiritual and supernatural order. That does not interfere with each man's civil duties to his earthly country and ruler. Christ Himself taught this when He said, "Render therefore to Caesar the things that are Caesar's; and to God, the things that are God's." Matt. XXII., 21. He would not admit that our duties to God superseded all duties to our country and nation. And the lawful authority of different rulers in the temporal sphere cannot but result in different civil allegiances. Since men go to war, not because they are sons of God in Christ, but because they are citizens of different earthly countries, all wars are not civil wars.

1201. *Is it not a fact that the early Christians refused to serve in the Army?*

It is not a fact. Thousands of Roman soldiers became Christians and remained Roman soldiers.

1202. *No nation ever wins any of these "just" wars. They all get deeper into debt to the International Moneymongers, who are the "real" enemies of all nations.*

Every word of that could be true, and not one word I have said on this subject would be affected. Take this case: If one nation attacked another suddenly, and without any provocation, merely through national pride, commercial greed, and blood lust, would the victim be justified in engaging in a war of self-defense or not? And if she were, would the justice of her cause be affected by victory or defeat? Or by the debts incurred? You know it would not. You may say that the war as a whole would be unjust. I grant that. You may say that, in such a case, the aggressor would be guilty of a very wicked thing in the absence of any provocation. I grant that. But how far does that get you? I merely maintain that it is not always unlawful to engage in war, and that a soldier is justified in taking up arms to defend his country. If he kills the invader, it is the invader's fault, and the defender is not guilty of murder. Will you say that he violates the commandment "Thou shalt not kill," and that he should rather allow himself to be shot, and the women and children of his native land to be gassed and poisoned? It is no use saying, "There could not have been any right to commence such a war." I agree. And I agree that if the aggressor did not commence it there would be no war. But my supposition is that he does villainously launch his attack. Is it lawful for the victim to take up the gauntlet or not? Is the defending soldier who takes up arms justified, or is he a murderer? If he is justified, then it is no use saying that it is never lawful to engage in war, and that all killing, without any qualification, is forbidden by the commandment, "Thou shalt not kill." If you wish, let us even suppose that the International Moneymonger, whom you call the enemy of all nations, is merely using the aggressor as a cat's-paw—that the big financiers have poured money into the country, and inspired the offensive, would the invaded country then be obliged to say, "War is evil." "Thou shalt not kill." "Our duty is to be slaughtered." I leave it to your own common sense.

1203. If war is, under certain circumstances, a justifiable business, why does not the Church allow priests to fight as ordinary soldiers?

War is not a justifiable business. Whenever it occurs, it supposes injustice on somebody's part, and even as that injustice is evil, so war is evil. Don't imagine that, because I protest against your violations of logic and reason, I do not protest against violations of peace and harmony between nations. I protest against war, and vehemently. But if warfare is unjustly forced upon a peaceful people, then that people is justified in defending itself by force of arms if necessary.

At the same time, whilst ordinary citizens are justified in the violent repulsion of violent aggressors, the Church forbids priests to engage in an occupation involving unavoidable bloodshed.

Even apart from war there are many occupations quite lawful in themselves, and to other people, which would be most incongruous for priests. For example, it is not sinful to be a bartender, but it would be most unbecoming for a priest to engage in such a duty. The Church forbids priests to engage in many forms of ordinary commercial and industrial activity normal to others. And above all, when war breaks out, and citizens enlist for the armed support of their country's cause, priests should abstain from active violence. By his very vocation the priest stands for unworldly ideals. Heart and soul he must labor for the eternal and spiritual rather than the temporal and material welfare of men. He is concerned with a heavenly rather than with an earthly Kingdom. He represents Christ and the claims of Christ rather than the demands of an earthly allegiance. And as, when men's worldly careers come to an end, they must turn their thoughts to another and higher realm altogether, so the priest must be one whom they have regarded as apart from worldly interests, and dissociated from their own earthly concerns. As they are ceasing to belong to the world about them, they find help in one who has already ceased to belong to this world in spirit and profession. Again, the priest represents the love of God, the peace of Christ, and the mercy of a Master who would far rather be crucified than crucify. And he should abstain from that active fighting in which ferocity and hatred are so easily enkindled as opposed to love; in which peace is destroyed by a storm of conflicting emotions; and in which man is the agent of death rather than of life. For even when a nation is justly at war, these sad consequences cannot but arise. Let the priest shed his blood, if necessary, for Christ and for souls; but let him not shed blood. The Church even goes so far as to forbid priests to engage in surgery. He must abstain from all unbecoming duties; be in the world, but not of it; fulfill his personal spiritual duties, destroying his enemy, sin, inculcating virtue, devoting himself to prayer and the worship of God; and be ready to assist any men, friends or enemies, who need his ministrations.

1204. Your Church seems to be "anti" every effort to give peace on earth and good will towards men in practice.

No one could write those words save one who has little or no knowledge of the attitude of the Catholic Church towards the problem of peace.

1205. Your Church is in a wonderful position to bring about peace, if it liked.

The Catholic Church could be in a wonderful position to do so, if only the nations would accept her advice and submit to her rulings. Don't forget that, at the beginning of the last war, the nations realized that the influence of the Catholic Church would be for peace, and that France, Russia, and England agreed with Italy to exclude any overtures for peace to be made by the Vatican, and to exclude the Vatican from any say in the terms of settlement after the war. If the nations won't have peace, they won't. But you cannot blame the Catholic Church to which they refused to listen.

1206. *By preaching submission to lawful authority I take it that you mean we must submit to whatever conditions the pig-headed and obstinate few choose to impose upon us.*

You are wrong. Civil rulers exceed the limits of their lawful authority when they violate the known law of God by their legislation. And in such cases, obedience is no longer due to them.

Where war is concerned, the Catholic Church says that no government has any right to declare war without just cause; and if a nation does so, those citizens who are aware of the injustice are guilty before God if they volunteer their services.

1207. *National authorities make wars and make the common herd do the fighting, and you say that we must submit.*

You must not make me say what I do not say. I have just said that if a country is not justified in engaging in war, then citizens are not justified in volunteering their services if they are clearly aware that the cause is not just. If it be just to take up arms, then citizens have a duty to obey lawful authority and assist in the war. For example, if some other nation, without any just cause at all, were to invade our country, the government here would have the right to organize armed resistance. And the duty of defense would fall on all citizens according to their capacity, and in their proper spheres of action. The trouble with you is that you have only half formulated the problem to yourself, and come to conclusions based on inadequate views.

1208. *Every obstacle is placed in the way of any anti-war movement, whilst authorities give the greatest freedom to warmongers. And you say we must submit.*

Obstacles are not placed in the way of "any" anti-war movement. Reasonable efforts to prevent war deserve all support. I have said over and over again that war must be absolutely the last resort, and then only when very grave injustice is involved. Unfortunately, many anti-war speakers manifest such ignorance and fanaticism that no reasonable man could support them. They spoil their own case. Often, too, the anti-war demonstrations are blended with Communistic propaganda which vitiates them by their very association with such destructive principles.

You say that, meantime, the authorities give the greatest freedom to warmongers, and that I hold that we must submit. Now, firstly, if the authorities are guilty in allowing munition factories without restriction, then State authorities are to blame for that; and I have not undertaken to defend the legislation of human governments. Nor do I say that we must submit to this particular phase of their policy. Citizens who disapprove such a policy are quite free to vote against such a government and if possible to vote it out of office.

1209. *The Church proclaims to the world that we must fight in a just war, such as a war of self-defense.*

She does not. If another nation unjustly decides to annex our country, we are free to allow ourselves to be annexed without firing a shot, if we are content to pass under an alien rule. We are not obliged, as a nation, to defend ourselves. But the Church says that it is certainly lawful for an attacked nation to defend itself; and that, if it be the national will to do so, then citizens have the national duty of patriotism to do all in their power to secure the welfare of their country.

1210. *But the Church says in a still, small voice that we are not bound to fight in a war prompted by the lust of conquest, or merely for territorial expansion.*

The still, small voice was apparently loud enough to reach you, despite the fact that you were not sufficiently interested and attentive to perceive the significance of its utterances. The Church says that no nation is justified in declaring an offensive war prompted by lust of conquest and expansion. If the authorities do declare war, however, then individual citizens are free to volunteer or not according to their individual knowledge of the justice or injustice of the cause.

1211. *Or does the Church now, as it always has done, maintain a cowardly silence, and so assist the warmongers in leading the people to the slaughter?*

Such a question is born of ignorance and folly. The Church must declare the moral law, and she does so without fear or thought of popular reactions to the law; and that, whether nations, or individuals are concerned. Where other Churches give way on such questions as birth control and divorce, the Catholic Church promulgates the demands of morality whether her decisions are popular or not. So, too, she lays down the principles governing the question of war. But when you come to the order of facts and of actual national disputes, you leave the question of moral principles, and come to the question of their application in a concrete case. Now here the attitude of the Church to nations is much the same as that of a priest to individuals. As a priest I may preach that injustice is wrong. But if a Catholic enters into litigation with a non-Catholic, and neither asks me to judge in actual fact as to who is guilty of injustice, it is not my business to decide the question of fact. I am not obliged to say to all-comers that the Catholic is right, and the non-Catholic guilty of injustice. Nor am I obliged to say that the non-Catholic is right, and the Catholic guilty of injustice. At most I can say, "If one is right, the other is wrong." But I have not the duty to judge which is right, and which wrong. If they come to me, and submit the facts to my decision, then it will be time to pass judgment. But to scatter denunciations of this one or that without having even been asked to decide the case would be absurd. Now transfer this to the Catholic Church, Italy, and Abyssinia. Call Italy the Catholic Nation, and Abyssinia the non-Catholic Nation. The Catholic Church said that the nation which unjustly commences a war is guilty of injustice. That is the principle. Italy accused Abyssinia of injustice sufficient to warrant war; Abyssinia accused Italy of similar injustice. Here was a question, not of principles, but of fact. Neither nation offered to submit the case for adjudication to the Catholic Church, and the Catholic Church was not called upon to decide it, and apportion the blame. You must seek a judgment in each actual case from that court to which the case has been submitted, and which has been provided with the evidence by the parties concerned.

1212. *If you can justify the attitude of the Church towards wars between men, you will do a lot towards enabling me to take up religion.*

Religion is a virtue which impels us to offer God due acknowledgment in religious worship for what God is. Now God is God independently of your opinion as to whether war between men can ever be justified or not. Even if you condemn all war, the fact that you thought men were not behaving well towards each other would not justify your refusal to behave well towards God yourself. You owe to God the debt of religious acknowledgment. Pay that debt, and then give your attention to the problem of war, trying to understand the ethics of the question.

1213. *I presume you believe the Pope to be the one authority who could give a sound judgment on international moral issues.*

Correct. And he would do so, were he consulted and did he have the facts submitted to him by the contending parties.

1214. *Then why do not Catholic nations consult him?*

Where is the nation today which would answer to the description of a Catholic nation? There are nations the bulk of whose members profess the Catholic Faith.

But that does not mean that the State as such professes the Catholic religion as an integral part of national administration. Even in the countries where Catholicism is not only granted liberty but also State protection and privileges, government policy abstracts from religion in its own deliberations concerning internal and foreign affairs. But were there a State today not infected by indifferentism towards religion, its failure to practice the principles it accepted would be accounted for just as one would account for the moral lapse of any individual—through weakness, or through malice on the part of those in charge of the nation's destinies.

1215. *If unity under the authority of the Pope is a fact why did Catholics fight against each other in the war?*

They did not fight against each other as Catholics. There happened to be Catholics amongst the various nations at war. But as members of their respective nations, they had the duty as citizens to defend the interests of their respective countries. But the political leaders of the countries themselves were not religiously united under the authority of the Pope. Protestants had the power in Germany. France was under an irreligious and Masonic government. Those in control of England's destinies were entirely Protestant in their outlook. The Czar of Russia owed no spiritual allegiance to the Pope. The Italian government of the day simply ignored the Pope. In the face of this, the religious unity of such members of these nations as were Catholics could not prevent their being drawn into war as citizens.

1216. *Where is the authority the Pope is supposed to be exercising, if he does not exercise it over Catholic nations?*

The authority of the Pope remains, whether men submit to it or not. Millions of Catholics throughout the world, of course, both acknowledge the authority of the Pope and submit to it. When we turn from individuals to nations, there are no Catholic nations in the full sense of the word. They do not, therefore, submit their policies involving moral issues to the guidance of the Church as they should.

1217. *Why does not the Pope do something about it?*

Because men who are not sensitive to their moral obligations will be moved only by physical compulsion. And it is not part of the Pope's commission to rule by physical force. After all, though God Himself has given the ten commandments, men still break them. You might just as well ask why God does not do something about it. But even God will not compel men by physical violence to observe His law. He will, of course, "do something about it" in due course. Men already endure many penalties at least as a consequence of their lapses; and they will endure more later on when they meet God in judgment. And we can certainly say that the nations which ignore the Pope as supreme moral arbiter are not a very happy lot. Their independence of him is their punishment.

1218. *Not one word came from the Pope to say that such conduct violated the commandment, "Thou shalt not kill," or that war was opposed to the law, "Love thine enemy," and that no sincere Christian could take part in it.*

The Popes protested again and again against the European war of 1914-18 as a violation of fraternal charity. Before the war commenced, Pope Pius X. circularized the heads of the nations, imploring them to avoid such a war, and foretelling all the miseries it would bring in its train. The nations would not listen. When Benedict XV. acceded to the Holy See, his first act was to try to bring about a cessation of hostilities. And again the national leaders would not listen. Yet the Pope continued his efforts until the Armistice in 1918.

At the same time the Pope could not say that no sincere individual Christian was not justified in defending the cause of his country, nor that such a Christian would be violating the commandment, "Thou shalt not kill." For neither of such statements would be right. A sincere Christian may take up his country's cause when it is in danger. And the commandment, "Thou shalt not kill" does not forbid one's undertaking the duties of a soldier.

1219. *The presence of any priest in the army as chaplain only serves to sanctify war, and the cause they are fighting for, no matter how bad.*

It does not. The chaplain's presence serves to secure the spiritual welfare of such unfortunate men as are wounded or dying, whether the souls appealing to him for help are friends or enemies from the military point of view.

1220. *The army is a body of men sworn to fight and obey their superiors, and their actions are not controlled by their own reason or conscience.*

Soldiers are subject to the demands of military obedience, but that very obedience is their reasonable choice, and their actions are very much subject to the control of their own conscience. Many soldiers are the most conscientious of men in the fulfillment of duties allotted to them by their military superiors.

1221. *The chaplain gives sanctity to such a body of men, becomes one of them, and commits himself to all future situations that may arise during his term of chaplaincy, because he could hardly be expected to induce the men to disobey.*

The chaplain would violate his own duties if he advised the men to neglect their obligations of obedience to lawful commands. But his presence is not for the purpose of securing military discipline. The officers attend to that. Granted that the country is at war, the least the country can do is to provide chaplains for the spiritual needs of those men who lay down their lives for their country's welfare. And the fact that chaplains are provided for this purpose does not identify them with the decisions of military authorities in the conducting of the war, nor does it commit them to all situations which arise. The effort to transfer the responsibility to chaplains is as foolish as it would be to blame the Ambulance Association for all the street accidents that occur. The chaplain goes on a spiritual mission of mercy to men in grave danger just as the Ambulance Officer goes on a temporal mission of mercy to any people injured, however they may be injured. And the chaplain is no more cause of the war necessitating his services than the Ambulance Officer is cause of the accident demanding his attendance.

1222. *How can you leaders bless war instruments, ships, submarines, planes and guns, which will be used to destroy men, women and children, even fellow Catholics?*

There is not a single thing which can be of use to man in the cause of justice and right which cannot be the object of a blessing. The blessing on military weapons is for the good use to be made of them insofar as they serve in the protection of one's country or in vindicating a just cause. The sad consequence to enemy countries with resultant loss of life is not the purpose of the blessing. If a man saw his mother being throttled by a murderer he could certainly ask the blessing of God on his aim as he fired a revolver that he might save his mother's life. That such a blessing would mean the death of the murderer would be an inevitable consequence, but not the primary motive of the blessing.

You may say, "But there the bullet will hit the actual and guilty murderer. What of innocent men, women and children in an enemy country?" To that I must reply that, when two nations are at war, they are to be taken as collective units. Non-combatant members of these collective units must be spared as far as possible, but where that is impossible, harm to them is an unintended and inevitable consequence. The weapons were not blessed for the purpose of these unintended and inevitable consequences. Another point to notice is this: The weapons could not be intended for the killing of fellow Catholics, or those using them would have to ask each enemy whether he was a Catholic or not before killing him, slaughtering him if he was a Catholic, sparing him if not. It may happen that amongst the enemies killed some are Catholics. But it is not the Catholic Faith, but the national welfare of the contending parties which is at stake. All along the line you are transferring your attention to aspects of the matter which are outside the real case to be considered.

1223. Can you see any sense in preaching, "Thou shalt not kill, and blessing those who shoot each other down in war time?

Of course I can. "Thou shalt not kill" is a commandment of God forbidding all unjustified taking of another's life on one's own individual authority. And that commandment must be preached. But that does not forbid our asking God's blessing on our soldiers who fight for their country's welfare from motives of duty. They do not take life, then, on their own individual authority, but act as units of a nation engaged in self-defense. If the cause of a nation is just, its soldiers are also justified.

1224. Is there any sense in claiming it to be the will of a just God?

There can be sense in claiming that. If another nation treats us unjustly, it cannot be the will of a just God that such injustice continue. And it can be His will that we ourselves repress this injustice. What would you suggest doing, if a man entered your home and began to carve up your wife and children? Can you see any sense in claiming it to be the will of a just God that you should defend your family, and carve up the aggressor, if there were no other way to stop him?

1225. In the last war, ministers of religion told the unfortunates who were dying in most degrading circumstances that a just God was with them.

Whether on the side of the Allies, or on the side of our enemies in the last war, no individual soldier who believed his cause to be just and gave his life for his people's welfare, died a degrading death. There are ideals more precious than earthly existence. And granting their good faith, and their repentance of their sins, these dying soldiers were rightly told that a just God was with them. What would you have told them? That the just God had abandoned them, despite their fidelity to what they believed to be right?

1226. Ministers of every nation claimed that God was on the side of the misguided men who shot each other down because of a quarrel between the blustering brass hats.

If the men were misguided, and thought they were doing their duty, they were personally right with God as far as the war was concerned. If a minister were personally convinced that the cause of his nation were just, he would be justified in giving it as his opinion that God was on the side of his nation. The minister might be mistaken in his judgment, and lack sufficient information; but his good faith would save him from personal guilt. Meantime, if you say that blustering brass hats were to blame, you must confine the guilt to the blustering brass hats. And you would do a service to the world if you could tell us which of the blustering brass hats were in the right, and which in the wrong. No one has succeeded yet in apportioning the guilt in the case of the last war. War is a curse on humanity. We all know that. No one wants to advocate or defend war in itself. But that does not say that all who take part in a war for what they believe to be grave and necessary rights are guilty.

1227. If God was interested in the great Mass Murder of 1914-18, He was certainly most impartial.

God is intensely interested in all the doings of humanity. But He has given man's management and destiny into man's own keeping, whether individually or socially. There is no more reason why God should step in miraculously to prevent one nation from attacking another nation in Europe, than that He should step in miraculously to prevent a gangster in Chicago from murdering a single victim. Both the murderer and the man he murders will be judged justly by God; and so, too, will each individual engaged in the war. And each will be judged according to his personal knowledge and responsibility. Meantime, whilst nations suffered from their own national folly, God permitted the calamity to fall on the participating nations impartially, for individual and national sins quite apart from the war were pretty evenly distributed. Which of the nations participating had been faithful to God's laws, and was without guilt before Him? Men ignore God, and mock God by their legislation; and then blame God for the just retribution which comes upon them. Let mankind succeed—great is the progress and the ability of man! God doesn't come into it then. Let mankind make a costly mistake, then comes the cry, "God is to blame for this."

1228. Do you imagine that God has a sense of humor?

I am not so foolish as to take anthropomorphic views of God, as though attributes proper to a human mind are equally proper to Him. But, in any case, there is nothing really humorous in opposed parties simultaneously asking the help of God. The superficial man might possibly confine his attention to the opposition between the objects for which they pray. But the wise man will view the convictions and the dispositions of those who offer the prayer. There is nothing humorous in opposed parties praying for what they think to be a just cause. One, or both of the parties may be mistaken. But there is nothing humorous in that.

So, too, as either side wins a victory, there is nothing humorous in thanksgiving to God that His Providence did not permit a defeat instead.

1229. The Cardinal Archbishop of Berlin brought God on to the Altar in Germany, and got a word in for the Germans. Simultaneously, Cardinal Bourne did the same thing in London, and got in a word for the British Empire. Is not this a mockery of religion?

The Mass is but a supreme form of prayer, and your difficulty is in no way affected by bringing in the Mass where before you mentioned prayer. The same solution avails. That two Cardinals prayed for their respective countries which were at opposition one with another was not a mockery of religion. If it were, I do not think that that would distress you greatly. For you are deliberately guilty of a mockery into which you think others to have fallen unconsciously; a thought which is erroneous, of course.

1230. "Using such great swelling words," says Judge Rutherford, "in support of their claims brings reproach on the name of the very God they claim to serve."

If ever a man's teachings brought reproach on the name of God, they are the teachings of Judge Rutherford. And your own thoughtless utterances also dishonor Him, when you deny His blessing and any prospect of heaven to soldiers fighting and dying in perfectly good faith for what they believe to be right. And after denying God's interest in mankind even during the great sufferings it brought on itself, you have no further right to accuse others of bringing reproach on the God they claim to serve. If you don't believe in God, you're a hypocrite whilst you plead tearfully on God's behalf. If you do believe in God, you are guilty of offering Him a greater insult than any of which you have pretended to complain, and speak of Him without a trace of reverence or respect.

1231. *You insist that the State has the right to inflict capital punishment.*

The State possesses the right on the same principle as an individual who may kill an unjust aggressor, if there be no other efficacious way in which to preserve his own life. Those whose crimes gravely threaten the well-being of society may be put to death by social authority when lesser penalties prove inefficacious as a control upon them. God Himself sanctioned this law in Hebrew society, and it is entirely reasonable. If the extreme penalty could not be lawfully inflicted by the State upon enemies of the common good, much greater and more widespread evils would ensue.

1232. *Is not the executioner guilty of murder? He kills an individual person whom he knows by name, and intends to do so.*

He knows he is hanging an individual person, and the name of the person. But he is not guilty of murder. Firstly, he acts not as a private person, but as the agent of the State exercising lawful authority. Secondly, his intention is not one of personal revenge but of doing a lawful act for the common good. His fulfillment of duty, far from being evil, could be quite meritorious. Motive makes morality.

1233. *I cannot admit your version of the commandment "Thou shalt not kill," except by lawful authority.*

The very Bible which gives you the commandment also records God's authorization of death as a penalty when inflicted by lawful authority.

1234. *Very often the voice of the government is not that of the people.*

Even were that so, the question of capital punishment is not affected. The State right to inflict the penalty of death is an inherent right of society as such, independently of those who are in actual authority. The government gets its mandate of ordinary temporal administration from the people. But the social right to self-protection does not come from the people. It is from God, and, therefore, is an inherent and natural right. The people can vote governments in and out of office, but this merely means that they decide who shall be the agents of social authority. The inherent rights of social authority remain unaffected.

1235. *A Nationalist Government applies the death penalty, whilst a Labor Government refuses to do so. It is a terrible thing that a man's life depends merely on a change of government.*

You are viewing only one aspect of the case. The normal law of the land—and it is just a law—is that the penalty for a capital crime is death.

That is, a man's life normally depends upon his avoiding those crimes which are classified as capital, and it depends, therefore, upon himself. If a government applies the law and inflicts the penalty—that is normal procedure. If a government commutes the sentence of death, that is abnormal—and we may say that those whose sentences are commuted are fortunate; though they may not be—and may endure far more bodily and mental anguish over a long period than one who suffers the extreme penalty.

But whilst we may congratulate those whose sentences are commuted, we cannot regard one whose sentence is not commuted as having been deprived of any just right.

The accidental change of government is external to the question. A man does not commit a crime relying on an accidental retention of a favorable government in power. I suppose had I gone to Napier, in New Zealand, just prior to the accidental earthquake and been killed, my friend who did not go, could worry that an accident alone made such a difference between our fates. But if I *knew* that an accident was more than possible, and I deliberately courted the danger, he would rather speak of my folly.

1236. Is it a crime to sympathize with the criminal going to his doom?

Not at all. Nor is anyone expected to be inhuman. But in this, as in many other cases, there are two sides to the question. It is quite possible to have great sympathy for an individual who encounters disaster, yet to experience a reasonable relief that other good ends have been attained; and that a sufficient sanction and deterrent has been upheld for the good of the community.

1237. Would you kindly explain in detail the aims and objects of Catholic Action?

The aim of Catholic Action is the same as that of the Church—the salvation of souls, and the establishing of the reign of Jesus Christ in all phases of individual, family, and social life, so that Christ is ever better known, loved, and served by men.

The object is to secure the co-ordinated action of the Catholic laity in union with, and under the direction of the Bishops for the defense of religious and moral principles, and for the development of a sound and beneficial social crusade outside and above all political parties and movements.

1238. Is not Catholic Action merely organized resistance to the alleged evil of Communism?

Communism is a real evil, not merely an alleged evil. But Catholic Action is not what you apparently think it to be. In reality it is a stimulation of vitality within the Catholic body to resist the Communistic contagion, on the principle that the building up of one's own health is the best safeguard against disease germs. The secondary effect of this will be a reaction upon society itself.

The multiplication of virile and healthy Catholic cells in the social body will counteract Communistic poison. But this policy of Catholic Action in opposition to Communism has nothing in common with the bloodthirsty tactics adopted by Communism in its efforts to destroy Christianity whenever the opportunity for murderous persecution presents itself.

1239. In the sermon on the Mount Jesus said that evil should not be resisted.

He was then giving lessons of personal and individual holiness. But here I will let one of the greatest real rationalists in history reply to you, even though he did live in the despised Middle Ages. I hope you will appreciate his clear thinking. St. Thomas Aquinas was faced with the objection that, on its own principles, the Christian religion could not organize any opposition to the forces that would destroy it. And the objector quoted your text where Christ said, "But I say to you not to resist evil." Matt. V., 39. Now here is the reply of St. Thomas Aquinas, "There are two ways in which one can refuse to resist evil. Firstly, one can forgive and overlook personal injuries, and that is virtuous when it can contribute towards the salvation of souls. Secondly, one could refuse to resist evil to other people, and this is a vice when one is able to restrain the aggressor. Much more would it be evil to refuse to resist injuries offered to God."

1240. Pope Pius XI. even said that those who attack "Catholic Action" strike at the Pope.

By that he merely wished to impress on Catholics that he personally inspired the movement called "Catholic Action," and identifies his authority with it. "Catholic Action," of course, is not a political, but a purely religious movement, calling on all Catholics actively to put their principles into practice. Politicians who fear that this will prevent multitudes from accepting their anti-Christian doctrines of absurd racialism and international hatred will naturally regard Catholic Action as a form of political opposition. But the Pope himself has replied to that by saying that, when political rulers themselves go beyond their rights, and invade both the moral and religious sphere, the Church is bound to defend her moral and religious principles.

1241. The Pope added, "He who strikes at the Pope dies. It is a truth which history has proved." Was that a threat?

No. It was a statement of fact embodied in a popular expression quite current in Europe. You must not let it bring to your imagination any crude ideas of poison or daggers, such as were popularized in previous and more prejudiced and credulous generations. The Pope was quoting an axiom which appears in various forms, and which embodies an historical fact. I remember hearing in France the same axiom in the words, "He who bites the Pope dies of it." It merely means that all who attack the great and fundamental moral and religious principles for which the Pope stands are bound to come off second best in the end. And the reference, of course, is not to the Pope personally, but to his supreme office in the Catholic Church. In the clash between Caesar and St. Peter we know who triumphed. Emperors and Kings in history who have opposed the Catholic Church since then have come and gone—but the Church remains. I could give you a formidable list of names through the ages—Attila, Genseric, Charlemagne, Henry IV. of Germany, Frederick Barbarossa, Philip of France, Napoleon, Bismarck, and a host of others who have found only ultimate disaster in their foolish opposition to the eternal principles of the Catholic Church.

1242. Is the Pope any different from other men?

By his office he is. For he is the supreme representative of Christ in this world, that Christ who promised with divine authority and power, that the forces of evil would never prevail against His Church. But quite apart from that, the position of the Pope is undoubtedly the greatest in this world. Papini, who recently wrote a "Life of Christ" which has become world-famous, has since published a remarkable estimate of the office held by the Pope. "For the historian," he writes, "the Pope is the unique witness of the remote past; the heir of Moses the legislator, the successor of the Caesars. For the philosopher he is the preserver of the living traditions of the human race. For the artist he has the majesty of Solomon, the authority of St. Peter, and speaks the language of Virgil under the dome of Michelangelo. For the politician he is the spiritual sovereign of over 300 million men. For the Catholic he is the follower of St. Peter and the Vicar of Jesus Christ. Human, he speaks in the name of God; of the earth, he speaks eternally of heaven; living, he is in constant communion with the dead; modern, he seems eternally ancient; Italian, he speaks to all nations; a sinner, he can wipe out all guilt and administer the patrimony of the Saints." So writes Papini. And even though a man did not agree with all that he has said, the mere fact that the Pope is one of whom such things could be said cannot but leave the impression that the Pope is somewhat different from other men.

See R. R., Vol. I., 1441-1588.

CHAPTER XIV

COMPARATIVE STUDY OF NON-CATHOLIC DENOMINATIONS

1243. How many were the major forms of defection from the Catholic Church since the time of the Apostles?

As a general estimate, I would say seven, namely, Gnosticism, Manichaeism, Arianism, Nestorianism, Eutychianism, Greek Orthodoxy, and Protestantism. I have given them in the order of their appearance on the stage of history.

1244. What was the principle cause of desertion in each case?

That is a very comprehensive question, and I can but give here a general answer. In each case the dissident movement began either in a denial of the teachings of the Catholic Church, or in a rebellion against her authority. Both aspects were always, of course, ultimately involved. Those who began by rejecting the teachings of the Church soon found themselves in rebellion against her authority; whilst those who began by rebelling against her authority soon found themselves denying her doctrines. The Gnostics, Manichaeans, Arians, Nestorians, and Eutychians, began with doctrinal error, and ended by defying the authority of Rome. The Greek Church began by defying the authority of Rome, and has ended in a denial of much Catholic teaching, today becoming more and more infected by rationalism and modernism. Protestantism began in Germany by Luther's rejection of Catholic doctrine and his subsequent rejection of the authority of Rome; whilst in England it began by Henry VIII.'s rejection of the Pope's authority, followed by Elizabeth's repudiation of Catholic doctrine.

1245. What was Gnosticism?

Gnosticism arose in the second century, being a blend of Greek philosophy and pagan mythology with Christian doctrine. It split up into many independent heresies such as Marcionism and Montanism, and lingered on until about the seventh century. The history of most of these heresies is much the same. Protected by civil authority in many cases, each became fairly widespread, or even very widespread; then split up into warring sections, and eventually died out, or lingered on in a state of stagnation.

1246. What was Manichaeism?

Manichaeism tried to blend Indian and Persian philosophy and mythology with Christian doctrine. It commenced in the third century, became very widespread, but split up, and lingered on until the thirteenth century in various forms, the chief of its later forms being Albigensianism. It therefore had a long run of nearly ten centuries.

1247. What was the heresy of Arius?

Arius was born in Lybia in 256 A.D., and was ordained a Catholic priest in 313 A.D. In the year 318, at the Synod of Alexandria, the Patriarch of that city gave a discourse on the doctrine of the Most Holy Trinity. Arius declared that the Patriarch had fallen into error, and proceeded to set out his own ideas of Christian doctrine. He denied that Christ was really the Eternal Son of God, equally sharing in the Divine Nature with the Father. According to him, the Person of Christ existed before all other created things, and was nobler than them all. But God had created that Person of Christ in eternity, and then through Him created all other things in time. Later that created Personality of Christ became man for the redemption of the human race. In 320 A.D. a second Synod of Alexandria condemned the doctrine of Arius as heretical because it made the Eternal Son of God a mere creature, denying that He was equally the uncreated God with the Father and the Holy Ghost. Arius would not submit, but went on teaching and publicly spreading his errors, securing many followers and causing immense disturbance in the Church, and also in the State. The Emperor Constantine demanded that a General Council be held to settle the matter, and in 325 A.D. the Bishops met at Nicea. They condemned the teaching of Arius because he denied the Deity of Christ, and he was excommunicated because he would not submit to the authority of the Church. His heresy led multitudes astray, and for over four centuries Arian heretics were proportionately as numerous as the various forms of Protestantism during the last four centuries. Arius himself died in 335 A.D., and his movement died out also in the seventh century. In modern times Unitarianism is really a revived form of Arianism, at least by its denial of the doctrine of the Trinity and of the Deity of Christ.

1248. Will you explain the teachings of Nestorius?

As opposed to the Arians who would not admit that Christ was God, Nestorius insisted that we must adore Christ as God. But in explaining how Christ is God, he fell into error; and as he had become Patriarch of Constantinople in 428 A.D., his very influence demanded immediate decision by the Church. Nestorius said that we must adore Christ as God because God dwelt in Christ. However we could not identify Christ with God, and apart from the indwelling of God within Him, Christ was a merely human Person. There were, therefore, two persons as well as two natures in Christ; not, as the Church held, the One Person of the Eternal Son of God who, possessing the Divine Nature from eternity, had assumed to Himself a human nature in time. Nestorius taught that Mary was the Mother of a merely human child whom God used as an instrument for our redemption. She may be called the Mother of Christ, but she must not be called the Mother of God. In the year 431 A.D., the Council of Ephesus condemned the teaching of Nestorius, and defined the doctrine that there is only one Personality in Christ, that of the Eternal Son of God who, after the Incarnation, possessed both a Divine and a human nature. Insisting that the Child born of Mary was truly God, the Council defined that Mary was the Mother of God insofar as God deigned to be born of her in human form, when the Word was made flesh and dwelt amongst us. Nestorius refused to accept the decision of the Council, was excommunicated, and originated the Nestorian Church which lingers on amongst groups of Eastern Christians to this day in a stagnant condition, and hopelessly bound up with national considerations. At no time was the Nestorian sect as numerous as the Arians in their day, but it has lasted much longer.

1249. What was the Eutychian heresy?

Eutyches was the Superior of a Monastery in Constantinople who strongly opposed Nestorius. Unhappily his reaction against the errors of Nestorius led him into an opposite error. The Catholic doctrine teaches that in Christ there is one Person only, that of the Eternal Son of God, and two natures, the one Divine and the other human. Nestorius had wanted two persons and two natures. Eutyches, to safeguard the one Person of Christ, taught that the human nature was so absorbed into the Divine Nature as to lose its identity, so that as a result there was but one Person and one Nature in our Lord. The Council of Chalcedon in 451 A.D. condemned this error of Eutyches as heretical, and redefined the Catholic doctrine of one Person and two natures in Christ. Eutyches, despite his first good intentions, manifested a great attachment to his own ideas, refused to submit to the decision of the Church, and gave to the world the Monophysite heresy. The Monophysites, or the "upholders of one nature," have persevered through history to the present day, forming various sects such as the Coptic and Ethiopian Churches in Africa, and the Jacobite Churches in Mesopotamia. National reasons account for their survival, but they are without vitality.

1250. Do not these wrangles seem a mere matter of words?

That is a very superficial estimate. These heresies struck at the essential doctrine concerning the very Person of Christ, and were destructive of the Christian faith in their ultimate consequences. The Church, which St. Paul calls the "pillar and ground of truth," was safeguarding the revelation of God given into her keeping by her Founder, being in turn safeguarded by the Holy Spirit in her work of preserving the faith intact.

1251. I have read recently that the Abyssinians belonged to the Coptic faith, the earliest sect of the Christian denominations, to which all the Christian world adhered until the rise of the Church of Rome.

It is true that the Abyssinians belonged to the Coptic Church. But the rest of the statement is erroneous. Firstly, a sect is a group of dissentient people who abandon a previous position in order to set up a new form of Church. If the Coptic Church were the original Church to which the whole Christian world adhered, then it is not a sect. All the newer and independent Churches which broke away from the original Church would constitute the sects. Secondly, we come to a question of fact. Was the Coptic faith the original faith to which all Christians adhered from the beginning? In other words, did St. Peter and the other Apostles belong to the Coptic Church? That is impossible, for the Coptic sect did not come into existence until the fifth century.

1252. It is said that the Abyssinians were converted to the Christian faith by St. Frumentius, who was consecrated Bishop of Abyssinia by the Patriarch Athanasius of Alexandria.

That is quite correct, but it spells death to the idea that the Abyssianian Coptic Church is the oldest form of Christianity, and to the notion that the Church of Rome was subsequent in origin. For St. Athanasius, who consecrated St. Frumentius, was in complete union with the Pope of Rome! In certain difficulties with his own subjects St. Athanasius appealed to the Pope, and Pope Julius I. wrote back to the rebels, "Do you not know that the ordinary practice is first to write to us, and from Rome to receive the decision as to what is right? Should any reproach fall upon the Bishop of your city, you must undoubtedly refer the case to this Church of Rome." How could St. Athanasius be subject to the Church of Rome if the Church of Rome had not yet arisen? And what religion would St. Frumentius preach save that professed by the Bishop who consecrated him? St. Frumentius preached the Roman faith, and lived and died without ever hearing of the Coptic Church.

1253. How did the Coptic Church come into existence?

Christianity was first preached in Abyssinia by St. Frumentius who had been consecrated Bishop by St. Athanasius in 341 A.D. He preached the faith of the Roman Church to which all the Christian world adhered insofar as it was the faith St. Peter himself had preached at Rome. Over 100 years after the consecration of St. Frumentius, Eutyches, an Archimandrite of Constantinople, was condemned as a heretic at the Council of Chalcedon in 451. Refusing to submit, Eutyches commenced the Monophysite heresy. Now some Bishops from the Abyssinian Church founded by St. Frumentius 110 years earlier were present at the Council of Chalcedon. They then acknowledged the jurisdiction of Pope Leo I. But they became infected by the Monophysite heresy, went back to their own country, broke away from the authority of Rome, and commenced that sect which today is called the Coptic Church of Abyssinia. The word "Coptic" means "Egyptian," and the "Copts" are simply the descendants of the Monophysite heretics in Egypt. As you will notice, the Coptic sect is very old. It is over a thousand years older than any Protestant sect. But still it did not begin until over 400 years after the foundation of the Catholic Church. And when you realize that it is now just about 400 years since Protestantism began, you will understand that the Catholic Church is a good deal older than the Coptic Church.

1254. What is the Greek Orthodox Church?

There are some 16 different Orthodox Churches existing independently of one another. After the first really definite break with Rome when Photius, Patriarch of Constantinople, left the Catholic Church in the ninth century, the Eastern Church followed in the path of all schismatical Churches, splitting up into further divisions. Eight of these separate sections of Orthodoxy have their own Patriarchs, namely, Jerusalem, Antioch, Alexandria, Constantinople, Bulgaria, Rumania, Russia, and Servia. The others lack definite rule. The term "Greek Orthodox Church" is popularly applied to any or all of these Churches; but strictly speaking it should be reserved for that section of Orthodoxy which acknowledges the Patriarch of Constantinople. This is really one of the smaller sections, for the Bulgarians, Rumanians, Russians and others of Slav nationality, are Greeks in no sense of the word. But it is clear that there is no one united Orthodox Church at all, any more than there is one united form of Protestantism. However, since the schismatic Orthodox Churches began with the rebellion of the Patriarchate of Constantinople against Rome in the ninth century, we can allude to all the Orthodox Churches as belonging to the Greek Schism.

1255. Was the Christian Church governed from the beginning with the Bishop of Rome as supreme and infallible head, or by a Council of Bishops?

The Church from the very beginning was governed by the Bishops, including the Bishop of Rome, all the other Bishops being in union with and subject to the universal jurisdiction of the Bishop of Rome. At times the Bishops met together in Councils for more important deliberations, and the decisions of these Councils were acknowledged as binding provided they were approved and sanctioned by the Bishop of Rome as supreme head of the Church.

1256. Did the Patriarchs of the Greek Orthodox Church at any stage after the death of Christ recognize the Pope as supreme and infallible head of the Church?

We cannot speak of the "Patriarchs of the Greek Orthodox Church" prior to the Greek Schism commenced by Photius in 867 A.D. Until then there were simply Patriarchs of Constantinople, presiding there and subject to the Pope. Dr. Orchard, when a Congregationalist, wrote, "An examination of the circumstances of the Great Schism shows that the Eastern Church did then repudiate a supremacy which it had previously been in the habit of conceding to the Roman Patriarchate." The First Council of Constantinople in 381, which only Eastern Bishops attended, demanded that the Bishop of Constantinople should rank next after the Bishop of Rome, and before the Bishops of Alexandria and Antioch. The Council of Chalcedon in 451, attended by the Eastern Bishops, ended its discussion with the unanimous cry, "Peter has spoken by Leo," when the Pope's decision was given. A century and a half later Pope Gregory I. could still write, "Who doubts that the Church of Constantinople is subject to the Apostolic See?" No one then doubted it; and no one disputed it until Photius came along in 867 to plunge the East into schism. The Patriarch of Constantinople, and all the Eastern Bishops signed the formula of Hormisdas, who was Pope from 514 to 523. That formula contained these words, "We follow the Apostolic See in everything and teach all its laws. I hope to be in that one Communion taught by the Apostolic See in which is the whole, real, and perfect solidity of the Christian religion." Dean Milman writes, "Before the end of the third century the lineal descent of Rome's Bishops from St. Peter was unhesitatingly claimed and obsequiously admitted by the Christian world."

1257. What reasons led to the breakaway of the Greeks?
The reasons were chiefly political. According to the most recent research work of Jugie, Grumel, Amann, and Dvronik, the schism commenced by Photius in 867 would never have happened had it not been for political rivalry concerning jurisdiction over Bulgaria. In 861 the Bulgarians were converted by missionaries from Constantinople. In 866 Pope Nicholas I. appointed Bishops for the Bulgarians in order to bring them under the jurisdiction of the Latin Patriarchate of the West rather than have them under the Patriarchate of Constantinople. The motive to maintain Rome's political authority over Constantinople was not absent, and from this point of view the move was a grave political mistake. The Greeks resented it, and Photius, Patriarch of Constantinople, wrote a reprehensible letter to the Pope in 867 in which he condemned the Catholic Church, and made various charges against her even from the doctrinal point of view. The undeniable provocation did not justify his doing this. The Pope excommunicated Photius, who retaliated by excommunicating the Pope, and the schism commenced. Photius made peace with Pope John VIII., and was duly recognized as Patriarch of Constantinople; and the reconciliation endured so long as Photius lived. But trouble had been set on foot; and intermittent difficulties with Rome continued until 1054 when Michael Cerularius, the then Patriarch of Constantinople, renewed the break with Rome, moved by sheer ambition to be universal Patriarch over the whole Church. He won the Emperor to his side by appealing to national pride in the political importance of Constantinople. From that time on, no Patriarch of Constantinople has sought confirmation of his appointment from Rome, nor submitted to the jurisdiction of the Pope. Greek Delegates to the Second Council of Lyons in 1274, and again at the Council of Florence in 1439, admitted that they should do so, and return to unity with Rome. But on each occasion on their return to the East their admissions were repudiated through national interests. So the Greek Churches continue in their schismatical state. Political quarrels and personal antagonisms, with faults on both sides, were the original cause of the schism, not dogmatic differences. But from a doctrinal point of view, the Eastern Churches are gradually drifting from othodoxy, and yielding to the inroads of modernist influences.

1258. I have been told that Greek priests have power to consecrate the Eucharist.
Priests of the Greek Orthodox Churches have valid Orders, and when they offer the Sacrifice of the Mass, they consecrate validly.

1259. As the Greeks are schismatics and heretics also, how can you admit their Orders whilst denying Anglican Orders?
The Greek Orthodox Churches are separated from the Catholic Church by schism, or division from its authority; and also by heresy, insofar as they refuse to admit certain Catholic dogmatic teachings. But these things do not necessarily affect the question of Orders. If, after leaving the Catholic Church, such ecclesiastical bodies retain the correct form of ordination, and administer the Sacrament of Holy Orders with the right intention, then the priests will be truly ordained, even though in a schismatical and heretical Church. This is the case with the Orthodox Greeks. And since Greek priests are truly ordained, they cannot be re-

ordained should they seek admission to the Catholic Church. Even in the Anglican Church, after its separation from Rome by Henry VIII., in 1534, the ordinations continued to be correct for the first sixteen years, until 1550. But in 1550, during the reign of Edward VI., the form for ordination was altered, and the intention of ordaining priests in the Catholic sense of the word was repudiated. From then on, Anglican Orders have been simply invalid, and converted clergymen from the Anglican Church must remain either as Catholic laymen, or be ordained as Catholic priests without any allowance being made for their previous ordination as ministers in the Church of England.

1260. If a married Greek priest became a Roman Catholic, would he be allowed to officiate as a priest and still live with his wife?

He could not do so if he adopted the Latin rite. But he could do so if, as would probably happen, he joined one of the Uniate Greek Churches which retain their Greek customs and Liturgy even whilst subject to the Pope.

1261. Do the Greek Churches believe that Christ is really present in the Eucharist? If so, do they celebrate a valid Mass?

The Greek Churches believe in the Real Presence of Christ in the Eucharist; and since their priests have valid Orders, they possess the power of consecrating the Blessed Eucharist in the true sense of the word. The Sacrifice of the Mass in Greek Churches is, therefore, every bit as valid as the Mass in the Catholic Church, even though it is not celebrated in Latin.

1262. May a Catholic hear Mass, then, in a Greek Church?

He may do so in a Uniate Greek Church, but not in any of the schismatical Orthodox Churches. Those Churches are not part of the Catholic Church, but are in a state of schism and of protest against the authority of Christ in His true Church. Churches separated from the unity of the Catholic Church are not according to the will of Christ, who demands that His followers should form one flock under one shepherd. No Catholic therefore may take part in, or sanction in any way, the services of the Greek Orthodox Churches.

1263. I have heard that, when a Catholic priest is not available, Catholics may receive the Sacraments from Greek Orthodox priests. Is that consistent?

When no Catholic priest is available, the Catholic Church permits a dying Catholic to receive one Sacrament only from a Greek priest, and that is the Sacrament of Confession. The very law of the Catholic Church forbidding participation in Greek rites during life is to preserve a Catholic from danger of schism, and within the true Church, for the sake of his very salvation. And if, at the hour of death, that salvation can be the better secured by the reception of absolution from a Greek priest rather than go without such absolution, the Church wisely and mercifully permits it. But, as is clear, this exception avails only in the case of extreme necessity, when no Catholic priest is available, and on condition that the Catholic merely accepts absolution from the Greek priest as a priest, and in no way approving his position as a schismatic.

1264. In what doctrines do the Greek Orthodox Churches differ from the Roman Catholic Church?

They differ on many essential points, although they are much nearer to Catholicism than they are to Protestantism, insofar as they retain the bulk of original Christian doctrine, and a valid priesthood. They acknowledge the doctrine of the Trinity, but deny that the Holy Ghost proceeds from both Father and Son. They deny the supremacy and infallibility of the Pope; the right of the Church to baptize by pouring the water instead of by completely immersing the subject; the right to give Communion under one kind only; the Catholic doctrine of the particular and general judgments; also the Catholic doctrine on the nature of purgatory, although they admit the existence of purgatory. Whilst believing that Mary was quite sinless, and maintaining a great devotion to her as the Mother of God, they deny the doctrine of the Immaculate Conception. This, however, is a more recent denial. The Greek Churches believed in the Immaculate Conception until the advent of Protestantism. Under pressure of Protestant opinion they wavered without denying it. The denial came when the Pope defined the doctrine in 1854, but merely because they were opposed to the Pope and wished to manifest their opposition. They have nothing against the doctrine in itself. The Greeks also differ from Rome concerning the nature of original sin, and of justification. These are the chief differences, some of them rendering the Greek Churches heretical as well as schismatical.

1265. *I belong to the Greek Orthodox Church, and regard my religion as identical with the Roman Catholic except for the fact that you acknowledge the Pope as head, whilst we acknowledge the Patriarch of Jerusalem.*

Even were that true, you are confronted with a great problem. Christ declared definitely that His Church would be one fold under one shepherd. And your duty would be to inquire as to the relative merits of the Pope and of the Patriarch of Jerusalem in their claims to be head of the Church. Both cannot be. But, as a matter of fact, you cannot speak of one Greek Orthodox Church with the Patriarch of Jerusalem as its head. The Rev. C. J. MacGillivray, in his book, "Through the East to Rome," 1931, says that, as an Anglican clergyman, he spent some years in the East amongst the Greeks and Syrians, working for the reunion of Greeks and Anglicans. He found it impossible, and in the end became a Catholic. On page 91 of his book he writes: "To begin with, there is no such thing as the 'Orthodox Church.' There is a group of some 15 or 16 independent Churches, recognizing no common authority, but loosely connected as being all 'Orthodox.' And again, if you leave out Russia, the whole number of the Orthodox is exceedingly small; and the Russian Church was only held together by the power of the State. Compared to the Roman Catholic Church the so-called Orthodox Church is just a collection of fossilized and moribund fragments of what was once a great and living Church. Indeed it seems to me to be a great object lesson in the disastrous consequences of abandoning the rock on which the Church of Christ was built. The Orthodox Church has ceased to be a living teacher. It is incapable of any sort of development, or of that constant advance in thought and undying vitality which are characteristic of the Roman Catholic Church. It is not, indeed, carried about with every wind of doctrine like the Protestant Churches. It has, in the main, kept the old Faith, but only at the cost of ceasing to think. On all the vital questions which have been discussed, and in many cases settled in the West, it neither has, nor can have anything to say." Such is the impression formed from first-hand knowledge by the Rev. C. J. MacGillivray during his sojourn amongst Eastern Christians as an Anglican clergyman. You cannot, therefore, speak of the Greek Church as one Church; and not all the groups comprising it acknowledge the jurisdiction of the Patriarch of Jerusalem by any means.

1266. *Even though in schism, the Greek Orthodox Church is at least an Apostolic Church.*

That cannot be admitted. The word "Apostolic" in general signifies the identity of a present Church with the Church of the Apostles. This identity can be either adequate or inadequate. Adequate apostolicity is present when a Church of today has not only the same doctrine and worship, and the same episcopal constitution, but also the same uninterrupted and lawfully transmitted jurisdiction or authority. Without this latter requirement, any vestiges of apostolicity are inadequate, and useless as a mark of identification. The chief thing, therefore, is the continued juridical succession of apostolic authority. Now this element precisely is missing from the Greek Orthodox Church. By the mere fact of being in schism, apostolic authority is forfeited. In addition, the Greek Church has not preserved the Faith intact in many points. The Greek Church cannot therefore be called apostolic in the technical sense of that word.

1267. Do you deny the Greek Church to be truly Catholic?

Yes. By Catholic we mean a given Church, i.e., one united Church, which remains everywhere essentially the same, and inherits the commission of Christ to teach all nations as a right, exercising that right by constantly propagating itself in continual expansion. Now, in the first place, there is no one Greek Orthodox Church. For example, there is no authoritative bond of union between the Greek Churches of Constantinople, Alexandria, Antioch, Russia, Servia, Rumania, Bulgaria, Ukraine, and Estonia, etc. Moreover, these Greek Churches are not even conscious of a Divine commission to teach all nations. They consent to be national in their outlook, and show no sign of the expansive power which seeks to propagate itself amongst all peoples. The Greeks declare the Latins to have fallen into schism, yet make no effort to convert them back to "Orthodoxy." Is it not significant that, whilst no Latins ever followed the Patriarch of Constantinople, many in the East, including many Patriarchs of Antioch and Alexandria, remained in Communion with Rome after the schisms of Photius and Cerularius? It is impossible to regard the Greek Orthodox Churches as Catholic in the true sense of the word.

1268. Since Greek Orthodoxy is so near to Roman Catholicism, why change from one to the other?

The mere fact that they are not identical is sufficient reason for a change from Greek Orthodoxy to Catholicism. It is necessary to be subject to the right authority. Obedience is the very heart of religion. We went from God by disobedience; the road back is by obedience. And the authority of the Pope is that of Christ. Of him Christ said, "He that heareth you, heareth Me; and he that despiseth you, despiseth Me." Lk. X., 16. Again, Christ said, "If a man will not hear the Church, let him be as the heathen." Matt. XVIII., 17. Our Lord could never have commanded men to obey two conflicting authorities. That would spell chaos. The very reasons the Greeks urge for not becoming Catholics show that they do not really believe their Churches to be as near to Catholicism as they pretend. Moreover, Greek priests are getting more and more into the habit of fraternizing with Protestants in common services. But no Greek Orthodox priest would be allowed to participate in any Catholic rites. The Greeks acknowledge a bond with definitely heretical Churches; but they have no real bond with the Catholic Church. They are outside Catholic unity.

1269. I was taught by my parents that the Church of England has always been a distinct Church on its own right from the second century.

Your parents apparently belonged to that school of Anglicans which refuses to admit that the Church of England originated only at the time of the Protestant Reformation. Those who belong to that school of thought persuade themselves that the present Anglican Church is one and the same as the Church which was established in England by the first Christian missionaries to that country. But this theory cannot stand the test of history.

1270. You insist that it originated at the time of the Protestant Reformation?

Yes, until the Reformation, England was a Catholic country. The first missionaries preached the Catholic religion, and were as subject to the Pope as I am. Henry VIII. was a Catholic, and subject to the Pope until 1534, when he rebelled against the Catholic Church, left it, and made himself head of his own new Church within his own kingdom.

1271. Is your verdict historical?

It is the normal and correct verdict of the ordinary historian who judges simply in accordance with the facts, and who has no particular ecclesiastical theory to maintain. Thus Lecky, an agnostic, in his "History of England in the Eighteenth Century," says that the Church of England was founded at the Reformation as an institution most intensely and distinctively English.

1272. The Church of England, then, is not one with the pre-Reformation Church in England?

No. If it were, it would still be subject to the Pope, one with the Catholic Church throughout the world, observing the same Canon Law, offering the same Sacrifice of the Mass, and teaching the same doctrines as those held by all Catholics today, whether in Italy, Spain, France, Germany, Austria, America, Australia, India, Africa, and elsewhere throughout the world. But on all points, doctrinal, devotional, and disciplinary, the Church of England is out of harmony with the Catholic Church. Any one who believes that the religion of England for over a thousand years prior to the Reformation was correct, has no option but to leave Anglicanism and return to the Catholic Church—as I myself did.

1273. Will you briefly explain how the Anglican Church came about?

Until the year 1534, Henry VIII., was in full communion with and subject to the Pope, and England was a Catholic country. In fact, after Luther in Germany had rebelled against the Pope in 1517, Henry wrote a book to refute him, and received in return for this from the Pope the title, "Defender of the Faith." Unfortunately Henry grew tired of his lawful wife Catherine of Aragon, and wished to put her away and marry Anne Boleyn. He asked the Pope to annul his marriage with Catherine; but, as his marriage to Catherine was quite valid, he failed to secure the favor he sought. He therefore broke with Rome, and had himself created head of the Church of England by the Act of Royal Supremacy in 1534. He thus set up the Church of England as a Church independent of the Catholic Church, and took the divorce he wanted. Whilst repudiating the authority of the Pope, however, Henry also repudiated the new Protestant doctrines apart from the denial of Papal authority. He insisted on all other Catholic teachings and practices, persecuting Catholics who denied the royal supremacy, and Protestants who denied transubstantiation and the Mass. After Henry's death, however, his new Church could not remain as it was, neither Catholic nor Protestant. Under Edward VI., who was but a boy, Cranmer protestantized both the doctrines and worship of the Church of England. Edward died before the work was consolidated, and was succeeded by Mary, who was an ardent Catholic. She determined to undo the work of both Henry and Cranmer, banishing the former's royal supremacy, and the latter's Protestantism. She restored the Catholic religion, and the deposed Catholic Bishops, and brought the Church once more into unity with Rome under the jurisdiction of the Pope. That ended the first phase of the Church of England as a separated Anglican Church. This was in 1554, twenty years after Henry's first break with Rome in 1534. Mary died, however, in 1558. And in the first year of her reign, 1559, Elizabeth renewed the Act of Royal Supremacy, and set up the independent Church of England again, this time on a definitely Protestant basis. The Protestant Church of England has continued unbrokenly since then, though it has exhibited an interior spirit of dissension and turmoil such as few other Protestant sects can boast.

1274. Anglicans deny absolutely that Henry VIII. was the founder of the Church of England.

That denial will not stand the test of history. It is certain that prior to 1534 the Church in England was subject to the authority of the Pope. After 1534, when Henry repudiated the authority of the Pope and set himself up as supreme head on earth of the Church in his realm, a new Church was the result—just as America became a new and separate nation when, in 1776, it repudiated the authority of the King of England, despite its retaining the same customs, traditions, language, and possessions as before.

1275. Henry insisted that the Church should remain just as it was.

You forget that the Church is essentially a unified society, and that it is utterly dependent upon the bond of authority binding it together. The authority and jurisdiction of the Pope is the very heart of the constitution of the Church. When Henry rejected the authority and jurisdiction of Rome, and declared these things to be centered in him as far as the Church in his realm was concerned, he dragged that Church into schism and altered its essential character, by the radical constitutional change he had imposed upon it. The Henrician schismatical Church was by the very fact cut off from, and outside the true Catholic Church.

1276. There was a true continuity with the previously existing Church in England.

The new Church continued to retain the Church property and buildings that belonged to the old Church, but did not retain identity with that Church. It could not break away from that Church and still belong to it. The Anglican Dr. Goudge rightly says, "The English Church has in England supplanted the Roman, and we hold the Cathedrals, the parish Churches, and the little that the State has left of the ancient endowments. . . . If English Roman Catholics were not hostile to the Anglican Church, it would be a miracle of grace."

1277. The continuity of the Church of England with the pre-Reformation Church is recognized by the law of England.

To that I will let Sir W. S. Holdsworth, K.C., D.C.L., LL.D., professor of English Law in the University of Oxford, reply. In his "History of English Law," published 1931, he writes that, because the Pope would not grant Henry VIII. a divorce, "a break with Rome became necessary. Although the break was accomplished with as little external change as possible, it necessarily involved an altogether new view as to the relations between Church and State. In the preamble to Henry's Statutes we can see the gradual elaboration of the main characteristic of these changed relations . . . . the theory of the Royal Supremacy. The dual control over things temporal and things spiritual is to end. The Crown is to be supreme over all persons and causes. The Canon Law of the Western Church is to give place to the 'King's Ecclesiastical Law of the Church of England'. . . . In the preamble to the Statute of Appeals in 1533 the relations between the new Anglican Church and the State were sketched by the king himself with his own hand . . . . Henry VIII. often inserted in the preambles to his Statutes reasoned arguments designed to prove the wisdom of the particular Statute. And . . . . he never hesitated to color facts and events to suit his purpose. But the preamble to this Statute of Appeals is remarkable, partly because it manufactures history on an unprecedented scale, but chiefly because it has operated from that day to this as a powerful incentive to its manufacture by others on similar lines. Nor is the reason for this phenomenon difficult to discover. The Tudor Settlement was a characteristically skillful instance of the Tudor genius for creating a modern institution with a mediaeval form. But, in order to create the illusion that the new Anglican Church was indeed the same institution as the mediaeval Church, it was necessary to prove the historical continuity of these two very different institutions. . . . It was not till an historian arose who, besides being the greatest historian of this century, was both a consummate lawyer, and a dissenter from the Anglican as well as the other Churches (i.e., F. W. Maitland, LL.D., D.C.L., late Downing Professor of Law at Cambridge) that the historical worthlessness of Henry's theory was finally demonstrated." Such are the words of Sir W. S. Holdsworth on the recognition of Anglican continuity by English Law. They will be found in his "History of English Law," 5th Edit., 1931.

1278. The Church of England is Catholic, because it holds to the old truths which are patently cardinal.

It permits the denial of those truths even by its own Bishops. In his book, "The Necessity for Catholic Reunion," published in 1933, the Rev. T. Whitton, M.A., an Anglican clergyman, writes, "The Anglican Communion is very unlike the Roman Catholic and the Orthodox Communions. Each of the latter are at least one in faith. In the Anglican Communion, on the contrary, there is no such unity. Not only are there at least three different and contradictory religions calling themselves 'Catholic,' 'Evangelical,' and 'Modernist,' but also these three religions are divergent."

1279. To these the Church of England is as a whole unalterably faithful.

The unalterable fidelity of the Church of England as a whole to the basic truths of Christianity is a mere dream. It is necessary to face realities. The Protestant Bishop Weston, of Zanzibar, published a book in 1914 entitled, "Ecclesia Anglicana." In it he wrote that the Church of England, of which he himself was a Bishop, is "puffed up with a sense of what she calls her broadmindedness," but that she "stands today at the judgment bar, innocent alike of narrowmindedness and broadmindedness, but proven guilty of double-mindedness. And until she recovers a single mind, and knows it, and learns to express it, she will be of use neither in the sphere of reunion nor in the mission field." He added that ministers of the Church of England treat "the fundamental articles of the Christian Faith as open questions."

1280. Neither by addition as some, nor by subtraction as others, do we allow the Apostolic deposit of Faith to be impaired.

Ideals, and not a vision of the real, dictate such statements. Deploring the different and contending parties in the Church of England, the Rev. T. Whitton, in the book above quoted, says, "In this confusion and contradiction what can be expected of the people? Seeing these differences, and the teachings of the Modernists, and that the Bishops do not repress these contradictions, they naturally conclude that the parsons themselves do not believe that Jesus Christ is God. They think that the Bishops would never allow these important doctrines to be denied if they believed them themselves. . . . The Church of England is simply unable to cope with a situation which is rapidly changing from bad to worse on account of these divisions. . . . There are Bishops and others who boast of their divergence from the Catholic Church even in the fundamental doctrines of the Holy Trinity and the Incarnation . . . and there is no court in the Church of England competent to declare the truth or condemn error." How can it be said that the Church of

England does not allow the Apostolic deposit of the Faith to be impaired? The safest position for an Anglican to adopt is to say that it does not matter whether his Church holds to the old truths or not; that those truths cannot be cardinal; and that it is the genius of Anglicanism to allow any kind of teaching at all.

1281. At the Reformation we brought back the doctrine of the sufficiency of Holy Scripture.

Anglicanism adopted that principle from the Continental reformers. But it no longer believes in that doctrine. The Rev. Mr. Whitton writes, "The real Evangelicals are in a difficult position, for the Church of England no longer believes in the Inspiration of the Bible, as she allows it to be denied by those who teach in her name." As for the Reformation, he says that the Anglo-Catholic or High Church clergyman "regards the Reformation as thoroughly bad. He yearns for the time when it shall be undone, and the Church of England be one in faith under the Pope as she was until the catastrophe of the sixteenth century, since when she has lost the mass of the people. He gradually learns to repudiate the whole of the present regime. He sees that the so-called Ecclesiastical Courts derive their authority from the State, and that there are no Spiritual Courts whatever left. He sees that the Book of Common Prayer is a schedule to an Act of Parliament, and that spiritual authority it has none except the promise made to use the form contained in it; also that this promise is made by order of, and to the State, and therefore is to be interpreted in a sense as strictly minimized as possible."

1282. Together with Scripture, of course, we accept the authority of the Church.

Mr. Whitton writes, "Membership in the Church of England determines nothing; in that comprehensive body all beliefs are called in question except perhaps the existence of God. No one can say that a man, just because he is a member of the Church of England, must hold any one doctrine. Anglo-Catholics and Evangelicals will probably dispute this." But the Rev. Mr. Whitton adds that each of these groups follows its own theory, and it is not in obedience to any authority of the Church. In fact, "they know that the Church of England does not demand it; that others in the same Communion believe and act quite contrarily, and are allowed to do so quite freely by their Church." How then can it be said that Anglicans believe in the authority of their Church?

1283. Anglicanism insists on belief in the Trinity, the Divinity of Christ, the uniqueness of the Incarnation, and the Holy Spirit as proceeding from the Father and the Son.

I would that the Church of England did maintain such Catholic teaching. But it does not. The Report of the Girton Conference of Modern Churchmen, 1921, records the words of the head of an Anglican Theological College as follows: "Christ did not claim Divinity for Himself.... I do not suppose for a moment that Jesus ever thought of Himself as God.... We must absolutely jettison the traditional notion that His person was not human but Divine." How can it be said that the Church of England insists on belief in the Trinity and the Divinity of Christ? In their book, "Is Christianity True," Cyril Joad, the rationalist, challenges Arnold Lunn, an Anglican at the time of their controversy, in these words, "The only branch of Christianity which has not declined is Roman Catholicism. Logical, coherent, definite, and above all, dogmatic, it offers a sure foundation to those whose feet are beset by the quicksands of modern doubt. I find it in the highest degree significant that, although you have so recently controverted against Father Knox and taken up the cudgels against Catholicism, when you come to a rough-and-tumble with me over the whole field of Christian controversy, you have over and over again adopted the Catholic point of view, and .... retreated in safety behind the ramparts of the citadel of Rome." So speaks the rationalist. And, as a matter of fact, shortly after this controversy with Joad, Arnold Lunn found no alternative save to be received into the Catholic Church.

1284. The Church of England retains the seven Sacraments.

Some Anglicans or Episcopalians venerate seven Sacraments; some venerate two; some have no faith in any. The 39 Articles declare that there are two Sacraments properly so-called, Baptism and the Eucharist. The other five are not to be regarded strictly as Sacraments. And, of course, even though the Holy Eucharist is declared to be a Sacrament, it is not accepted in the orthodox sense, and that it contains the Real Presence of the Body and Blood of Christ is denied. Both the Catholic Church and the Greek Orthodox Church have retained seven Sacraments as coming down from the very beginning, and as instituted by Christ Himself.

1285. The Church of England believes in the Real Presence of Christ in the Eucharist.

At the Reformation the Church of England abolished that doctrine. Thomas Cranmer, who had gone to the Continent and absorbed the spirit of Protestantism in Germany, decided after the death of Henry VIII. to protestantize the Church of England. And one of the foremost planks in the new Protestant platform was the rejection of the Catholic doctrine of the Mass, and of the Real Presence of Christ in the Eucharist. As Archbishop of Canterbury under the boy king Edward VI., Cranmer had practically a free hand to do as he pleased. And having lost the Catholic Faith himself, he made the fullest use of his position to rob the English people of that same faith. Rejecting any idea that the bread can actually become the Body of Christ, the Anglican Articles have to find some other explanation of the Eucharist. They say that the Body of Christ is received by faith. The bread still remains bread after the consecration. There is no trace of Christ's Body in the bread, or under its appearances. At most the bread is but a symbol of Christ's Body. If the one receiving the bread has faith, it will be as if it were Christ's Body for him, though it isn't in itself. That is the authentic Anglican doctrine, invented as a substitute for the Catholic and Greek Orthodox doctrine of the real objective Presence of Christ's Body. John Jewel (1571), Bishop of Salisbury, wrote: "The bread we receive with our earthly mouths is an earthly thing, and therefore a figure, as the water in Baptism is also a figure ... the Sacramental Bread is bread; it is not the Body of Christ." In 1898, April 4th, the then Anglican Archbishop of Canterbury, Dr. Temple, wrote to a lady who asked him whether the doctrine of the Real Presence were according to Anglican teaching: "Dear Madam, The bread used in Holy Communion is certainly not God, either before consecration or after; and you must not worship it." Bishop Barnes, of Birmingham, repeats the same doctrine today: "There is no real objective Presence of Christ attached to the bread and wine used in Holy Communion."

1286. I have attended Anglican Churches in which Mass is celebrated and the blessed Sacrament reserved for the adoration of the people.

Both practices are quite out of harmony with Anglicanism or Episcopalianism. The 31st Article of Religion, setting forth Church of England doctrine, says, "The sacrifices of Masses, in which it was commonly said that the priest did offer Christ for the living and the dead to have remission of pain or guilt, were blasphemous fables and dangerous deceits." In his book, "What We Owe to the Reformation," p. 19, Dr. Ryle, Anglican Bishop of Liverpool, says, "The Reformers found the Sacrifice of the Mass in our Churches. They cast it out as a blasphemous fable and a dangerous deceit.... The Reformers found our clergy sacrificing priests, and made them prayer-reading, preaching ministers—ministers of God's Word and Sacraments. The Reformers found in our Church the doctrine of a real corporal presence of Christ in the Lord's Supper under the forms of bread and wine, and laid down their lives to oppose it. They would not even allow the expression 'real presence' a place in our Prayer Book."

1287. Is there much difference between the High Church section of the Church of England and the Roman Catholic Church?

There is a profound and radical difference. For High Church Anglicans equally belong to the Church of England with Low Churchmen who hold the Protestant teaching and outlook; and equally with them repudiate the divinely-given authority of the Catholic Church. No introduction of similar forms of worship could make the High Church section of the Church of England identical with the Catholic Church. For the essential thing in religion is obedience. We went from God by disobedience. Our way back is to retrace our steps by obedience. And if religion is to get us back, it must essentially demand obedience. So Christ said, "If you love Me, keep My commandments." Jn. XIV., 15. And again, "If a man will not hear the Church, let him be as the heathen." Matt. XVIII., 17. Similar rites and ceremonies can no more make an Anglo-Catholic a member of the Catholic Church than the similar language makes an American a member of the British Empire. For the United States repudiates the unifying bond of authority proper to the British Empire. The profound and radical difference between High Church Anglicans and the Catholic Church will cease to exist only when these High Churchmen sever their connection with the Anglican Church and submit to Rome.

1288. Whatever her doctrinal differences, the Church of England has never failed in her moral witness.

Writing in the "Hibbert Journal" for July 1930 apropos of the Lambeth Conference of that year, the Rev. J. M. Lloyd Thomas, a Protestant minister of Birmingham, said, "We can all be magnanimous enough to recognize that Rome in a uniquely tenacious temper, is a steward of the mysteries and of the moral witness of the Christian Church. The supreme attraction of Rome is to be found in its ethical rigorism. Rome is the one uncompromising corporate witness to that moral code of Christendom which preserves Western Civilization from final collapse. It represents the last loyalty of the human race to its own highest moral standards. It is the iron bulwark of Christianity against the overwhelming invasion of the corrupting neo-paganism of our times. There is no authoritative moral theology which can tell us what is the final judgment of Anglicans and Free Churchmen on questions such as marriage, divorce, birth control, companionate experiments, abortion, euthanasia, suicide. Only Rome speaks with one voice on such themes, and these are the issues of life and death, of the survival or decline of the West." After the Lambeth Conference of that year, the London "Daily Express," Aug. 15th, 1930, said that the Anglican Church "could not hope to control the conduct of men by debated measures conceived in fear and born in compromise." And the Anglican Rev. T. H. Whitton wrote in 1933, "So the defense of Christian morals is left to Rome, and the Anglican Communion, and all of us within it, stand disgraced before the world . . . the only remedy, and the only safeguard against other breaches in the Christian moral code, is Catholic reunion." "The Necessity for Catholic Reunion," pp. 116-117.

1289. I have heard it said that the Free Churches could not have withstood the onslaughts of Rome had it not been for the Anglican Church.

Never was a statement farther from the truth. The very term "Free Churches" arose from a refusal to submit to Elizabeth's "Act of Uniformity in Religion" by which she tried to make all Englishmen submit to the Anglican Church. Protestants who refused to submit were called "Nonconformists." They would not conform to the Established Church any more than Catholics. They wanted Churches free from Rome, but also free from domination by the Crown. They suffered persecution together with Catholics and, as the "Pilgrim Fathers" fled from England to America to escape the State-established Church of England. The truth, therefore, is not that the "Free Churches" withstood the onslaughts of Rome with the help of the Anglican Church, but that both Catholics and Nonconformists have survived the onslaughts of the Anglican Church in England. All that, of course, is past history; but it is past history which should not be forgotten whilst such things as you have heard are being said.

1290. *How did the Free Churches originate in England?*

Their origin can be traced back as far as 1567, when there were small independent congregations of religious people, strongly Protestant, who rejected not only Catholicism, but also the very idea of an established and national Church. In 1593 Henry Barrowe and John Greenwood were put to death for denying that the national Church of England was the true Church of Christ, that the Queen could make laws for the Church, and for insisting that each particular Church should govern itself. This idea of independent Churches gave rise to the Congregational Churches of today.

1291. *Whence came Presbyterianism?*

Presbyterianism was founded by John Knox in Scotland. John Knox was a Catholic priest who had thrown in his lot with John Calvin at Geneva. He began to preach Calvinistic Protestantism in Scotland about the year 1555. He was expelled from the country, but returned in 1559. By Acts of the Scottish Parliament Protestantism under the form preached by John Knox was made the established religion of Scotland in 1560. Presbyterianism, therefore, was founded by John Knox, and dates from 1560 as an organized Church.

1292. *Are not Methodists very sincere people?*

Many of them are. There are sincere people in every Church. But the Methodist Church cannot be the true Church of Christ. Traced back historically, it merges into Anglicanism. In 1728 John Wesley was ordained as an Anglican clergyman. He gathered together a group of earnest Anglicans who met for study and prayer, and who lived according to such strict rules that they were called "Methodists." They had no intention of leaving the Church of England. In 1738 John Wesley began his campaign as a revivalist preacher, and the hostility of Anglican authorities who resented his unorthodox ways led to the establishment of the separate "Wesleyan" or "Methodist" Church. Methodists teach salvation by faith in Christ and an experienced interior conversion. Apart from that they do not stand for any distinctive point of teaching or Church discipline. Formal Creeds and set forms of worship have little appeal for them.

1293. *Is not the "Church of Christ" the only true name for a Church mentioned in the Bible?*

No. Christ described His Church in very many significant ways—all of which apply to the Catholic Church, and the Catholic Church only.

1294. *The "Church of Christ" was established on the Day of Pentecost.*

The true Church of Christ commenced then, but not what are called the Protestant "Churches of Christ." These can be traced back to a Rev. Alexander Campbell, who was born in 1788, and who was originally a Presbyterian. As Mr. Campbell grew up, he pressed the Protestant principle of "The Bible Only" to its extreme limits, and repudiated all creeds or statements of doctrine. He therefore felt compelled to leave the Presbyterians who clung to the Westminster Confession, based on Calvinism, and became a wandering preacher affiliated with the Baptists. However he was never strictly a Baptist, and soon began writing and lecturing as a free lance religious teacher. He soon gathered some devoted followers, and in 1827 these followers formed themselves into a sect called the "Disciples of Christ." The Rev. Mr. Campbell died in 1866, and his followers fell into disputes concerning methods of organization. As a result two sections arose, calling themselves respectively the "Progressives," and the "Conservatives." The "Progressives" retained the title "Disciples of Christ," whilst the "Conservatives" took the new title "Churches of Christ." As the division took place about the year 1900, the "Church of Christ" as an independent body dates from the beginning of this century.

1295. What are the doctrines of the Church of Christ?

Since those who form what are called the "Churches of Christ" repudiate creeds, it is not possible to state their doctrines very clearly. They say at least that people must be Christians, but they will not state what Christians must believe. They demand, of course, that the Bible be accepted as God's Word, but no exact statement of what the Bible means can be imposed on anybody by those who maintain the right of private interpretation. Probably the members of the "Churches of Christ" would like to be described simply as "Bible Christians," and nothing more.

1296. On what grounds do you reject the claim of the "Churches of Christ" to be the true form of Christianity?

On the score that they ignore or reject the faith, worship, and discipline Christ intended to prevail in His Church. Also their basic principle, held together with other Protestants, that the Bible only is the one rule of faith is false. Moreover, a Church which cannot trace back its history beyond 1827 is 1827 years too late to be the Church founded by Christ Himself. We have seen the force of that reason when dealing with the truth of the Catholic Church.

1297. I am a Baptist, and I believe that St. John the Baptist himself was the founder of our Church.

You are mistaken in that; and in any case such an origin would be of no real value for one who professes to be a Christian. The New Testament insists that we must follow Christ, not St. John the Baptist. For the preaching of John the Baptist was essentially a preparation for Christ. He himself told his followers not to remain his disciples, but to become disciples of Christ. "He must increase," he said, "and I must decrease." To inquirers he said clearly, "I am not the Christ." In Acts XIX., 3-5, we find the Apostles baptizing again in the name of Christ those who had received only John's baptism. However, as a matter of fact, the Baptist Church cannot trace itself back to St. John the Baptist.

1298. How and when did it begin?

The first traces of the Baptists appeared in 1521. Martin Luther began the Protestant revolt against the Catholic Church in Germany in 1517. In 1521 a certain Thomas Munzer set up as a prophet on his own account, claiming that Luther did not go far enough in abolishing former ideas. He taught that no one who had been baptized as an infant was really baptized at all. His adherents, therefore, had to be baptized again. From this his followers got the name of "Anabaptists," or the "Rebaptizers." It was almost 100 years before this movement spread from the continent to England, although the English Baptists disclaim any connection with the Anabaptists. The first English Baptists were John Smyth and Thomas Helwys; and the first Baptist Chapel was commenced in London in 1611. John Smyth had been an Anglican minister prior to his becoming a Baptist, which he did in Germany through his association with the Anabaptists there. The Baptist Church, therefore, traces itself back to 1611 in England, and indirectly to 1521 on the Continent. Prior to that it was non-existent.

1299. How many Baptists are there in the world today?

The Baptists have gone off into many independent subdivisions, but all told they would number about 12 millions.

1300. What are their doctrines?

They are much like the Congregationalists or the Methodists, save in their main point of adult baptism only, and by immersion. For the rest, Baptists are required to accept the Bible as the Word of God and as the only and sufficient rule of faith; and, of course, they must believe in the Divinity of Christ and the atonement for sin wrought by His death on the Cross.

1301. In observing Sunday instead of Saturday the Roman Catholic Church is at variance with Scripture.

If Holy Scripture insisted that followers of Christ must observe Saturday, and not Sunday, then the Catholic Church would indeed be at variance with Scripture. But the Bible nowhere so much as hints that the followers of Christ must observe Saturday.

1302. If one wants the religion of Christ, he must become a Seventh Day Adventist.

If one really wishes for the religion of Christ, he certainly could not become a Seventh Day Adventist. If you believe in Christ, you must believe that He kept His promises. Now He said, "I will build My Church, and the gates of hell will not prevail against it." His true Church must have been founded by Him personally, and it could never go wrong. But who commenced the Seventh Day Adventists? And when? Certainly Christ did not establish that sect. It began in the 19th century —19 centuries too late to be the work of Christ. The Seventh Day Adventists are simply an offshoot of the Millerites, the followers of William Miller who began to give his religious ideas to the world in 1831.

1303. What is the significance of the word "Adventist"?

William Miller, born in 1782, was an uneducated American farmer who took to Bible reading, and got wrapped up in the idea of the Second Coming or Advent of Christ. In 1831 he believed he had discovered that the Second Advent of Christ was due in October, 1843. He began to preach this, gained some disciples, and they received the name of "Adventists." When Miller's prediction failed in 1843, he declared that Christ would come in the spring of 1844. When the end of the world did not come then, Miller apologized to his followers for the mistake in his calculations, and told them that the end would come in the autumn of 1844—to be precise, on October 22nd of that year. When that date failed, Miller washed his hands of the whole movement, admitted that he was wrong, and declared that he had no confidence in it. But a prophetess arose named Mrs. Ellen G. White, who consolidated the movement, adding the Seventh Day doctrine.

1304. Are there other Adventists besides the Seventh Day Observers?

Yes. It was Mrs. Ellen White who discovered that all Christians had fallen into error by their observance of Sunday. She declared that she had been taken up into heaven and shown the truth—that Saturday was the day to be observed. In 1845 she and her followers organized themselves into a body called the "Seventh Day Adventists"—"Seventh Day" because they insist on observing Saturday instead of Sunday; and "Adventists" to show their retention of the idea that the Second

Coming of Christ is near at hand. Other forms and offshoots of the Millerite movement are, "The Life and Advent Union," 1848; "The Advent Christian Church," 1861; "Church of God, Adventist," 1865; and the "Churches of God in Christ Jesus," 1888. Needless to say, all these sects fail with Protestantism, just as all other forms of the Protestant religion.

1305. Who founded the Plymouth Brethren?

This sect owes its origin to a Rev. John Nelson Darby, who was an Anglican clergyman in Ireland. He was an extremely Low Churchman, very Protestant in his outlook, and with a horror of the Catholic Church. Disgusted by the growing High Church tendencies associated with the Oxford Movement, he left Anglicanism in order to become a Protestant evangelist unattached to any Church. A pronounced "Bible-only" man, he began to preach a strict literalism in the interpretation of Scripture, even of the most mystical and symbolical passages. In 1827 he began to plead with people to separate from all Churches, whether Protestant or Catholic, and to reject ecclesiastical authority of any sort. In 1830 he went to Plymouth, and there founded his sect of the "Brethren." Hence the name, "Plymouth Brethren." But they were also known as the "Darbyites." Any brother was allowed to pray or preach, but those not gifted with utterance were discouraged from officiating. Despite the rejection of all ecclesiastical authority, however, the "Brethren" were expected to adopt the teachings of Darby himself; and the refusal by some to do so led to their excommunication. Various subsequent disputes have led to the formation of four different branches, at least, of the "Brethren."

1306. What are their doctrines?

They hold that the whole Christian body throughout the world fell away from the truth, and was rejected by God. They themselves are the "Lord's People" now. Darby taught strict Calvinism. For him, some people were predestined to hell; others to heaven. Personal merit makes no difference. Prayer must be chiefly the praise of God. Prayer of petition is not of much value. The Lord's Supper is celebrated every week. The Second Coming of Christ is likely to occur at any moment now, when He will inaugurate the Millennium, or His reign on earth for a thousand years. During that time the devil will be bound, and people will get a second and better chance of salvation. But the Brethren differ among themselves as to the nature of this Millennial reign of Christ.

1307. Are the Plymouth Brethren of any importance numerically?

They number about 11,000 throughout the world. The sect cannot expect to grow. The very doctrine of predestination, and the necessity of being elected by God, discourages efforts to convert others. If a man is predestined to join the Brethren, he will do so; if not, no preaching will persuade him to join. The members are not very interested, therefore, in the gaining of converts, and they profess to welcome only those whom the Lord sends them. They are not in the least disconcerted by the fact that the Lord inspires few to join their ranks, for they are essentially the "chosen few" as opposed to the multitudes whom God rejects. The Catholic Church knows, on the other hand, that she has been commissioned by Christ to go to all nations, and to "preach the Gospel to every creature."

1308. Do you recognize the "Catholic Apostolic Church" of the Irvingites?

We recognize it merely as a comparatively new Protestant sect which really commenced its existence in 1835.

1309. How did this Church originate?

Its history must begin with the Rev. Edward Irving who was born in 1792. Irving became a Presbyterian minister who preached with great success in Glasgow and London. He was of a mystical turn of mind, and got deeply interested in Biblical prophecies. As a result he began to preach the imminent coming of Christ, enkindling considerable excitement. In 1833 he was deposed and expelled from the Presbyterian Church for heretical teachings about Christ, but the majority of his congregation adhered to him, and a new form of Protestantism was developed. Irving thought that the special gifts of the Holy Ghost to the early Christians, and even the Apostolate itself, were restored to him and to his followers as a preparation for the Second Coming of Christ. He died in 1834. In the following year his followers organized what they called the "Catholic and Apostolic Church," under the fond delusion that the mere taking of these names would indeed render them Catholic and Apostolic. In reality, as I have said, they but formed a new Protestant sect.

1310. *What are their main doctrines?*

The Irvingites accept the Bible as the inspired Word of God, and the Apostles', Nicene, and Athanasian Creeds. They believe also in the gift of tongues and the spirit of prophecy in their midst, and live in expectation of the early coming of Christ. Tithing is part of their religion, or the giving to the Church by every member of one-tenth of his earthly goods. Their worship is based on the Eucharist, but they deny the Catholic doctrine of Transubstantiation. In 1842 they drew up a liturgy based on Greek, Roman, and Anglican rites, making use of Catholic Mass vestments.

1311. *If it is an Episcopal Church, are its Orders valid?*

The Irvingites are vaguely episcopal, though they have no Bishops in the ordinary sense of the word. They believe in a fourfold ministry of prophets, apostles, evangelists, and pastors. According to them, their apostles alone can minister the Holy Ghost by the laying on of hands, and alone have final doctrinal authority. Their apostles, therefore, would be equivalent in their view to Bishops. They claim that this ministry is valid if only by virtue of the direct communication of the Holy Spirit, independently of any need of uninterrupted transmission from the Apostles. But the whole thing is a structure of religious imagination opposed to the teachings of the New Testament. And the Catholic Church certainly rejects their Orders as invalid, and the sect as but another peculiar form of Protestantism.

1312. *Does the Catholic Church recognize the Salvation Army as in any way representative of genuine Christianity?*

No. As a religious body the Salvation Army is a form of Protestantism which the Catholic Church cannot but reject. It was founded by William Booth, an ex-Wesleyan minister. Disagreeing with Methodist ways, he left the Wesleyans in 1861 to become an independent evangelist. In 1865 he and his wife began to devote themselves to street preaching and rescue work in the slums of London. In 1877 he organized his converts into the Salvation Army, with himself as General, with the avowed purpose of working for the conversion of the poor and the alleviation of their temporal needs. But the whole movement is characterized by an un-Catholic, and even an anti-Catholic outlook.

1313. *Does not the Army agree with the Catholic Church that men owe their redemption to the Precious Blood of Christ?*

Yes. But the Salvation Army has an extremely Protestant view of the nature of the Christian religion in other vital points—a view radically opposed to the Catholic concept. Where the Army preaches, "Believe on Christ and be saved," the Catholic Church insists that no one, whilst still in this life, can actually be termed "saved"; and that it is the will of Christ that all should believe in the Catholic

Church, accepting all that she teaches and commands in the name of Christ. This involves acceptance of the Catholic Faith, the worship of God by assistance at the Sacrifice of the Mass, the reception of the Sacraments instituted by Christ, and the fulfillment of those good works for the love of God which are demanded by Christian virtue.

1314. *Through the Salvation Army God provides for a certain class of people not reached by the Catholic Church.*

God does not need the Salvation Army for that. He can provide by divine grace for men outside the fold of the Catholic Church in a thousand and one ways. He does so for infidels, Mahometans, Anglicans, Presbyterians, Methodists, Adventists, and a host of others. If the apparent good done by the Salvation Army is proof that God Himself inspired its creation, then the apparent good done by all other Protestant organizations is proof that He inspired them also. And we cannot admit that God inspired all these conflicting religious bodies—bodies, also, which unite in denying the claims of that Catholic Church which Christ did undoubtedly establish.

1315. *Are not Salvation Army methods preferable for simple people incapable of intellectual study to the Catholic Sacramental system?*

Under no circumstances could we say that. For, firstly, we can never admit that any means devised by men could be preferable to those instituted by Christ Himself. Secondly, we cannot say that the Catholic Sacramental system is in any way unsuitable for simple people; for Catholic children are well able to appreciate the significance of the Sacraments and to benefit by them. The value of the Sacraments does not depend upon the intellectual capabilities of the recipients. Thirdly, you seem to argue on merely natural grounds, not making sufficient allowance for the fact that Catholic Faith is a gift of divine grace, which is as difficult for intellectual people to attain as for simple people, and as easy for simple people as for intellectuals.

1316. *The Catholic way may be better for some types of people, but the Salvation Army way is superior for others.*

Our Lord gave His religion for all mankind, and that religion is the Catholic religion. Had He thought variations necessary for different types, He would have incorporated them in the religion He established. He did not do so. Nor can a way which involves the preaching of heresy be better for anybody in reality and absolutely speaking, whatever good it may accidentally accomplish or occasion. I am discussing the matter from the viewpoint of principle, of course. Though I do not think the Salvation Army justified as a substitute for the true Catholic Church, I have an immense admiration of the zeal and sincerity of its members; their demonstration of the courage of their convictions, and the sacrifices they make; the indifference to the world on the part of women members exhibited by their modest dress and behavior. But, with all their good will, they support and continue a movement which ignores and is independent of the true Church established by Christ.

1317. *The conclusion would be that the Salvation Army has a God-appointed, and not merely a man-designed place in this world.*

Though the Salvation Army has the best of intentions, there is no doubt that it is a man-designed enterprise for religious purposes. General Booth was a good man who wanted to do something for God and the salvation of souls. Being a stranger to the Catholic religion, and not satisfied with any other Church, he had to fall back on his own ideas. But they were very much his own ideas. However, though not God-appointed, the Salvation Army has resulted in much good, and in many genuine conversions from evil ways of living. And the explanation of that is simply this: Many a good man mistakenly does what is wrong with the best of intentions. In such cases, God overlooks the mistake, and even in spite of it blesses that man, and makes his work an occasion of blessing to others. But it always remains true that the work itself was really in opposition to God's will. Such is the position of General Booth and the Salvation Army. We Catholics rejoice at the sight of any good the Salvation Army may accomplish. But we are compelled to regret that it should be regarded by its members as a sufficient form of the Christian religion, and be allowed to occupy that place in the lives of its adherents which should really be held by Catholicism only. Many are thus contented to remain outside the Catholic Church, and to have so much less than our Lord really intended them to possess.

1318. *How does the Roman Catholic Church view Spiritualism?*

On April 24th, 1917, the Holy See issued the following decree: "It is not lawful to assist at any spiritualistic meetings, conversations with spirits, or manifestations of spirits. It matters not whether a medium be present or not, nor whether the meeting seems to be above board and apparently conducted from motives of piety. A Catholic may not be present at such meetings even as an onlooker, let alone asking questions of departed spirits and listening to their supposed replies."

1319. *How do you account for the supernatural powers of some spiritualistic mediums?*

Some of the phenomena produced by spiritualistic mediums are due to dexterity and fraud; some to natural clairvoyant and telepathetic powers; some to the influence of evil spirits. None can be ascribed to good spirits. God does not work that way, nor do His good ministering angels.

1320. *Do departed souls return to speak at spiritualistic meetings?*

No. With God's special permission, and by His power, it would be possible for a departed soul to communicate with those still in this world. But I deny that this occurs at spiritualistic seances. Supposed communications from deceased people at such weird gatherings are due to fraud on the part of the mediums; or are only imaginary and due to mental suggestion imposed by a medium; or are created by some dupe's own excited and expectant psychological state; or due to impersonation, some evil spirit exerting its influence and pretending to be this or that departed personality. Not only the Catholic Church condemns spiritualism. No professing Christian should have anything to do with it and its occult practices.

1321. *Catholics believe in the communications of the Saints.*

We do not believe in any communication with the souls of departed human beings in any spiritualistic way. Those souls are not in a condition of life adapted to such communication with us in this world. If God wishes, He can by a miracle permit such communications, but that very rarely happens and is quite abnormal. The Communion of Saints means simply that we who belong to the same Christ as fellow members of Him can benefit by the merits of the Saints and by their intercession. Communication with them is by prayer on our part. We are certain that they enjoy the very Vision of God, in which Vision they are aware of our prayers to them. But souls which have not attained to the Vision of God have no normal medium by which they can be aware of our doings in this world.

1322. *By not believing in spiritualism the Church discourages inquiries which could lead to the discovery of knowledge not possessed by herself.*

The Church does not believe in spiritualism as a semi-religious cult. She does believe in the existence of a spirit-world. God Himself is a pure spirit. Angels are spirits. So, too, are departed souls, and likewise devils. But the Church does not rely on spiritualism to provide her with the truth she must teach to mankind. She has received that truth from Jesus Christ who commanded her to teach mankind all that He had taught her. In the natural order the Church encourages men to discover all that science can teach them. In the supernatural order, she remains strictly faithful to the teachings of Jesus Christ. And she condemns spiritualism as a movement with all its works. If men want supernatural progress, let them seek to unite themselves with God by prayer and by the Sacraments of Christ, not with spirits by superstitious incantations in dark corners, moved rather by a morbid curiosity than by any desire to serve God and sanctify their souls. Baron Von Hugel rightly said, "One never gets any spiritual ideas out of spiritualism."

1323. *The Bible speaks of visions received by men, and of voices heard prompting to a certain course of action.*

The Bible records that such things happened at times to certain people. But it does not say that they will happen to all. If you came to me to say that you had received a vision of some departed person, you would not convince me by producing documentary proof that St. Paul had a vision whilst on the way to Damascus. His vision would not prove yours; and I would certainly not take your mere word for it.

1324. *Why do you doubt visions today, or treat them as being of the devil, or as due to insanity, or a temporary delusion?*

The presumption is against God's departure from His ordinary ways. And the giving of visions is not God's ordinary way of acting. Therefore I would take it for granted that a supposed vision would be due, not to God, but to some physiological or psychological cause, or to the influence of some evil spirit. Certainly all such causes would have to be positively disproved before I would go on to consider the vision in a supernatural light. That is ordinary prudence, from which the Christian religion dispenses no one. If a case were submitted to me, I would first weigh very carefully all the natural qualities of the person concerned. Is he neurotic, nervous, hysterical? Or is he of a calm, well-balanced temperament, and in good bodily health? Is he normal mentally, or endowed with an extravagant imagination? I would weigh well his virtue. Is he utterly sincere and humble, or eaten up with pride, and given to vanity, boasting, and untruthfulness? Then I would examine the nature of his vision, and ask myself whether it in any way conflicted with the doctrines of Christian Faith already revealed by God; or whether it was in strict accordance with Christian holiness and moral decency. I would note also its effects upon himself —good, or bad. The Catholic Church has laid down many such tests. She does not deny the possibility of such things; but she does deny the right of any man to accept them as from God with blind credulity.

1325. *The Bible prophesies that such things will be.*

The Bible does not say that such things will occur always to everybody. Nor are they at all necessary. Visions do not make the recipient of them any better or holier. God may grant visions at times to the Saints because they are Saints. But they are not Saints because they have visions. They are Saints because they avoid sin as a very plague, and courageously practise Christian virtue. It is virtue and goodness that matter, not visions.

1326. *The Bible should at least dispose you to accept spirit manifestations claimed by spiritualism.*

That is not so. The evidence produced by spiritualists has nothing like the value of the evidence of Sacred Scripture. I do not deny that, at times, spirit-beings may be responsible for some of the manifestations at spiritualistic seances. But, if they are, they are not good, but evil spirits. God has given His complete revelation through Christ. Also, since good spirits are in perfect accordance with the will of God, they could not be sent by Him to reveal the contradictory and often blasphemous doctrines claimed by spiritualists to come from the spirit-world. Moreover, if Scripture has any authority, we must obey its precepts. What are they? "Let there not be found among you anyone that seeketh the truth from the dead." Deut. XVIII., 10. In Lev. XX., God absolutely condemns the man or woman who claims to have a "divining spirit"—not a very comforting reflection for the modern medium. The Prophet Isaiah (VIII., 19) says, "When they shall say to you: Seek of people with a prophesying spirit and of diviners who mutter in their enchantments, should not the people seek of their God instead of seeking comfort for the living from the dead?"

1327. *I John, IV., 1, tells us to "try the spirits, if they be of God."*

St. John is not referring to spiritual beings of another world than this. He is speaking of impulses and inclinations which come into our minds, and which can lead to disaster if people insist on following private judgment. He also refers to the spirit of other people's teachings. Immediately he makes this clear. "Believe not every spirit," he says, "for many prophets have gone out into the world." I Jn. IV., 1. We must try the spirit of these teachings to see if they be in conformity with the true doctrine revealed by Christ. How are we to know that true doctrine? If every man is to decide for himself what that true doctrine is, we are back in chaos again. Christ knew this, and took the precaution of establishing the Catholic Church, promising to preserve it from error till the end of time. If any doctrine contradicts the authentic teaching of the Catholic Church, it is false.

1328. *What is your judgment of Christian Science?*

I regard it as a violation of Christian teaching as well as of science and reason. Those good people who take it up so enthusiastically have not lost their attachment to a vague Christian sentiment, but they have lost their grip on the fundamental truths of Christianity, and have no real idea of science and the demands of logic. Mrs. Eddy, the accepted prophetess who gave this new religion to the world in 1875, denied that Jesus is the Eternal Son of God made man. Mr. H. A. L. Fisher, Warden of New College, Oxford, is right when he says that "for the Christian Scientist, a brilliant pioneer in drugless healing has taken the place of the suffering Figure on the Cross." The whole religion depends on faith in Mrs. Eddy as a substitute for faith in Christ. As for science, when a woman rules out anatomy and physiology on the score that they suppose matter, and that matter is unreal and non-existent, she stands condemned as the very embodiment of the unscientific. And the system is absurd, because the absurd violates reason and logic. Mrs. Eddy tells us that "matter is an erroneous belief of mortal mind." Then she declares that "mortal mind is nothing." How nothing can begin thinking, and produce a real thought, even though it be an erroneous thought, is beyond all comprehension. Page after page of her book "Science and Health" is filled with similar nonsense. It simply doesn't make sense. And it is an insult to the God of Truth to assert that such a religion is His responsibility. The only excuse for good and sincere people who take up Christian Science is that they are incapable of logical thought, and do not understand Sacred Scripture.

1329. *Christian Science is based absolutely on the teachings of the Holy Bible.*

It is based on the unchristian and unscientific nonsense written by Mrs. Mary Baker Eddy, and falsely ascribed by her to the Bible.

1330. *Jesus meant all generations of His followers to have the power to heal the sick.*

Had He intended that, you can be quite sure that all His followers would have possessed the power. For Christ, being God, could undoubtedly accomplish His designs. The fact, therefore, that not all His followers have possessed the power is indication enough that such was not His intention. Any explanation which does not fit in with the known facts must be rejected. But, in reality, there is not a text in the New Testament which implies such a continued power to be manifest in all followers of Christ. He came to save men from sin, and to induce them to live holy lives. He did not come to bestow upon all men the powers of miracles. Holiness does not consist in doing startling things, or in seeking an escape from the cross of suffering.

1331. *Jesus said, "He that believeth on Me, the works that I do shall he do also." Jn. XIV., 12.*

Jesus had just told the Apostles that He would soon leave them, but He consoled them by saying that He was going to the Father whose work He had come to accomplish, and who would continue to work through them in their task of establishing the Church He had inaugurated. And He promises that the power of God will not be less evident in their work than in His. But there is no suggestion whatever that the special providence watching over the initial stages of the Church would continue to operate always and in the same way through all generations. And, as I have said, the facts themselves exclude the possibility of such having been the intention of Christ.

1332. *He mentioned the signs that would follow those who believe.*

The signs He mentioned did follow the first believers in Jesus, being verified now in this individual, now in that. And they contributed greatly to the solid establishing and rapid expansion of the infant Christian Church. But it is going far beyond anything contained in the text to suggest that such signs were meant always to follow all believers in all ages, so that they should be a permanent feature in the lives of all who profess the Christian religion. Moreover, once more, the facts of history exclude such an interpretation.

1333. *St. James says, "The prayer of faith will heal the sick man." Jas. V., 15.*

Those words occur in the midst of a passage describing the Sacrament of Extreme Unction. Immediately prior to them, St. James declares that the priests of the Church should anoint the sick with oil in the name of the Lord. And he adds that, if the sick man be in sin, his sins will be forgiven him. There is no reference to an infallible and ever-ready panacea for all temporal ills. The idea of holding out the recovery of bodily health as a bribe to attract recruits is utterly foreign to the religion of Christ Who said, "If anyone will come after Me, let him deny himself, take up his cross, and follow Me." Matt. XVI., 24. Christian Science, with its impression that Christ came to the world primarily to heal the sick, labors under a complete misconception of the nature of His life-work on behalf of humanity. Jesus came to teach us to avoid sin and all moral evil, and to practice virtue in the midst of the trials of this life. And He died on the Cross to expiate our sins, and to make a heavenly and eternal destiny possible to us as the result of our efforts to serve Him.

1334. *Catholics say that sufferings can't be helped, and that it should be our joy to suffer; but Christian Science says it is one's own fault if one suffers.*

Suffering has ever been a problem to man. Deeply sensitive to this problem, some people have cried out that there is no God. But that does not better things.

They have their sufferings just the same, and merely forfeit the one source of consolation. As G. K. Chesterton remarks, "These people say: Grin and bear it like a Stoic. But the trouble is that if you bear it like a Stoic, you don't grin." Other people, religiously-minded, insist that there is a God, but deny that there is any real suffering. Thus the Christian Scientist will tell you that suffering is unreal, a mental mistake. You wrongly think you are suffering, and if only you decide to think that you are not suffering, you won't suffer. But this fantastic solution does not solve the problem. It merely violates common sense, leaves people suffering just the same, and dries up the wellsprings of human sympathy. Compassion is necessarily lessened by a mental contempt for those we do not believe to be really suffering at all, but who have merely given way to a weakness of mind. It is hard to respect one whom we think to be a sham. On the other hand, Catholics deny neither God nor suffering. They say that a genuine love of God will give peace in the midst of suffering, and that this alone can do so. Genuine love of God always means happiness. It does not always mean pleasure. It is as much at home with pain as it is with pleasure, for it proves itself by self-sacrifice. Catholics see the love of Christ choosing such intense suffering for them on the Cross, and their love of Him makes them glad to share in suffering, blending their pain with His. And that gives the peace of Christ in their souls, a peace the world can neither give nor take away from them. And it is this attitude which gives the power to communicate peace to others.

1335. *I have been asked to join the Christadelphians. Could you give me some information concerning them?*

The Christadelphian sect was founded in America by a man named John Thomas, who lived from 1805 till 1871. He was a member of an American sect called the "Disciples of Christ" or the "Campbellites," founded by Alexander Campbell, an ex-Presbyterian minister, in 1827. Thomas, reading the Bible with his own peculiar mentality, decided that the whole of Christendom had gone astray, including the Campbellites, and therefore decided to become a freelance Bible teacher. He taught that the doctrine of the Trinity is erroneous; that Christ was a prophet but not the Son of God; that man has not an immortal soul but just ceases utterly to exist at death. However, the Christadelphian will be restored to life in this world and will live forever on earth when Christ returns to be King of this world with His headquarters at Jerusalem. Thomas predicted that Christ would return in 1910 but his present-day followers are not disconcerted by the non-fulfillment of that prophecy. Their title "Christadelphians" signifies "Brethren of Christ," and they still await, in suspense and hope, the early return of Christ. They call upon all to "come out" of the "iniquitous system of the Papacy and its offspring, the Anglican Church," as well as from all the Protestant sects. Since the present state of human society is, in their idea, hopelessly corrupt, they do not engage in any works of social or political betterment. They wait simply for God to come to judge it. There is no need for me to add that the Christadelphian religion is not that of either the Old or New Testaments, but the fruit of the personal imaginations of the founder, John Thomas, of Brooklyn, N. Y.

1336. *What is your opinion of British Israelism?*

It is a non-Christian substitute for religion based upon an unbridled imagination, a denial of history, and a perverted sense of patriotism which would like to exalt the British Empire and the United States of America at the expense of other nations. It is really a freak religion which goes to the opposite extreme from the position adopted by Judge Rutherford. Where Judge Rutherford declares that the British Empire and America are Satan's oganizations, the British Israelites declare that they alone constitute God's chosen people on the face of the earth.

1337. What do British Israelites teach?

They teach that, with the coming of Christ, the Jewish religion was not abolished in favor of Catholicism. The true religion was preserved amongst ten tribes of Israel who got lost, and wandered far afield to the British Isles. As descendants of these lost tribes the British nation and the United States of America constitute God's chosen people today. Those who want to belong to the true "Israel" today must, therefore, belong to one of these two nations by blood relationship. There is no need to belong to any Church. Needless to say, the British and American Governments are blissfully unconscious of the sublime dignity and greatness which the British Israelites wish to thrust upon them. In 1932 the British Israel World Federation issued as a National Message that the end of the world was coming in 1934, when God's people, the British Empire and the United States, would be arrayed in warfare against the rest of the world. The final battle of Armageddon would then occur, when the English and the Americans would triumph over God's enemies, the French, Germans, Italians, Russians, Spanish, and other peoples.

1338. Why do you disagree with the system?

Because it is absolutely opposed to the teachings of Christ, to the facts of history, and to the ordinary laws of logic and reason. Christ sent His Apostles to teach all nations. The Jews were the chosen race for the preservation of God's revelation until the coming of Christ. But there is no chosen race in any national sense since the coming of Christ whose religion is for all men of good will. The British Israel Theory is a denial of Christ, and of His work of redemption. Again, that the British people are descendants of the lost tribes of Israel is quite unhistorical, and without any foundation other than the fantastic dreams of the originators of this absurd doctrine. Reason, too, is violated by the ridiculous arguments so often put forward in its favor, arguments based on verbal quibbling in the English language which depend for their success on the reader's ignorance of Hebrew. For example, to prove British descent from Israel, we are invited to consider the word "Saxon." Compare with that the two words, "Isaac's son." Cut out the "I," and you have "Saac's son" or "Saxon." There is scarcely need to comment upon such a travesty. 1934, when the world should have come to an end, has come and gone. And with the failure of that prediction, belief in British Israelism, which should never have come, should at least have gone. But there will always be people in whose credulous souls hope springs eternal, and who can forget yesterday in the glorious prospects of tomorrow. At any rate, no Christian could adopt the British Israel religion without denying the mission of Christ, and abandoning the Christian Faith.

1339. Is there nothing in the claim that the British constitute the lost tribes of Israel?

None whatever. The theory is based on guesswork, misinterpretation of Scripture, and the violation of history. Professor Rawlinson rightly remarks that the theory can appeal only to the ignorant and unlearned, or to those "who are unaware of the absolute and entire diversity in language, physical type, religious opinions, and manners and customs, between the Israelites and the various races from which the British can be shown historically to be descended." The British Israel Theory sets at defiance all ethnological and linguistic evidence. Sir E. B. Tylor remarks that "there is indeed no doubt that this abject nonsense has a far larger circulation than all the rational ethnology published in England."

1340. Is it possible to trace the lost tribes to any country?

There are no lost tribes to be traced. The whole idea of the lost tribes is based on absurd mystical interpretations of a few passages in Scripture; and on the conditions proposed by the exponents of the "Lost Tribe" theory, any one nation or country would do as well as any other. Remnants of the tribes are supposed to have been found marauding in the Afghan passes, wandering with the reindeer in Lapland, or slaughtering human victims in ancient Mexico. Deluded people have found the "Lost Tribes" wherever they have wanted to find them.

1341. Do you deny that the king of England is directly descended from David of Israel?

I do. And there is not a member of the Royal Family who would not repudiate the notion. Nor is there a reputable historian who would not reject the idea the moment it was put before him. As one distinguished scholar has said, "The theory could have been invented only by persons equally uncritical in history and etymologies, and to whom the history of nations was quite unknown." It is self-evidently false to suppose an earthly throne to be the throne of David, and an earthly kingdom restricted to a section of the peoples of the earth to be the essentially spiritual and universal kingdom of Christ predicted in the Old Testament. Christ, of David's line, is He who is now reigning in the universal Church He established; and the substitution of the king of England for Christ is a blasphemy which the king of England would be the first to disclaim.

1342. According to the British Israelites, the Great Pyramid is shrouded in mystery.

There is much that is mysterious about the pyramids. But, religiously unbalanced people have tried to attach to the pyramids a lot of mysteries of their own making.

1343. There are marks on the Great Pyramid whereby dates of happenings past and future can be determined.

That is not true. There are no intelligible inscriptions on the Great Pyramid. Religious eccentrics have, therefore concentrated on the formation of the interior passages, working out from their angles, direction, and length, all kinds of predictions of the future.

1344. What is the Catholic belief concerning these historical and prophetic markings?

There are no such markings, and Catholic belief is not concerned with the pyramids. Matters of purely geographical, anthropological, and historical interest are to be sought in their proper place, the textbooks of explorers, archaeologists, historians and others. The Great Pyramid is not an integral part of the Christian religion; and that it is a kind of Bible in stone inspired by Almighty God is too absurd and farfetched to merit discussion.

1345. I might mention that Catholics are excluded from the inheritance of British Israel.

Catholics desire to be excluded. Christ died for all mankind, and the Catholic Church prefers fidelity to Christ. Once the word "British" is introduced, that is the end of any claim to catholicity of outlook. The soul of a Negro, or of a Japanese, or of a German, is as dear to the Catholic Church and to Christ as that of a British or an American subject. Christ abolished the restriction of the true religion to the chosen people of Israel, and extended it to all mankind.

1346. Was the lapse of the Liberal Catholics from Roman Catholic unity a recent event?

The so-called "Liberal Catholic Church" never lapsed from unity with Rome for the simple reason that it never was in union with Rome. Its origin was as follows:

HOLY ORDERS OF LIBERAL CATHOLICS

In 1875 a Colonel Olcott and a Madame Blavatsky founded a Theosophical Society in New York. Later this society was joined by a Mrs. Annie Besant, and still later by a Mr. Leadbeater, an ex-Anglican clergyman. The doctrine of these Theosophists at first was very nebulous, and incorporated much from ancient Indian philosophies. In the beginning Theosophy claimed to be outside and above all religions, and to be the key to the whole mystery of existence. Yet all must remain mystery, so that whilst members might believe what they liked, they ought not to maintain that they have the truth, nor to admit that anyone else has it. But Mr. Leadbeater, who had been expelled from the society in 1906 but was readmitted later on, decided to "religionize" Theosophy; and it was he who commenced the Liberal Catholic Church. He chose this name because he grafted on to his Theosophical ideas forms of worship which he borrowed from the Catholic liturgy. From this you can see that the "Liberal Catholic Church" has no more connection with the true Catholic Church than the king of Siam would have with the king of England, were he to model his coronation robes on those worn by the English king.

1347. Have not the Liberal Catholics valid Holy Orders derived from the Roman Catholic Church?

They claim a succession of valid Orders ultimately traced back to Rome. In 1870, at the time of the Vatican Council, a few Bishops left the Catholic Church and became schismatics. They set up what they called "The Old Catholic Church" in Holland. By these an Anglican minister got himself consecrated as a Bishop. This reverend gentleman, a Mr. Willoughby, in turn consecrated a Mr. Wedgewood, who styled himself the first "Presiding Bishop of the Old Catholics" in Great Britain. In 1916 this "Presiding Bishop Wedgewood" consecrated Mr. Charles Leadbeater as "Regionary Bishop of Australia," presumably with the idea of founding the "Old Catholic Church" in that country. But Bishop Leadbeater was not true to his trust. He was a dreamer of weird dreams, and envisaged a new religion altogether. He invented a blend of Theosophy, Spiritism, and an incredible number of superstitions, merged with Catholic forms of worship derived from the Roman liturgy. In 1918 the title "Liberal Catholic Church" was adopted for this new cult of astral, etheric, and from the Catholic point of view, blasphemous nonsense.

1348. Do you deny that the Liberal Catholic priesthood is valid?

I do. It is certain that Christ never intended His priesthood to be transmitted for such purposes as these Liberal Catholics have in mind. Bishop Leadbeater, of course, wanted to say that he had incorporated the very essentials of Catholic liturgy in his religious services—and above all, that he possessed a valid Eucharist. There is scarcely need to remark that, whilst Theosophists regard Bishop Leadbeater's Liberal Catholicism as a wholesale corruption of Theosophy, we ourselves regard it as a still more serious corruption of the Catholic liturgy.

1349. Liberal Catholics say that Rome itself recognizes their Orders as valid.

That is not true. No declaration or document from Rome acknowledging the Orders of these Theosophical Liberal Catholics as valid has ever been given. If a Liberal Catholic Bishop became a convert to the Catholic Church, he would find himself unacceptable either as a Bishop or as a priest to the Catholic authorities. Were he otherwise eligible, and wished to be a priest, he would find himself compelled to submit to ordination at the hands of a Catholic Bishop. If the Liberal Catholics dispute this verdict, let them submit their case to Rome, and ask for a Decree acknowledging their Orders as valid. In the absence of such a decision they have no right to say that Rome recognizes their Orders.

1350. What Catholic articles of belief are rejected by the Liberal Catholics?

All of them. Whatever Christian ideas the Liberal Catholics may profess to accept, it is certain that they do not accept them as orthodox Christians understand them. Mr. Leadbeater denied the divine inspiration of the Bible, declaring that science has rendered it incredible. But he asserts that there is an underlying element of truth in Christianity which can be understood only by a special gift of clairvoyance. His writings give us an extraordinary mixture of Indian philosophy, modern Theosophy, Spiritualism, and distorted Christian teachings. Liberal Catholics deny the absolute, final, and unique validity of Christianity, and claim to find in it a weird and mysterious significance which all genuine Christians must repudiate.

1351. Are the Witnesses of Jehovah an offshoot of the Russellites?

They are rather a continuation of the Russellites. The present leader of the Witnesses of Jehovah, who calls himself Judge Rutherford, is but the successor of Pastor Charles T. Russell, who founded the movement.

1352. Russell was a pious, devout Christian, and a faithful follower of Christ.

Pastor Russell was born in America in 1852. He was first a Congregationalist, then dabbled in Seventh Day Adventism, and finally set up for himself as a prophet announcing the Second Coming of Christ. His piety was not true piety. It was an unbalanced religious mania centered entirely in himself. He set himself up on a pedestal as the sole object of his worship. Nor was he a Christian, for he denied the divinity of Christ, declaring that Christ was really Michael the Archangel who came in the flesh to redeem mankind. That is not Christian doctrine. Nor was Russell a follower of Christ in practice. His wife divorced him for infidelity; and he made money by selling what he called "miracle wheat" at sixty dollars a bushel to credulous farmers, the fraud being eventually stopped by the Federal authorities, who made him refund the money.

1353. No one wants to hear scandalous incidents in Pastor Russell's life. We could dig up scandals amongst Roman Catholics.

Without any digging at all the writers in Russellite books and papers delight in inventing scandals about Catholics. But do not think for a moment that I have any idea of retaliation. I do not believe in arguments against a religion which are drawn from unworthy conduct of members belonging to that religion. If a man does not live up to a religion, it is proof only that he does not live up to it. It is not necessarily proof that his religion is bad. It may be that he has not really practiced his religion. And one judges the value of a medicine from people who take it, not from those who neglect it. But Pastor Russell himself is in a very different position from that of subsequent followers. He offers himself to the public as a prophet, and as the founder of a new religion. And as he wants his religion to be public property, he is a public figure whose life should be an open book. Christ is the Founder of the Catholic Church, and we are willing that men should examine both His teachings and His life. But, in the same way, we claim the right to test both the life and teachings of all other founders of religions offered to the public.

1354. Pastor Russell was as well able to interpret Scripture as anyone.

How do you know that? What knowledge have you of Scripture by which you can check his interpretations? Russell traded on the ignorance of simpletons; and his followers still do the same. Throughout his books Russell pretended to deep learning, quoting Greek words, and frequently attributing a special sense to them which they never possessed in the original language at all. Challenged in an American Court, he had to admit that he did not know Greek, and he was unable to name the letters of the Greek alphabet. Russell poured out page after page of arrant nonsense which he tried to support by myriads of texts torn from their context and forced to mean whatever he wanted them to mean. If ever a man misused and abused Sacred Scripture, that man is Pastor Russell, although his successor, Judge Rutherford, runs him a very close second. Seldom have men given to the world a better example of those whom St. Peter describes as "wresting the Scriptures to their own destruction."

1355. What was Pastor Russell's doctrine?

He taught that the Second Coming of Christ began to take place, not visibly, but invisibly, in 1874. From that year commenced the "Millennium," or the reign of Christ in this world for 1000 years. At the end of the "Millennium" this earth will be turned into a vast garden of Eden. The wicked will be finally annihilated, and the good will inhabit this earthly paradise for all eternity, earthly rulers being abolished in favor of Christ, the King of the world. Religion, for him, was but a means to magnificent material prosperity.

1356. Who is Judge Rutherford?

He is the successor of Pastor Russell as leader of this fantastic movement—a kind of Elisha upon whom the mantle of the original prophet has fallen. Pastor Russell died in 1916, and Mr. Joseph Rutherford, one of the editorial committee of Russell's paper, "Zion's Watch Tower," secured control of the movement.

1357. Does Rutherford teach the same as Russell?

He teaches the basic ideas of Pastor Russell, with additional ideas of his own. He declares that the 1000 years' period is going on apace, and being rapidly inaugurated. In 1914 God handed over to Christ full authority over this world. A war at once took place in heaven between Christ with the good angels, and Satan with his evil gang. How Satan got back into heaven Mr. Rutherford does not say. However, Satan was cast out, and at once plunged "Christendom" into the World War of 1914. God stopped that war in 1918 for the express purpose of allowing Rutherford's agents to travel about distributing Rutherford's books by the millions, giving testimony of the approaching end. Rutherford has changed the name of the organization from that of the "Watch Tower Society" to that of the "Witnesses of Jehovah"—he being the Chief Witness. An additional contribution to the cause on his part is a still more fervent denunciation of all Christian Churches, Catholic and Protestant, as being in the hire of the devil; and more exact descriptions of the imminent and final catastrophe about to overwhelm mankind.

1358. Do not Judge Rutherford's books explain the Bible to the people?

No. He has deluded many people into distributing his books which explain what he mistakenly thinks the Bible to teach. In reality he teaches what is directly opposed to the Bible. He proclaims that some leader is to set up a kingdom in this world to the destruction not only of the Churches of all kinds, but of all present forms of government. He denounces all authority, civil or ecclesiastical, teaching principles of anarchy opposed to the explicit doctrine of Christ and the Apostles. St. Paul wrote to the Romans, "Let every soul be subject to higher powers, for there is no power but from God; and those that are, are ordained of God. Therefore he that resisteth the power, resisteth the ordinance of God." St. Paul therefore insisted on obedience to lawful civil authority, even in pagan Rome. St. Peter said, "Be ye subject, whether to the king as supreme, or to governors sent by him. For so is the will of God. Honor all men. Fear God. Honor the king." Yet Judge Rutherford tells us that "Christendom" is Satan's organization, and chiefly America and the British Empire. And in his fanaticism he promises the nations and the Churches a war such as has never been seen on the face of the earth, with all the forces of heaven pitted against his adversaries. He declares that "the worst tribulation that has ever afflicted mankind" is to come upon organized Christendom; and that the nations will get a "terrible drubbing." Of course he declares that he is not inciting sedition, and that he is merely advocating the cause of Christ who is to become the temporal king of this world—a title Christ indignantly repudiated and refused. "My kingdom," He said, "is not of this world."

1359. Is Judge Rutherford an accredited legal Judge?

No. He has no real title to call himself a judge at all. He was originally a court reporter at Boonville, Cooper County, Missouri, U. S. A. Familiar with court procedure, but without any formal training in law, he managed to get a license to practice as a lawyer in the State of Missouri, U. S. A. in 1892. Four times in Cooper County his turn as a local lawyer came to preside over the local court owing to the absence of the regular judge. And on each occasion he presided for one day only. The other local lawyers also took their turn on other occasions, and if Mr. Rutherford is entitled to claim to be a judge, then every lawyer in the State of Missouri is a judge! Every other lawyer rejects the idea; and "Judge" Rutherford, never officially appointed to such a position in his life, is masquerading under a title to which he has no real claim at all.

1360. At least he was engaged in a respectable and responsible profession before he was converted.

His record is not very impressive. In 1894, 1895, and again in 1897, he was in legal trouble himself, accused of sharp practice and unprofessional conduct. Later he was employed by Pastor Russell who was frequently involved in litigation, and thus came into contact with the Russelite organization. In 1916, as I have already said, he succeeded to the full control of that organization. In 1918 he was sentenced to twenty years' imprisonment for conspiracy and disloyalty in promoting military revolt in America, but was released with many other prisoners by an amnesty in 1919, after having served nine months in Atlanta Penitentiary.

1361. What is the trend, gist, and authority of Rutherford's teaching?

Its trend is to turn people into simple fools, impelling them to wander about, calling themselves Witnesses of Jehovah, and selling Judge Rutherford's booklets. Its gist is this: Civil governments, and all Churches, in fact, all religious, political and commercial powers in this world organized before the new commercialized religion of Judge Rutherford are the work of Satan, and under the control of Satan. Any day now—and so soon that "Millions Now Living Will Never Die"—God is going to smite all except those who accept Joseph Rutherford as their infallible guide and teacher. Of what authority is all this? Of none whatever. God neither invited Rutherford and his dupes to be His "Witnesses," nor did He dictate their "message."

1362. In Isaiah XLIII., 10, you will find the words, "Ye are my witnesses."

The Russellites do not prove their claim by pointing triumphantly to such a text. What they have to prove, if they wish to establish their case, is that those words were written of them, and truly apply to them.

1363. Do you consider the movement harmful?

It is harmful from almost every point of view. It is not in the least constructive. It is destructive, not only of Christianity, but of all lawful civil authority. Recently in Canada two distributors of Rutherford's books were sentenced to two months in jail and a fine of three hundred dollars. They appealed against the sentence, but their appeal was dismissed. The presiding judge said, "I find in these pamphlets a sapping of all authority, to be replaced only by anarchy and mob rule, unless some despot should present himself. The language, repeated and again repeated is grossly insulting." He added that their contents were beyond all permissible fair comment on other people's political, social, and religious tenets.

1364. Who is Rutherford's "Jehovah"?

Rutherford uses the term "Jehovah" for God. The word "Jehovah" is an English misspelling for "Jahveh" or "Yahweh," the Hebrew word for God. As the Mahometans say, "There is no God but Allah, and Mahomet is His prophet," so the Witnesses of Jehovah believe that there is no God but Jehovah, and that Rutherford is His prophet. Rutherford's main prophecy is that the end of the world is at hand, and that the only means of escape from the impending disasters is to join his Witnesses of Jehovah and sell his books from door to door.

1365. What is the religious character of his movement?

Rutherford declares that he does not believe in religion of any kind. He says that Satan invented religion, and that his own followers will have no religious obligations save to help him attack and denounce religion, sell his literature, and play his gramaphone records wherever possible.

1366. What is Satan's visible organization on earth?

Satan has no visible organization on earth. Christ has a visible organization —the Catholic Church. But Satan is the adversary of Christ, and adopts quite other methods. As Christ remarked, "Those that love the works of darkness come not to the light." Jn. III., 20. Satan is not so foolish as to betray his hand in his nefarious schemes. He is essentially a hidden worker. But whilst he has no visible organization of his own, he subtly makes use of organizations ostensibly established by men for commercial or other purposes. He inspires the daily press to give publicity to antichristian theories; he relishes the sight of publishing houses deluging the world with the thinly-veiled immorality of novels and other literature; birth-control clinics and easier divorce are favorable to his cause; and he influences political regimes to try to legislate religion out of existence. But, whilst with devilish cunning Satan makes a parasitical use of various human organizations, he has no visible organization of his own.

1367. Why is Judge Rutherford so opposed to "Christendom"?

Because that is the peculiar form in which the religious fanaticism of Mr. Joseph Rutherford happens to manifest itself. No mania, whether it be religious or otherwise, has any real reason other than the fact that it does break out as it does. Lunacy follows no set laws. Financially, of course, Rutherford's lunacy is very profitable.

1368. I agree with Judge Rutherford that the soul is not immortal. All ends for each of us with the grave. And on the Judgment Day only the good will rise. Satan's agents will remain utterly destroyed.

Rutherford's doctrine is self-contradictory. If we are completely extinguished by death, there will be no "you" to stay in the grave. Nor will the non-existent "good" be able to rise again. Being non-existent, they won't be able to do anything. They won't "be." Resurrection supposes some kind of continuity of existence. Complete cessation of existence denies the possibility of resurrection. God could choose to create other beings, but they would be other beings, and not the previous beings who had been completely annihilated. God will not utterly destroy any soul. The human soul is immortal of its very nature, and it is an insult to God's wisdom to suggest that He purposely endowed the soul with an indestructible nature only to undo His work in millions of human beings.

1369. *At least Judge Rutherford tells the truth about the Roman Catholic Church.*

Surely I, as a Catholic priest, should know what the Catholic religion really is. And I can assure you that Judge Rutherford has no idea of the Catholic religion. Of course you may doubt my honesty, and believe that I am only saying what I have to say. But if so, you will not doubt the verdict of the Anglican Bishop of Ballarat, Victoria, Australia, to whom the Witnesses of Jehovah submitted some of their literature, hoping that this Protestant Bishop would sympathize with their anti-Catholic bias. The Bishop wrote back to them, "I most strongly condemn the literature which you are distributing and selling. It is not, as you claim, Bible truth. It is most bigoted and dangerous error. You left me a booklet called "Uncovered," in which Judge Rutherford purports to deal with the teachings and claims of the Roman Catholic Chuch. This book is dangerously misleading on account of Judge Rutherford's profound ignorance of theology, and his gross misrepresentation of Bible truth. As an attempt to deal with the Roman Catholic position it is worthless. The books are so full of dangerously misleading matter that I feel they should be destroyed." There is no need for me to add anything to that verdict of the Anglican Bishop of Ballarat, who is no more inclined to accept the Roman Church than Judge Rutherford.

1370. *In vain Judge Rutherford has challenged members of the Catholic Hierarchy to public debate, so that the people can decide for themselves who is right.*

No sane person would humor an ignorant, deranged, and abusive charlatan whose one craving is publicity. Rutherford is as ignorant of his subject as he well could be. His challenge is as absurd as would be that of a child who is just commencing school, yet who would challenge Einstein to a debate on relativity. Again, Rutherford's books are filled with scurrilous abuse of the Catholic Church. Imagine a man calling another an unmitigated liar, and then calmly inviting him to a debate as to whether he is really an unmitigated liar or not!

1371. *By accepting, the Hierarchy could at least expose the wily influence of this so-called deceiver.*

Rutherford is not wily. He is but persistent and noisy. And his books can safely be left to the common sense of the average reader. If a person is so unintelligent that he cannot perceive their absurdity at a glance, he would certainly lack sufficient intelligence to see the force of any reply given during a debate.

1372. *Judge Rutherford has even challenged the Pope to debate with him.*

I gravely doubt whether the Pope is aware of that. But Judge Rutherford should not be upset. He is not the only one to be deprived of such a glorious experience. Even Aimee MacPherson has not had the honor of a debate with the Pope on the respective merits of Catholicism and the "Hot Gospellers."

1373. *How do you account for so many adopting Rutherford's teaching?*

By their ignorance and superstition, and by Rutherford's publicity methods. If you were to apply an intelligence test to the average simple soul engaged in tramping from door to door with Rutherford's books, the results would not be very impressive. In the midst of the misery resulting from economic distress and disastrous wars, there is a vast field for such exploitation amongst thousands of people who lack any real knowledge of religion yet are religiously inclined. A man who comes with the doctrine that Satan is directly responsible for the things they hate and dread is sure of disciples. And above all when he trades on their fears of a still more dreadful catastrophe in the near future, continually asserting that he alone knows the secret by which it can be escaped.

1374. Are not the Witnesses persecuted because they are showing that the Catholic Church does not teach the truth?

No. In many countries the civil authorities are beginning to realize that Rutherford's doctrines are anarchical and subversive of all lawful authority. When a man scatters far and wide throughout the land streams of booklets urging people to detest, hate, and fight against the "Beast," and then identifies the "Beast" as the United States of America and the British Empire, those responsible for the welfare of those countries are not doing their duty if they allow such propaganda to continue. Then, too, the fanatics who peddle the books from door to door disturb the peace and comfort of their fellow citizens, and constitute a public nuisance. People have the right to complain and ask protection from it. The Witnesses of Jehovah, of course, make capital out of this by calling it persecution. But because one who tells the truth may be persecuted, it does not follow that all who suffer opposition are telling the truth. There is scarcely a lunatic in an asylum who does not regard the restrictions placed upon him as a form of persecution. But sane people cannot help that, and they are quite justified in restraining a dangerous maniac. And the religious mania of Judge Rutherford is contagious among simpletons, and dangerous to the welfare of the State.

1375. I have been asked to join the Group Movement for the discussion of religion and the sharing of problems. Could you tell me something about this Movement?

Members of the "Oxford Group Movement" go in for what they call "Life-changing," or rapid emotional conversions. Small groups meet together and share out their personal and individual religious experiences, even to public confession of secret sins. Each is expected to be guided by the Holy Spirit in future conduct, and to aim at "a maximum experience of God." The movement is really a new form of Quakerism, with a few additions invented by the founder, Frank Buchman.

1376. Could you give me something of its history?

It is American in origin, having been started at Princeton, New Jersey, by the Rev. Frank Buchman, a Lutheran minister, in 1909. Frank Buchman was ordained as a Lutheran minister when he was 24 years of age. After four years of the ministry, he resigned from the American Lutheran Church, and went to England. There, one day, he went into a small Pentecostal Church during a service, and heard a woman preacher addressing a congregation of about 17 people. During the lady's discourse, he felt a wave of strong emotion welling up within him, and experienced a "very mighty change" in himself. After that he found that he had an uncanny and half-hypnotic influence over young men. He went back to America, and became a Y. M. C. A. secretary for a time. But, before long, he began experimenting as a "Life-changer," working among groups of young people for rapid, emotional, revivalist conversions. This he accomplished at what he called "House Parties" rather than revivalist meetings. The movement was suppressed in Princeton because it led to immoral excesses and fanaticism. Buchman went back to England with some American converts, and in 1921 began revivalist "House Parties" at Cambridge. The movement was then simply called "Buchmanism"; but later the name was changed to the "First Century Christian Fellowship." Buchman then conducted similar "House Parties" at Oxford, and in 1928 shrewdly took the name "Oxford

Group Movement," knowing that the publicity and reflected glory of Oxford, and association with the reputation of the famous Oxford Movement, would be no disadvantage.

1377. What is meant by "Life-changing"?

"Life-changing" consists in stimulating or receiving a new surge of religious sentiment, which gives the conviction that whereas you were a sinner you have become good, and that henceforth you will be able to remain good. It is a purely natural excitation which Mahometans, Hindoos, Buddhists, or any others could experience, and which has no necessary connection with Christianity. Where the old Revivalists asked, "Brother, are you saved?" Buchmanism asks, "Brother, are you changed?"

1378. What is "Sharing"?

"Sharing" is a kind of public confession of religious experiences and past sins. It is a form of community psycho-analysis. Not contrition, but "hilarity" is expected to accompany the admission of how far one has dared to go in iniquity. In a leading article the London "Times" rightly remarked that this "hawking" of past sins will tend to pride and boasting in the sharer whilst besmirching the minds of the listeners.

1379. What do "Groupers" mean by "Guidance"?

"Guidance" is an emptying of the mind and a waiting for an impulse from God. Frank Buchman says that such "guidance is available at every moment." But the scope for self-deception is immense. There is no test as to whether the impulse really comes from God or not. Frank Buchman says that individual ideas must be submitted to the "Group" for guidance and direction. But the "Group" is no safer as a guide than the individual. The following of blind impulses can ruin one's character, and make people creatures of every caprice and stray inclination. One "Grouper" publicly declared that she received "Divine Guidance" to get sausages for dinner! The Holy Spirit is Wisdom itself, and He does not stultify Himself, nor contradict Himself. He is not in any movement which would drag Christianity into disrepute, and even drag people from Christianity.

1380. I must say that I believe in the "Four Absolutes" as advocated by the Oxford Group.

No one could disagree with the ideal that one should be absolutely truthful, or honest, or pure, and so on, with all the Christian virtues. That is but an application of Christ's appeal that we should be perfect as our heavenly Father is perfect. However, it is not necessary to go to Buchmanism to learn that one should aim at perfection of life. It must be noted, too, that to profess belief in absolute standards is not to prove that one has attained them. Human nature being what it is, many will always fall short of their ideals. In fact, the majority of men will, and it is for the majority that provision must be made. Christ came to save, not the just, but sinners. And the Catholic Church makes room for both saints and sinners, cherishing the former, and laboring to convert the latter. She is not a select society for those only who can qualify by a complete and revolutionary change overnight into saints.

1381. Especially I admire the doctrine of restitution in part, if not in full.

Why "in part"? If harm has been done to others, restitution must be made in full. And until it has been made, the obligation remains. That, at least, is the Catholic doctrine.

1382. *This is better than the Catholic way of saying certain prayers to get forgiveness.*

That is not the Catholic way. A Catholic must be genuinely sorry for his sins against God's laws, confess them to a priest, make reparation to God by saying certain appointed prayers in a penitential spirit, and repair whatever harm his sins may have caused to his neighbor. The restitution idea which you have discovered in the Group Movement has been known and applied in Catholic theology for all the centuries of its existence.

1383. *What do you think of the "Oxford Group Movement"?*

It is a movement which every professing Christian should absolutely reject. Firstly, it violates its own principle of absolute honesty by its very title. It has no real connection with Oxford, and it is not honest to trade upon a similarity of sound in a title so closely resembling the "Oxford Movement." Oxford University is proud of the real Oxford Movement. It repudiates the "Oxford Groupers." Turning to its own inherent characteristics, it fails by default from the Christian point of view. One could be a "Grouper," yet not be a Christian at all. The Group imposes no doctrinal standards. In practice it preaches not the Way of the Cross, but "the joy, the thrill, and the fun" of a new religious experience. An American paper called the "New Yorker" defined the Movement as "a form of evangelism which combines the advantages of mysticism, mesmerism, spiritualism, eroticism, psychoanalysis, and high-power salesmanship." It plays with religion as with a new toy. We are told that Buchman himself is "a piece of divinity hungering and thirsting for expression"; that the word to pray consists of four letters—P-R-A-Y—and that these letters mean, "Powerful Radiograms Always Yours." Even the holy name of Jesus is not free from this grotesque mockery. J-E-S-U-S has been discovered to mean, "Just Exactly Suits Us Sinners." The element of irreverence is clear to those who have some understanding of what the Christian revelation really is. The Rev. C. M. Chavasse, an Anglican lecturer at Oxford says, "We are filled with grave misgivings about this cult, which we have watched closely for five years; and our misgivings are shared by practically all religious leaders and responsible persons in the University."

1384. *Are the laws of the Catholic Church opposed to the Group Movement?*

Yes. It is essentially a religious, yet a non-Catholic sect; and no Catholic may join it. Did a Catholic do so, he would be regarded by the Catholic Church as having joined a heretical sect, an act which carries with it excommunication from the Catholic Church.

1385. *But the Oxford Group forbids sectarianism.*

You ignore the primary meaning of the word sectarian, and fall back on a secondary meaning adapted to the viewpoint of the Group. The Groupers profess to welcome all, no matter to what Church each may belong. But in reality the Group is a religious society claiming that it not only does not matter to what Church you belong, but that it does not matter whether you belong to one at all. Dr. Buchman tells us that it would be quite sufficient to belong to his movement alone. Now if the Group is sufficient in itself as a substitute for other religions, it is already a religion; and it is not the Catholic religion. It must therefore be ranked as another Protestant sect, even though the members may say that they do not wish to "feel" in any sectarian way.

1386. *It does not ask a man to change his religion. It does ask a man to allow his religion to change him.*

That is a clever turn of speech; but it is not true. And where Catholics are concerned it is an impossibility if one is to be also a Grouper. If the Group seeks recruits from among Catholics it asks those Catholics to change their religion. For they would find themselves cut off from the Catholic Church in order to embrace Buchmanism! If a Catholic allowed his religion to change him he would cease being careless and become fervent. But the fervent practice of his religion would compel him to wash his hands altogether of the religious meetings of the Group. The Group is destructive of all true faith in Christ and substitutes a vague religious emotionalism. The truth revealed by our Lord is ignored or despised; the Mass is regarded as worthless, and the Sacraments as unnecessary. The authority vested by Christ in the Catholic Church is not acknowledged, and private judgment reigns supreme under the pretentious claim that it is Divine Guidance received from the Holy Spirit. The "Oxford Group Movement" is the very essence of Protestantism stripped of all definite statements of doctrine or creed.

1387. *The "Oxford Groupers" refer repeatedly to the fact that Catholics belong to it.*

Enthusiasts are given to exaggerated statements based upon what they would like to be true. The claim that Catholics belong to the Group is not justified. There is not an instructed Catholic in the world who does not know that active participation in non-Catholic religious movements is strictly forbidden by the Catholic Church. A Catholic who would join the Oxford Group would either be very ignorant of his own religious obligations, or else would be consciously renouncing his Catholic Faith.

1388. *Why are you so particularly hard on Protestantism?*

I have no more reasons for the discussion of Protestantism than for the discussion of any other form of religion. But Protestants are more numerous than others in this country, and consequently more questions are submitted from the Protestant viewpoint than from others. Were I in a country where the Greek Orthodox Church is in the ascendancy, my discussions would have to do chiefly with the differences between Greek Orthodoxy and Catholicism. The Catholic Church is the same everywhere, but she has not the same problems to face everywhere. Conditions are much the same now as when St. Augustine wrote in the fourth century: "You will not find the same heretics everywhere, but still you will find heretics everywhere. Heresies are never wanting; but you will find one type of heresy here; another there. So you will find one sect in Africa; another in the East; another in Egypt; and yet another in Mesopotamia. But the heretics of one region have no connection with the heretics of another region."

1389. *If faith has its rights, has not charity its duties?*

Undoubtedly. But the demands of charity are not overlooked merely because the things that divide other Churches from the Catholic Church seem to be insisted upon. My particular duty happens to be to explain and defend the accuracies of faith; and the duties of charity do not diminish the rights of truth. In fact, in so grave a matter as religion, any tampering with truth would violate charity; for men have a right to the truth, and the truth in turn will be most beneficial to them. If, by clearing away misconceptions, I can help men to the realization of the truth of the Catholic Church as the one true Church of Jesus Christ in this world, then I have rendered them the greatest possible service—as those who have become Catholics so gladly and gratefully admit.

1390. Why do you prefer the Catholic Church to Protestantism?

The reasons are legion, whether from God's point of view, or from my own point of view, or from the viewpoint of Protestantism itself, or from the aspect of the Catholic Church. I shall try to summarize them for you.

From God's point of view, He certainly has the right, not only that I should acknowledge and serve Him, but that I should do so in the way He commands. Not any way of my own choosing will do. And as He has commanded the Catholic way, I am obliged to serve Him in that way.

From my own point of view, I want a religion that can really substantiate its claim to be the one true form of religion in this world; that knows its own mind, and can tell me definitely what is to be believed and what is to be done; and which can offer me the necessary spiritual helps in the way of guidance, inspiration, and assistance, to do these things. Catholicism alone can comply with these requirements.

From the viewpoint of Protestantism, its origin in the sixteenth century was sixteen centuries too late to be the religion given to the world by Christ; it has no consistent doctrinal teaching; its services vary with the idiosyncracies of individual clergymen; those clergymen have no valid Orders in the Christian sense of the word, and therefore they lack the Real Presence of Christ in the Eucharist, and the power to destroy sin by sacramental absolution in Confession. In a word, historically, Scripturally, and logically, no form of Protestantism can stand.

On the other hand, from the aspect of the Catholic Church, historically, she alone goes right back to Christ, and can alone inherit His promise to be with His Church all days from His time till the end of the world; Scripturally, she alone is in complete accord with God's revealed word; logically, she alone is thoroughly consistent; as a teacher, she alone claims to know her own mind infallibly; and as a guide, she alone knows what discipline really means.

CHAPTER FIFTEEN
TO AND FROM ROME

1391. Did not Cardinal Newman lose faith in the Catholic Church before he died?

No. During his own lifetime the rumor was published by the "Globe" newspaper that he had been disillusioned by Catholicism, and was going to return to the Church of England. Newman at once had his denial published in the same paper. He wrote saying, "I have not had one moment's wavering of trust in the Catholic Church ever since I was received into her fold. I have no intention, and never have had any intention, of leaving the Catholic Church and becoming a Protestant again. And I hereby profess ex animo with an absolute internal assent and consent that the thought of an Anglican service makes me shiver, and the thought of the Thirty-Nine Articles makes me shudder. Return to the Church of England! No! I should be a consummate fool (to use a mild term) if in my old age I left 'the land flowing with milk and honey' for the city of confusion and the house of bondage." He added, in a later letter to a friend, that he hoped he had settled all such rumors once and for all, but said that he might not be alive by the time a new denial became necessary. I have hereby made it for him.

1392. If the truth of the Catholic Church is so clear, why did such an intelligent man as W. E. Gladstone remain entrenched in Protestantism?

It was certainly not because Protestantism is true, nor because Catholicism is false. Nor was it because Gladstone was intelligent. Both Newman and Manning, fellow Protestants with Gladstone, were equally intelligent, yet both became Catholics. We must remember that religion implies much more than merely intellectual conviction. It is deeply psychological, involving a yielding of mind and heart and will. Reluctance on the part of any one of these factors can prevent a clear sight of one's obligations. Pascal has rightly said that "the heart has reasons of which reason knows nothing." Gladstone had many more motives for remaining a member of the National Church, and less knowledge of the ecclesiastical issues involved than either Newman or Manning. And I believe these prevented his giving full intellectual attention to aspects of the problem which led in a direction he was not willing to follow.

1393. Why did not the late Lord Halifax, though apparently so near to Rome, become a convert to your faith?

I admit that his case is more difficult than that of Gladstone. Lord Halifax was a convert to Catholic teaching and forms of worship. But Catholic discipline and jurisdiction were beyond him. He was so absorbed by the idea that the Anglicanism he loved was somehow or other part of the Catholic Church that his judgment was clouded on the one point as to whether he should abandon the Church of England and submit to Rome, or not. He was a wonderfully good man; but wonderfully good men can make mistakes. Certainly he never saw clearly the obligation of joining the Roman Church, or he would have done so.

1394. He must have been conversant with all the Catholic arguments, for he was in constant touch with Cardinal Mercier.

I am sure he had considered all the main arguments. And they quite convinced him that the Roman Church was the true Church. Had you asked him, "Is the Roman Catholic Church in error?", he would have declared that she was not! He constantly deplored the fact that the Church of England was not in visible communion with the Holy See. But he would rather see the whole of the Church of England seek unity with Rome than go over alone. He knew that Rome regarded him as an outsider so long as he remained an Anglican, and this hurt him very much. In a letter to the Abbe Portal he wrote, "How can I make it clear in Rome that I believe in one only Church, and that my one aim is to work for the return of the Church of England into the fold of Catholic unity, and to restore the relations which must necessarily exist between the English bishops and the Holy See?" A man who can write like that is certainly convinced that the Roman Church is the true Church. From our point of view, of course, any man who admits that the Church of England should be within the fold of Catholic unity and is not, and that its bishops should be subject to the Pope but are not, surely has the obligation personally to go over to Rome. Yet that is precisely what Lord Halifax did not see. He knew the arguments in favor of this obligation, but apparently they did not impress him. It is a lack of insight for which I am not prepared to blame him. As G. K. Chesterton has said, "When you look at a thing for the hundredth time, you are in great danger of seeing it for the first time." To know, and to realize are very different things.

1395. *If such people as these were not convinced, how can you hope to convince people of ordinary mental caliber? You will never reason them into the Church.*

I do not hope to convert people by reason. In itself reason cannot be the road to the faith, or else brainy people would have a better chance of attaining religious security merely because more intelligent. After all, intellectuals have no greater claim upon God than the dull-witted. What I do hope to do by reason is to clear away misapprehensions and prejudice, show the rational foundation for belief, and bring out the impossibility of conflicting statements of doctrine being equally true. Then I can show that the characteristics of the Catholic Church alone fit in with those intended by Christ. After that, I must leave it to each man's good will and the grace of God. I can explain the faith; but I cannot give the gift of faith. The suggestion that because some intelligent men are not convinced it will be impossible to convince less intelligent men is without weight. The intelligent men who are convinced more than offset the ones who are not, whilst your fears concerning people of ordinary mental caliber are excluded by the fact that such people are convinced and converted daily. As a matter of fact, simpler people often see more clearly than the learned whose minds are tangled with hosts of ideas which get in each other's way. Where these men cannot see the wood for the trees, less distraught minds have an intuitive perception of the vital truth. And always, of course, allowance must be made for the grace of God which follows no law of man's own devising.

1396. *Gibbon, the historian, became a Catholic despite parental opposition.*

He did, and apparently sincerely. He was but sixteen years old at the time.

1397. *Yet he went back to Protestantism, and then to a vague sort of atheism.*

He did, but I deny that he did so because he really proved the Catholic Church untrue.

1398. *Was his a guilty renunciation of the true faith?*

Yes. Horrified by his conversion to Catholicism, his father packed him off to Lausanne to board with a Swiss Calvinist pastor named M. Pavillard. M. Pavillard loyally set to work to bring Gibbon back to Protestantism; and his work was made easier by the fact that Gibbon fell in love with Susanne Curchod, daughter of a neighboring Protestant pastor. Had Gibbon fulfilled his duty in the first place he would have refused to go to board with M. Pavillard, and enter into circumstances expressly designed to destroy his faith. Nor would he have met Susanne. Even after his weak yielding to that, he could have obtained sufficient grace from God to persevere in his faith in the Catholic Church, and to resist the influences he encountered, had he prayed as fervently as he should to God. There is a sequence of stages in a man's driftage from the Church. But that sequence begins at least with a deliberate infidelity in his own will. God never withdraws from a soul unless that soul first withdraws from Him. It is worth remarking that Gibbon went back to Protestantism, and then to a loss of faith altogether. He saw, as every reasonable man must see who has ever really known both Catholicism and Protestantism, that if there is any true and complete Christianity, it can only be Catholicism. So the choice is Catholicism or nothing.

1399. Father Chiniquy found the Catholic Church to be false, and left it to become a Protestant.

Father Chiniquy did not voluntarily leave the Catholic Church, but was suspended and degraded for misconduct on many occasions, and excommunicated despite repeated piteous appeals for reinstatement as a priest.

1400. Catholics say that Pastor Chiniquy was expelled from their Church, but Archbishop Bruchesi, of Montreal, wrote as follows on Jan. 10th, 1899, to Chiniquy's son-in-law, the Rev. J. L. Morrin:

Sir:

I hear that Mr. Chiniquy is very seriously ill, and that he may soon die. Although he separated from us a long time ago, I cannot forget what he always remains in the eyes of the Church; and I consider it a duty of my pastoral charge to write to you that, should he desire to see me, I would feel happy to comply with his wish. Kindly make known to the patient that I have taken this step, and accept the expression of my devoted feelings.

Paul—Archbishop of Montreal.

That is one of the noblest letters that has ever come from any man's pen. There have been few priests in history who have proved so unfaithful to their office as Father Chiniquy. He not only failed to live up to his obligations; he also gave great disedification and scandal by his manner of life. After the expulsion from the Catholic Church his conduct brought upon him, he indulged in a bitter campaign of vilification against the Church—so bitter and untruthful that, when he came to die, the normal human reaction would be to let him die in whatever dispositions he might choose. Or the Archbishop might reasonably say, "If he wants the last Sacraments of the Church, and to be reconciled to God, let him ask for a priest. If he sends for a priest, a priest will be put at his disposal." But the Archbishop was a man of great faith. His faith shines out in his letter. No one can doubt his sincere and utter conviction of the priestly dignity indelibly impressed upon the soul of Pastor Chiniquy. No one can doubt his deep appreciation of the intense significance of death, of judgment, of the vital necessity of securing one's salvation. And Archbishop Bruchesi was so much a man of God that he felt it his pastoral duty, not only to leave the 99 and seek out the one sheep in danger of being lost. He sought not only one who had gone astray, but one who had consistently reviled and attacked all that was most dear to him. If ever a man put into practice the command of Christ, "Love your enemies," it was Archbishop Bruchesi. And it was not for anything he personally had to gain, but for Father Chiniquy's own sake. The good Archbishop really dreaded the thought that even a Chiniquy should go to his judgment unrepentant and unforgiven. That is why he wrote such a letter.

1401. ***You will notice that your Archbishop says, "He separated from us."***

In such a letter at such a moment, harsh terms would be quite out of place. And it is true that Father Chiniquy severed his connection with the Catholic Church insofar as he was personally responsible for conduct meriting his excommunication. Chiniquy was a French Canadian who was ordained a priest in 1843. On Sept. 28th, 1851, he was suspended from priestly duties by his bishop for immoral conduct. He left Canada for the United States, and persuaded a bishop there to give him another chance. But that bishop had to expel him on Nov. 20th, 1856. At once Chiniquy wrote to his former Canadian bishop as follows: "My Lord, as my actions have given scandal, and caused many to believe that sooner than obey you I would consent to be separated from the Catholic Church, I hasten to express my regret. To show the world my firm desire to live and die a Catholic, I hasten to write that I submit to your sentence, and I promise never more to exercise the sacred ministry in your diocese without your permission. So I beg your lordship to take off the censures you have pronounced against me, and against those who have communicated with me in things divine. I am your most devoted son in Jesus Christ, Charles Chiniquy, Nov. 25th, 1856. Chiniquy's conduct even when writing this letter was such that no bishop could accept it. And the bishop rightly refused to reinstate him as a priest on active duties. In 1858, he persuaded the Bishop of Chicago to accept him, but almost at once was again expelled. Then, having made himself impossible to every Catholic bishop, he went to a hotel, and after a night of agony and distress over his abandonment by the Catholic Church, he says that the light of heaven dawned upon him, and he saw clearly that the Church of Rome was false, and that salvation was with the Protestants. But they had trouble with him also. In 1862, the Protestant Synod of Chicago expelled him for misappropriation of money he collected on false pretenses in Europe on behalf of a non-existent Protestant charity. The American Presbyterians then accepted him, but before long had to expel him for embezzlement. After that, the Orangemen took him up, and he became a lecturer against Rome on the Protestant platform. Thus he spent the rest of his days till he came to die. It was then that the Archbishop of Montreal most charitably extended to him the offer of forgiveness and reconciliation with his Church in the spirit of Christ's own forgiveness at the last moment of the repentant thief on Calvary. In the light of all this, it cannot be said that Father Chiniquy voluntarily left the Catholic Church; nor does his conduct in any way prove that Church to be erroneous.

1402. ***Will you insist that there was something wrong with Father George Tyrrell, the ex-Jesuit, rather than with the Catholic Church he left?***

Yes. No man who has ever had the Catholic Faith can ever leave the Catholic Church save through an abuse of grace for which he himself is responsible.

1403. ***Tyrrell not only embraced Catholicism, but joined the Jesuits.***

It is true that Tyrrell was a convert from Protestantism to the Catholic Church, and subsequently became a Jesuit.

1404. ***Surely if Catholicism were true, he would not want to leave it.***

In the introduction to his book, "Hard Sayings," Tyrrell wrote: "It is to the Church that we must look for our guidance. The minds of her children will ever press on towards a fuller intelligence of the mysteries of faith, turning back at times to receive her approval, or to receive her rebuke, or to listen to her counsel. To whom shall we go but to her who has the words of eternal life, who for two thousand years has kept all these sayings and pondered them in her heart?" Tyrrell published that statement of his convictions in 1898. Yet a few years later he was expelled from the Catholic Church for deliberately refusing to obey those convictions. When the Church withdrew her approval from his modernist teachings, rebuked them, and offered her counsels, he obstinately maintained that he knew better than the Church. Pride gripped his soul. He never returned to Protestantism. He still vehemently claimed to be a Catholic. But he wanted Catholicism to be what he thought it ought to be, not what it is. And he refused to submit his judgment to that Church which St. Paul declares to be the "pillar and the ground of truth." And in doing so, he resisted God's grace.

1405. *No man prayed harder than Tyrrell for the guidance of God.*

Tyrrell was a profoundly religious man. And pride is a subtle force which adapts itself to men as they are, not eliminating inborn tendencies, but warping them, and diverting them from their proper direction. And pride also has a peculiarly blinding effect upon the soul, urging it never to admit its error. Tyrrell went on with his prayers as an expression of his religious feelings; but if by those prayers he was trying to secure guidance from God, he wanted a guidance in accordance with his own desires, and interpreted all his inner experiences to suit his own theories.

1406. *He did his best, and kept on praying, despite ecclesiastical persecution.*

There was no ecclesiastical persecution. The Catholic authorities merely said to him, "You cannot go on teaching a modernism quite opposed to Catholic teaching, and continue to function as a priest of the Catholic Church." The Church merely asked him to put into practice his own principles, and submit to her counsels. He refused to do so, and was expelled from communion with the Catholic Church. No one could call that persecution. The Catholic Church has as much right to say, "If you want to enjoy my privileges, you must undertake also the obligations of a Catholic" as the State has to say, "If you want my privileges you must obey my laws." The trouble with Tyrrell was that he wanted the privileges of a Catholic without the obligations. And he protested against his exclusion from the Catholic Church which he would not obey. Writing on Nov. 25th, 1908, Cardinal Mercier of Belgium said to Bishop Hedley, "I do not know whether or not I should reply to that poor Tyrrell. Is it not better to ignore his insolent tone, the theatrical affectation with which he complains of being accused of modernism, and of openly denying the Papal infallibility and the decision of the Vatican Council! If I reply, he will answer again. Where shall we end? If there remain some hope of seeing him return to the Church, is it not better to leave him to reflect in silence?"

1407. *Why did Bishop Julio Garrett, of Cochabamba, Bolivia, leave the Catholic Church, if it is so true?*

Bishop Julio Garrett did not voluntarily leave the Catholic Church. Because he was not true to his charge, he was deposed and excommunicated by the Pope in December, 1929.

1408. *He joined the Anglican Church, and gave as his reasons for leaving Rome the avarice and immorality of Latin America, and his inability to accept the infallibility of the Pope.*

Naturally Bishop Julio Garrett had to give reasons for his change of allegiance, and he was not likely to give the real reasons. His first excuse will not impress thinking people. If sin is prevalent in a given locality, a good bishop whose mission it is to labor for the conversion of sinners knows that that place is just where he is needed. And as a good shepherd he does not desert his post merely because there are more sinners than he thought who badly need converting to Christ. But, as a matter of fact, Julio Garrett was not a good bishop. If avarice and immorality were too prevalent, the example he gave, far from checking it, would only tend to increase it. He was reported to Rome for his scandalous conduct, cited before an ecclesiastical court, found guilty, and expelled from the Catholic Church.

The second reason, that he could no longer accept the infallibility of the Pope, is not surprising. The only thing to be noted is that he gave no hint that he could not accept the infallibility of the Pope until after the Pope refused to accept him any longer as a bishop in the Catholic Church.

1409. *It is not often that a Catholic Bishop loses faith in the Catholic Church.*

Correct. But, if Bishop Garrett has lost his faith in the Church, he lost much else before he came to such a stage. Refutations of this kind are not very pleasant. But if a man is held up as a living argument by Protestant papers that Rome is wrong, it is necessary to examine the value of that living argument. Listen to the calm, measured, and dignified language of this cable from Rome concerning Bishop Julio Garrett. "The reason, and the sole reason, for the deposing by the Holy See of Julio Garrett as Bishop of Cochabamba, Bolivia, in December, 1929, was the proving by judicial and exact procedure of offenses both against the commandments of God and the laws of the Church. To safeguard charity, the decree of deposition, with its reasons, was not made public at the time; but the bishopric was merely declared vacant. However, since Protestant periodicals have published statements that Julio Garrett came to Rome, and became convinced that the Catholic Church was in error, whereupon he went over to the American Episcopal Church, the Holy See has caused the decree of his deposition to be published in Bolivia and to the world. Henceforth only ignorance or bad faith can repeat the assertion that Julio Garrett left the Catholic Church of his own accord, or that he was a faithful bishop in that Church."

1410. *Are those who leave your Church a thorn in your side?*

Not as regards the effect of their defection upon the Church they have left. The value of the evidence for the truth of the Catholic Church remains unaffected by the lapse of individuals from her fold. And the loss of faith by such individuals cannot possibly interfere with the continued existence of the Catholic Church. If I myself were to renounce the Catholic Faith, and spend the rest of my life lecturing against the Catholic Church, my conduct would neither prove that Church wrong, nor result in its collapse. From the viewpoint of the Church, therefore, ex-Catholics are not a thorn in my side. At the same time, I regret to hear of any Catholic forsaking his or her religion both because such a soul forfeits immense spiritual blessings and privileges, and because such defections set a bad example to other individuals. You would rightly blame me were I indifferent to the spiritual welfare of others, whoever they may be.

1411. *Is everyone who leaves the Catholic Church a scoundrel?*

No. People who have never forfeited their right to an honorable and unblemished reputation in the eyes of their fellow men have drifted from their faith in the Catholic Church; some because not well instructed in that religion; others because, although intelligent enough in other directions, they have been unable to take an intelligent attitude where religion is concerned; others, again, have abandoned their religion for the sake of worldly advantages which do not seem in the least evil to the majority of worldly-minded people. Not everyone, therefore, who leaves the Catholic Church could be called a scoundrel according to the ordinary standards accepted by public estimation. But it remains true that no adult Catholic can lose his faith in the Catholic Church without some degree of moral responsibility before God.

1412. *Have all who leave a poor weak intellect?*

No. Some are very intelligent, but have proved to be out and out scoundrels. Others, very intelligent, have devoted their intelligence to all subjects save their religion, of which they have known little or nothing; or else they have devoted it to the discovery of excuses to leave their religion because they found it uncomfortable. Others again, as I have already remarked, are psychologically unable to reason clearly where religion is concerned. Many people, Catholics and non-Catholics alike, tend to become quite unreasonable once religion is involved, however reasonable they may be in other matters. For example, a very highly educated woman who professed to be an agnostic once showed me a photograph of Herbert Spencer, and challenged me to say that a man with such a kindly face could teach wrong ideas about religion. I might mention that this woman was very religiously inclined, and found a relish and a devotion in declaring herself to be an unbeliever which it would be hard to better in the most fervent of revivalist meetings.

1413. Are not those who leave as convinced in their own minds as you are in yours?

Some are as convinced as I am that the Catholic Church is indeed the true Church. I have met many such people, and have been told by them that they hope to return to their Church some day. Others attain to a genuine conviction that the Catholic Church is wrong. But usually this conviction is due to some form of mental aberration. People can convince themselves, and most intensely, of almost anything. If you visit a lunatic asylum you may find an inmate most intensely convinced that he is Napoleon. In the clash of divergent convictions, you must first sort out the sane people from the insane. Then you must take the convictions of the sane ones, and examine carefully the evidence for them. If this is done impartially, it will be found that other forms of religion are not based upon sound foundations, whilst the Catholic position is impregnable. Were I myself, by some drastic infidelity on my part, to lose my faith and become an atheist, I would still maintain that if there were anything in the Christian religion, the Catholic Church could alone justify itself as the true Christian Church in this world.

1414. Are people heroes only if they turn from Protestantism to Roman Catholicism?

Not necessarily. The taking of such a step does not always require heroic courage. At times it does. There are many people who would become Catholics tomorrow only for the fact that they have not the heroism to face the consequences of taking such a step. However, heroism is not manifested only in the religious field. It is quite often manifested in other fields also.

1415. Why are not the Protestant clergy as anxious to convert Catholics as you are to convert Protestants?

At the time of the Protestant Reformation, of course, the early reformers were anxious to convert as many Catholics as possible to their new Churches. And the Catholic Church was denounced as the work of Satan, whilst the Pope was branded as the Beast. This idea of the Catholic Church still persists amongst some of the smaller and narrower Protestant sects. A Seventh Day Adventist booklet in my possession declares the "great Roman System" to be Antichrist, and appeals most fervently to Catholics to leave it. This booklet tells Catholics that God is crying out to them, "Come out of her, my people." Judge Rutherford's "Witnesses of Jehovah" adopt the same attitude. But these are relics or revivals of an ancient superstition. The Protestant tradition is dying fast, and more and more Protestant clergymen are deprecating efforts to convert Catholics to Protestantism. Where once they declared that they had left the Catholic Church, they now wish to say that they never really left it at all, and that they still belong to it. And that makes it rather absurd to try to convert Catholics from a Church to what these clergymen claim to be really the same Church.

1416. *How many Protestant clergymen would agree with you in this?*

Thousands. For example, Dr. Percy Dearmer, an Anglican, wants to hold that all professing Christians are really one. In his book, "Our National Church," p. 160, he writes, "We are not divided; all one body we. We have to say this, and to mean it. And the acid test is that there should be no proselytism." In other words, this Anglican Canon says that it is definitely wrong to try to convert a Catholic to any other form of Christianity. Dr. R. G. Macintyre, a Presbyterian, in his book, "The Substance of the Christian Faith," pp. 81-83, says, "We have laid far too much stress on the form, the organization of the Church. . . . Each of us may find that a particular form suits us. Well and good. But . . . we are sharers in one common life, and union with Christ implies union with one another. There is no narrowness comparable with that which unchurches any section of Christians because they follow not with us." On such principles, Dr. Macintyre is quite content that Catholics should remain Catholics. And he is not moved by any desire to convert them.

1417. *A little over a year ago I joined the Catholic Church against the wishes of my family.*

You did the right thing in following your conscience. Since the others in your family did not perceive the truth of the Catholic religion as you did, they could scarcely be expected to wish you to become a Catholic. But at least they should wish you to do what you yourself thought to be right.

1418. *I would not leave the Church I have grown to love so much, even for my mother whom I love very dearly.*

That is the correct attitude to adopt.

1419. *My mother says that, if I did love her, I would do what she asks, and even have no religion rather than belong to the Catholic Church.*

She knows quite well that you love her. She is merely trying to use your love for her to persuade you to abandon the Catholic Church. But she is asking too much. Love for one's mother should impel us to give her all the lawful happiness we can. But no love for any human being can justify our offending God and violating our conscience. If a mother said to her child, "If you love me you will steal $5,000 for me," the child would be obliged to refuse. That is not a lawful test of one's love. Now religion is one's duty to God. Yet your mother would have you acknowledge no duty to God at all, rather than see you a Catholic! She would not mind your doing what you believe to be sinful before God provided she gets her own way. It is her love for you that is deficient, for if she loved you rightly she would think of your good, and she would not have you incur the guilt of sin before God for any earthly consideration. Only selfishness, based on wounded pride, human respect, and prejudice, could make such demands.

1420. *She says I am disobeying the commandment, Honor thy father and thy mother.*

You are not doing so. That commandment, as all other subsequent commandments, is regulated by the preceding commandments which deal with God's rights. God comes first. "I am the Lord thy God. Thou shalt not have other gods before Me." Duties to parents can never come before duties to God. "Thou shalt love the Lord thy God with all thy heart and with all thy soul" leaves no room for conflicting loves, though it can include lesser loves. So Christ said, "If anyone love even father and mother more than Me, he is not worthy of Me." He knew that, for His sake, many would meet with opposition from their own parents, and would have to choose between pleasing them and pleasing Him. And when a conflict arises, He must come first.

1421. *Is she right? Or am I justified in my action?*

She is not right. You are justified in your action. You can but say to her, "Only for God you would not be my mother, nor I your child. I must do God's will. In fact, the more I love you, the more grateful to God I am that He should have given you to me as my mother; and the more grateful I am to Him, the more obliged I am to do His will. I will do anything I can for you, except what I know will offend God." In standing to a principle like this, of course, you are not unaware of the fact that she does not see things as you do. You do not forget that she can have little sympathy with the step you have taken; and that it causes her a very real suffering. Appreciating that, you should be twice as kind and devoted to her in all the ways you can be to make up for the pain your necessary fidelity to God inflicts upon her.

1422. *Is it not God's will that all should be Catholics?*

It is. For Christ established the Catholic Church, and bade her go and teach all nations, baptizing them in the name of the Father, and of the Son, and of the Holy Ghost. But He said also, "He that believes and is baptized shall be saved; he that believes not shall be condemned." He thereby tells us that not all who hear the truth will accept it. He Himself did not convert all to whom He preached; and we must not be surprised if we ourselves have the same experience. In individual cases, however, we must refuse to judge as to the degree in which even those who have heard the truth concerning the Catholic Church apprehend its significance. Their responsibility in remaining non-Catholics must be left to God. Meantime we can but pray for them, patiently bearing the trial that those we love show no present signs of conversion to Catholicism, or the fact that they are not converted as quickly as we could wish. God's time is the best time. It is for us to plead that He may give them the grace of the Catholic Faith, and that they may correspond with that grace despite all difficulties when it becomes clear to them whither God is calling them.

ALPHABETICAL INDEX

Numbers refer to paragraphs

Abortion, 1000 ff.
Abraham, 570.
Absolute State, 1167 ff.
Absolute Truth, 200.
Absolution of the dead, 1071 ff.
Abstinence, Friday, 1068.
Abyssinian Christians, 1251 ff.
Access to Christ, 261, 308.
"Action, Catholic," 1237 ff.
Actual sin, 607.
Adam, 567 ff., 617 ff.
Adrian VI., Pope, 241.
Adultery, 982 ff., 1014.
Adventists, Seventh Day, 1301 ff.
Age of Christ, 475; of man, 567; of world, 538.
Albertus Magnus, on astrology, 942.
Albigensianism, 1246.
Alexander II. and England, 354.
Alexander VI. and America, 357.
Allegiance, divided, of Catholics, 352 ff.
Alphonsus Liguori, St., 759.
Angels, 513, 547 ff.; sin of, 559, 876.
Anglican Church, 250, 1269 ff.; origin of, 1270 ff.; continuity of, 1271 ff.; doctrine of, 1278 ff.; worship of, 1284.
Anglican Orders, 1259.
Anglo-Catholicism, 1287.
Anointing of sick, 823 ff., 1333.
Antichrist, 234, 392 ff., 565 ff.
Antioch, See of, 351.
Apostles, equality of, 340 ff.; teaching of, 429.
Apostolicity of the Church, 246 ff., 428 ff.
Apotheosis of Christ, 628 ff.
Aquinas, St. Thomas, on astrology, 944; on resisting evils, 1239.
Arianism, 1247.
Aristotle, 37.
Armageddon, 1337.
Art treasures in Rome, 408.
"Articles of Religion," Anglican, 471.
Ash Wednesday, 1063 ff.
Assumption of Mary, 695 ff.
Assurance of salvation, 1009 ff.
Astrology, 934 ff.
Athanasius, St., 1252.
Atheism, 1.
Atonement, the, 609 ff.
Attendance, at Mass, 964 ff., 1046 ff.; at non-Catholic services, 274.
Augustine, St., on astrology, 941; on heresies, 1388; on miracles, 86; on predestination, 709.
Authenticity of the Gospels, 91 ff.
Authority, of the Church, 286, 365 ff., 472 ff., 1005, 1254; of St. Peter, 317 ff., 923 ff.; of the State, 1126 ff.
"Authorized Bible," 458 ff.

Bacon, Roger, not "persecuted," 507; on astrology, 943.
Bad Catholics, 754 ff.; Popes, 382 ff.; Priests, 399 ff.
Baptism, 716 ff.; of desire, 722; by immersion, 731; necessity of, 735; of Protestants, 271.
Baptists, the, 1297 ff.
Barnes, Bishop, on the Eucharist, 1285.
Beads, Rosary, 1076 ff.
"Beast," the, 234, 392 ff., 565 ff.
Behaviorism, 489.
Benson, R. H., on Catholic Unity, 181.
Berg, Prof., on evolution, 546.
Bergson, Prof., on creation, 536.
Besant, Mrs. Annie, and theosophy, 1346.
Bias, historical, 226 ff.; of the Press, 1150 ff.
Bible, errors in, 114 ff.; as foundation, 452 ff.; inspired, 105 ff., 452 ff.; lost Books of, 96; obscure, 467 ff.; and Protestantism, 257, 452 ff.; reading of, 454 ff.; as rule of faith—see Private Judgment; truth of, 537.
Bible Societies, 455 ff.
Bibles, Protestant, 457 ff.
Biblical account of creation, 120 ff.
Biblical criticism, 94 ff.
Biology, teaching of, 974 ff.
Birth prevention, 988.
Bishops, 289 ff.
Bismarck, attack on the Church, 436.
Blavatsky, Madame, and theosophy, 1346.
Blessed Sacrament, 761 ff.
Blood of Christ, in the Eucharist, 771.
Body of Christ, in the Eucharist, 761 ff.
Body, resurrection of the, 877 ff.
Book of Enoch, 101.
Booth, Gen. William, 1312 ff.
Brethren of Christ, 680 ff.
Briggs, Prof., on Church Unity, 194; on Papal history, 430; on the Petrine text, 328.
British Israelites, 1336 ff.
Brown Scapular, 1082 ff.
Bruce, Dr. James, 101.
Bruchesi, Archbishop, and Father Chiniquy, 1400 ff.
Bruno, Giordano, 500.
Buchmanites, 1375.
Buildings, ecclesiastical, 1041 ff.
Burial, rites for, 1070 ff.; of suicides, 1035 ff.
Cabot, Dr., on sex instruction, 976.
Caiaphas and Christ, 160.
Cain's wife, 576 ff.
Calendar, the Christian, 474 ff.
Calvinism, 709.
Campbell, Rev. Alex., and disciples, 1294.
Candles, 1074.
Canon of the Bible, 459 ff.
Capital punishment, 1231 ff.
Capitalism, 1099 ff.
"Catholic," as title, 252, 416 ff., 1267.

Catholic Action, 1237 ff.
"Catholic Apostolic Church," 1308 ff.
Catholic Church, origin of, 283 ff., 430; founded by Christ, 287; truth of, 288, 480, 1390; unity of, 90, 181, 386 ff.; 471 ff.; Holiness of, 754 ff.; Catholicity of, 415 ff.; apostolicity of, 246 ff., 428 ff.; authority of, 286, 365 ff., 472 ff., 1017, 1266; infallibility of, 361 ff.; indestructibility of, 435 ff.; exclusive claims of, 274 ff.; necessity of, 202, 1422; spirit of, 265; prospects of, 438 ff.
Catholic countries, 1090 ff.
Catholic historians, 226.
Catholic priesthood, 260.
Catholic standards, 396 ff., 754 ff.
Catholicism and civilization, 503; and reaction, 498 ff.
Catholicity of the Church, 415 ff.
"Catholics, Liberal," 1346 ff.
Catholics, number of, 417.
Cause of religious divisions, 178.
Causes of the Reformation, 237.
Celibacy, 401 ff.
Celsus the pagan, 689.
Censorship of books, 917 ff.
Ceremonial, 1047 ff.
Cerularius, Michael, and Greek Churches, 1257.
"Chair of Peter" at Rome, 351.
Chalcedon, Council of, 1249, 1256.
Chalice and laity, 789.
Chaplains in war time, 1219 ff.
Charity, virtue of, 905; necessity of, 703, 1389; towards Protestants, 273, 915 ff., 1388, 1421 ff.
Chastity, 401 ff., 976 ff.
Chesterton, G. K., on suffering, 1334; on knowledge and realization, 1394.
Children, and morals, 970 ff.; fate of unbaptized, 723 ff.
Chiniquy, Ex-priest, 1399 ff.
Christ, divine origin and character of, 137, 159, 622 ff., 630 ff.; genealogies of, 137 ff.; age and year of birth, 475; establishes the Catholic Church, 284 ff.; ethical teaching of, 624 ff.; attitude to Judaism, 150 ff.; entry into Jerusalem, 146 ff.; fulfillment of prophecies, 134 ff.; rejected by Jews, 158; mediation of, 307 ff.; mystical body of, 786, 805; attitude to war, 1178 ff.
Christadelphians, 1335.
Christian Science, 22, 1328 ff.
Christians, divided, 178 ff.
Christianity, defined, 176; reasonable and credible, 166 ff.; relation to Judaism, 150, 153 ff., 163 ff.; relation to Greek philosophy, 151; relation to paganism, 152; propagation of, 152, 168 ff.
Chrysostom, St., on St. Peter's supremacy, 342.
Church, sense of the word, 280 ff.; origin of, 283 ff., 430; nature of, 193; Modernist interpretation, 283 ff.; Kingdom of Christ, 284 ff.; constitution and government, 289 ff.; unity of, 90, 181, 386 ff., 471 ff.; Holiness of, 388 ff., 414, 754 ff.; Catholicity of, 415 ff.; apostolicity of, 246 ff., 428 ff.; wealth of, 407 ff., 1041 ff., 1143 ff.; social influence of, 1098 ff.; attitude to peace and war, 1181, 1204 ff.
"Church of England." See Anglican Church.
Church, "Orthodox Russian," 1153 ff.

Church "Teaching" and "Taught," 363.
Church-buildings, 1041 ff., 1143 ff.
Church-unity, 386 ff.
Churches, dying, 245.
"Churches of Christ," 1293.
Civil authority, 1126 ff.
Civilization and Catholicism, 503.
Clayton, J., on the Reformation, 225; on Protestantism, 262.
Columbus and the discovery of America, 357.
Coming of Christ, 883 ff.
Commercialism and religion, 70 ff.
Communion, Holy, 761 ff.; under one kind, 789.
Communion of Saints, 668 ff., 865 ff., 1070, 1321.
Communism, 1099 ff., 1139 ff.
"Companionate Marriages," 999.
Compromise, spirit of, 196.
Conception, moment of, 1004.
"Conception, Immaculate," of Mary, 675 ff., 1004.
Conditions of salvation, 447, 651 ff., 697 ff., 710 ff., 843 ff., 855 ff.
Confession, St. Peter's, 324.
Confession, Sacrament of, 736 ff.
Congregationalists, 250, 1290.
Conscience, nature of, 901 ff., 970 ff., 1162 ff.
Consciousness after death, 35 ff.
Conservatism, Catholic, 502 ff.
Consistency and truth, 200.
Constantine, Emperor, 165, 1247.
Constitution of the Church, 289 ff.
Continuity, Anglican, 1269 ff.
Contraception, 988.
Contradictions, Biblical, 114 ff.
Conversion and reason, 1395; an obligation, 1422.
Co-operative State, 1133.
Copernicus, 508.
Coptic Church, 1249, 1251 ff.
Co-Redemptress, Mary as, 674, 696.
"Corpus Christi," Feast of, 1069.
Corruption, of the Church, 237, 391 ff.; of the Confessional, 760.
Cosmogony, Mosaic, 120 ff.
Council, of Chalcedon, 1249, 1256; of Constantinople I., 1256; of Ephesus, 1248; of Florence, 1257; of Jerusalem, 343 ff.; of Lyons II., 1257; of Nicea, 1247; of Trent, 240, 260.
"Counter-Reformation," 240 ff.
Countries, Catholic and Protestant, 1090 ff.
Cram, R. Adams, on Ritual, 1052.
Cranmer, Archbp. of Canterbury, 1273.
Created things limited, 8-11.
Creation, 2, 534 ff.; a free divine act, 899; Biblical account of, 120 ff.
Credibility of Christianity, 166 ff.
Credulity, 173.
Creed, necessity of, 489 ff., 971.
Criminology, 49 ff., 56.
Critics, modern, 94 ff., 802 ff.
Cross, necessity of, 647 ff.
Culture and Catholicism, 505 ff. See also Faith, Reason, Science.
Cup-reading, 951 ff.
Curse, nature and effects of, 957 ff.
Cyrinus, Governor of Syria, 143.

Darby, Rev. J. N., 1305 ff.
"Dark Ages" the, 512.
Day of Judgment. See Judgment.
Dead, prayers for, 1070 ff.
Dearmer, Dr., on proselytism, 1416.
Death, 588 ff., 678 ff.; inevitable, 27 ff., 64, 785; of Christ, 658; of Mary, 678 ff.
Death-bed repentance, 710 ff.
Death-sentence by State authority, 1230 ff.
Decay of Rome, 438 ff.
Definition, of God, 11; of the Church, 193, 280 ff.
Deity of Christ, 159, 630 ff.
Delage, on evolution, 541.
Denominations, variety of, 178 ff., 1243 ff.
Descent of man, 575 ff. See also Evolution.
Destiny of man, 26, 61 ff., 446, 587 ff., 613, 828 ff., 868 ff., 1137.
Determinism, 45 ff. See also Free Will.
Devil, the, 555, 615; influence of, 562.
Diabolical influence, 561.
Dictatorships, 1167 ff.
Diet of Spires, 219 ff.
"Disciples of Christ," 1294.
Discipline of the Church, 932.
Dispositions for faith, 159.
Disraeli, on Catholicism, 438.
Divided allegiance of Catholics, 352 ff.
"Divine," sense of the term, 8.
Divinity of Christ, 159, 630 ff.
Divisions of Christians, 178 ff., 1243 ff.
Divorce, 794 ff.; of Marconi, 816 ff.; of Napoleon, 814 ff.; and Protestants, 272.
Dogma, 472 ff., 484 ff.
Douay Version of the Bible, 463 ff.
Dreams, reliance upon, 954.
Duty to parents, 1417 ff.

Easter, date of, 1062.
"Ecclesia," 281 ff.
Ecclesiastics, 293 ff.
Eddy, Mary Baker, 1328 ff.
Education, Catholic, 1092 ff.; on sex matters, 974 ff.
Edward VI., of England, 1273.
Elizabeth, Queen of England, 1273.
Emerson, on beautiful Church-buildings, 1044.
End of the world, 886 ff.
Enoch, Book of, 101 ff.
Environment, influence of, 50.
Ephesus, Council of, 1248.
Episcopal Church. See Anglican Church.
Equality of men, 1096, 1115 ff.
Errors in Scripture, 114 ff.
Eternal happiness, 867 ff.
Eternity, a mystery, 872 ff.; of matter, 3.
Ethical instinct, 969 ff.
Ethical teaching of Christ, 624 ff.
Ethics, medical, 1002 ff.
Ethiopian Church, 1249.
Eucharist, 486, 493, 761 ff.; in the Church of England, 1285; and "Liberal Catholics," 1346 ff.
Eusebius, on St. Peter at Rome, 350.
Eutychian heresy, 1249, 1253.
Eviction of unemployed, 1122 ff.
Evidence, intrinsic and extrinsic, 6.
Evil, problem of, 12 ff., 1334.
Evolution, 534 ff.
"Ex Cathedra" utterances, 380 ff.

Ex-Catholics, 1391 ff.
Exclusive claims of Catholicism, 274 ff.
Existence of God, 1 ff.; tested by science, 4.
Expiation of sin. See Atonement, Penance.
Externalism in religion, 1048 ff.
Extreme Unction, 823 ff., 1333.
Faith, nature and necessity of, 166 ff., 491 ff.; dispositions for, 159, 1395; a divine gift, 491 ff.; harmony with reason and science, 88, 166, 495 ff., 513 ff., 537 ff., 923 ff.; rights of, 1389; salvation by, 447, 489, 651 ff., 697 ff.; loss of, 1398.
Faith-healing, 1330 ff.
Fall, of the Angels, 556 ff.; of man, 609 ff.
Fascism, 1167 ff.
Fear and religion, 64, 847 ff., 966 ff.
Felder, Dr., on the Gospels, 92.
Fidelity of Catholics, 390, 850, 1046 ff.
First parents of mankind, 131.
Fisher, G. P., on Calvinism, 709.
Fisher, H. A. L., on Christian Science, 1328.
Fleischmann, Prof., on origin of life, 541.
Fleming, Sir Ambrose, on origin of life, 541.
Flirtation, ethics of, 991 ff.
Florence, Council of, 1257.
Foerster, Dr., on sex education, 975.
Foreign missions, 268 ff., 423 ff.
Foreknowledge of God, 707 ff.
Forgiveness of sin, 736 ff.
Fortune tellers, 947 ff.
Foundation of morality, 60 ff.
"Free Churches," the, 1289 ff.
Free Love, 982 ff.
Freedom, religious, 197 ff.
Free Will, 24, 38 ff., 612 ff.
Friday abstinence, 1068.
Friday, Good, 1066 ff.
Frumentius, St., 1252 ff.
Fundamentalists, 111.
Future Life. See Immortality.
Galileo case, 367 ff., 920.
Garrett, Bishop Julio, 1407 ff.
Genealogies of Christ, 138 ff.
General Judgment, 831 ff., 884 ff.
Genesis, 113 ff.
Gentile Christians, 165.
German Naziism, 1170 ff.
Gibbons' conversion and lapse, 1396 ff.
Gladstone, W. E., and Catholicism, 1392.
Gnosticism, 1245.
God, existence of, 4 ff.; defined, 11; not identified with universe, 8-10; freely creates, 899; omnipresent, 10, 645-6, 775, 836; omniscient, 707 ff.; will of, positive and permissive, 13 ff.; providence of, 12 ff., 40 ff., 1227 ff., just and merciful, 618, 837 ff.; source of man's happiness, 867 ff.
Golden Rule, the, 626.
"Good Catholic," the, 397.
Good Friday observance, 1066 ff.
Good works, necessity of, 489, 699 ff.
Gospels, authentic history, 91 ff., 660 ff.
Gospel, of St. Mark, 322; of "Nicodemus," 687.
Goudge, Dr., on Church Unity, 194; on continuity, 1276; on meaning of Protestant, 215; on Reformation history, 230.
Government of the Church, 289 ff.
Grace, dispensation of, 267; life of, 718.
Great Pyramid, 1342 ff.

Greek Orthodox Churches, 250, 1254 ff.; not apostolic, 1266; not Catholic, 1267; not united, 1265; heretical, 1264; schismatical, 1254 ff.; possess the Holy Eucharist, 1261; Catholics forbidden to attend, 1262.
Greek Orthodox priesthood, 1258 ff.
Greek philosophy and Christianity, 151.
Gregory I., Pope, 1256.
"Group Movement," Dr. Buchman's, 1375 ff.
Guardian Angels, 554.
Guidance, spiritual, 605.

Halifax, Lord, and Catholicism, 1393.
Happiness, 64; eternal, 867 ff.
Hatred of Protestants, 915 ff., 1388.
Healing of the sick, 1330 ff.
Heaven, 867 ff.
Hell, 36, 653 ff., 916 ff.
Helwys, Thomas, 1298.
Henry VIII., 222, 1270 ff.
Heredity, 46, 50 ff.
Heresies, 434, 1243 ff.
Hierarchy of the Church, 289 ff.; and Protestantism, 259 ff.
High Church Anglicans, 1287.
Historians, bias of, 226 ff.
Historical method, 186.
History and the Gospels, 92.
Holdsworth, Sir W. S., on Anglican continuity, 1277.
Holiness of the Church, 388 ff., 414, 754 ff.
Holy Communion. See Eucharist.
Holy Days, 964 ff.
Holy Orders, Sacrament of, 791 ff.
Holy Spirit, guidance by, 192, 291.
Hormisdas, Pope, 1256.
Host, the. See Eucharist.
Hugel, Baron Von, on Spiritualism, 1322.
Human soul. See Soul.
Humanitarianism, 905.
Humility of Christ and Mary, 677.
Huxley, T. H., on evidence, 541.
Hypocrisy, 968.

Idealization of religious leaders, 628 ff.
Idolatry and Mary, 670 ff.
Incarnation, 622 ff.; necessity of, 647 ff.
Indestructibility of the Church, 435 ff.
Index of forbidden books, 917 ff.
Indifference, religious, 187 ff.
Indulgences, 863 ff.
Infallible Church, 212, 361 ff., 453, 486 ff., 509 ff.
Infallibility of the Pope, 362, 373 ff., 382 ff.
Infant Baptism, 722 ff.
Infidelity, marital, 997 ff.
Influence of the Church, 358 ff.
Innocent III., Pope, on abuses in the Church, 235.
Inquiry, duty of religious, 364 ff.
Inquisition, 929 ff.; and Galileo, 370.
Insanity and religion, 69.
Inspiration of the Bible, 105 ff.
Intercession of the Saints, 668 ff.
International Law, 1183.
Interpretation of the Bible, 364 ff., 453 ff., 466 ff., 478 ff., 1067. See also Private Judgment.
Interpretation of Civil Law, 1017.

Intolerance, Catholic, 274 ff., 498 ff.; Protestant, 249.
"Imitation of Christ," 233.
Immaculate Conception, 675 ff., 1001.
Immersion, Baptism by, 731.
Immorality, 969 ff.
Immortality, of body, 27 ff.; of soul, 31 ff., 588 ff., 1368.
Impeccability, 362, 382 ff.
Irvingites, 1308 ff.
Isis, 671.
"Israelites, British," 1336 ff.

Jacobite Church, 1249.
James, St., at Council of Jerusalem, 343 ff.
Jerrold, Douglas, on Middle Ages, 293.
Jerusalem, Council of, 343 ff.
Jesus. See Christ.
Jewel, Bishop, on Eucharist, 1285.
Jews, 158, 570.
Joad, Prof., on determinism, 55; on logic of Catholicism, 1283.
John the Baptist, St., 144.
John VIII., Pope, 1257.
John XXII., Pope, 312.
Joseph, St., foster-father of Jesus, 139 ff.
Judaism and Christianity, 150 ff., 163 ff.
Judas, and freedom of will, 43.
"Judge" Rutherford, 1230, 1336, 1351 ff.
Judgment, Private. See Private Judgment.
Judgment of mankind, General, 831 ff., 884 ff.; Particular, 828 ff., 885.
Julius I., Pope, 1252.
Jurisdiction in the Church, 1265.
Justice of God, 618 ff.

Karl Marx, 1128, 1135, 1140.
Kepler and Galileo, 369.
Kidd, Dr. B. J., on St. Peter in Rome, 348.
"Kingdom" established by Christ, 285.
Kirk, Dr., on freedom of will, 55.
Kissing, morality of, 996.
Klausner, on ethics of Jesus, 627.
Knowledge of God by man, 4; in heaven, 874.
Knox, John, bigotry of, 1291.
Kuinoel, on Petrine text, 330.

Labor, rights of, 1116 ff.
Lagrange, M. J., on dishonest Biblical criticism, 684.
Lambeth Conference and moral laxity, 1288.
Lamps, votive, 1075.
Last Judgment, 831 ff.
Last Supper, 761 ff.
Law, International, 1183.
Law, interpretation of civil. 1017.
Laws of the Church, disciplinary, 932.
Lazarus, return from the dead, 590.
Leadbeater, Bishop, and "Liberal Catholics," 1346 ff.
Leaders in religion idealized, 628 ff.
Learning and Catholicism. See Culture, Faith, Reason, Science.
Lenin, on religion, 1153.
Leo X., Pope, 241.
"Liberal Catholics," 1346 ff.
Liberal critics, 94.
Liberty, limits of, 925.

Liberty and Protestantism, 219 ff., 258 ff.
Lie, nature of, 903 ff.
Life, origin of, 541; on other worlds, 572; purpose of, 61 ff., 446, 869, 1137.
Life, supernatural, 718, 733.
Life of the Pope, 412.
Liguori, St. Alphonsus, and moral theology, 759.
Limbo, 723 ff.
Limitations of creatures, 8 ff.; of reason, 19 ff., 60, 80.
Liturgy, 1047 ff.
Lloyd Thomas, Rev., on Anglican ethics, 1288.
Loss of faith, gradual, 1398.
Lost Books of the Bible, 96.
Lost souls, 621.
"Lost Tribes of Israel," 1337 ff.
Lourdes, 90; water from, 1081.
Love, nature of, 991 ff.
Love-making, 991 ff.
Loyalty, 1163 ff.; of Catholics, 352 ff.
Lowliness of Mary, 674.
Lunn, Arnold, 506, 1283.
Luther, Martin, 220 ff., 240 ff.
Luxury of the Popes, 413.
Lyons, Second Council of, 1257.
MacGillivray, Father, on Greek Churches, 1265.
MacGregor, Sir W., on Christian Missions, 427.
Macintyre, Dr. R. G., 1416.
Maitland, F. W., Prof., on Anglican continuity, 1277.
Man, origin of, 131, 567; nature of, 25 ff. See also Destiny of man.
Manichaeism, 1246.
Manning, Cardinal, 1392.
Manson, Dr. T. W., on the Petrine text, 333.
Marcionism, 1245.
Marconi divorce case, 816 ff.
Mariolatry, 670 ff.
Marital infidelity, 997 ff.
Marriage, Sacrament of, 793 ff.; effected by consent of parties, 821 ff.; permanency of, 821 ff.; privileges of, 984 ff.; between Protestants, 272, 795; "Companionate," 999; annulment of, 813 ff.; Napoleon's, 814 ff.; Marconi's, 816 ff.
Martin Luther, 219 ff.
Mary, Mother of Christ and of mankind, 674; immaculate, 675 ff.; ever a virgin, 680 ff.; co-redemptress, 674, 696; subject to death, 678 ff.; assumption of, 695 ff.; intercession of, 668 ff.; glory of all women, 674.
Mary, Queen of England, 1273.
Marx, Karl, 1128, 1135, 1140.
Mass, Sacrifice of, 398, 781 ff., 1047; Catholic attendance at, 964 ff.; offered in the Greek Orthodox Church, 1306 ff.; claimed by Anglo-Catholics, 1285 ff.
Materialism, 516 ff., 548.
Matter, reality of, 516; not eternal, 3.
Matthias, election of, 342.
Mediaeval Church, 506.
Mediation of Christ, 307 ff.
Medical ethics, 1002 ff.
Mediums, spiritualistic, 1319.
Mercier, Cardinal, and Lord Halifax, 1394; and George Tyrrell, 1406.
Mercy of God, 618 ff., 754 ff., 837 ff.

Methodists, 1292.
Middle Ages, 293.
Millennium, the, 1306.
Miller, William, founder of Adventists, 1302 ff.
Milman, Dean, 1256.
Miracles, 82 ff.; demanded unreasonably, 288.
"Missing Links," 546.
Mission of St. John the Baptist, 144.
Missions, Catholic, 423 ff.; Protestant, 268 ff.
Modernism and George Tyrrell, 1402 ff.
Modernists, 94; attitude to the Church, 283 ff.; attitude to marriage, 802 ff.
Modesty, virtue of, 976.
Mommsen, and Gospel of St. Luke, 143.
Moncton, Capt., on Christian missions, 427.
Money and religion, 70 ff., 1041 ff. See also Wealth and the Church.
Monophysites, 1249, 1253.
Montanism, 1250.
Moral sense, 970 ff.; definite standards necessary, 982 ff.; teaching of Christ, 624 ff.; teaching of Anglicanism, 1288.
Moral training, need of, 972 ff.
Morality, foundation of, 60 ff.
More, St. Thomas, on evils in the Church, 233.
Mortal sin, 599 ff.; 1034.
Mosaic Cosmogony, 120 ff.
Mother of God, 1248. See also Mary.
"Mother's Day," 1054 ff.
Munzer, Thomas, originates Baptists, 1298.
Murder, 1000 ff.
Murray, Sir Hubert, on Christian missions, 424 ff.
Mussolini, 1169.
Mysteries in religion, 74 ff., 174.
Mystical Body of Christ, 786.

Napoleon's marriage and divorce, 814 ff.
Napthali VI., 133.
Nativity stories, 141 ff.
Nature, defined, 8; not God, 9, 84.
Nazi regime in Germany, 1170 ff.
Necessity of religion, 57 ff.; of Catholicism, 202, 444 ff., 1422.
Nestorianism, 1248.
Newman, Cardinal, on origin of Catholicism, 433; unwavering faith of, 1391.
Newspapers, bias of, 1150 ff.
Nicea, Council of, 1247.
Nicholas I., Pope, 311, 1246.
Nicodemus, Gospel of, 687.
Nonconformists, 1289 ff.
Norway and Protestantism, 223.
Nullity, marriage decrees of, 813 ff.
Numerical strength of Catholicism, 417.

Oaths, 963.
Obedience, necessity of, 1268, 1287.
Obligation of Catholicism, 202, 444 ff., 1422.
Obligations, religious, 964 ff.
Obscurity of Scripture, 467 ff.
Olcott, Colonel, and theosophy, 1346.
"Old Catholic Church," 1347.
Omnipresence of God, 10, 645 ff., 775, 836.
One religion not as good as another, 187 ff.
Orchard, Dr., on Papal supremacy, 1256.
Orders, Sacrament of, 791 ff.; in Greek Church, 1258 ff.; in Anglican Church, 1259 ff.
Origin of the Church, 283 ff.; of human race, 131, 567, 575.

Original Sin, 175, 607 ff.
Orthodox Greek Churches, 250, 1254 ff.
Orthodox Russian Church, 1153 ff.; 1265.
"Outside the Church no Salvation," 202, 444 ff.
Ownership, rights and duties of, 1115 ff.
"Oxford Groupers," 1375 ff.
Pacificism, 1187 ff.
Paganism and Christianity, 152.
Pantheism, 10, 646.
Papal supremacy, 1255 ff. See also Pope.
Papini, on unique position of the Pope, 1241 ff.
Parallelism between Old and New Testaments, 132 ff.
Parents, duty to, 1417 ff.
Particular Judgment, 828 ff., 885.
Pascal, on belief in God, 1; on psychological factors in belief, 1392.
Passion of Christ foretold, 134 ff.
Passions, the human, 977 ff.
Patriotism, 1163 ff.
Peace and the Church, 1181, 1204 ff.
Penances imposed in Confession, 746.
Permissive will of God, 13 ff.
Perpetuity of the Church, 435 ff.
Persecution of the Church, 404 ff., 435 ff., 439 ff.
Personal trust, 261.
Peter, St., rock-foundation of the Church, 317; supremacy as Vicar of Christ, 316; first Pope, 314 ff.; at Antioch, 351; as Bishop of Rome, 348 ff.; called "Satan" by Christ, 335 ff.
Peter's confession, 324.
Petrine text, 316 ff., 324.
"Petros" and "Petra," 326.
Petting, ethics or morality of, 991 ff.
Pharisees, 625.
Philanthropy, 905.
Philosophies, divergent, 7.
Photius, Patriarch of Constantinople, 1254 ff.
Physicists and free will, 47.
Pius X., Papal claims of, 310.
Pius XI., on Communism, 1158 ff.; on the priesthood, 402; on social justice, 1131.
"Plagiarism" of New Testament writers, 132 ff.
Plato and the doctrine of the Trinity, 522.
Plummer, Dr., on the Petrine text, 328, 339.
Plymouth Brethren, 1305 ff.
Pollen, on the reformation in Scotland, 225.
Poor, care of the, 412.
Pope, Head of the Church on earth, 297 ff.; not God, 309 ff.; Vicar of Christ, 314 ff.; succeeds St. Peter, 314 ff.; supreme, 1163 ff., 1255 ff.; infallible, 373 ff.; temporal ruler of Vatican City, 352 ff.; duties of, 412; unique position in the world, 1241 ff.; international significance, 1222 ff.
Popes, personal lives of, 382 ff.
Positive will of God, 13 ff.
Possession, diabolical, 561.
Poverty of the masses, 1099 ff.
Power, of the Church, 358 ff.; of priests, 762 ff.
Prayers, for the dead, 859 ff.; 1070 ff.; to Mary and the Saints, 668 ff.
Pre-Adamites, 569.

Predestination, 707 ff.
Pre-existence of souls, 37.
Prejudice, of historians, 226 ff.; of Protestants, 477.
Presbyterianism, 250, 1291.
Presence of God, 10, 645 ff., 775, 836; of Christ in the Eucharist, 761 ff.
Press, bias of the, 1150 ff.
"Priestcraft," 293 ff.
Priesthood, Catholic, 260, 762 ff., 791 ff.
Priesthood and Protestantism, 259 ff.
Priests, authority of, 289 ff.; failures amongst, 399; spiritual guides, 605; forgive sin, 736 ff.; duties in war time, 1203 ff.
Priests, Greek Orthodox, 1258 ff.
Primacy of St. Peter, 316 ff.
Private interpretation of the Bible, 1067. See Private Judgment.
Private Judgment, right of, 364 ff., 453 ff., 466 ff., 478 ff.
Private property. See Property.
Problem of evil and suffering, 12 ff., 612 ff., 1334.
Procter, on Galileo case, 369.
Prohibited books, 917 ff.
Propagation of Christianity, 152, 168 ff.
Property, rights and duties of, 1115 ff.
Prophecy, miraculous, 90; of Christ's passion and death, 134 ff.
Prospects of Catholicism, 438 ff.
Protestant, Reformation, 214 ff.; baptisms, 271; Bibles, 457 ff.; countries, 1090 ff.; historians, 226; marriages, 272, 795; sincere ministers, 193; missions, 268 ff.; services, 274.
Protestantism, unjustified, 243 ff.; causes of, 237 ff.; spirit of, 265; not apostolic, 246 ff.; divided, 182 ff.; teachings of, 256 ff., 697 ff.; attitude to the Bible, 257. See also Private Judgment. Attitude to the priesthood, 259 ff.; boast of liberty, 219 ff., 258 ff.; fruits of holiness, 395; relation to divine grace, 267; failure of, 244 ff., 256 ff., 262 ff., 479 ff.
Protestants, not heathens, 273; not Catholics, 249; not hated by Catholics, 915 ff., 1388.
Providence of God, 40 ff., 612 ff., 1227 ff.
Psychological determinism, 45 ff.
Psychology of sex, 969 ff.
Punishment, capital, 1231 ff.
Purgatory, 727, 851 ff.
Purity, virtue of, 976 ff.
Purpose of life, 61 ff., 446, 869, 1137.
Pyramid, the Great, 1342 ff.

"Quadragesimo Anno," Encyclical of Pope Pius XI., 1131 ff., 1158 ff.

Rabbinical writings, 625 ff.
Racketeers, religious, 70 ff.
Rational foundation of faith, 166 ff.
Rawlinson, Prof., on "British Israelism," 1339.
Reactionary, Catholicism, 498 ff.
Reading of the Bible, 454 ff.
"Real Presence," doctrine of the, 761 ff. See also Eucharist.
Reason, power and limitations of, 19 ff., 60,

80, 1033; and faith, 166 ff., 495 ff., 1395.
Redemption, 609 ff.
Reform, social, 1096 ff.
Reformation, Protestant, 214 ff.; history of, 226 ff.; causes of, 237 ff.; unjustified, 238, 243; effects of, 232, 1052.
Reformation, Catholic, 240 ff.
Reincarnation, 592 ff.
Religion, necessity of, 57 ff., 964; revealed, 74 ff.; not a racket, 70 ff.; not "opium of the people," 1120 ff.; influence of fear, 64, 847 ff., 966 ff.; attitude to science, 68; to superstition, 64; to Communism, 1144 ff.
Religious freedom, 197 ff.
Religious leaders idealized, 628 ff.
Religious sects, 178 ff., 1243 ff.
Renaissance, 512.
Renan and morality, 62.
Renegade Catholics, 1410 ff.
Repentance at death, 710 ff.
Reparation of sin. See Atonement. Penance.
Resurrection of Christ, 659 ff., 770.
Resurrection of the body, 588, 877 ff.
Revelation, 74 ff.
"Revelations, Book of," 234.
Revolution, 1096 ff., 1126.
Rights of man, 1115 ff.
Ritual, 1047 ff.
"Rock" of St. Peter, 324 ff.
Roger Bacon, on astrology, 943.
"Roman Catholic" as title, 252, 418 ff.
Rome and St. Peter, 348 ff.
Rosary, 1076 ff.
Rule of Faith, 471. See also Private Judgment.
Russellites, 1351 ff.
Russia, 1129, 1142.
Russian Orthodox Church, 1153 ff., 1265.
Rutherford, "Judge," 1230, 1336, 1351 ff.
Ryle, Bishop, on Anglican doctrine of the Eucharist, 1285.

Sabbatine Privilege, 1082 ff.
Sacramental System, 715.
Sacraments, 398, 715, 1315; all Catholic, 271; number of, 1284; effects of, 720; Baptism, 716 ff.; Confession, 736 ff.; Eucharist, 761 ff.; Holy Orders, 791 ff.; Matrimony, 793 ff.; Extreme Unction, 823 ff.
Sacred Heart Missions, 427.
Sacred Scripture. See Bible.
Sacrifice of the Mass, 398, 781 ff.
Saint Mark's Gospel, 322.
Saints, all Catholic, 390, 394 ff.
Saints, Communion of, 668 ff., 865 ff.
Salvation, necessity of, 64 ff., 175; conditions of, 447, 651 ff., 697 ff., 710 ff., 843 ff., 855 ff.; not by faith alone, 447, 489.
Salvation of Catholics, 444 ff., 202.
Salvation Army, 1312 ff.
Satan, 555.
Satan's organization, 1366.
Satisfaction for sin by penitent, 746 ff.; by Christ. See Atonement.
Scandals, 224 ff., 294, 414, 906 ff., 1353.
Scapular, 1082 ff.
"Scarlet Woman," the, 392 ff.
Schisms, 434, 1243 ff.

Scholasticism, 513.
Science, and God, 4; and religion, 68; and death, 27 ff.; and faith, 495 ff., 513 ff., 537 ff., 923 ff.; and Genesis, 123 ff.; and miracles, 87.
"Science, Christian," 1328 ff.
Scientists, unreliability of, 496.
Scotland and Protestantism, 224.
Scripture, Sacred. See Bible.
Seal of Confession, 749 ff.
Second Coming of Christ, 883 ff.
Secrecy of Confession, 749 ff.
Sects, religious, 178 ff., 1243 ff.
See of Antioch, 351.
Self-defense, killing in, 1007 ff.
Self-existence of God, 11.
Septuagint Version of the Bible, 459 ff.
Services, non-Catholic, 274.
Seventh Day Adventists, 1301 ff.
Sex education, 974 ff.
Sex psychology, 969 ff.
Sick, anointing of, 823 ff.
Sin, Catholic view of, 175, 754 ff.; original, 607 ff.; actual, 607 ff.; divisions of, 596 ff.; forgiveness of, 596, 736 ff.
Sin of the Angels, 559, 876.
"Sinaitic Syriac" text, 684.
Sinners, Catholic, 390, 394 ff.
Sixtus V., Pope, and Spain, 356.
Slavery, 1104 ff.
Smyth, John, 1298.
Social Reform, 1096 ff.
Socialism, 1139 ff.
Soldiers, justified, 1184 ff.
Son of God, Christ, 630.
Soul of man, 25 ff.; not pre-existent, 37; immortal, 584 ff., 1368; when created, 37, 1004.
Souls, lost, 621.
Space, notion of, 515.
Species, origin of, 541.
Spires, Diet of, 219 ff.
Spirit, teaching of Holy, 192, 291.
Spirit of man, 25 ff., 584 ff.
Spiritual guidance, 605.
Spiritualism, 1318.
Spontaneous generation, 541.
Spread of Christianity, 152.
Standards of conduct, Catholic, 396 ff., 754 ff.
State Absolutism, 1167 ff.
Stead, W. F., on beautiful Churches, 1044.
Substitutionary expiation of sin. See Atonement.
Suffering, problem of, 13 ff., 1334.
Sufferings in Purgatory, 852.
Suicide, 1034 ff.
Sundays, observance of, 964 ff.
Supernatural, reality of, 74, 514 ff.
Supernatural Life, 718, 733.
Supernatural outlook of Catholics, 265.
Superstition, 67, 511 ff., 934 ff.
Supremacy of St. Peter, 316 ff.; of the Pope, 1255 ff. See also Peter, Pope.
Survival of the soul, 31 ff., 588 ff., 1368.
Sweden and Protestantism, 223.
Synagogue repudiated by Christ and the Apostles, 163 ff.

Teaching of Christ, 624 ff.
Teaching authority of the Church. See Authority.
Temple, Archbishop of Canterbury, on the Eucharist, 1285.
Temporal power of the Pope, 352 ff.
Temptation, 562 ff., 615 ff.
Theosophy, 1346.
Thomas Aquinas, St., on astrology, 944; on resisting evils, 1239.
Thomas, John, founds Christadelphians, 1335.
Time, notion of, 515, 535 ff., 845, 872.
Tolerance, 273, 915 ff.
Totalitarian States, 1167 ff.
Tradition, 472 ff.
Transcendence of God, 10.
Transformism, 542.
Translations of the Bible, 463 ff.
Transmigration of souls, 592 ff.
Transubstantiation, 766 ff.
Trent, Council of, 240, 260.
Trinity, 519 ff.; 632 ff.
Truth, nature of, 485 ff.; consistent, 200; of the Bible, 105 ff.; of the Catholic Church, 288, 480, 1390.
Truthfulness, 903 ff.
Tylor, Sir, E. B., on "British Israelism," 1339.
Tyrrell, Father George, 1402 ff.

Unbaptized, fate of, 722 ff.
Unction, Extreme, 823 ff., 1333.
Uniate Greek Churches, 1260.
Unitarianism, 1247.
Unity, of God, 519 ff.; of the human race, 575 ff.; of the Church, 90, 181, 386 ff., 471 ff.

Van Zeeland, on Social reform, 1138.
Variations in religion, 176 ff., 1243 ff.
Vatican City State, 352 ff.
Venial sin, 599 ff.
Veracity, 903 ff.
Vicar of Christ, 315. See also Pope.
Vicarious death of Christ, 658.
Violence by unemployed, 1122 ff.

Virgin birth, 137 ff.
Virginity of Mary. See Mary.
Vision of God in heaven, 867 ff.
Visions, 1323 ff.
Von Soden, 684.
Votive Lamps, 1075.
Vulgate Bible, 464 ff.

Wafer, Eucharistic, 761 ff.
War, 1178 ff.
War-chaplains, 1219 ff.
Water, Lourdes, 1081.
Wealth of the Church, 407 ff., 1041 ff., 1118 ff., 1143.
Wedgewood, Bishop, and Liberal Catholics, 1347.
Wells, H. G., 541.
Wesley, John, 1292.
Weston, Bishop of Zanzibar, on divided Anglicanism, 1279.
White, Mrs. Ellen G., 1303 ff.
Whitehead, Prof., on Scholasticism, 513.
Whitton, Rev. T. H., on Anglican divisions, 1278, 1280 ff.; on Anglican moral standards, 1288.
Will of God, 12 ff.
Will, freedom of, 24, 38 ff., 612 ff. See also Determinism.
Willoughby, Bishop, of "Liberal Catholics," 1347.
Wilson, Prof., on free will, 47.
Witnesses of Jehovah, 1351 ff.
Women in Church, 1053.
Women, Mary the glory of, 674.
Word of God, 105 ff.
Workers and the Church, 1122 ff.
Works, necessity of good, 489, 699 ff.
World, age of, 538; end of, 886 ff.
Worship, obligation of, 964 ff.; and ritual, 1047; of Mary, 668 ff.

Zachary, prophecy of, 146 ff.
Zumpt, on accuracy of St. Luke, 143.

If you have enjoyed this book, consider making your next selection from among the following . . .

Ven. Francisco Marto of Fatima. *Cirrincione,* comp.	1.50
Ven. Jacinta Marto of Fatima. *Cirrincione*	2.00
St. Philomena—The Wonder-Worker. *O'Sullivan*	7.00
The Facts About Luther. *Msgr. Patrick O'Hare*	16.50
Little Catechism of the Curé of Ars. *St. John Vianney*	6.00
The Curé of Ars—Patron Saint of Parish Priests. *Fr. B. O'Brien*	5.50
Saint Teresa of Avila. *William Thomas Walsh*	21.50
Isabella of Spain: The Last Crusader. *William Thomas Walsh*	20.00
Characters of the Inquisition. *William Thomas Walsh*	15.00
Blood-Drenched Altars—Cath. Comment. on Hist. Mexico. *Kelley*	20.00
The Four Last Things—Death, Judgment, Hell, Heaven. *Fr. von Cochem*	7.00
Confession of a Roman Catholic. *Paul Whitcomb*	1.50
The Catholic Church Has the Answer. *Paul Whitcomb*	1.50
The Sinner's Guide. *Ven. Louis of Granada*	12.00
True Devotion to Mary. *St. Louis De Montfort*	7.00
Life of St. Anthony Mary Claret. *Fanchón Royer*	15.00
Autobiography of St. Anthony Mary Claret.	13.00
I Wait for You. *Sr. Josefa Menendez*	.75
Words of Love. *Menendez, Betrone, Mary of the Trinity*	6.00
Little Lives of the Great Saints. *John O'Kane Murray*	18.00
Prayer—The Key to Salvation. *Fr. Michael Müller*	7.50
Sermons on Prayer. *St. Francis de Sales*	4.00
Sermons on Our Lady. *St. Francis de Sales*	10.00
Passion of Jesus and Its Hidden Meaning. *Fr. Groenings, S.J.*	15.00
The Victories of the Martyrs. *St. Alphonsus Liguori*	10.00
Canons and Decrees of the Council of Trent. *Transl. Schroeder*	15.00
Sermons of St. Alphonsus Liguori for Every Sunday.	16.50
A Catechism of Modernism. *Fr. J. B. Lemius*	5.00
Alexandrina—The Agony and the Glory. *Johnston*	5.00
Life of Blessed Margaret of Castello. *Fr. William Bonniwell*	7.50
The Ways of Mental Prayer. *Dom Vitalis Lehodey*	14.00
Catechism of Mental Prayer. *Simler*	2.00
Fr. Paul of Moll. *van Speybrouck*	11.00
St. Francis of Paola. *Simi and Segreti*	8.00
Abortion: Yes or No? *Dr. John L. Grady, M.D.*	2.00
The Story of the Church. *Johnson, Hannan, Dominica*	16.50
Reign of Christ the King. *Davies*	1.25
Hell Quizzes. *Radio Replies Press*	1.00
Indulgence Quizzes. *Radio Replies Press*	1.00
Purgatory Quizzes. *Radio Replies Press*	1.00
Virgin and Statue Worship Quizzes. *Radio Replies Press*	1.00
The Holy Eucharist. *St. Alphonsus*	10.00
Meditation Prayer on Mary Immaculate. *Padre Pio*	1.25
Little Book of the Work of Infinite Love. *de la Touche*	2.00
Textual Concordance of The Holy Scriptures. *Williams*	35.00
Douay-Rheims Bible. *Leatherbound*	35.00
The Way of Divine Love. *Sister Josefa Menendez*	18.50
The Way of Divine Love. (pocket, unabr.). *Menendez*	8.50
Mystical City of God—Abridged. *Ven. Mary of Agreda*	18.50

Prices subject to change.

Title	Price
Hail Holy Queen (from *Glories of Mary*). *St. Alphonsus*	8.00
Novena of Holy Communions. *Lovasik*	2.00
Brief Catechism for Adults. *Cogan.*	9.00
The Cath. Religion—Illus./Expl. for Child, Adult, Convert. *Burbach*	9.00
Eucharistic Miracles. *Joan Carroll Cruz*	15.00
The Incorruptibles. *Joan Carroll Cruz*	13.50
Pope St. Pius X. *F. A. Forbes*	8.00
St. Alphonsus Liguori. *Frs. Miller and Aubin.*	16.50
Self-Abandonment to Divine Providence. *Fr. de Caussade, S.J.*	18.00
The Song of Songs—A Mystical Exposition. *Fr. Arintero, O.P.*	20.00
Prophecy for Today. *Edward Connor*	5.50
Saint Michael and the Angels. *Approved Sources*	7.00
Dolorous Passion of Our Lord. *Anne C. Emmerich.*	16.50
Modern Saints—Their Lives & Faces, Book I. *Ann Ball*	18.00
Modern Saints—Their Lives & Faces, Book II. *Ann Ball.*	20.00
Our Lady of Fatima's Peace Plan from Heaven. *Booklet*	.75
Divine Favors Granted to St. Joseph. *Père Binet*	5.00
St. Joseph Cafasso—Priest of the Gallows. *St. John Bosco.*	4.50
Catechism of the Council of Trent. *McHugh/Callan.*	24.00
The Foot of the Cross. *Fr. Faber.*	16.50
The Rosary in Action. *John Johnson*	9.00
Padre Pio—The Stigmatist. *Fr. Charles Carty*	15.00
Why Squander Illness? *Frs. Rumble & Carty.*	2.00
The Sacred Heart and the Priesthood. *de la Touche*	9.00
Fatima—The Great Sign. *Francis Johnston*	8.00
Heliotropium—Conformity of Human Will to Divine. *Drexelius*	13.00
Charity for the Suffering Souls. *Fr. John Nageleisen*	16.50
Devotion to the Sacred Heart of Jesus. *Verheylezoon*	15.00
Who Is Padre Pio? *Radio Replies Press*	1.50
Child's Bible History. *Knecht.*	4.00
The Stigmata and Modern Science. *Fr. Charles Carty*	1.25
The Life of Christ. 4 Vols. H.B. *Anne C. Emmerich*	60.00
St. Anthony—The Wonder Worker of Padua. *Stoddard*	5.00
The Precious Blood. *Fr. Faber.*	13.50
The Holy Shroud & Four Visions. *Fr. O'Connell.*	2.00
Clean Love in Courtship. *Fr. Lawrence Lovasik.*	2.50
The Prophecies of St. Malachy. *Peter Bander.*	7.00
St. Martin de Porres. *Giuliana Cavallini*	12.50
The Secret of the Rosary. *St. Louis De Montfort.*	3.00
The History of Antichrist. *Rev. P. Huchede.*	4.00
St. Catherine of Siena. *Alice Curtayne*	13.50
Where We Got the Bible. *Fr. Henry Graham*	6.00
Hidden Treasure—Holy Mass. *St. Leonard.*	5.00
Imitation of the Sacred Heart of Jesus. *Fr. Arnoudt*	15.00
The Life & Glories of St. Joseph. *Edward Thompson.*	15.00
Père Lamy. *Biver.*	10.00
Humility of Heart. *Fr. Cajetan da Bergamo*	8.50
The Curé D'Ars. *Abbé Francis Trochu.*	21.50
Love, Peace and Joy. (St. Gertrude). *Prévot*	7.00

At your Bookdealer or direct from the Publisher.
Call Toll-Free 1-800-437-5876.

Prices subject to change.